The Israeli-American Connection

AMERICA-HOLY LAND MONOGRAPHS

Editors
Jonathan D. Sarna, Brandeis University
Moshe Davis, The Hebrew University of Jerusalem

The Israeli-American Connection

Its Roots in the *Yishuv*,
1914–1945

MICHAEL BROWN

Wayne State University Press
Detroit

Copyright © 1996 by Wayne State University Press, Detroit, Michigan 48201. All rights reserved. No part of this book may be reproduced without formal permission.

The publication of this volume in a freely accessible digital format has been made possible by a major grant from the National Endowment for the Humanities and the Mellon Foundation through their Humanities Open Book Program.

LIBRARY OF CONGRESS CATALOGING-IN-PUBLICATION DATA

Brown, Michael (Michael G.), 1938–
The Israeli-American connection : its roots in the yishuv, 1914–1945 / Michael Brown.
  p. cm.—(America-Holy Land monographs)
Includes bibliographical references and index.
ISBN 978-0-8143-4459-0 (paperback); 978-0-8143-4458-3 (ebook)
1. Zionists—Palestine—Biography. 2. Zionism—United States. 3. United States—Relations—Palestine. 4. Palestine—Relations—United States. I. Title. II. Series.
DS151.A2B76   1996
320.5′4′095694092—dc20
[B]   96–5939

Wayne State University Press thanks the following individuals and institutions for their generous permission to reprint material in this book: Gordie Frimerman; Bettman Collection of Getty Images; Central Zionist Archives; and the Pinhas Lavon Labor Archive, Tel Aviv.

Exhaustive efforts were made to obtain permission for use of material in this text. Any missed permissions resulted from a lack of information about the material, copyright holder, or both. If you are a copyright holder of such material, please contact WSUP at wsupressrights@wayne.edu.

http://wsupress.wayne.edu/

In grateful memory of
my parents,
Albert Brown (1908–1963)
and Eunice Levy Brown (1908–1987)

and my wife,
Francine Nison Brown (1943–1994)

Their love, nurture, and encouragement are sadly missed.
May their memory be for a blessing.

Contents

Preface 9   Acknowledgments 11   Abbreviations 13

1
Introduction
The *Yishuv* Discovers America   15

2
Vladimir Jabotinsky
A Politician Who Missed the Boat   35

3
Chaim Naḥman Bialik
America, A Cultural Wasteland with Promise   69

4
Berl Katznelson
A Man of the Spirit Confronts the Land of Dollars   101

5
Henrietta Szold
Health, Education, and Welfare, American-Style   133

Contents

6
Golda Meir
"Minister of American Affairs"   161

7
David Ben-Gurion
Building the American Alliance   197

8
Afterword
241

Notes 247   Glossary 353   Selected Bibliography 357

Georgraphic and Name Index 379   Subject Index 389

Preface

EVERY BOOK has its own peculiarities of style and form. This one is no exception, and readers may appreciate knowing what they are—at least those that are the result of conscious decisions by the author. The first and most important of these idiosyncrasies is that the book deals primarily with six builders of Israel, each in a separate chapter. These six individuals confronted many of the same issues and interacted with many of the same people. In order to avoid duplication, people and issues are introduced at length only in the chapter where they are most fully discussed. A curious, confused, or impatient reader may want to look ahead—or behind—using the index.

The main characters in this book are referred to in ways that may seem inconsistent. Berl Katznelson and Golda Meir are often called by their first names, as they were during their lifetimes, and not only by their friends. David Ben-Gurion and Henrietta Szold, on the other hand, were almost never called by their given names and therefore are not here. Szold was Miss Szold to almost everyone, although that formality has been dropped. A short glossary identifies some groups and institutions and offers definitions of some terms which, because they are familiar to many readers, are not explained more fully in the body of the text.

What may jar some readers is the use of the term "Palestine" to denote the pre-1948 territory that is today Israel, the West Bank, and Gaza. In the pre-state era, however, that was the term in general English use; before 1922 it included what is now Jordan as well. Then it was only a geographical, not a political, term. And "Palestinians" then invariably meant Jews and not Arabs, as it is used here. Some people prefer the Hebrew term "Eretz Yisrael" or its English translation, "land of Israel." I have rejected it here, because it is clumsy and anachronistic in English.

Readers may note, as well, that the term "America" is used in different, although connected, ways in the text. At various times it refers to the American Jewish community, to the American government, to American society and culture, or to the United States as a country. All of these uses are, I believe, legitimate. I hope that the meaning is clear in all cases from the context. I find justification for the multiple uses in James Baldwin's observation that "America's history . . . [is] so profoundly and stubbornly unique that the very word 'America' remains a new, almost completely undefined and extremely controversial proper noun. No one in the world seems to know exactly what it describes."

Finally, there are here many names and terms in languages other than English, particularly Hebrew and Yiddish. In general, the names of people and organizations appear as they were written by the people and groups themselves. Hebrew and Yiddish terms that are in fairly common use in English, such as "aliyah" and "kibbutz," appear in their most common English form. Others are written as phonetically as possible. The standard scholarly transliterations of Hebrew have been largely ignored, because they are confusing and awkward-looking to the general reader, while the specialist can get along quite well with phonetic spellings. Every attempt has been made to be consistent.

Acknowledgments

THERE ARE many people to whom I owe thanks for their assistance with this volume. Without their kindness, patience, encouragement, and generosity my task would have been very much more difficult. I appreciate all that they have done.

First are my colleagues at York University in Toronto who released me from teaching and administration for research and writing. I benefited from sabbatical leaves and from several research fellowships. I am especially grateful to my colleagues, Professors Sydney Eisen, Martin Lockshin, and Bernie Zelechow, who took over some of my accustomed duties so that I could complete the project, and to my departmental chairs, Professors Margo Gewurtz and Susan Ehrlich, for their cooperation and encouragement. Profesor Eisen, my very dear colleague, deserves to be singled out. As director of the Centre for Jewish Studies, he provided succor in many different ways. As a friend, he has been unfailingly encouraging. As the project neared completion he uncomplainingly read the entire text and offered innumerable judicious comments which have strengthened it immeasurably. Thanks are also due to Susan Rainey and the staff of the Academic Technical Support Group of the Faculty of Arts, the staff of the Scott Library, Daphne Lazar who assisted in preparing the bibliography, and Professors Richard Pope and Mark Webber who helped with translations from Russian and German.

Much of the research for the book was done in Israel, and I am grateful to many people there for their assistance. Professor Moshe Davis, of blessed memory, the founder of the Institute of Contemporary Jewry at the Hebrew University and the founder and long time director of the America-Holy Land Studies Project, provided inspiration for the volume and gave generously of his wise counsel over the years. A fellowship from the Project helped to facilitate the research. Dr. Menahem Kaufman of the Institute and the Project provided advice and assistance, as did a number of other colleagues at the Institute and Professor Allon Gal of Ben-Gurion Univer-

Acknowledgments

sity. Mention must be made of the staffs of several archives as well as others, who graciously answered questions and helped me track down sources. The archives include: the Central Zionist Archives; the Jabotinsky Institute, especially Rachel Halperin and Yehuda Ben-Ari; Genazim; the Ben Zvi Institute, especially Shimon Rubenstein; the Mapai and Katznelson Archives at Beit Berl, especially Baruch Tor-Raz; the Labor Archive, especially Ilan Gal-Pe'er and Meir Galperin; the National and University Library; and the Ben Gurion Archive. Also, portions of chapter 5 were delivered at the conference "Envisioning Israel" at Ben-Gurion University of the Negev in June 1993, and may be found in the conference volume, *Envisioning Israel: The Changing Ideals and Images of North American Jews*, ed. Allon Gal (Jerusalem: Magnes Press, 1996); an earlier version of chapter 2 appeared in *Modern Judaism* vol. 9 (Winter 1989), pp. 71–99; portions of chapter 6 appeared in *Jewish History* vol. 6 (1992), pp. 35–50; and much of chapter 3 appeared in *Jewish Political Studies Review* vol. 6 (Fall 5755/1994), pp. 47–105.

A number of people on both sides of the ocean, including Emma Ehrlich and Lou Kadar, who are no longer living, Dr. S. Zalman Abramov, Professor Moshe Davis, Sylva Gelber, Judy Hollander, Regina Medzini, Mrs. Shulamith Nardi, and Sarah Rahabi, were kind enough to share with me personal reminiscences about the subjects of this book and the findings of their own research. In addition, Yehuda Ben-Ari, Raḥel Halperin, Jack Chodoroff and Jacob Goldfein helped with translations; Susan Feibus, Cheryl Belkin, Nancy Schwartz, and Rabbi Yaakov Rone located materials in Washington, Paris, Cleveland, and Scranton.

Much gratitude is due to Professor Jonathan Sarna of Brandeis University, the editor of the series in which this volume appears, and to the staff of Wayne State University Press. Arthur Evans, the director of the Press, and Lynn H. Trease and Kathryn Wildfong, who worked with me in editing the book, are owed special thanks. Their valuable suggestions have significantly enhanced the text.

My sons Josh and Matthew read large portions of the book and offered significant insights and helpful stylistic comments; Matthew painstakingly prepared the index; and my daughter Abby patiently endured years of conversation about the project and offered her encouragement. Unfortunately, my wife Frankie did not live to see the completion of the book. During the long years of research and writing, she provided reassurance and inspiration. As she always did, she read the work in progress and tactfully made invaluable suggestions, most of which I eventually accepted. Most importantly, she spurred me on when I flagged. I miss her sunshine, her love, and her wisdom, but I am thankful for the years we shared together.

Abbreviations

General
- **AZC** American Zion Commonwealth
- **AZMU** American Zionist Medical Unit
- **FDR** President Franklin Delano Roosevelt
- **HEC** Histadrut Executive Committee
- **HMO** Hadassah Medical Organization
- **JDC** American Joint Distribution Committee
- **WZO** World Zionist Organization
- **ZOA** Zionist Organization of America

Notes and Bibliography
- **ABTA** Genazim, Machon Bein-Bibliografi al Shem Asher Barash, Tel Aviv
- **BGA** Ben-Gurion Heritage Institute, Sde Boker
- **BGD** Ben-Gurion Diaries
- **BKL** *Iggrot Berl Katznelson* [Letters of Berl Katznelson-Hebrew]
- **BZA** Ben-Zvi Archive, Jerusalem
- **CZA** Central Zionist Archives, Jerusalem
- **GMM** Golda Meir Memorial Association, located in the Lavon Institute, Tel Aviv
- **HC"** Histadrut Council Minutes
- **HVHP"** Histadrut Executive Committee Minutes
- **ISA** Israel State Archives, Jerusalem
- **ISAHC** Words of Golda Meir at the Histadrut Council, ISA
- **ISAHVHP** Words of Golda Meir at the Histadrut Executive Committee, ISA
- **ISAMP** Words of Golda Meir at Mapai Party Meetings, ISA
- **JAE"** Jewish Agency Executive Minutes
- **JTSA** Jewish Theological Seminary Archives, New York
- **KABB** Katznelson and Mapai Archives, Beit Berl
- **KBK** *Kitvei Berl Katznelson* [The Writings of Berl Katznelson]
- **LAT** The Pinhas Lavon Labor Archive, Tel Aviv

Abbreviations

MC"	Mapai Party Center Minutes
MHP	Moetzet HaPo'alot [Working Women's Council]
MJ	Machon Jabotinsky, Tel Aviv
MPC"	Mapai Party Political Committee Minutes
MS"	Mapai Party Secretariat Minutes
PRO	Public Record Office, London
WAR	Weizmann Archive, Rehovot
YIVO	YIVO Archive, New York

CHAPTER

1

Introduction

The *Yishuv* Discovers America

SINCE 1948, and even more since 1967, an intimate Israel-America connection has been so much a part of the international scene that it is hard to imagine a time when it did not exist. In fact, the relationship is not very old, and the alliance is not altogether natural. In the past, oil, geopolitics, and antisemitism have invited United States patronage of the Arabs or at least neutrality in the Arab-Israeli dispute. The European origins and socialist ideology of many Israeli leaders, moreover, pointed them away from America.

From the inception in the late nineteenth century of the modern movement of Jewish return to the land of Israel, the Promised Land of the New World and that of the Old World have been unequal competitors for the allegiance of Jews and for Jewish immigrants. The land of Israel was small and poor in resources; until 1918 it was one of the more backward areas of the Ottoman Empire. Under both the Turks and the British, Jews had only limited access to it. The vast United States, on the other hand, was the fabled *goldene medine*, the "land of unlimited opportunities," as Golda Meir used to call it. More important, it was the land of freedom, where inherited privilege and prejudice counted for little, at least in theory. Until after World War I, Jews—and other whites—had almost unlimited access to it; and they flocked there from all over the Old World, creating the world's largest Jewish community. The Jews of Palestine were typical in their response to the promise of America. In 1891, the United States consul in Jerusalem, Selah Merrill, reported to his superiors that Jewish newcomers to the land of Israel often used it as a stepping-stone to America. Even "those who were born in the country or who spent here most of their lives, [yearn] to go to . . . America, with a view to better[ing] their circumstances."¹

As might be expected, this lopsided competition has sometimes provoked a negative reaction in residents of the Holy Land. In 1881, Eliezer Ben-Yehuda, the Hebrew lexicographer who was instrumental in reviving the ancient Jewish tongue as a modern spoken language, himself an immigrant to Palestine from Russia, published an essay entitled "Palestine or America?" in the Jerusalem journal, HaHavatzelet. It was a year of Russian pogroms which served as catalysts of the mass exodus of Jews from eastern Europe. That Jews should "settle in a strange land very far from their place of birth, when the land of their fathers beckon[ed] to them to partake of its goodness," seemed regrettable to Ben-Yehuda.² He and his fellow returnees and many of the native Jews of Palestine agreed with Consul Merrill about the reason. As the German-born Arthur Ruppin, who headed the Palestine Settlement Office of the World Zionist Organization, put it almost three decades later: "Those emigrants whose aim it was to make much money in a short time, either did not go to Palestine at all, or, having tried it, left it soon. . . . [Palestine attracted only] persons devoted more to the pursuit of an ideal than . . . of money."³

But the money was not free in America. Yosef Feinberg, a founding settler of Rishon LeZion, one of the first Zionist agricultural colonies in Palestine, raised a red flag in 1882 for Jewish émigrés contemplating a new life in the New World. "America," he warned, "requires of immigrants total assimilation; one must become there an American, body and soul."⁴ Three decades later, Rabbi Abraham Isaac HaCohen Kook, then chief rabbi of Jaffa and later chief Ashkenazi rabbi of Palestine, was asked by a rabbinical colleague in Europe whether he should encourage his son to emigrate to Palestine or to America. Kook acknowledged that many of the young pioneers in Palestine were godless. Still, he said, "there is more hope for [the boy's] spiritual condition in the Holy Land." In the same year, one of those godless workers, Ya'akov Zerubavel, undertook a fund-raising mission to America on behalf of HaAhdut, a Palestine Labor journal. No less than traditional Jews, Zerubavel was appalled at how public schools in the United States "succeeded in alienating the child not only from the old country, from his people, but also from his parents who still maintained their spiritual independence in the American melting pot."⁵

1

The Israel-America nexus, as it took root in the apparently infertile soil of the *yishuv* during and between the world wars, is the subject of this book, which examines the American experiences of six of the foremost leaders of Jewish Palestine. Because it has been thoroughly studied by others, the American side of the relationship is not dealt with here.[6] The period was chosen because it was in these years that the framework for statehood and, to a large degree, for the new Hebrew-speaking society was erected. Europe and its centuries-old Jewry, with its rich and variegated culture, were in eclipse; the United States and its young and still raw Jewry were on the rise. Many in the *yishuv* and elsewhere, however, did not discern what was happening or refused to draw the implications. The men and women studied here reflect this changing world. During these years they could— ostensibly—still choose their cultural and political mentors and allies; after 1945 there was really only one option. This book is about the choices they made and the consequences of their decisions.

The six were selected because of their prominence but also because through them can be seen the impact on Israel—still in the pre-state period—of American technology and culture, of American political and social theory and practice, and of American mores and attitudes, to say nothing of American money. The six leaders, who represent different fields of endeavor, crossed paths with one another, especially the three Laborites, Katznelson, Meir, and Ben-Gurion. Yet each wove his or her own network of ties with the New World into a patch in the quilt that became the Israel-United States relationship. A common aspect of their careers is that their authority rested primarily on a power base in the *yishuv* itself.

After 1930, the center of Zionist gravity shifted from Europe to Palestine, as the Jewish population there grew, and because the major issues facing the movement played out there.[7] The Palestine Zionist leaders became the on-site authorities of the state in the making. Chaim Weizmann, the other larger-than-life Zionist figure of the immediate pre-state era, remained staunchly loyal to Britain and was largely indifferent to the potential advantage for Zionism of American connections. Stationed in London, he acted rather like an imperial minister for the colonies, seeking to influence the course of affairs from abroad. As a result, he never succeeded in forming a personal power base in the *yishuv*. When Israel achieved independence in 1948 he became its first president; but he could be no more than a figurehead. To be sure, Jabotinsky lived in Palestine only for two relatively brief interludes, and, from the late twenties, derived much of his political strength from his popularity in Poland. His Palestinian supporters, however, accepted his absentee leadership to an astonishing degree until shortly before his death, regularly electing him to the Va'ad Le'umi (the Representative Council of the *yishuv*), even though the British forbade him entry to the country. No local leader even approached his command of the Palestine Revisionist movement.[8] These six men and women, then, together with their compatriots, laid the groundwork not only for Israel's American alliance but for the state itself.

2

While the friendship between the *yishuv* and the United States required development and nurturing during the interwar years, earlier events had helped to create an appropriate atmosphere for it. American interest in the Holy Land, rooted in Christian theology but with a unique American dimension, dates from the earliest days of European settlement in the New World.[9] A permanent American presence there was established in the mid-nineteenth century with the arrival of the first consuls and the first American settlers, and with the institutionalization over the years of charitable contributions. Documented interest of Holy Landers in America dates from the mid-eighteenth century. Jews in Palestine and in the Diaspora were aware of the America-Holy Land relationship almost from its genesis.

Beginning in the early 1830s, the United States posted a minister to Constantinople whose jurisdiction included Palestine and maintained consular agents, most of them not Americans, to look after visiting citizens in Jerusalem, Jaffa, and Haifa. In 1844 the United States appointed its first resident Holy Land consul, Warder Cresson. An exotic personality who converted to Judaism as Michael Boaz Israel and spent the rest of his life working for the return of the Jews to their ancient homeland, Cresson was never confirmed in his consular nomination. The first bona fide American consul arrived in Jerusalem only in March 1857, establishing a presence that has existed since then except for a few short interruptions.[10]

Peculiar—but not exclusive—to the Ottoman Empire was the system of "capitulations," which granted to the representatives of foreign powers extraterritorial privileges applicable not only to their citizens but also to adopted protégés. Over the years, the United States became ever less enthusiastic about assisting anyone other than its native-born nationals; and, like the representatives of other countries, American officials were often biased against Jews. On the whole, however, American officials proved less inimical to Jews than those of other countries. American protection was particularly prized in Palestine in the nineteenth century, because only the United States retained "exclusive jurisdiction over both trial and punishment," and because, at least after 1887, the Americans generally refused to permit the Turks to discriminate among United States citizens.[11] By 1899 the Jerusalem consulate had eight hundred protégés under its wing, a large number of whom were naturalized Jewish Americans and their children, who had no intention of returning to the United States. It was not uncommon by then

Introduction

for consular officials to become involved in the political and social affairs of the Jerusalem Jewish community.[12]

Often the minister in Constantinople directly influenced events in Palestine. General Lew Wallace, the author of the epic novel, *Ben Hur*, who occupied the post from 1881 to 1885, gained permission from the Porte for Jews to settle in the empire, although not in Palestine; and the American community in Jerusalem asked his support in their efforts to gain a larger slice of the American Jewish charitable pie. But he was labeled "a republican despot" in *HaHavatzelet*, because of his support for Christian missionaries to the Jews, among other reasons.[13] With the appointment of Oscar Straus as minister in 1887, Palestine's Jews gained a valuable friend. Straus, whose family controlled Macy's Department Store in New York, was a wealthy and prominent Jew. At first he hesitated to become involved in issues concerning his coreligionists, claiming he had been sent to Turkey as the American minister, not as a Jew. As American minister, however, he found himself duty-bound to insist on the equality of Jews before the law; and shortly he became drawn into their affairs. In 1888, he visited Palestine and received an impassioned welcome from local Jews who, along with their gentile countrymen, understood the force and significance of the statement made by "the government of the enlightened American republic," when it "appointed a Jew . . . to represent its interests at the Sublime Porte."[14] Straus served two terms as minister (1887–89, 1898–99), and another after the position had been upgraded to ambassador (1909–10).

By the last decades of the nineteenth century, the work of the consuls and ministers, especially Straus, had led many traditionalist Holy Land Jews to look upon the United States as the guarantor of their safety, and they took upon themselves a reciprocal obligation. In 1881, when President Garfield was shot, Sir Moses Montefiore, the venerable English philanthropist, appealed as a matter of course to "the Spiritual Heads of the Spanish and German Hebrew Congregations of Jerusalem" to pray for his life.[15] In 1898, the United States embarked on its "splendid little" imperialist war against Spain. Jews of Jerusalem crowded into the Beit Ya'akov Synagogue in the presence of Consul Merrill, himself a Protestant minister, to pray with Shmuel Salant, the chief rabbi of the city's German, Russian, and Palestinian Jews, for the welfare of the aggressors. No American jingoist could have written a more one-sided supplication than Salant, who believed the United States was redressing the wrong done to Jews when they were expelled from Spain in 1492. The rabbi begged "compassion" for the people in whom "the love of Liberty and Humanity [was implanted] more than in any other [who] . . . went out to battle against a mighty foe, not to widen territory . . . [but] to bring eternal justice." He invoked God's favor on "the army . . . actuated by the feelings of righteousness," but besought Him to "annihilate the . . .

power" of their "adversaries," thereby avenging "the blood of thy servants that has been shed by a cruel nation."[16]

3

Another American presence in nineteenth-century Palestine was exerted by gentile expatriates, whose efforts at colonization sparked the interest of contemporary Jews abroad and later Jewish settlers in Palestine.[17] In 1851 and 1866 two groups of millenarian American Protestants attempted to establish agricultural colonies. Although they failed at farming, some of them remained in the country; one colonist, Rolla Floyd, became the first local representative of Thomas Cook's tours and then a popular dragoman, hotelier, and omnibus operator. In 1908, Yitzhak Ben-Zvi boarded at his hostelry in Jerusalem. The pioneer and future president of Israel was unaccustomed to luxury; Mr. Floyd's, however, he considered a rabbit "warren," and its denizens "a cluster of sharks."[18] In 1881 a small group of Americans with idiosyncratic notions about religion and collective living established the American Colony in Jerusalem to bring education, faith, and medical care to the natives. Their ideas and life style aroused the suspicion of traditionalist Jerusalemites, including Consul Merrill. But Rahel Yana'it, Ben-Zvi's future wife and, like him, a socialist, was very favorably impressed by their dedication and sharing, and in "later years . . . became friendly with members of the Colony."[19] Eventually the American Colony achieved bourgeois respectability; and during the Mandate its hotel became a meeting place for government officials and the Jerusalem upper crust, a status it has maintained until the present day.

American Jews, also motivated by religion and a desire to rebuild the Holy Land, followed their gentile countrymen, with similar results in the nineteenth century. In 1870, Simon Berman, who was Polish-born but had lived in the United States for eighteen years, sought without success to establish an agricultural colony. The 1890s saw at least two more abortive attempts at settling North American Jews on the land.[20]

The new century brought a change in fortune. The number of Jews and gentiles from America grew steadily, although numbers remained quite modest. On the eve of World War I there were about 85,000 Jews in the country out of a total population of less than 700,000, of whom only a very few were Americans. The Jews from the United States included both pietists who came to live out their years in the Holy Land and young Zionists eager to rebuild the Jewish homeland. In 1910, a few Russian-born *olim* who had lived for some time in the United States and acquired agricultural training at the Jewish farm schools in Doylestown, Pennsylvania, and Woodbine, New Jersey, arrived in Palestine. Two years later the "Young Farmer[s]," as

Introduction

they called themselves, led by Eliezer Lippe Yoffe, arrived at the Kinneret Training Farm operated by Ruppin's Settlement Office. There they were known as "the American Group," and with their technical training and modern equipment they almost succeeded in making the farm profitable for the first time in its history. Yoffe, in particular, tried to demonstrate to the undisciplined, angry young Russian Jews of the Second Aliyah that a new society could be built "in an orderly fashion with [scientific] methods."[21] The approach was seen as typically American by others at the Farm, including Berl Katznelson, one of the subjects of this study. Eventually they scattered, but most remained in the *yishuv*; Yoffe became the moving force behind the *moshvei ovdim*, or smallholders' settlements.[22]

The Achooza movement was an early twentieth-century colonization project that spanned Europe and North America. The fourteen American societies formed between 1908 and 1914 were composed of middle-class American citizens, recent eastern European immigrants, and former residents of Palestine, with enough means to contemplate purchasing their own farms and emigrating. They were not "rich Americans," as some of the penniless pioneers from eastern Europe thought.[23] Copious publicity in the *yishuv* about the American Achooza notwithstanding, only two of the groups succeeded in establishing colonies (Saint Louis at Poriya, and Chicago I at Sarona); and those two settlements were abandoned in the early postwar period. After the war most of the remaining societies in the United States were folded into the American Zion Commonwealth, a semipublic settlement company under the aegis of the Zionist Organization of America. The AZC was successful in aiding and establishing urban and rural settlements in Palestine, including Kibbutz Merḥavya, where Golda Meir lived for a time, and Herzliya, where her parents made their home.[24]

As noteworthy here as the settlement endeavors themselves is the assistance provided by American consuls and ministers directly to American citizens and indirectly to all Jews immigrating to Palestine in the pre-World War I years. The Americans were friendly towards Turkey. Yet they naturally "opposed an Oriental regime inherently suspecting and condemning anything . . . foreign." United States diplomats considered it "a sacred mission to uphold the principles of freedom and democracy abroad"; more specifically, they helped in obtaining the removal of restrictions on land acquisition directed at non-Muslims and in many other ways.[25] Such activities served to heighten the impression that the United States could be counted on to protect Jewish interests in the Holy Land.

Another of the prewar Palestine ties to America related to agriculture was of a different nature and, although involving in the main one person, Aaron Aaronsohn, had broad ramifications. Aaronsohn's family was among the founders of the agricultural colony, Zichron Ya'akov, in 1882. His brother, Alexander, worked for the American Department of Agriculture for a number of years and even took out naturalization papers, although he did not remain in the United States long enough to become a citizen.[26] Aaron himself was a trained agronomist who, by the early years of the century, had earned a considerable scholarly reputation for his research into dry farming and wild wheat. In 1909–10, at the invitation of the Department of Agriculture, he visited the United States, touring areas of the country where dry farming was practiced and lecturing in scholarly forums on the strain of wild wheat that he had discovered in the Galilee. He also arranged for his *Agricultural and Botanical Explorations in Palestine* (1910) to appear as an official United States government publication.

Thanks to his official connections, Aaronsohn was introduced to a number of America's most prominent Jews, both Zionists and non-Zionists. During his stay, his Agricultural Experiment Station at Athlit near Zichron Ya'akov was incorporated in the United States with a number of Americans as directors, including Henrietta Szold, who also served as secretary, and Julius Rosenwald, a noted philanthropist, who controlled Sears Roebuck. The directors and their friends advanced twenty thousand dollars for start-up costs and promised ten thousand dollars annually for the running expenses of the station.[27] Later, Jacob Schiff, one of the wealthiest Jews of his time and a non-Zionist, although a rather traditional believer, offered to support five Palestinians for two years to "be educated in American agricultural methods."[28] Along with the American Exploration Society and the American School for Oriental Studies, Aaronsohn's Agricultural Station and his Hebrew Health Station for Bacteriological Research, established in 1911 with the help of Nathan Straus, the philanthropist brother of Oscar Straus, represented the first significant America-Palestine cooperative scientific ventures.

On his several trips to the United States, Aaronsohn involved himself in Zionist affairs, as well as advancing his research activities. In 1910 he met with the Young Farmer society and urged them to complete their studies before heading for Palestine; and he tried to discourage the Achooza movement, which he considered "naive and ill-founded."[29] In early 1912 at a dinner given by the Rosenwalds, he met Louis Brandeis, then a Boston lawyer prominent in Progressive circles. Brandeis thought Aaronsohn's talk on wild wheat "the most thrillingly interesting" he had "ever heard, showing the possibilities of scientific agriculture and utilization of arid or supposedly exhausted land."[30] The meeting took place during the period of Brandeis's conversion to Zionism; and Aaronsohn's vision of the potential contribution of the Zionist enterprise to the betterment of humanity probably played a role in that process.[31] Had he not been killed in a plane crash in 1919,

Introduction

Aaronsohn would undoubtedly have figured prominently in the America-*yishuv* relationship in subsequent years.[32]

One other important aspect of the pre-World War I American presence in Palestine was charitable funds. The Jews of the Old *Yishuv* were, for the most part, pietists who saw their task in life to be prayer and contemplation, not for themselves alone, but on behalf of the entire Jewish people. Most of them refrained from gainful employment which might detract from their sacred vocation; they considered it the obligation of fellow Jews to support them in this enterprise. In the nineteenth century they organized themselves in *kolelim*, that is, communities based on their lands of origin, largely for the purpose of tapping the charitable resources of their native countries more efficiently.

From the mid-eighteenth century, Palestinian Jewish institutions had been sending fund raisers to North America with varying degrees of success. A century later, several American organizations were collecting money on a regular basis for the maintenance of the Old *Yishuv* pietists. In 1854, Judah Touro of New Orleans bequeathed sixty thousand dollars, an enormous sum at that time, for Jews in the Holy Land, to be disbursed by Sir Moses Montefiore. The Englishman used the funds for the construction of new neighborhoods in Jerusalem, for which he, rather than Touro, was given credit. In the same year, the North American Relief Society for the Indigent Jews in Jerusalem was founded; and *The Occident* carried one of the first appeals in print to American Jews on behalf of the poor of the Holy Land.[33] The next two decades saw considerable bickering in Palestine over the riches of America.[34]

By the mid-1890s, American donations had become an important source of funds for the pietists; some groups, however, mainly the Sephardim and Jews with a personal connection to North America, felt they were receiving less than their share. In order to ensure that American expatriates would get their due, Kolel America was organized in 1897 with the aid of the American consul in Jerusalem, Edwin S. Wallace. In subsequent years the American *kolel* not only disbursed funds to individuals, but also built housing for its members and provided burial plots for them on the Mount of Olives.[35]

Zionists from abroad, as well as the native Jews who joined their ranks (the New *Yishuv*, generally referred to herein, simply as the *yishuv*), objected strongly to the notion of living on welfare in order to serve God. Many were not believers; but the religious Jews among them thought that the Divine would be best glorified by the renewed vitality of the Holy Land. They set as principal goals for themselves the productivization and self-sufficiency of Palestinian Jewry. Unfortunately, in such a poor country, those goals were readily perceived to be beyond immediate reach; in fact they have been only partially attained even today. As a result, these groups also began looking to America for help. By the turn of the century both *yishuvim* were heavily dependent on foreign funds; and America was on its way to becoming their chief financial backer.[36]

4

The onset of World War I proved disastrous for the Jews of Palestine, and no boon for the other residents of the country. The fragile economy deteriorated immediately with the interruption of the flow of remittances from abroad and of exports from Palestine. Suspicion of foreigners inevitably becomes heightened in wartime, and the Turks had a proclivity to xenophobia even in peacetime. That many Jews in the *yishuv* came from Russia, Turkey's traditional enemy with which she was once again at war, endangered their position. In such a situation, the United States was propelled to the forefront of people's consciousness. America remained neutral until 1917, and although it broke relations with Turkey, it never declared war. That made it possible to intercede repeatedly on behalf of Palestinian Jews (and their institutions), large numbers of whom became American protégés when the British, French, and Russian ambassadors left Constantinople at the start of the war. During the war, the material and manpower resources of the United States, which was untouched by the fighting, were drawn upon to sustain the already dependent community in the Holy Land in unprecedented ways. And many more Palestinians than usual now planned to emigrate to North America.

Two dramatic American interventions in wartime Palestine were the Jewish Legion and the American Zionist Medical Unit (AZMU). Their story, however, properly belongs to later chapters, and only a word of introduction can be included here. The Legion brought about 1,500 North American soldiers to Palestine in all-Jewish units of the British army. Most of them returned to North America after the war, but their willingness to volunteer for service in Palestine left a memory of American Jewry's concern for the fate of the Zionist enterprise. The AZMU marked the beginning of a prominent and permanent American presence in the health care system of the *yishuv*.

American diplomatic activities on behalf of the *yishuv* were no less remarkable than the Legion and the AZMU. The last two American ambassadors in Constantinople before the interruption of relations in 1917, Henry Morgenthau and Abram I. Elkus, were Jews; and that fact proved to be of inestimable importance to the welfare of their coreligionists in the Holy Land. Their presence, which implied great Jewish power, together with the good offices of the German ambassador to the Porte, may have ensured that

American soldiers in the Jewish Legion in Palestine shortly before their return to the United States. (Courtesy of the Central Zionist Archives, Jerusalem.)

Jews would not suffer the fate of the Armenians in wartime Turkey. President Wilson apparently intended his representatives to look after their fellow Jews. He advised Morgenthau before he left for the Middle East that "anything you can do to improve the lot of your co-religionists is an act that will reflect credit upon America, and you may count on the full power of the Administration to back you up."[37]

Morgenthau was not himself a Zionist; in fact he later became an opponent of the movement, although his wife had been an early donor to Henrietta Szold's Daughters of Zion group in New York.[38] One of his first official acts in Turkey was a 1914 Passover pilgrimage and grand tour of the Jewish communities in the Holy Land. He visited Jaffa, Hebron, the colony of Petaḥ Tikva, the American Achooza settlement of Poriya, and other places. In Jerusalem he hosted an official banquet for the local governor and other dignitaries. At the dinner, which was held in a kosher hotel, he recited the traditional blessing over the wine, and pronounced himself "happy, as a Jewish ambassador, to break bread with his guests in the ancient capital city of the kingdom of Israel."[39] Palestine Jewish leaders "recognized at once that his hand and heart would be extended for their welfare and salvation," as President Wilson had instructed.[40]

Within months of the ambassador's triumphal tour came war and privation. In late August, Jacob Schiff received a communication from Secretary of State William Jennings Bryan, relaying a cablegram from Morgenthau which advised "that the Jewish charities and colonies in Palestine require[d] immediate assistance." Morgenthau requested that Schiff and their mutual friends "raise and send funds with [a] warship." Bryan was willing to help with the ship.[41] Thus began one of the more extraordinary episodes of America-Holy Land relations.

In early October the USS *North Carolina* arrived in Jaffa harbor with money and supplies provided by Schiff, the American Jewish Committee, and the Provisional Executive Committee for General Zionist Affairs, then acting for the WZO, which had been rendered impotent by the war. In charge of the shipment was Morgenthau's son-in-law, Maurice Wertheim, whose detailed "Report on the Condition of the Jews of Palestine" provided American Jewish leaders with a firsthand description of the suffering in the *yishuv* from "one of their own."[42] A later consignment was brought by Louis Levin, a Baltimore Jewish community worker and a brother-in-law of Henrietta Szold. Until the winter of 1916–17, when submarines made eastern Mediterranean waters too dangerous, more than a dozen such trips were made by American warships. The food, fuel, funds, and medical supplies they brought, not only for Jews but for other residents of Palestine as well, helped greatly to alleviate suffering there and to enhance the reputation of America, the bountiful. Abraham Elmaleh reported that some twenty-three

The World War I Provisional Executive Committee for General Zionist Affairs. Seated second from right is Committee secretary Henrietta Szold. At her left is Louis Brandeis; at her right, Rabbi Stephen S. Wise. Standing second from left is Louis Lipsky. (Courtesy of the Central Zionist Archives, Jerusalem.)

thousand people in Jerusalem received an allotment of food from just one ship in 1915.[43]

In Jaffa the warships took on a return cargo: refugees, almost all of them Jews. Some, like Rabbi Yehuda Leib Maimon, the leader of the Mizraḥi Orthodox Zionists, had been expelled as "dangerous enemy aliens," and others were voluntarily fleeing the hardships of war. (Ben-Gurion and Ben-Zvi were expelled, but they left on a commercial vessel.) In late 1915, Mordecai Ben-Hillel HaCohen of Tel Aviv, whose diaries provide the most complete contemporaneous chronicle of the war period in Palestine, lamented that "a thousand Jewish souls had left the country in one day" on board the USS *Tennessee*, a naval cruiser. Like the other ships, the *Tennessee* took its passengers to Egypt, where some remained throughout the war, and others booked passage abroad. Many eventually went to the United States.[44]

The ships were an advertisement for America. Among their most vital functions was providing a means for uncensored communication between Palestine and the outside world. Captain Decker of the *Tennessee*, who made a number of runs to Jaffa, interviewed leaders of the *yishuv* and submitted to the State Department an accurate assessment of the dangers facing the Zionists. His report motivated the government to intensify its aid efforts.[45] After the first months of the war, the American ships were the only ones available to transport passengers to a neutral port. The sailors acquired instant fame for treating their charges with exceptional "politeness, friendliness, and humanity."[46] According to Alexander Aaronsohn, "the natives were especially impressed by the manliness and quick action of the American boys. Frequently a few sailors were involved in a street fight with scores of Arabs, and they always held their own. In a short time the Americans become feared, which in the Orient is equivalent to saying they were respected [sic]."[47] Aaronsohn also claimed that the ships had saved "the Russian Jews in Palestine" who had all been marked for "massacre and outrage like the Armenians."[48] To Jews, these were "ships of salvation," but also "ships of exile." The *Tennessee* was "our good angel"; to Arabs, it was "the Jews' frigate." When it sank in 1917, Mordecai Ben-Hillel HaCohen gave it the traditional benediction for the dead: that its "memory . . . be blessed for all eternity."[49]

The Jews of Palestine appreciated not only the exploits of the navy but also the generosity of their coreligionists who footed the bill for the supplies and for other relief efforts. Julius Rosenwald, for example, pledged one thousand dollars a month for Palestine relief for the duration of the war and for a year afterwards. Abraham Elmaleh, a member of the native Sephardi community, praised American Jews' "substantial and speedy aid," while the *Luaḥ Eretz Yisrael* compared them to the Israelites in the desert who responded with alacrity to Moses' call for donations to God's Tabernacle.[50]

Refugees on board the USS *Tennessee* at Jaffa, late 1914 or early 1915. (Courtesy of the United States Naval Historical Center, Washington, D.C.)

In his account of the wartime travails of his city, the longtime mayor of Tel Aviv, Meir Dizengoff, expressed gratitude for the "American Fund" (he meant the American Assistance Council), which filled the void left when remittances from Europe ceased in 1914.[51] The pioneering Laborites, mostly immigrants from eastern Europe, criticized the hoity-toity manner of American donors and their failure to meet all needs. But they, too, acknowledged that the American Jews were "fulfilling a function that would never be forgotten. . . . American assistance," wrote one author in the Labor journal *HaPo'el HaTza'ir* in July 1915, "is what has saved the *yishuv* [from] . . . hunger and destruction."[52]

Besides the supply ships, Ambassador Morgenthau assisted the Palestinians in a number of ways. The fear of a massacre was never far from Jews' minds; even Morgenthau is said to have thought it likely. Acting on Secretary Bryan's instructions, he urged the Turkish government time and again to safeguard the lives of both Zionists and Armenians.[53] Whether the Turks had intended to slaughter the Jews of Palestine is a moot point. But they did expel large numbers at the beginning of the war, a process that Morgenthau, together with the German ambassador, was able to halt, at least temporarily. In 1917, with the British armies moving up from Egypt, there were new expulsions from Jaffa and Jerusalem conducted with considerable harshness. By then the American ambassador had left Turkey. But as Jabotinsky and others recognized at the time, there could be no doubt that the Turks had been impressed by the nature of the American interposition on behalf of Palestine's Jews.[54] The forthright advocacy of Morgenthau and his successor may well have influenced the behavior of the Turks.

What the *yishuv* recognized as special about Morgenthau himself was the attitude with which he approached his task. In late 1914, Arthur Ruppin wrote to thank him and Schiff for the first allotment of funds. In his gracious response, the ambassador reflected a Jewish patrician's understanding that *noblesse oblige*, and he affirmed his pride in the connection to fellow Jews. "I do not know," he wrote, "whether you and your friends or I have to be grateful for the fact that I am ambassador. It makes me feel that I have been the chosen weapon to take up the defense of my co-religionists, and that I have been blessed with the opportunity to render them some service. So I really believe that I am the one who should be the most thankful and not the beneficiaries."[55]

Unfortunately, the relationship soured soon after Morgenthau left his post. In the spring of 1916 he returned to Turkey, at the behest of the American government, ostensibly on an investigatory mission to prevent further depredations against Jews. The real goal was to find grounds for detaching the Ottoman Empire from its alliance with Germany and Austria. When he returned to the United States, Morgenthau reported in a public

Introduction

speech in Cincinnati that he had proposed to the Turks selling Palestine to the Jews in order to liquidate the Turkish debt. (The next day in Chicago he gave a somewhat different version of his proposals.) The Turks were embarrassed and wreaked vengeance on Zionist officials whom they banished from Palestine. The British, by now secretly planning to invade Palestine, opposed a separate peace with Turkey; and Weizmann (and the Armenians) feared that maintaining the Ottoman Empire in any form would hinder plans for Jewish (and Armenian) autonomy. The government disavowed the initiative. Morgenthau was left looking as though he had embarked upon a foolish personal embassy, which may, in fact, be the case. Unfairly, he held the Zionists mainly responsible and felt they had repaid him ill for his exertions on their behalf. Ever after he was numbered among their outspoken opponents.[56]

One other aspect of American wartime diplomacy in Palestine deserves mention here: the work of the consulates in Jerusalem and Jaffa. Although not as dramatic nor as public as Morgenthau's interventions, the activities of Otis Glazebrook, the consul in Jerusalem, who was a personal friend of President Wilson, served to enlarge the fame in the *yishuv* of the country he represented. Ruppin considered him "the most helpful of all" in directly alleviating suffering, "a thoroughly decent man . . . averse to all bureaucratic measures."[57] Alexander Aaronsohn called him "a true American . . . rendering at Jerusalem the same sort of service that Ambassador Morgenthau has rendered at Constantinople . . . practically the only man who stood up for the poor, defenseless people of the city."[58]

The two consulates assisted in the distribution of the money and supplies sent from America and supported Russian nationals waiting to be expelled from Palestine.[59] When Eliezer Ben-Yehuda and his family left for America, Glazebrook took charge of his manuscripts. When Ruppin resigned from his position with the Palestine Settlement Office in 1916 because of Turkish objections to his activities, Glazebrook put an apartment at the American Archaeological Institute in Jerusalem at his disposal. And when Aaron Aaronsohn, operating as a British spy unbeknownst to the consul, sought an interview with the governor, Jemal Pasha, Glazebrook arranged the meeting. What most Jews probably did not realize at this time was that Glazebrook was an anti-Zionist, although he seems to have rendered service to all in need regardless of his feelings. This was less the case when he returned to Jerusalem after the war.[60]

The prewar and wartime diplomatic and consular assistance rendered to Jews in Palestine by the United States became a precedent only in a very limited way. Isolationism, increased antisemitism in government circles (especially in the State Department), trust in Britain, a feeling that it was inappropriate to badger the British as they had hounded the Turks, and improved conditions in Palestine served to restrain the Americans from intervening in Palestine in the interwar period. In the *yishuv*, however, the earlier period was not forgotten; the leadership continued to hope for renewed help from Washington, which eventually was forthcoming. Memories of the early patronage, moreover, served to reinforce positive attitudes towards the United States.

5

One way in which the *yishuv* became further acquainted with the United States during the World War I years was through American activities in Palestine. Another was through the prolonged stay in the United States of exiles and refugees from the Holy Land, and of Europeans who would later emigrate there. As already mentioned, Ben-Gurion, Ben-Zvi, and Rabbi Fishman (Maimon) were among the exiles. Another was Ben-Zion Mossinsohn, principal of the Herzliya Gymnasium in Tel Aviv, the country's first modern Hebrew secondary school. Among the refugees were the Ben-Yehudas; Israel Belkind, one of the pioneer Zionist settlers; and three members of the Aaronsohn family, Alexander and, for a time, Aaron, and their sister Rivka. Europeans who found themselves in America during the war but who were destined to play a major role in *yishuv* affairs included Shmaryahu Levin and Rabbi Meir Berlin (Bar-Ilan), the Mizraḥi leader.

Their stay in America enabled the Palestinians to get acquainted with their future partners. All of them participated in American Jewish life, especially in Zionist affairs and the Hebrew and Yiddish press. Ben-Gurion and Ben-Zvi were active in the Poale Zion Labor Zionist party, wrote and published prolifically, and recruited for the Jewish Legion, all of which will be discussed later. Levin played a key role in the Provisional Executive Committee for General Zionist Affairs; Berlin published and edited *Halvri*, a significant Hebrew weekly for which Fishman wrote frequently, while providing dynamic leadership for the Mizraḥi. Ben-Yehuda wrote and published in Hebrew, lectured to various audiences including the American Oriental Society, and launched an abortive "plan for securing restoration to Palestine of important archaeological treasures" looted by the Turks.[61]

In retrospect, Ben-Zvi claimed that his three years in America had taught him "much about life in the Atlantic republic."[62] Rabbi Fishman's daughter and biographer said that his years of exile "enriched his conceptual world and taught him a lesson in practical affairs," although he himself would never have admitted it.[63] There is little evidence, however, to suggest that many of the Palestinians acquired much of a sense of non-Jewish America. The Aaronsohn brothers were exceptional, because they had been in the United States before, knew English well, and mixed with gentiles. In

Introduction

his diaries, Aaron comments on American cuisine ("very thoroughly bad"), on an Arkansas congressman ("ignorance ... regarding the most elementary matters concerning Europe ... beyond the bounds of the permissible"), on President Wilson ("doctrinaire"), and on the American people (they have "their own good, healthy logic").[64]

For the most part, the America that the Palestinians came to know was Jewish America, which they found wanting—although not altogether. Ben-Zvi thought Jewish workers in America lacking in revolutionary spirit, "more superficial and more mechanical" in their approach to life than Europeans. American Zionists, he said, made "a sport" of their beliefs, a common refrain of Palestinians.[65] Rabbi Fishman found "cause to worry" when he surveyed "the spiritual state of our brethren" in the New World. And Menahem Sheinkin was shocked by "the neglect, the foolishness, and the apathy" of the "virtually petrified" American Jews, so different from the patriarchs of ancient Israel with their deep sense of purpose.[66] But Sheinkin also realized that, unlike other countries of the Diaspora, America sometimes evoked in "children and young people a natural religious and national instinct."[67] And Ben-Zvi was heartened by the Zionist revival that occurred in labor circles in the wake of the Balfour Declaration in 1917, which committed the British government to the Zionist dream.[68] His experience with fellow Jewish Legionnaires from America encouraged him further.

For the most part, their American exile weighed heavily upon the Palestinians. Rivka Aaronsohn longed to return to "the sweet, warm sun-kissed little home," she wrote to Henrietta Szold, as her train to California sped past scenery that bore "the same relation to our country, as a homely looking face bears to a handsome looking one." Ben-Zvi could not wait to "shake the dust of America from ... [his] feet," he wrote to Rahel Yana'it on the eve of his departure in 1918.[69] The Palestinians returned home with mixed, but generally negative, impressions of the United States. Most of them had seen only a narrow slice of American life; and they had experienced only a moment of a society that was in rapid and constant flux, something they would not always remember when dealing with Americans in the future. What they saw had neither tempted them nor distracted them from their Zionist mission. Yet their knowledge of the New World and its ways, however limited, as well as experiences with Americans in Palestine itself in the prewar decades, ultimately helped to prepare the way for the more extensive and deeper contacts between leaders of the *yishuv* and Americans in the interwar years. Although it has not been much noticed by observers and analysts, it was those latter contacts which laid the groundwork for the America-Israel alliance of more recent times.

CHAPTER
2
Vladimir Jabotinsky

A Politician Who Missed the Boat

MAVERICK, MILITANT, MAXIMALIST Zionist Vladimir Jabotinsky was in many respects a pioneer, proposing policies others would adopt only years later. In some ways though, he was a man of his time, no more visionary than his opponents, or even less so. His views of the United States were both more and less perceptive than those of other Zionists. Like them, the spiritual ancestor of Israel's right-wing Likud Party found he could not ignore the New World in the interwar period; but he became seriously interested in North America only in his dying days, long after others had established a foothold there. Although he knew a great deal about America and had an affinity for aspects of its politics and culture, he put little stock in that country's potential for Zionism.

1

Most of the early eastern European Zionists grew up in traditional Jewish surroundings; Jabotinsky came from an assimilated family, although his mother was Yiddish-speaking and rather observant. As a child he received a Russian education but little Jewish education; one of his American antagonists, Zionist leader Louis Lipsky, remarked that "he had a *goyish* head."[1] Jabotinsky spent some time in an Italian university. His early interests in literature and politics put him in touch with America.

Among his early heroes Jabotinsky counted Abraham Lincoln, "the most straightforward, the most noble, the most honest statesman in the world," a person who, like Garibaldi, Victor Hugo, and Theodor Herzl, "believed in the natural goodness of man" and was willing to fight for his principles.² Although he was known to describe himself as a Jeffersonian democrat, "first on . . . [Jabotinsky's] list of American presidents" was Theodore Roosevelt, "a sober man with a simple, healthy, straightforward mind," one of the most "famous lion hunters" of the world.³ Admiration for Roosevelt, the "rough rider," was less common among Jews than adulation for the "great emancipator" Lincoln, but not unknown, especially among Zionists.⁴ Roosevelt represented to the young Jabotinsky the American dream of adventure and daring, the conquest of uncharted lands. Not only Roosevelt awakened in Jabotinsky the pioneering spirit. Among his favorite early authors were the American writers of the frontier, James Fenimore Cooper and Bret Harte, as well as the Englishman, Mayne Reid, who also wrote about the American West.⁵ For Jabotinsky, a pioneer was a "person who did not accept boundaries," who desired "to keep on going, to investigate and to experience God's creation from the other side of the border."⁶ And it was that spirit which he believed to be characteristically American. He found Jules Verne's tales of undersea and space adventure "American" and appealing.⁷ While still in his teens he was drawn to Edgar Allan Poe, the pioneer of the spirit, the explorer of the dark side of the human psyche, whose poem, "The Raven," young Jabotinsky translated into both Hebrew and Russian.⁸ And he read Mark Twain, undoubtedly attracted both by Huck Finn's search for spiritual freedom and by the later, darker tales of psychological searching.⁹

Jabotinsky's interest in America was not based on blind affection. From the press, the movies, and from literature, he became familiar with "the American dilemma." Like almost all of Zionism's founding fathers he read *Uncle Tom's Cabin*, the single "book which most directly influenced history."¹⁰ D. W. Griffith's film, *The Birth of a Nation*, impressed upon him the complexity of the Civil War and Reconstruction periods;¹¹ but he never overcame the conviction that there was not "anywhere in the civilized world," including Russia and Rumania, "the kind of inequality" that "democratic" America imposed upon its black population.¹²

He was appalled by the race riots that broke out following the Johnson-Jeffries prize fight in 1910.¹³ Johnson became the first black heavyweight champion, and within hours of his victory seven blacks had died at the hands of whites in various parts of the United States. White bands had "formed apparently for the sole purpose of beating up whatever negroes they could get their hands on" to revenge the defeat of the popular Jeffries. In the days following there were more deaths and injuries, and in many places movies of the fight were banned in order to prevent further violence.¹⁴ Jabotinsky wrote in 1910, that American lynchings were worse even than the barbarous pogroms in Kishinev, which had shaken the world only a few years earlier. He attributed the behavior of white Americans to a perverse physical-psychological revulsion for blacks, as opposed to European feelings about Jews, which he found more rational, although no more acceptable.[15] In a bizarre story set in the pre–Civil War era Jabotinsky attempted himself to explore the aberrations inherent in black-white relations. "Virginia" is the tale of a Southern woman raped by a black during a slave rebellion, whose Swedish husband comes to loathe her for having been defiled by a black.[16] Here was an aspect of the underside of American psychological "exploration," which led Jabotinsky ultimately to regard Poe and some other American writers as "unhealthy," perhaps worthy of rejection.[17]

As a young man, Jabotinsky shared some of the negative views of America held by many early twentieth-century European intellectuals. Americans could be forgiven their off-putting, nasal pronunciation of English, but other unpleasant characteristics, such as their penchant for empty-headed "entertainments" and "soul-less," assembly-line uniformity, were less pardonable. The United States had not produced even "one true genius," he asserted in 1910.[18] Its "melting-pot" ethos, a by-product of the impulse to standardize life, was contributing to the country's ruin. That ethos, he said, stressed "America before all, America after all, and America in between, as well, America and nothing else"; he believed it stifled creative powers, which only individualism and ethnic particularity could release. It was an ethos especially dangerous for Jews and other small minorities. In this respect, he felt Jews were better off in the Russian empire before 1914 than in America.[19]

All of these notions were developed before Jabotinsky had met many Americans and with relatively little reference to Jews. War brought him into contact with Americans. The opportunities it offered for altering the situation of Jews in Europe and the status of Palestine presented an occasion to test some of his earlier views about the United States.

2

When the war broke out, Jabotinsky became a correspondent for a Russian newspaper. He soon found himself in Alexandria, Egypt, where he met the Jews who had been expelled from Palestine by the Turks. A veteran of several years of active involvement in the Zionist movement, Jabotinsky consulted with a number of people in Alexandria in search of an appropriate response to the crisis facing the Jews of Europe and Palestine. He settled on a plan, which he believed should become Jews' principal war effort: the creation of a Jewish fighting force to serve in a campaign to free Palestine from Turkish rule.

It was in connection with this scheme that Jabotinsky's interest in America was aroused. Undoubtedly, he was drawn to the idea of a fighting force for the same reasons he was attracted to the frontier, to American pioneering, to Theodore Roosevelt. Not in psychology and emotions, however, but in politics lay the rationale of his project. He believed that Jews' participation in the armed struggle would give them a claim to the spoils of war. In fact, they would have participated in the battle for the one prize they wanted, the land of Israel. It took almost three years of single-minded effort on Jabotinsky's part and of much agitation on the part of others to bring the Jewish Legion into being. In that initiative American public opinion played a role which has, until now, been virtually unnoticed by historians of the period.[20]

The Legion was not intended by Jabotinsky to address only the issue of the ultimate disposition of Palestine. On both sides of the lines in World War I Jews rallied to the colors with the same enthusiasm as other citizens. In neutral countries, and principally in the United States, opinion was divided. In eastern Europe, Germany was liberating Jews from Russian oppression; in the Jewish world, in general, Germany had long been admired for her "superior culture"; and in the United States there was considerable sympathy for Ottoman Turkey to which the American government had posted two Jewish ambassadors over the years, including the incumbent. On the other hand, German ambivalence regarding Jews was well-known, while Turkey opposed Zionism and was treating the Jews of Palestine harshly. Britain, however, had been politically active on behalf of beleaguered Jews for many years and was considered most likely to promote the goals of Zionism. And it was known as a very hospitable country to Jews and Judaism. But the British were allied with Russia, the country most oppressive to Jews, and the place from which a large number of North American and British Jews had fled. Both the Germans and the British expended considerable effort in trying to overcome their negative image and in wooing American Jews, partly because of an exaggerated estimation of Jewish power.[21] Jabotinsky envisioned the Legion as a valuable propaganda weapon for the British, whom he favored in the war, as well as a desirable political instrument for the Jews.

By the spring of 1915 Jabotinsky was in London lobbying for the Legion. A relentless campaigner, he badgered politicians, fellow Zionists, people of the press, and others likely to help. In December 1915, he wrote to C. P. Scott, editor of the Manchester *Guardian*, Liberal politician, and friend of Zionism, that among "the Jews of America . . . the Jewish Legion would be . . . a powerful means of propaganda for the Allies." He reminded Scott of Jews' "influence" in the United States and went on to suggest, that "the only way to counter-balance their ill will towards Russia was to appeal to their attachment to Palestine."[22] A copy of that letter with a covering explanation was sent a few days later to Lord Robert Cecil, the parliamentary undersecretary for foreign affairs.[23]

Early in the new year Jabotinsky spelled out his case in full in his yet imperfect English to C. F. G. Masterman, the director of Wellington House, which oversaw Britain's war propaganda. In what sounded like a veiled threat, he invoked the specter of Jewish power, rather as Ambassador Morgenthau was doing implicitly in Turkey to defend the embattled *yishuv*. Jabotinsky recounted to Masterman American Jews' alleged power, not only in their own country but also in "international politics. I have to remember here," the journalist wrote, "only one fact: it was their influence which led to the rupture of the commercial treaties between the United States and Russia." He described the "Jews of America" to Masterman as "utterly democratic and pacifist . . . [and] by nature essentially anti-Russian." Still, he claimed, they were drawn to Britain because of her long-standing support of Zionism. And that was the only possible "lever" England might use to win them over wholeheartedly to the Allied cause. Jabotinsky offered to organize Allied propaganda among American Jews, if the British government would agree to form the Legion. By 1917 Chaim Weizmann was using similar arguments in his negotiations with the British government. Zionists in America, such as Jacob De Haas and the Palestinian Eliyahu Lewin-Epstein, confirmed the claims.[24]

On occasion Jabotinsky used a somewhat different approach. The pacifism of American Jews—including prominent Zionists, such as Rabbi Stephen S. Wise, Henrietta Szold, and Rabbi Judah Magnes, later the founding president of the Hebrew University and a leader of the movement for a binational, Arab-Jewish state—was well advertised.[25] (In 1929 Jabotinsky would assert that Magnes's "whining" pacifism, steadfast even in the face of Arab terror, "nauseate[d]" him.[26]) In England the unwillingness of Jewish immigrants of Russian origin in London's East End to volunteer for service in either the Russian or the British army became less and less tolerable to public opinion as the war dragged on and losses mounted. The resourceful lobbyist argued that if Jews were marked as pacifists or as lukewarm patriots, then antisemitism would increase in both the United States and Britain. Jews would then be increasingly unwelcome immigrants to America. That, he implied, would make their evacuation from Britain after the war less likely and might result in more Russian Jews immigrating to Britain rather than to the United States.[27]

Even after the entry into the war of America, Jabotinsky was asserting that only the Legion and the promise of Palestine could overcome American Jews' deep-seated pacifism.[28] He informed British policymakers that "the Zionist Organization in the U.S. . . . under the chairmanship of Mr. L. Brandeis (Judge of the Supreme Court), is the strongest of Jewish organizations in the world."²⁹ And there is evidence to suggest that his rhetoric carried some weight.³⁰ Later, he would claim to British politicians, with some exaggeration, that the Legion together with the Balfour Declaration and the campaign for Palestine had won over American Jewry to the Allied cause and propelled the United States into the war.³¹ Implied, of course, was a reminder of the debt owed to him and to Zionism by Great Britain, a debt the British became ever more reluctant to repay.

The Legion was the first issue in which America figured as a major political factor for Jabotinsky. It also provided his first extensive contact with Americans: one of its three battalions of Royal Fusiliers was manned largely by North Americans, most of them immigrants without Canadian or American citizenship, a number of whom had come from Palestine. Although no exact figures are available, it seems that some 1,500 Jews from North America served.³² The Legion, in which Jabotinsky held the rank of lieutenant, participated in the latter phases of the Palestine campaign as a unit of the British army, just as he had originally imagined.

The cessation of hostilities, however, brought disillusionment to its founder, who had imagined that the foreign Legionnaires would settle in Palestine after demobilization and that the Legion would remain as a Jewish unit within the permanent British force there.³³ But the battalions were disbanded. Neither the British government nor the Zionist Commission, which had come to Palestine to administer the *yishuv* on behalf of the World Zionist Organization (WZO), was of much help in promoting the settlement of discharged soldiers.³⁴ Most of them returned to Britain and North America, leaving behind in Palestine a sense that "the most magnificent vision of our times had come to an end."³⁵ A few months earlier the Legionnaires had been greeted with eager expectation. Now they were regarded by many veteran settlers as having committed an act of "national treachery."³⁶

Even before the soldiers began to return, rumblings about them could be heard among Palestinian old-timers. David Ben-Gurion found his soldier comrades from America too doctrinaire in their socialism and too immersed in Yiddish culture for life in Hebrew-speaking Palestine. Columnists in *Ha-Po'el HaTza'ir*, the Palestinian Labor journal, complained about the "childish," "whining" Legionnaires from America, who "wanted the table set for them, so they could 'make whoopee.' "³⁷

Although he had to deal with the Americans at their most difficult, Jabotinsky usually refrained from criticizing them. In the spring and summer of 1919, with Palestine secure, with the British ever less enthusiastic about the politics of a Jewish fighting force, and with the separation from family becoming harder to bear for the men in uniform, several nasty incidents occurred, including two mutinies that resulted in courts-martial and unreasonable punishments. Jabotinsky acted as lawyer for the accused, almost all of whom were North Americans. He had counseled the soldiers to endure the harshness of military life for the good of the *yishuv*, but he did not fault them for rebelling against what he described as "the anti-Semitism which has been cultivated for so long a time by higher ranks [and which] seems to have now reached the private soldier."[38] If anything, Jabotinsky appreciated the Americans' unwillingness to tolerate British racism. He agreed that they had been duped into a "swindle" of the American-Jewish public, who believed that the British unequivocally backed the Jewish cause, when, in fact, many of them harbored deep-seated animosity towards Jews.[39]

Jabotinsky greatly regretted that more of the North Americans did not remain in Palestine. Nonetheless, he later recalled them as an admirable lot, in contrast to the British Legionnaires. The American volunteers, he said, were rather like the pioneers of whom he had read in his youth: quick-witted and "strictly practical," eager to fight, "of a high order of intelligence, of bravery, and of physical development." On the other hand, the British Jews, who were conscripts, had a Latin, "*mañana*" mentality and preferred training for battle to fighting.[40] When they returned to North America, many of the ex-Legionnaires remained close to Zionism and to Jabotinsky personally. A few, such as Elias Ginsburg, eventually formed the American nucleus of the militant Zionist-Revisionist movement. Others could be relied upon for donations to Revisionist causes, to form an honor guard when Jabotinsky came to town, or a bodyguard to strong-arm his opponents, as proved necessary during his 1922 visit to Toronto. Even people peripherally involved in the Legion assisted their charismatic lieutenant in his later ventures. Some of the veterans eventually returned to Palestine as settlers.[41]

There were other North American twists to Jabotinsky's involvement with the Legion and his acquaintance with the North Americans in its ranks. At the outset he had sensed how America might be used as a stick with which to beat the British into forming the Legion. Still in 1919 he was reminding the peacemakers that the English-speaking peoples had no moral grounds on which to oppose Zionism, since Jewish colonization of Palestine was no less just than British colonization of Canada, Australia, and the United States. At first, the American argument had been a stick used to complement a number of carrot arguments in favor of the Legion. Later, American support became vital to the very life of the Legion. Jabotinsky solicited funds in America for soldiers' welfare. He pleaded for the support of the Zionist Organization of America (ZOA) in pressing Britain to remove antisemitic officers from their commands and to compensate its American soldiers at the same rate as British soldiers to prevent their disaffection. He wrote to Brandeis that the Legion could become a significant institution, a real instrument of Zionist policy, only if it were "openly supported by American friends."⁴² When that support was not forthcoming, the Legion indeed ceased to exist.

There were other blows dealt by Americans in these years. In early 1919 in one of several changes of the guard at the Zionist Commission, Jabotinsky was pushed out of his position as head of the Commission's political department. Although Chaim Weizmann seems to have orchestrated the change from London, those who carried out the orders were two Americans: Dr. Harry Friedenwald, the acting chairman of the Commission, and Robert Szold, who replaced Jabotinsky as Commission spokesman. When Brandeis visited Palestine in July 1919, Jabotinsky met him together with Szold. The soldier tried to convince the jurist of the need for speaking out forcefully against the incipient hostility to Zionism of the military authorities in Palestine and of the government in London. Brandeis was not persuaded. Inclined still to trust the British, he declared the warrior unfit for Zionist service in Palestine.⁴³

A year later another *contretemps* further poisoned relations between the two. Jabotinsky, Ginsburg, and a number of others had been imprisoned for participating in the unauthorized armed defense of Palestine Jews during Arab riots. The American Zionist journal *The New Palestine* called for their release, as did a special meeting of the ZOA. Philanthropist Nathan Straus offered Jabotinsky a loan for the support of his family. Louis Lipsky and others proposed that American Zionists organize mass protest meetings. The British ambassador in Washington, sensitive to public opinion, reported to the Foreign Office that Jabotinsky's release would make "an excellent impression" in the United States. Brandeis and his followers, however, objected to the protests, fearing that the mob might get out of hand. Then the new British high commissioner, Herbert Samuel, eager to appear evenhanded, decided to amnesty the Palestinians together with Arabs who had been convicted of raping Jewish women during the riots. Jabotinsky wanted Brandeis, then chairing a conference of world Zionist leaders in London, to protest Samuel's equating Jewish self-defense with Arab rape and terror. Apparently Brandeis never received Jabotinsky's request for help; but Jabotinsky assumed the judge had ignored it. Relations between them would never again be cordial.⁴⁴

Jabotinsky was a manic optimist and a forgiving man, who took account of political realities when it suited him. Although American Jews had let him down, he remained an admirer of their virtues and accomplishments. He championed the American Zionist Medical Unit, which, like the Legion, was greeted with tremendous enthusiasm by the war-ravaged population when it arrived in Palestine. Its arrival was looked upon as a sign of the growing commitment of American Jewry to the Zionist enterprise. Within a short time, however, the Unit and its sponsoring organization were embroiled in local politics, in particular with the socialist Zionists. The Americans were accused of medical imperialism and of the arrogance typical of Europeans bearing the "white man's burden" in what was not yet known as the "Third World." Jabotinsky agreed that local control of medical institutions was desirable; but he recognized that the local doctors, practicing as they were in a provincial backwater, had lost touch with recent medical advances and lacked the resources to establish an effective health-care system. The Unit, or Hadassah Medical Organization, as it came to be known, represented, Jabotinsky asserted in 1919, "a very great step . . . forward" for Palestine; both the Americans and the Palestinians ought "to be proud" of it. For the moment, at any rate, it was irreplaceable.[45]

Jabotinsky was generous in his postwar evaluation of the United States and its role in the momentous events of the recent past. He believed the American Senate's refusal to ratify the Treaty of Versailles and to permit the United States to enter the League of Nations signified "the moral collapse of America" and rendered her participation in the war no more than "a strange mistake, a laughable misunderstanding." But he recognized that some Americans opposed the League out of noble motives. Leftists, he wrote in a late 1919 essay in Hadshot HaAretz, the Palestine daily, wanted a peace based on mutual forgiveness, not on the submission of Germany. He presciently agreed with their assessment that the treaty, as it stood, did little more than sow the seeds of future war.[46] Some years later he wrote even more magnanimously, if rather naively, of America's role in World War I, perhaps recalling her early interventions in Palestine. America went to war, he said, "in an exemplary fashion. There was no material aspect to her act, neither economic nor political. America entered the war because of the pure, passive pressure of the masses: because of a sense of 'mission,' because of an undefined but powerful desire for sacrifice, for making the world a better place."[47] America, for Jabotinsky, was still the land of Lincoln and Teddy Roosevelt. And its Senate, if it sometimes acted foolishly, wisely isolated America from "the riff-raff of other nations" by limiting immigration, and from the encroachments of foreign countries by enforcing "the Torah of Monroe."[48]

3

It was not without preparation, then, that Jabotinsky boarded the ship for America in early November 1921. He went, not as a tourist to view the frontier that had occupied his imagination, nor as an old soldier to renew contact with his former comrades in arms, but as a member of both a five-man fund-raising delegation of the Palestine Foundation Fund (Keren

HaYesod) and the WZO executive. It was less to the land of the pioneers that he set out than to the land of dollars.

Money seems to have been one aspect of American life that occupied Jabotinsky but little, before he assumed an official position in the Zionist movement. As a member of the Foundation Fund board of directors, however, he shared responsibility for finding the resources to finance the rebuilding of Palestine, a hoped-for £25 million by 1925. In addition, the WZO sought $12 million to cover its expenses in Palestine and London between 1921 and 1924.[49] These were sums unprecedented in Zionist fund raising. They were needed desperately and quickly, and there was little chance of finding them anywhere but in North America. Russian Jews were without funds and lived under the Bolsheviks, who were unsympathetic to Zionism. Poland was impoverished. German, French, and British Jewries were beginning to recover from the war but were still—and, as it turned out, permanently—weakened. Jabotinsky wrote to his mother in Jerusalem from the ship taking him to New York, that the WZO "would have had to declare bankruptcy, if it were not for the opportunity" in America.[50] At least three-quarters of its budget would have to be raised there "for obvious reasons," and as large a proportion of the Foundation Fund.[51] Jabotinsky and the other members of the delegation spent about half a year at their task. They followed on the heels of Chaim Weizmann and Albert Einstein, who had devoted their efforts to the Foundation Fund just a few months earlier.

In an exhausting series of one-night stands across America from Omaha to Norwich, Connecticut, in synagogues, homes, and New York's huge Lexington Avenue Armory, "Jabotinsky, the orator, the linguist, the publicist, the poet, . . . the statesman,"[52] spoke effectively in Hebrew, Yiddish, and English to young people and adults, in mass meetings and intimate gatherings. Nahum Sokolow headed the delegation; and it was he who was received at the State Department and at the White House by President Harding, perhaps rankling the ambitious and more dynamic junior delegate. Jabotinsky was also absent from a national ZOA convention in Philadelphia in March 1922.[53] Wherever he did go, however, the Legion hero was "received with enthusiasm" by the Jewish public. In Chicago, "the audience rose to its feet and greeted . . . [Jabotinsky] with shouts of 'Hurrah!' and prolonged, stormy applause." Among the admirers of his performance in New York's Carnegie Hall in November was Berl Katznelson.[54]

Jabotinsky found fund raising preferable to sitting in his London office. Like others before and after, however, he was disappointed by the results of his labor.[55] Donations were forthcoming, but "not nearly enough." The "world crisis" that had also depressed the American economy was part of the problem, as were "the inertia and lethargy which . . . had reigned supreme for so long" in American Zionism.[56]

Vladimir Jabotinsky

Another difficulty was posed by civil war in the Zionist camp. Weizmann had just succeeded in deposing Brandeis and his associates from their offices in the ZOA. Many of the potential major donors and the best fund raisers were allied with Brandeis and were not now inclined to cooperate wholeheartedly with the Europeans. An important aspect of the struggle between the Weizmann and Brandeis forces, moreover, had to do with the management of funds. Weizmann and his American associates were regarded by their opponents—and others—as having little competence in that area.[57] Jabotinsky supported the Weizmann coup, in part, no doubt, because of his earlier encounters with the judge. More to the point, he very strongly disagreed with Brandeis's conviction that in the post-Balfour Declaration era, Zionist political activism was outmoded; and he feared the domination of the movement by the Americans, who were expected to provide some 80 percent of Palestine development funds.[58]

Still, he tried during his visit to establish a liaison with Brandeis and his friends through Julian Mack and Rabbi Stephen Wise. An opening was provided by his agreement with the judge on the strict construction of the Zionist mission, in opposition to Weizmann's vision of the WZO as the representative body of world Jewry on all matters of national importance. Brandeis, however, would have nothing to do with the "Jewish Garibaldi."[59]

A political problem of his own making also plagued Jabotinsky. Following the Bolshevik Revolution, Ukraine enjoyed independence for a short time, always under Russian siege. The protracted fighting was marked by a series of bloody pogroms, for which Jews held the nationalist leader, Simon Petliura, responsible. By 1921 the Ukrainian nationalists had been defeated, but it was thought that with Western aid they might stage a comeback. Shortly before sailing for the United States, Jabotinsky entered into negotiations with a representative of Petliura of his acquaintance, to ensure that any future Ukrainian army would include a Jewish self-defense force. Many Jews, especially on the Left, felt it was inappropriate to negotiate with the perpetrators of pogroms. The American Labor Zionists waged war against Jabotinsky in their new Yiddish-language daily, *Di Tsayt*, urging him to resign his post on the Zionist Executive. By early 1922, the acrimony had abated somewhat, although the effectiveness of the hero of the Legion in Labor circles had been seriously undermined.[60]

A further complicating factor was the fund drive itself. What must have been most painful to Jabotinsky was that he had foreseen many of the technical problems. A year before coming to America, he had cautioned the directorate of the Foundation Fund against "planless and confused appeals." He insisted that no campaign get under way before the method of collection and the manner of distributing the proceeds had been decided upon.[61] He urged that propaganda and fund raising be separated; that house-to-house canvassing be instituted as the chief means of collecting money; and that the innovative methods used successfully by the Hadassah organization in the United States be adopted by other Zionist groups.[62] Instead, his trip was plagued by "the same old mistake with which we have to struggle in England: relying on propaganda, public meetings, and banquets instead of personal canvassing . . . all our experience here has amply proved that in America, more than anywhere else, only the fringe of the Jewish population can be reached through these methods." Jabotinsky submitted to the Fund a detailed plan for house-to-house solicitation in the New York area, which was later implemented partially with some success; and he conducted at least one workshop for volunteers.[63] He conceded that in America large public meetings might be necessary "to create an appropriate atmosphere." But he remained generally dissatisfied with American planning and methods.[64]

Especially unsatisfactory was the approach to the "business class" of American Jews. "The reason," the swashbuckling Legion veteran reiterated to his London colleagues, was "the way in which our Palestine work is being carried on . . . without system and without understanding, in an old-fashioned, romantic and disorderly way."[65] Similar complaints would be voiced in subsequent years by many of the Palestinian emissaries to North America: Yitzhak Ben-Zvi, Arthur Ruppin, Golda Meir, and others.[66] Those who directed the campaigns in America and Europe and those who spent the money in Palestine, however, preferred receiving less to succumbing to American efficiency. For them, Zionism was a romantic enterprise, not a business. The solution to sluggish fund raising offered by Louis Lipsky, the new head of the ZOA and Weizmann's lieutenant in America, Jabotinsky found chilling. Lipsky thought a spring pogrom in Palestine would be just the thing to "increase the collections."[67] Jabotinsky, who professed to "believe in private enterprise in Palestine," preferred the establishment of a club of one thousand merchants and industrialists, each of whom would donate one thousand dollars to the Foundation Fund; and he looked forward to the success of "the Brandeis Group and other [business] groups." He also proposed a policy he would soon repudiate: alliance with the wealthy, acculturated non-Zionists.[68]

Besides his fund-raising tasks, Jabotinsky found time for other activities during his first North American visit. He participated in the negotiations between the American Zionists and his friend Pinhas Rutenberg, who was raising capital for Palestine's first hydro-electric station.[69] Politics were always his concern; and he discovered that his notion of America as a lever with which to move the British, and now the League of Nations, was still useful. It was Weizmann who urged using the ploy during the debate in Palestine and in Britain, which culminated in the issuance of the white paper of 1922. That document reiterated the Balfour Declaration but limited its application geographically and politically. Its proclamation was part of the process of gaining League ratification of the Mandate. Jabotinsky wrote Weizmann that the ZOA should "inform" the British ambassador that the situation in Palestine was harming fund raising in the United States and causing antagonism towards Britain. A delegation to President Harding was planned, as well as mass meetings of sympathetic gentiles and acculturated Jews to stir up American public opinion. In April Weizmann requested that Jabotinsky marshal all the support he could for American adherence to the Mandate. The politicking included lobbying for the pro-Zionist, Joint Congressional Resolution, which was passed while Jabotinsky was in the United States in 1922. The usually dauntless Jabotinsky had at first been "uneasy" about the resolution, fearing that it might "do the cause more harm than good," should it fail.[70]

His official duties left Jabotinsky little time for private affairs. But he was by now a family man with a wife and son in Europe to support and a mother and sister in Palestine whom he helped from time to time. Before the war he had earned his living as a journalist. Under the Bolsheviks, however, Russian papers would not employ him; and the *émigré* press to which he contributed did not pay. In early 1918, when he was still in uniform, he had been approached by the *Morgn Zhurnal*, one of New York's largest Yiddish-language dailies. He turned the offer down, partly because he felt it might contravene military regulations.

By early 1920, however, he was endeavoring to make contact with American papers in the hope of putting his personal finances in order. During his imprisonment in Palestine, he had begun a Hebrew translation of *The Divine Comedy* at the request of a New York publisher, but the project was stillborn, because his knowledge of Hebrew was inadequate. Toward the end of his North American visit, he received an offer from Dr. S. M. Melamed, editor of the Chicago *Daily Jewish Courier*. Melamed agreed to accept his submissions, provided they were "not a learned and sociological [sic] treatise, but a series of interesting stories." Jabotinsky did not usually produce light-hearted stories. Melamed's words undoubtedly reminded him of his earlier perception of Americans as addicted to frothy "entertainments." He commented disdainfully that every issue of every American newspaper had an interview with "some Peaches," but seldom a full account of affairs in Washington. Some time later Jabotinsky referred to Melamed as a "tasteless, slum language" journalist. A year after his return to Europe, Jabotinsky accepted an offer from New York's *Di Warheit*. After three articles, however, the editor canceled the contract, complaining that Jabotinsky was recycling his essays, which were, in any case, too difficult for the paper's readers.[71]

All in all, Jabotinsky's first visit to North America ended on a low note. Of the United States he remembered little that was positive. He met with old friends in California and Texas; he was greeted in many places by Legion veterans, attended a Legion ball in New York, and addressed a reunion in Philadelphia. But while the former Legionnaires displayed warmth and nostalgia, they failed to heed his call to erect a concert hall in Palestine as a memorial to the fallen of the World War and to settle the country's dangerous border regions.[72]

Most American Jews he found dull and provincial, except for a few, like Brandeis and Mack, with whom he did not get on. American Zionism he thought disorganized, no better than that of prewar Odessa. And it was being destroyed by its overwhelming concern with fund raising, which was not even that successful. He saw no chance of American aliyah, the supposed goal of Zionists everywhere.[73] He visited Mormon leaders in Utah and was impressed with their system of tithing. But he knew Jews were too individualistic to submit to it, despite its biblical origins. He took note of Prohibition and other Blue Laws, which he read as retrograde inversions of America's pioneering spirit and willingness for sacrifice. Jabotinsky had never forgotten his reservations about the United States based on the treatment of blacks. In prison in Palestine in 1920, he had lectured about it to fellow inmates. Now in Texas he witnessed a parade of the Ku Klux Klan, which convinced him that both Jews and blacks in the United States would one day have to undertake their own physical defense.[74] About a year after he returned to Europe, Jabotinsky pronounced the final judgment on his trip. He declared that future visits by Zionist leaders would be "futile" and doubted that even "a successful *tournée* . . . in America" could save Zionism "for long."[75]

4

Jabotinsky's pessimism regarding North America was, no doubt, partly a function of his growing misgivings about the Zionist movement in general. In early 1923 he dramatically resigned not only his executive position but even his membership in the WZO, in disgust with Weizmann's leadership. Subsequently he resigned as a director of the Palestine Foundation Fund, as well. In time he would become the leader of the main opposition to the Zionist establishment. For now, however, he was a free man; and the freedom allowed him to reassess some of his political and intellectual positions. Included in the reassessment were his views of America. It is probably not unfair to say that Jabotinsky's temperament was better suited to opposition than to team play, and to leadership rather than power sharing. Some of his long-held notions, moreover, fitted well into the framework of his new political stance.

Vladimir Jabotinsky

One area in which he revised his views was economics. For a time he had been quite close to socialism in his essential outlook, although he sometimes nodded in the direction of free enterprise. Now he developed a thoroughgoing appreciation of capitalism and the bourgeoisie, partly in reaction to developments in Russia. "The real beggars' kingdom," he wrote, "is in Soviet Russia, not in England, nor in France, nor even in America."[76] He maintained that the bourgeoisie was the only creative element of society. To prove that dubious thesis, he rewrote Jewish history, depicting the ancient Israelites as shopkeepers rather than the farmers and shepherds portrayed in the Bible and other sources.[77]

The American business ethos looked better from this new perspective. Sinclair Lewis's quintessential bourgeois boor, George Babbitt, Jabotinsky described as "lively, thriving, [and] vigorous."[78] American "pioneering," he asserted, "had not come to an end, it had merely taken on another form," big business. Years after the inner circle of President Harding—all businessmen and their associates—had been exposed as corrupt mediocrities, Jabotinsky, without a trace of irony, extolled those "self-made men" and the system that had propelled such "excellent people" to the fore. On the eve of the Great Depression, he acclaimed Herbert Hoover as a stalwart opponent of "both socialism and that public phenomenon known in America as radicalism." Hoover, he said, like Harding, exemplified American individualism at its best. While socialism and autocracy stifled the individual and, therefore, production, the American business ethos allowed a person "to develop his aspirations ... and his mind" to the full. In 1987 the *Wall Street Journal* enshrined Jabotinsky in the capitalist pantheon by reprinting his sixty-year-old essay, "We Bourgeois."[79]

His new esteem for American capitalism promised to make the United States a more congenial sphere of activity, especially since wealth there was now also buying culture. By the early 1920s, Jabotinsky noted, the United States had well-endowed universities with some 600,000 students and "some of Europe's best professors"; New York's Metropolitan Museum of Art was one of the finest in the world; and its Metropolitan Opera boasted "all the best voices of Europe" including Caruso.[80] American Jews might, perhaps, be weaned of their mindlessness.

Jabotinsky was not prepared to embrace capitalists unconditionally. Once he had thought that the "Yahoodim" of America, the prosperous, acculturated Jews of German extraction, were different from "the assimilating Jews of Europe," more "prepared to work for the rebirth of the land of Israel even though to a man they fail to understand the concept of nationalism."[81] Now, perhaps because of his objections to Weizmann, he declared unalterable opposition to his former colleague's pet scheme, an enlarged Jewish Agency for the development of Palestine, which would include in its directorate wealthy Jews, most of them Americans. Jabotinsky argued that coopting money moguls, who were prepared to finance the rebuilding of the Holy Land although they opposed political Zionism, was an antidemocratic measure that would result in relinquishing control over activities in Palestine to the non-Zionists. Although his objections were chiefly political, his perfervid rhetoric sounded like that of an angry Marxist.[82] He inveighed against the fat-cat "mulattoes and mongrels oscillating between 'pro-Palestine' and 'contra-Palestine' " positions, the "Fifth Avenue ghetto" crowd, as he would later call them, who, he suggested on one occasion, "should drown themselves together with their banking accounts."[83]

He began to articulate a philosophy of financing the *yishuv* that called for investment on a business basis rather than charity and for the aggressive marketing in North America of Palestine products. Earlier he had come to the conclusion that the unbusinesslike behavior of Zionist leaders was self-defeating. Now he began to move close to the Brandeis-Mack position on financial matters, which he had rejected by backing Weizmann only a few years before. By the late twenties he was arguing that "the secret of successful colonization" in Palestine lay in attracting private capital. These notions were not unique to him. Socialist Zionists were also beginning to move in some of the same directions in these years. And, like them, Jabotinsky maintained that the WZO "should have a monopoly on the management of natural resources" and communications.[84]

But it was less in economics than in culture that Jabotinsky saw America in the "roaring twenties" taming the frontier and leading the way for the Old World. He took note of *Mantrap*, a novel by Sinclair Lewis set on the "northwest frontier" of North America, in Canada. The book's characters he perceived as rugged, old-fashioned American heroes, "extraordinarily brave, noble, and strong."[85] In American music, dance, and film, new frontiers were opening up; undreamt of boundaries were being crossed; old codes of behavior could be broken publicly. "Jazz, the fox trot, and Harold Lloyd" he saw as expressions of "a philosophy . . . not far from that of . . . the pioneers," a philosophy of breaking through established norms. Once the purpose of the dance had been to suggest the erotic; in its latest American versions, Jabotinsky the culture critic wrote, it had become itself an erotic act.[86]

To be sure, such revolutionary energy could be dangerous. The forces loosed might never be harnessed. America was a country "looking for some dragon, some evil witch" to slay, "some battlefield on which to venture" forth. She had no direction yet and could easily be led astray. Her "tremendous ethical ardor" was already being channeled in frivolous, sometimes ominous, directions, like the Scopes Trial, Prohibition, vegetarianism, and the Ku Klux Klan. That fervor inspired the imaginations of Europe's young fascists, stirred by the world they viewed in American films, to demand a bigger slice of the economic pie; and it led them to believe that brute force was a morally acceptable way of achieving their goal.[87] On the whole, however, American adventurousness, which encouraged opposition to traditional and received wisdom, was promising for the world, Jabotinsky believed.

In the eagerness to disregard old norms and break through into uncharted terrain he perceived a lesson for American Zionism and, through it, for the Zionist movement as a whole. He had "complete faith in 'the third generation' of the American Diaspora."[88] Youthful leaders of American Zionism, unfettered by hoary tradition, could "play a leading part" in revivifying the WZO, and "not only in financial matters." Conditions in America were right. "The very atmosphere of this country, the magnificent sweep of its initiative ought to prompt the American organization to lead . . . every movement intended to rejuvenate Zionism, to instill courage instead of timidity, to broaden the avenues we have to trudge."[89] America was "the richest, the youngest, the most vigorous" of the world's countries, with "a tremendous amount of energy."[90] Just as American film had become "the greatest revolutionary influence in the world," so American Zionism could again "actively encourage . . . revolutionary propaganda," which he saw as vital to a stagnating movement.[91] There was danger for Jews, too, in the cowboy spirit. The pragmatism and "the flexibility" of American Zionism had so far amounted to little more than a lack of principles. The movement lurched from program to program, from ideal to ideal, embracing each in turn with intense but misplaced and thoughtless vigor. Often, he said, it threw its "spineless" weight behind causes of little merit in a destructive way. On balance, however, the American spirit of rebellion offered hope to the "tired and weary" Jews of the Old World, just as it did to the gentiles.[92]

5

By the end of 1923 Jabotinsky had returned to the political fray and within a few months was organizing a new movement soon to become known as Revisionist (and later, New) Zionism. Although he regarded North American support as "pivotal" to the success of Revisionism, he had not maintained his contacts there and needed to seek out allies.[93] As might be expected, he began the search among Legion veterans.[94] Probably through the auspices of one of them, Joseph Brainin, he received an offer from impresario Sol Hurok to tour North America in early 1926. The reborn politician was so eager to garner support there that he accepted Hurok's offer in preference to one for the same honorarium but only half as many lectures in Poland.[95] A number of establishment Zionists eager to inject some "excitement into the[ir] quiet, complacent camp" helped to underwrite the trip.[96]

Jabotinsky's five-and-a-half-month-long itinerary included meetings with old friends and a few media celebrities, and visits to the movies and to the theater "to see nude girls," who, he felt, were not presented "as well . . . [in New York] as in Paris." He corresponded with a Jewish inmate in New York's Attica prison.[97] Apparently he cooperated with Yitzḥak Ben-Zvi, who also "toured" North America in 1926, in the procurement of arms for the nascent Jewish self-defense forces of the *yishuv*.[98] He was invited to address a Jewish National Fund mass meeting in New York along with Chaim Naḥman Bialik. Years before he had translated some of Bialik's poems into Russian; and as a welcome for the bard he published an article on his "poetic range" in *The New Palestine*, the English-language organ of the ZOA. In a public debate in New York's Town Hall, however, the two clashed over the role of Hebrew in the Diaspora; and Jabotinsky's opponents had good reason to believe that Bialik had joined their ranks.[99]

The most time-consuming of Jabotinsky's extracurricular activities were connected with publishing and journalism. He negotiated with American firms regarding the publication in English of some of his own works. He sought backing for Hasefer, a company he hoped would publish Hebrew translations of some of his favorite American authors, such as Cooper, Harte, Stowe, and Zane Grey, whose books he had "really understood . . . felt [and] . . . digested" as a young lad. His goal was to provide for youngsters in the *yishuv* muscular role models different from the more pacific heroes of rabbinic literature. His "pet project" was the *Hebrew Geographical Atlas*, on which he collaborated with Dr. Samuel Perlman of the Boston Hebrew Teachers' College, whom he had first met in Alexandria during the war. Jabotinsky passionately solicited support for his publishing ventures from "notables," such as Nathan Straus, and Rabbis Abba Hillel Silver and Stephen S. Wise; but Hasefer went bankrupt even before he left America.[100]

The lack of an alternative led Jabotinsky to regard the American-Jewish press as his "last [possible] source of [a secure] income."[101] Journals, including the *The New Palestine*, *Der Tog*, *Der Morgn Zhurnal*, and the Jewish Telegraphic Agency *Bulletin*, now sought him out; and he successfully concluded long-term agreements with the latter two. Even before the editor of the *Morgn Zhurnal* whittled down the agreed-upon fee, however, he had noted that the arrangements were not likely to make him "a rich man." Still, they provided some income during the remainder of the decade and an American platform for his views, not only on Zionist politics and world affairs but also in the broad area of culture, about which he so much enjoyed writing. From time to time he commented insightfully on aspects of Ameri-

Vladimir Jabotinsky

can Jewish life which would not have interested a less curious and wide-ranging visitor, such as Hebrew-speaking summer camps.[102]

The chief motivation for this second American tour was the lectures arranged by Hurok; and Jabotinsky devoted most of his attention to them. At first, he sent upbeat reports to his mother and sister in Jerusalem that the "lectures [are] going well [and] paying me well, [and the] press [is] treating me well," that his appearances had "been very successful, more so than in Europe."[103] To his wife, however, he admitted the truth: he was being greeted by "empty halls." At the opening lecture in New York only one seat in three was filled. He complained to Rabbi Abba Hillel Silver of Cleveland, that "nobody [in your city] seems to want me."[104] Hurok lost money on the tour; and Jabotinsky did not make much, which he greatly regretted. He had hoped to use the proceeds of the lectures to put Revisionism on its financial feet. In March he cabled his wife to tell his coworkers that there was "no money here."[105]

The explanation for his poor reception lay partly in the fact that many American Zionists were unnerved by outspoken opposition to the Zionist establishment. Robert Silverman claimed, albeit after the fact, that in sponsoring Jabotinsky's visit, he and his friends had "not intend[ed] to become parties to . . . a new movement to talk out Dr. Weizmann [sic] from the leadership of the World Zionist Organization."[106] At times Jabotinsky and his supporters complained of a "boycott." And, indeed, a number of people—including David Remez and Avraham Harzfeld, Palestinian labor movement leaders then on their own "tour" of America—lobbied against him. So, too, did Louis Lipsky, who, according to Jabotinsky, was "too slippery" and just "didn't understand which way the wind was blowing."[107] Shmuel Katz claims that ZOA stalwarts pressured potential supporters into backing off and cites the case of Nathan Straus. According to Katz, Straus had promised twenty-five thousand dollars for the New Zionist Party but reneged after being convinced of the danger to Zionism of Jabotinsky's maximalist plans and intemperate language.[108]

But the visitor recognized that his lack of appeal in America also had something to do with his not having done his homework before coming. Most American Zionists, he felt, were callow "youths or people of the past generation," who were simply unprepared for his message. They were not cut from the same yard of cloth as his literary and historical heroes. They were, as he put it some time later in a retrospective evaluation of the tour, "less Jewish" than Europeans, who understood him more readily, and "less Jewish" than he had expected.[109]

After fulfilling his obligations to Hurok, Jabotinsky, who was never down for long, turned renewed energies to political organizing. He detected encouraging signs, only some of them products of his imagination. In fact,

Zionist officialdom had not been unalterably opposed to him until he attacked its "blind and stupid bosses" head-on. As one observer noted, prominent ZOA members "coquetted" with Jabotinsky until he posed a threat to them all.[110] Although Katz suggests that the flirting was designed only to prevent the establishment of an alternative Zionist organization,[111] opposition had smoldered in the ranks of the ZOA since the days of the Weizmann coup. As time went on, Lipsky's lackluster leadership fanned the flames of discontent. By 1926 the Brandeisists were emerging from their long sulk and starting to reassert themselves. Jabotinsky thought that Mack "and his friends were beginning to draw close," that Maurice Samuel and Meyer Weisgal, two well-known Zionist figures, were on the verge of an alliance, and that even "Lipsky more or less" agreed with his program.

In the years immediately following, cooperation with the Brandeis Group seemed increasingly to be a possibility. Revisionists participated in Group conferences. The weak response by Britain to the 1929 Arab riots in Palestine prompted several Brandeisists to express preference for Jabotinsky's more forceful style to Weizmann's wishy-washy leadership. Brandeis himself now thought the "Revisionists . . . right in . . . much." He still doubted Jabotinsky's judgment and urged his followers "to go slow on hitching up" with him. But he refused even to discuss a proposal for Arab-Jewish power sharing suggested by Judah Magnes with the backing of Felix Warburg and other non-Zionists active in the enlarged Jewish Agency.[112]

In a surge of hopefulness, Jabotinsky wrote to his wife in 1926 that he was looking forward to "a Zionist revolution greater than I achieved in Europe." But he conceded more realistically, that he might be "mistaken." A few Zionists, most of them old cronies, who "treated [him] . . . with respect," provided "the opportunity for organizing a [Revisionist] party" in America.[113]

Jabotinsky's major triumph came with the Sons of Zion, a Zionist fraternal order and mutual aid society, which had been founded some years earlier and already served as a focus of dissidence within the American Zionist movement. Following his own prescription for success during his first American tour, personal canvassing, Jabotinsky doggedly campaigned in the local lodges of the order. Although its annual convention at which a formal vote on Revisionism would be taken was to be held only in June, he was reporting to family and associates in Europe and Palestine as early as April that he had succeeded in capturing the group.[114] When convention time came, he was proved right. By an overwhelming vote, and despite the very strong objections of Lipsky and others, the Sons of Zion elected a Revisionist executive of which Jabotinsky was made an honorary member. The exultant politician reported to his wife that he "was happy as a kid, not just because of winning over [the order to Revisionism], but because I was able to give . . . [Lipsky] a bop on the head in his own country. I was a hero."[115] Ironically, the pacifist Judah Magnes had been the founding chairman of the Order in 1907, and Lipsky would become its *nasi* or president in 1944. Jabotinsky expected the Sons of Zion to provide a springboard for a takeover of the entire American Zionist movement. Lipsky and his supporters were so fearful of such a development that they prevented the interloper even from speaking at the convention of the ZOA, which took place just after that of the Sons of Zion. But even without appearing, Jabotinsky exerted a considerable presence at the later convention.[116]

Winning the Sons of Zion was important because the group added several thousand members to Revisionist ranks, because it might serve as the catalyst of further North American conquests, and because it offered the prospect of a substantial, regular subvention to underwrite Revisionist work. Of "primary importance" were the activities of the order "in Palestine, which consisted of sponsorship of the Tel Aviv Exposition and the Judea Insurance Company," the sort of middle-class, business investment that Jabotinsky was beginning to promote as essential to the development of the *yishuv*.[117]

Friends and enemies alike warned him that a threat of scandal hung over the Judea. Weizmann suspected that the company was not "a good business" and thought it "a great pity that Jabotinsky [had] . . . linked himself up" with it. Accusations of fraud and mismanagement would soon prove to be well-founded.[118] Hard-pressed for funds, however, and perhaps a bit naive, Jabotinsky accepted the offer in 1928 to become Judea vice-president and managing director in Palestine at an annual salary of six thousand dollars, enough to restore the fortunes of his family. He was also desperate to return to Palestine; and it is doubtful that the British would have granted him a visa if he had not been employed by the American firm.[119] Most important to him, his contract allowed him to participate freely—after working hours—in publishing and political activities.

Two months after his arrival, he became editor of the daily *Do'ar HaYom*, replacing Itamar Ben-Avi, one of the country's foremost journalists and literary figures, the son of Eliezer Ben-Yehuda. An ardent admirer of Jabotinsky, Ben-Avi had toured the United States earlier in 1928 promoting fascism "as a new plan for upbuilding Palestine."[120] He stepped aside to provide a platform for the Revisionist leader, perhaps motivated in part by the fact that the Judea was a major advertiser in the paper. During his short tenure, the new editor used the paper, which had previously covered American affairs rather fully, to propagate American culture and to tout the virtues of American free-enterprise and the pioneering spirit.[121] He was less generous towards American Jews. He catalogued the weaknesses of American Zionism; he argued strenuously against the enlarged Jewish Agency during the visit to Palestine of Felix Warburg, one of its architects; and he aimed barbs at Lessing Rosenwald of Sears Roebuck, one of the "fat cats" he hated, for giving munificently to causes in Egypt and Lebanon but parsimoniously to Palestine.[122] The paper avoided mention of the American connections of the Judea and of its editor's ties to it, but perhaps such public information required no comment.[123]

Jabotinsky's career as insurance executive and editor was cut short after a year by the Mandatory government, which refused to renew his residence permit because of his political activities. He had been in the country long enough, however, to reassert a personal presence and to catalyze the local Revisionist movement. And American Zionists had made those developments possible![124] That one result of his 1926 North American tour justifies his only positive (prophetic?) assessment of it as "the most successful [visit] to any country to date."[125]

For a time in the mid-twenties, then, Jabotinsky seemed to have become intimately connected with America. His long-standing intellectual interests dovetailed with his political aims. Some American Zionists found his talents and program appropriate to their needs and goals. The American Jewish press became a mainstay of his income and offered a prominent platform for his views. A company owned by American Zionists enabled him to return to Palestine. On the face of it, the second tour of North America, which had begun inauspiciously, seemed to have turned to gold in the land of dollars. For a brief period, Jabotinsky became dependent—at least financially—on America.

What is rather surprising about Jabotinsky's 1926 American visit is his failure to follow up his gains. He recognized even before leaving America that making the victory permanent or enlarging its impact would necessitate returning in subsequent years.[126] At his parting dinner, he spoke explicitly of "next season's campaign in America." By early 1927 he had laid out plans for apportioning the proceeds of such a trip, following his early dictates for successful fund raising.[127] But the next year he headed for Palestine and refused to visit North America on the way. In 1929 he once again contemplated a North American trip and rejected the idea.[128] In fact, he would not set foot there until 1935, by which time the achievements of 1926 had largely dissipated and an entirely new situation in North America and in the world in general formed the background of his visit.

The reasons Jabotinsky elected not to consolidate his 1926 victories are not entirely clear. Undoubtedly they have partly to do with his mercurial temperament. He began more projects than he could ever hope to complete. It may be that he was reluctant to commit scarce financial resources to an American trip. And, as already noted, in the 1920s he could earn more money and gather larger crowds in poverty-stricken Poland than in affluent

America. In Poland, where Jewish life was increasingly bleak, many more people were open to his strong rhetoric and his seemingly simple solutions to their suffering than in the land of George Babbitt and the Jewish "all-rightnik."[129] But it seems also that Jabotinsky reverted at this time to some of his early negative notions regarding America. Despite his attraction to aspects of American culture, he still tended to feel, like so many intellectuals in Europe, that America had no soul and only half a brain. It was a place where all too often "ideas are manufactured, and vital decisions can be produced by machine methods."

For Jabotinsky, reading and theorizing about America was more congenial than dealing with real-life Americans. In the United States people with Revisionist leanings did not follow their heads and hearts but held back, waiting "for the bandwagon." The American Zionist movement had much potential but for the moment seemed to be realizing none of it, while Revisionism by 1927 was nowhere "in a more . . . dishevelled state of no cohesion . . . [than] in America." Even the Sons of Zion, he felt, were lapsing into "passivity," their promising enterprises mired in controversy.[130] David Levinsky and Sammy Glick, he discovered, were only distantly related, at most, to Natty Bumppo and Huck Finn, to say nothing of Abraham Lincoln and Theodore Roosevelt. And if American Jews listened to jazz and danced the fox trot, such "revolutionary, pioneering" deeds barely affected their attitudes to Zionism, if, indeed, to anything other than getting ahead and having a good time. Pioneering had given way to decadence on the cultural frontier.

Jabotinsky took to comforting from afar his few loyal American supporters, who were growing dispirited, and to urging his European stalwarts not to despair entirely of the Americans. But he did not come to terms with the fact that his own absence from America contributed to demoralization in the ranks. At times he grew impatient with the Americans, who now seemed to him a whining lot. He wrote to one of his closest followers in New York in 1927, that the Americans' troubles were

> just child's play compared to the difficulties with which we [in Europe] are confronted. Busy as all of you are, you are none of you "refugees"— and if you do not realize what it means in terms of dollars and cents and every second's worry, the better for you. Yet we carry on. . . .
> We in Europe are doing our duty under the bitterest of handicaps. But the worst of the handicaps, the one that paralyses [sic] our influence even in the remotest Orient, is the absence of a Revisionist organization in America.[131]

Jabotinsky felt strongly, then, the need for an American support group. He knew that the way to build such a group was to attract "indigenous" Americans and to garner influential allies. But either he did not know how to do these things, or he preferred to spend his energies on more congenial tasks.[132] At the end of the 1920s he seemed no further along with his program in the United States than at the start of his career in opposition to the Zionist establishment. And he seemed less interested in the American government or public than he had been during World War I, when he had first recognized the potential usefulness of their intervention in Zionist affairs.

6

The last decade of Jabotinsky's life was also the most turbulent. Opening with the economic collapse of western Europe and North America and closing with the early battles of World War II, it marked the beginning of the end of the Jewish world as it had been for centuries. By 1945 European Jewry would be decimated, a development that neither Jabotinsky nor anyone else had foreseen. In these events Zionists found confirmation of their convictions and reacted in a variety of ways. Most grew increasingly impatient and radical. In Palestine the Arabs staged anti-Jewish riots in 1929 and a full-scale revolt starting in 1936. The British responded by backing away from their commitment to Zionism, closing the doors to the country just when Jews were most in need of a place of refuge.

Even more restive than other Zionists, Jabotinsky and his followers adopted as their models in style and, to a degree, in substance the fascists of Europe. In 1932 they seemed poised to gain control of the WZO in the not distant future. Yet Jabotinsky led them out of the organization and down a separate path, although some of their policies were less exceptional than he and his followers cared to acknowledge. From 1934 the Revisionists promoted a scheme for a worldwide petition to the British government for a Jewish state. In Poland and elsewhere in eastern Europe they backed a plan for the large-scale "evacuation" of Jews to Palestine, in pursuit of which they allied themselves with fascists and antisemites eager to rid their countries of Jews. In the late 1930s they were active in assisting illegal immigrants into Palestine, although others, especially the labor parties, led the movement. In conjunction with a government academy in Mussolini's Italy, the Revisionists conducted the Jewish Marine School to train seamen for the future Jewish navy; and in a number of places, they trained youngsters for the future Jewish army and in the meantime for local self-defense. In the United States, they recruited as a trainer a Jew on active duty in the army who was threatened with court-martial for his extracurricular involvements.[133] After the invasion of Poland, Jabotinsky dusted off the World War I Legion plan and renamed it "the Jewish Army." Somewhat earlier he had begun planning a coup in Palestine to be financed by donations from America, an idea he abandoned when war broke out.[134] In Palestine militant Revisionists acting independently of the leader declared war on the British notwithstanding the crisis in Europe; and others plotted a coup in alliance with the Germans. Everywhere young party members—and sometimes adults—attended official functions in uniforms resembling those of the Italian and German "shirts." Within the New Zionist Organization itself the leader refused to tolerate opposition.

Jabotinsky's view of the United States in these years matched his mood: crankier, more somber, and less sanguine than before. The "colossal work which both we and the period demand from Revisionism" was, he wrote to his old comrade in arms Elias Ginsburg in 1932, impossible "without a great deal of money." He "demand[ed]" that Ginsburg "undertake the raising of funds," even though associates had warned him that "the Jews of America . . . [were] flat" broke.[135] He still found Americans "energetic . . . fervent . . . and capable," but in a mid-1930s essay published in Palestine, the United States, and Poland, he echoed the racists of Europe in attributing those qualities to Americans' "superior blood"; elsewhere, he noted that "the chosen of . . . twenty Aryan races" were blended together in the American "race."[136] Earlier and later in the decade he sounded more like his former self, criticizing American racism directed at blacks, Indians, Okies, and Jews.[137] In a 1940 review published in a Tel Aviv Revisionist paper of recent works by American Jewish novelist Edna Ferber, Jabotinsky described the characters in her *Cimarron* as genuine pioneers,

> not in any way resembling the pioneering race of this generation [in Palestine, who are little more than] . . . silk stocking[s] or yeshiva student[s]. . . . The whole content, tone, and climate [described in *Cimarron*] . . . are closer to those of the biblical book of Judges than to the account books of the Palestine Foundation Fund.[138]

But this was surely rhetoric, meant less to praise America than to damn his Zionist opponents, both the Laborites in Palestine and the WZO officials.

A review of Steinbeck's *The Grapes of Wrath* in the same paper was less disingenuous. There he praised the American *Weltanschauung*, which he perceived as similar to the Jewish in its "idea of social justice [and] hatred of [both] poverty and . . . wealth," and distant from that of gentile Europe which, he said, values "order, beauty, and logic" above all.[139] In Jerusalem's *HaYarden*, also a Revisionist paper, and elsewhere, he described Franklin Roosevelt as "an American . . . looking for his own individual Mount Sinai [from which] to rescue the world." But he saw the president as one of a multitude of American reformers, many of whom, such as Aimee Semple MacPherson, Huey Long, and Father Charles Coughlin, were eccentrics, charlatans, or villains. He found the New Deal old-fashioned compared to Europe in its approach to social legislation and overblown in importance. "The more [he] read about it, the less . . . [he could] understand it."[140] And he had little use for the Jewish—and gentile—"tuxedo leftists" who abandoned their capitalist ideals to support it.[141]

Jabotinsky's one unequivocally positive assessment of a Roosevelt policy turned out to be based on a misapprehension. Like most people outside of government—certainly most American Jews who tended to trust the president more than almost any other politician of the day—he took for granted FDR's good intentions in calling the conference at Evian-les-Bains, France, in 1938 to discuss the plight of refugees from Nazi Europe. Its failure he attributed to "powerful interests" in Europe, especially "official London . . . [with its] deliberate policy of scuttling the chances of Jewish salvation." In fact, however, the Americans had all along intended a smoke-and-mirrors conference which would give the appearance of concern without requiring them or any other country to admit Jewish refugees.[142]

Roosevelt's most prominent Zionist supporter was Rabbi Stephen S. Wise. An erstwhile Brandeisian of independent mind who served as president of the ZOA between 1936 and 1938, Wise often differed with Weizmann and his associates, preferring a firmer stand towards the British. In the mid-1920s Jabotinsky came to see him as an ally and even thought of him as a possible president of the WZO, although he harbored "misgivings [as] to the durability of Dr. W.'s moods."[143] When the rabbi turned sixty, Jabotinsky eulogized him as

> a man constantly seeking justice . . . proud of our own Jewish Torah but at the same time . . . ready to understand the spiritual value of other religious doctrines . . . a builder of a Jewish State and at the same time one of the best citizens of the "youngest State of God" . . . a passionate political fighter and a pure humanist.[144]

Wise seems to have liked Jabotinsky, as well; he invited him to speak at his rabbinical seminary, the Jewish Institute of Religion in New York; he and his wife sent him not inconsiderable donations (Ben-Gurion was also a recipient of their largesse); and for a time, *Opinion*, a journal founded by Wise's son James, gave him favorable publicity.[145] By late 1934, however, the relationship was cooling, as the Wises became more and more "deeply concerned and unhappy about the Fascist tendency in Revisionism."[146] In 1935 Jabotinsky paid his third visit to the United States; and Wise lent his name to the reception committee. But his real greeting was a withering attack in a sermon to his New York congregation, the Free Synagogue, which met in Carnegie Hall. In the talk, which was reported in the American-Jewish press and in Palestine, Wise compared Jabotinsky to Father

Vladimir Jabotinsky (fourth row center) with a group of supporters in Toronto, 1935. The young people are all in Betar uniforms. (Courtesy of Harry Frimerman, Toronto.)

Coughlin, the antisemitic "radio priest" and demagogue. He described Revisionism as "a species of Fascism in Yiddish or Hebrew" and pronounced it "immeasurably imperilling . . . to the future of the Jewish people," contrary to their "every ideal and idealism."[147]

Jabotinsky responded with an ad hominem attack on Wise, calling him a liar and a *"führer,"* a man "who says what he thinks, but unfortunately never thinks," rather startling comments in light of the encomia he had heaped upon the rabbi's head less than a year earlier. The ZOA's other leaders and the rank and file the Revisionist firebrand dismissed as "salon socialists."[148] The break with Wise was total and irrevocable.

Brandeis and the Palestinian Laborites rejoiced. In the early 1930s Jabotinsky's enemies were apprehensive about a possible "big victory" for Revisionism in America.[149] The Labor Zionists feared that as economic conditions worsened, American Jews might go the way of their Polish cousins. In the Brandeis camp, Jacob De Haas, Abraham Tulin, and others, in addition to Wise, were becoming increasingly disgruntled with the leadership of Weizmann and Lipsky, and warming to Jabotinsky. De Haas, an early intimate of Theodor Herzl who had helped to bring Brandeis to Zionism, coauthored with Wise *The Great Betrayal* (1930), which detailed the stages of Britain's backing away from her commitment to Zionism. In 1935, he formally joined the Revisionists.[150]

The 1935 tour might have given Revisionism a major boost. Instead, it was a dismal failure. In New York nearly four thousand people overflowed the Mecca Temple to hear Jabotinsky; and in Montreal the hall was full. Elsewhere, however, half the seats were empty, he reported to the Revisionist Executive Committee in Paris. In Detroit, Ben-Gurion was told, half of the small audience left in the middle. Jabotinsky achieved "neither moral nor financial success" and sailed from "America disgruntled, tired and depressed," although he was soon revived in "the fountain of youth": Poland, Lithuania, and Czechoslovakia, where he was greeted with "incredible . . . rejoicing."[151]

Familiar excuses were offered to explain the debacle: no organizer had traveled with Jabotinsky; the few American Revisionists lacked influence; the Brandeis Group was "tired, inactive, and largely inclined to flirt with the left . . . thanks to Roosevelt"; America was "the hardest place . . . to conquer," because the approach of Revisionism was "extraordinarily serious [and] . . . intolerant of [the kind of] recreational or consolatory Zionism . . . [that views] nationalism . . . as a flower show."[152]

Jabotinsky's American followers were, indeed, "second-raters." That, however, did not mean they could not accomplish their goals, as he himself noted.[153] More of a hindrance was the atmosphere of "relative paradise" in which all Americans lived. Even in the midst of the Great Depression, they were too optimistic and too safe to comprehend the hopelessness and desperation that thrust eastern European Jews into the arms of Revisionism, or the pessimism that propelled other Europeans into the arms of fascism and Nazism.[154] And as one of his apologists has pointed out, although Jabotinsky "realized the tremendous political, economic, and cultural significance of the great American Democracy," he was unwilling to tailor Revisionism to suit the American market.[155] Abraham Tulin tried to convince him in 1931 that the "psychology and methods" of the Revisionists were "foreign to America, just as young Moseley is foreign to England," that the style and approach "of continental Europe . . . simply cannot take root in an Anglo-Saxon country."[156] Illustrative was a resolution adopted at the New Zionist congress held in Vienna shortly after Jabotinsky returned from the United States in 1935. The congress voted to establish "an international army to combat oppression of the Jews throughout the world." The American Revisionists "retained some last glimmering of sanity" and voted against the provocative proposal, which had no hope of being implemented.[157] The eastern Europeans, however, would grasp at any measure which offered a ray of hope, even if that hope was no more than fantasy.

7

Had he been able to do so, Jabotinsky would probably have forgotten about the United States after his experiences there in 1935. He conceded that "there would not soon be" a viable American Revisionist movement and lost patience with his followers who fell to squabbling.[158] By 1938 he had virtually ceased publishing in the United States, preferring instead friendly journals elsewhere in the English-speaking world. On occasion he still read American novels and scholarly works; and he remained a fan of American movies, such as *Gone with the Wind* and *Northwest Passage*.[159] But the bloom was off. In 1930, in response to a suggestion of Wise that the WZO headquarters be moved from London to Washington, Jabotinsky had demurred: "If we decide that we are done with England, we should make sure of her successor before we process the divorce." By 1936 he was thoroughly disillusioned with England, but the United States did not appear to him a likely bride.[160]

And yet, the last act of Jabotinsky's dramatic life was to be played on the American stage. By the end of 1939 he was shut out of his accustomed theaters of operation: in eastern Europe by Germany and Russia, in Palestine by England. Only in the United States was there a possibility of raising funds and of recruiting replacements for the "prisoners of war" behind the lines. Only in America, he wrote in March 1940, was there "a chance to . . . rebuild our lost fortresses of Poland."[161]

Even before the onset of hostilities, Jabotinsky had begun again to acknowledge the importance of America in the volatile world political arena. As early as 1937, the Revisionists under his direction were actively lobbying American diplomats and politicians with regard to their scheme for the mass evacuation of Jews from eastern Europe to Palestine (the Nordau Plan). As with the Legion in World War I, the hope was that Washington would pressure the British to cooperate. Also, he pointed out to Americans and other Westerners that their desire to bar Jewish immigrants from their countries would be more justifiable "from a moral perspective" if they supported Jewish immigration to Palestine.[162] Interestingly, during a discussion of the Nordau Plan with a Revisionist lobbyist, Herbert Feis, a Jewish academic who served as an advisor in the American State Department, offered the "dark prophecy that the Jewish question in Europe may be liquidated simply by the Germans' killing out all the Jews." This was a much more bleak vision than that of Jabotinsky, who spoke only of the displacement of unwanted Jews in eastern Europe.[163]

With war came the unwelcome realization that "the center of our national political activities has shifted to America."[164] The Revisionists were still "zero," and it might be "no use to attempt anything there";[165] but Jabotinsky hoped to reverse that situation. He arrived in the United States in mid-March 1940, without his wife, for whom he was unable to secure a visa. It was to be his last journey.

His political objectives were to build an American party, to raise money for Revisionist work in Palestine and Europe, and to promote the Jewish Army. He instructed Elias Ginsburg to lay the groundwork for his visit and to ensure there would be follow-up, otherwise he would not come.[166] To a supporter in Haifa, he wrote that he planned "to begin [political organizing and fund raising] . . . with a propaganda campaign of major proportions."[167]

His correspondence regarding that campaign reflects wild mood swings, perhaps manic depression. He suffered frequent "grey and sad" moods, but at other times was "full of big hopes."[168] Soon after his arrival, he noted that it had been "colossally wise and lucky that we did not ask for any financial help from here," that "the boycott in the usual circles . . . [was] tighter than ever," and that even Tulin had not phoned.[169] A week later he reported to his wife: "the Jewish press is all with me."[170] In mid-June, he wrote to supporters in Buenos Aires and Johannesburg that American Jewry would surely accept Revisionist ideas and leadership in the near future, that he had been

> met with [an] incomparably greater welcome than ever before . . . that here in the United States . . . our possibilities are vast and solid. There

Vladimir Jabotinsky (standing) talking to Colonel John Henry Patterson at mass meeting in New York's Manhattan Center in support of a Jewish army, 19 June 1940. (Courtesy of UPI-Bettman.)

is almost unanimous dissatisfaction with "all and everything" of the present leadership in the Old Zionist ranks.[171]

And just ten days later, he told his wife there was no use "lying, . . . the whole New Zionist Organization and I together are not wanted by anyone" here.[172] The reality according to Benjamin Akzin, one of Jabotinsky's closest collaborators during this period, was that he was able to do virtually nothing for the party; and no money could be raised.[173] In America there was affection for Jabotinsky, the man, and attraction to his charismatic personality. His organization and many of his quixotic policies, however, were not popular. And perhaps the source of his contradictory readings of his reception lay in that dichotomy.

A particularly bedeviling aspect of the party work was unaccustomed rebellion within the ranks. Since 1938 tension had been growing between the National Military Organization (the Irgun), the Revisionist military arm in Palestine and Poland, and the veteran politicians, including Jabotinsky. Although the Irgun leaders agreed not to act independently of the New Zionist Organization leadership, by late 1939 they had set out on their own course, establishing independent offices in Geneva and New York, raising funds in competition with the party, and ignoring Jabotinsky's counsel.[174] In March he "had a long talk with the American Friends" of Jewish Palestine, as the New York Irgun group was called, and came away convinced that there was no need to "fear any separation on their part."[175] Yet by early June, the Friends were "not behaving as they should." They not only rebelled against their beleaguered putative leader, they treated him shabbily. Requesting that his old war buddy Colonel Patterson not address an American Friends' gathering, he complained that "Neither I nor any of my colleagues have been invited to that convention, nor to the dinner to which they sent out dozens of invitations. It matches with the fact that the only Jewish publication in the USA which did *not* mention my visit was the 'Friends' bulletin." Jabotinsky forbade the Irgun "to engage in any [further] independent political action" in America, but he had lost his authority over them.[176] After his death the Irgun representatives would have considerable success in garnering support in the United States and collecting funds for their program, although most mainstream Zionists shunned them as terrorists.

Jabotinsky's efforts on behalf of the Jewish Army also failed. At times there seemed to be hope; the Laborites also favored the scheme. But it was not quite the case that "American public opinion [was] literally seething with [the] Jewish Army plan," as the Johannesburg *Jewish Herald*, a Revisionist paper, claimed in June, and as Jabotinsky and Colonel Patterson cabled to Churchill.[177] Akzin and Patterson lobbied in Washington and

Ginsburg in Ottawa. Jabotinsky corresponded with American, British, Canadian, and French government officials and contacted the Polish and Czech governments in exile.[178] Some of the arguments were identical to those used twenty-five years earlier on behalf of the Legion: Here was a ready supply of needed manpower; antisemites would be won over by Jewish soldiers; American Jews would be moved to sympathize with the British, and their gentile countrymen would be swayed by them.[179] The old soldier spoke of the army as a "challenge to America's Jewish manhood." Volunteers, some of them veterans of the American forces or of European armies, presented themselves at Revisionist offices. Influential gentile journalists, such as Claire Booth (later, Luce) and John Gunther, expressed sympathy. (Gunther's wife was a Jew who had earlier been won over by the Revisionists.)[180] Lord Lothian, the British ambassador in Washington, was quite positive at first, but Rabbi Wise and others persuaded him that the Revisionist Army plan would sabotage the unity of American Jewry just when it was most necessary.[181] Late in the war the British would include in their European army the Jewish Brigade, which had been raised in Palestine. That force, however, owed little to Jabotinsky, except, perhaps, the precedent set by the World War I Legion.

Not only political rebuffs but trying personal problems plagued Jabotinsky in his last months. Perhaps fearing that he would attempt to remain permanently, the American authorities refused until shortly before his death to grant Mrs. Jabotinsky a visa. His son Eri had been imprisoned in Palestine by the British for his role in Aliyah Bet, the illegal immigration movement. And the wolf was at the door. As Eri later wrote, in his last days in bounteous America his father lived with only "pennies in his pocket . . . [worried about] his wife in London which was being bombed and about me in prison needing legal defence."[182]

Jabotinsky died on August 3, 1940, while visiting a summer camp for Revisionist youth in upstate New York. It seemed an incongruous end for "one of the heroic fighters for the honor and the future of the Jewish people."[183] He died far from the action in Europe and Palestine, in a country where he had enjoyed little tangible success. To be sure, he was not unloved in America. Thousands "of ordinary" New York Jews, "long-time residents and recent refugees," attended his funeral. His antagonists mourned, as well. Lipsky came, although Akzin made it known that Rabbi Wise would not be welcome.[184] Labor Zionists remembered a man "who naively believed, above all, in the basic goodness and dignity of the individual human being." Socialist editor Abe Cahan "sincerely admire[d his] . . . talent."[185] He was a man whose temperament and ideas had led him out of the mainstream. Perhaps it was not altogether inappropriate that he should die on the periphery.

Jabotinsky, the man, appealed to pragmatic Americans more than his ideas; and the idea of America appealed to the dogmatic Jabotinsky more than real-life Americans. He understood—and appreciated—American culture better than most European and Palestinian Zionists, better, for that matter, than many well-educated Americans; and he identified with American historical experiences and heroes. He wrote about American literature and culture, making them familiar to his followers, especially in Palestine. I "am, in the final account," he declared in 1926, "an American!"[186] More than most other Zionists, he recognized the political, financial, and cultural potential of the United States and American Jewry for Zionism. And on occasion, during World War I with the Legion and in the late 1920s with the Judea Insurance Company, he exploited that potential. On the whole, however, for reasons of ideology, temperament, and expediency, unlike his political rivals, he neglected the United States and American Jewry until it was too late. And he rigidly refused to pander to American sensibilities by altering his message, methods, or tone. In late September 1939, Jabotinsky met Berl Katznelson in London. It was a moment of truth. "You have won," Jabotinsky conceded. "You have America, the rich Jews. I have only Polish Jewry, and now it is gone. I have lost the game!"[187] His successors would eventually learn how to play the American game; and in his own reluctant and contrary fashion he had taught them the rules.

CHAPTER
3
Chaim Naḥman Bialik

America, A Cultural Wasteland with Promise

WHAT A foreign poet who died in the mid-1930s thought of the United States would seem to be an arcane, if not altogether frivolous, question. In many cultures, however, writers exert considerable influence on public affairs. Witness, for example, the position of Vaclav Havel in postcommunist Czechoslovakia, or that of Sartre and Camus in postwar France. Jews, "the people of the book," may be somewhat more open to the influence of the literati than others. Especially in the period between the Emancipation and the birth of Israel, when their political life was circumscribed and the influence of religion declining, they filled some of the void with culture. They accepted poets, essayists, and novelists as tastemakers and looked to them for guidance in setting the communal agenda.

1

Of those who achieved a position of prominence in Jewish letters between 1750 and 1948, Chaim Naḥman Bialik ranks first. It is not much of an exaggeration to say that he occupies a position in modern Hebrew literature analogous to that of Shakespeare in English literature, as his contemporaries already recognized. Few of them would have disagreed with the judgment of the *The Washington Post*, which described him in 1926 as "the greatest of living Hebrew poets."[1] Most also appreciated the significance of his public and even his personal activities: his virtual abandonment of poetry for the task of collecting the literary treasures of the Jewish past and publishing them; his departure from Russia in 1921; his immigration to Palestine (aliyah) in 1924.[2]

Long before his aliyah, Bialik enjoyed a reputation among the Jews of Palestine. The revival of Hebrew as the spoken language of the Jewish people in its old/new homeland was both a goal and an instrument of Zionism. The lion of modern Hebrew literature naturally occupied a respected place in the communal pantheon. Aliyah ensured his primacy. Ben-Gurion recalled that on the day Bialik arrived in Palestine, "the whole city [of Tel Aviv] celebrated." Within a year of his immigration, noted Chaim Weizmann, Bialik had become "the most valuable man in Tel Aviv" and the "one who may have the greatest influence."[3] When, less than two years after his remove to Palestine, the poet journeyed to the United States on a cultural, fund-raising, and personal mission, the daily *HaAretz*, remarked that his absence, however brief, would be deeply felt.[4] And when he died in 1934 at the age of sixty-one, the *yishuv*—along with Jews outside of Palestine—was gripped with a sense of incomparable national loss.[5]

2

As might be expected of a European-Palestinian writer in Hebrew, Bialik did not concern himself a great deal with the United States. His writing was influenced by Russian and German novelists and poets; he understood that modern Jewish schools had to teach "the culture of the new Europe." But he knew no English and even after his visit to America had but little appreciation of American culture. Unlike some of his contemporaries, such as the poet Saul Tchernichovsky, who had studied medicine and literature in Germany and acquired a taste for European and American literature (he translated Longfellow into Hebrew, as well as Homer, Goethe, Shelley, and Molière), Bialik had almost no acquaintance with American literature, even in translation. His cultural and literary interests remained focused on the Jewish world throughout his life. His Hebraism and Palestinocentric Zionism were tempered only by rootedness in the Yiddish-speaking Diaspora and the Russian landscape, and by feelings of kinship with all Jews.[6]

During his formative years, Bialik acquired the parochial and rather stereotypical views of many cultured Europeans regarding America, views which he never overcame entirely. Like other eastern European Jewish writers and intellectuals of his day, he tended to regard the Western world, in general, as an insecure place for Jews, destructive of their authentic roots.[7] America, in particular, was unformed, uncultured, unscrupulous, and unserious.[8] As a young writer in Odessa, Bialik shared with his friend the comic Yiddish writer Sholem Aleichem (the pen name of Sholem Rabinovitch) the belief that American Jewish writers were all "total ignoramuses, tailors, and peddlers," who would corrupt any genuine talent that came into their midst from Europe.[9] None of the enthusiasm for America of Jabotinsky, his occasional translator, rubbed off on him.

Later, too, the poet tended to associate America with "noise, confusion, ta-ra-ram, . . . with those things we condemn in strongest terms: bluff, . . . 'business,' etc." In America, Bialik was known to assert, it was not literature that flourished but advertisements, "inflated, hollow, and lacking in content."[10] Such views were not confined to Europeans. American Hebraists of Bialik's day, themselves of European origin and nurtured on the same genteel stereotypes, tended to look down their noses at "the national and cultural degeneration of the [Jewish American] masses," at their alleged "licentiousness, ignorance, rudeness, and . . . materialism." Many gentile American intellectuals agreed.[11]

To an extent the Hebrew writers can be excused their provinciality, for behind their prejudices and Eurocentrism lay an important reality. Before World War I the heartland of Jewish culture was eastern Europe, especially Russia. Life there was not easy nor pleasant, and conditions did not improve as time went on. Jews suffered discrimination, at best, physical violence, at worst. The writers Sholem Aleichem, S. Ben Zion (Simḥa Alter Gutman), and Mendele Mocher Sforim (Shalom Jacob Abramovitch), all members of Bialik's Odessa literary circle and among his closest compatriots, fled the violence, the first to America, the others to Switzerland. Yet Russia remained home to the Jewish cultural and intellectual elite, because only there could they find peers and an audience conversant with their languages. In Russia, where there was no possibility of assimilation, Jewish culture was safe, even if Jews were in danger.

Odessa, as Bialik observed, served "as a campground and meeting place of Hebrew writers for decades, . . . [even] in the most difficult period for Jews and Jewish culture in Russia and the Ukraine."[12] In the turn-of-the-century years, the city was home to an incomparable Jewish literary and cultural circle. Besides Bialik, Sholem Aleichem, Mendele, and Ben Zion, there were the historian Simon Dubnow, the essayist and philosopher Aḥad HaAm (Asher Ginsberg), and a host of lesser lights. Understandably, Bialik regretted the departure of any of them, especially to America, where Jews were safe but Jewish culture was thought to be in mortal danger, in part because of the freedom and openness which characterized that country. That is why he sounded "a note of lament in his [1905] letter of farewell to Sholem Aleichem." In fleeing to the safety of America, his friend was "uprooting himself from the source of his vitality," Bialik said. He added that "no country was as good [for Jews] as Russia, no city as good as Odessa," a wild assertion that makes sense only as a statement of cultural context, especially in that year of pogroms.[13]

Bialik believed that language was the only possible replacement for religion in a post-religious age and that Hebrew was the only language that could "serve as the foundation and root" of Jewish civilization.[14] After World War I, the center of Hebrew culture shifted to Palestine, reinforcing the Palestinocentrism of Hebraists, who now had a growing audience there.[15] The dislocation severely undermined Bialik's interest in the Diaspora, interest that had been sustained earlier by his ties to Russia. In this he resembled most other writers and public figures in Palestine, even new immigrants, who, as Shimon Halkin, the American Hebrew poet and critic noted in 1929, quickly came to look upon the *yishuv* and its concerns as "altogether paramount" in importance.[16]

Bialik's hesitations regarding the United States stemmed from another source, too: his own personal experiences. Born in a Ukrainian village and reared in the town of Zhitomir, the poet remained a "small-town boy" all his life. He found it difficult to tolerate the noise and confusion of the big city. Although Odessa, where he spent many of his most productive years, was a metropolis of sorts, the poet was at home in the Russian language and, in any case, functioned within the confines of the city's Jewish community. But even Odessa had frightened him at first. He was eighteen years old when he arrived there; yet he drifted "for six months . . . like a lost lamb" in the "big city."[17]

Large foreign cities he found still more daunting. Although he spoke German, he never overcame the sense that Berlin, where he lived between 1921 and 1924, was entirely "foreign," a city whose byways he "would never know." Berlin Jews he found alien; they had, he said, "eyes and heart only for corruption."[18] London, which he first visited in 1926, was "depressing" to the "virtual village boy," as he referred to himself. Despite its grandeur, he saw it as inferior in many ways to Jewish Palestine. Four years later on another visit, Bialik felt no more at home and still needed the help of Shmaryahu Levin, the Zionist publicist and his friend and partner in the Dvir publishing house, to help him "find [his] . . . hands and feet." In 1926 he thought London's Jews "petrified." His friend and mentor Aḥad HaAm, who had lived in England for a number of years, described English Jewry as a "cemetery . . . dotted with grand artifacts and yet devoid of the . . . human tension that makes life bearable." By 1931 Bialik saw the English Jews as "uncircumcised of heart," people worthy of "Sodom and Gomorrah, among whom the God of Israel does not dwell." Exasperated after a lengthy and unproductive stay, he wrote to his longtime collaborator, Yehoshua Ravnitzki, that he hoped to "blot" London out of his "book and heart."[19] In the last year of his life Bialik found even Tel Aviv, then hardly more than an overgrown village, unbearable; and he fled to the sleepy suburb of Ramat Gan in search of peace and solitude.

That he would have been intimidated by the size and tumultuousness of America, then, and that he considered the prospect of visiting teeming New York and its vast hinterland with "fear and trembling," is not surprising. And, when he did consent to go, that he insisted that Levin, a seasoned American traveler, be "his eyes in the New American World" and his "guide to the etiquette of English dining" was altogether in character.[20]

3

Whatever Bialik's predilections, America could not be ignored. The mass emigration of Russian Jews began when he was still a child and swept up family members, friends, disciples, and colleagues.[21] Like Jabotinsky, he recognized that the material and political support of American Jewry had become crucial to the success of Zionism in the postwar era, perhaps to its very survival, as well as to the survival of Europe's Jews, increasingly threatened by poverty, Bolshevism, fascism, and, finally, Nazism. Over the years Bialik learned more about America from the press and from reports of trustworthy associates who visited there or emigrated. And he encountered American scholars, Hebraists, and Zionist leaders, such as Judah L. Magnes, the Zionist Reform rabbi and communal worker and future founding chancellor of the Hebrew University. Magnes was one of the few people Bialik met at the 1907 Zionist Congress at The Hague whom he found impressive enough to mention by name in a letter to his wife. An article by Magnes contrasting Bialik's creativity with the barrenness of American-Jewish culture may have predisposed the poet towards him.[22]

After Sholem Aleichem left for the United States in 1906, Bialik followed his career there with interest, rejoicing in "the great honor America [sometimes] bestowed upon" his friend, and railing when their shared prejudices regarding the New World proved correct.[23] Bialik enlisted his aid—and that of Shmaryahu Levin, also then in New York—in raising funds for the publication of the complete works of their mutual friend and mentor, Mendele Mocher Seforim. "American Jews had a duty to provide the funds," Bialik claimed, because they had pirated Mendele's works and paid him no royalties.[24] Neither Levin nor Sholem Aleichem could help, however; and the project was only completed years later.[25]

Y. D. Berkowitz, the son-in-law and translator of Sholem Aleichem, shuttled between Europe and America from 1906 until 1913, when he settled in New York, providing another living link with the New World. (Years later he joined Bialik in Palestine.) Over the years, the poet encouraged Berkowitz, an author in his own right, whose classical, rather fustian prose style Bialik considered "first class."[26] In 1915 the younger writer became editor of *HaToren*, America's foremost Hebrew journal, a sign to Bialik, no doubt, that even vulgar America recognized talent.[27] Before then, only a few of Bialik's poems had been published in the United States in Hebrew or in Yiddish or English translation. Berkowitz used his position to acquaint Americans better with the poet whom he held in unbounded admiration,[28] dedicating an entire issue of *HaToren* to him on the twenty-fifth anniversary of the publication of his first poem.[29] Hebraists on both sides of the ocean belonged to a kind of global Jewish village, and Bialik was aware of his growing fame in America. Although he eschewed lionization, he surely appreciated the recognition, as well as the expansion of the world of Hebrew letters that it signified.

Bialik's literary disciples, Benjamin Silkiner and Simon Ginzburg, also settled in the United States in these years, pursuing successful careers in Jewish education and participating in the nascent Hebrew culture movement. Still in Odessa, Ginzburg had translated some of Bialik's poems into Yiddish; and the great bard tried to interest him in a job at the Moriah Publishing House which he controlled. An editor of *HaToren* before Berkowitz, Ginzburg was to have a long scholarly and publishing connection with his former mentor, of which more below.[30] Silkiner, who also served as an editor of *HaToren* for a short time, had had only slight contact with Bialik in Odessa, although the older poet certainly knew his long poem, "Mul Ohel Timura," depicting the clash of Indians and Spaniards in the New World. Dvir would become the publisher of Silkiner's volume of collected poems, *Shirim* (1927), and of the bestselling Hebrew-English dictionary, which he coauthored.[31]

David Neumark, who taught medieval Jewish philosophy at the Hebrew Union College in Cincinnati after emigrating to America in 1907, was an established scholar whose work Bialik held in high esteem.[32] In Europe, he had published some of his research in *HaShiloah*, arguably the most important turn-of-the-century Hebrew literary-cultural journal, a publication with which Bialik was intimately connected from 1903 to 1919, off and on as an editor. Later he published a major study with Moriah. From America, he continued to contribute to *HaShiloah*, now helping to familiarize Europeans with the achievements of American Reform Judaism.[33]

The pages of *HaShiloah* provide a partial inventory of Bialik's early knowledge of America. Among the American-based academics who appeared there besides Neumark was Henry Malter, another German-trained scholar of medieval Jewish philosophy who taught at Hebrew Union College and, from 1909, at the new Dropsie College for Jewish studies in Philadelphia.[34] The work of Malter and Neumark demonstrated that America could foster Jewish scholarship, as did the monumental *Jewish Encyclopedia*, which was reviewed favorably in 1907.[35] Abraham S. Waldstein, an academic and Labor-Zionist activist before his aliyah in 1912, wrote unflatteringly of American Jewish literature and scholarship but more positively about American Zionism.[36] His first article praised Yankee ingenuity and energy, and pointed to American practicality as a cause of the distance between the immigrant generation and their children. Bialik proposed a simple, perhaps simplistic, way to bridge the gap: "Let the child drink at the fountain from which his father has been nourished," he wrote in *The New Palestine* some years later, "and the rift will be healed."[37]

Other *HaShiloah* authors, including Simon Ginzburg, focused on American materialism, crime, and alienation. A review of higher education was more mixed, pointing both to discrimination against Jews and to growing opportunities for them in American universities, some of which, the author noted, already rivaled the best in Europe.[38] In 1904, when Bialik was literary editor of the journal, Max Raisin, the American Hebraist and Reform rabbi, published a long article about Mordecai Manuel Noah, "the great American prophet" who proposed to establish a Jewish state on Grand Island in the Niagara River. (Years later Bialik read Raisin's Hebrew-language history of the Jews in America approvingly.) Another author in that same year discussed "the advantages of the United States" as a land of immigration.[39] The American Hebrew and Yiddish journals which his friends and former colleagues sent him and firsthand reports from American Jews and transplanted Europeans together with *HaShiloah* and other European journals provided Bialik with diverse views of the New World.[40] To a degree in these years, the negative stereotypes on which he had been nurtured were challenged. Willy-nilly, his ideas about America became more nuanced.

4

Bialik's poetry, most of it written in the two decades before the outbreak of World War I, reflects acute awareness of the breakdown of the traditional foundations of Jewish life. Often the poet seems himself to be encouraging, if not demanding, that very breakdown, although at other times he laments the loss of a coherent world.[41] Even at his most rebellious, however, Bialik, who wrote in Hebrew and spoke Yiddish, assumed the existence of the Jewish people as an enduring national and cultural entity. They were, perhaps, a people in flux, undergoing the agonies of entry into modernity, like other European peoples. If the new contours of Jewish nationhood and culture were not altogether clear, there was confidence in a future "slouch[ing] . . . towards [Jerusalem] . . . to be born." Like most Europeans on the eve of the war, Bialik did not suspect the dimensions of the catastrophe that lay ahead. Retrospectively he described the period just before the war as a time when all the newly erected "fortresses" of Jewish national life appeared to be "standing strong. Russian Jewry was vital and productive, at the height of its power. The [glittering] exterior of German Jewry masked its inner poverty . . . [while in] America a period of growth and development had begun. It seemed that in those strongholds we should be able to hold our own, even in the Diaspora."[42]

The war and its aftermath, however, swept away the existing European-Jewish world no less completely than it did the Russian, Ottoman, and Austro-Hungarian empires. As Bialik lamented at an international meeting of Hebraists in Carlsbad, Czechoslovakia, in 1921, "this whole, beautiful, magnificent structure was razed . . . to the ground . . . and on the pile of rubble stands Jewry, broken and shattered."[43] Polish Jewry had been ravaged by the war and then by the postwar disturbances. Like their governments, the Jews of Britain, France, and Germany would never recover their prewar prosperity. In the Soviet Union, Jewish culture in general was coming under proscription; and Hebrew, the language of Palestine-centered Jewish nationalism, was particularly threatened. The Bolsheviks forced Moriah to cease publishing. Together with a number of other writers, Bialik was allowed to leave Russia in 1921 only after Maxim Gorky interceded with Lenin. The less fortunate were imprisoned. But Bialik was not thankful; he compared the national Jewish loss to the destruction of the ancient Temple by the Romans, and he acquired a lifelong hatred of the Bolsheviks.[44]

The cataclysm brought about radical changes in Bialik's life and attitudes. After a three-year interlude in Germany, he settled in Palestine in 1924; and, as noted earlier, his sense of the importance of the land of Israel to the Jewish people grew stronger. No longer, he declared in 1921, was there "any hope for [Jewish] property or the [Jewish] heritage in the Diaspora. . . . [An evil] spirit was uprooting and obliterating them."[45] Whereas once he penned fiery, sometimes subversive poetry, now he devoted himself almost entirely to salvaging the Jewish literary and religious treasures of the past and making them accessible to present and future generations. He permitted himself, albeit reluctantly, to be harnessed to the national bandwagon as a cheerleader and fund raiser for Zionism. And, not surprisingly, he began to look upon America through different spectacles. He poignantly cautioned against dependence on the New World, since Jewish history had seen "great Diaspora centers that had disappeared completely." Nonetheless, he told a London audience in early 1926, "America is now our only comfort."[46]

A number of people on both sides of the ocean encouraged Bialik to participate in the search "for the Golden Fleece," as Weizmann referred to the Zionist fund-raising delegations that made their way to the United

States in the postwar period. Weizmann personally urged him to help, as did Shmaryahu Levin, and the executive of the American Keren Hayesod, which was charged by the WZO with making arrangements on the American end for its delegations. In the summer of 1921 the Americans listed Bialik fifteenth on a list of fifteen desirable visitors.[47] Worried about his health, preoccupied with the affairs of Moriah and Dvir, ever shy of big cities, and reluctant to allow himself to become a national icon, the poet had doubts about such a trip. "The ways and customs of America" he still considered an "abomination, ... its crowds and confusion and the noise of its gears" detestable. Publicly debating with himself in a two-hour speech in Berlin that same year, he declared, probably with irony, that he was "not, by nature, an agitator." Nonetheless, he felt a responsibility to undertake the journey "at this difficult hour ... [when] the nation is gripped by [the kind of] apathy that leads to decay and death."[48] In early November, the New Yorkers were preparing for Bialik's arrival. He never went, however, mostly because the Americans and the London headquarters of the WZO decided in the end that the visit would not be "worthwhile." Bialik was delighted with the reprieve. The following summer the Americans again considered inviting him and again decided against it.[49]

During the next few years, Bialik became better known in America, although from afar. The first edition of his collected works, published in Berlin in 1923, had sold more than eight hundred copies in America by 1926; his essays and poetry, and articles about him, now appeared regularly in American Hebrew-language journals and the Yiddish and Anglo-Jewish press.[50] In early 1922 Daniel Persky, the "totally dedicated" Hebraist whose "sometimes exaggerated honesty" appealed to the older poet, sent him a packet of laudatory clippings from American publications, which "touched [him] to the depths of ... [his] soul." He was undoubtedly also pleased by celebrations of his fiftieth birthday, which included a special jubilee issue of *HaDo'ar*, the American Hebrew journal, and a mass meeting addressed by Weizmann at the Apollo Theater in New York's Harlem, only recently a middle-class, Jewish neighborhood. Ripples of the growing recognition included the establishment in Worcester, Massachusetts, of Agudat Bialik, a group that aimed to foster Hebrew-speaking among young people.[51]

During these years, it began to seem plausible for the first time that America might succeed eastern Europe as the center of a vibrant Jewish culture and Hebrew-language movement. For several months in 1921 and 1922, when Warsaw's *HaTzefira* had temporarily ceased publication, the United States was home to the only Hebrew-language daily appearing outside Palestine. And, as Bialik noted, the New York *HaDo'ar* was exemplary "in its content, its language, and its excellent style." He felt kinship with the paper's sponsors, who shared his goal of "revivif[ying] ... the nation of

God" through the medium of the Hebrew language. He viewed them as lonely knights "fighting mightily for the establishment of our tongue in the land of dollars . . . among the walls and pillars of iron America."[52] Another indication of America's growing promise was the Hebrew-language children's magazine, *Eden*, published in New York from 1924 by Batsheva Grabelsky with Persky, and later Y. D. Berkowitz, as editor. Bialik found the early issues of *Eden* in need of "improvement upon improvement." Still, he responded positively to Persky's diffident invitation to contribute some of his stories and poems for children; and he became more eager to participate when Berkowitz took over. It was an innovative venture; education was one of Bialik's primary concerns; and Grabelsky, Persky's student who bankrolled the venture, agreed to pay the poet twenty-five dollars a month (not always done promptly) for his labors. Between 1924 and 1926, ten children's poems and a story by Bialik were published first in *Eden*.[53]

Dvir had some success in selling its books in the United States in these years. But the poet complained in 1922 that the Americans were hurting his never adequate income by purchasing his volume of collected poems at a discount made possible by the weak German mark. He tried himself to take advantage of cheaper printing costs in Germany; but he proved to be a poor match for the denizens of the land of business and dollars.[54]

Several of Bialik's business and professional dealings with the United States during the early 1920s were complicated by tangled personal relationships. His friendship with Simon Ginzburg had cooled, although he commended novelist Yoḥanan Twersky to him when the latter headed for the "strange land" of America in 1924. The breach was repaired, when Dvir undertook to print Ginzburg's edition of the works of the eighteenth-century, Italian-Jewish mystic and poet, Moshe Ḥaim Luzzato. It was a project the older poet and his partner Ravnitzki had themselves begun in Odessa but abandoned because of war and revolution. Bialik graciously yielded to Ginzburg, taking care to praise the younger scholar's "good and faithful work." When he read in *HaDo'ar* that Ginzburg's wife had died, he consoled him and urged him to come to Palestine and renew their working relationship.[55]

Business led to temporary estrangement from Berkowitz, who failed to persuade the "brigands and thieves" of the Hebrew Publishing Company of New York to pay royalties on works pirated from Moriah. A proposal of Berkowitz's to copublish an illustrated children's pamphlet series seems to have been stillborn; he was slow in paying a debt to Dvir; then Bialik expressed less than wholehearted enthusiasm for his new Yiddish drama, "Under the Cross." The relationship improved when Bialik decided to let the Dvir office worry about the debt, while committing the company to publishing a new fifteen-volume edition of the works of Sholem Aleichem with Berkowitz's translation.[56]

Shalom Ber Maximon was another American Hebraist with whom Bialik had an uneven relationship, largely because Maximon ignored deadlines. Like the others, he was forgiven. In 1926 Bialik interceded with Rabbi Stephen Wise in an effort to have Maximon reinstated as a lecturer at the Jewish Institute of Religion. (The touchy writer accused Bialik of not trying hard enough with Wise.) When he died, Bialik noted magnanimously but not effusively, that Maximon had been "an important Hebrew writer."[57]

Bialik established a more fruitful long-distance relationship with Israel Davidson, a professor of medieval literature at New York's (Conservative) Jewish Theological Seminary, some of whose work in the field of medieval poetry paralleled his own. By 1925 the two were carrying on a regular correspondence about scholarly matters and exchanging publications. Davidson's "magnificent craftsmanship" as well as the extraordinary Seminary library served as further evidence that America was not entirely a cultural and scholarly wasteland.[58]

The long, Yiddish narrative poem, "Kentucky," sent to Bialik in 1925 by its author, I. J. Schwartz, however, suggested that everyday Jewish experience in America bore little resemblance to life at the Seminary. Schwartz's Yiddish and Hebrew writing was heavily influenced by Bialik, one of whose poems he had translated into Yiddish; and it was natural that he should send the bard a copy of his magnum opus. Schwartz's American works reflected his broad experiences in the New World. In "Kentucky," he chronicled the progressive dilution of Jewishness from generation to generation. Bialik could not put the book down until "he reached the last page." The poem surely rekindled his doubts about the United States as a new home for Jewish culture and reinforced his conviction that the *yishuv* was now of supreme importance.[59]

By 1925, then, Bialik knew a great deal about America's Jews, although not about American civilization in general. He was well acquainted with the gains of American Hebrew letters; and he had extensive contacts in the American Jewish cultural world. He was not unmindful of America's shortcomings; but he was painfully aware of the devastation of the old European-Jewish heartland and of the massive assistance needed by the *yishuv* if its culture and society were to become viable. At the same time, American Jews had come to regard Bialik as a major Zionist figure. A word of encouragement from him could now serve to "strengthen the hand of" the American Zionist leadership, whom he had erroneously come to perceive as "energetic and dedicated," ready to lead in financing "the redemption . . . [of] our national land."[60] He was gradually overcoming his reluctance to solicit funds; and the Americans now seemed prepared to extend a measure of support to the cultural institutions with which he was most concerned.⁶¹ The moment was ripe for closer involvement with American Jewry; and the poet was ready, more or less.

5

Bialik's 1926 American tour is the only aspect of his connection with the New World to which scholars have paid much attention; and it has usually been treated as a dramatic turning point in his relationship with the United States.⁶² As the foregoing indicates, however, the tour followed almost naturally from the poet's experiences, from his changing attitudes towards a changing world, and from Americans' growing acquaintance with him. The trip came about as a result of the confluence of a number of forces.

By the second half of 1925 the treasury of the Zionist movement was empty and the future of the *yishuv*, which depended on outside funds not only for growth and development but also for the maintenance of many of its institutions, was endangered. Matters grew more desperate as the weeks went by. Weizmann refused to travel to the United States in search of funds; instead, he declared the "presence" in North America of Shmaryahu Levin, who was recuperating from a severe heart attack, to be "imperative," and suggested he "use all [his] influence" to induce Bialik to go along. Aware of how "difficult the time [is] for our [Zionist] Federation and the *yishuv*," Bialik, like Levin, responded affirmatively to Weizmann's command and to the pleading of Ahad HaAm, the grand old man of Hebrew letters, now Bialik's friend and neighbor in Tel Aviv. Weizmann and other European Zionist leaders were "grateful" to them both for undertaking "the mission," and to Bialik for overcoming his "discomfiture" in "deal[ing] with matters of the pocket."⁶³

This time the Americans were also eager. They were attempting to raise an unheard-of $5 million and faced stiff competition for the Jewish charitable dollar from Yeshiva University, which had embarked on a major building fund campaign, and from the American Joint Distribution Committee, which was seeking $25 million to aid Jewish farming colonies in the Crimea. The Joint appealed not only to its wealthy non-Zionist and anti-Zionist supporters but also to socialist Jews who regarded the Soviet Union, rather than the *yishuv*, as the fulfillment of messianic prophecies. Zionist campaigns in America were based on the "star system." For the 1926 campaign to succeed, a major star would be needed; and Emanuel Neumann, the director of the American Keren Hayesod, "was running out of 'stars.'" Neumann, who seldom underestimated his own importance, claimed that he "hit on the idea of inviting" Bialik independently of Weizmann.⁶⁴

The poet had his own reasons for wanting to go now. In mid-1925 he wrote to Batsheva Grabelsky that he "wholeheartedly wished to visit America, just once, to witness the life of our brethren there." Some months later he spoke of his "natural desire to see with [his] . . . own eyes the largest Jewish aggregation" in the world.[65] As the symbol of renascent Hebrew culture and its best known spokesman, he felt a strong personal obligation to perform not only "the material task" but also "the spiritual task"—to strengthen Jewish culture and education and Hebrew letters in America. As Levin put it at a "state" send-off in Tel Aviv attended by Mayor Dizengoff: "Without a nation, there can be no poetry. Bialik must go to America in order . . . to elevate [Zionist] propaganda so that it can speak to the soul . . . . Our brethren there . . . thirst for vision."[66]

Curiosity and culture were not all that motivated Bialik to put aside his "longstanding inner fear of American Jews" and a newly acquired anxiety that they would "desecrate his . . . honor."[67] He needed now to consider his own "matters of the pocket": Dvir, which required an infusion of funds, and his shaky personal finances. The Keren Hayesod agreed that Bialik and Levin could take time during the tour to attend to the affairs of Dvir. Bialik, moreover, was paid five thousand dollars by the American Keren Hayesod and Levin one thousand—tidy sums in 1926—for their five months of labor. As well, short-term loans, which were repaid promptly, were arranged with the Keren Hayesod head office in Jerusalem for Dvir and for Bialik himself. Neumann labeled the generous arrangements and the negotiations "sordid," perhaps because he felt artists should not have material concerns; others seemed to feel they were justified.[68]

Whatever the reservations before the start of the tour, once it was under way, spontaneous American enthusiasm combined with painstaking orchestration by Neumann, Meyer Weisgal, the secretary of the ZOA and future head of the Weizmann Institute in Rehovot, and others to give it the dimensions of a triumphal state visit. When the Labor Zionists or Jabotinsky came to America in these years, their "tours" consisted of gruelling one-night stands with stays in inexpensive lodgings. Bialik, his wife, and Levin, in contrast, were given red-carpet treatment befitting "the poet-laureate of the Jewish people," as the *New York Times* called him. The poet paid a courtesy call on London Jews when he passed through Britain. There he was joined by ZOA president Louis Lipsky, an honor guard of one, whose task it was to part the Atlantic's waters before the visitors. Lipsky, however, was not Moses; and the Bialiks spent most of the journey in bed seasick.[69]

In the meantime, Jewish America was preparing for the poet with unprecedented media hype.[70] The Histadruth Ivrith, the association of American Hebraists, distributed "campaign buttons" with Bialik's picture and published a biographical pamphlet by A. R. Malachi "to serve as a worthy introduction to the minstrel of the Jewish Renaissance." *The New*

Palestine published his *Selected Poems* newly translated by Maurice Samuel; the press was flooded with information; and on the sabbath before his arrival sermons about him were preached in synagogues across the land. The week of his advent was declared "Bialik Week" (to be followed soon after by "Bialik Month"). *HaAretz* reported that "the men of 'business,' " inspired by the poet, had begun "to prophesy."

The achievements of the publicity buildup were dramatic. During his stay Bialik would be hailed and heard by thousands of Americans, most of whom had only the vaguest notion of what he had to say or even who he was. He complained of being led "like a circus elephant to places where [his] . . . name was unknown." On one occasion he was introduced as "[King] Balak," a character in the Bible who sought the destruction of the Israelites. In the midst of the "roaring twenties," in America with its insatiable appetite for flagpole sitters, goldfish swallowers, and other curiosities, the Hebrew-speaking poet was a nine-days' wonder, even to President Coolidge, whom he met at the White House. The all-Jewish HaKoach soccer team from Palestine that toured the United States at the same time may have aroused more enthusiasm. More than fifty thousand people came to see them play the final game of their series at New York's Polo Grounds in April; and Coolidge sent them a farewell telegram. For a poet, however, he generated enormous excitement; and those who did know something about him were overwhelmed at meeting a classic face-to-face.[71]

The ballyhoo came to its first climax when Bialik and his entourage reached New York harbor. Strings had been pulled in Washington to waive normal immigration procedures; and the party was greeted on board ship by an all-star delegation of Jewish notables. On shore a band waited. New York's mayor, Jimmy Walker, ill with bronchitis and unable to attend the reception, lent a launch. A parade had to be canceled because of snow and the late arrival of the ship; but the "ta-ra-ram" was hardly over.

The poet's first major public appearance the next night drew a sellout crowd of more than three thousand to the Mecca Temple in midtown Manhattan. Another thousand stood in the cold outside. The event united, at least for the moment, Hebraists and Yiddishists, Zionists and non-Zionist Jewish labor leaders, the Weizmann camp in the ZOA and their Brandeisist opponents, Orthodox, Conservative, and Reform Jews. Judge Julian Mack, who probably knew little, if any, of Bialik's poetry, opened the evening with a speech in English, which the poet could not understand. He was followed by Nahum Sokolow, the number-two person in the WZO, Lipsky, Yehoash (Solomon Bloomgarden), the Yiddish poet and Bible translator, Rabbi Stephen S. Wise, and others. Bialik's Yiddish-language speech failed to meet the expectations of the charged audience, which gave him a twelve-minute ovation nonetheless. The tour had begun.[72]

6

During the next five months the poet became a fixture of the New York Jewish community. Fund raisers called upon him freely, sometimes arranging events without his permission. He spoke at grand charitable happenings on behalf of the Jewish National Fund (Keren Kayemet) in the Hotel Astor and the auditorium of Cooper Union, and at modest events in local synagogues, sharing the platform with everyone from Congressman Sol Bloom to Yossele Shlisskey, "the Yascha Heifetz of the vocal artists."[73] A few weeks after his arrival Bialik was dispatched on a by-then familiar mission to Boston, where he appeared together with Professor Nathan Isaacs of Harvard University. April and May took him to several of the large Jewish communities in the Northeast, Midwest, and South. In one of his few contacts with non-Jewish people of letters, journalist Norman Hapgood shared the podium with him in Baltimore. In Cleveland the poet was welcomed at "a grand reception." Featured on the program were "tableaux [with a musical background] presenting pictures of four [of his] great poems" and Cantor Kanter singing a poem authored by a local writer and set to music. The tableaux were intended to give "a living picture . . . of the genius of Bialik" to "the thousands assembled in the Masonic Temple," few of whom had heard of the poet even three months before. During his stay in the Ohio city, Bialik planted "cedars of Lebanon" in the Hebrew poets section of the Shakespeare Garden (now the Hebrew Cultural Garden). His visits were all well publicized in advance; and the financial results were satisfactory. By April he felt sufficiently knowledgeable about fund raising in America to proffer advice regarding the large loan which the Keren Hayesod hoped to negotiate.[74]

Bialik did not limit himself to money raising. He had some involvement with the affairs of the ZOA, "endear[ing] . . . himself," as Louis Lipsky inelegantly put it, to "Zionists who were never aware of the deep sources of Hebrew tradition and had never seen or heard a personality of such varied Jewish quality." (Lipsky himself was American-born and knew no Hebrew.)[75] Bialik intervened with the National Executive Committee of the ZOA to prevent their making an accommodation with the ultra-Orthodox Agudath Israel movement, which, he claimed, had done "practically nothing" for the *yishuv*. Henrietta Szold and Rabbi Stephen S. Wise were among those present at that meeting; Abraham S. Waldstein, known to Bialik from *HaShiloah* and now back in America, sent his regrets. A few days later the poet held a press conference to a "packed house" at the ZOA offices, in which he offered an update on conditions in Palestine.

His most significant political activity was the White House appearance, which can be seen as part of the campaign to enlist the support of the

A rather unhappy-looking Chaim Naḥman Bialik with his wife, Manya, as they arrived in New York on the SS *Mauretania*, 9 February 1926. (Courtesy of UPI-Bettmann.)

United States government for Zionism. Undoubtedly well coached, Bialik took the opportunity to thank the president for the nonbinding Congressional Resolution of 1922 in support of the Balfour Declaration and the British Mandate. After he left the White House, he was entertained by the British ambassador, which seemed to indicate that His Majesty's government appreciated the potential political import of the meeting of poet and president. Following his return to Palestine, Bialik maintained only slight interest in the political affairs of American Zionism.[76]

More important than his political involvement and perhaps even than his fund raising were Bialik's cultural activities, "the spiritual task" he had set out for himself before leaving Palestine. These included ceremonial functions, such as accepting honorary degrees from the Jewish Theological Seminary and the Jewish Institute of Religion. (Perhaps jaded by all the adulation, he sent identical letters of acceptance to both institutions describing the honor as "a sign of the renewed covenant between scholars of Judaica . . . and Hebrew writers.") He delivered formal addresses on aspects of Jewish culture to the national conventions of the Young Judaea youth movement, of Avukah, the student Zionist association, of the Keren Hayesod and the ZOA, and to a mass meeting of Hebraists held in his honor in New York. And there was the staged public debate with Jabotinsky on the importance of Hebrew to the national revival.[77]

Chaim Naḥman Bialik planting a tree in the Hebrew Cultural Garden in Cleveland, 1926. (Courtesy of The Hebrew Writers Association, Tel Aviv.)

In talks at dozens of less formal events—a visit to the National Hebrew School on New York's Lower East Side, a faculty-student lunch at the Hebrew Union College in Cincinnati, a gathering of young intellectuals in Cleveland, an evening for Hebrew writers at Lipsky's home—he spread his aura over those with whom he came in contact. In fact, his mere presence in the United States energized Hebraists and teachers from Wilkes-Barre to Waco and beyond. With great fanfare the ZOA launched a National Cultural Corporation at a special conclave in New York with Bialik in attendance, the goal of which was to raise the cultural level of American Jewry; but it quickly proved a failure.[78]

In addition to his public appearances, Bialik spent a great deal of time meeting informally with American Hebrew and Yiddish writers and with scholars of Judaica. He was able to renew contact with old friends and associates, such as Simon Ginzburg, Berkowitz, Silkiner, and the family of Sholem Aleichem, who had died a decade before. He met Max Raisin, Persky, and others with whom he had corresponded over the years, and established valuable contacts for the future with other Hebraists. His visits to the Hebrew Union College and the Jewish Theological Seminary also sowed the seeds of future cooperation. At the Seminary he had hoped to meet Israel Davidson, "the only person [in the world] able to lend much assistance" to his Spanish poetry project; but the two crossed paths in mid-ocean, as Davidson headed for a visiting post at the new Hebrew University in Palestine.[79] Bialik met Joseph Marcus, his American research assistant who acted as the liaison with Davidson, and Professor Alexander Marx, the Seminary librarian whom he also knew by correspondence, as well as other members of the Seminary faculty. He luxuriated in the "uniquely rich" Seminary library, buttressing the self-assurance of the seminarians, still not altogether confident of their standing in the world of Jewish letters.[80]

Contacts with Yiddishists were less pleasant. He was disturbed by the crassness of much of the American-Yiddish press, especially by advertisements in at least one Yiddish paper, which appropriated his name to promote Palestine land sales ("Bialik says: . . . 'Buy land . . . in *Eretz Yisroel!*' "). The ads cheapened his image, as he had feared might happen, and awakened his old prejudices about the United States.[81] Bialik disagreed passionately with the Diaspora nationalism of the American Yiddishists who negated the value of the Hebrew language and of Zionism and looked to the Soviet Union as a model for the Jewish future. The largest Yiddish-language daily in the country, the socialist New York *Forverts*, was politely, but predictably, noncommittal about his visit. At a banquet ostensibly tendered in his honor by New York's Y. L. Peretz [Yiddish] Writers' Association, several people, including a journalist with the communist daily *Di Frayhayt*, who were, no doubt, aware of Bialik's hatred for Bolshevism, accused him of "selling himself to the devil." They meant the moneyed American Jews underwriting his tour. Although he answered in kind with a vigorous defense of his principles, the incident left an unpleasant aftertaste.[82]

The work for Dvir brought mixed results. Bialik left America with "a box full of new manuscripts" for publication. Together he and Levin had some success in arranging for better distribution of Dvir books and for regular reviews. Money, however, had been the real concern. Levin, the more businesslike of the two, had set a goal of twenty thousand pounds to ensure the company's solvency.[83] As his contribution to the effort, Bialik published a piece on Dvir and Moriah in Hebrew and in English, in which he surveyed the history of his publishing endeavors. He emphasized, quite truthfully, that his "main object" had never been profit but rather the revitalization "of Hebrew education, which," he feared, "was gradually becoming emptied of its national and humane content."[84] The "lion's share of the worry," that is, the actual money-raising, Bialik left to Levin, as the latter remarked with some annoyance. The poet's *amour propre* made any fund raising difficult for him; solicitation for his own company was particularly distasteful. Levin labored arduously; and they delayed their departure from late April to early July because of Dvir. Levin worried that they would return to Palestine without sufficient funds to guarantee the existence of the company. Bialik feared that the company's workers and management would assume "there was no limit" to American largesse and waste whatever they received. Both were right. The original goal was not met; by late 1926 Dvir was on the brink of bankruptcy; and support had to be sought elsewhere than the United States.[85]

7

Assessing the results of Bialik's American foray requires a consideration of its effects on America, on Bialik himself, and, in the longer term, on the *yishuv*. In general, the trip's American sponsors, as well as the leaders of international Zionism and of the *yishuv*, pronounced themselves satisfied with the visit, which "ushered in a feeling of joy and renaissance in American Zionism." *HaDo'ar* described the tour as "days of blessing," especially for Hebrew culture aficionados. Levin wrote to Weizmann, that the "visit . . . had brought tremendous benefits"; and Emanuel Neumann conceded that the poet had "served our practical purposes well." The United Palestine Appeal raised over 80 percent of its quota, "the largest sum ever secured [in any place to that date] in one year for Palestine." Americans were particularly pleased by the impression Bialik, unlike most Palestinian emissaries, gave, of being eager "not only to teach [about Palestine], but also to learn" about America. A few naysayers felt the "mission had not been much of a success," perhaps because the American-Jewish community had not been culturally transformed during those five months. The continuing interest in Bialik after his departure, however, can be appreciated from the intense and widespread enthusiasm generated by his sixtieth birthday in 1933 and the deep sense of communal loss when he died a year later. Even in the land of dollars, according to Rabbi Stephen Wise, "one Bialik" was now worth a "thousand Warburgs."[86]

The poet left America, as he had come, ambivalent; but the scale tipped farther to the positive side than before. He had experienced American-Jewish life firsthand and become very minimally conversant with the culture of the United States. He renewed acquaintance with former schoolmates and others from Europe; and he met Americans, such as writer and translator Maurice Samuel, who "tried to give him some sort of insight into the nature of American civilization." If his former notions about America did not lose all their weight, they were now well balanced by knowledge of aspects of American life with which he had not previously been familiar. Rarely in the future would he lose sight of America as a significant factor in Jewish life, particularly in the welfare of the *yishuv*, his mixed feelings notwithstanding.[87]

Just after leaving New York, Bialik wrote to Ahad HaAm summing up his recent experiences in well rehearsed terms. During his stay, he complained, tongue-in-cheek, he "had not found [even] a [single] free moment to read about himself in the American papers," so busy had he been with "meetings, banquets, . . . parties, interviews, discussions, visits, declarations, proclamations, commencements, [and a hundred other meaningless activities, all of them accompanied by] . . . American noise, confusion, tumult, ta-ra-ram, bluff, and humbug."[88] He struck some similar, if more oblique, notes in a long poem penned in New York and published in *HaDo'ar* just after his departure.[89] Elsewhere, he even cast doubt on the physical security of American Jews. Their future, he asserted, was no more certain than that of Jews elsewhere, their achievements no more than "a soap bubble."[90]

Regarding the future of Jewish culture in America, the poet remained ambivalent. His most profound prejudices had related to American Jewry; and they were not entirely dispelled during his stay. After five months in America, he was painfully aware that "American Jews produced . . . [little] distinctive Jewish art and literature," that they talked "glibly about Jewish culture" but remained largely ignorant of "the original sources of our spiritual treasures." He was "deeply shocked" to discover on a visit to the home of Professor Louis Ginzberg of the Jewish Theological Seminary, one of the world's greatest Talmudists, that the scholar's children "knew no Hebrew." Reform and Conservative rabbis, he asserted, had contributed "no new or original ideas whatsoever" to Jewish culture; Hebrew letters in the United

States were in a "degraded condition," the teachers "over-Americanized" and ineffectual. In any case, he declared, Jewish culture in America could never be more than a pale imitation of the holistic cultural life that had once existed in eastern Europe and now was achievable only in the all-Jewish society of Palestine.[91] Zionism, which in other countries offered the greatest promise for a creative Jewish existence, amounted to little more than sterile philanthropy in America, according to Bialik. "Most of the leaders" of American Zionism, like Louis Lipsky, were "steeped in alien culture," hardly able to arouse "hunger for Hebrew" learning.[92]

On the other hand, Bialik acknowledged publicly that his longstanding apprehensions regarding America had been exaggerated and admitted to Ahad HaAm and others that he "had no regrets" at having undertaken the trip.[93] Although he knew no English and spent almost all of his time in the United States within the confines of the Jewish community, Bialik had come to sense the vitality and potential of America. He arrived convinced that America was "the apotheosis of a mechanical civilization, a machine itself," but discovered "living organisms, alive and awake," continually renewing themselves. Like Jabotinsky and many other Europeans, he was attracted by the "unlimited power" of America enhanced by freedom from "the spiritual and cultural baggage of the past." He recognized the opportunity for Jews inherent in the absence of European social and religious traditions and in the new notions of cultural pluralism espoused by Ralph Waldo Emerson [?] and John Dewey.[94]

He recognized, too, "the revival of interest in Jewish culture" in the New World, the "undefined longing for stature and self-recognition, . . . [the] firm will to . . . emerge out of spiritual penury onto the . . . 'royal highway' of Jewish history." Bialik sensed the benefits for Jewish creativity inherent in the well-being and prosperity of the United States. To an extent, he could excuse the spiritual shortcomings of American Jewry because of its "relative youth and newness." He asserted the notion that the first period of American-Jewish history, "the period of adaptation to the living conditions of the new country," was ending; he came to perceive the Jewish community of the United States as "fallow soil," which, if "properly cultivated, . . . [would] yield rich harvests."[95] In his farewell to America delivered at the ZOA convention in Buffalo in June, the convention at which Jabotinsky was prevented from speaking, Bialik reiterated the statement he had made in London at the beginning of his trip. "American Jews," he declared in words tinged with despondency and dependency, but also with expectancy and faith, are "the sole hope of the Jews of the world; . . . the Jewish homeland . . . [will] be restored and rebuilt" by them. On a number of occasions before he left the United States and afterwards, the poet went even further, characterizing American Jewry as less than "total compensation for the destruction of our life in the other countries of the Diaspora—but [certainly] partial compensation." This was great praise, indeed, although hardly unqualified.[96]

Regarded as a pundit, Bialik's opinions on any topic evoked considerable interest in the Jewish world at large, and especially in the *yishuv*, where "culture rotated about his personality." He broke the return trip in London, where he reported to the executive of the World Zionist Organization.[97] His views received their most dramatic airing in Tel Aviv, where he addressed a crowd of several thousand at the outdoor Beit HaAm on October 6. The large audience—perhaps one of every ten Tel Avivians—and the extensive coverage in *HaAretz* and *Davar* testify not only to the prominence of the speaker but also to the importance of the topic.[98] The speech, which represents Bialik's fullest exposition of the meaning of America, highlighted the question of the relationship of the *yishuv* to the New World and its Jewry. The poet repeated much that he had said before in other forums, but he sounded a new, more positive tone, altogether different from the resignation which had marked his send-off nine months earlier.[99]

Although the talk contains some curious misreadings of the American scene (an assertion that Americans had demonstrated little nationalistic sentiment before World War I, for example) and errors of fact, it is essentially perceptive, if somewhat over-optimistic. Like foreign visitors from Crèvecoeur and de Tocqueville to Jabotinsky, Bialik spoke of the United States as "the land of unlimited possibilities," which was giving birth to "a new life" and "a new type of human being," free of the constraints of Europe. He spoke of American youth, energy, and plenty, and of the willingness even of writers and intellectuals to dirty their hands with daily affairs, making it possible to accomplish things undoable elsewhere. Rather than uncultured brashness, American "naturalness" was the "most legitimate and beautiful" character trait. American bluster he now considered the "clean, pure" self-expression "of youngsters"; in "bluff" he recognized Americans' sense of "playfulness." Ever the small-town boy, he seemed almost in awe of Americans who were able effortlessly to negotiate their vast, populous country. Americans were "generous of spirit" and remarkably peaceful; the "near absence of crime in New York" he found incredible. (This in the Prohibition Era!) And Americans were not without cultural attainments. Especially in the applied arts and sciences, such as psychology, "Torah would come forth from America." Americans had their culture heroes, such as Washington and Lincoln, who already served as "examples with respect to matters of the spirit"; and in the future strong indigenous traditions would develop.[100]

Turning the tables, Bialik declared American Jews one of the "wonders" of the universe. Their arrival in the New World he pronounced "a mini-exodus from Egypt," a compliment fraught with implied meaning, although he feared they remained precariously camped on the political and economic shores of their land of milk and honey. The struggle to become established had "dulled them" spiritually; but unlike other Americans, they had not entirely thrown off the yoke of the past. They retained strong Jewish loyalties and were eager to create a viable, vital, "communal, Hebrew life." They possessed "special sentiment" for the land of Israel. Appropriate emissaries, "who would take them to heart and seek to draw them near," could create "an enthusiastic [Zionist] movement."[101] In short, whatever its failings, America was a land of great promise for all, including the beleaguered Jews of the *yishuv*, so much in need of moral support and funds in their epic struggle to create a renewed Jewish society and culture.

8

Bialik's trip and subsequent reconsideration of America had consequences for the relationship of the *yishuv* to the New World. That he proposed reevaluating some of the basic negative notions of Palestinians about America at a mass gathering organized by the Hebrew Writers' Association, a group known for strong nationalistic sympathies and suspicion of the Diaspora, especially the United States, gave his comments added bite. It may also have contributed to the cooling of his relations with some members of the Association.[102] In the years following his trip, Bialik worked to realize his rosy prognosis. He did what he could to further the development of Zionism and Hebrew culture in the United States; he exploited the contacts he had made with American Hebraists, Yiddishists, and scholars; and he acted as an intermediary for American philanthropists interested in the *yishuv*.

In the United States the afterglow of Bialik's visit lingered even beyond his death in 1934, helping, according to Morris Rothenberg, erstwhile president of the ZOA, "to give new direction to . . . Jewish destiny and new courage to . . . Jewish character."[103] He continued to be written about often in the American Jewish press; and his own essays and poetry appeared in print frequently in Hebrew and in English and Yiddish translations, and even in a medium which the "village boy" had "never imagined," a phonograph record.[104] His ongoing popularity despite the occasional gaffe, such as forgetting to greet the sensitive Lipsky on his fiftieth birthday, emboldened Bialik to intervene from time to time in American Zionist affairs on behalf of the *yishuv*, albeit not very effectively. In late 1927, for example, he appealed—without result—through Henrietta Szold to the executive of the ZOA and to a national United Palestine Appeal conference "to avert [through increased remittances the] calamity" of bankruptcy and collapse then facing the educational network of the *yishuv*.[105]

Two years later Bialik became embroiled in a nasty squabble involving both American and Palestinian Zionists and their opponents. Reuben Brainin was a veteran Hebrew writer and a longtime vice-president of the ZOA, with whom the poet had had considerable contact over the years. In the mid-1920s Brainin began to exhibit interest in the communist experiment in Russia, and especially in the Crimean Jewish agricultural colonies. The American Jewish philanthropists bankrolling the colonies coopted him for publicity and fund raising, exploiting his Zionist connections. In the *yishuv*, which he had visited about the time of Bialik's sojourn in America, and in the United States, Zionists wished either to silence Brainin or to distance him from the Zionist movement. His public attacks on Bialik, as well as the latter's passionate Zionism and fierce antagonism to Bolshevism, brought the poet into the fracas in 1929, when, after a tour of Russia, Brainin wrote glowingly of what he had seen without mentioning Soviet oppression of Zionism.[106] "The battle of the books" was joined in several arenas: the press in America and Palestine; a Tel Aviv meeting of "activists and writers," chaired by Bialik, which acted as a kangaroo court; and, finally, a hearing held in Berlin by a World Zionist Congress tribunal, with Bialik as plaintiff and Brainin as defendant. Bialik was vindicated. The court and many other Zionists seemed to feel, however, that the poet and his colleagues had overreacted; and the feud was allowed to recede into history without final resolution.[107]

Bialik's heightened involvement with American Jewish cultural affairs between 1926 and 1934 proved more rewarding and constituted an important link in the chain connecting the *yishuv* to the New World. Building on old relationships and on the new connections established during his trip, Bialik began to work closely with a number of American scholars, especially those of the Theological Seminary and the Hebrew Union College, notwithstanding his strictures regarding Reform and Conservative rabbis. He read the publications of the latter institution with approval, although he believed its *Annual* (*HUCA*) should contain more articles in Hebrew. Neumark had died in 1924; but Bialik established ties with other scholars at the College, such as Zvi Diesendruck, the linguist and philosopher whom he had met during the latter's brief tenure at the Hebrew University. From the College's eminent musicologist, Abraham Zvi Idelsohn, and others, he solicited manuscripts for Dvir and contributions for the journal, *Reshumot*, which he had founded together with Ravnitzki and Alter Druyanov. Bialik was excited about Diesendruck's book on the Hebrew language, *Min HaSafa VeLifnim*, which Dvir published in 1933; but he condescendingly told Idelsohn, who had lived and taught in Jerusalem for many years before Bialik had come to Palestine, that his works might "satisfy the needs of the American Jew" but not "our clientele."[108] Scholars affiliated with the Reform wing of Judaism—but not the College—with whom Bialik corresponded in these years, included Max Raisin, Ḥaim Tchernowitz (Rav Tza'ir) of the Jewish Institute of Religion, a former Odessa friend and colleague, and Hyman G. Enelow, whose critical edition of the fourteenth-century work, *Menorat Ha-Ma'or*, the poet recognized as "precious and wonderful, incomparable," in fact.[109]

Although most of the American Reformers with whom Bialik was in close contact were transplanted eastern Europeans, he seemed to have more in common with the scholars at the Conservative Seminary. He admired the work of Marx, Ginzberg, Shalom Spiegel, Michael Higger, and, of course, Davidson. He saw to it that the Seminary library received the books published by Dvir; and he attempted unsuccessfully to persuade Ginzberg to remain in Palestine, when the latter visited there in 1928 and 1929.[110] Joseph Marcus, his poorly-and-not-always-regularly-paid research assistant and scribe in the field of Spanish Jewish poetry, has already been mentioned. Isaac Rivkind, another habitué of the Seminary library, assisted Bialik in a number of ways and contributed to *Reshumot*.[111] The scholarly collaboration begun earlier with Davidson remained particularly close. Their work on the medieval Spanish poets overlapped; they shared material and critiqued each other's research; through Davidson the Seminary "opened to [Bialik] . . . the gates of its book treasury." But the relationship was not always amicable, partly because of the unavoidable element of competition. The prickly Davidson accused Bialik on several occasions of overlooking his works and Marcus's contributions; the poet felt slighted, at times, by Davidson, who probably regarded him as lacking in scholarly methodology. Apparently, though, their long-distance relationship survived until Bialik's death.[112]

There were also exchanges with Orthodox scholars, such as Rabbi Yekutiel Greenwald of Columbus, Ohio, and with several Jewish academics.[113] Bialik felt particular closeness to people who had lived in Palestine, such as Samuel Faigin and Israel Eitan of Pittsburgh and Nehemiah Samuel Libowitz, a Brooklyn dealer in precious stones and an enthusiastic amateur researcher, who published more than twenty books on mysticism and rabbinics over the years. Bialik encouraged Eitan to write in Hebrew and to contribute to the new linguistic and academic journals of Palestine; and he maintained a lively correspondence with Libowitz, although he kept his "exalted and precious [jeweller] friend" at arm's length from Dvir.[114] Bialik concluded an agreement, sight unseen, with Simon Bernstein, the longtime editor of *Dos Iddishe Folk*, the Yiddish organ of the ZOA, for Dvir to publish his critical edition of unknown Italian Jewish poems. Although Bernstein had a doctorate and other academic credentials, when the manuscript arrived, Bialik adjudged the poems to be "garbage." He asked to be released from his commitment, even though Bernstein had agreed to pay the initial costs of publication himself.[115]

Simon Ginzburg linked the worlds of scholarship and Hebrew belles lettres of Odessa, New York, and Tel Aviv. His reunion with Bialik in America reinvigorated their friendship and literary collaboration. Between 1927 and 1933 Dvir published three works of Moshe Ḥaim Luzzato edited by Ginzburg and two volumes of the latter's own writing, as well as the Ḥaverim series of books in Hebrew by young American authors (Silkiner, Avraham Sho'er, Ephraim Lissitzky, and Simon Halkin), of which Ginzburg served as the American coordinator.[116] The two exchanged publications, comments on current events, and gossip; Bialik confided to Ginzburg that the American Hebrew poet, Hillel Bavli, a Seminary faculty member, was a "bag of wind." The senior poet responded with measured words to his sensitive colleague's requests for a critique of his poetry (on one poem: "excessive muscularity"; on the full corpus: "your own singular voice"). In 1933 Ginzburg followed Bialik to Palestine, although he returned to the United States in 1939.[117]

During these years Bialik served as a bridge between the cultural worlds of America and the *yishuv*. He felt a responsibility to fulfill the obligation with which he had been charged in 1926 by Simon Bernstein, "to lay the broad spiritual groundwork for . . . a Hebrew renaissance" in America, which many Palestinians were increasingly recognizing as the only viable Diaspora community.[118] Hebrew and Yiddish writers in the New World sought Bialik's stamp of approval, which he conferred generously; he helped to promote writers and artists from the *yishuv*, such as painter Pinḥas Litvinovsky, in the United States; and in absentia he was called upon for such tasks as judging the annual *HaDo'ar* writing contest.[119]

His most sustained undertaking was the publication of American works through Dvir, especially in the Ḥaverim series. The American authors shared publication expenses; but hard pressed themselves, they often failed to meet their obligations on time. Bialik persevered. He found some of the young writers "imitative." Others, however, such as Yoḥanan Twersky, he recognized as "first-rate" talents, who would be a credit to the firm; even the "derivative" Americans, he averred, exhibited "richness of content, form, and style." The extent of the talent pool he found staggering, especially in light of his previous assumptions—accurate enough for an earlier era—about its small size and the cultural poverty of Jewish America. (He was reduced to asking the author of a praiseworthy collection of "authentic" Yiddish poetry in 1929, "Who are you?")[120]

That Dvir published American authors served not only to strengthen Hebrew culture in America. It enlarged the company's list of authors and gave it added variety. More importantly, it worked to broaden the scope of the emergent culture of the *yishuv* by connecting it with the much larger American Jewish community, which Bialik and others hoped would become its hinterland. And it made the American experience accessible to Hebrew readers. In addition, although the publishing company had quickly become rooted in Palestine, like other institutions there, it rested upon a shaky financial foundation. That it survived during these years was in large part due to the volunteer assistance and financial support of Jews "all over the world, including America," who "felt [love] for the poet."[121] Not only did American authors—or their well-wishers—subsidize their own books. As the economic and political situation in Poland deteriorated, the United States became the principal Diaspora market of Dvir. Vigorous efforts were now made to sell the firm's books—and shares—in the New World. By 1929 about a third of the shares not held by Bialik, Levin, and Ravnitzki had been purchased by Americans, while almost half of its outstanding accounts were owed by one American bookseller. A year later, when "crushing debts . . . and interest were devouring" the concern, Bialik appealed to Levin, who was again in New York, "to become the redeemer of Dvir" by negotiating an interest-free loan, no easy task in Depression-Era America.[122]

If Americans' devotion did not bring instant relief for Dvir, it did smooth the way for several cultural and charitable enterprises in Palestine. American philanthropists had shown little interest in Bialik before meeting him; and he had expressed disapproval of their values. During his New World sojourn, however, the man of letters learned to value practical entrepreneurs. He would never suffer gladly those he considered to be rich fools. Witness the snappish letter to Robert Marwill in 1929, in which he declared that "only the blind would fail to recognize the great things we have done in this small land," and his annoyance with Lessing Rosenwald's openhandedness towards blacks and lack of generosity towards Jews! Still, he came to believe that the wealth of the United States was of such magnitude and so easily obtained that there the rich would one day free themselves of the possessiveness that gripped even the fabulously wealthy in the Old World. Americans, he now asserted, "would be the first [ironically] to break the thrall of the dollar fetish." Unlike Jabotinsky and others, he trusted non-Zionist, American millionaires sufficiently to support Weizmann in his efforts to enlist them in the service of Zionism in the reorganized Jewish Agency.[123]

There were several American "Maecenases" with whom Bialik became closely connected, among them the Rosenbloom family of Pittsburgh and Nathan and Lena Straus. More important to Bialik personally were his connections to Israel Matz, head of the Ex-Lax Company and a generous supporter of Hebrew culture in the United States and elsewhere, and to Samuel Simon Bloom, a Philadelphia manufacturer of false teeth who moved his factory to Palestine in 1926. Through Bialik, Matz and Bloom became significant contributors to the development of culture in the *yishuv*.

Probably because of Bialik's iconoclastic past, Sol Rosenbloom, an early munificent supporter of the new Hebrew University, expressed doubt in 1923 that he could "be entrusted" with overseeing Jewish studies there. Rosenbloom's widow, however, decided, after meeting him in America, to support the poet's appointment to the committee administering her $500,000 gift to the university in memory of her husband.[124] Bialik headed the building committee for the Nathan and Lena Straus Health Center in Jerusalem in 1927 and then for a similar center in Tel Aviv. Straus provided some support for indigent writers; and Bialik entertained hope that funds would be forthcoming for a writers' residence. His ties to Straus, whom he described as a "sensitive, old man, [who had] endeared himself to all residents of the *yishuv*," brought the poet into close contact with Henrietta Szold, who provided yet another window onto America.[125]

Matz established a foundation "for the promotion of Hebrew literature and culture and for [the] relief of Hebrew writers" in 1925, with Bialik as a member of its advisory council. Until his death the poet acted as an advocate for indigent writers and their survivors in Palestine, the United States, and even Russia, and for the cause of Hebrew letters, in general. Usually his pleas received a favorable hearing, although at times the foundation applied criteria more stringent than Bialik thought appropriate. In 1933, for example, he had difficulty in securing support for a new monthly publication of the Palestine Writers' Association.[126]

Bloom was "an ordinary Jew, a simple businessman" with healthy "Jewish intuition," according to Bialik. By his own description, he was an idealist who had come to Palestine "to lend a helping hand to the upbuilding of our beautiful land" after thirty years of "personal sacrifices [in America] for Zionism." He financed the erection in 1928 of Ohel Shem, a community center in Tel Aviv, which had been a dream of Bialik, who hoped it would provide educational and cultural programming for secularized adults, especially on the Sabbath, and serve as a model for similar centers elsewhere in the country. Bloom felt betrayed and unappreciated in Palestine by what he perceived to be a lackadaisical Zionist administration, unacquainted with American standards of efficiency, despite the participation of Henrietta Szold; and he felt exploited by workers, whom he believed to be lazy, greedy, and overprotected by a union unaccustomed to American standards of productivity. Bialik's depiction of Bloom indicates no deep mutual understanding between them. Still, the industrialist was attracted by the poet's plans and volunteered his aid. Later he attempted to raise funds in America to expand the programming of Ohel Shem. Their cooperation is an indication of how successful Bialik had become over the years, not only in strengthening the cultural bonds connecting American Jewry and the *yishuv* but also in garnering the support of wealthy Americans for his pet projects.[127]

9

During a period of some three and a half decades, Bialik had partially and gradually overcome the prejudices of a small-town, European-Jewish intellectual regarding America. He became involved in certain facets of American Jewish life and drew Americans into the cultural orbit of the *yishuv*. With him one sees that aspect of life in Palestine which should have been least amenable to American influences becoming intertwined with the affairs of that country's Jewry. Especially in the last two decades of his life, the poet became increasingly aware that the *yishuv* would never realize its potential, even in the realm of culture with which he was most directly concerned, without massive assistance from the American Diaspora. That understanding, together with a growing appreciation of positive aspects of America, led Bialik, the outstanding cultural and literary personality of the *yishuv* and a sharp critic of the shortcomings of the United States, to become intimately connected with Americans.

And yet, however closely Bialik worked with Americans, and however much he revised his early preconceptions, he never became a wholehearted enthusiast of the New World. He remained sceptical about American culture and character. His optimism regarding the prospects of American Jewry was ever guarded, his efforts to strengthen the community and his sense of its importance to Zionism notwithstanding. He never faltered in his conviction that the *yishuv* would be the only viable center of Jewish culture in the long term, and perhaps the world's only viable Jewish community.

Towards the end of his days Bialik was again expressing deep reservations about the United States. He thought the contemporary generation there "degraded." He could appreciate the movie *Ben Hur* and the work of George Foote Moore, the gentile Harvard rabbinics scholar; but he continued to find the "sensational" American press well below any acceptable journalistic standard. He deplored the way in which American Jews had reduced Weizmann, "the leader of the generation," to little more than "an itinerant beggar." He was appalled that the Hebrew poet, Menaḥem Mendel Dolitzky, who had once dwelled on "the heights of 'Parnassus' " as the chosen successor to the remarkable Yehuda Leib Gordon, had been condemned in the United States first to "the cellar of the Yiddish-language, yellow press" and then to death "in a poorhouse." When he heard that Y. D. Berkowitz was at last coming to Palestine to live, he rejoiced and allowed himself the wish that one day "all of our worthy comrades who are laboring faithfully at God's work [that is, the Hebrew writers of America], will become rooted here in the land of Israel."[128]

If it was "partial compensation" for the Jewish civilization of Europe that had been destroyed in World War I, America was still *galut* (exile) to Bialik. To him it was a land, like any, other than Palestine, of exile and alienation for Jews, of "weakening of the national will. . . . Nothing in the Exile has happened," he wrote to American Jews in 1929, "to modify our belief, that it is the scene of our nation's degeneration, a blind alley with no hope or way out, whereas in Palestine, everything we dreamt of is coming true to an unhoped-for degree."[129] Whatever Jews do in the Diaspora "in the fields of science and culture," he told an American audience on another occasion, "belongs to strangers." During the years "in the Exile," the Jewish people had "produced men with great ideas that embrace the whole universe." To Bialik, however, "the smallest creation in the land of Israel" was worth more than all that, because of the direct benefit to the Jewish people.[130] Even after Hitler had come to power, Bialik remained convinced that the New World was only marginally different from other lands of the Diaspora, if at all.[131] In 1927, soon after his return from the United States, the erstwhile iconoclastic poet penned some words of old-fashioned faith to an American journalist with the hope that he would convey them to his readers. Palestine, Bialik said, is "the single, central location, towards which God has pointed His finger . . . saying: 'This is the only place where you will find rest; and there is no other.' "[132]

Bailik's coffin arriving at Ohel Shem, 1934. Ohel Shem was the Tel Aviv cultural center built with the help of the American false-teeth manufacturer Samuel Simon Bloom. (Courtesy of the Central Zionist Archives, Jerusalem.)

CHAPTER
4
Berl Katznelson

A Man of the Spirit Confronts the Land of Dollars

EXCEPT FOR Ben-Gurion, Berl Katznelson may have wielded more influence in the *yishuv* during the interwar period than anyone else. The guru, conscience, and thinker of the labor movement, he took an active role in its affairs and in those of the *yishuv* at large. As editor of the movement's weekly *Kuntres* and daily *Davar* and founder of its Am Oved publishing house, he had platforms for making his voice heard. Anita Shapira, his definitive biographer, has called him, "the architect of Palestinian socialist society";[1] and in these years the *yishuv* and that socialist society were in many ways one.

The outstanding pioneering institutions of the *yishuv*—the *kibbutzim* (collectives) and *moshavim* (smallholders' settlements), the Histadrut national labor union, and HaMashbir, the consumers' cooperative—were established by the labor movement; and Katznelson helped to shape them. From Labor's ranks came much of the political leadership of Jewish Palestine; many of its foremost intellectuals were card-carrying members or sympathizers like Bialik. Berl was mentor to all, even if they frequently disregarded his somber, principled, demanding counsel. He declined high political office and refused to join the Zionist Executive, the Jewish Agency Executive, or the Jewish National Council in Palestine (the Va'ad Le'umi). Yet his strong personality, uncompromising principles, and enormous creativity made him *primus inter pares* in the Zionist body politic.

Katznelson was an intense patriot with loyalties to the Jewish people, Jewish culture, and aspects of Jewish tradition. As a young man, he flirted with several varieties of radicalism, eventually settling into an eclectic, non-

Marxist socialism suffused with Jewish values. He was a militant Zionist, who "rebelled against the servility and cultural poverty" of the Diaspora.[2] After his aliyah to Palestine, his deepest concerns were the internal affairs of the *yishuv*. He lacked enthusiasm for the gentile world, in particular for the United States, which he saw as the epitome of capitalism and an alternative place of settlement to Palestine that invited assimilation. Of those who contributed most significantly to molding the *yishuv* in its formative period and preparing it for statehood, Katznelson may have been the least curious about the United States, although by the 1920s, he exhibited considerable knowledge of events there.[3] Until the late 1930s, he limited his interest in America almost entirely to its Jews but generally avoided involvement in their affairs. Often he addressed American issues in asides and parenthetical comments; but his extraordinary position in the *yishuv* gave even his casual views considerable weight.

1

Berl spent most of his early years in Bobruisk, the Belarus town where he was born in 1887. In the turn-of-the-century years, Bobruisk Jews were on the move. Like others in the Pale of Settlement, they lived in poverty, feared pogroms, and resented the lack of civic rights. America, Katznelson later wrote, appeared to be both "a haven" and "the land of gold."[4] His younger brother, Isser, "hoped" it would "rescue [the Katznelson family] . . . from [their financial] . . . troubles."[5] His step-brother, Ḥaim, and brother, Israel, as well as friends and more distant relatives headed for the *goldene medine*. In early 1908, not altogether sure of his ultimate goals, Berl thought America might "straighten out a hunchback" like himself.[6] Later that year, however, he headed south to Palestine rather than west to the United States.

Katznelson had limited formal education, although he read widely; he learned English as an adult, but imperfectly. Before leaving for Palestine he had seen nothing of the world outside Russia. He may have gleaned some knowledge of America from the books and journals to which he had easy access as librarian of the Bobruisk Jewish library. The works he recommended to his sister, Hannah, in 1912, however, do not indicate familiarity with the New World. They included only two American selections, Mark Twain's *Tom Sawyer* in Hebrew translation, and Max Raisin's Hebrew biography of Mordecai Manuel Noah.[7]

From the European-Palestinian Hebrew writer, Yosef Ḥaim Brenner, a friend whose works he admired, Berl got a mixed view of America. Brenner's 1911 novel, *Mikan u-miKan*, presents a rather bleak portrait of American "laborers [who] do their jobs like automatons, while buried up to their necks in muck and rags and yarn and scraps of cloth . . . and [then fritter away] their leisure hours" on worthless pursuits. But in *HaAhdut*, the Palestinian Poale Zion journal, he observed approvingly that hundreds of thousands of Jews who had been unemployed in Russia "make a living" in America and, as a result, had acquired power. In addition, they had "created the [American] Jewish press and [Yiddish] literature."[8]

Emigré family members and friends also depicted life in America with ups and downs, as in Russia.[9] Mostly they reported the downs. When they could find work at all, Berl's brothers and other Bobruiskers labored at tedious jobs in dehumanizing conditions for skimpy wages. None had realized the American dream. One of his friends there committed suicide. Katznelson feared for his brothers' health, and even more for their souls. He chided Israel for "following the strange American custom . . . of bluffing," thus erecting a barrier between members of the once close-knit family. And he scolded him for lodging with a Bobruisker whom missionaries had induced to "sell out his honesty and people."[10] Palestine appeared to be a healthier place to live.[11] Berl was fortified in his decision by the writings of his socialist-Zionist "mentor and comrade," Nahman Syrkin, who imbued him with "hatred of the Diaspora and its degradations."[12]

Katznelson belonged to the pre-World War I "wave" of Palestine immigration, known as the Second Aliyah. Most of the newcomers were young idealists, socialist pioneers determined to build a new society through physical labor. In 1911 he joined a cooperative housed at the Kinneret Training Farm of the Palestine Settlement Office. The members of the spartan group saw their ideals as the antithesis of American materialism and wastefulness. Not only their spiritual condition but even their economic circumstances seemed superior to those of Jews in the United States. Echoing Brenner, Berl wrote to his brother, Israel, from Kinneret that in Palestine "it is possible to live, to work without the suffocation of the shop [that is, the clothing factory], without fear of the eternal 'slack' " season, in which no work was available.[13] As a popular Zionist song of the day went, the pioneers were helping "to reconstruct" the Jewish land and people, and in the process were themselves "being reconstructed." In America, where "time was money," his brother's "health," Katznelson feared, "was being eroded and his years used up without purpose."[14]

Although Berl missed his family greatly and hoped they would join him in Palestine (Israel and his wife came from America in 1912 and others at the same time or subsequently from Europe), he did not paint an unrealistic picture of life there. Nor was he altogether blind to positive aspects of the New World. He admired American technology, especially what might be of use in Palestine. He studied American farming manuals, although able to understand "only the . . . drawings and pictures." (Even *Der Yiddisher*

Farmer with its Americanized Yiddish was hard for him to read.)[15] In the first essay he published in Palestine, he praised "the men of good will, the seekers of greatness, redemption, and a field of opportunity for their uncontainable energy . . . [with their un]conventional ideas . . . [who] had created . . . America and Australia and given the world" its most significant social experiments. Without people like that, he asserted, there would be "no hope for the redemption of Palestine."[16]

Jewish life in the United States was not as rich nor as polished as in the Russian Pale, but Yiddish and Hebrew culture were being transplanted with some success.[17] Katznelson recognized the merits of American Zionism, which many Europeans and Palestinians regarded with total disdain. Syrkin, "the only man in the Diaspora," according to Berl, with "a feel for Palestinian affairs as well as deep historical understanding," emigrated to America in 1907 and flourished, although he was not uncritical of his new home.[18] Among Second Aliyah pioneers were some who had come from America, including the group led by Eliezer Yoffe, with whom Katznelson worked in Kinneret. Although they would later become ideological antagonists, Katznelson noted in 1911 that Yoffe "had [already] earned considerable admiration" in the *yishuv* and was "apparently . . . a good fellow." Years later he listed the desirable "American" attributes that Yoffe had brought to the *yishuv*: his familiarity with American scientific literature, "his clean clothes, good grooming, . . . [and] politeness."[19]

Whatever the virtues of America, by 1911 Katznelson already looked upon himself as a "citizen" of Palestine. For him, the United States, no less than other countries of the Diaspora, was a dead end. By contrast, the "old-new land" of Israel had become once again a "land of the living."[20]

2

Towards the end of World War I, Katznelson had his first extensive contacts with Americans; and only then did events in America begin to impinge upon his world. In the Jewish Legion he met American and British soldiers, including Ben-Gurion and Yitzḥak Ben-Zvi, who returned from their American exile with the Legion, and some old friends from Bobruisk. Like Jabotinsky, Katznelson found "the [conscript] English Legionnaires" apathetic about army service and Zionism. The Americans, however, "had enthusiastically enlisted of their own free will." Among them were "comrades" whose goal was to come "to Palestine as pioneers."[21] The Americans were "good Jewish boys," he said, "loyal, special soul mates, the likes of whom" he had seldom met. Ben-Gurion thought them unregenerate Yiddishists, but many were studying Hebrew in preparation for settling in Palestine. Here, at last, Katznelson wrote exuberantly, was that first wave of the mass immigration "for which we have been waiting all our lives!"[22] The Legionnaires gave him "an entirely different kind of connection with America." In the fall of 1918 he held talks with the Americans, probably to encourage them to remain in Palestine after demobilization and to enlist them for his "non-party [political] party."[23] Later, he joined with Ben-Gurion, Ben-Zvi, and other Legionnaires in "overcoming the fractiousness" of some of the Second Aliyah old-timers to form Aḥdut HaAvoda, "a kind of Palestine council of workers and soldiers." Eventually the new party (a forerunner of today's Labor Party) would unite most Jewish workers in Palestine under its banner.[24]

Like Jabotinsky, Berl was greatly disappointed that most of the Americans returned to the United States. In its straitened circumstances, the WZO did not realize the veterans were "its principal asset." Katznelson accused the Zionist establishment of squandering "national energy" by allowing the Americans to leave. They would have to be brought back at greater expense later, if they were still interested in aliyah. He also feared that embittered, "trashy Legionnaires" might seek to damage the reputation of the *yishuv* in America. "Encouraging the emigration from Palestine of thousands of young men, was," he declared at the time, "a terrible, shameful business."[25] The Americans had forsaken their fleshpots in order to share in the great task. The shortsighted Zionist leadership had rejected them; and the movement would suffer immeasurably. More than two decades later Katznelson recalled the events as "a tragic nightmare." Those few Legionnaires who had stayed in Palestine, he noted, retained "the spirit of the Legion from those days" and marshaled it to deal with the crisis of World War II.[26]

Katznelson did not initially react to the American Zionist Medical Unit as he did to the fighting force. Like most *yishuv* Laborites, he was aware that local medical services compared unfavorably with those in the developed world. Still, he resented what appeared to be the maternalistic imperialism of Hadassah. Before seeing the Unit in operation, he declared it "almost unbelievable that [it could do] anything worthwhile." A few months later, he disdainfully observed that few of the Unit's original personnel remained in the country and recommended that the WZO withdraw support. The "great dedication, alacrity, loyalty, and tenacity" of the HMO staff during the 1920 Arab riots changed his mind, demonstrating, as he wrote in *Kuntres*, that Hadassah "had struck roots" in the *yishuv*. Although he originally advised his sister not to enroll in the new HMO nursing school, by her graduation in 1923, he was a fervent supporter.[27]

In the area of Zionist affairs closest to Katznelson's heart, Labor Zionism, Palestinians and Americans seemed to be forging a significant alliance in the immediate postwar period, he noted in a letter to his Labor comrades.[28] At its international conference in Vienna in 1920, the Poale Zion

Party split into two factions. The leftists, most of them eastern Europeans, unconditionally agreed to join the Third [Communist] International. Supported by the Americans and British, the Palestinians conditioned their membership on the acquiescence by the International in the establishment of a Jewish socialist society in Palestine and upon adherence to the principle of national rights, neither of which was acceptable to that body. During their World War I stay in the United States, Ben-Gurion and Ben-Zvi had become disillusioned with the American Poale Zion, largely because of what they considered a halfhearted commitment to Palestine. In 1920–21, however, the Americans demonstrated devotion to their confrères, not only supporting them in Vienna, but also organizing a successful "Tool Campaign" to provide advanced agricultural, woodworking, and road-building machinery for the *yishuv*. After the split of the international party, Katznelson wrote to Baruch Zuckerman, a New York Poale Zion activist: "Palestine and America are obliged to stick together."[29] When the party, which in the *yishuv* had merged into Aḥdut HaAvoda, started the daily, *Di Tsayt*, in New York, Berl assumed the paper would bring Palestinians and Americans "a great deal closer" and make them "much more than two allied parties."[30]

In subsequent years the dual alliance solidified, although the Americans would frequently disappoint their partners. Already in early 1921 they annoyed Katznelson by using funds collected for the *yishuv* to pay for running the American office and campaign and for *Di Tsayt*. He had hoped the paper would supplement the income of penurious Palestinian writers; but it lost money and became a serious drain on party resources, of which more below.[31]

If Americans in the Legion, HMO, and the Poale Zion impressed Katznelson favorably, others in the immediate postwar period aroused negative feelings. Like Jabotinsky, he grew to dislike Brandeis, although for his own reasons. During his 1920 Palestine tour Brandeis pronounced the country not yet ready for settlement, largely because of its rudimentary sanitary and medical facilities. Berl felt the aristocratic judge had no feel for pioneering and had gratuitously given the British an excuse to prohibit aliyah.[32]

Brandeis and his coworkers in the ZOA crossed swords with Katznelson at a London conference later that summer. World Zionist leaders had last met before the war. Now they were confronted with a promising new political reality but also with the WZO's shortage of funds. One of the thorniest questions was Palestine settlement. Two years earlier "in thunder and lightning the American [Zionists] had given the world the Pittsburgh Program . . . overflowing with radicalism and socialism," Katznelson wrote in *HaAdamah*. In London, however, in the hope of attracting wealthy—and conservative—donors, they advocated private property rights and opposed the nationalization of land, as he and other Laborites were demanding.[33]

Berl Katznelson

By 1920, Berl claimed, an imperialistic and paternalistic mentality reigned in the Zionist movement. "Notables and clerks from London and New York," who were "altogether without daring national ideas and had no courage for serious initiatives," sought to impose their rule on the "natives" in Palestine. The movement, he feared, was selling its soul in the vain pursuit of "large private investments." Perhaps because he felt they had repudiated their own progressive, democratic, American ideals, Katznelson focused his attack on the patrician Zionists from the United States. In the press and privately he condemned not only Brandeis but also Robert Szold, Harry Friedenwald, and Eliahu Lewin-Epstein, who had been working with the Zionist Commission in Palestine since 1918.[34]

The far left of Jewish America Katznelson found even more problematical than its bourgeois elements. He expected but refused to condone the unsympathetic attitude towards the *yishuv* of the Bundists with their Marxist, Yiddishist orientation: New York's *Forverts*; the protean Ḥaim Zhitlovsky ("a socialist, revolutionary, assimilationist, nationalist, autonomist, territorialist, Zionist, Yiddishist"); and the Left Poale Zion, which, he claimed, "deliberately misled the public" with exaggerated tales of a war on Yiddish-speakers in the *yishuv*.[35] He was especially vexed by Zionist journals, such as *Dos Iddishe Folk*, an official organ of the ZOA, and even *Di Tsayt*, which lent occasional support to the Yiddishists.[36]

Notwithstanding his dislike of the money-oriented Zionist captains, money drew Berl in the direction of America. Even the idealists recognized that the *yishuv* could only be built up by significant infusions of funds; and once he joined the leadership ranks, Katznelson had to face the community's financial crises. In a 1920 letter to Baruch Zuckerman, he posed what he called the "principal question" of the day: "What financial means are available to us for Palestine?"[37] With few resources of their own, the Labor Zionists were particularly hard hit by the postwar turndown. Towards the end of 1920, Katznelson commented despairingly that budget reductions by the official Zionist bodies removed "any possibility of [creating new] agricultural enterprises or employment opportunities" in Palestine; Ben-Gurion warned him that the entire Labor Zionist movement "faced bankruptcy."[38] Money, however, meant America! In the aftermath of the war, Katznelson recognized, Jews "in the countries of eastern and central Europe were altogether unable to assist [the Zionists] . . . and the entire movement [had become] . . . dependent upon the good will and understanding of America."[39]

Since England and America, he believed, were given over to materialism, Zionism there could in any case only "start with serious money raising"; and he encouraged Zuckerman not to be embarrassed by the task.[40] Some years later he would assert that "popular cultural work" could only be done in the United States, if it were stimulated by fund-raising activities.⁴¹ American Jews, "the only ones spared the terrible destruction" of war and pogroms, had "an obligation," he said, to fund the rebuilding of Palestine for all Jews; and he did not hesitate to tell them so.⁴²

Still, the reality of solicitation could be embarrassing; dependence on charity was debilitating; and Americans were not reliable. Their methods of handling money disturbed Berl.⁴³ Although sometimes generous, they employed tasteless fund-raising stratagems, often resorting to "bluff."⁴⁴ "The way they organized the distribution" of funds, he asserted in a 1920 *Kuntres* article, was demeaning. The wartime American Relief Committee had sent to Palestine its own charity wardens, who, unlike their clients, he noted sarcastically, "could be trusted by all of Columbus's countrymen" to oversee distribution of the largesse.⁴⁵

By 1921, American Zionists "were not meeting any of their obligations" to the Zionist movement, Ben-Gurion wrote to Katznelson. Early that year the American Poale Zion cut off funds for the party's London office, which had served as Labor's representative to the WZO. Katznelson maintained "a spark of hope," that if the Americans knew how "murderous [a] blow" they had dealt, they would make up the shortfall. His pleas, however, fell on deaf ears and empty pockets.⁴⁶ The Americans would not even support the movement publications with which Katznelson was closely connected and which perennially hovered on the brink of insolvency.⁴⁷ Despite his misgivings about the Brandeis group, Berl turned to them—unsuccessfully—for help in obtaining a substantial sum to train agricultural experts and acquire up-to-date farm machinery.⁴⁸

However distasteful or unreliable American philanthropy was, and whatever the dangers of dependency, American funds were indispensable. To secure them it was "essential to send people [and] to concentrate energy" there.⁴⁹ Although he preferred to work in the *yishuv*, Berl acceded in mid-1921 to the call of Ben-Gurion and others "to fortify the home front" (that is, the Diaspora Zionist organizations). He feared that failure in America, where "the danger and the rot were very great," could deliver "a mortal blow to" Labor's cause;⁵⁰ but he agreed to participate in the first fund-raising mission of the Histadrut. His recent experiences in the Legion may have made the decision somewhat easier. A workers' bank, the primary object of the trip, moreover, could, in the long term, help to end dependence on charity by creating an instrument for productive investment.⁵¹

3

The Histadrut founding conference in December 1920 discussed sending a delegation to America, since Labor's priorities were unlikely to be met soon by the WZO. Berl, who understood that the fate of Labor institutions "depend[ed on] . . . America," was considered a likely emissary.[52] A practical, pragmatic man, he had demonstrated ability to "extract . . . funds from the settlement institutions of the [World] Zionist Organization . . . [and] donors" in Europe for Poale Zion projects.[53] Earlier the Party had tried to send him to America; and Pinḥas Rutenberg, the promoter of electric power in Palestine, had sought his help in raising capital funds there.[54]

The Histadrut leaders dithered over the delegation; the political parties haggled over its composition and agenda; and likely candidates refused to go. The May 1921 Arab riots in Palestine, and Britain's failure to back the Zionists unequivocally, catalyzed the Laborites. But even after a delegation was in place (Berl and Manya Shoḥat from Aḥdut HaAvoda and Yosef Baratz from the non-Marxist party, HaPo'el HaTza'ir), it could not "plan its work," according to Katznelson, because of the "chaos in the Zionist movement" in Palestine and abroad. When they left, the trio knew for certain only that they were to raise investment funds for the nascent Histadrut institutions, "most especially, the Workers' Bank," for which a charter had just been received from the WZO. On the other side of the ocean, "no preparations . . . were made" by the hosts, the Poale Zion Party of America.[55]

Katznelson arrived in New York in early November. Perhaps because of the urgency of the hour and his uneasiness in the United States, perhaps because he felt it appropriate in materialistic America, he determined upon a business-only trip, although normally when traveling he indulged his broad cultural interests. His goal, he wrote his sister, Hannah, was to "disturb the usual complacency" of the Americans, to disabuse them of their "illusions and idle consolations."[56] He restricted off-hours activities to those likely to confirm his negative views of the New World. Except for the dictaphone, which caught his attention during a factory tour in Columbus, Ohio, he ignored the natural and technological wonders of America, barely taking note of Niagara Falls or the Ford factory outside Detroit. The occasional movie or museum visit gave no pleasure. He did go to the theater and was surprised at the level of sophistication. The Yiddish plays, however, served to remind him of "the glory and the grandeur" that had been Jewish eastern Europe, now in ruins. A visit to the Yiddish poet, Shmuel Niger, whom he had once admired, left him saddened by the "weakness and submission" which had overtaken Niger in America.[57]

A loyal friend and relative, he visited family, Bobruisk friends, relatives of Palestinian comrades, and Legion veterans, including Jabotinsky's friend Elias Ginsburg and journalist-historian Louis Fischer. Everyone, he wrote to his wife, greeted him with "exaggerated honor," although his concerns seemed "foreign" to most; even once close associates treated him like a "creature of another species." Such contacts provided a window on the day-to-day life of the immigrants, most of whom appeared no better off than they had been in Russia. "God's leftovers," he called them. His step-brother, Haim, seemed now "an old man, broken and miserable." The prosperous had degenerated into "status-conscious allrightniks;" but even the allrightniks had lost confidence during the postwar recession. One exception was a Bobruisk friend married to a farmer, who lived "a truly wonderful" life, "a kind of idyll" in rural isolation.[58]

Katznelson construed his task in America in the narrowest terms, unlike other Labor emissaries, including his partners. He had planned "to do something for aliyah . . . the most important aspect of [Zionist] work." Syrkin urged that it be one of the delegates' main concerns.[59] Katznelson matched a few prospective settlers with institutions in the *yishuv*; and he helped a group of Jews from the Ukraine arrange the aliyah of recent pogrom victims; but he did not recruit *olim*.[60] He also did not urge the Palestinian emigrants whom he met to return, and only canvassed them for funds. He had moral qualms about advising people who were adjusting to America "to exchange their life" for one less certain and may have considered them "unfit" for life in Palestine. He was surely mindful of the demobilized Legionnaires' experience.[61]

Once, he took an active role in a cultural event unrelated to fund raising, a memorial meeting for the Hebrew writer, Michah Yosef Berdichevsky, where he flayed his listeners for their superficial attachment to Hebrew culture.[62] In England he had made special efforts to cultivate labor leaders; and he knew the American Federation of Labor was friendly towards Zionism. Yet he ignored American labor leaders, except for Jewish union activists who raised money for Palestine.[63] He met with the head of the Cooperative League only, apparently, in the hope of gaining entrée through him to wealthy Jews.[64]

Money alone was the object of this trip! Katznelson felt "upon him the eyes of the Palestine workers" who were interested in funds to run their settlements and institutions, not in laying the groundwork for the future.[65] From Europe he warned Zuckerman that there "would be no time for discussions." From New York he reported to his Ahdut HaAvoda colleagues that "any meeting with us . . . immediately turns into a serious Zionist session," which meant solicitation for the bank.[66] Following a call on his revered mentor, Syrkin, the singleminded emissary recorded in his diary only that he had "invited [Syrkin] . . . to throw himself wholeheartedly into work for the bank."[67]

Baratz and Shohat had come to the United States before Katznelson, but only when he arrived was a welcome meeting held in New York's Cooper Union Hall. At the impressive reception Berl renewed old friendships and met some of those with whom he would work in the coming months: union leader Joseph Schlossberg, *Di Tsayt* editor David Pinsky, Judah Magnes, Haim Zhitlovsky, Syrkin, and others.[68] The gathering served to reinforce his sense of Americans as fluffy and insubstantial. The bank campaign had not yet been organized; so the reception was all show and no money.[69]

It took about a month to assemble broad-based sponsorship and almost another month to map out the campaign, tasks which fell on Katznelson.[70] Meanwhile the delegates obtained the agreement of Zionist and non-Zionist labor groups in the New York area to sell bank shares to their members.[71] They also approached the Joint Distribution Committee (JDC) for an investment in the bank's capital fund. Those discussions introduced Berl to upper-middle-class, non-Zionist Jews, including Louis Marshall, the acknowledged leader of American Jewry, Herbert Lehman, the future governor of New York, and Felix Adler, founder of the Ethical Culture Society. He wrote home that "Marshall quoted Lehman to Magnes to the effect that the impression [he had] made was formidable." No JDC funds were forthcoming, however. No doubt "Columbus's countrymen" trusted more the Central Bank for Cooperative Institutions [in Palestine] sponsored by the Brandeis group and managed by Americans.[72]

At the "enthusiastic [campaign] kickoff" on New Year's Day at the Manhattan Opera House, Katznelson, who was not very effective before large crowds, received "a tremendous ovation," when he spoke of "another kind of life" in Palestine, "a Jewish workers' economy." Between eight and ten thousand dollars in bank shares was pledged or sold that evening.[73] Then the delegates took the show on the road, assisted by Magnes and Poale Zion stalwarts.[74] By early February, Katznelson had spoken in Rochester, Buffalo, Syracuse, Catskill farming communities, Hamilton, Toronto, Detroit, and Chicago. Later he visited Pittsburgh, Cleveland, Columbus, South Bend, Rock Island, Milwaukee, Minneapolis, Duluth, and other communities.[75] In Chicago he made sales to professionals, as well as to blue-collar workers; at the Talmud Torah in Minneapolis he peddled bank shares to schoolchildren, amongst whom he sensed "an inclination towards pioneering."[76] From "the provinces" Katznelson sent articles to *Di Tsayt*, provided raw material for other journalists, and prepared a brochure on the bank.[77] In mid-April he returned to New York to supervise the collections, lest the money be diverted for local needs and "all the propaganda and fund raising across the country have been done for nothing."[78] It was ironic that Berl resented American donors who did not trust their Palestinian clients, although he did not trust even his own comrades in the American Poale Zion Party.

In a letter to his wife written towards the end of his stay, Berl reflected upon the "gruelling labors of this year that we sacrificed."[79] The results seemed modest, indeed. Ben-Gurion, whose call to arms Katznelson had answered in going to America, initially declared the mission a failure, although he would later sound a more positive note. Katznelson, usually the less upbeat, recognized that there had been intangible gains. The mission earned heightened "prestige" for the Histadrut in American-Jewish labor circles;[80] and valuable new friends had been acquired. These included Magnes ("the man for whom we have been looking");[81] Max Pine, "a pillar of the *Forverts*" and longtime opponent of Zionism, whose "respect and affection for Berl" led him to become an ardent supporter of the Histadrut;[82] and Joseph Schlossberg ("a willingness to know and to help"), from 1914 to 1940 secretary of the large and powerful Amalgamated Clothing Workers of America, another anti-Zionist converted by Berl.[83] Without those three the campaign would never have gotten off the ground; the last two would play an invaluable part in later Histadrut campaigns. Also promising was future ZOA president Solomon Goldman, a Conservative rabbi. Although Katznelson remained attached to Jewish tradition and looked askance at Conservatism and Reform, he respected Goldman's "spirituality and traditional learning."[84]

On the minus side of the ledger was the principal goal of the tour and Berl's only real interest: money. Accountings of share capital raised range from $17,000 to $60,000;[85] but even the higher figure is only a fraction of the goal of $200,000–$290,000.[86] Net proceeds were lower. The mission had faced a set of probably insurmountable obstacles. These bear enumeration here, because they help to explain Katznelson's subsequent reticence regarding American Jewish affairs.

As in the case of Jabotinsky, much of the failure resulted from lack of preparation. "We are," Berl wrote to his wife in March 1922, "three people without any talent" for our job.[87] The scale of operations demanded by the United States amazed them. The country was so dauntingly huge, Berl remarked, that "good, precious people, who . . . could do a great deal, . . . get lost" in the crowd.[88] Because they knew—and cared—little about America, the emissaries refused to tailor their pitch to suit local sensibilities, again rather like Jabotinsky. Katznelson sensed early on that his listeners might respond favorably, if he would "say a few flattering words"; but he regarded them as "unworthy" of kid-glove treatment.[89] He opted for an "argumentative, chastising" stance and actually sought "to cast a pall over" his audiences.[90] The problem was not only attitude. Katznelson, Baratz, and Shoḥat said repeatedly that they had come to America "not as recipients, . . . but as donors."[91] What they had to give, however, was unclear; and even Jews who felt responsible for their less fortunate brethren did not wish to think of themselves as milk cows whose only purpose was to sustain the *yishuv*. Not surprisingly, Berl found himself "alienated and isolated," unable, he lamented to his wife with some slight exaggeration, "to get close to a single person in America."[92]

His calculated bad temper—if it was that—was aggravated by bouts of illness and by living conditions "even less settled than in Jaffa."[93] On the road he was "adversely affected by the [winter] climate," and forced to resort to beggary for his personal needs by the Poale Zion office in New York, which otherwise squandered its resources. By January he was seriously ill. The next month he had to interrupt his trip in Pittsburgh and Cleveland, where he was hospitalized. In March he collapsed in Rock Island.[94] Even a sunnier person might have succumbed to dampened spirits under such circumstances.

Poor planning was the tour's nemesis. The postwar recession was not over. Yet the Histadrut mission arrived at the same time as the WZO mission of which Jabotinsky was a member.[95] In the battle for media attention and money, the fledgling, class-based Histadrut was at a disadvantage, although relative to their goals, the Laborites proved the more successful fund raisers.[96] Berl needed up-to-date information on the *yishuv* "even [to] begin [work] properly." On arrival in New York, however, he found that nothing had been sent, not even stock certificates, making it difficult to approach wary purchasers, many of whom had been sold worthless Palestinian stocks in the past.[97] Ben-Gurion tried to intercede, but the budding Histadrut bureaucrats offered no concessions to American ways of doing business.[98] Over a year after returning to Palestine, Katznelson was still trying to persuade the Histadrut to set up a foreign desk.[99]

Berl and his partners had not anticipated the extent of their hosts' ineptitude. He would eventually conclude that one could raise "significant amounts of money" in America, but only with the aid of "an energetic organization."[100] In 1921, however, "the only force ready to help" was the Poale Zion, whose "shortcomings" Ben-Gurion and Ben-Zvi had observed years before.[101] Ideological disputes were tearing the leaderless, disorganized party asunder. Berl considered its officials "vacuous" mediocrities "without any concept" of the larger Zionist issues or of developments in the *yishuv*;[102] he thought campaign head Hirsch Ehrenreich "the least appropriate choice" for the task.[103] Not only were no preparations for the campaign made before the delegates arrived, but afterwards, instead of "helping us to make the right contacts," Berl charged, the Poale Zion actually "impeded us."[104] Confusion and ill will produced half-empty halls. In Rock Island and South Bend Katznelson's hosts "behaved in a most ugly fashion." In Buffalo, like Ben-Gurion before him, he arrived as an "unwanted guest."[105] Most painful of all, there was no one to inherit the Palestinians' modest organizational achievements.[106]

The most troublesome problems besetting the mission related to ongoing debates in the immigrant community over Yiddish language and culture, and socialism. These "lay like a wolf in ambush," a potential threat to any

Berl Katznelson (seated) with Yosef Hagai in Detroit, 1921. (Courtesy of the Central Zionist Archives, Jerusalem.)

advocate of Zionism and Hebrew culture, as Bialik was to learn, but especially to socialists unenthusiastic about the Bolshevik experiment in Russia. Early on, Katznelson realized they had been caught "in the teeth" of the wolf.[107] While the Palestine labor movement in general was accused of persecuting Yiddish language and culture, Manya Shohat was charged with having been an *agente provocatrice* who betrayed Jews to the czarist secret police.

The attack was led by Vladimir Medem, a sworn anti-Zionist, who, although raised a Christian, had become one of the foremost leaders of the Polish Bund before fleeing to New York in early 1921. In the *Forverts* he answered Magnes's call to American-Jewish workers to support the cause of Palestinian Labor by pointing to Shohat's alleged treachery. He insisted, moreover, that the Palestinians were entitled only to a share of Labor's charitable dollar proportional to their numbers, not to the large amount they sought in order to prepare the infrastructure for the future.[108] Katznelson perceived immediately the implications of Medem's "*Forverts* bomb." He had been anxious about Shohat because of her background but also because she was easily distracted by irrelevant issues.[109] He and Baratz remained on the sidelines of the skirmish, in the hope, undoubtedly, of salvaging the bank campaign.[110] In the end, the affair was less damaging than feared at first, as Shohat successfully redirected her fund-raising efforts to middle-class groups. Still, the scent of scandal dogged the delegates until their return to Palestine.[111]

In part, the assault on Shohat was a screen for the general opposition to Zionism of the Yiddishist, radical Left, which Katznelson believed to be taking direction from communists in Palestine.[112] Despite friendly representations to Abe Cahan, the editor of the *Forverts*, and a secret night meeting between him and Katznelson, that paper led the war against the mission. It carried derogatory articles, ignored the delegates' activities, and even refused to accept paid advertisements for public events.[113] Within the Poale Zion Party, Yiddishists directed the faithful "into the trap of the Zion-haters."[114] Zhitlovsky undercut the Palestinians with direct assaults in *Di Tsayt* and with pointed silence,[115] as did Abraham Revusky, a Palestine-based correspondent affiliated with the Left Poale Zion, once vice-minister for Jewish affairs in the Ukrainian counter-revolutionary government under Petliura. Revusky's colorful reports about the persecution of Yiddish speakers in the *yishuv* amounted to "insidious fabrication," Berl charged. Years later he made peace with a repentant Revusky and invited him to write for *Davar*. Now, he fought back vigorously in *Di Tsayt*, although the New York *Morgn Zhurnal*, which had no connection to the Poale Zion, was more hospitable to his rejoinders.[116] The struggle was the more demoralizing, because Katznelson was a moderate on the language issue, who, as he jested to a friend, would never "breakfast on a Yiddishist."[117]

Di Tsayt became a real thorn in the flesh. As noted above, the Palestinians, most of whom opposed strengthening the Diaspora at the expense of the *yishuv*, understood the need for a party organ to propagandize American-Jewish workers. Many American Zionists believed the fortification of their own institutions justifiable—even at the expense of Palestine—for without a strong Diaspora to lend it support, the *yishuv* would be imperiled. Berl thought that rationalization to be "empty, superficial, [and] foolish," another form of American assimilationism, little more than an excuse for not giving financial assistance to Palestine.[118]

Under any circumstances he would have resented the diversion of energy and money to *Di Tsayt*. Now, however, the daily tottered towards bankruptcy in the midst of the bank drive; and rescue efforts detracted from "work on behalf of Palestine." In January the party mounted a fifty-thousand-dollar campaign for the paper. Katznelson believed the closing of *Di Tsayt* would be a "disaster" for the Labor Zionist cause, but the competing campaign, which turned "friends" into "enemies," made him bitter.[119] When the paper folded in the spring of 1922, after "swallowing three-years of Poale Zion work," Katznelson regretted most that his mission had been robbed of considerable resources.[120]

He returned to Palestine exhausted and dispirited. In over half a year he had achieved little in the United States, which lived up to his preconceived notions. In his diary he recorded admiration of the "innocence, intelligence, self-confidence, and self-knowledge" of American Jews, and of their sympathy for religious tradition.[121] But he accused them of preferring talk "about uplifting, spiritual subjects" to dealing with the concrete political and economic problems of the *yishuv*, on which he wished to focus. When he raised these issues, Katznelson said, the Americans would turn the discussion to pseudo-spiritual problems: contravention of the kosher laws, the alleged dictatorship of the proletariat, and the suppression of Yiddish.[122] He was convinced that American Jews' raison d'être was to support the *yishuv* financially; and this he had not motivated them to do. He perceived no irony in the failure of an intellectual with deep spiritual concerns to communicate effectively with supposedly materialistic Americans about wordly concerns.

4

After his searing experiences Katznelson lost interest in the United States. (Such disengagement was not unique to him;[123] nor was this the only issue from which he would withdraw in his career.) From 1925, *Davar*, which quickly became a major voice in Palestine, occupied much of his time and energy. When he directed his attention to American matters, he exhibited aloofness and irritability. In public speeches and articles in *Davar*, he took favorable notice of such American phenomena as women's liberation, Jewish mutual-aid associations, municipal federations, and trade union control over production through the "union label."[124] He was more impressed, however, by the hollow rituals of American Jewish life ("New York banquets") and the assimilatory power of the melting pot; and he poked fun at "modern" (Conservative) American rabbis, who presumably fell prey to both. With less charity—and less knowledge—than Bialik, he mocked American Hebraists, whose work he found pretentious and derivative. Nonetheless, he invited several of them to write for *Davar*, and, no doubt mindful of his own disappointment with *Di Tsayt*, promised them a small honorarium.[125] Returning to an old theme in a 1928 *Davar* editorial, he reminded "the people of 'donating' America" of their odious image in " 'recipient' Jewish communities."[126] In *Kuntres* he decried the impotence of the American Jewish Congress and other institutions, which appeared to be "no more than a front for resolutions, without any financial clout."[127]

American Jewish labor circles and the American Federation of Labor exhibited an increasingly positive attitude towards Zionism in the 1920s, especially towards the labor sector of the *yishuv*. Thanks to Max Pine, Joseph Schlossberg, and others, the United Hebrew Trades conducted a campaign for Labor Palestine, the Geverkshaften (that is, Trade Union) Campaign, annually from 1924. In 1927, without acknowledging the turn of the tables, Berl suggested that proceeds of the Geverkshaften Campaign be used to rescue *Davar* from crushing indebtedness.[128] Abe Cahan visited Palestine in 1925 and 1929; and "a breach . . . appeared in the iron wall called, *Forverts*."[129] In 1928 *Davar* secured a linotype machine at a considerable discount through Baruch Charney Vladeck (a brother of Shmuel Niger) of the *Forverts*. Katznelson was not altogether unappreciative of the changing atmosphere in America; and he understood the growing importance of American Labor to the welfare of *yishuv* workers.[130] Still, when Cahan arrived in Palestine in 1925, he seized the opportunity to chide him for the quality and anti-Zionism of his journalism, although he also mustered some flattering words for the dean of American-Jewish newspapermen.[131] Only grudgingly did Berl accept the linotype, insisting that even at no charge, a "luxury" American machine might cost the paper more in maintenance than it could afford.[132]

In the 1920s Katznelson no longer saw much positive in American Zionism. In a speech to the Zionist Congress in Carlsbad in August 1923 he carped at the inability of the ZOA to comprehend the most fundamental facts about the *yishuv* and claimed that the organization actually damaged the cause of Zionism on occasion.[133] He recognized the continuing partnership of Aḥdut HaAvoda with the American Poale Zion but could not forget that the "same party in the same uniform . . . produced people" such as Medem and Zhitlovsky, "who vilified" the *yishuv* and its workers. He now concluded that the American Poale Zion would never achieve power, and implausibly attributed their past successes to having ridden the coattails of Aḥdut HaAvoda.[134] By 1927 he was becoming apprehensive that the anti-Labor Revisionists might sweep the United States as they had Poland.[135]

The Brandeisists with their notions of scientific management, technical expertise, and "efficiency," earned special opprobrium in these years from him and other Laborites for their supposed lack of humanity and Zionist commitment. In the summer of 1923, Judge Julian Mack, who headed the Brandeis group after Brandeis had retreated to the cloistered sanctum of the Supreme Court,[136] came to survey the progress of the *yishuv*, especially the projects in which his group was involved. Berl greeted him with a "success story" in *Kuntres*, about their Central Bank for Cooperative Institutions, "one of the [few] remnants of the lofty aspirations from the days of the Pittsburgh Convention of blessed memory, the golden age . . . of Brandeisian Zionism." Success, however, was relative. The generously capitalized bank, Katznelson pointed out, lent far less than the undercapitalized Workers' Bank, which the Brandeisists sought to undermine at every opportunity; the American manager of the Central Bank, Harry Viteles, earned an exorbitant salary for Palestine; and the bank's overhead in the previous year had amounted to fully a quarter of the sum lent. With unsubtle sarcasm, Katznelson wondered if the time had not come "at last, to learn how to build from our big brothers, with their imagination and practicality."[137] A few years later he editorialized against the bank in *Davar*, because its annual report was published in English for the benefit of directors "who sit abroad," and of Viteles, who still did not know Hebrew. Confident that they would not understand, he used Bialik's words to describe bank officials as "pigs fattened on foreign cultures."[138]

As noted above, the Brandeisists lost the struggle for power in the ZOA and the WZO to Weizmann and his followers in 1920–21 and withdrew from active involvement in "official" Zionism. By 1927, however, the Weizmannites and their allies, including the Labor Zionists, had proved incapable of obtaining adequate funding for the *yishuv* or of managing on what they had. There was no money for new settlement projects, not even enough to pay teachers or deal with growing unemployment. Assuming that Americans would respond to scientific management, the Zionist Congress that year embraced Brandeisist ideals and chose an Executive that would implement them. "Brandeisism without Brandeis," Katznelson griped in *Davar*, "the same tune, but different trumpeters."[139] Henrietta Szold, who had close ties to Mack and other Brandeisists and a reputation for efficiency and hardheadedness, became one of three members of the Palestine Zionist Executive. The Laborites did not oppose the change at the Congress, but they rebelled vigorously when the Executive tried to carry out its mandate of balancing the budget. Typically, Katznelson expressed controlled scepticism regarding "the new American regime" at first but later, in *Davar*, castigated an administration which, he said, attached "the emblem" of Zionism "to an empty shell." Justly enough, he pointed out that the Americans withheld financial support from this, their own administration, as they had from earlier ones, and, while preaching probity and economy in Palestine, did nothing about corruption and the mismanagement of Zionist affairs at home.[140]

Katznelson looked rather more favorably than most other Laborites on one American-Zionist project of the 1920s, the American Zion Commonwealth land-purchase and settlement company. Between 1924 and 1927 the company acquired large tracts from absentee Arab landlords on which the towns of Herzliya and Afula would be built, and in the Haifa Bay area. By 1926, it was experiencing financial difficulties, only partly because of bad management. Although it was a private initiative established to compete with the settlement activities of the Jewish National Fund, now the Fund had to save the AZC, lest lands revert to their former owners, creating a scandal in America harmful to the entire movement.[141] Laborites were outraged that national funds were being used to rescue a private company, especially because the bailout caused their priorities to be ignored.[142]

Perhaps because he believed so strongly in the necessity of American funding, and because most AZC investors were of modest means, Katznelson took a moderate approach to the problem. He advocated Histadrut cooperation with the AZC if workers were not exploited; and he praised decentralized settlement. As a director of the Keren Hayesod in 1928 and 1929, he supported a bailout, which would leave the National Fund in control of most AZC lands, remarking sardonically that private initiative seemed to succeed in Palestine only with the aid of public funds.[143]

To Berl in the 1920s money was the only unequivocally positive feature of America. In *Kuntres*, he waxed euphoric over Weizmann's "material success" there in 1923.[144] He would not consider another trip himself but urged Ben-Gurion, Dov Hoz, and others to seek American funds for "a number of small—and perhaps large—undertakings."[145] He could not easily shed his suspicion of wealthy, American, non-Zionist "big fish" (that is, Louis Marshall and his cronies) and, like Jabotinsky, feared partnership with them in the enlarged Jewish Agency sought by Weizmann.[146] By the end of the decade, however, he knew his fears were a luxury that neither Labor nor the *yishuv*, as a whole, could afford.[147] In any case, he said to Ben-Gurion, there was probably "no more to fear from the very rich of America than from the petty bourgeois of eastern Europe." The money of both was vital; the overlordship of either would be destructive. The enlargement of the Agency was a positive step, so long as the Zionists—especially those in the *yishuv*—maintained control.[148]

As he had asserted years before, accepting money from America was to confer a favor upon the benefactors. Taking it legitimated the donors' wealth and assuaged their feelings of guilt for having grown rich, while friends and relatives in other countries languished in poverty. "When," Katznelson asked in 1923, "has the dollar" (a derogatory metonymy for American Jews?) "ever enjoyed such moral stature as now, when it can justify its existence through redemption of the soil, building workers' quarters, and opening the gates [of Palestine] for tens of thousands of expellees from Poland and Rumania?"[149]

5

As a journalist and politician Katznelson was called upon to respond to the dramatic events of the decade from 1929 to 1939. As a militant and maximalist Zionist and a practical thinker in the changing world of the 1930s, he found himself reviewing attitudes and operating assumptions regarding the United States, which he now began to view rather more positively. At a time "when our regular political cane [that is, Britain] is broken," he remarked on the eve of war in 1939, "it is necessary . . . to reexamine . . . this [American] Diaspora, its power, its value, and our contribution to it. To my sorrow, I must admit that in this matter we have been neither broad of vision nor farsighted."[150] In fact, he had begun the reevaluation years earlier.

Katznelson never abandoned the negative attitudes towards America rooted in his generalized hostility to the Diaspora. The land of Israel would remain for him "forever the one and only homeland." Except in Palestine, he claimed, Jews had run out of creative steam.[151] In America, no less than in Germany and Poland, they faced "catastrophe," he prophesied to the Mapai Party directorate with a startling lack of prescience two months after Hitler's accession to power![152] (Founded in 1930, Mapai was the successor to Aḥdut HaAvoda and the immediate forerunner of today's Labor Party.) A few months later he told delegates to the fourth Histadrut convention that the United States remained the land of puffery and bluff, where "success" was "a cult."[153] Now he saw it also as a place where violence was endemic,[154] and where Jews were menaced by antisemitism—even by Nazis—as in Europe, despite the country's efforts at "total isolationism."[155]

American Jews, Berl still maintained, could never achieve spiritual fulfillment. As prejudice mounted and the immigrant generation began to die off, assimilation was becoming an ever more serious problem. He returned from his second trip to the United States in 1937 with tales of self-abnegating Jews threatening to apostatize if a Jewish state were established in Palestine.[156] American Jewish workers lived in a spiritual ghetto; but in the New World melting pot, he told a conference of young workers, they could never have "an autonomous cultural life."[157] The American "Jewish labor movement lacked imagination," he admonished a visiting delegation of American labor leaders in January 1937, and "only Palestine could lend it substance." The American movement, he charged, failed utterly to recognize its obligations to the workers of Palestine and to "the Jewish people."[158]

Now America was not even the *goldene medine*, which had once beckoned to him and other Russian Jews. Stricken by the Great Depression, American Jews, he feared, stood at the brink of the same abyss that had opened under unsuspecting Russian Jews after World War I. Once the economic "shield and salvation" of their fellows everywhere, some American Jews, he noted in a 1931 Jerusalem speech, were now considering aliyah to save themselves from financial ruin and possible future oppression.[159]

And yet, despite the logic of the situation as Katznelson saw it, American Zionism languished. Like Bialik, he expressed pity for Weizmann, who had to go cap in hand to "the crumbling, disintegrating" American Zionist "camp," which resembled nothing so much "as a rotting tree."[160] He continued to chide American Zionists for armchair progressivism. At the 1933 Zionist Congress he accused Rabbi Stephen S. Wise, who had disparaged the Histadrut, of favoring "freedom, progress, workers' rights, and democracy" for gentiles only. Other Laborites apparently now persuaded him that the AZC bailout amounted to a giveaway of public funds to people who should bear the burden of their investment follies.[161] He complained to the 1932 Mapai Party conference that the Brandeis group's Palestine Economic Corporation subverted socialist ideals through its investment policies and undermined the national principle, even when it supported projects backed by Labor.[162] During his 1937 stay in America he observed that "no young leadership worthy of the name" existed in any Zionist organization, while the older leaders, from Louis Lipsky of the Weizmann camp to Judge Mack and Rabbi Wise of the Brandeis group, "were unable to initiate any activity." That, he reported to the Mapai leadership, constituted "the tragedy of American Zionism, which has great opportunities for action not present anywhere else in the world, and which could garner strength from the tremendous shift in Jewish opinion in favor of Palestine . . . but is just incapable."[163]

At the twenty-first Zionist Congress, held beneath war clouds in August 1939, he experienced his deepest disappointment with American Zionism. Rabbis Solomon Goldman, whom he had earlier admired, and Abba Hillel Silver, the outstanding leaders of the ZOA, spoke in opposition to illegal immigration to Palestine. Katznelson held major, although unofficial, responsibility in the *yishuv* for illegal immigration, which offered one of the few escape routes open to European Jews. In one of his most effective speeches, he called Silver's words "a stone cast at our refugees on the seas and a knife in the back of Zionist policy."[164] Secure in their bastion, American Jews failed to comprehend the desperate imperative to become "law breakers" rather than abandon the Jews of Europe to their destruction, he wrote a few months later in the (American) *Pioneer Woman*.[165] In this case, time proved him tragically insightful; both rabbis would soon recant.

As the decade closed, Katznelson, unlike Ben-Gurion who thought him unduly pessimistic, still "viewed the future of Judaism and Zionism in the United States through a glass darkly."[166] That outlook continued to dull his interest in the New World. Moshe Davis, the founder of the Institute of Contemporary Jewry at the Hebrew University, relates an illustrative encounter with Katznelson. Davis, who had been president of the Hebrew Youth Association in the United States (Histadrut HaNo'ar HaIvri), arrived in Palestine in 1937. Leaders of the *yishuv*, including Ben-Gurion, considered the Hebrew-speaking American *rara avis* and met with him to discuss how his peers might be attracted to aliyah. Katznelson also requested an interview. When Davis arrived from Jerusalem at the *Davar* office in Tel Aviv, however, he found a scribbled note on the door: "Do not disturb! I am preparing the lead editorial for tomorrow." The young graduate student realized the brush-off was not a personal snub but rather an indication of how indifferent the editor was to American developments.[167]

If America left Katznelson generally unimpressed in the 1930s, it also began to pique his interest again. Times and needs had changed; the memory of his experiences in 1921–22 had faded. He came now to appreciate certain aspects of the American past about which he had known nothing earlier: the nineteenth-century Jewish and Christian Americans, including President Grant, who contributed to the rebuilding of Palestine, as well as the "vigorous, idealistic, and courageous young people" who had brought "*ideology and organization*" (italics his) to American-Jewish immigrant workers, like his own two brothers, in their "cellars and sweatshops." Those young Jewish socialists, Berl remarked, had taught the "exploited, defenseless" masses of America to defend their economic interests, serving as an inspiration to Jewish working people everywhere.[168]

The present, he realized, was also not entirely barren. He valued from afar the plenitude of the United States, even in the Depression Era, as well as its civility and tolerance.[169] Benny Applebaum (later, Ben-Zion Ilan), an American-born disciple with whom Berl felt special "closeness," helped him to see that the "pioneering will . . . [and] spirit [were] not yet maimed . . . [in America, that the] vision [was] still fresh."[170] Shmaryahu Levin, the consummate Zionist fund raiser, taught him that through "love of fellow Jews," rather than angry, uncompromising speeches, it was possible not only to extract money from American Jews but also to ignite "that nobility of spirit which smoulders under the embers of business and 'all right.' "[171] There were now a few bright lights on the American Jewish cultural stage, such as Labor Zionist thinker Haim Greenberg ("not boring, even from a purely journalistic point of view"), whom he deemed worthy of being printed in *Davar*.[172] He recognized the meaningful changes undergone by the American Jewish labor movement since he had observed it firsthand in 1922. It was no longer, he noted already in a 1930 *Davar* editorial, "a limp limb," with a membership of "refugee tailors" and a leadership of "wardens from the temple of ignorance."[173] Abe Cahan exemplified the change. Although still "no Zionist and altogether different in outlook" from the pioneering Jews of Palestine, he had been spurred by the 1929 Arab riots, Katznelson observed, at last "to state [publicly] his sympathy for the *yishuv* and his pride in it."[174]

This tentatively more positive appraisal of the United States led Katznelson to a modest reassessment of his working relationship and that of *yishuv* institutions with American Jews. He came to realize, as had some of his more Diaspora-oriented colleagues years earlier, that the *yishuv* had been remiss in "never having attempted any systematic work" to stimulate Zionist sentiment in America and that his own purely instrumental approach had proved unappealing.[175] He agreed to head the new Youth Department of the Histadrut, which was established to provide Palestinian leaders for Diaspora youth groups. From Yitzhak Chizik, Golda Myerson (Meir), and other young Palestinians who visited the United States, he had heard that the best young people there were being attracted to communism, while Zionism was the preserve of immigrant oldsters.[176] Exchanges with "groups of Hebrew-speaking, American young people" at the Boston Hebrew Teachers' College and elsewhere in 1937 led him to believe the trend could be reversed.[177] Although the Youth Department proved a failure, Berl's concern for Diaspora youth grew. He cautioned Mapai leaders in the spring of 1939 regarding "the fate of Zionism when the present generation will have descended from the stage."[178] At the outbreak of World War II, he was involved in discussions about the proper preparation of emissaries to the young people of America.[179] Something had been learned since 1922!

In these years Americans sought Katznelson's intervention or offered advice on issues ranging from Zionist youth to the possible appointment of Rabbi Joseph Soloveitchik of Boston as chief rabbi of Palestine.[180] He offered counsel in articles in the American Jewish press, although poor health prevented him from responding favorably when Abe Cahan finally invited him to contribute to *Forverts*.[181] In 1937 his pamphlet *Revolutionary Constructivism* appeared in the United States, translated by Benny Applebaum and Shlomo Grodzensky. An abridged version of an essay published in Hebrew three years earlier, it provided Americans "insight into [his] . . . unique approach" to Zionism, as well as instruction in analyzing "socialist and Jewish problems without fear of gentile reactions."[182]

Berl's involvement with American Zionism reached its peak during his 1937 visit to the United States. Like the journey of sixteen years earlier, this was a business trip. Now, however, he was more experienced and better prepared, older and more willing to meet Americans halfway; and he knew some English. He showed interest in the New York municipal elections; he went to the theater, on one occasion as Golda's date; and he toured the sights of Washington and New York, including the Metropolitan Museum of Art, the Library of Congress, and the Arlington National Cemetery. He made time for family and friends, although the tie with former Bobruiskers had frayed beyond repair.[183] He visited the Jewish Theological Seminary more than once, like Bialik taking special interest in its library; and he spent time in discussion with Hebrew teachers.[184] With sceptical satisfaction he observed that American Hebraists no longer seemed "isolated, orphaned, and emasculated"; and with mild surprise, he acknowledged that at least "at certain moments ethical issues count for something" in the land of dollars.[185]

Katznelson promised Menaḥem Ussishkin of the Jewish National Fund that he would endeavor to raise money in America for land purchase and the expansion of Jewish settlements, as he had been doing in England.[186] He also wanted to promote understanding of the implications of partitioning Palestine into Jewish and Arab states, as the British were now proposing. To accomplish these tasks he devoted attention to the broad spectrum of Zionists.

Well before 1937, Berl began to mend his fences with the "progressive" Brandeis group, good relations with which were, he now came to believe, "of inestimable importance to the future of Zionist work."[187] During his second American sojourn he met with Professor Felix Frankfurter of the Harvard Law School, Brandeis's close collaborator who would soon join him on the Supreme Court, and Brandeis himself; and he dined with the executive of the American Economic Committee for Palestine, an organization sponsored by the group.[188] Those exchanges resulted in admiration all around, if not in tangible accomplishments. Subsequently Brandeis proffered financial aid to the Arabic-language newspaper and other projects of the Histadrut; and the Brandeisists looked to *Davar* for public recognition of their activities.[189]

On his first American foray Katznelson had contact mostly with Yiddish-speaking, immigrant workers. In 1937 he addressed the national board of Hadassah, an English-speaking, mostly second-generation, middle-class organization, and traveled to Atlantic City for its national convention. In vain, he tried to persuade the women of the virtues of partitioning Palestine into Arab and Jewish cantons; he also sought to direct their attention away from politics and towards a sales campaign for Palestine products. The Hadassah members, however, saw in the battle against partition "their great educational role in the [Zionist] movement" and resisted his approaches.[190] Not without irony, he observed that Hadassah and the Geverkshaften Campaign, with their philanthropic orientation, had become the two most actively Zionistic organizations in the United States.[191]

Katznelson had come to America chiefly to finalize terms for the merger of the American Poale Zion-Zeire Zion with the non-Zionist, National Jewish Labor Committee. As will be discussed below, Ben-Gurion had shortly before concluded an agreement in principle with Baruch Charney Vladeck, the *Forverts* journalist who had once aided *Davar*, now a New York City politician and chairman of the Labor Committee. To Katznelson fell the task of selling the pact to both sides.[192] Although he proceeded with tact and diplomacy, the assignment proved "to be much more difficult than Ben-Gurion had imagined."[193] The unionists "knew," he confided to his wife, "that one day they would have to succumb to Palestine."[194] To his amazement, some opponents of the agreement were themselves considering aliyah; but they were unwilling, for personal reasons, to give Vladeck the satisfaction of having engineered the arrangement.[195] Katznelson attempted to salvage the trip by persuading International Ladies' Garment Workers' Union secretary David Dubinsky, one of the most powerful union leaders in the United States, to invest three million dollars from union reserve funds in Palestine. Here, too, he failed, in part because Dubinsky, along with several other Jewish labor leaders, felt he had been slighted by Histadrut officials over the years.[196]

Americans' sense of the importance of the *yishuv* in the geopolitical context of the late 1930s led to the only real successes of the tour. These came in the realm of public relations, which Katznelson tended to devalue. As noted above, he was well received by Hadassah, even if many of the women disagreed with his views. The National Arbayter Farband and the New York Jewish Educators' Council responded enthusiastically to his softened rhetoric; other groups, including the veterans of the Jewish Legion and an association of nutritionists, invited him to speak. During an address to the thirteenth annual convention of the Geverkshaften Campaign, in which he reviewed the situation in Palestine and Europe and took to task the leaders of "certain Jewish socialist organizations" who still refused to climb aboard the Zionist bandwagon (meaning, of course, Vladeck and his compatriots), "everyone hung on his every word."[197] His departure from America in December 1937, unlike that fifteen years earlier, was not unlamented, especially within the Labor Zionist movement. The *Iddisher Kemfer* captured his essence, albeit in the florid language that he disdained as American bluff. All during his trip, the journal observed, Katznelson had spoken "without one word of empty propaganda, without one false note . . . , with a firmness whose great magic and forceful power lie in the gentle humanity of the person."[198] If he remained ambivalent about America, some Americans had learned to appreciate him. Ironically, his voice would henceforth carry more weight in the United States, while in the political arena of the *yishuv*, events were beginning to pass him by.

The most significant consequence of Berl's encounter with America and its Jewry in the 1930s was a moderate and conditional revision of the role he envisioned for them in the Zionist enterprise. In line with Ben-Gurion, he now accorded America a political as well as an economic function. American Jewish workers, who in the past had "left" the workers of Palestine to themselves, could, he realized, smooth the way in international labor and socialist circles and garner left-wing support for Zionism. He told visiting union leaders in January 1937 that "the influence of [the workers of] America must" be felt.[199] More important was the political task he now assigned to American Jewry, at large, which he began to envision as a counterbalance to the increasingly anti-Zionist British government. Those Jewries, especially in the English-speaking world, which were least committed to the personal fulfillment of the Zionist ideal, he told the Mapai Party Council in the spring of 1939, were well placed to become not only "the financial reservoir" of the *yishuv* but its "political crutch" as well.[200]

Like Jabotinsky and Ben-Gurion, Katznelson was aware of British sensitivity to American opinion on the Palestine question and less inclined even than his Mapai colleague to expect fair play from England. In March 1930, the British government officially received the Shaw Commission report, which placed a considerable measure of blame for the 1929 riots on Jews' displacement of Arabs from their ancestral lands. Shortly thereafter Sir John Hope-Simpson was dispatched to Palestine to study the question of land transfer. Katznelson feared the worst and suggested to the Mapai Party Center that a delegation of "Palestinians [be sent] to New York . . . to stir up the Jewish public." In that election year, he asserted, "every senatorial candidate would express his sympathy for Zionism"; and a skillful delegation "would know how to exploit" such statements;[201] but the deputation was not sent. The initial sympathy of the American public for the *yishuv* in the wake of the riots quickly dissipated; and the isolationist American government quietly acquiesced in Britain's restrictive measures against the Jews.[202]

During the first days of the 1936–39 Arab insurrection, Katznelson again urged upon party leaders "serious action in Washington," such as an official warning that additional restrictions on the *yishuv*, "would make a bad impression in America."²⁰³ He proposed that President Roosevelt be urged "to make America the guarantor of Jewish interests in Palestine. A country with a Jewish population of four million, which was a partner in the establishment of the Mandate, and which has a treaty with Britain regarding Palestine issues, is certainly entitled to become involved."²⁰⁴ Unlike others, he did not perceive any special affinity of the United States for the *yishuv*. He wished merely to exploit the potential of American Jewish political power. Less than a year later he predicted to his friend and physician in London that neither "America nor France would assist . . . [in forcing Britain] to maintain the Mandate faithfully," although he seems not to have discouraged Mapai and the Histadrut from seeking the support of organized Labor in the United States and Britain.²⁰⁵ During the debates over partition and immigration restriction that raged between 1937 and 1939, Katznelson again reminded his colleagues of the importance to British "government circles of the American reaction" and urged Weizmann and Ben-Gurion to secure the support of the Zionist hinterland in America.²⁰⁶ On occasion, usually in private, he attributed Zionist political victories to "the unprecedented unity of American Jewry."²⁰⁷

The importance that Katznelson came to attach to American political activity on behalf of the *yishuv* in the 1930s reflects the changes that occurred in the Zionist movement, in the geopolitical context, and in Katznelson himself during that troubled decade. As the French proverb has it, however, "*Plus ça change, plus c'est la même chose.*" In fact, he continued to look upon money as "the principal factor" in the America-Palestine relationship. "I know of nothing," he declared to a Histadrut Council meeting in 1936, "more important than saving workers from the affliction of unemployment."²⁰⁸ Without funds the Zionists could not fight for their goal. In America there was money in relative abundance, even in the Depression Era; and he understood better than most that time was running out. Now more than ever the *yishuv* needed money to build. That it should look to America was natural and necessary.²⁰⁹

Katznelson expected financial backing for all the projects of the labor movement, which depended upon American funds for a major portion of its budget in the 1930s. Like Bialik, he solicited money for the Hebrew University and for the subvention of Hebrew writers coming from Europe. For *Davar* he sought backing and subscribers.²¹⁰ Most especially, he was eager to raise funds for illegal immigration. He tended to ignore the Depression, probably on the assumption that however difficult conditions were in America, they were worse in Palestine.²¹¹ If America was no longer the *goldene medine* for individuals, it had to remain that for Zionist institutions.

Berl saw "nothing wrong with . . . repeated requests for money." Not only did the ends require means but he remained convinced that "depriving the American Jewish public of its fund drives would impoverish [it spiritually] rather than enrich it." His own experiences in the New World notwithstanding, he still believed that fund raising was the only way to prepare the ground for cultural and educational activities among America's money-oriented Jews. He claimed American and western European Jews had forgotten "what poverty was," and—contrary to evidence—that American gentiles were more generous than Jews. Since, he averred, *"giving ennobles the donor"* (italics his), through their financial demands the Palestinians were contributing to the character development of American Jews.[212] America was still chiefly a cow to be milked. Berl did not lose sight of the dangers of dependency, but he regarded the Geverkshaften Campaign, Labor's mainstay, as benign. Unlike the "well-known personalities" who had highhandedly doled out American relief funds during World War I and after the 1929 riots, or the "money moguls" of the enlarged Jewish Agency, Geverkshaften Campaign leaders, he claimed, never tried "to assert control over expenditures or over cultural affairs or politics. . . . [They] do not attempt to impose [upon us] the ways . . . of Warsaw or New York."[213]

6

The war years were the last of Berl's life. Although he was only fifty-two years old in 1939, his physical health and morale were declining. He now became something of an elder statesman, and gradually ceased to play the central role in the political life of the *yishuv* that had been his for so long. He remained very active in the Histadrut "study month," which he organized for the first time in 1941, in Mapai Party seminars and other teaching settings, to an extent in *Davar*, and, most of all, in the Am Oved Publishing House established by the Histadrut in 1942 with him as director and general editor. These forums enabled him still to function as the spiritual mentor and intellectual preceptor of mainstream Laborites, and, to a degree, of the entire *yishuv*.[214] His voice was still heard everywhere. His opinions still carried weight with close associates like Ben-Gurion, with the Labor leadership, and with many others. Once again, he manifested apathy and negative feelings towards America; but building upon the reevaluation he undertook in the 1930s, he came to recognize its enormously increased importance to the free world and to Zionism in the wartime period. As teacher and editor he voiced those contradictory sentiments.

To Berl, America was still the place where people worshiped success, where those who had not prospered materially were deemed to have led worthless lives.[215] In a letter to the Chicago Hebrew poet and critic, Shimon Halkin, he mourned the Hebrew writer, L. A. Orloff, who, he said, had possessed "the true spark" but, like so many others, was "shunted aside" in

America.[216] Capitalistic society, which was "fundamentally anarchic," he claimed, "promised individuals freedom, but absolved itself of any responsibility for their . . . welfare." By contrast, he told a Labor conference in 1942, at the heart of the socialist society for which they were striving "was the question of human beings within society."[217] His views in this regard seemed to have changed little since the days at Kinneret. At its best, the freedom of America promoted homogenization, as the fate of Jewish labor movements illustrated. American Jewish unions, he told the twentieth-anniversary celebration of the Histadrut, shed their commitment to the Jewish people, as their members climbed the ladder of success. Only in Palestine was it really possible "to share in the fate of the reborn nation."[218]

In the early days of the war, Eliezer Kaplan, the treasurer of the Jewish Agency, Manya Shoḥat, his old comrade in American arms, and others reported to him on the infighting in American Zionism, which was undiminished by the threat to Europe's Jews. He "could not come to terms" with the failure of the Americans to rise above their usual behavior, but the news was not surprising.[219] Like Jabotinsky, he longed for the good old days of World War I and hoped American Jews could be recruited for a new Jewish Legion to serve in Palestine. He understood, however, that "many *American* [legal] obstacles" (italics his) stood in the way; and he doubted the will of American Jews.[220] In a vastly overgenerous evaluation of the role of Ben-Gurion and Ben-Zvi during the earlier emergency, he asserted before a gathering of Palestinian Jewish soldiers that only the miraculous presence of "a few Second Aliyah" exiles, who "lit the Zionist torch," had brought American volunteers to the Legion in 1917.[221] He refused, however, to provide such a presence now himself.[222] This exaggerated compliment to his colleagues constituted an unfair devaluation of the contribution of Americans to the Legion, a contribution which, as noted above, he had acknowledged two decades earlier.

By early 1940, Berl already perceived the Nazi "crusade" as the worst in history; in the hour of crisis the Jews of the world were looking desperately to their prosperous and more secure American brethren for leadership. But Hitler's influence was felt even in Russia and the United States, still untouched by the war. America's once "assertive and proud" Jews, he averred in a 1940 speech, were frightened "to speak out" against the Nazis, "lest they be suspected of desiring war."[223] After Pearl Harbor American Jews still seemed more "fearful" and less nationalistic than during the First World War, he remarked in 1942. Even Professor Salo Baron of Columbia University, the respected historian of the Jews, failed to grasp the gravity of the situation. In an essay that appeared in *Davar*, Baron expressed the hope that after the war, Europe's displaced Jews could return to their former homes. To Berl that was the sort of cowardice, naiveté, and blindness to the proper role of Palestine, characteristic of "the respectable Jews of America."[224]

In September 1941, he answered Baron in an essay in the *Jewish Frontier*. "Whatever the general atmosphere following the war," Katznelson proclaimed, "we can expect only defeats unless the Zionist movement makes a firm stand on its full platform. This means the full solution of the Jewish Question, the transformation of millions of homeless and defenseless Jews into a population that is not dependent on the love or hatred of others." It was a call for the establishment of a Jewish state and a vote of unequivocal no-confidence in the Diaspora. He issued it in the United States, moreover, where, until then, even Zionist leaders who favored a state usually refrained from forthright language.[225]

As always, however, his attitude was ambivalent. One senses that in the early forties Berl was setting his house in order by making peace with some of his American adversaries, perhaps with America itself. As he withdrew from active political involvement, he devoted less attention to financial matters. Although he never lost sight of the importance of American money to the *yishuv* nor abandoned the notion that American Jews had a duty to bankroll Zionism,[226] he now showed interest in other aspects of American Jewish life.[227] He expressed regret for "the catastrophe" wrought by "the lack of understanding" between Western Jews and eastern Europeans in the Zionist movement. The tragic split after World War I between Brandeis and Weizmann, he wrote in *Davar* in 1940, had been caused not by conflicting interests but by "the inability [of the two camps] to communicate with each other."[228] In 1942 he sent warm greetings for a volume honoring David Pinsky, the former editor of *Di Tsayt*, on his seventieth birthday. Pinsky's "literary and public creativity," he asserted, was "intimately connected . . . with the flowering of Zionist and socialist consciousness."[229] Katznelson had been in the United States when the Poale Zion celebrated Pinsky's fiftieth birthday. Then he had conspicuously avoided sending even a perfunctory greeting. In 1943 Am Oved began the publication of the complete works of Abraham Liessin (Walt), the Yiddish poet, editor, *Forverts* journalist, and socialist, who was one of Berl's heroes. In the introduction Berl acknowledged that America had not snuffed out Liessin's spark nor his commitment to the Jewish people during the forty-one years he lived there.[230] Shortly before his death Katznelson seemed ready for reconciliation even with the American Jewish communists. Golda warned him that they were unregenerate in their opposition to Zionism, but he preferred to believe otherwise, despite his strong dislike for their Moscow masters.[231]

The war forced him to come to terms with America as a political power and moral force. "We are more interested in the victory of the democracies," Katznelson declared in a June 1940 speech to the Mapai Party

Council, "than they are themselves."[232] Considering the enemy about whom he harbored no illusions, it could hardly have been otherwise. By mid-1941, along with Golda, Ben-Gurion, Moshe Shertok (Sharett), and others, Katznelson recognized that Zionism's "front line was in London and America" and that the welfare of the *yishuv* now depended in no small measure upon the political clout of American Jewry.[233] As a non-Marxist socialist, he had long before perceived the danger of "the romantic pro-Soviet" outlook of many Palestine Laborites, which led to admiration for Russia's anti-Zionist tyranny. Appreciation of America, he now hoped, might counteract that potentially destructive sentiment.[234] He expressed special contempt for leftist American intellectuals whose love affair with communism blinded them to their own country's moral promise and political responsibilities. Roosevelt, he wrote in *Davar* in September 1941, had comprehended the threat posed by the Axis well before Pearl Harbor but had been unable to rouse the nation, in part because of the activities of the leftists.[235]

To foster the reorientation of the Palestine labor movement Berl sought American books about politics, art, and society by authors such as Lewis Mumford, Max Lerner, and Alan Moorehead, for publication in translation by Am Oved.[236] He brought out an anthology of British thought concerned with wartime issues and hoped to publish a complementary volume of American thought.[237] He eagerly searched for suitable works of American Yiddish and Hebrew writers and of refugees from Hitler's Europe living in the United States.[238]

Central though the United States may have been to his concerns in the early 1940s, Berl remained characteristically wary. Anxiety about the Soviet Union could not move him to unqualified endorsement of capitalist, materialist America; and American Jews, with their Diaspora values, could never earn his unreserved acceptance. His ambivalence manifested itself in a number of ways. At Mapai seminars, he refused to experiment with the modern pedagogy pioneered in the American-Jewish teachers' seminaries because the youth of Palestine, who could "live Hebrew literature," supposedly required a different approach.[239] In politics, he reminded Histadrut members and *Davar* readers in the spring of 1942, America was not thoroughly reliable. During World War I, she assented to the Balfour Declaration. But after the 1920–21 riots came the American King-Crane investigatory commission, which sided with the Arab perpetrators.[240] Still, America's workers, the "vanguard of tomorrow," were sympathetic to Jews;[241] and the country was the best—if not the only—hope the world then offered. His reservations were fewer. His early awareness of the value of American technology and funds was now enlarged by recognition of the political and moral role that only the United States could play in a world threatened by unprecedented tyrannies. His approbation of America was greater; but it could never be total.

Katznelson's death in 1944 shook the entire *yishuv*. A commanding leader and moral visionary who had remained uncompromised by eschewing political office and its emoluments was gone. The conscience of the *yishuv*, the voice that had cautioned against both American materialism and bluff and Bolshevik tyranny, while waving the banner of the Jewish people and of a humane socialism infused with Jewish values and tradition, was stilled. Ben-Zion Ilan was overcome by a "feeling of personal orphandom";[242] but even political opponents would miss Berl's guidance and reproof. His appreciation of the importance to the *yishuv* of American money and political power would prove to be a significant and so far permanent legacy. His no less well-placed anxiety regarding many American values would be less long-lasting. Across the ocean, his loss was felt most deeply by those Labor Zionists who shared his vision of America, those who also saw the United States and its Jews largely as financial and political resources to be exploited for Zionism. To them Berl was "essentially a man of thought and expression" who exemplified the highest aspirations of the Jewish people, the most exalted ideals of the human race.[243] Soon after his death, his Labor colleagues decided to establish a teachers' seminary and retreat center in his memory. The funds for the institution that came to be known as Beit Berl were to be raised in the United States.[244]

CHAPTER
5
Henrietta Szold

Health, Education, and Welfare, American-Style

ONLY A FEW of the immigrants to Palestine in the pre-state period came from the United States. Among the leaders of the state in the making, the American presence was correspondingly minimal. Surprisingly, however, three of the most prominent figures of the *yishuv* came from the New World: Judah Magnes, Golda Meir, and Henrietta Szold. That two of the Americans were women who rose to the pinnacle of the male-dominated *yishuv* leadership cadre is also rather startling. Magnes's American habits and mind-set, together with his rather unbending personality, have been interpreted, with considerable justice, as having contributed to his increasing marginalization in Jewish Palestine. Szold, his veteran associate in the American Zionist movement and then in the *yishuv*, is, however, often read incorrectly. She was the founding president, organizer, and visionary of Hadassah, the American women's Zionist organization, certainly the most powerful Zionist group in the United States and arguably the most successful Jewish organization of all time. In Palestine, she was an outsider as a woman, as a person whose family did not come from Yiddish-speaking eastern Europe, and as an American. To a degree and for a time there, she served as the representative of Hadassah and of other organizations and wealthy individuals in the United States; eventually she emerged as the representative of the *yishuv* to America.

Her achievements in America, especially Hadassah, as well as her American upbringing, her attachment to her family in the United States, and her nostalgia for the American landscape were widely recognized in her own day.[1] So, too, was the fact that she grew apart from her American roots over time,[2] although the extent to which she overcame her "outsiderness" was often overlooked, at least by American observers. Her Americanizing influence on the *yishuv* and the nature of that influence have not been at all adequately considered by her biographers. Nor has the degree to which Szold helped to make America, its Jews, and its ways less alien to the Jews of Palestine. This she did through her forceful, charismatic personality and the institutions she molded.[3]

Ernst Simon, Szold's coworker in education, compatriot in politics, and close friend, remarked in a eulogy soon after her death that her "life's work" had been built upon three foundations: "her family heritage, Lincoln's America, and her encounter" with eastern European Jews.[4] In fact, Szold's responses to situations in Palestine, especially to the Arab-Jewish conflict and to the refugee crisis of the 1930s, were in large part conditioned by her earlier experiences with outsiders in the United States: women, blacks, and eastern European Jewish immigrants.

A very significant element in her background, which Simon and others did not recognize, was American Progressivism, what Richard Hofstadter defined as the broad "impulse toward criticism and change that was everywhere so conspicuous [in the United States] after 1900." In those years "the already forceful stream of agrarian discontent was enlarged and redirected by the growing enthusiasm of middle-class people for social and economic reform." Although "rather vague and not altogether [a] cohesive or consistent movement," Progressivism promoted the use of science to bring order to a society perceived as increasingly chaotic and to improve it. Progressivism affected "the whole tone of American political life" in the turn-of-the-century years.[5] To it can be attributed the advanced technology and the notions of bureaucratic thought and scientific method[6] which Szold brought to the health, education, and welfare institutions with which she was associated in Palestine.

Although she became a Palestinian heart and soul, Szold never overcame or abjured her American upbringing. Many of her coworkers, especially those of eastern European origin, resisted her American ways, at least at first. Over time, however, her sensibilities became better understood; her approach mellowed; her charisma won her friends and allies; and the presumably superior technology she introduced was accepted, at least in part. Willy-nilly—but often consciously—in both her faith and her "works" Szold served as an apostle of Americanism.

1

Henrietta Szold was born in Baltimore in 1860. Although learned and scholarly, her formal education ended with high school, except for courses in Talmud and Bible, which she took at the Jewish Theological Seminary after moving to New York in 1902. Among her formative experiences were the Civil War and the issue of black slavery, the Spanish-American War and World War I, and especially the immigration crisis which lasted from 1881 to 1914. Another was the Westernized Judaism of her Hungarian-born, German-educated father, Rabbi Benjamin Szold, who practiced a moderate traditionalism that emphasized spirit rather than letter. Rabbi Szold had been one of the few supporters of Lincoln in Baltimore, a border city with Southern sympathies. From him she acquired an approach to religion which stressed broad tolerance towards all people, including blacks and other minorities.[7] Her memory of viewing Lincoln's bier while perched on her father's shoulders acquired the status of personal myth.[8] Books, such as *Up from Slavery* by Booker T. Washington, the black American educator and social reformer, and *The War-Time Journal of a Georgia Girl, 1864–1865* by Eliza Frances Andrews, helped to form her adult consciousness.[9] She rejoiced at the victories of black American athlete Jesse Owens at the 1936 Olympics in Berlin, hoping that "Herr Hitler's race-conscious soul . . . [was] squirming."[10] At one of her last Passover seders, the ceremony ended—at her request—with the singing of Negro spirituals.[11]

Only somewhat less influential in Szold's development was the "wicked, wicked war" of 1914 to 1918, perpetrated, she believed at the time, by "poor old wicked Francis Joseph."[12] In 1917, as war fever gripped the nation, she declared herself "anti-war, and anti-this-war, and anti-all-wars." Even after the United States entered the melee, she refused to budge from her absolutist position, to the chagrin of Louis Brandeis, head of the wartime Provisional Executive Committee for General Zionist Affairs with which she, too, was associated, and of other Zionist leaders, who feared that their movement would be branded as unpatriotic.[13]

Most indelibly inscribed in her memory was the era of mass immigration to America, "when the doors of the country stood wide open and the disinherited of many nations were permitted to crowd in."[14] That period she saw as a golden age, when the United States was living up to its highest ideals and being invigorated by the vitality of the newcomers. Her vision of America as "a composite of nations" was similar to that articulated by Brandeis in *The Jewish Problem and How to Solve It* (1915) and by other advocates of the new doctrine of cultural pluralism. Szold believed that "each nation" or immigrant group represented in the United States "should apply the fundamental ideals common to civilized peoples in the way its history and traditions teach. That," she said, and not material prosperity, is "what is meant when . . . [America] is called the land of unlimited possibilities."[15] She herself worked with the immigrants as a teacher. Americanization, she declared, was not "the opposite . . . to Jewish living and thinking." It meant simply the "process of acquiring [the] power of realizing [the] fundamental ideas and ideals of the Republic,"[16] the empowerment of the disfranchised, in the language of a later day.

From these experiences Szold emerged as a fairly typical American Progressive with radical leanings in some areas and rather conservative views in others, a genteel reformer with robust notions colored by a strong sense of both morality and aesthetics, "a liberal of the old school, a defender of the rights of the individual."[17] To her last days she admired "the abolitionist spirit—unflinchingly just and true in the fashion of the day when the spirit of the champions of a great cause lingered in the air."[18] She read *The Nation* and followed the influential social-work journal, *The Survey Graphic*, *de rigueur* for a Progressive, although by 1930 she had canceled her subscription to the *The Nation*, disillusioned with its "superficialities" with regard to the Palestine issue.[19]

America to Szold was not the wild, open frontier so admired by Jabotinsky. Like Bialik, she had ambivalent feelings about New York with its "telephonic, tumultuous life in the dust and noise." She was attracted to Boston with its "machinery well oiled and in good condition," its "simply exquisite" public park, "walks and promenades . . . lined with benches, where workmen eat their dinner and read their paper." The New England metropolis, with its order and grace she thought "the most distinctly, characteristically American city" of any she knew.[20] And she tried to imbue all her works with similar "American" order and grace.

Szold held Justice Brandeis in high esteem; and Brandeis, who paid her salary for years through a private arrangement with the ZOA, much admired her.[21] Szold shared with the judge, a leading Progressive and an early proponent of the notion that "small is beautiful—and efficient," an appreciation for the little man, respect for labor organizations, a suspicion of great wealth, and a sense that "prosperity [had] . . . something vulgar and repugnant about it."[22] She deplored "America's business greed [which] has deprived us of" beauty in our lives;[23] and she was outraged when the United States withheld its assent to the British mandate over Palestine and Mesopotamia "in order to protect the interests of the Standard Oil Company."[24]

Szold's political tastes, although reformist, were decidedly middle-of-the-road. To her, Bolshevism and fascism were "both ugly [and] inconceivably barbarous."[25] When conservative Republican William McKinley, during whose first term the colonialist Spanish-American War had been fought and won, was reelected president in 1900, she could find no "reason to rejoice."[26] In later years, she found Franklin Delano Roosevelt too radical. Like many other Progressives, she considered him unacceptably unsystematic in his approach to the Depression ("too 'jumpy' for my taste," as she put it) and cavalier with regard to individual rights. On one occasion, she compared him to Hitler.²⁷ When, in 1935, the Supreme Court declared the National Recovery Act, one of the keystones of FDR's New Deal program of economic regeneration, to be unconstitutional, Szold "wasn't surprised." She had disapproved of the president's "antics" from the start and believed that in politics, as well as economics, "he was acting impulsively to the point of irresponsibility."²⁸ Wendell Willkie, the unsuccessful progressive Republican candidate for president in 1940, seemed to be an accurate "interpreter of [her own cherished] principles and attitudes,"²⁹ although she was not blind to Roosevelt's "extraordinary ability and his great human qualities."³⁰

In religion Szold was also a centrist. Despite her affinity for eastern European Jews, she rejected their Orthodoxy, which she saw as turning away from the modern world. But she also rejected Reform Judaism, which appeared sterile and removed from Jewish life and learning. A "deeply religious" person,³¹ she was for many years close to the modernizing traditionalists at the Jewish Theological Seminary in New York, people such as Solomon Schechter and his wife, Mathilda, Louis Ginzberg, whom she assisted with his research and for whom she developed a romantic attachment that he did not reciprocate, and others. She enrolled in classes at the Seminary, but as a woman she was required to make a public declaration that she did not aspire to the rabbinate.³²

2

Her Americanized values and faith equipped Szold with guidelines and a mind-set with which to approach the political, religious, and economic mine field of the *yishuv*, not necessarily with success. Religion was a particularly thorny area. Although she recognized the intense commitment and humane values of the labor leaders of the day, she was uncomfortable with the propensity of many of them to devalue religion altogether. She sought "a Zionism which stressed the positive worth of a living and growing Judaism"; but only Haim Arlosoroff, who had been educated in Germany, and a few others in the labor movement sympathized with that goal.³³ The traditionalists, on the other hand, were foreign to her enlightened and scholarly spirit. Rabbi Kook, the chief rabbi of the Ashkenazi community from 1921 to 1935, was regarded by many, even by secularists, as saintly. Szold, however, could see in him "not an iota of grace or even human-ness," she declared in 1922.³⁴ The Orthodox Zionists of the Mizrahi movement were closer to her in spirit, but not quite to her liking, nor she to theirs.³⁵ She was "disappointed" that the Orthodox of the *yishuv* contributed little to the development of Jewish religious law, especially in areas "touching women," where she found the tradition "very reprobate."³⁶

In her early years in Palestine she and a few American friends, including Magnes, gathered together on sabbath mornings for the study of sacred texts or for an informal worship service. Those sessions, she wrote to the mother of poet Jesse Sampter, one of her American acolytes who also immigrated to Palestine, "save[d her] . . . from [spiritual] homesickness."[37] In later years she attended the partially modernized Yeshurun Synagogue in Jerusalem, where a small circle of followers looked to her for spiritual guidance.[38] At the same time, she began to show increasing impatience with the "clap-trap" of Westernized Judaism.[39] On the whole, her Americanized religious sensibility proved irrelevant in the *yishuv*.

Although pacifism cannot be considered typical of Americans, it was a philosophy that Szold, together with many of her contemporaries in women's movements, had espoused in the United States; she brought it with her to Palestine. Despite the dangers of life in the *yishuv*, she did not abandon the notion easily. The Palestine reality did, however, force her to reevaluate her uncompromising stance. In 1939 she wrote to the Hadassah National Board that she concurred with their opposition to military training in Youth Aliyah villages. The "international relations of recent years," however, and "the state of Palestine itself, no longer allow[ed her] . . . to see things with the simple, single-minded directness with which [she had] . . . once happily looked upon them."[40] Palestine in the late 1930s and 1940s was not the United States of 1917. Still, in 1941 she insisted on the right to help a young man withstand pressure to volunteer for the British army by securing a position for him as a clerk in the Youth Aliyah office.[41] As a result of such actions, many *yishuv* militants considered her, along with Magnes, Martin Buber, and their associates, nothing less than "quislings."[42]

In the area of Arab-Jewish relations Szold's American baggage was most evident and also ultimately irrelevant, if not misguided. Her pacifism, her commitment to cultural pluralism, and her empathy for blacks all came into play on this issue. Although she supported the idea of a binational, Jewish-Arab state in Palestine, she often felt that her official positions constrained her not to "go beyond the expression of platonic sympathy."[43] Already at the time of the 1921 Arab anti-Jewish riots, she came to believe that Jews bore some responsibility for Arab discontent. Two years later, she secured from Nathan Straus a sum of money "to be spent for the benefit of Moslem children."[44] In the 1930s she lent tacit approval to the Brit Shalom organization, which sought to foster Arab-Jewish rapprochement; in 1937 she wrote to Judah Magnes, concurring, in general, with the approach to Arab-Jewish relations which he had outlined in a speech at the recent Zionist Congress. She cautioned her old colleague, however, that she did not agree that "the consent of the Arabs" needed to be sought in advance of any Zionist initiative and that she was uncertain of her response should negotiations with the Arabs fail.[45]

In the 1940s, when the Iḥud was founded to promote the idea of a binational state, she served on its executive committee along with Buber, Magnes, and others. (Many members of both the Brit Shalom and the Iḥud were intellectuals or technocrats who had come to Palestine from the English-speaking countries or from central Europe. Both groups exhibited many of the patrician reforming characteristics of American Progressives.) Together with the writer S. Y. Agnon, the philosopher Shmuel Hugo Bergman, and others in 1939, Szold signed the self-critical Manifesto Against Internal Terror, which circulated in the *yishuv*. Of the leaders of the Labor faction with whose approach to Arab matters she often agreed, only Berl Katznelson signed. Two years later she angered many friends by issuing a public statement equating stink bombs thrown by Jews at Arab targets with explosive bombs thrown by Arabs at Jewish targets. In 1942 she proved less than enthusiastic about the assertive Biltmore Program for achieving Jewish statehood authored by Weizmann and Ben-Gurion, of which more below.[46]

Szold perceived the Arab-Jewish conflict in Palestine to be analogous to black-white friction in the United States; the solutions she favored were also American-made. In a 1934 article published in the United States in Yiddish on the first anniversary of the murder of Ḥaim Arlosoroff, the Labor leader and "foreign minister" of the Jewish Agency, she remarked that "the fulfillment of the Jewish-national ideal on the soil of Palestine is altogether bound up with the solution to the Arab problem."[47] Two years later she wrote despairingly to her sisters of the joy and alacrity with which the residents of Tel Aviv constructed a new harbor in response to the Arabs' having closed the Jaffa port to them. "Matters are not going to be mended," she asserted "if the alienation between us and the Arab population is emphasized. . . . It is not the way—this way of creating race-tight compartments—of healing the breach, of destroying the seeds of race-hatred."[48]

In these years she expressed fear that "racial pride" among the Jews in Palestine would "lead to Nazi-ism."[49] Some time later she referred to the Arab-Jewish standoff as "a racial problem" and declared Jews "not to have stood the acid test of finding the way to [its] . . . solutions."[50] These were unmistakably the words of a Progressive who had experienced "the American dilemma" at first hand. Zionists of eastern European background also deplored the fate of America's blacks, as noted earlier. They, however, viewed it as analogous to the fate of Jews in czarist Russia and vowed to avoid being placed in a similar position in Palestine.[51] Ernst Simon noted the connection between Szold's American experience and the Palestine reality. "She, herself," Simon asserted, "had pointed to the source of her extraordinary sensitivity to the Arab problem" in the " 'anguish and injustice and [the] exalted efforts to free the slaves.'" Simon felt that Szold "erroneously (but naturally, for an immigrant from America) considered . . . [the Arab-Jewish conflict a] 'racial problem.'" He agreed with her, however, that it was "the most important of the political questions" in Palestine.⁵²

Like many genteel Progressives in America, but unlike most Palestinian Jews, Szold tried to remain above politics, or at least nonpartisan, "Not because I don't consider politics important or interesting, but because I trust my judgment on political matters even less than on others."⁵³ She particularly "hated [the kind of] acrimony which carries political strife into personal relations." But she discovered early on that such "relations [were the norm] in Palestine."⁵⁴

As overseer from 1920 to 1923 of the American Zionist Medical Unit-Hadassah Medical Organization, she encountered considerable opposition from Laborites who assumed her to be a political foe. In December 1923, by chance, while sailing toward Palestine, she met Ben-Gurion, who was returning from a mission to Moscow. Perhaps inspired by Soviet equality, the labor leader noted with scorn that Szold, by then a woman of sixty-three, was traveling in first class. When she told him that American Jews were unlikely to meet their fund-raising quotas that year, he responded furiously, albeit to his diary, with a general diatribe against the "unimaginative [American] blockheads who think that the messianic dream of generations sated with suffering and oppression is nothing but an empty illusion."⁵⁵

As a Hadassah insider remarked retrospectively, the period was characterized by "an extreme distrust of Americans, both individuals and institutions."⁵⁶ The Laborites, who, as noted earlier, feared that their fledgling medical institutions could not withstand what they perceived as Hadassah's colonialism and imperialism, were especially hostile.⁵⁷ Between 1927 and 1930 Szold was one of three people on the Palestine Executive of the World Zionist Organization, which had been charged with making ends meet on a starvation budget. At first, she was the object of frequent "fierce denunciation[s]"⁵⁸ by disgruntled Laborites, who, like Berl, felt that she and her compatriots were insensitive to the needs of working people, insufficiently Zionistic, and shortsightedly tightfisted. In a confrontation between the leadership of the Histadrut and the Executive a short time after Szold's arrival, Ben-Gurion, then secretary general of the Histadrut, accused her to her face of stalking "the teachers and workers of Palestine dagger in hand." Behind her back, he said she exhibited "the sadism of a hangman."⁵⁹ The labor leaders also resented her inability to extract funds from her fellow Americans, most especially the ZOA, which consistently reneged on its obligations, to her chagrin as well as theirs.⁶⁰ Before her departure, her American Zionist colleagues had acknowledged that not enabling Szold "to grapple with . . . [her] task adequately [by remitting the promised funds] would be a sort of personal betrayal of one who had merited the love and help of every Jew and Jewess in America."[61] Once she was out of sight, however, they "fail[ed] ... to keep [their] pledge";[62] and, as their representative, she was held accountable by the Palestinians.

As the writer Moshe Smilansky noted, Szold's longstanding distrust of "'Wall Street,' ... the bank trusts, and the industrial cartels that enslave peoples ... to the god, Mammon"[63] made her a natural ally of organized labor. So, too, did her idealism and her Brandeisian affinity for unions. Already during her first months in Palestine in 1921, she felt attracted to "the almost unparalleled idealism of the Haluz [that is, pioneer]."[64] Her life style there resembled that of the spartan pioneers; she had virtually "no possessions."[65] Despite her professed impartiality, her aversion to the militant, anti-Labor Revisionists was well known. In the 1930s she steadfastly refused to allow Youth Aliyah immigrant children to be placed in their settlements; and the Revisionist press regularly snubbed her.[66]

Eventually most of the Laborites came to see in her a kindred spirit. An American commentator affiliated with the Palestine labor movement remarked in 1931 that because of "Miss Szold's broad sympathy and understanding ... today the working element of Palestine look to her as their friend in the Palestine Zionist Executive."[67] By 1931 she could write in response to the seventieth birthday greetings of the HEC, "Happy am I, who has had the privilege of joining with you in the great task of fulfillment that lies before our generation." The men and women of the Histadrut, she said, "know from their lives and souls ... the meaning of daily labor and genuine creative efforts that seek to make aspirations reality."[68] A few years later, another commentator writing in *Davar* acknowledged that Szold's "organizational achievements had been extraordinary and that her human qualities had endeared her to the entire *yishuv*."[69] In the internal politics of the *yishuv*, if not in religion or Arab-Jewish relations, her American experiences and vision served her well.

3

Like Magnes, her fellow American Progressive, Szold went to Palestine "because of an inexorable passion to serve, to fashion ... a useful destiny, on the pattern of the Quakers, the Social Gospelists, the Social Reformers."[70] According to Ernst Simon, as a child she wished nothing so much as to become "a Quaker lady," a goal achieved in part through her dedication to pacifism and to a life of good deeds.[71] Towards the end of her life, she modestly claimed but "one distinction, a strong sense of duty."[72] She was not, however, "the obedient slave of her assignment, ... the [happy] humble housewife whose work is never done," as Louis Lipsky fatuously described her.[73] She enjoyed music, books, theater, and movies; she had a passion for flowers; and she exhibited a measure of vanity with regard to her appearance.[74] In 1923 she complained to an old friend: "I never do the things I want to do—not the good things, not the useful things, not even the naughty things. Alike in America and in Palestine, fate has ordained that I must do what is thrust upon me from the outside."[75]

In Palestine she devoted her energies and talents to medical and social work and to education through the Hadassah Medical Organization, through Youth Aliyah, which established villages and training schools for refugee children during the Nazi period and for local children with special needs, and through the education and social welfare agencies of the *yishuv*. On all of these "works" she left the mark of her American background. Sara Feder, an active American Labor Zionist and longtime friend of Golda Meir, wrote in 1941 that Szold "belongs to that group of American liberals who built many of our great social service institutions [and] settlement houses, and encouraged labor and adult education."[76] Here her American experience proved most adaptable to Palestine and her American connections extremely useful.

As a prelude to her career in Palestine, Szold had founded and organized Hadassah, the Women's Zionist Organization of America, an organization that exemplified in many ways the Progressive spirit. Channeling women's activities into the areas of social and medical work and child care was typical of the Progressives, who maintained "the traditional image of women as tender mothers, angels of mercy, and keepers of the morals," but liberated at least some of them from the traditional role of homemaker.[77] In 1896 Szold argued that "sexless work [that is, gender free] is the great desideratum";[78] later she willingly accepted certain endeavors as appropriate for women.[79] Brandeis and others strongly believed in a special role for women. The "supreme task" in Palestine, he asserted in 1921, was "the moral regeneration of the Palestinians. That task," he said, "was the reason why Miss Szold's going there was significant. . . . Our meagre forces on the firing line should be strengthened by other women of the right calibre as soon and so far as this is possible." Brandeis feared that Szold's return to America "even for a brief visit," might endanger the character of the Palestine work.[80]

As Carol Bosworth Kutscher has observed, Hadassah "modeled itself after . . . prestigious American women's organizations, rather than . . . [male] Jewish religious or Zionist groups with European origins. . . . [From those women's organizations came its] practical . . . emphasis on health, hygiene, and sanitation. . . . The Hadassah leaders were ardent believers in [Progressive] American [methods and] institutions; they sought efficiency of operation, while enforcing strict financial accountability."[81] Szold herself was

Henrietta Szold (standing center, with lace collar) with the staff of the Safed Hadassah Hospital at the hospital, 1926. (Courtesy of the Central Zionist Archives, Jerusalem.)

acutely conscious from the first of the differences between her women's group and the disorganized, male-dominated American and international Zionist organizations.[82] From its founding in 1912, she remarked some years later, Hadassah was characterized by its "achievement, its trained and willing forces, [and] its tested organization."[83] In 1926, she proudly described the organization to Irma Lindheim, her successor as president of Hadassah who also followed her to Palestine, as "a sharp knife set into a finely-turned handle" that could "be used" effectively "to exert weight in Zionist circles on all issues."[84]

In Palestine she discovered that the ethos of the *yishuv* resembled that of Diaspora Zionist organizations. The "systemless" eastern European immigrants "hate[d] efficiency," she wrote to her sister Adele in 1921, making it difficult for her to "accept them," at least at first. "Disorder," she declared, "nauseates me."[85] Some months earlier she had remarked that American salaries were "the only American element that is acceptable over here. American brains, American efficiency, American system are spurned."[86] Szold readily assumed the task of imposing "order and [the] disciplined acceptance of rules of precedence upon the workers," although she believed "a regiment of Hoovers [might be needed] for this stupendous piece of organizational work."[87] (In 1927 the future president, Herbert Hoover, an outstanding Progressive, was still best known as the successful organizer of American relief to Belgium during the World War I.)

To all of the endeavors with which she was associated in Palestine Szold brought the Progressive notions of sound financial practices, scientific management, and hard work. When anyone asked her support for a new project, her inevitable reply was, "Where is the money to come from?"[88] She took special pride in her early days in Palestine that Hadassah paid its salaries on time, unlike other Zionist enterprises;[89] and she implored the WZO to manage its affairs and its funds with good sense and probity.[90] On one occasion she lent two thousand pounds of her own money to the Palestine Zionist Executive, so that it could meet its obligations.[91] When Szold agreed to serve on the Executive in 1927, she did so with the conviction that "in competency it is essential at this moment that we American Zionists should attain and hold the hegemony."[92] She had come "to the conclusion that an American system of administration must be introduced." By that she meant "a small, non-partisan Executive" similar to the city manager plans promoted by American Progressives. This was not to be "an Executive of experts, [but one] . . . that can supervise and manage the work of the experts."[93]

Like other American reformers of her day, she regarded highly honesty, intelligence, and good sense, as well as expertise. She remarked to a friend in 1943 that she did not believe in courses "in administration [although] . . . doubtless there are techniques which [it] would be well to know and acquire." Most important for an administrator, she maintained, were "a sense of organization and, above all good common sense and interest in and knowledge of the work in hand."[94] No less, Szold valued hard work, a concept then associated with America. In fact, despite her cultural interests, she was a workaholic, who, at the age of seventy-six, slept only three to five hours a night and spent all her "waking hours . . . strenuously at work . . . never, never relax[ing]."[95] At an eightieth birthday celebration for her in 1940, Laborite Moshe Shertok (later, Sharett), then head of the Political Department of the Jewish Agency and later foreign minister and prime minister of Israel, remarked upon Szold's "enormous capacity for work, her perseverance, her ability to get to the bottom of a matter, her thoroughness, [and] her concern for performance and for finishing a job." In many ways "she has enlightened us," he said, "but chiefly through" her seemingly inexhaustible energy for work.[96]

4

As noted earlier, Progressivism was characterized by the desire to apply the methods of the natural sciences to most areas of human endeavor; and Szold's first arenas of service to the *yishuv* were in the areas of scientific agriculture and medicine. Between 1909 and 1919, she served as a member of the board of directors and secretary of Aaron Aaronsohn's Jewish Agricultural Experiment Station. In 1913, Aaronsohn addressed the Daughters of Zion, as Hadassah was first called; and Szold, whom he considered "the greatest Jewess [he had] . . . ever had the opportunity to meet," helped him to raise funds for the Station.[97] Although she remained interested in the agricultural colonies of the *yishuv* (one was named for her), Szold's involvement with scientific farming seems to have ended with Aaronsohn's death.

Public health was one of the most important concerns of American Progressives in the turn-of-the-century years;[98] and, as already observed, it was a field for which women were presumed to be particularly well suited. The American Red Cross was founded by Clara Barton in 1882 and chartered by Congress in 1905. Other health-care organizations also came into being in these years, which saw feverish activity designed to improve the physical well-being of Americans. Influenced by the concerns of their time and place, the women of Hadassah under "the leadership of Henrietta Szold . . . [made] available [to Palestine] the best of American medical standards and practice."[99]

What sparked this thrust was Szold's trip to the Holy Land, in 1909, during which she was struck by the widespread incidence of trachoma.[100] With the help of Nathan Straus, Szold and her Hadassah sisters dispatched two American nurses in 1913 to "instal [sic] a system of American District Visiting Nurses in Palestine."[101] The guidelines for the nurses' activities were essentially those of the state of New York. Among other things, the nurses would "train helpers and probationers and organize 'Little Mothers' circles" like those run by the New York City Board of Health.[102] Shortly after the nurses began their work they were visited by Jane Addams, the settlement house pioneer from Chicago, and Rabbi Stephen S. Wise, who "heartily expressed their appreciation of the work being done."[103] When she returned to Chicago, Addams, one of the country's foremost Progressives, tendered Szold (to whom Brandeis and others referred as "the Jane Adamms [sic] of our Jewish world") a "big luncheon" at Hull House and presented her with a copy of her memoirs.[104]

As described earlier, the First World War caused considerable dislocation and suffering in Palestine, especially for the Jewish community, which had always depended upon outside aid. At Brandeis's suggestion in 1916, Hadassah took upon itself the task of organizing the American Zionist Medical Unit (AZMU), including doctors, nurses, a field hospital, and dentists, to be sent to Palestine. Soon after the arrival of the AZMU there in August 1918, it began to revolutionize medical care by introducing American methods and technology. It took over the new nursing school and the Rothschild Hospital in Jerusalem and opened clinics and hospitals elsewhere; it established a Schools Hygiene Department and an X-ray clinic in Jerusalem, dental clinics in Jerusalem and Jaffa, and infant welfare stations in a number of communities; and it mounted a Medical Sanitary Expedition "to visit all the Jewish villages and the Jewish communities in the cities." Even its hospital laundry was innovative, the first steam laundry in the country. And in the absence of municipal garbage collection in Jerusalem, Hadassah organized the city's first sanitation service, which was turned over to the municipality in 1920.

Between the summer of 1919 and that of 1920, when Szold arrived in Palestine to take personal charge of the Unit, the AZMU recorded almost 400,000 visits to its clinics.[105] In 1921 with money donated by Brandeis, the Unit, now renamed the Hadassah Medical Organization, undertook a program of malaria control, "which closely resembled the methods of the International Health Board of the Rockefeller Foundation."[106] Aside from its personnel and technology, the AZMU could be identified as a liberal American institution in the spirit of Szold, by its rule, "that no discrimination be exercised in any of its . . . branches of service as to race, creed, or colour," a policy maintained to the present by the HMO.[107]

Although on several occasions she was called upon to take a more active role, after 1923 Szold served largely as a watchdog or advisor to the HMO, albeit one whose advice could not be easily ignored; and in 1925 she returned to Palestine as resident mentor to the new HMO director, Dr. E. M. Bluestone, an American. The organization continued to adapt recent American medical innovations to Palestinian needs, often at her suggestion. Among these were the first hospital social service department in the country in 1934, the first medical social worker in 1937 (an idea still very new in America), and the medical center concept for the new Hadassah Hospital opened in Jerusalem in 1939.[108] In 1944, only months before her death, Szold coauthored with the then HMO director, Dr. Haim Yassky, a proposal for the control of venereal disease, an outbreak of which was expected with the return of Palestinian soldiers from the war in Europe.[109] The goal of all these undertakings, as Szold told a Hadassah reception in New York in 1923, was the "development of public health work to the same degree of efficiency attained by our [that is, American] hospitals."[110] By 1940 it was widely recognized in Palestine and in the United States that the goal was on the way to achievement, that thanks to Szold and Hadassah the *yishuv* enjoyed

"American standards of health and hospitalization" to an extent unparalleled in other developing countries.¹¹¹

5

The second major area of Palestine life in which Szold became involved was education, yet another of the central concerns of American Progressives, and one to which she had already given considerable attention as head of the Education Department of the ZOA from 1918 to 1920 and in her Hadassah work. Alexander Dushkin, an American Jewish educator and close friend of Szold, noted that one of "the fundamentals of" the "pedagogic credo which guided her throughout her long and blessed life [—even in Palestine—was the] . . . complete integration of Jewish and American traditions."¹¹²

One of Szold's first acts as director of the AZMU was to revamp the school for nurses to bring their "training . . . up to the point at which it stands in the United States."¹¹³ Another early foray into Palestine education was the endorsement of the progressive school founded in Jerusalem in 1920 by Deborah Kallen, an immigrant from America and the sister of Horace Kallen, the theoretician of cultural pluralism who had had much to do with Brandeis's conversion to the Zionist cause.¹¹⁴ Just a few months after her arrival in Palestine, Szold expressed the hope that wealthy parents there, like those in the United States, "would make demands which the public school system could not satisfy." That would make "it possible for progressive teachers" like Kallen to offer children the kind of [private] education they deserved.¹¹⁵

In 1922 Szold brought Dr. Frances Cohen, assistant to the director of school inspection in New York City, to Palestine as a consultant to the HMO school hygiene program. Cohen taught her that Americans did not always have useful advice to offer. Szold wrote to her sisters that the New Yorker, who spoke only English, "came to our work for 10000 or 12000 children, in inadequate, rented school buildings under teachers for the most part not trained professionally, from a system that deals with 930,000 children under luxurious, regulated American conditions." Szold found it "interesting" that Cohen "often did not realize that we were already doing the very things she advocated, in a modified form, adapted to the Palestinian peculiar [sic] situation."¹¹⁶

On the Palestine Zionist Executive, Szold held the health and education portfolios. Since the HMO had already brought some order to the medical system by the mid-1920s, she devoted most of her time to education, at least at first. When she arrived in the country in late 1927 the Jewish education system was in total disarray; the WZO was on the verge of bankruptcy;

and most of the Mandatory government's education budget was reserved for Arab schools. There was no money for supplies or even to pay the teachers, who were resorting to strikes; and there was little sensible structure in a system riven by political and religious disagreements.[117] "My cursory examination," Szold wrote in controlled understatement to the New York Junior Hadassah on New Year's Day in 1928, "indicates that a very thorough reorganization will be necessary."[118]

Already when elected to the Executive the previous summer by the Zionist Congress, Szold had resolved to secure expert American assistance for her educational work. She turned to two friends, Alexander M. Dushkin, an erstwhile Palestinian who then headed the Chicago Board of Jewish Education, and Isaac B. Berkson, the school and extension program supervisor at the New York Bureau of Jewish Education.[119] Berkson—a follower of the educational theories of W. H. Kilpatrick, "the father of progressive education," and of philosopher John Dewey—was the author of *Theories of Americanization* (1920), in which he proposed applying the notions of cultural pluralism to Jewish education. He agreed to come to Palestine to conduct a survey of the education system. "Objective, experienced, [and] calm," like "every expert," Berkson sailed with Szold. Their "discussions [during the journey] . . . of the education problems ahead . . . had the tendency to tranquillize . . . [Szold] concerning the task . . . thrust upon [her]."[120]

When he had completed his survey, which included recommendations for the future, Berkson was invited by the Executive to remain in Palestine as the director of its Department of Education. Although "his candidacy was met openly and secretly unsympathetically, beginning with his rumored salary up to his knowledge of Hebrew [sic]," he accepted the "challenge." At the time of Berkson's appointment, Szold noted, there was "no restored confidence as yet; . . . [and] our [American] methods and outlook are as unpopular as ever."[121] She understood well that her "attitude toward educational reforms as expressed through the person of the new director of my choice, Dr. Berkson," would cause her more than "a few private difficulties."[122]

In his first year as director, Berkson and Szold "worked out the Education Budget [together], reducing it and reducing it to a minimum beyond which reduction is not possible if the existing system is not to be broken up completely."[123] Substantial gifts for education were solicited by the Zionists from Baron Rothschild and from Felix Warburg, an acquaintance of Szold. Salaries were to be paid on time but only by firing teachers; and nonessential institutions, such as the Bezalel School of Art, were to be closed.[124] Szold realized that sound budgetary principles were "forcing the educational system into [a] . . . straight-jacket," and that "high excitement" would result.[125]

As director of education of the *yishuv* from 1928 to 1935, Berkson—

and indirectly Szold, his "minister" until 1930—succeeded in imposing a degree of American Progressive reform. Besides balancing the budget, Berkson had American books on school architecture, pedagogy, and education translated into Hebrew, and introduced into the *yishuv* the philosophy of Dewey and Kilpatrick and the Thorndike-Terman measurement systems. "He continued with . . . reorganization, eliminating duplication and needless expenditures," and raised teachers' salaries "through more efficient" collection of tuition and other means.[126] Some of his ideas for reform were not successful, however, such as the suggestion in the name of efficiency to close the Haifa Technical Institute (Technion) and send engineering students to the United States for training. He also failed to gain approval for the establishment of a teacher-preparation institution like his alma mater, Columbia University's Teachers' College, or of a model school along the lines of the Horace Mann School in New York.[127]

By 1930, if not earlier, Berkson and Szold were having their differences. Szold came to suspect that Berkson had "always [been] restive under [her] leadership."[128] In any case, with the reconstituted Jewish Agency now in place, the temporary suspension of party politics in the Zionist Congress, which had allowed a nonpartisan Palestine Executive to be chosen in 1928, ended. Moreover, the American non-Zionists who wielded considerable power in the Agency, most especially Warburg, its chairman, insisted upon trained managers, rather than self-taught amateurs such as Szold. Warburg was also eager to purge the Agency of Zionists and to replace them with non-Zionists who would ostensibly ensure its nonpolitical character. Szold and her compatriots were fired unceremoniously. "Here is my summary of . . . [Warburg's dismissal] letter," she wrote to her sisters: "Damn the Zionists, and as for you, get thee to a Home for Genteel Old Ladies."[129]

She returned to the United States, leaving behind, Berkson acknowledged, a "school system [that] had not only been lifted out of the hollow of the wave of depression, but . . . set on the way to orderly and effective administration and financing."[130] As the educational publisher and Tel Aviv municipal councillor Shoshana Persitz wrote in the teachers' journal, *Hed HaḤinuch*, Szold had managed to get education legitimized in the *yishuv*, despite the high value the Palestinians placed on productive labor. Her insistence on sound financing, Persitz asserted, had freed education officials from fund raising and enabled them to devote their attention to pedagogy.[131] In less than three years Szold had had a major impact on Palestine education. She had successfully battled widespread anti-American prejudice and the animus of the labor movement and succeeded in opening the door to Progressive American educational thinking and practice.

If the Zionist politicians abroad and the wealthy non-Zionists participating in the Jewish Agency did not appreciate her accomplishments, the *yishuv* did.[132] Even Berkson felt "an inner compulsion [guilt?] to join" the public outcry against Szold's dismissal;[133] and she would shortly be called back to Palestine to serve the newly organized Jewish community in the area of social work. Although she did not have official responsibility for education in subsequent years, she continued to function as a conduit for American educational ideas. In 1934 she opened Palestine's first school of social work under the aegis of the Knesset Yisrael, the quasi-governmental representative body of the *yishuv*. The school, funded at first by contributions from wealthy American admirers of Szold, was headed by an immigrant from Germany; but it was heavily influenced by developments in America.[134] In the early 1940s, at her suggestion, Hadassah supported the establishment in Jerusalem of a trade school for girls, the first in the country.[135] Some years later at the age of eighty-three, Szold was still interested in bringing the latest American educational developments to the *yishuv*. She explored the possibility of adapting methods for teaching basic English developed in the United States, for the teaching of Hebrew to immigrants from Nazi Europe.[136]

6

Social work was the third area of life in the *yishuv* to which Henrietta Szold made a significant and lasting contribution. Here perhaps even more than in other fields, American Progressive precedents exerted a paramount influence. From afar she perceived similarities between the problems of Palestine and those of the United States. There is no "hope," she asserted in 1913 sounding as if she were a reformer speaking of New York or Chicago, of building "up a sane, healthy life" in the Holy Land "until the problems of the cities . . . are . . . corrected in a modern, systematic, organized way."[137] Years later, when living in Palestine, she set about solving those problems by reorganizing along advanced American lines social service, which "in the sense of family welfare work, was not known"; and she oversaw the institution of "modern, American-style casework."[138] Still in America, Szold had sensed the need to improve the lot of the women of Palestine and proposed that

> a few American women go to the colonies and do settlement work there. They can teach modern housework and other domestic industries . . . so that hand and head are developed. The chief thing that the settlement worker should do is rouse a noble discontent among them. The women are too patient! If they had only risen up and demanded better sanitation and better living conditions.[139]

Soon after she arrived in Palestine in 1920, she visited with young pioneers at work in the fields and discovered that the lot of men was also harsh. She felt a need to arrange "some lightening up of their monotonous, hard lives. . . . When I am with them," she wrote to her sister, Rachel, "I realize what I never realized before, that the Y.M.C.A. activities are a great need for young men and young women gathered in camps."[140] Her experience in organizing American women volunteers prompted her to coax into existence in that same year the Histadrut Nashim Ivriyot (the Federation of Hebrew Women) to engage in social work activities in the *yishuv*.[141] As she noted some years later, she hoped that American Jews' ability to unite for the good of the Jewish people would serve as an example to the Jews of Palestine.[142]

Already in the prewar era Szold was aware of the "lack of system" that made "it almost impossible to do anything comprehensive for a Palestinian [welfare] institution."[143] During the 1920s she advised Americans how to support social work projects in the *yishuv* and on occasion acted on their behalf. In 1926 when Israel Belkind asked the ZOA for a contribution to his orphan home, her account of his incompetence, which, she felt, actually endangered the children in his care, persuaded them to refuse.[144] As a member of the Palestine Executive she received funds from Hadassah for the Hadassah School Luncheon Fund, which provided food for "undernourished children" in a number of communities.[145] More extensive was her involvement with the Nathan Straus Soup Kitchen and its successor, the Nathan and Lena Straus Health Center. For many years the Soup Kitchen fed large numbers of Jerusalem's poor, most of them pietists who lived in the adjacent neighborhoods. Soup Kitchen personnel were unacquainted with newfangled notions regarding the distribution of charity; and its clientele had come to accept the dole as their due. At the request of the Strauses, who were eager to upgrade the facility, Szold was involved in an extensive investigation in 1926–27, which led to reforms and the building of the Health Center.[146]

A few years later Szold returned to the Soup Kitchen and Health Center at the request of Mrs. Irving (Sissie) Lehman, the Straus's daughter and heir. The Great Depression in the United States affected Lehman's fortune; and she had requested that costs be pared. In any case, she was less committed to the Zionist enterprise than her parents. Szold had never been satisfied that the operation had been sufficiently streamlined.[147] She suspected that it encouraged "people to look upon free food as a general right" rather than engaging in "constructive social work" to help them "become self-supporting," a criticism that resembled the standard accusation leveled by Zionists of the New *Yishuv* against the *ḥalukah* (that is, the charity system of the Old *Yishuv*).[148] In 1931–32 a second, more "thoroughgoing," more "scientific" investigation of the facility was undertaken by "a trained corps of investigators," although eliminating cases "from the Soup Kitchen rolls

... elicited such warmth," that Szold felt obliged to tread lightly lest other projects be endangered.[149] She was caught, she said, between "the modern outlook and the medieval," but she concluded, as might be expected, "that the Soup Kitchens are not a constructive activity" and "that there should be a rapid elimination of all rehabilitable cases."[150]

Szold's most important contributions to social work in the *yishuv* were made between 1931 and 1939, during which time she held the social welfare portfolio for the Knesset Yisrael. As noted earlier, her expertise had become so widely recognized by 1931 and her ability to function in the hurly-burly of Jewish Palestine so greatly admired by the once suspicious Palestinians that they summoned her back from the United States, where she had retired after her summary firing from the Jewish Agency. (Her valuable connections with American donors, especially the Hadassah women, were also appreciated.) In her new post she would deal with three main issues, all of them related: the institution of scientific social work; immigrant aid; and the problems of young people, especially those who came to Palestine as refugees from Nazi Europe without their parents. Although no one could foresee the social problems that lay just ahead for the *yishuv*, her appointment proved to be most fortuitous.

Her work on the Palestine Zionist Executive, as noted earlier, had focused mainly on education. But social welfare was also a "matter... which ... received the special attention of Miss Szold" during those years. She was prodded along by the American Zionists, who sought assurance that their meagre funds were being well used.[151] One of her main goals had been to end the dole system for the unemployed and to persuade the government to institute a system of public works.[152] In her 1930 report, "The Future of Women's Work for Palestine," she acknowledged that the *yishuv* had "developed a long series of social service agencies and institutions" and was "alive to needs and generous in meeting them." What was still lacking, however, was "a systematizing, strengthening, stimulating instrumentality."[153] There was, moreover, considerable resistance to the whole issue of social welfare. As Szold recounted a few years later in a speech to the Hadassah National Board in New York, the "Zionists," by whom she meant chiefly the Laborites, had "dogmatically opposed" social work at first. In their eagerness to replace the life of the Diaspora, which they saw as "base[d] ... on charity" with "justice and social righteousness," the Palestinians had refused to undertake "this nasty piece of work." Despite a high incidence of broken homes and the poor health of immigrants, the leaders of the *yishuv* insisted that employment would solve social problems.[154]

By 1931 dogmatism and optimism were being eroded by stark reality. *Yishuv* leaders viewed Szold's return and her new post as "important steps that will restore hope."[155] She set out to persuade the Laborites that social work was not "non-productive" labor, but rather, "a public welfare undertaking," like education and medicine.[156] And she succeeded, becoming in the process "one of the leaders of the *yishuv* in the fullest sense of the word."[157]

She came "set [in] her heart on introducing modern reforms in the various social [welfare] activities."[158] Although she took a year to learn about social work and was in touch with Jewish social service agencies in many places,[159] her model from the beginning was Progressive America. Soon after arriving back in Palestine, Szold wrote to Mrs. Lehman: "Until we have in each center, what in America used to be called United Hebrew Charities, that is to say, an organization prepared to do 'case work,' to deal with the rehabilitation of the family, no sort of modern social service will be possible." The existing arrangement, she said, "is the old Lady Bountiful system, based on hysteria and not on justice to the unfortunate."[160]

In 1932 Szold started to organize local social welfare agencies with the help of "a small fund secured for me through Judge [Julian W.] Mack."[161] Two years later there were agencies in Jerusalem, Tel Aviv, Haifa, and Petaḥ Tikva, although not yet the hoped-for federated charities, their "corollary."[162] In 1933 she established the Social Service Department of the Knesset Yisrael, which was maintained for its first two years by a grant from the Nettie Lasker Foundation of New York.[163] The next year came the social work school mentioned earlier. By the end of the decade, "a comprehensive network of local social welfare offices had been established" throughout the country; and, as a Labor observer noted, the Social Service Department had become "one of the most vital instruments" of the *yishuv*.[164] "An efficient and well-organized body," it was "equipped with [all the latest American tools:] records, a library, a bulletin, and a statistical section."[165] For most people by 1939 it had become "impossible to imagine life in the country without [either] the 'Hadassah' [that is, the HMO] . . . or the many social welfare institutions" Szold "had initiated."[166] The "model" for all these accomplishments had been "chiefly that of American" practice and experience.[167]

Thanks to Szold's persistence, aspects of immigrant-aid work became an integral part of the activities of the Social Service Department. As with social work in general, the *yishuv* was not predisposed to offer special aid to immigrants. Those who had come in the early years of the century and risen to leadership positions had succeeded by dint of hard work and perseverance; and they tended to think that those who came after them could and should do the same. There was awareness that immigrants, like veteran settlers, needed jobs, medical treatment, and schools. The general assumption, however, was that newcomers unable to look after themselves could be served within the mutual-aid frameworks in place for the whole population of the *yishuv*. Szold, however, recalled what had happened "half a century ago in America, when the early stream of immigration came from Eastern Europe." Even though the United States then had been "the land of unlimited [economic] opportunities," unlike Palestine in the 1930s with its very limited resources, the immigrants had needed considerable special assistance, "and it was not withheld."[168] She was not unmindful, however, that by the 1930s the United States was no model haven for immigrants. The *yishuv*, she told the *Survey Graphic* associates in 1936, was keeping "its gates ajar if not wide open," while the United States barred entry to most Jewish refugees.[169]

"When the Hitler business was threatening," Szold understood immediately the promise and the challenge to the *yishuv*. She recalled a few years later having warned her "associates on the Va'ad Le'umi" that her Social Service Department was "going to have . . . [its] hands full with the immigration when it comes." She reminded Ben-Gurion, the outstanding Labor leader who was also a member of the executive of both the WZO and the Jewish Agency, that she had "come from a country of immigrants—America—and," as a result, knew "that there is no immigration without social service."[170] What she saw "in Palestine and in the classical land of immigration—in America—demonstrated to . . . [her,] that any person moving from one place to another . . . needs . . . emotional and intellectual support." She proposed the creation of "an advising center, an address for anyone overwhelmed by his difficulties [and] . . . a special immigration department."[171]

Although she did not succeed in concentrating general immigrant-aid work in the Social Service Department, Szold did bring youth immigration and settlement under her wing, despite her initial hesitations regarding the project.[172] From 1932 Youth Aliyah brought thousands of refugee children to Palestine, settling them in youth villages, usually adjacent to kibbutzim, and overseeing their education and acclimatization. It was an aspect of her work, which in substance owed little to her American roots, although she was familiar with American methods of dealing with child welfare cases and young deviants.[173] Szold did bring to Youth Aliyah her usual "American . . . love of order [and] . . . systematisation."[174] To the annoyance of Ben-Gurion, who on one occasion in 1942 considered wresting control of the organization from her, she remained true to her Progressive ideals in limiting the intake of children to ensure that only "professional personnel" would care for them. Ben-Gurion, who then headed the Jewish Agency, seemed to be at least as interested in enlarging his empire as he was in accommodating more children. Golda Meir backed him, although Katznelson and others blunted his attack on Szold, reminding him that, unlike the bureaucratic and anonymous Agency, she genuinely cared for children. Ben-Gurion, who knew how to hold a grudge, may have harbored resentment against Szold for not including his wife, a nurse, in the original AZMU, despite her energetic entreaties, or for her tough stance vis-à-vis Kupat Holim in 1923 and the unemployed workers in 1927. In 1942, moreover, Ben-Gurion feared that Szold, the erstwhile pacifist who still sought accommodation with the Arabs, might try to rally American Jews against the Biltmore Program and his aim of immediate Jewish statehood. He may well have hoped that by clipping her wings within Youth Aliyah he could neutralize her political influence in the United States.[175]

The most American characteristic of Youth Aliyah was its financing. As conceived, the organization was to have been funded by the German Jews for whom it was intended. Beginning in 1935, however, the American Hadassah began to contribute to its budget; Szold, of course, was the link with Hadassah, as Katznelson reminded Ben-Gurion.[176] Like the practiced fund raiser she was, Szold praised the women for assuming an additional burden and for meeting their "new commitment brilliantly." On the other hand, she let them know that they were fulfilling a responsibility and benefiting themselves. "To its healing activities Hadassah . . . added a creative activity," Szold wrote to the organization's convention in 1936, and in doing so "itself has been rejuvenated."[177] By 1941 Hadassah was supplying 75 percent of the Youth Aliyah funds; and Szold repeatedly told the women how "filled with admiration" she was at their "courage and unfaltering energy" in raising large sums even in depression times, not only for Youth Aliyah, but for the HMO, as well.[178]

7

What emerges, then, from a consideration of the faith and works of Henrietta Szold is a portrait of a woman shaped to a great degree by America, who brought with her to Palestine American ideas, some of which proved uncongenial to the new setting and others that guided her most successful endeavors. Szold was not, however, an uncritical admirer of the United States. Throughout her life she was acutely aware that "Anti-Semitism [was] . . . pervasive everywhere—[the] U.S.A. not excepted."[179] Moreover, with all of her closeness to American Jews in general, to Brandeis, and especially to the Hadassah women, she was often quite disappointed in them. As she put it in 1918, her "Jewish experiences . . . made a hardened Zionist" of her. "We in New York," she wrote from Texas to her friend, Elvira Solis, "haven't a conception of Jewish laxity—the distance between the Jew and Judaism. It is not a question of reform and orthodoxy—it is Judaism and non-Judaism. Zionism is the only anchor in sight."[180]

She had an aversion to the bluster, bluff, and dishonesty that Bialik, Katznelson, and other Palestinians found so offensive in Americans. When in 1927 the ZOA perpetrated a publicity stunt designed to create an image of solvency, she protested mightily. "Can't you see," she wrote to her former coworkers in New York, "that my method of telling the truth is the proper one, even from the propaganda point of view?"[181] American tourists were a reminder of what Szold liked least about her native land; and her reaction to them was as negative as that of any native-born Palestinian. Often she poured out her exasperation to her sisters. After an encounter with "Hadassah members from the Middle West and from New York" in 1935, she wrote:

> To me there are no tourists, but the Tourist. He is a type, almost an abstraction. In his collectivity he is stupid, uninformed, hasty in judgment, has pettifogging interests, won't let you either praise or criticise or even analyze. And if he stays only two days, he possesses all these qualities to the nth degree.[182]

In 1920–21, at the outbreak of the conflict between the forces of Weizmann and Brandeis over the shape and control of the Zionist movement, Szold was "arraigned . . . on the side of 'business Zionism,' " that is to say, of Brandeis.[183] Even then, however, she disagreed with the Brandeisists' desire to remove cultural and educational work from the agenda of the Zionist movement; and she perceived "tactlessness" and "unwisdom" in many of their actions.[184] By the late 1920s she had come to view the seven-year-long, "holier-than-thou" aloofness from active involvement in the ZOA of the Brandeisists as destructive.[185] Over the years, she also drew apart from the Hadassah women, although she never severed her ties, because she realized their economic importance to the *yishuv*.

To her sister, Bertha, she admitted that the decision to return to Palestine in 1931 stemmed, in large part, from her alienation from America and its Jews. America, she said, now meant to her little more than "desultory speechifying, eating dinners and luncheons, attending meetings and teas, and being 'inspirational.' I am not in tune with the powers that be either in Hadassah or in the Z.O.A."[186] To her former associates in Jerusalem she wrote sadly that she could find among American Jews "no cohesion, no well-directed effort to change sentiment into action. And the young," she noted, "have been allowed to drift away."[187] She came to resent especially Hadassah's "ruthlessness in exploiting . . . [her] as propaganda material."[188] On a fund-raising tour of the United States in 1937 primarily for Youth Aliyah, she remarked to Berl Katznelson that she "wanted to kill" a Hadassah woman who had boasted of having traveled from California "just for her." Katznelson, himself no admirer of American "bluff," was both shocked and amused at the vehemence of her reaction.[189] In 1943 Szold wrote to Rose Jacobs, her longtime coworker in Hadassah, that she had completely "lost touch with . . . [her] own Jewish America."[190]

Henrietta Szold

Szold traveled with American baggage. She could wax nostalgic about the American landscape and long for her family. Although she spoke Hebrew fluently and was deeply rooted in Judaism and Jewish culture, she remained attached to American culture and was always most at home in English. (She was elected a life member of the International Longfellow Society in 1916.) After all, her first extended stay in Palestine occurred when she was sixty years old! And although she was not blind to American antisemitism, she "reached Zionism, not by the road of anti-Semitism" but through her own deep roots in the United States and those of her family.[191] Ben-Gurion, Katznelson, Bialik, Jabotinsky, and even Golda Meir, all came to Palestine with personal memories of anti-Jewish violence in Europe. Szold, on the other hand, could recall a memorial in New York for the victims of the 1882 Russian pogroms in which gentiles marched beside Jews, while the bells of Grace Church peeled in sympathy.[192]

If she "brought America to Palestine,"[193] less and less over the years did she seek to make the *yishuv* into an American outpost. In 1920, as overseer of the AZMU, Szold acted like an apostle of Americanism, although even then she recognized that the AZMU's "ultimate success depend[ed] . . . upon . . . having a Palestinian head-nurse."[194] By 1926 she saw her task to be "to translate Palestine statements of fact into Americanese" for Dr. Bluestone, the new HMO director, so that he could adapt himself to local conditions.[195] When she appeared most out of step with the *yishuv*, while trying to balance the budget of the Palestine Executive in 1927 and 1928, she was still much more critical of American Zionists than of the Palestinians. "I wonder whether anyone in America," she wrote to the Executive Committee of Junior Hadassah in early 1928,

> has a notion of what [it] . . . means when the budget is so curtailed that no piece of new work [however] infinitesimally small can be begun. I wonder whether anyone over there knows what it means to balance the budget when even the curtailed budget does not . . . [arrive from America]. To us in the Executive it means the summoning of every power of resistance we are capable of, only to fall back in despair when we find that our heroic efforts at resistance to demonstrations . . . of empty stomachs resolve themselves into futility.[196]

To the ZOA she wrote more bluntly: "While you have sent us here to be stern for twenty-four hours of the day, you follow the line of least resistance. You have deserted the Executive of your choice."[197] By 1939 she seemed to have lost patience with American "business principles" altogether, at least as applied by Berl's bugbear, Harry Viteles of the Palestine Economic Corporation. Only after much pleading on her part, she complained, did Viteles "pull . . . the ramrod out of his back" and make possible a loan for the building of Youth Aliyah facilities.[198]

THE ISRAELI-AMERICAN CONNECTION

In the early 1920s one of Szold's chief concerns was maintaining the organizational independence of Hadassah from the ZOA and its financial independence from the Keren Hayesod. By 1930, she had come to "respect the inclusive character and integrity" of the Keren Hayesod and "the centralized expenditure of its funds by the Executive of the Jewish Agency."[199] In 1923, she instructed the Hadassah women: "You must have your own representative in Palestine . . . [to] keep you informed of what is happening to your work," although she insisted that that representative "be a Palestinian from the moment she sets foot on Palestinian soil."[200] Five years later, she still agreed with Gertrude Rosenblatt, a fellow founder of Hadassah, that the American organization should have a resident representative in Palestine to monitor its contributions.[201] Two years after that, however, she had come to "see the evils of . . . [Hadassah's] system of absentee government" which "insist[ed] upon holding a community of 160,000 [Palestinian] Jews in tutelage." The members of the "Hadassah National Board," she remarked with asperity in 1930, "at a distance of six thousand miles . . . know it all."[202]

She came to favor local control over Hadassah hospitals and programs and even of the Straus Soup Kitchen, although she recognized the need for Americans to fund those institutions for years to come and believed they had an obligation to do so.[203] Over time her view of the proper relationship of American donors to the *yishuv* came to resemble closely that of Katznel-

Henrietta Szold talking to Rabbi Stephen S. Wise at a Hadassah Convention in Atlantic City, New Jersey, 1937. Rose Jacobs is at right. (Courtesy of the Central Zionist Archives, Jerusalem.)

son. About other aspects of life in Palestine she became even more adamant. To Rose Jacobs, the president of Hadassah, she asserted in 1930 that she would "never consent to do anything that will give a body outside of Palestine anything but advisory powers on educational matters."[204] Her appreciation of Hadassah's fund-raising efforts on behalf of Youth Aliyah notwithstanding, she was "definitely and unalterably opposed to [its] . . . having a voice in the management" of that organization.[205] After the sinking in 1940 off the shore of Palestine of the *S.S. Patria*, a ship carrying illegal Jewish refugees, the chairman of the National Youth Aliyah Committee in New York wrote to Szold instructing her in the future to use Youth Aliyah funds to save children's lives first. Szold replied in fury: "Will you understand that if there had been a possibility of transferring them from the vessel or from the port . . . it would have been done whether your '250000 Dollar commitment' had been made or not?"[206]

From the ship taking her to the United States in 1937, she wrote to the Jewish Agency Executive in Jerusalem that she fervently hoped she could "increase the sense of responsibility [of] American [Jews] . . . towards Palestine."[207] In 1940, when "many Americans [in Palestine, including veteran residents, were] . . . planning their return home" to the safety of the United States, Szold "consider[ed] it right and proper that I stay with the community I have lived with these last twenty years."[208] She had cast her lot irrevocably with the *yishuv* despite the pain of being cut off from her surviving family.

Although one of her biographers has claimed that Szold remained an unloved outsider in the *yishuv*,[209] the evidence is contrary. As *HaAretz* noted shortly after her death, she became over the years "one of the few [genuine] bridges between . . . [the *yishuv*] and American Jewry,"[210] in the end, much more the representative of Palestine to America than of America to Palestine. On her seventieth birthday in 1930, a writer in *Moznayim*, the journal of the Hebrew Writers' Association, described her as "our righteous grandmother" and noted that the *yishuv* regarded her as "one of its own." *HaAretz* declared in a front-page editorial on the same occasion that "for generations .... there has been no Jewish woman as great and outstanding in Torah, wisdom, and human qualities, as vital, active and sagacious as Henrietta Szold."[211] In 1935 the Tel Aviv Council made her an honorary citizen of that city, the first woman to be so honored. And in the same year, a writer in *Do'ar HaYom*, the Revisionist-leaning daily that sometimes derided her pacifism and Labor sympathies, acknowledged that it was she who "had breathed enthusiasm and dedication to [Zionist] work into the women of America."[212] In fact, she was much loved in the *yishuv* and better accepted than any other American of her time.

From the earliest days of Zionism, Palestine was, for Szold, "the central

Jewish undertaking, which alone" held "the promise of quickening Jewish life," as she wrote in 1929.[213] Twenty years earlier on her first trip to the Holy Land, she had remarked that whatever the difficulties of life in Palestine, in America Jews "could not keep the Sabbath. And," she added with prescience, "how long will America take them?"[214] Szold acknowledged that Palestine in the interwar period depended "upon the Diaspora for material aid; tomorrow, [however,] Palestine, resplendent intellectually, will pay back to the Diaspora its whole investment, capital and interest, in terms of spiritual succor, stimulation and strength." Hers was a magnificent vision of mutuality between America and Palestine, one in which the Americans would be the donors at first, but finally the recipients. For its own "salvation," she asserted in 1930, "the Diaspora . . . should prolong the period of its attachment to Palestine as much as possible."[215] There might be "disappointments in Palestine"; and she retained "optimism about the Jewish people" everywhere, including the Diaspora, together with a conviction that they "have the greatest possibilities of all peoples." Nonetheless, she averred in words that echoed those of Bialik, "philosophically considered, there is nothing but Zionism for us to save us."[216]

Long before she lived there, Szold considered Palestine, not America, the indisputable center of the Jewish world. She devoted the last quarter century of her long life exclusively to strengthening that new center. She contributed to the *yishuv* what she had: her American connections; American work habits, sensibilities, and beliefs; Progressive American notions and technology which, in the areas of health, education, and welfare, were widely regarded as the most advanced available. Most generously, she gave herself. And as she did, she seemed to fulfill her own vision, becoming ever more the Palestinian and ever less the American. She brought to the *yishuv* what she believed to be the best America had to offer. Although some of her most American beliefs were rejected, most of her gifts were gratefully received.

CHAPTER
6
Golda Meir

"Minister of American Affairs"

BY HER OWN admission, Golda Meir never shared the American "taste for parlor Zionism."[1] Unlike Judah Magnes and Henrietta Szold, Meir,[2] went to Palestine when she was young and almost unknown, and the relevance of the United States to her career in the *yishuv* is not obvious. Friends, colleagues, and biographers have often considered her American background all but incidental to her life, claiming, in the main, that she was an eastern European Jew who merely passed through the New World on her way to the land of Israel. Even the degree to which her later "tours" in America boosted her political career has been downplayed. Others, writing mainly for an American audience, have stressed her affinity for America and commitment to its values, sometimes citing the rather dubious evidence of the close relationship between the United States and Israel that developed during her term as prime minister.[3] In fact, Meir's American experiences were a critical component of her power and influence, although perhaps not in the manner suggested until now.[4]

1

Born in Russia, she was taken to the United States by her mother (her father had immigrated a few years earlier) in 1906 at the age of eight, after having endured experiences that were in no way unusual for Russian Jews of the day: poverty, dislocation, and fear of pogroms and of the arrest of a revolutionary sibling. In later life Meir remembered that her father had gone to America planning to accumulate a nest egg and return to Russia. Her sister, Sheyne, claimed that already in 1906 the family was planning to settle in Palestine.⁵ These memories, however, can be viewed with some scepticism. At the least it must be noted that by the time mother and children arrived in the United States, Moshe Mabovitch (Meir's maiden name) was becoming rapidly Americanized and attached to his new homeland.⁶ In Milwaukee, where Meir's father had settled some time before, the Mabovitch family lived in straitened but steadily improving circumstances. All of them, including Sheyne who was least enthusiastic about America, came to view it as "the land of unlimited possibilities," if not quite the *goldene medine* of which they had heard.⁷ After the poverty of Pinsk and Kiev, even an immigrant ghetto in America seemed promising.

More importantly, they came to see America as the land of freedom, the opposite of oppressive Russia. One of the mythic tales of Golda's childhood was of a Labor Day parade in which her father marched. She marveled that American police escorted the marchers instead of trampling them as the Russian police would have done. Some years later, she was surprised when "many non-Jews participated" in a demonstration she helped organize to protest the post-World War I pogroms in the Ukraine.⁸ Although the more revolutionary and more prickly Sheyne records incidents of antisemitism in America, Golda insisted later in life that growing up she had never experienced any at all. She did notice America's color bar; and one of the plays that shocked her as a young girl was *Uncle Tom's Cabin*. Jabotinsky, Ben-Gurion, and other visiting Zionists from Europe and Palestine perceived America's attitude towards blacks as analogous to Russia's attitude towards Jews, and feared that Americans would come to treat Jews as they did blacks. She, however, seems to have viewed color prejudice through American eyes. The shortcoming was deplorable; but no general conclusions about American society could be drawn from it.⁹

Trust of America and distrust, even hatred, of czarist Russia—and communist Russia, as well—became part of Meir's mind-set. During World War II, many labor leaders in the *yishuv* lobbied strenuously for sending aid to the embattled Russians. Meir resisted, unless the assistance could be given jointly with American Jews. She wanted the Russians to know that Jews were treated well in America and that the United States did not suppress Zionism, as the USSR did. In 1947, when the *yishuv* was growing desperate for manpower, she lectured her colleagues on the meaning of "volunteer" in the USSR and turned to the United States for funds and volunteers.¹⁰ That she, in particular, went to Moscow in 1948 as Israel's first ambassador was a signal to both sides in the Cold War of the new country's future orientation.

Understanding the extent to which Meir's *Weltanschauung* and her future actions were influenced by her American experiences depends in part upon an evaluation of the extent of her acculturation during the fifteen years she spent in the United States before making aliyah. These were her formative years—childhood, teenage, and early adulthood. They included all of her formal education, which took place in the public schools of Milwaukee and Denver and the Milwaukee normal school affiliated with the University of Wisconsin.

Apparently, Meir, like most other young immigrants, became rapidly Americanized. She excelled as a student and learned English well enough to teach it briefly in the United States and in Palestine. It became the language of communication with many of her closest friends who came from Yiddish-speaking families similar to hers.[11] On leaving America in 1921 she was bilingual, although in both Yiddish and English she spoke much better than she wrote. There is no evidence, however, that she had read American literature or history widely or that she had acquired broad American cultural interests. In the pre-state era, she often reminded her coworkers that she knew more than "a little about America," and she exhibited considerable knowledge of the American-Jewish scene. But she possessed scant acquaintance with general American affairs before the mid-1940s.

Her acknowledged early mentors were neither teachers nor authors, nor were they Americans. Rather, they were Zionist activists and thinkers, such as Baruch Zuckerman and Naḥman Syrkin, both also immigrants to the United States from Russia, and David Ben-Gurion and Yitzḥak Ben-Zvi, whom she met during their World War I exile in America.[12] Essentially, the America which she experienced was immigrant Jewish America; and her American culture was a rather thin veneer.[13] Her Jewish education was even less complete than her American. She had no formal Jewish schooling. Before her aliyah, she did not know Hebrew, the language of the new *yishuv* (she never lost her strong American accent); her knowledge of Zionist theory was rudimentary; even her familiarity with the Jewish religious tradition was superficial. In terms of education and culture, she was as much American as anything else, as Zuckerman later observed.[14]

Early on Meir came to feel that her own self-fulfillment and that of all Jews could occur only in Palestine. Only there could the Jew speak and act as a Jew. "The more than five million Jews in America live in a free and democratic country," she remarked in 1944; but they cannot "say what they think nor demand their due without fear."[15] Only in Israel, she reiterated a quarter century later, was there "the possibility of living a full Jewish life, proud and secure." For her and for many other Jews, that country was the place that was "the best, the most beautiful, and the only one for them."[16] She believed the land of Israel to be "a necessity to the . . . spiritual life of the Jewish people" everywhere. There they could "*hope* to create something finer and better," she told American Jews in 1932 (emphasis hers). Jews in the Diaspora could never achieve their full potential. At most, working for Zionism and coming into contact with Palestinians might help them to make something of their wasted lives. Never, she declared some forty years after leaving the United States, did she feel she was making a sacrifice or giving "anything to anyone" by living in Israel. Rather, she felt that in the land of Israel she just "received and received."[17]

When she left the United States, Meir seemed to do so with "no nostalgia, no regrets."[18] She burned her bridges, surrendering her passport when the ship docked in Naples (although she and her compatriots did later appeal to the American consul in Jaffa for help in retrieving their misplaced luggage).[19] From then on the land of Israel was "home"; and to her the new home was preferable to the old, despite the necessity "to suffer a lot economically" and the danger of "pogroms again."[20] In subsequent years she often admitted to having affection for the United States, but she felt increasing "hatred towards exile."[21] On the eve of World War II, she rhapsodized over the good fortune of Palestinian Jews whose "notion of 'home,' be it a shack or even a tent, is that of a true home and . . . not that of an anchorage in the Diaspora."[22] Just after the war, she remarked that what united "the people from various countries" including the United States who had come to live in the land of Israel was their desire "to build with their own hands" a home that would be really "dear to their hearts."[23]

Her rejection of the United States and the seeming superficiality of her acculturation to America notwithstanding, Meir took with her some weighty baggage when she emigrated: fundamental American values, characteristics and habits acquired during her sojourn, and ties to family and friends left behind. She departed a liberated woman and a confirmed democrat, who had little use for European notions of hierarchy and protocol.[24] Her personality was in many ways an American one. She was blunt and outspoken. She "never disguised her meaning with flowery words," seeking to "put an end to Jewish apologetics."[25] She was a pragmatic person, who shared the characteristic American suspicion of theory. (Europeans often accused Americans of making a "sport" out of serious issues, such as Zionism.)[26] Meir liked to think of her practicality as representative of the Third Aliyah, the wave of immigration that had come from Poland and Russia in the 1920s. Although it coincided with some of the traits of the eastern European *olim* of that period, it was, of course, quintessentially American. She herself remarked in a 1932 letter to Chaim Arlosoroff that an American was "seldom . . . a scholar and a profound thinker."[27] In 1940 she described American youth in terms that suggested as much about her as about Americans. The main difference between American young people and Europeans, she said, is that Americans cannot be fed abstractions. "Only through concrete demands can one educate American youth."[28]

Although she was only twenty-three when she left America, Meir had already acquired some training in the conduct of public affairs. Hers was the

Goldie Myerson (far right) with the staff of the Jewish People's School, Milwaukee, 16 July 1916. (Courtesy of the Golda Meir Memorial Association, Tel Aviv.)

experience of the grassroots politician, not that of the social worker; and in some ways it was more appropriate to Palestine than the genteel, philanthropic experiences of Henrietta Szold. As a teenager she raised funds for immigrant relief and to buy schoolbooks for fellow pupils. She delivered streetcorner orations on socialism and Zionism, "as was the custom in America."[29] She fought for the Zionist cause among anti-Zionist Jewish workers and got herself elected a delegate to the American Jewish Congress in 1918, when she was only twenty years old. And she proved herself an indefatigable fund raiser for the Poale Zion Party in a campaign trip undertaken just a few weeks after her marriage. In the rough-and-tumble of America, where energy and talent counted for much, there were "boundless opportunities" for capable people, men and women alike, as Meir put it in one of her stock phrases. In the immigrant ghetto, the older generation often lacked the skills for success. Their children, however, retained the drive of their parents while learning the ways of American society; and parents "were willing to sacrifice everything to ensure" that their children forged ahead. Golda was one of those children; and the lessons she learned in America would serve her well in her new home.[30]

On another level entirely, Meir had become an American. She was "steeped in the spirit of expansiveness, that America . . . radiates."[31] In her later years she liked to stay in the best hotels; and she often yearned for a good corned-beef sandwich.[32] But even in her earlier, spartan days in Palestine, she maintained the habits of America: promoting nutritious oatmeal as a breakfast food instead of herring, insisting on clean, ironed clothes even when doing field work and on window screens to keep out the flies. Such habits may seem inconsequential, but to her fellow pioneers they were the "strange . . . way[s]" of "American aristocrats"; and they had the effect of separating Meir and her group from the *olim* who had come directly from eastern Europe.[33]

American plenty was also the source of inner conflict. Marie Syrkin, a close personal friend of Meir as well as her biographer and the daughter of her mentor, Naḥman Syrkin, observed that one of the push factors in Meir's aliyah was the feeling of guilt for the good fortune she had enjoyed in America, while Jews in Europe were suffering deprivation and depredation.[34] Reflecting in 1941 on the events of the First World War, Meir recalled that "Every one of us then lived with the feeling that he had no right to exist, no sanction for continuing to live a peaceful life while all of Jewry was expiring. . . . We felt it our duty to be together with the Jews of Pinsk and Proskerov."[35]

Emigration would prove insufficient as a means of assuaging such guilt feelings, because many of those she met in Palestine refused to believe that America had been left behind. On the voyage over, Meir and her fellow travelers found themselves in the company of a group of Lithuanian pioneers who disdained them as "soft, spoilt" Americans. At Qantara, when they crossed the border into the Promised Land, a customs official told them that Palestine was not a place for "young Americans." In Tel Aviv the almost destitute newcomers were welcomed as typical American "millionaires."[36] Such reminders reinforced Meir's guilt and created another legacy, a strong need to live down her Americanness, to prove that she had not been spoiled by life in the *goldene medine*. On board ship, she insisted that the members of her group abandon their accommodations and sleep on deck to demonstrate their toughness.[37] Berl Repetur, one of Golda's close coworkers over the years, has noted that in the 1920s everyone in the *yishuv* was convinced that "those who would build the land ... were the Russians .... They were [considered to be] the [real] Jewish nation, not the Americans." Golda was determined, however, that the *yishuv* would come to recognize that there were genuine pioneers in America and that the land of Israel would be built by them too. From her, Repetur and others learned that "it was [simply] incorrect [to assume] that America didn't produce pioneers."[38] It was a point Meir would feel the need to make over and over again. As late as 1942 in an angry exchange, she challenged a Mapai Party colleague who had questioned her labor *bona fides* to compare "pioneering records," hers and his.[39]

In values and culture, in habits and hangups, then, there was much about Golda Meir that marked her as an American when she arrived in Palestine. Although she would work hard in subsequent years to overcome her background, much would remain ineradicably with her. At least some of what she had learned in America would serve her well, as she herself acknowledged. Moreover, as she could not have known in 1921, her American experiences were far from over. And in the years to come, America would, in some ways, loom even larger in her life.

2

For more than seven years after coming to Palestine, Meir did not set foot on American shores. At first she was very much a private person; but gradually she began to participate in the affairs of the *yishuv*. The period from 1921 to 1928 is a kind of dark ages in her biography, both because of the dearth of sources and because of the repetitive and stereotypical nature of the material that exists. Still, some information is available, and from it patterns emerge.

Apparently Meir had decided while still in the United States to settle on the land in Kibbutz Merhavya. The choice reflects both her desire to live down America and her continuing tie to the country she had left. Living on the land was surely the most difficult option available. Her husband opposed the move and was altogether unsuited to kibbutz life; even her ideologically oriented sister, Sheyne, did not go along. Golda, however, was determined to realize the pioneering ideal of the *yishuv*. At first the young couple was not accepted by the kibbutz. Although eager for new members, the veterans feared, as Meir later remembered, "that an American girl would [not] do the hard physical work required," that she would look upon kibbutz life as "a sport."[40] She set out to prove them wrong, being "careful not to make any slip expected of an American girl." She shunned no task as too difficult, mastered the art of poultry raising despite her fear of chickens, and forced herself "to eat every kind of food . . . , even if it was hard to look at."[41] Meir might have considered pioneering in the land of Israel as related to the experience of American frontiersmen. There is no suggestion, however, that she did. For her the abstemious life on a struggling commune was as far from bourgeois America as she could get.

And yet Merḥavya was not all that far from America! Its members included a number of American veterans of the Jewish Legion. One, Meir Dubinsky, had been Golda's "closest [male] friend"; and it was he who had drawn her interest to the kibbutz.[42] Another was Neḥemiah Rabin, whose son Yitzḥak served as army chief of staff and then as Israel's ambassador to Washington before becoming prime minister. Merḥavya members were suspicious of Americans, in part because they were familiar with them; undoubtedly, as former Americans, they also felt the need to prove themselves unspoiled by the Golden West.

Merḥavya was not Golda's only contact with Americans during the years of acclimatization in Palestine. She kept in touch with the friends with whom she had come, especially Regina (Hamburger) Medzini. And there was her family. Her husband, Morris, was also a Russian-Jewish immigrant to the United States. Self-taught but steeped in Western culture, he was more deeply rooted in English than his wife. Although in the early years, when the family was still together, Morris and Golda spoke Yiddish to their children and perhaps between themselves, English was his preferred language and was surely heard at home.[43] While the Myersons were at Merḥavya there was relatively limited contact between them and Sheyne's family in Tel Aviv. Because of Morris, they returned to town. Then they lived for a time with Sheyne, whose husband had originally remained in the United States to earn a grubstake for his family. In later years he would return there, when making a living in Palestine proved difficult. In Tel Aviv, Sheyne found housing in buildings erected by Americans (the "old-boy tie" and an appreciation of American construction standards) and work with the Hadassah Medical Organization. In later years, Golda, like other Laborites, would be critical of Hadassah, especially in the late 1930s when she served as chair of Kupat Ḥolim. Now, perhaps because of Sheyne, perhaps because she appreciated the high quality of American medicine, she had words of praise for the organization.[44]

Originally the two sisters had expected that Clara (Zipke), their youngest sibling, would join them in Palestine. Although Clara never came, the parents made aliyah in 1926, settling in Herzliya, a new town developed by the American Zion Commonwealth.[45] (Despite her parents' connections, Meir shared the generally negative attitudes of most Laborites towards the AZC.)[46] During these years, then, the members of the Mabovitch/Myerson family reinforced the Americanness of one another through a variety of "old-country" connections which helped to sustain them in their new life.

At work during the 1920s and in public life in the Histadrut and its women's affiliate, the Working Women's Council, Meir also felt an American presence. In 1924 she was employed by the Histadrut construction firm (later called Solel Boneh). One of her coworkers was the wife of Nehemiah Rabin, Rosa, with whom Golda did not get along, despite their common American bond.[47] Even earlier, the Histadrut leaders, who needed workers fluent in English to deal with the Mandatory government and for propaganda and fund-raising work among English speakers, had sensed her potential usefulness. In 1923 Meir acted as guide for the first time to a bigwig visitor, the wife of Phillip Snowden, the British labor leader. Despite her initial reluctance, her success in "igniting" VIPs, especially Americans, ensured that she would frequently be called upon for such tasks. She came to realize that anti-Zionists who had the right sort of experience in Palestine "of necessity alter their views," and that "members of our movement" also needed to be guided carefully around the *yishuv* if they were to return home as ambassadors for the cause.[48] Even when she had no specific job to perform, she was often present at Histadrut events related to America, such as the reception held in Tel Aviv in 1925 for *Forverts* editor Abe Cahan.[49]

Meir's activities in the Working Women's Council and the Histadrut during these years led her to be recognized as a person of some promise by the leaders of the Palestine labor movement: Ben-Gurion, Katznelson, Ada Maimon, David Remez, and others. Partly as a result of their influence, her ideas about the United States and about almost everything else began to crystallize, although America remained a peripheral concern, at most. As early as 1922, she may have begun to voice the notion that American Jews had a duty to support Jewish institutions in Palestine if they were not coming on aliyah themselves.[50] Three years later during an HEC discussion of the parlous financial condition of Solel Boneh, she asserted a principle which she would espouse for more than a decade, although it was one of the few that she would eventually renounce. In contrast to Yitzhak Ben-Zvi and others, she insisted that the Histadrut had the moral right to use American funds as it pleased, even if the money had been solicited for a different purpose. That way independence from the American donors could be maintained. "The comrades in America," she mistakenly assured her compatriots, "will understand us."⁵¹

The year 1928 marked the end of Meir's period of integration into the *yishuv*. She was by then rather well known in labor circles, a leader of the second rank, at least. She was serving on the secretariat of the Working Women's Council and had achieved a position of some power in that organization. The Histadrut leaders recognized her as a suitable international spokesperson for Palestine Labor. Twice they chose her as a delegate to an international conference, in 1924 to a labor conclave in Vienna and in 1928 to a women's conference in Brussels. She did not attend the 1924 gathering, perhaps because she was pregnant with her first child. At the second meeting she apparently acquitted herself well, although the event went largely unnoticed.⁵²

More significantly, Golda's Labor comrades began to see her potential for propaganda and organizational work in the English-speaking world, especially in the United States. In December 1928, they dispatched her to America for the first time since she had left on aliyah. Having proved to herself and others that she was not a "spoilt" American, she was prepared to go. Between then and mid-1938 she would spend a part of every year in the United States (except for 1930, when she undertook a mission to England instead), in total, almost four years. On these trips, she worked closely with fund raisers, youth, women's organizations, and the League for Labor Palestine, all within the Labor Zionist ambit. These tours of duty would provide the decisive push in her rise to power in the *yishuv*, by offering an optimum forum for the demonstration of her considerable political and fund-raising talents, and by allowing her to develop a power base in America. Her activities, moreover, led naturally to new responsibilities related to the United States and its Jews, first within the Palestine labor movement, then in the official institutions of the *yishuv*.

3

To finance its burgeoning activities, the Histadrut had been conducting fund-raising campaigns in North America since the time of Katznelson's trip in 1921–22 (annually from 1924 under the aegis of the non-Zionist federation of Jewish trade unions, the United Hebrew Trades [in Yiddish, Geverkshaften], and hence, the name, Geverkshaften Campaign). Like most Zionist institutions the Histadrut was chronically short of funds; and as the tempo of its activities heightened in the 1920s, it came to depend upon America for most of its operating budget. To many this dependency was particularly unwelcome, because bourgeois America represented, as it did to

Golda, the antithesis of their values. Yosef Sprinzak, the future speaker of the Israeli Knesset, expressed a common sentiment in 1923 when he declared his "organic antipathy to America."[53] David Remez, however, Golda's chief sponsor and longtime lover, noted at an HEC meeting in September 1928, that the organization "was standing on its [financial] head. We have dived into a sea of troubles," he said, "and the only breathing tube [available] is the Campaign [in America]."[54] Antipathy to America had become an unaffordable luxury. Throughout the fall of 1928 the Histadrut Executive was increasingly preoccupied with American affairs, especially the Campaign.[55] Eliyahu Golomb, the future military leader, tried to comfort those who were anxious about the growing dependency. "It has become accepted in the Zionist world," he said, "that the *yishuv* can be built [only] with the help of the Diaspora; and the Histadrut Campaign in America is one of the ways [of mobilizing that help]."[56]

Notwithstanding their eagerness to distance themselves from all aspects of the life style of the pietists, Zionists of all stripes, including the Laborites, adopted the tried-and-true means of financing their work: fund raising abroad, especially in the New World. For the "delegates" from Palestine it was an exhausting and often frustrating exercise in public relations for which many had no talent. Moreover, absence from home for such long periods was often detrimental to family life and career. Not surprisingly, there were few eager volunteers, although some, like Golda, probably preferred to be away from their families.

Despite the desperate financial situation, 1928 was a year in which the Histadrut found it almost impossible to draft a delegation. Rahel Yana'it Ben-Zvi had just completed a stint with the Pioneer Women's Organization, the women's arm of the American Poale Zion-Zeire Zion Party, which was insisting on a replacement in time for their October convention. The Gevershaften Campaign leaders urged that a strong delegation be sent to them even earlier. Likely candidates were reluctant, however, and needed considerable persuasion. Golda arrived only in early December, and her coworkers, David (Blumenfeld) Bloch and Israel Mereminsky (Merom), even later. Chaim Arlosoroff was already in the United States and was co-opted by the newcomers. The Americans, who had little understanding of the personal hardship that the tours involved, were put out. The Palestinians were unable to understand why schedules could not be altered to accommodate them. They had little appreciation of American notions of planning and efficiency; and they often seemed to disdain their benefactors.[57] Golda learned quickly to do business in the American manner. After her return to Palestine, she entreated her colleagues to respond promptly to requests from the United States. In later years she earned kudos for her promptness.[58]

The Americans' annoyance melted away when Meir, who came as

very much an unknown quantity, set to work immediately and made "an excellent impression overall."⁵⁹ As the year was ending, she earned her fund-raising spurs. At the closing session of the National Labor Committee for Palestine convention in New York, the thirty-year-old woman, who had not seen American shores for seven years and had never appeared before a major American organization, addressed the 585 convention delegates, most of whom were male and organization veterans, very much her senior. But it was she of all the speakers who "brought the convention to its highest pitch of enthusiasm."⁶⁰

For the next six months she traveled across the country speaking to Campaign rallies, writing the occasional article, and working closely with Labor Zionists. She devoted much of her attention to the Pioneer Women's Organization, which had been founded four years earlier. Now it was providing almost 95 percent of the budget of the Working Women's Council and had begun to send *olim* to Palestine.⁶¹ Golda grasped intuitively the special problem of the wives of working-class American Jews, who had no public outlet for their Zionist enthusiasm. She sought to give "the intelligent Jewish woman in America . . . an opportunity to give the best that is in her." She carefully delineated her goals for the Pioneer Women and distinguished them from those of the well established, enormously successful, middle-class women's organization, Hadassah. Hadassah, she said, offered aid to the needy and the sick. The Pioneer Women would concern themselves with the healthy, helping them to become useful and productive; they would "work *with* the Chalutzoth of Palestine," not for them (emphasis hers). She pointed out to her audiences that "the agricultural enterprises of the [Palestine] working women . . . [were] all self-sustaining." And she aimed her pitch at "the younger, English-speaking generation," the only ones, she believed, who could build a working-class women's group in America.⁶² "In every place she . . . visited . . . [she was] very successful," so much so that the American Poale Zion-Zeire Zion Party placed her name in fourth place on their list of candidates for the upcoming World Zionist Congress, ahead of the few other nonresident candidates, all of them male.⁶³

Golda's achievement was rooted in her earlier experiences. She had a good working knowledge of America. The stress on health, youth, and financial success struck a responsive chord with her audiences; and her expansiveness allowed her to see the bright, promising side of American life in those last days of prosperity before the Great Depression. There is no evidence that she paid much attention to America at large; and what little she saw was not tempting. She boasted that in Palestine, unlike America, life had a high tone; it was not a sport: "There are no gangsters, policemen, or flappers."⁶⁴

Her America was still that of the immigrant Jews; and it was still the "land of unlimited possibilities," including Zionist possibilities, for those with energy and know-how. The Pioneer Women she found to be "idealistic, politically committed, liberal young women to who [sic] what was happening in Palestine really mattered."[65] Some might think forty thousand donors to the Geverkshaften Campaign a small number in a Jewish community of some four million. She, however, accentuated the positive, focusing on the growth of the Campaign since its inception.[66] Some of her colleagues saw a great gap between themselves and American Jews and were especially pessimistic about the prospect of getting support from the non-Zionist Jewish workers in America. She, however, exulted that "the Palestinian workers have begun to dig a tunnel to reach their American brothers and . . . the American Jewish workers have heard the chop of our hammers. . . . The wall of separation is being broken down and the union is coming."[67]

Others had ceased to believe that American Jews would go to Palestine. She, however, found "many who looked upon their residence in the United States as temporary" and were ripe candidates for aliyah.[68] She felt close to American Jews and refused to see them as a lost generation. She—and her family—were, after all, partly products of America and proof of the hope it offered to Zionism. The Americans reciprocated the affection and responded to her charisma and to her upbeat approach. As a result, she could "dare . . . to hit hard and to make demands," in a way that other emissaries, less in tune with America, could not.[69] (Raḥel Yana'it, no minor leaguer, complained in 1928 that often on her recent tour of America "the comrades shut their ears" to her pleas.)[70]

Not all was rosy in America for Meir. Her sister, Clara, and brother-in-law had been lost to communism; and there was a danger that many more American Jews, who might otherwise be Zionists, would go the same way.[71] At the other end of the social spectrum, she doubted any good would come from "the men of the salon," the wealthy, acculturated American Jews, such as Louis Marshall and Felix Warburg. She met some of them on her way home from the United States during her stopover in Europe for the Zionist Congress; and like many other Palestinian Jews, she came to fear that their non-Zionism would hamper the settlement work of the newly reconstituted Jewish Agency.[72] She sometimes despaired of convincing the veterans of the Pioneer Women's Organization that to keep the group viable they would have to attract young people and abandon Yiddish. It also proved difficult to convince her colleagues in Palestine, who preferred to work with the semi-Americanized, Yiddish-speaking oldsters, that they needed to develop propaganda materials in English.[73] Unlike many of the non-American emissaries, Golda believed these problems could be overcome through intimate "internal work," at which she was a master, rather than the usual "large public gatherings" to which her colleagues less familiar with America were limited.[74]

On the personal level, this first trip back enabled Meir to develop a new means of dealing with her guilt for having had a secure American childhood and teenage. She began to channel the guilt into making America, the bountiful, into an institution for upbuilding the *yishuv*. Whatever was necessary to enhance that institution would be done, including long absences from Palestine. Visits to America, though, were business, not pleasure, trips. The pattern was established in 1921 during her stopover in New York to earn money for the passage to Palestine. Morris had sought out the "theater, music, and book stores" of the metropolis. Golda had spent her leisure hours at "constant meetings with Labor Zionist colleagues."[75] During her extended stay from 1931 to 1934, she took her children to see the sights of New York; and in 1937 she found time to attend the Yiddish theater.[76] Such jaunts, however, were exceptions. In these years, at least, Golda abjured American pleasures. Ironically, for her, returning to the United States was to be another way of renouncing America.

On the professional level, the 1928–29 tour of the United States allowed Golda's talents for fund raising and organizational work to shine. Overnight she became by far "the most popular" Histadrut figure in America, as her comrades in Palestine quickly recognized.[77] In fact, she became so popular that in subsequent years the Americans—especially the Pioneer Women—would often insist that she was the only acceptable emissary. The result was that other potential emissaries acquired a "fear of America."[78] In the spring of 1930 the Pioneer Women pleaded for her return. "The extraordinarily good mood and impression" she had created the previous year led them to believe that with her help they "could capture an unprecedented number of . . . English-speaking young people, who would certainly become involved in our work [and] . . . help . . . greatly [to] broaden our influence."[79] In August the Americans declared peremptorily "that the least she must remain with us is five months and that is not enough."[80]

Meir's successes in America provided her with the beginnings of a power base in the United States, which, in turn, "gave [her] . . . an entry ticket" to the upper echelons of the Palestine labor movement.[81] Like her, the comrades had come to understand that the "work" in Palestine "was made possible only thanks to the funds from America."[82] Because she proved so good at fund raising, her colleagues now came to value her very greatly indeed. Soon after her return to Palestine in the late summer of 1929, Meir was made a member of the active secretariat of the Working Women's Council, its inner circle. The labor leadership now saw her as someone who could bear major responsibility both in Palestine and in the English-speaking world. Her presence was deemed essential whenever American affairs were under consideration, and that was more and more often.[83] When the Mapai Party was established in 1930, Meir was one of the founding leaders. In the same year, along with Ben-Gurion and Dov Hoz, she was chosen to represent the Palestine labor movement at the Imperial Labor Conference in London.

That conclave held considerable significance for the Histadrut leaders, who sought to gain friends for Zionism from among the working people of the Empire. Golda's presence there was a sign of her growing stature in the *yishuv*; and she did not disappoint her mentors. Ben-Gurion reported that her speech "shook the Conference," that it was delivered with "genius, forcefulness, bitterness, pain, and taste." Golda was proving she could serve as spokesperson to the world at large, not just to American Jews.[84]

4

In the summer of 1931 the Working Women's Council, the Mapai Party, and the Histadrut finally acceded to the importuning of America and ordered Meir to undertake a second tour of duty there.[85] She would remain until the summer of 1934, except for a two-month home leave in July and August of 1932 to report to the comrades, recharge her batteries, and fetch her two children. Meir had personal reasons for agreeing to the long stay. Her daughter, Sarah, required medical treatment not available in the *yishuv*. Her marriage now was quite shaky; and Zalman Rubashov (later, Shazar), the journalist and future president of Israel with whom she was then romantically involved, would also be in the United States.[86] During this extended visit, she firmly established herself as a power to be reckoned with on both sides of the ocean.

Before leaving Palestine, she asked her colleagues for a plan of action. Ben-Gurion refused, realizing that it was "impossible . . . to dictate directives to America" from Palestine. He undoubtedly also knew that Meir could be trusted to act in Labor's interest.[87] She arrived in October with a clear sense of purpose, "at an extraordinarily difficult, and therefore demanding, time," as she asserted on her arrival, confident that the *yishuv*, "together with" American Jewry, would achieve "ultimate victory [in] . . . the struggle . . . still ahead."[88]

She explained to her children that "it was her job . . . to tell some of the Jews of America to come and help and to tell others to give money so we can help ourselves."[89] Aliyah took a back seat to fund raising, because immigration certificates were rationed by the British; and Jews in America, unlike those in an increasingly unstable Europe, were safe, if less prosperous than before. (Of the certificates it was allocated for pioneers in 1935, the Jewish Agency apportioned 1,250 to Berlin and 2,250 to Warsaw, but only

55 to New York.)⁹⁰ She sought to promote aliyah by assisting the "many comrades from America [who were eager] to get to Palestine" but appreciated the need to foster the allegiance of those who "will never come to live in Palestine, but whose hearts are with us and who understand us."⁹¹ For a resolute Zionist with maximalist commitments, that was a most unusual concession to European and American—and Palestinian—realities. Aliyah might be deferred, but Golda could no longer "imagine a Palestine workers' movement without a campaign" in America, although she believed that campaigns needed "positive content." By that she meant "concrete," specific projects for which gifts could be designated. These could arouse "the enthusiasm" of donors, in contrast to debt service, which, however necessary, dampened their spirits.⁹²

Officially, Meir came as a "delegate" to the Pioneer Women's Organization. She determined to make the still rather disorganized group into an efficient Zionist instrument. As its secretary (in effect, the executive vice-president), Golda sought "to bring order and system to the educational work [of the women], to deepen the[ir] political understanding, and to enrich the[ir] organizational experience."⁹³ She undertook to visit "most clubs" in the United States and Canada at least once, conducting "three or four meetings every day, followed by discussions until the wee hours." Many groups she visited several times. "Very often [she] . . . was exhausted."⁹⁴ In addition to her other tasks, she organized conferences and a summer encampment for youngsters and acted as an ambassador to other women's groups, especially Hadassah and the non-Zionist National Council of Jewish Women. From them, too, she secured financial aid for the Working Women's Council.⁹⁵ Although she later remembered having edited the *Pioneer Woman*, its masthead never carried her name.⁹⁶

As a result of her labors, membership in the organization rose to more than four thousand, including, for the first time, "young American women" seeking "solution[s] to various national and social problems and content for their lives."⁹⁷ She managed to maintain the level of giving, "despite the hard times."⁹⁸ Yosef Sprinzak wrote to the Mapai Center in the summer of 1934 that by then the Pioneer Women was "the best organized" group in the Labor-Zionist camp, thanks to Meir. Early in her mission, Meir herself proclaimed the significance of her accomplishments. She told the Americans that "Hearing the notes of thousands of comrades from the coldest points of western Canada to Texas, from the noisy and tumultuous New York to California of marvellous beauty similar to that of Palestine—provides extraordinary encouragement for the comrades in Palestine." Under her tutelage, she noted, the Pioneer Women's Organization had become "the most vital element of the [American Labor Zionist] movement," although she viewed that fact as a "sad" commentary on the rest of the movement. It was a judgment with which her American coworkers concurred.[99] By 1934, she could claim that the group had become "a substantial political force." She considered it a major achievement to have harnessed that force for the common Zionist good by discouraging the women from turning the Pioneer Women into a radical feminist splinter group. At the same time, she established the principle that any Labor mission to America must include a woman prepared to deal with women's concerns.[100]

When she returned to Palestine, Golda "left [behind] her influence everywhere on everyone" in the organization.[101] Her "simplicity and logical way of thinking" had made "the greatest impact" on the Pioneer Women, creating "a magical, holiday atmosphere" that continued to inspire maximum output long after her departure. To them she was "our Goldie . . . one of us, reared and trained in America."[102] Groups from Omaha to Washington perpetuated the memory of her visit by adopting her name. In the *yishuv*, her accomplishments were widely recognized, although female coworkers, perhaps out of jealousy, were less enthusiastic than the men. When asked to take Golda's place in the United States, Ada Fishman (Maimon), the sister of Rabbi Y. L. Fishman, replied disparagingly that she "had no faith in the work in America." Some months later, Elisheva Kaplan, then in the United States, remarked that as yet the Working Women's Council exerted influence there only within a very narrow circle and that "changes needed to be made" with regard to the delegate's role. Ben-Gurion, however, accepted Golda's self-evaluation. He echoed her words in describing the Pioneer Women as "the most significant part of our movement in America, deserving of nurture and care." Characteristically, he declared his own opinion to be "the consensus."[103]

After leaving the United States in 1934, Golda's interest in the Pioneer Women diminished, in part, no doubt, because she began again to focus largely on the *yishuv* and, as a result, to readjust her priorities. In a retrospective speech to the Histadrut Council in 1941, she described the Pioneer Women as "a magnificent movement," which had succeeded in "putting an end . . . to the loneliness of the Jewish mother" and in harnessing her energies for Zionism.[104] But during her 1936 "tour" of America, she found relatively little time for the organization; and in the years following, the records indicate few contacts between her and her erstwhile American comrades. She firmly refused to travel to America for their 1947 convention, despite the hard-sell of Bert Goldstein, who was convinced that an appearance by Golda could transform the group into "the most important woman's Zionist organization" in America. But by then Meir had to attend to more pressing matters at home, where the Arabs were attempting to strangle the as yet unborn Jewish state.[105]

Her duties with the Pioneer Women might have constituted a full workload for someone less energetic or less committed. Meir, however, labored almost as hard raising money for the Geverkshaften Campaign and for Labor institutions, such as the Kupat Holim health insurance scheme and its clinics and hospitals, and Yachin, the Histadrut settlement company.[106] Her fund-raising coworkers included Rubashov, Israel Mereminsky, Shimon Kushiner, and Yosef Sprinzak.

"The terrible economic conditions," which, Meir noted, "deteriorated by the day," caused a radical decline in donations to the Keren HaYesod and the Keren Kayemet.[107] The Laborites, however, believed that their campaign served as "the front line of the nation," not only providing needed funds but also "conquering [the] hearts" of American Jews for Zionism.[108] They sympathized with unemployed workers and the "even worse-off middle class" in the United States; but in light of the economic collapse of the capitalist world and the resurgence of antisemitism in central Europe, they felt more the urgency of the situation in Palestine, where the "need of the hour [was] as never before."[109] Despite some reticence about "appearing with their hands out" in depression times,[110] they put forth an extraordinary effort. Rubashov visited some four hundred cities and towns for the Campaign in 1931–32. Sometimes Golda combined work for the Pioneer Women with Campaign duties; sometimes she traveled exclusively on behalf of the Campaign.[111] Thanks to the efforts of the Palestinians and their American colleagues the Geverkshaften Campaign sustained a better level of giving than most drives during those years.

The comrades in Palestine were not always appreciative of the hard work or the hard times. In November 1932, Eliyahu Dobkin wrote to Mereminsky on behalf of the Histadrut Executive that he hoped "for more income" from the Campaign; he also suggested "additional cutbacks" to the already lean fund-raising budget. And there were repeated complaints that Golda did not report often enough on her comings and goings.[112]

Another area of intense involvement for Meir during these years was youth work. Others had given up on American youth; and, as noted earlier, she, too, recognized the emptiness of the flapper age and the lure of both communism and Revisionist Zionism in those depression years. Together with Mereminsky, however, she was convinced that the early 1930s offered unprecedented "opportunities to capture the youth in America" and expressed confidence that "the Labor movement in Palestine . . . [could] serve as a guide to the troubled minds and souls of Jewish Youth [sic] in America." In 1930 she reminded her colleagues in the Mapai Center that young Americans were coming to Palestine "as pioneers, despite . . . [the party's] lack of energy" in recruiting them.[113]

As a youth worker, even in a summer camp setting, her programming was sometimes "too heavily laden"; she was occasionally hampered by the inability to relax and to deal openly with young people; and she did not always take account of the differences between Americans and Palestinians. In 1932, for example, she told the American Young Poale Zion convention that "the individual who must, for some reason beyond his control, remain outside of Palestine must feel that great personal misfortune has occurred in his life." Not surprisingly, the young people were "dissatisfied."[114] Even so, she understood the importance of English-speaking leadership; she was willing to allocate scarce manpower for youth work in America; and her energy and can-do personality proved appealing to young Americans.[115]

During her first American trip, Golda had addressed the Boston and Ann Arbor chapters of Avukah, the student Zionist group. In 1931–32 she reached out successfully to the student elite, appearing before Avukah groups at Harvard and the University of Chicago and at the national convention of the organization. In the summer of 1933 she taught at the Avukah Summer School, together with Professor Shalom Spiegel of the Jewish Theological Seminary, Rabbi Simon Greenberg, and others, impressive colleagues for a graduate of the Wisconsin Normal School. She retained a long-distance relationship with Avukah for a number of years.[116] In November 1932, she was one of the instructors of a five-week course given by the Menorah Society at the City College of New York; and in May 1933 she lectured on "idealogy and leadership technique" [sic] to the Central Community Younger Clubs of Brooklyn. Meir also helped to organize the summer encampments of Labor Zionist youth groups, at which she aroused yearning for the "healthy society . . . in Palestine."[117]

The HeHalutz youth movement occupied much of her time. A fairly loose aggregation of groups dedicated to pioneering settlement in Palestine, the organization had been one of the projects promoted by Ben-Gurion and Ben-Zvi during their World War I sojourn in the New World, of which more below. Although it prospered elsewhere, HeHalutz had languished in America. In late 1932 there were fewer than one hundred members in all of North America, as opposed to some forty-one thousand in Poland a year later.[118] The more left-wing HaShomer HaTza'ir youth organization was somewhat more successful in reaching out to Americans.

As was the case with most aspects of American Zionism, Golda evaluated "the pioneering commitments" of young Zionists there "more highly" than did her Histadrut colleagues from eastern Europe. Some time earlier she had accused the Histadrut of having "sinned" in not promoting HeHalutz in America, as it had in Poland and Rumania.[119] From 1932 to 1934 she sought to strengthen the organization through the merger of HaShomer HaTza'ir and other Labor-affiliated youth groups, including Gordonia and the Young Poale Zion, into a unified American HeHalutz. (The HaShomer HaTza'ir leadership complained of her partisanship in favor of groups associated with the Palestine Mapai Party and remained independent until 1939.) She also helped to organize HeHalutz activities, spoke to young pioneers at the group's training farm in New Jersey, and served as a member of its adult council. The result was a steady, but not spectacular, increase in membership.[120] In 1936, the American HeHalutz "was still not a large movement," although Meir claimed that a discerning observer could detect "signs of growth." By 1945 she had to admit that the American Poale Zion "had not succeeded in spawning a mass pioneering movement, for whatever reasons," but she gave them considerable credit for their more limited achievements in the relatively uncongenial American setting.[121]

An aspect of American Zionism which did not seem promising to Golda was the Labor Zionist political parties. The natural allies of Mapai and the Histadrut, the American Poale Zion and the smaller parties had an aging membership uninterested in aliyah. In fact, Golda charged in 1932, they were generally uninterested in any meaningful activity. The party's leaders, she reported to her colleagues in Palestine, were "not the most talented" and not united. Ostensibly the heads of a socialist-Zionist organization, they seemed disengaged from both socialism and Zionism. It was "clear" to her that "no activities could be undertaken given the present situation [and] that only a prolonged war for the sake of the party" could bring about change. Over two decades later her bleak assessment remained unchanged.[122]

The League for Labor Palestine provided an alternative to the political parties, and it was yet another focus of Golda's attention during her 1931–34 American tour of duty. It was an institution she helped to found. Conceived as the "iron front" of American Labor Zionism the purpose of which was "to create a periphery" for the movement, the League was essentially a "front organization" modeled on the communist leagues in the United States and on established support groups for Palestine laborers in Europe.[123] From 1931, Meir worked on the League together with Mereminsky and others. She addressed League chapters across the country, adding them to her crowded itinerary. Through the League she hoped to "make Eretz Yisrael [Palestine] popular among the Jewish masses [in America] . . . , just as the communists [had done with] . . . Russia," although she refused to assume an official position in the new organization.[124]

By mid-1937 the League had enrolled almost three thousand members in seventy chapters around the country, including intellectuals, staid Hadassah women, and non-Zionist members of the National Council of Jewish Women brought on board by Golda, whose "brilliant lectures . . . created a wonderful sentiment." As intended, the League made Zionism respectable to "groups which had [previously] been inaccessible" to the movement. (One St. Louis "lady" was so taken by Meir's discussion of the League that she volunteered her support, if the organizers would agree to "omit . . . two words [from its name]: 'Labor' and 'Palestine.' ") There was even a chapter at the Hebrew Union College in Cincinnati, where some students and faculty members maintained the staunch anti-Zionism of classical Reform Judaism. The League's upper-middlebrow journal, *Jewish Frontier*, was endorsed by Justice Brandeis. In 1937 it claimed a circulation of eleven thousand and had become so successful that some of the Palestinians proposed removing it from League control and turning it into a Labor-Zionist movement journal.[125]

Despite the anxiety of some American Labor-Zionist party stalwarts about competition from the League and the scepticism of some of her Histadrut colleagues regarding its worth,[126] Meir took justified pride in its success. She believed that "the scope of work and the people that have been drown [sic] into it certainly make one certain that at last we are beginning to build something serious and worthwhile." *Jewish Frontier*, she declared in 1935, "is something that our movement in the States never dared to attempt before." Its advent, she asserted, marked a timely departure from "our kindergarden [sic] stage." Never much of a reader, she had "managed to read several articles."[127] In subsequent years Meir remained a staunch supporter of the League. Although she refused to heed a summons to serve it as a special emissary, and only reluctantly agreed to support its activities at the expense of remittances to Palestine, she acted as an advisor from afar and made herself available to chapters when she returned to the United States.[128]

Golda's other major activity during this extended stay was acting as an ambassador of Labor Zionism. Her tasks were ceremonial and political. In addition to participating in movement gatherings of all sorts, she appeared at conventions of the Socialist Party of America, the International Ladies Garment Workers Union, the Workmen's Circle, and other non-Zionist organizations giving the Palestine workers and Zionism, as a whole, much favorable exposure.[129] Meir took part in negotiations with Jewish labor leaders in an effort to bring non-Zionist workers into the Zionist orbit.[130] And she assumed a major role in the battle against Revisionism, lecturing to more than one thousand New York Poale Zion in November 1932 on the evils of Jabotinsky and his followers. She took to task the president of Hadassah who encouraged supporting the Revisionists at the 1933 Zionist Congress, and denounced the New York *Morgn Zhurnal* for its "vicious" pro-Revisionist, anti-labor stance.[131] Her Histadrut colleagues wanted even more vigorous action. They urged her and Mereminsky to charge the Revisionists with slander before a Zionist court for having claimed in the *Morgn Zhurnal* that Revisionists were excluded from Histadrut elections and discriminated against in the workplace, and that Palestine Laborites had beaten a Revisionist to death.[132] Some months after her return to Palestine in 1934, Golda was dismayed to discover that "organized" Labor gangs had in fact been attacking Revisionists and that she "had told a lie" in America when she denied that possibility. She swore never again to "travel abroad" on behalf of Labor, a vow she did not keep for long.[133]

It is perhaps something of an exaggeration to say that during her 1931–34 sojourn in America, Meir succeeded in creating there an effective Labor-Zionist infrastructure, and in transforming Labor Zionism into an "American" movement. The Pioneer Women, the League for Labor Palestine, and *Jewish Frontier* were not her brainchildren; they were not the only viable Labor-Zionist institutions; nor was she alone responsible for their newfound popularity and effectiveness. But she played a major role, perhaps the major role, in strengthening those institutions and enabling them to supplant, as the standard-bearers of the movement, the ineffectual political parties, always viewed as "foreign" transplants with appeal only to immigrants. In so doing she had become herself an American Labor Zionist leader. The American Poale Zion-Zeirei Zion again chose her as one of their delegates to the World Zionist Congress. This time, too, she was fourth on the slate. Ben-Gurion, by contrast, was ninety-ninth and last.[134]

Meir's triumphs in the United States in the early 1930s are attributable to her personality, her organizing talents, her tremendous energy, her earlier American experiences, her unwavering faith in Zionism, and her confidence in the Zionist potential of America, which she knew how to exploit. More than anything else, however, her achievements were connected to her extraordinary ability to communicate with ordinary American Jews. Towards the end of her life, Meir wrote a foreword to a biography of Yisrael Merom (Mereminsky), her fellow Histadrut emissary in the United States in the early 1930s. Her words apply to her no less than to him. Merom, she said, had "the ability to talk to simple workers . . . in a way that made them feel that a fellow-worker was sincerely sharing with them the needs and problems which confronted [both] them in America and their counterparts in the Histadrut."[135]

One further aspect of Golda's mission requires comment. Her stay in the United States coincided with one of the most turbulent periods of American history. These were the years of the Great Depression, the banking crisis, the election of Franklin Roosevelt as president, the beginning of the New Deal. Curiously, there is no echo of these earthshaking happenings in Meir's letters, her oral and written reports, or her articles, other than terse references to the "hard times" being experienced by individual Jews and Jewish organizations. Her later reflections on the period are similarly silent. Apparently she did not recognize any relevance then or later in the events of those days to the *yishuv*. Nor did she discern anything translatable

Goldie Myerson (second row, fifth from left) with the members of the Pittsburgh chapter of the Pioneer Women's Organization, 20 February 1934. (Courtesy of the Golda Meir Memorial Association, Tel Aviv.)

to Palestine, although, at the least, some of the New Deal innovations might have provided instructive models for dealing with chronic unemployment.

Meir's America remained circumscribed by the borders of the Jewish community. And even then, her vision was selective. In 1941 she addressed the Histadrut study seminar on the subject of "Mutual Aid in Times of Crisis." Only the Histadrut, she claimed, cared about its members' needs; union members elsewhere "felt no responsibility for each other" and limited their interest to wages.[136] But American unions, particularly those with heavy Jewish involvement, such as the International Ladies Garment Workers and the Amalgamated Clothing Workers, had pioneered in the areas of health care, subsidized housing, unemployment and disability benefits, adult education, and cooperative banking.[137] Golda could not have been unaware of these activities. The knowledge might have been of use to her, if not immediately, then after 1935, when she held responsibility in the Histadrut Executive for the social services sector, or later, when she served as Israel's second minister of labor and social welfare. In the 1930s, however, her sights were fixed firmly on the *yishuv*. America could provide financial aid for Palestine and *olim;* it could not be a model. An interesting exception to the rule occurred in 1942 during a discussion in the Mapai Party Center of a new law forbidding wartime strikes. Golda cited the example of John L. Lewis, the head of the United Mine Workers of America, who promised Roosevelt there would be no coal strikes during the war, even though he was an implacable foe of the president.[138]

5

Yosef Sprinzak put a somewhat different spin on Meir's sensibilities. She was, he wrote to his wife in 1934, "the most successful" Histadrut emissary to America and the "best suited to that place and its conditions," and yet she remained "immersed [in] . . . the [Labor] movement in Palestine."[139] In appreciation of her ability to function in both worlds, and perhaps also of her Palestinian blinders, Golda was invited to join the secretariat of the HEC and the Mapai Central Committee soon after her return to Palestine. In effect, she became Labor's "minister of American affairs." Mapai was by then the dominant party in Palestine; and Ben-Gurion headed the Jewish Agency. Golda now belonged to the policymaking elite of the *yishuv*.

The rise of Hitler, moreover, as well as the deteriorating situation of Polish Jewry, and Britain's steady backing away from its commitment to Zionism in the mid-thirties propelled America to the forefront of Zionists' consciousness. With Polish Jewry leaning heavily towards Revisionism, the Palestine Labor leadership was coming to see America as "the single . . . most important Jewish center . . . upon which depends the realization of [our kind of] Zionism."¹⁴⁰ The United States, Golda reminded the Histadrut National Council in 1937, was home to "the largest and strongest and politically most powerful" Jewish community in the world.¹⁴¹ For the *yishuv* as a whole, America had become "the place to which we shall look in wartime and from which we shall expect protection, supplies, and manpower," David Remez acknowledged in 1938.¹⁴² American experience no longer aroused suspicion; in fact it now conferred prestige and power. As Labor's most qualified expert on American Jews, Meir inevitably found her power and prestige enhanced.

One of the less glamorous tasks that fell to Golda as head of the Histadrut American desk was looking after visitors and prospective settlers from America, much as she had done for years without an official post. Setting up a special tourist department had been suggested by Mereminsky, Eliezer

Goldie Myerson at Camp Kvutzah in New York State, summer 1934. (Courtesy of the Golda Meir Memorial Association, Tel Aviv.)

Galili, and other Palestinians, as well as American Zionists. They were weary of Americans with "inflated" notions about accommodations and travel, who did not receive "appropriate guidance" in Palestine and, as a result, "returned home with mistaken impressions," often disappointed and angry. The danger of making enemies through tourism and failed attempts at aliyah made the idea of a visitors' bureau palatable to the Laborites, who tended to disdain comforts and luxuries, at least in theory, and, like Szold, to regard tourists as little more than voyeurs.[143] In one of her first reports to the HEC after her return in 1934, Golda proposed the establishment of a Labor tourist agency. The suggestion was adopted, and Tiyur veTiyul (Sightseeing and Touring) was launched with her at the helm.[144]

As head of the agency in 1935–36, Golda preached "the importance of well organised tours to Palestine" and practiced what she preached.[145] She set up trips for Americans connected to Labor and occasionally herself acted as guide for a VIP, such as (Reform) Rabbi Edward L. Israel of Baltimore, a League activist and a supporter of Labor causes in the United States and Palestine.[146] To groups of teachers, young people, and synagogue members whom she hoped to instruct and inspire, she paid special attention. She arranged for youngsters to "spend their time *living* the life of the country—not only *seeing* it" (emphasis hers). She "warn[ed youthful clients] against demands of unnecessary comfort or luxury," and endeavored to offer them "a fine serious Zionist education," whether they wanted it or not, as well as an "enjoyable" experience.[147] She also acted as advisor to Americans planning aliyah, some of whom toured the country in preparation.[148] One of her innovative suggestions was that visitors should experience pioneering life firsthand in kibbutz and moshav guest houses with modest accommodations.[149] The educational tour and the kibbutz guest house were ideas ahead of their time. In subsequent years, especially from the mid-1950s, they would be very widely accepted, although few, if any, remembered then that Golda had offered similar suggestions two decades earlier.

It was expected in these years, too, that Golda would take part in events relating to American visitors; even after she had left Tiyur veTiyul, she continued to help with arrangements. She both welcomed and scolded visitors. She "marvel[ed at] . . . the patience" of visiting Geverkshaften Campaign leaders in the summer of 1937 "to persevere in their hard work." But she "wished many of . . . [them] would come . . . to settle, [or] at least come . . . often" to visit.[150]

Earlier that year a high-level National Labor Delegation, representing groups which had become valuable allies of the Palestinian Laborites, had come from the United States. A few months before, during the Arab riots, some of their number had successfully interceded at Golda's request with the British Trade Union Council on behalf of the *yishuv*.[151] Isaac Hamlin, the [executive] secretary of the National Committee for the Jewish Workers in Palestine who had organized the trip in New York, implored the HEC and Golda to roll out the red carpet, and, indeed, they did. Anxious about the Palestinians' lackadaisical, if not hostile, attitude to visitors, he issued detailed instructions to be "follow[ed] . . . exactly." He pleaded, among other things, that the union leaders meet all the "right" people. He implored the Palestinians to do "everything that will put the delegation in the eye of the local Jewish reader and [also] make a strong impression when they return to America [as well as to] . . . make sure they see the institutions built with American campaign funds."[152]

Hamlin was heeded. *Davar* reported every move of the delegation. Golda and others greeted them at the ship and accompanied them almost everywhere. They met Weizmann, the high commissioner, and Menaḥem Ussishkin, the head of the Jewish National Fund; they planted trees in memory of an American labor leader and a Jewish pioneer killed in an Arab attack. Golda accompanied them home from Palestine to continue their "education" and to ensure that they would lobby for Zionism in London.[153]

The planning and the efforts were rewarded. Max Zaritsky, president of the Hat and Capmakers' Union of America and, according to Hamlin, the key person on the trip, had wanted to "live the atmosphere of the land of Israel," not just to tour. And "the loveable Comrade Golda" had made that possible, just as she regularly did for younger tourists.[154] In her usual way Meir praised the unionists for their support of the Geverkshaften Campaign, which provided, she said, "vital pioneering capital" without which the Palestine laborers could do nothing. At the same time, she reminded them of the need for more money, for immigrants, and for political support.[155] In London, they submitted a strong pro-Zionist statement to the Trade Union Congress and to the Labour Party. Back home, Golda reported, they demonstrated "exceptional dedication and loyalty . . . appear[ing] . . . at . . . meetings and . . . [making] heartfelt statements about the Histadrut."[156]

Another Histadrut activity with which Meir was connected in these years was the promotion of Palestine-made products (Totzeret HaAretz). In American Labor circles the sales campaign was conducted through the Consumers' League of the Pioneer Women.[157] Meir became involved in 1938, when the Pioneer Women despaired over shoddy, poorly packaged merchandise, bills for goods never received and perhaps never sent, cottonseed oil masquerading as olive oil, and a refusal on principle to label kosher products as such, and begged for her intervention. When approached in New York, Meir agreed to serve on the committee in Palestine that selected items to be sent. Back home, however, she proved uneager to be involved in such a prosaic task. Uncharacteristically, she ignored the angry letters from New York. Some of Golda's colleagues thought a major opportunity which held the promise of increased self-sufficiency was being missed, but she apparently disagreed.[158] Wartime disruption of shipping put an effective end to the project in any case.

In addition to looking after Americans in the *yishuv* in these years, Meir remained the Histadrut's most effective emissary to American Jews. In 1931 with more on his mind undoubtedly than politics, Rubashov argued that Golda should be sent to America, because she was "the only man [!]" in the Histadrut who knew the "ways" of the New World. Seven years later, with war clouds on the horizon, Pinhas Lubianiker (later, Lavon), the future government minister and secretary general of the Histadrut himself the son of a Jewish Legionnaire from America, claimed there was still "no possible suggestion [for an emissary] other than Golda." No one disagreed.[159]

Meir was the most capable American fund raiser of the Histadrut, although her strength lay in dealing with people of modest means; and she was still reluctant to approach the "men of the salon."[160] In 1936 she returned home to report that American Jews had been most favorably impressed when the anti-Jewish outbreaks in Palestine of that year did not prompt a request for additional financial aid.[161] But in general, the *yishuv* could not afford to go it alone, and Golda knew how to inspire Americans to help. Although she did not obey the call of Geverkshaften Campaign leaders to become Campaign director for a year at a reasonable salary, she spent much time on every trip raising funds.[162]

In late 1937 she told 1,500 campaign workers at New York's Hotel Pennsylvania that if Palestine were to be partitioned by the British into an Arab and a Jewish state, "the Jews alone" would be "responsible." With "Jewish hands to colonize more territory," she declared,

> to fertilize and cultivate more land, . . . no power in the world would be able to uproot Jews from the land. But for long years the Jewish masses have been apathetic regarding the reconstruction work which has been going on in Palestine, and that has brought us to the present plan to partition the land and allot Jews only a small part of it.
>
> Young Jewish idealists have come to dry the swamps of Hadera and plant . . . eucalyptus trees. Now those trees have grown and they make Jewish ships. Jewish pioneers have enough courage to settle . . . surrounded by Arabs; but their courage places upon us a great obligation.

"Often their security hinges on several factors" related to adequate funding, she told her rapt listeners, adding, "One must give them the vital needs."[163] It was "a masterly speech,"[164] typical for Golda, that aroused enthusiasm and guilt by evoking the most positive images of the *yishuv* while stressing its dependence on America. In 1948 she would play on the same themes in her dramatic speech to the Council of Jewish Federations, threatening the Americans that "the youngsters . . . in the front line . . . [might] fail because money that should have reached Palestine today will reach it in a month or two months from now."[165]

Her most intensive fund-raising effort in these years was conducted on behalf of Naḥshon, a new maritime venture of the Histadrut. The idea of developing the shipping and fishing industries in Palestine emerged in the mid-1930s from a number of sources. In the spring of 1935 H. M. Caiserman, the general secretary of the Canadian Jewish Congress and a Poale Zion activist, offered several ships to the Histadrut at a bargain price. In an article and an address to the Zionist Congress that same year, Ben-Gurion showed an interest in the maritime frontier. The Arab blockade of Jaffa in 1936 gave the notion a further boost; and that year David Remez and others proposed a major undertaking.[166]

Meir was naturally drawn into the project, because its success depended upon American funds. In late 1936 she exchanged letters on behalf of the Histadrut with Alfred J. Miville of New York, who had "been asked to head a five million dollar steamship company operating between New York and Jaffa."[167] Towards the end of that year the Histadrut decided to create a "special company for [its] . . . maritime activities," to be financed through the sale of thirty thousand shares priced at five dollars each.[168] Since its experience with shares for the Workers' Bank in the early 1920s, the labor federation had generally eschewed stocks as a way of raising capital.[169] Times now seemed ripe to try again. Golda was to be the chief salesperson.

She employed her tried-and-true approaches and some newer ones. There were two major whirlwind tours of the usual kind. From March to July 1937 and from November of that year to July 1938 she visited Scranton, Binghamton, Waterbury, Omaha, and other smaller Jewish centers, as well as all the large communities, speaking to working people's groups. She also appeared at the usual conventions, although not at the United Palestine Appeal gathering in Washington, perhaps because the ZOA leadership was annoyed with her for conducting the Naḥshon campaign while their drive was in progress.[170] By Golda's earlier standards this was a short, easy trip; and she reported to the Histadrut that she had visited only a few cities.[171] For the first time, Meir turned also to a few wealthy "private people" whom she knew, some of whom "had not previously supported a [Labor] undertaking."[172]

All of her efforts were rewarded with success. "Real encouragement came from the public," she told the HEC; never before in her work in America had she "seen such readiness."[173] She sold almost forty thousand shares and could easily have sold more. She made useful contacts with people in the shipping industry who were eager to help, including a Jewish executive of the giant United Fruit Company. Meir's enthusiasm for passenger ships seemed to grow by the day, and it was infectious. Her colleagues in Palestine, however, were getting cold feet, fearing they might be over their heads in a project that could prove to be a very expensive failure. When they refused to allow her to proceed with the purchase of ships, she returned home in a huff.[174] In a reversal of her earlier position, she objected strenuously when the other members of the HEC decided to develop the fishing industry with the funds she had raised for a passenger line. She protested to no avail that this meant breaking faith with the American donors.[175] The onset of war also decided this issue and allowed for face saving.

Throughout the 1930s Meir was involved mostly with working- and middle-class American Jews. Sometimes, however, she was required to deal with gentiles; and she began to gather some confidence in doing so. In 1936 the Histadrut appointed her, along with Rubashov and Professor Chaim Feinman, an American, as delegates to the annual meeting of the American Academy of Political and Social Science. That year she began to monitor the general American press, although she proved unable to place articles favorable to Labor Zionism. She also assumed responsibility for maintaining contact with American labor leaders, such as William Green, president of the American Federation of Labor. She persuaded Green to prod British Labor leaders and Roosevelt to press the British government to keep the gates of Palestine open for Jewish refugees.[176]

6

Meir's focus with regard to America shifted considerably during the war years, although her goal of securing effective support for the *yishuv* remained the same. She took much more interest than formerly in world events: the course of the war, the fate of Europe's Jews, and the international politics of creating a state, in particular. During part of the war she held the foreign affairs portfolio of the Histadrut; in 1946, when the more experienced statesmen were either jailed by the British or outside Palestine avoiding arrest, she became acting head of the foreign affairs desk of the Jewish Agency, in effect, the foreign secretary of the state in the making. Some scholars view Meir's rise through the ranks into the field of foreign relations as an example of the Peter principle;[177] it might better be seen as recognition of the growing importance of the United States, her area of special competence.

In July 1938, Meir sat as a nonparticipating observer at the international conference in Evian-les-Bains, ostensibly called by President Roosevelt to find a solution to the problem of Jewish refugees from Nazi Germany. There she came to "realize . . . that [even] a world which was not . . . anti-

Semitic . . . could stand by" while Jews were "victimized."[178] Like Jabotinsky, Ben-Gurion, and so many others, Golda "believed in Roosevelt's good intentions." She attributed the failure of the conference to his not having prepared for it adequately.[179] "Sitting there in that magnificent hall listening to the delegates" explain why they could do nothing for Jewish refugees was a shattering, "terrible experience" for Meir.[180] No other country offered more than did America; most offered the Jews nothing. Golda resolved, she told a press conference at Evian, that the Jewish "people should never again need declarations of support."[181]

In the meantime, the Jews desperately needed support, not declarations. Like her close associates, Katznelson and Ben-Gurion, Meir realized that meaningful assistance could come only from the United States, that the battle for Palestine had to be waged in the American political arena. Jabotinsky had said as much during World War I.[182] Never much of an Anglophile, she predicted with prescience in early 1941 that the United States would play a much more important role in the Second World War than it had in the First. And "the front in America [had to be] . . . an extension of [the] . . . front in Palestine." She exhorted the Laborites and the *yishuv* as a whole to improve their "ability to influence" American public opinion.[183] The rationale for action in the *yishuv* or in America was twofold: improving the political situation, and strengthening the Jewish community for the struggles ahead. Ever the woman of action, never the theorizer, she urged the Palestinians to focus on what they could actually do.[184]

In response to the British White Paper of 1939, which limited further Jewish immigration to Palestine to seventy-five thousand and severely restricted Jews' rights to acquire land there, Golda took her cues from Ben-Gurion, of which more below. She proposed a general strike in the *yishuv* and demonstrations in the United States. The British, she believed, might be susceptible to pressure because they needed good relations with Washington. She doubted Roosevelt would be influenced by marchers, but demonstrations in America would showcase Jewish solidarity for the British and remind them of the potential clout of American Jewry. Such political agitation would stiffen the political backbone of the American Jewish community and revive the interest of pro-Zionist gentiles.[185] It was the same sort of reasoning she used with regard to aid to the USSR from the *yishuv* during the war, when she argued that joint action with American Jewry would demonstrate American solidarity with Zionism to the Russians.[186]

In 1943, when the Final Solution was becoming known and the Americans were planning another international conference on refugees (also designed to be unproductive), Meir and Remez dusted off an old Revisionist proposal for a petition to the Allies to be signed by every Jew in Palestine and then by the Jews of the English-speaking countries. The suggestion was rejected, like its Revisionist predecessor, as too time-consuming and not likely to succeed. Instead the two frantically cabled labor and political friends in the United States and England asking them to mobilize public opinion in favor of "immediate energetic action."[187] Some months later Meir insisted that the Histadrut send a strong delegation to an international labor congress in England to lobby for Jewish statehood. She found it hard to believe that "what has happened to the Jewish people during the war had happened" without the revolt of the British and American labor movements and of Russia. But she remained convinced that Labor held the key to government action. In the summer of 1944 she was gratified to learn that both the American Federation of Labor and the Congress of Industrial Organizations, the two national American labor groups, had endorsed the concept of Jewish statehood.[188]

Considering Golda's great concern for the Jews of Europe, the guilt which always plagued her when she escaped misfortune, and her appreciation of the importance of America in international politics, the record of her wartime activities seems scant. One reason is that she remained caught up in local *yishuv* affairs and did not visit America during the war. But she may have stayed home, because there did not appear to be much she could do in the United States, despite her enhanced stature and new political role. The United States, as opposed to Jewish America, was not yet familiar territory; and it appeared rather less hospitable to Jews and less open to their concerns than earlier.

Since the late 1930s she had been uncomfortably aware that antisemitism was on the rise in America.[189] There was, she admitted in 1939, "a hard and bitter truth" with which the *yishuv* had to come to terms. Zionists had

> relied not a little on public opinion in the different countries for support . . . [believing] that in every nation . . . labor movements, liberal movements, intellectual circles . . . would come to our aid at the critical moment. We [assumed]. . . that . . . countries with large and powerful Jewish communities . . . would come to our help.

Now, things had changed. In fact,

> there isn't much help to be hoped for from these quarters. Although there still remain a few . . . countries where Jews live in considerable numbers, and to us here they seem strong and influential and certainly able to help us—let us not deceive ourselves. There is no Jewish community in the world today, not even in the most liberal and democratic countries, where the Jew doesn't feel . . . that he himself is sitting on a volcano.[190]

By 1944 her outlook was even dimmer. She compared the future of American Jewry to that of the Jews of Europe. "Many millions of Americans" were "being sent to war against Hitler," she noted in a speech to the Histadrut Council; but "a Jewish child was not safe walking to school in New York, Boston, or Detroit." Impending danger in America made it imperative "to bring the maximum number of Jews" to Palestine from there "in the shortest time."[191] Never before had she felt this way.

The American Zionist movement was hardly equal to the task of inspiring and organizing a new aliyah. Already in 1936 Golda had pronounced the ZOA and its newly elected president, Rabbi Stephen Wise, hopeless. She claimed "there were no people fit for office" in the ZOA, that the best were "mixed up in petty politicking related to personal squabbles." Her longstanding conviction, that the *yishuv* should provide leadership for America, seemed confirmed. More than Ben-Gurion and Bernard Joseph (later, Dov Yosef, the military governor of Jerusalem during the War of Independence) she doubted the ability of the wartime American Emergency Committee for Zionist Affairs to conduct effective propaganda and urged her colleagues in Palestine to send an emissary to do the work properly.[192] Her opinion of American Labor Zionist politicos was, as noted, no more sanguine. Although often third-rate, they had once guarded the interests of the little man, the ordinary Jew. Now they had delusions of grandeur and sought "independence" from Palestine and "Americanization," although, she acidly remarked, it is "quite certain that their parents . . . did not come to America on the *Mayflower*."[193] The Laborites were still the best of the American Zionist lot, Golda conceded in late 1945. But the gap between the devoted rank and file and the mediocre leaders who had "not even an elementary understanding of what we need in America," who "live[d in their minds and hearts] outside of America," was lamentable, she asserted with unintended irony.[194]

The Americans themselves were not entirely at fault. "We are reaping . . . what we sowed," she acknowledged, having always treated America as "spoils to be plundered. . . . We thought . . . [that] we could receive money for our . . . work in Palestine year after year without ever giving back anything at all." Having been unwilling to send enough first-rate people to America to revolutionize its Zionist groups, and having insisted that every penny collected be remitted to the *yishuv* leaving little for programming in the United States, the Palestinians had undermined American Zionism. Now, at a time of great need and great danger, they would suffer from the Americans' weaknesses.[195] Meir had given of her talent and energy to the movement in America; her colleagues, as a group, had been less generous. But even she had always put the immediate interests of the *yishuv* first.

And yet, at this moment in history, American Jews had to take the place of the millions in Europe, the foot soldiers of Zionism, "from whom the possibility of life was being snatched away," Meir remarked with frightening foresight in early 1941. While she believed that Americans now needed to save themselves through aliyah, the *yishuv* needed them as *olim* to help "the broken and crushed from the lands of blood," or to replace them altogether.[196] In 1939 she thought it might be possible to recruit twenty thousand volunteers in America for service in the *yishuv*, although she knew a major effort would be needed to do so. The United States, she remarked in 1941, was "the only country left" where "large-scale, systematic" youth work could be undertaken.[197]

At the end of the war, knowledge of the Holocaust and the lack of support for Zionism in England and the United States left Meir disillusioned with both countries. The American president (by then, Harry Truman) and all the parties there, she charged, "had only shortly before . . . promised full support for all our demands." Now they were reneging. Still, she refused to despair and clung to vestiges of her more optimistic, pre-war hope, that "in the United States and in the . . . Labour Party in England there would [yet] be found an echo to our demands . . . a pure conscience."[198]

She was also somewhat disillusioned with American Jews and pronounced it a blessing that no one from the *yishuv* had had to endure service among them as an emissary during the war years.[199] But regarding them, too, she refused to despair. She rejoiced when eight hundred American war veterans registered for study in Palestine, expecting that their number would increase and that many of them would remain in the country. Golda was no longer satisfied with donations from America; now she demanded aliyah. "If American Jewry," she declared in 1945, "says, 'We stand with you,' that [declaration] is meaningless, unless they . . . marshal all their energy, strength, and money to establish a pioneering [settlement] movement of many thousands . . . who will come here [to Palestine]."[200] Two years later she would tell visiting Histadrut (Geverkshaften) Campaign leaders that it was their "duty" to return to America and spread the word that the *yishuv* needed more Jews. "The Jews of America must come" to settle she asserted; and "hundreds" of them should arrive on an illegal immigration ship to demonstrate that aliyah is not for the poor and homeless alone. She was convinced that "for this purpose it was possible to recruit the cream of American Jewish youth."[201]

7

In World War II the Jewish people lost a third of its numbers. To Zionists, and even to many not previously sympathetic to the movement, the message of the Holocaust was clear. Only a Jewish state could guarantee Jews' safety. It was also clear that without the support of the United States there would be no Jewish state. The funds for state building could only come from there. British enthusiasm for Zionism had all but evaporated, and Britain was becoming a second-rate power. American political opposition would ensure that the enemies of Zionism in Britain and the Arab world would gain the day. American backing might win it.

With the United States now indisputably the key to Zionist success, Golda's command of English and her American experiences automatically made her an important player in the drama about to unfold. As noted, however, she was more ambivalent about America and its Jews in the mid-1940s than she had ever been. And she was still inexperienced in dealing with wealthy American Jews and with gentiles, and unsure of her abilities. In September 1947, she urged the Jewish Agency executive to send Ben-Gurion there.[202] But he was needed at home; and in January 1948, she set out again for New York. As had been the case from the start, she rejected America and was at the same time propelled towards it.

It was zero hour for the *yishuv*. Arab armies were poised to attack the ill-equipped, ill-trained Jewish forces few in number. The Palestinians were certain they could "establish" themselves, but they needed "between twenty-five and thirty million dollars" for weapons and supplies, unheard of sums in Zionist fund raising. "You cannot decide whether we should fight or not," Golda told the Council of Jewish Federations and Welfare Funds in Chicago, "we will!" Wealthy American Jews could "only decide one thing: whether we shall be victorious in this fight or whether the Mufti [the religious leader of the Palestine Arabs] will be victorious."[203] She returned home with fifty million dollars.

Her triumph restored her faith in American Jewry.[204] The support of the American public and government for the new state would restore her faith in the United States. She had proved more than able to communicate with wealthy American Jews, which boosted her stock in the new state. She had labored to make American Jewry a cornerstone of Zionism. Her progress through the political ranks in the *yishuv* was in no small part the result of her American connections and vision. In 1957, Ben-Gurion described her as "the most precious gift that American Jewry has given to Israel."[205] With only slight exaggeration, he might have said that American Jewry was the most precious gift that she had given to Israel.

CHAPTER

7

David Ben-Gurion

Building the American Alliance

DAVID BEN-GURION was a diminutive man who towered over his contemporaries in the *yishuv*. He did not grow up in the United States like Golda and Henrietta Szold; and he set his sights squarely on Palestine earlier in life than Jabotinsky, Bialik, or Berl. He rejected the Diaspora at least as vigorously as any of them and sometimes scorned the American Jewish community. The Diaspora has "deprive[d] us of independence, security, self-respect, and the respect of others, and perverted . . . our image," he declared in 1944. Jews there, he asserted some years later, "as Jews, are [but] human debris."[1] Yet, of the *yishuv* leaders under consideration here, it was he who grasped most clearly the importance to the Zionist cause of the United States and American Jewry and who acquired the widest circle of admirers among American Jews and gentiles. He was also the most instrumental in laying the foundations of the political alliance of the *yishuv* with American Jewry and with the United States. His vision encompassed many of the most trenchant insights of his colleagues and adversaries. During the years under review, he became a master in dealing with Americans.

This relationship has not gone unnoticed.[2] Popular and scholarly biographers are generally agreed that, by the early months of World War II, at the latest, Ben-Gurion was firmly oriented towards the United States and that by the fall of the following year his policies presupposed eventual American support for the *yishuv* in its struggle for independence. Unresolved questions remain, however: When did he discover America, and what did he find there? What prompted him to pursue a trans-Atlantic tie, when Weizmann and others continued to count on the backing of Britain? How sensitive was he to the implications of reliance on America? The answers to these and other questions are important for understanding the origins of the Israel-America nexus.

1

Ben-Gurion (then Green) was born in 1886 in Plonsk, a town northwest of Warsaw with about five thousand mostly poor Jews and a larger number of mostly poor gentiles. Knowledge of his childhood is sketchy, because the future prime minister of Israel was given to weaving myths about his early life to enhance his image. He seems to have learned Hebrew from his grandfather at the age of three and the "love of Zion" from his father not much later. He was an energetic youngster and a voracious reader. Among the books which left a lasting impression was *Uncle Tom's Cabin*. One of the few novels he ever read, it "aroused [in him] . . . a deep revulsion against slavery, servitude, and dependence."[3] As a teenager, he spent much of his time with Ezra, a young people's Zionist society which he organized with his two best friends, Shmuel Fox (Fuchs) and Shlomo Zemah. Zemah, later a noted writer and literary critic, left for Palestine two years before Ben-Gurion. Fox emigrated to the United States, where he became a dentist.

For a time Ben-Gurion sought to study engineering in Warsaw. There he became a somewhat superficial convert to Marxism in 1905 and a member of a Poale Zion club. At the end of that year he returned to Plonsk, where he had a short career as a union organizer and, together with other young revolutionary Zionists, formed a band that extorted funds for Palestine from wealthy Jews, at gunpoint, if more temperate measures of persuasion did not work. In 1906 he left for Palestine, riding the crest of a large wave of emigration from Russia whipped up by the collapse of the 1905 revolution. In Palestine he worked as an agricultural laborer for more than three years before joining the editorial staff of *HaAhdut*, the new Poale Zion journal. During 1913 and 1914 he and Yitzhak Ben-Zvi, the future president of Israel, studied law in Constantinople.[4]

Focused as he was on Palestine, and determined as he was about building the *yishuv*, Ben-Gurion had relatively little head space for America during his early years in the land of Israel. He corresponded with his friend Fox from time to time; he undoubtedly came in contact with some of the *olim* from America, including the longtime business manager of *HaAhdut*; and he read *Der Iddisher Kemfer*, the Yiddish-language journal of the American Poale Zion. His first words in print were a letter to the *Kemfer* asking support for the newly founded Poale Zion group in Palestine.[5] More information came from the pages of *HaAhdut* itself and of *HaPo'el HaTza'ir*, the Palestinian publication of the non-Marxist labor party of the same name.

HaAhdut, to which Ben-Gurion contributed frequently from 1910 to

1914 and which must be seen as reflecting his views to some extent, carried rather a lot of news and commentary about the United States. In general, the Palestine Poale Zion tended "to look down upon" the "rich aunt" across the water, as would "a learned, impoverished blue blood at his wealthy lout of a father-in-law."[6] *HaAhdut* was keenly alert to the injustices of the country that was home to a huge and growing Jewish diaspora and that was seen as the embodiment of capitalism. Ben-Zvi charged in an early issue that "every school boy" knew the source of "America's gigantic wealth: . . . millions of miserable blacks who irrigated her soil with their blood."[7] Others commented on capitalist sins such as war profiteering, imperialism in Panama on the part of "the insatiable 'Yankees,' " alienation, intellectual superficiality, and a lack of hospitality towards immigrants stemming from unwillingness to share the wealth.[8]

Only Palestine offered Jews "a secure foundation for the future," it was argued, especially in the face of threatened limits on immigration to America; and yet, the New World lured them away from the *yishuv*. On the other hand, American immigrants to Palestine took opportunities away from those who had come before them and were more deserving.[9] Affluent American Jews were depicted as assimilating, as a matter of course, and acting without regard for their poor brethren.[10] They also subverted the virtue of the *yishuv*. When "the rich Jew," Julius Rosenwald, arrived in Palestine on a visit in 1914, *HaAhdut* reported with mocking bitterness that "the notables of the new Jerusalem *yishuv*," lexicographer Eliezer Ben-Yehuda and his wife, and " 'the learned' careerist, the champion of the experimental Arab [agricultural] station [sic!] at Athlit," Aaron Aaronsohn, had rushed to do obeisance in the hope of patronage.[11]

These were not mere pro forma criticisms. On the other hand, with regard to the United States, at least, the editors and contributors of *HaAhdut* were not blinded by Marxist-Zionist ideology. They celebrated the election of Woodrow Wilson in 1912, a "scholar and university president" who appealed to "people of the book." In Mexico, "American politicians, the faithful servants of American capital, came to the aid of the revolutionaries" against President Huerta, who had been bought up by the Japanese, according to Ben-Zvi's brother, Aharon Reuveni. And those same capitalist lackeys renounced the Russian-American trade treaty in 1911 because of Russia's treatment of its Jewish population, demonstrating that there was a "place in the world where . . . we [Jews] are considered humans, citizens."[12]

As Europe slid into war and chaos, America seemed to *HaAhdut* a more likely "Hebrew [cultural] center" and "national haven" for the endangered Jewish people. There, Jews were returning "*en masse* to the ranks of the proletariat" for the first time in history; and "the American edition of assimilation [was proving] less craven and submissive" than the European.[13]

Zionism in America was reported to be poised for takeoff. Achooza societies for agricultural settlement were forming in many communities;[14] among some Americans there was growing awareness that their "energy and abilities" ordained for them a special role in "the development of [Palestine] industry";[15] and in the last two years before the war Jews from America were a perceptible minority among *olim*.[16] When war came, "American Zionists understood the[ir] obligation . . . to provide for the institutions of the *yishuv*."[17] Relief funds caused dependency and "demoralization" and were often administered in a highhanded manner, but the need for them could not be denied.[18]

Particularly heartening to *HaAhdut* readers was the reported progress of the Poale Zion party in the United States. In 1910 Americans contributed over half the money collected worldwide for the Palestine Workers' Fund. Although it had "to fight the party of petrified Orthodoxy" while "bearing proudly aloft the flag of Hebrew socialism amidst the . . . hurly-burly of assimilationist [socialist] vandalism," the American cadre was gradually "growing . . . [and] penetrating the young generation."[19] Inspired by such upbeat reports, the Palestinians dispatched Ya'akov Zerubavel to "the overflowing spring" in 1912 in search of funds for *HaAhdut*, which threatened to drain their meager resources. It was the first Palestine-Labor fund-raising mission to America; and it secured the future of the journal until it was closed by the Turks in the early days of the war.[20]

Although he was not unreservedly enthusiastic about the American brethren, Zerubavel believed that their "distance from local issues" made them ideal allies for the Palestinians. They were, he said, "nourished either by [memories of] the old home in Russia or [dreams of] the new home in Palestine."[21] By 1914 Ahva, a scheme conceived in the United States for cooperative settlement in Palestine, was growing apace. Nahman Syrkin, no fan of the Diaspora, suggested that prospective European settlers come first to America for a few years to save up the investment needed to participate in the Ahva project.[22] To Ben-Gurion the American Poale Zion had become a model for others to emulate. In a speech to the fourth world conference of the party in Cracow in 1913, he urged that groups like the Ahva be established in Europe "to attract worker-power to Palestine."[23]

War evoked mixed emotions among the Jews of Palestine, as it did elsewhere. Some, like the Aaronsohn family, cast their lot with the British. Others, including Ben-Gurion and Ben-Zvi, believed that "only one country in the world" deserved their unqualified support: Turkey, which had welcomed Jewish exiles from Spain in 1492 and now provided a nurturing home for Jewish "national consciousness."[24] They were prepared to fight in the Ottoman army, although their Russian origin and the suspicion of Zionism harbored by many Turkish officials blocked that path.[25] The arrest of the editorial board of HaAhdut for having contravened censorship laws and the threatened expulsion from Palestine of Zionist Congress participants prompted the adoption of an alternative wartime agenda: work in the United States on behalf of the *yishuv*. According to Ben-Zvi, he, Ben-Gurion, and their compatriots "decided that if we should be expelled from Palestine—we would go immediately to America to begin preparing for the future together with party members [there] with whom we were in close contact."[26]

On 21 March 1915 the expulsion order was carried out. On the eve of Pentecost "the two Bens" arrived in New York inspired by the glowing accounts in HaAhdut and full of optimism regarding the possibilities of Zionist achievement in the New World. Ben-Gurion, who had spent his "time on the boat learning English,"[27] bubbled over in his diary about the adventure ahead:

> For some time I've dreamt about a trip to America. [The] teeming, noisy, ... modern, acquisitive life of the most developed and democratic country has attracted me. ...
> Besides, I have wanted to see the friends I parted from twelve years ago. ...
> And I—how many times—I have dreamt, and now suddenly, ... I'm coming to America.

This was more than a young man's caper. For the Zionist visionary, America was a model pioneer society; those "who seek to build a new country in the desolate wilderness and arid land need to see how the hounded, exiled emigrants from England established a wealthy, mighty state, the resources and creative powers of which are incomparable." At the same time, he proclaimed to his diary the imperative at that "great historic moment ... to repair the historical distortion of the Diaspora" by ending it.[28]

2

In some ways the New World lived up to Ben-Gurion's expectations. The shoreline parks of New York were as beautiful as "the Golden Horn"; the "proud Statue of Liberty" was breathtaking. "Of the gigantic splendor of Niagara Falls" it was "possible to absorb only a tiny bit." In his entire life, "he had never seen magnificence like that" of Buffalo.[29] "Americans knew the secret of speed" and efficiency, although the "noise, bustle, confusion, excitement, and running about" of New York were bewildering. A Salvation Army girl was "stunning." The United States had "already" spawned 401 labor-oriented Jewish schools and, "for the first time in Hebrew history, a book of poetry for children."[30] Even later in life, weighed down with the burdens of office and jaded by extensive travels, he could be moved to lyrical ecstasy by the sights of America. In 1935 he flew from Chicago to New York and recorded the following in his diary:

> A magical sight like that I shall never forget. The houses can't be seen in the murkiness, the ground is wrapped in black, but a sea of lights twinkles below, spots of fire spread over a vast area, squares and diagonals and lighted towers as if on a lower heaven, black and unseen, together with this ship floating on the darkling air, as if plucked from a fairy tale.[31]

The high hopes were a setup for disappointment, which came quickly. A few days after his arrival, Ben-Gurion visited a cousin whom he hadn't seen since leaving Europe. His relative's "thin face and somewhat bent frame" made him almost unrecognizable. That his children could "barely speak Jargon" (that is, Yiddish) was a further shock. A get-together with acquaintances from Plonsk who had also lived in Palestine was even more disturbing. Young people who had been among the most ambitious and "the most creative" in their home town and in the *yishuv* had become "in America—vacuous hobbledehoys, hollow, without substance or aspirations."[32]

When Ben-Gurion and Ben-Zvi plunged into Zionist activities, the disillusion mounted. Their principal goal, as Ben-Zvi stated it, was "to awaken among the Jewish workers in America, in general, and among our [Poale Zion] comrades, in particular, an orderly aliyah movement to Palestine once its doors opened [again]."[33] The instrument they created for this purpose was HeHalutz, a semisecret paramilitary organization akin to the youth associations of central Europe. Before his arrival, Ben-Gurion had targeted for enrollment "the many young people who had been workers in Palestine and, for a variety of reasons, departed" without severing their ties altogether. Later the pool was widened to include anyone who would adhere to the group's demanding principles. To promote *HeHalutz* Ben-Gurion planned to publish a Hebrew newspaper, something he mistakenly believed Americans "were unable" to do on their own. Hebrew, he wrote in his diary as his ship sailed past the fabled coast of Spain, "required a romantic atmosphere," not the "materialistic culture" of the New World.[34] It was an odd observation for a Marxist Hebraist.

Although Ben-Gurion would remember the American Poale Zion leadership as apathetic towards HeHalutz, even towards Palestine altogether, and uncooperative with him and Ben-Zvi during their stay,[35] in fact the veteran party officials seem to have been reasonably accommodating, at least at first. The newcomers' arrival was widely announced; the party's Central Committee endeavored to arrange speaking engagements for them and agreed to establish a Palestine Committee with Ben-Gurion in the chair.

David Ben-Gurion

In his first few weeks in the new country, Ben-Gurion spoke to Poale Zion branches in the New York area about events and conditions in Palestine and wrote the occasional article.[36] In early July he set out on his first "round" of recruiting, inauspiciously missing the train to Rochester. At Buffalo, the next stop, no one met him at the station; lodgings had not been arranged; and the comrades appeared "too apathetic and laid back" for HeḤalutz. The trip was interrupted when he fell ill with diphtheria on a return visit to Buffalo later that month and had to remain for weeks, first in hospital, then recuperating in the home of Jewish farmers.[37] In early August the missionary for Palestine arrived in Detroit. Since there was already "a fair [sized] Aḥva group" there, he assumed there would be interest in HeḤalutz. But only twenty people came to a meeting; of those only six signed up, none of them Aḥva members. By the end of August, the Bens had visited more than a score of cities between them; but they had enrolled fewer than one hundred HeḤalutz members.[38] A second tour a few months later was no more successful. Several branches refused outright to receive Ben-Gurion. In Canton, Ohio, four people came to hear his talk, only two of them Zionists. The Cincinnati audience made a better "impression, even upon" the increasingly dispirited emissary, although they, too, seemed "to lack a Poale Zionist sensibility." Back in New York the HeḤalutz group organized months earlier had "yet to meet even once."[39]

What caused the Palestinians' tribulations is not hard to imagine. For one thing, they had misread the news from America, taking at face value the enthusiastic reports in *HaAḥdut* and elsewhere. They may not have understood Americans' tendency to self-congratulation and bluff; and they did not realize that the American comrades were measuring small gains for Labor-Zionist values and institutions in the inhospitable "land of business" against their earlier failure to accomplish anything. Perhaps, too, the Palestinians missed the implicit warnings in the accounts they read because they had no alternatives to America at that time. The dearth of organizational skills among the American Poale Zion was a contributing factor, as was Ben-Gurion's own approach. Goldie Myerson met him when he was "on tour" in Milwaukee, as noted earlier. Much later in life, she would recall that, eager, ardent, and fearless though she was in 1916, she found him "one of the most difficult people to . . . approach." He made few friends during his three years in America, although he did find a wife, Paula Munweis, a European-born New York nurse. The party leaders thought him pushy; most believed his obsession with Palestine and lack of concern for the Diaspora to be wrongheaded and insensitive to their needs. He confided to his diary in September 1915 the attitude they suspected: "If we want to solve the problem of the Hebrew nation in Palestine, why bother with the Diaspora?"[40]

Another impediment to success, before late 1917, was Ben-Gurion's stance towards the Jewish Legion and the Jewish Congress movement.

At the time, he understood his difficulties differently. More than a year after his arrival, the discouraging recruiting missions notwithstanding, he remained very sanguine regarding American Zionism, which he found to be "unlike that of any other country." He marveled naively (and mistakenly) that "the American Jew

> who has never known any religious or national oppression, who has never been . . . discriminated against because of his Jewishness [sic!], a Jew who enjoys all rights and full equality in the most free and democratic of countries . . . [has been drawn] to Zionism . . . [only by] national consciousness and a desire for national freedom.

Moreover, Jews who strayed from the fold and then found Zionism, "such as Brandeis and Mack," retained, he noted with wonder, "the inner bond connecting them to the American people."[41] Zionism, he was sure, could be marketed in America with the proper techniques.

Ben-Gurion believed the cause of his failures was ignorance of the *yishuv*, which he set out to correct.[42] He and Ben-Zvi published a number of propaganda pamphlets in Yiddish;[43] and they wrote for the Yiddish press. Although for a time Ben-Gurion boycotted *Der Iddisher Kemfer* because its editor refused to print one of his articles, his long essay, "The Labor Problem in Palestine," was serialized there in the summer of 1916.[44] Even though the potential readership and the honoraria were much smaller, he preferred writing in Hebrew, the classical tongue of the Jewish people, to writing in Yiddish. One of the pleasant surprises about America was that there was no need to found a new journal, because the Hebrew press was flourishing. He and the other Palestinian exiles became its mainstays.[45]

The most "vital need," as he came to see it, was a book "explaining Palestine problems."[46] Three volumes in Yiddish were the result: two editions of *Yizkor* [Remember], and *The Land of Israel in Past and Present*. The first *Yizkor* was edited by Ben-Zvi, Zerubavel, and Alexander Ḥashin, a comrade who returned to Russia after the Revolution and was murdered in the purges of the 1930s. In part a revision of a 1911 work published in Palestine as a memorial for the martyrs of the *yishuv*, it included a new piece by Ben-Gurion, "Selected Reminiscences—From Petaḥ Tikva to Sejera," and easily sold out its run of 3,500 (according to one report, 5,000) copies. The second edition was edited by Ben-Gurion and Ḥashin, ostensibly because the other two were unavailable, perhaps because Ben-Gurion pushed them aside. It had a press run of more than 14,000 copies. *The Land of Israel* was authored by the two Bens and dealt with the history, geography, economics, and politics of the Holy Land. Like the others, it was a best seller.[47]

David Ben-Gurion

In addition to his missionary efforts and writing, Ben-Gurion engaged in other public activities during his first American sojourn, not all of them directly related to Palestine. Until he became thoroughly disaffected towards the end of his stay, he was involved with Poale Zion Party affairs, not only as head of the Palestine Committee but also as secretary of its Workers' Council. As a Party representative or in his own right he participated in meetings of the New York Kehilla (the organized Jewish community), the Provisional Executive Committee for General Zionist Affairs, and the Histadruth Ivrith.[48] Together with Rabbi Fishman, he founded an association of Palestinian exiles in 1916. He took part in the first national conference of the People's Relief fund for Jewish war victims. He lent his support to the notion of "a great national institution" to train Hebrew teachers in the United States, and raised his voice in opposition to socialist Congressman Meyer London of New York, who had spoken out against Zionism.[49]

By the last year of his stay, Ben-Gurion had learned to emphasize to good effect those of his character traits that were most appealing to Americans: "energy, efficiency, ambition, and resourcefulness"; and he had honed his leadership skills. As head of the Palestine Committee, he "organized ... lecture tours, mass meetings, and local Action Committees all over the United States," signed up 1,500 people for aliyah, and accumulated a substantial reserve fund for Palestine. He learned how to deal with the patrician Jewish fund-raising organizations, and together with Ben-Zvi secured a promise of ten thousand dollars from the Joint Distribution Committee in 1918 for a *yishuv* labor office.[50] His oratory had also improved. In late 1917, he was a featured speaker at celebrations of the Balfour Declaration: at a Hebrew-speaking gathering in the Bronx, at a "demonstration" held by a Hebrew-speaking branch of the Poale Zion, and at a mass meeting sponsored by his own Palestine Committee at New York's Cooper Union Hall. At the last event, the assembly adopted by acclamation a resolution urging "every Jew to devote all his energies, 'and if necessary, his life' to the establishment of a national home" in Palestine. A second resolution drafted by Ben-Gurion, in which "Jewish socialist workers and revolutionaries pledge[d]" themselves "to aid the immediate enlistment of the Jewish proletariat *to* Eretz Israel, *for* Eretz Israel, and *in* Eretz Israel," (emphasis added) echoed in Yiddish the cadences of Lincoln's "Gettysburg Address."[51]

According to his biographer, Shabtai Teveth, Ben-Gurion's triumphs alarmed the shortsighted, small-minded American Poale Zion leaders who became jealous of their power, apprehensive regarding his charisma, and anxious about the impending disintegration of their organization as a result of large-scale aliyah.[52] One might note, as well, the inherent contradiction between Zionism and aliyah. For the *yishuv* to prosper and for *olim* to be attracted to it, vigorous Zionist societies in the Diaspora were essential. But a thriving organization requires a considerable investment of time and emotional involvement which together engender loyalty to the group itself. Had the Poale Zionists ignored the immediate concerns of members and group dynamics to focus solely on the long-range goal of aliyah, they would surely have put their group at risk and jeopardized the prospects of aliyah, as well. In any case, the party stewards removed Ben-Gurion from the Palestine Committee on trumped-up charges of inactivity and refused to appoint him and Ben-Zvi as delegates to the Zionist Commission about to leave for Palestine, where it was to represent Zionist interests to the military authorities. A furious Ben-Gurion, by then familiar with the seamy side of America, charged that he had been euchred by politicians schooled at "Tammany Hall."[53]

Not only his latter-day successes caused friction with the local Poale Zion. An earlier contentious issue was the American Jewish Congress movement. As noted above, the Congress was intended as a grassroots, Zionist-oriented organization to unite and represent American Jewry, to coordinate public community activities in wartime and beyond, and to defend the interests of Jews in distress beyond the borders of the United States. The American Jewish Committee and others opposed it, because they objected to Zionism, because they feared antisemitic reactions to the image of a united Jewry, and because they sought the mantle of leadership themselves.

Some Zionists, however, including a number of Poale Zion leaders, gave the Congress only lukewarm support, but for another reason: it would inevitably provide a platform for the public condemnation of Russia. Although outraged by the pogroms, they soft-pedaled their criticism in the belief that it was in the Jewish and Zionist interest to side with the Triple Entente, which would be endangered by highlighting Russian atrocities. Ben-Gurion, the Turkophile, tended to favor the Triple Alliance. As such, he was "persuaded that it would amount to shameful treachery . . . towards the Jewish people if the Congress were not to come about."[54] Ironically, there was also anxiety in pro-German quarters. Their fear was that the constraints regarding Zionism imposed on Germany by Turkey would be denounced by the Congress. And in the *yishuv*, it was feared the new group would not be Zionist enough.[55] Ben-Gurion, Ben-Zvi, and other Palestinians took part in the Congress preparations. But the opening session was postponed until the end of hostilities, and convened after the Bens had left the United States. There is scant evidence to substantiate Ben-Zvi's later claim that they "exerted a very great deal of influence" in the movement.[56]

Ben-Gurion's involvement with the Legion was somewhat more complicated. Soon after his arrival in New York, he met Pinḥas Rutenberg, Jabotinsky's ally who had come to the United States to agitate for a Jewish fighting force. Rutenberg explained the proposal to the newcomer who re-

David Ben-Gurion (second row, fourth from left) at a convention of the Poale Zion in Boston, 1916. (Courtesy of the Pinhas Lavon Labor Archive, Tel Aviv.)

mained impassive.⁵⁷ Here, too, the war was at issue; and here, too, Ben-Gurion clashed with Poale Zion leaders. Those who were not pacifists or persuaded that patriotism demanded lip service to American neutrality, favored the Legion, because they supported the Entente. He opposed it, because he stood behind Turkey and thought she might win. In fact, he seems to have harbored thoughts about a pro-Turkish Jewish battalion, despite the Turks' growing unfriendliness to Zionism. After the Balfour Declaration, the picture changed. Some of the Poale Zion stuck to the socialist line of opposition to the "imperialistic war"; the Central Committee neither endorsed nor condemned the Legion.⁵⁸ Ben-Gurion, on the other hand, became its advocate. In later years he would sometimes claim to have founded the force together with Ben-Zvi. This was certainly untrue, as earlier chapters here indicate. In 1920 Jabotinsky referred to Ben-Gurion as "one of the chief organizers of the volunteers in America,"⁵⁹ an assertion closer to the truth but also exaggerated. Still, he did employ his considerable persuasive powers in the recruiting drive; many of those who had enrolled in HeHalutz enlisted in the Legion. Over the objections of his pregnant wife, he volunteered himself, when the Poale Zion closed off the only other early return route to Palestine by refusing to nominate him to the Zionist Commission.⁶⁰

When the time came for the inductees to report for duty, the Poale Zion tendered them a farewell dinner in New York's Clinton Hall; and *Der Iddisher Kemfer* devoted a lead article to them "emphasizing their great contribution to the American party and to the Legion, and wishing them safety from hostile bullets." At the banquet Hirsch Ehrenreich remarked that "their entry into the Legion . . . [constituted] liberation," freeing them from exile and setting them on their way to the Promised Land. He was undoubtedly less than sincere in questioning how the Americans would "manage without" the Palestinian presence.⁶¹ It is safe to assume that Ben-Gurion was eager not only to return to the *yishuv* but also to leave the New World behind—especially the Poale Zion—his new wife notwithstanding.

A quarter century later in the midst of another war and facing the decimation of European Jewry, Ben-Gurion took courage from the promise America held for Palestine. He recalled that "the first large-scale aliyah after the Balfour Declaration had come from America, *olim* in uniform."⁶² At the time, however, he was not as enthusiastic about the Legionnaires, certainly far less enamored of them than either Jabotinsky or Katznelson. At first he had been close to his American comrades in arms. He was all but commanded to accept the rank of corporal, because his superiors believed his popularity would make control of the independent, if not ornery, troops easier. But where Katznelson admired their efforts to learn Hebrew, he became increasingly disturbed by the propensity of the men to speak Yiddish and by their inability to close the book finally on the Diaspora. One of his motivations for merging the Palestine Poale Zion into the new Aḥdut Ha-Avoda labor grouping was a desire to reduce the potential influence of the American Legionnaires in the party, to protect its Hebraic character and Palestine orientation from their Diaspora focus and from Yiddish.[63]

Still, like Jabotinsky and Katznelson, he endeavored to find the money needed to settle the Legionnaires, and begged the Zionist Commission to create jobs in Palestine rather than acquiesce in the soldiers' repatriation. In the fall of 1919 he demanded that the Central Committee of the American Poale Zion "attend to . . . [the] task" of fund raising for the veterans "immediately." And he berated Nellie Strauss (later Mochenson), the Palestine representative of the American Zion Commonwealth, for the colonial mentality of her group. The AZC was underwriting the settlement of demobilized soldiers in what was to become Merḥavya, the kibbutz where Golda would settle. Ben-Gurion not only demanded their money, he insisted on complete Palestinian control over the colonization process. Like her Zionist mentor Henrietta Szold, Strauss had a Progressive American's sense of proper procedure and thought the AZC should have some control "over what is being done . . . so that there may [be] no surprises later on." To get his way Ben-Gurion publicized the dispute in *Kuntres* and elsewhere, naturally from his own partisan point of view.[64]

Back in Palestine after the war, Ben-Gurion manifested considerable disenchantment with the United States. His initial optimism inspired by reading and hearsay seemed to have foundered on the shoals of reality. In June 1921, a few months before Katznelson's departure for America on his fund-raising mission for the Histadrut and the Workers' Bank, Ben-Gurion issued a grim warning regarding the difficulties that awaited him there. "America," he said, "will shorten our lives."[65] But in fact, Ben-Gurion's notions of the New World had never been one-dimensional; nor were they now. His disappointment was chiefly related to the Poale Zion, not all American Jews nor the country itself. It would take some time yet for him to formulate a coherent, workable American policy based on a realistic assessment of New World realities. For now, experience had been gained, tools acquired, and seeds planted. One of those tools was a library of almost 350 books in English, which he would update regularly.[66]

3

Ben-Gurion returned home to major responsibilities. From the inception of Aḥdut HaAvoda, he served on its secretariat, at first *primus inter pares*, then as the acknowledged party leader. In November 1921, just a few months after the founding of the Histadrut, he became a member of its secretariat as well, and in 1925 secretary general, a post he would occupy for a decade. Yisrael Kolatt has written that "Ben-Gurion's leadership aimed at changing . . . [the] fate of a people and a social regime." Towards that end he developed "a comprehensive vision of a new and better society," which, as a political and labor leader, he attempted to implement.[67] Shlomo Avineri and others have observed that "pragmatic considerations" almost invariably caused the man of action to alter his original "ideologically determined goal."[68] In that, Ben-Gurion had an American sensibility. He himself observed approvingly that in the New World "dogmatism did not rule; and the approach to matters . . . [was] practical."[69]

Not once during the 1920s did he visit the United States.[70] But that did not mean that he had lost interest in the country or given up on American Jews as allies of Zionism. Berl's 1921-22 mission with Manya Shoḥat and Yosef Baratz he described as "the first important" attempt of the new Histadrut to "establish ties with Jewish workers abroad." The destination, he noted in 1923, had not been an arbitrary choice:

> In America there are half a million organized Jewish workers. Their unions are the largest and most secure in the worldwide Jewish labor movement. The[ir] . . . daily paper—*Forverts*—has half a million readers and over 200,000 subscribers. A workers' life insurance and mutual aid society—the Arbayter Ring—has 80,000 members. They constitute a gigantic national political and economic force, and its sway over all Jewish affairs in the New World is enormous. Many [workers] . . . had been estranged from Zionism. But the events of the war, the destruction of European Jewry, [and] the growth of Zionist hopes have awakened the masses. . . .
>
> To influence the Jewish worker in America, to draw him near to our philosophy and our work—was the main goal of our delegation.[71]

Ben-Gurion visited the Soviet Union in 1923 in conjunction with an exhibit of Palestine agricultural products. He came away with high regard for Soviet egalitarianism and economic planning. Jabotinsky could discern no good in the new Russia and tended to see good where there was none in the United States, as with President Warren Harding. Ben-Gurion, however, admired Lenin for his decisive style of leadership, and perceived the contrast with President Harding, who, he observed, had the "good fortune" to die before being fully exposed as the "characterless and mediocre" man he was. In Russia, Ben-Gurion averred, were to be found "the best [of Jewish] youth," who combined "the beautiful tradition of the Russian revolutionary movement with great dedication to the land of Israel." But Russian communism was the rival of socialist Zionism for the loyalty of left-leaning Jews. He rightly suspected that antisemitism would not disappear under the Soviets, and the suppression of Zionist organizations and the Hebrew language, as well as the refusal to allow the emigration of that "best youth" or of anyone else to Palestine, dimmed the luster of the USSR.[72]

During these years, Ben-Gurion never lost sight of the "virgin territory" that awaited Labor Zionist conquest in eastern Europe and America, if only "sufficient forces [could be found] to do that great work." Labor emissaries in the United States repeatedly confirmed his vision of its prospects; and discussions at the Histadrut Executive Committee often focused on American affairs. Avraham Harzfeld, for example, while participating in the mission that bedeviled Jabotinsky in 1926, urged Ussishkin to plough "the wide field" of America for the Palestine Foundation Fund. David Bloch (Blumenfeld) thought "the Reform rabbis" with their "richer temples" likely sympathizers. As "they become disaffected with tradition," they often turn to Zionism, he noted perceptively.[73]

Despite the sour note on which his relationship with the American Poale Zion had ended in 1918, Ben-Gurion respected "the extraordinary continuing efforts" of the group "to maintain the party apparatus" in the face of financial constraints. The party had "a reserve of excellent manpower dedicated to . . . [its] cause," he asserted in 1921, even though his old nemesis, "that creature" Party Secretary Hirsch Ehrenreich, "injects poison" into the organization, while "broken-down . . . machinery undermines its ability to act." It was necessary, he maintained, to revitalize the faltering American party, since all of Labor's "economic efforts in Palestine depend[ed]" on it.[74]

An American organization for which he developed grudging respect in the early 1920s was Hadassah, with its "considerable accomplishments . . . in the fields of medicine and sanitation." Ideology told him that "only an independent labor institution based on *mutual* [aid] and self-help [emphasis his] could fulfill the very responsible function of providing medical assistance to workers."[75] He championed the cause of Kupat Holim, the Histadrut health care system. But when his daughter Renana fell ill with meningitis in 1925, and when he and his family and Katznelson were injured in an automobile accident three years later, they were treated in Hadassah hospitals. In the spring of 1927 a Histadrut delegation which he headed and a Hadassah delegation led by Henrietta Szold hammered out an agreement for the treatment of Kupat Holim patients in Hadassah institutions whenever that should prove appropriate.[76]

While Ben-Gurion's enthusiasm for the United States survived, his understanding of its relevance to the *yishuv* changed somewhat. Before the war he had viewed Jewish workers everywhere in the Diaspora as a reservoir for aliyah and as partners in the worldwide class struggle. Now American aliyah became much less of a concern. With "the closing of the gates" to the United States and Canada in the early 1920s, Ben-Gurion observed, eastern European Jews desperately needed the scarce Palestine immigration certificates issued by the Mandatory authorities. Americans could wait, and Palestine could wait for them.[77]

The *yishuv* could not wait, however, for increased financial support, as has been noted repeatedly. In the 1920s the Labor leadership sought the rapid and wide-ranging expansion of their institutions; and Ben-Gurion was particularly eager to free the movement from its dependency on the WZO.[78] From London, where he was working with the Poale Zion and WZO offices in 1920, he wrote to Syrkin in New York, that starvation was prevalent in the *yishuv*; conditions were worse than during the war. "Just . . . at this point in time," when there "are great opportunity [sic] for wide-ranging activities . . . we lack the means. . . . There is no word from America; in [the last] six months not even a penny has been sent from there."

Almost half a year later, "telegram after telegram from Palestine demanded money," but in London the coffers were "empty." Towards the end of 1921, the People's Relief sent the Histadrut £1229.40 and a large shipment of old clothes. The clothes were refused. Early the next year, the HEC requested assistance from the Zionist Executive, but Ben-Gurion was certain it would not be given and considered resigning. In 1924, with several Histadrut enterprises, including the Workers' Bank, the Solel Boneh Construction Company, and the marketing cooperative HaMashbir, about to topple, Remez and others wanted to seek aid in America. Ben-Gurion preferred Europe, where donors would be less inquisitive about management practices; but in the end, the dimensions of the crisis required fund raising on both continents.[79] When Solel Boneh collapsed in 1927, it had to be rescued by a loan from the Zionist Executive secured by future donations to the Histadrut from the United States. That year and the next, unemployment soared in Palestine, pushing the labor federation to the wall. In May 1929, Ben-Gurion wrote to Mereminsky in New York that "the financial condition of the Histadrut was disastrous." Salaries were unpaid; creditors were suing; in March the phone had been cut off.[80]

By then, the Histadrut secretary-general had come to see Diaspora Jewish workers—especially the Americans—primarily as "suppliers of the means for the upbuilding of socialist Palestine, and as a support system for the WZO."[81] Virtually without local resources, certainly in the early 1920s, he "pinned his hopes . . . on the Jewish workers in America."[82] The annual Histadrut missions, which Berl inaugurated and in which Golda took part, have already been discussed. Ben-Gurion took them very seriously; and in that era of inveterate amateurism urged that emissaries be trained for their task.[83] Later, he felt the Geverkshaften Campaign, the principal instrument of Palestine Labor for fund raising in the United States, had done "a great service to the Zionist Movement" by winning "the sympathy of . . . leaders of the Jewish labour movement in America . . . for Palestine labour . . . [and] for Zionism" in general.[84] In the 1920s, though, he seemed more appreciative of "the decisive role of the [American] Jewish worker[s]" in ensuring through their donations that "socialist values" would triumph in Palestine.[85] On occasion, he advocated soliciting aid from middle-class Zionists rather than non-Zionist laborers; but the "dangerous decline" of the ZOA in these years blocked that route.[86] The idea itself, however, indicates the relative value he assigned to Zionism and to socialism.

Ben-Gurion was almost always willing to sacrifice a principle for the sake of a more important one; and he understood the necessity of nurturing potential allies and donors. Although a patriotic and even abrasive champion of Hebrew over Yiddish, he expressed willingness in 1927 and 1928 to accede to requests from America for a Yiddish-language paper to communicate Labor's message. On many occasions throughout the twenties, he reminded his colleagues to look after important visitors; and he encouraged American labor leaders to tour Palestine.[87]

Although he preferred to raise money "from the Jewish people at large," he discovered already in 1920 that Weizmann's policy of turning to the wealthy few who had the resources was unavoidable.[88] There were problems with such bedfellows. Louis Marshall and his associates in the American Jewish Committee often failed to see the need for things Ben-Gurion thought essential, such as Labor-run elementary and secondary schools. Marshall, however, he believed to be "a warm and dedicated Jew" with whom he could work.[89] Sometimes reluctantly, more often with a sense of entitlement, he and his compatriots turned to the Zionist Executive, the Jewish Agency, and the WZO's Keren HaYesod during the 1920s for what they considered to be a fair share of the funds raised in America. In addition, they appealed directly to the Joint Distribution Committee, to Brandeis, and to other American individuals and agencies to supplement the inadequate funds they raised themselves from the common folk in the Geverkshaften Campaign.[90] As secretary general, Ben-Gurion considered turning Histadrut enterprises into joint stock companies in order to attract American investors.[91]

The inclusion of well-to-do non-Zionists in the Jewish Agency, the plan so despised by Jabotinsky, gained Ben-Gurion's initial approval. After seeing the "Jewish plutocrats" in action, however, he admitted to having made "a criminal error," to feeling "shame . . . at the lowering of the national flag . . . and the surrender and toadying before the servants of the masters of great fortunes who [in any case] don't give [us] their money." He urged, without success, that non-Zionist socialists be added to the Agency Council and Executive as a counterweight.[92] In every political crisis before 1939, Ben-Gurion found the non-Zionists—most especially the Americans—unhelpful, often harmful to what he believed to be the interests of the *yishuv*. In the midst of the partition debate in 1937 he had a surprisingly encouraging interview with Osmond d'Avigdor Goldsmid and Lionel Cohen, two of the British non-Zionists on the Council. He confided to his diary afterwards that "there was a difference between fair-minded, cultured non-Zionists and American non-Zionists."[93] Still, the chairman maintained a measure of equanimity in dealing with the moguls, such as Felix Warburg, and their designated civil servants, such as Maurice Hexter. Occasionally the money men proved to be useful window dressing; and their appointees were usually skilled professionals. But he stoutly resisted their demand for equal representation with the Zionists on the Executive, because they abjured responsibility for political affairs and frequently avoided their financial obligations, as well.[94]

Important as it was, money was by no means all that Ben-Gurion saw in America in these years. After he became a member of the Jewish Agency Executive in 1933, he began to develop a concept of world Jewry—and after the Nazi conquest of Europe, of American Jewry alone—as the hinterland of the *yishuv* with a legitimate interest there parallel to or greater than that of the Arab world in Palestine's Arab community. What followed from that notion was the right—even the obligation—of American Jews, the American public, and the United States government to interfere in Palestine affairs, as had been done during the Ottoman era.[95] By the eve of World War II, this theory would be elaborated in full. It had been present in adumbrated form much earlier, perhaps from the moment he heard Weizmann's report of the assistance rendered the Zionist cause by Secretary of State Lansing at the Versailles Conference. In response to anti-Zionist remarks by the French Jew, Sylvain Lévi, Lansing had invited Weizmann to define the "Jewish National Home" and then backed his maximalist interpretation. "America extricated us from our difficulty," Weizmann said later to a Zionist gathering in London. "We owe them a great debt. We shall at no time be able to repay it." Although Ben-Gurion was never eager to enlarge Weizmann's reputation, he included the full account in his reminiscences. It had obviously made an impression.[96]

It was more this conception of their political role than their potential as an economic resource for the *yishuv* that lay behind Ben-Gurion's cultivation of American Jewish and gentile workers in the 1920s. In 1923 he drew a comparison between American Jewry and the *yishuv*, two immigrant societies capable of mutual understanding. The "Hebrew laborer in . . . Palestine," he wrote,

> is deeply conscious that he is only the vanguard of the world Hebrew worker. . . .

> Our firm belief is that our Jewish laboring comrades all over the world will cooperate with us during the difficult hours of struggle and suffering and will extend to us moral, material, and personal aid. It has fallen the lot of the Jewish worker in America to assume the major role in this cooperation and aid. Into his hand Jewish history has delivered the power and the means needed to perform the task begun by the Jewish worker in Palestine.[97]

Support from the American Federation of Labor aroused in him "deep feelings of spiritual satisfaction" and reinforced his "faith in the worldwide solidarity of the working class in its struggle for liberation."[98]

Several times during the postwar decade Ben-Gurion attempted to pressure the Soviets, Britain, and even his opponents in the *yishuv* through America. In early 1924, for example, he requested that Judah Magnes use his influence with the editor of the *Nation*, Oswald Garrison Villard, to place an exposé of the Soviet suppression of Hebrew culture and Zionism in that journal, in the hope of stirring up American public opinion. On another occasion, he suggested to the HEC that American pressure might be one of the only means of prying open the doors of the Soviet Union for Zionist emigration.[99] During the 1920 Arab pogrom, he sent letters and telegrams to the American (and British) press, in the hope that an aroused public would bring about the appointment of a more friendly Palestine administration. And in 1927 he publicized widely in America and Britain a strike of farm laborers against Jewish orange grove owners, who preferred Arab workers to Jewish, in the hope of coercing the owners.[100] Little resulted from these efforts, although in retrospect they can be seen as trial runs for more successful initiatives to be undertaken in the years to come.

4

In Palestine the 1920s began and ended with violent Arab riots against the Jewish presence. The intervening "seven years of plenty" were also not without problems, most notably the severe downturn in the economy in 1927–28 already mentioned. But their relative tranquility afforded a nurturing setting for the dramatic growth and development of the *yishuv*.

By contrast, the tumultuous thirties witnessed crisis upon crisis. The decade opened with a white paper which responded to the Arab riots the previous year by restricting Jewish immigration. That led to a battle with the British government which would not end until Israel became independent in 1948. The Great Depression in North America reduced contributions and exacerbated the financial difficulties of the *yishuv*. It was another problem that would not go away. From 1933 the Nazis menaced European Jewry. The Palestinians sought to respond by accepting more *olim* but were seriously hampered by Britain's policy of keeping peace with the Arabs by limiting the number of Jewish immigrants. All during the decade the Laborites and Revisionists fought, usually with great acrimony, sometimes with violence. In 1935 the British proposed to grant Palestine a measure of home rule. Central to the proposal was a legislative council with proportional representation, which would have the power to restrict Jewish immigration and development. It had to be contested, even at the cost of appearing to oppose democracy. In response to the Arab rebellion of 1936 a royal commission suggested partitioning the country into a small Jewish state and a larger Arab one. Ben-Gurion was prepared to accept even a mini-state with control over immigration. Others were not; and considerable division in the *yishuv* ensued. A new white paper issued on the eve of war in 1939 capped Jewish immigration and interdicted land purchases by Jews. It pointed the way to permanent minority status for Jews in the land of Israel.

As the leader of Mapai, the largest political party in the *yishuv*, as secretary general of the Histadrut until 1935, and as chairman of the Jewish Agency Executive in Palestine from that year, it fell to Ben-Gurion, in effect, the prime minister of the *yishuv*, to lead the fight on all of these issues. His focus shifted in these years from Labor to the *yishuv*, as a whole, "from class to nation," as he titled a 1933 manifesto. He told a Cleveland audience in 1930 that the *yishuv* thrived on crisis.[101] But the Palestinians could not do battle on their own; and increasingly during the 1930s they turned to America for help. Ben-Gurion assiduously maintained old alliances there and cultivated new ones to help meet the challenges.

Aliyah from the United States ceased altogether to concern him in these years. Many of the Histadrut emissaries still believed, like Golda, that "*for the sake of Palestine* it was definitely worthwhile to bring people from America" (emphasis in original). Poale Zionists complained to Ben-Gurion in 1930 about the Palestinians' lack of "concern [whether] . . . the members in America . . . settle in Palestine."[102] He remained unyielding. "We do not need American *ḥalutzim* of the usual kind," he wrote to his wife in 1937, although he conceded that it might be wise to open the doors to young Americans with "military, aeronautic, and naval training."[103] Until the end of the decade, he remained committed to selective aliyah, which would bring to Palestine young, able-bodied pioneers. "Jewry as it is constituted now," he told readers of *Jewish Frontier* in June 1935, is not "ready for Palestine. A people of middlemen, trades people, professionals, spiritual and sociological *luftmenschen* cannot emigrate *en masse*."[104] In any case, European Jews, who were "being strangled and destroyed," took precedence over Americans. "Germany is only the prelude," he wrote to Weizmann in 1933: "I saw the situation of the Jews in Poland, Lithuania, Latvia. It is impossible to exist this way. Not only the poverty, the lack of a job, the political pressure, the growing antisemitism. Worst of all is the hopelessness."[105] In early 1936 he told the Mapai Political Committee that the German situation was making it necessary "to begin . . . turning Palestine into a . . . haven for masses of Jews." But as late as 1938 he did not advocate indiscriminate aliyah, even for the endangered Europeans.[106]

Money remained a paramount concern. Without it, the new chairman of the Agency Executive acknowledged in 1936, "there will be nothing" in Palestine. And, of course, the "main front in this respect" was America. Any "hope for swift" change in Palestine rested on "a major campaign" in the United States; but no one seemed capable of mounting it.[107] On his four trips to North America during the 1930s, Ben-Gurion did what he could. In December 1930, he conducted parlor meetings at the homes of labor leaders and well-to-do sympathizers, addressed conventions and banquets, and negotiated with Felix Warburg, chairman of the Jewish Agency Council.[108] In the spring of 1935, there were the usual banquets for the Geverkshaften Campaign and visits with individuals. He also tried to convince Rabbi Wise and Judge Mack to conduct a campaign for Palestine outside the United Jewish Appeal. The UJA, which collected money for a variety of community needs, invariably shortchanged the *yishuv* in times of crisis, Ben-Gurion felt, because "the non-Zionist" partners "were unenthusiastic" about Palestine as a solution to Jewish distress. On a quickie trip in January 1939, he failed again to effect separation.[109] During his 1937 stay, he was unsuccessful in persuading the Americans of the wisdom of mounting an emergency campaign for the *yishuv*, which was faced with large numbers of immigrants from Germany and increasing defense needs.[110]

In 1938 Ben-Gurion proposed an alternative means of raising revenue: a tax that Jews everywhere would levy on themselves, the proceeds to be used for Palestine settlement. Fearing that European Jewry might soon be cut off by war, he suggested focusing on America. Katznelson and others felt it was irresponsible not to concentrate on rescuing the Europeans and recovering their assets before they disappeared.[111] By 1939 Ben-Gurion had found several American friends, including Brandeis, to help defray the costs of illegal immigration and defense; but his urgent requests for major assistance elicited nothing more than sparse words of encouragement from the ZOA president, Rabbi Solomon Goldman.[112]

Among the few financial bright spots were Hadassah and the Brandeis group. In 1936, Hadassah refused to hold an emergency drive but responded immediately to Ben-Gurion's plea for aid with ten thousand dollars "to ease the situation for the Executive under the present stress and strain."[113] Brandeis was personally generous; and the institutions maintained by his group now became very responsive to the needs of the *yishuv*, particularly the Labor sector. Grants were given for a number of initiatives, including the

Histadrut Arab newspaper and the purchase of land on which the city of Eilat now stands.[114] Brandeis considered Ben-Gurion (and Moshe Shertok) "practical leaders of great ability, men of understanding, vision and wisdom rare in government," who deserved "unqualified, ardent support." So complete was his trust that he occasionally sent undesignated funds to be spent "as Ben-Gurion may direct."[115]

5

More and more in the 1930s, Ben-Gurion devoted his attention to realizing the political potential for Zionism of the United States and its Jewry. He set two main goals for himself in this area for the decade and beyond. One was to strengthen American Jewry in order to maximize its Zionist promise; the other was to marshal its resources to influence the course of events in Palestine. One major concern was to ensure that the Revisionists would not gain the upper hand at the Zionist Congress or in the *yishuv*. In America there appeared to be "no conception of the danger from Revisionism," which to him in 1933 seemed "no less than that to the labor movement in Germany from Hitler."[116] A second vital concern was to obtain support for open immigration and—sooner or later—statehood.

In the early fall of 1930, Ben-Gurion presided over the World Congress for Labor Palestine in Berlin. The Congress, his brainchild back in 1919, was an attempt at Labor-Zionist political theater on the world stage. The intended audience included Revisionists, Bundists, the British government, and, of course, like-minded Labor Zionists, although each group was meant to draw a different lesson from the pageant. It took Ben-Gurion years of lobbying in the *yishuv* and abroad to bring off the project. It had been "clear" from the start that "without America there [would be] no value to the Congress,"[117] although the haphazard way in which it took shape militated against significant American participation. In the end, the Americans came, as did others, but the event proved less spectacular than Ben-Gurion had hoped or than he claimed afterwards. Of particular note here is his exaggerated estimate of its impact on America.[118]

His trip to the United States at the end of 1930 may be seen as an attempt to impart substance to his claims regarding the Congress. His natural starting point was the Poale Zion, which had "captured an important sector of America's workers" but remained peripheral to the Jewish labor movement. The Histadrut secretary general looked forward to the eventual enrollment in the Labor Zionist party of tens of thousands of workers sympathetic to Zionism but still reluctant to join a group outside the socialist mainstream. He advocated two contradictory strategies: uniting all American Zionist parties including the Poale Zion in a single organization; and merging the Poale Zion with non-Zionist socialist groups such as the Arbayter Ring, the union/*landsmannschaft*/mutual-aid society. The achievement of either goal would have been acceptable; both proved elusive.

He opened his campaign with a suggestion that the party outflank the anti-Zionist Bundists by becoming "the Jewish branch" of the Socialist Party of America, thus gaining a seal of approval in wider circles. At the same time, he urged courting the Bundist group associated with *Forverts*, a task in which he participated himself during the next few years by cultivating a warm relationship with the paper's editor, Abe Cahan.[119] In early January 1931, he met with the Arbayter Ring national board and excoriated them for extending a hand to workers in all countries, but "excluding the Hebrews" of Palestine. To underscore their self-hatred and soften them up for a merger with the Poale Zion, he said that last phrase in Russian, although the rest of his speech was in Yiddish.[120] He was unsuccessful on all counts except personally with Cahan.

When Ben-Gurion returned to America in 1935, he tried again. This time he sought an agreement with Baruch Charney Vladeck, the *Forverts* journalist and municipal politician who headed the Jewish Labor Committee. He and Vladeck negotiated a ten-point program for joint Zionist-non-Zionist action in the United States and Palestine to which the Poale Zion leadership as well as some Arbayter Ring and Jewish union leaders agreed in principle.[121]

When Rabbi Stephen S. Wise, who was head of the United Palestine Appeal, president of the American Jewish Congress, the initiator of the World Jewish Congress movement, a member of the governing council of the ZOA and soon to be its president, and a member of the Actions Committee of the WZO, got wind of the agreement, he exploded in high dudgeon. For his own partisan purposes, Ben-Gurion had made a pact with the "most bitter and virulent foe of our ideal of a Jewish National Home," a deed incomprehensible to Wise. The rabbi upbraided him for failing to distinguish between "his status as a socialist and . . . [his] position as one of the leaders of the Zionist Movement." He had, Wise charged, done "no good to Palestine and . . . infinite harm to our Jewish democratic point of view as against the grand dukes and their associates [that is, the wealthy non-Zionists, such as Warburg] with whom . . . Vladeck has consistently associated himself for twenty years."[122] Israel Mereminsky, one of the most knowledgeable members of the HEC on American affairs, also opposed the agreement but for other reasons. He believed that merging the Geverkshaften Campaign with the fund-raising efforts of the non-Zionist labor groups would result in reduced donations and the disappearance of a valuable pro-Zionist institution.[123]

Vladeck visited Palestine in 1936 and in an interview with the high commissioner proved himself a faithful confederate of the Laborites by asserting that non-Zionists in America also expected Britain to keep open the doors to Palestine in those troubled times. Rubashov and others backed Ben-Gurion; but more than two years after the nuptials, the marriage remained unconsummated.[124] During his brief visit to America in September 1937, Ben-Gurion renegotiated the deal, this time taking care to obtain Wise's approval and that of the Poale Zion leaders. In the end, as noted earlier, when Katznelson and Vladeck could not persuade the non-Zionist workers to accept the accord, organizational unity on the Left became a dead letter.[125]

During the war, American Labor—both Jewish and gentile—came generally to favor the Zionist cause and Jewish statehood, although Ben-Gurion believed the leadership to be more strongly supportive than the rank and file.[126] The kind of institutional integration he had sought in the 1930s proved unnecessary in terms of securing Labor backing. And yet, probably more out of old bitterness than cold analysis, he continued to accuse the Poale Zion of having prevented genuine unity. They wanted, he claimed, "to exploit the labor movement for their own party ends, without participating in general labor matters . . . moving away from both Zionism and socialism, with no trace of true creative or revolutionary content, . . . as Jews or workers, . . . Zionists or socialists."[127] This was a harsh and—considering his own willingness to compromise when necessary—unfair pronouncement on a group that had attracted him to the New World thirty years earlier. Like other organizations of working-class, immigrant Jews, the Poale Zion had, indeed, allowed its socialism to be tempered by middle-class American values; but it had remained steadfast in its commitment to Zionism.

Ben-Gurion's second strategy for augmenting the political clout of American Zionism was his unity scheme; again the starting point was the Poale Zion. In 1930 he proposed its merger with a smaller socialist Zionist society, Zeire Zion, most of whose members in the *yishuv* were affiliated with HaPo'el HaTza'ir. That group had just recently joined with Ahdut HaAvoda to form the Mapai Party. Shortly after his arrival in America Ben-Gurion all but ordered a Zeire Zion convention to close up shop. This time he achieved his goal.[128]

Further efforts at Zionist amalgamation proved less rewarding. He had no success in bringing about a consolidation of pioneering youth groups in 1930 and abandoned the task to others, including Golda.[129] Beginning in 1935 he pursued a grand union of all Zionist parties in the United States. As chairman of the Agency Executive, Ben-Gurion now had broader concerns, although he had hardly become nonpartisan. He believed the party structure of American Zionism to be an impediment to mass recruitment; but he also expected that union "would enable [his Labor] . . . comrades to influence the proceedings of the entire movement," as he explained to a sympathetic Brandeis.[130] To the realistic—and therefore sceptical—leaders of the Poale Zion, the Pioneer Women, and the League for Labor Palestine in Chicago, New York, and Milwaukee, he held out the prospect of becoming "the ruling party in Zionism destined to impose Zionism on the nation."[131] The Hadassah women, whom Jabotinsky had courted a few months before, agreed with Ben-Gurion about the desirability of unification but were adamant about retaining their independence. The ZOA men were even less open to his blandishments. In disgust, the visitor declared their president, Morris Rothenberg, to be "a non-Zionist with zero political value"; and he showed little regard for the "politicians" on its Executive Committee who, he claimed, greeted his recommendations with "obstructive discussion."[132]

Debate over the proposed legislative council in Palestine and preparations for the upcoming Zionist Congress required the Agency chairman's hasty return home. He left the United States convinced that "only . . . help from the outside," by which he meant the *yishuv*, could bring about the required restructuring of the American Zionist movement.[133] At a Mapai Party Center discussion in July, he noted that 23 percent of Latvian Jews were dues-paying Zionists, but only 1 percent of American Jews. "The difference," he asserted, "did not stem from American Jewry's having no interest in Palestine. On the contrary—except for Poland, no country was as interested . . . as America. . . . The only reason [for the poor showing] was that no Zionist movement [to speak of] existed [in the United States]." In early 1936, Rubashov reported from New York that he was making no progress towards union.[134]

The outbreak of the Arab rebellion in Palestine later that year made a strong American Zionist voice even more desirable. It turned out to be wishful thinking, but Ben-Gurion at first believed the crisis would provide "an opportunity . . . to put [the American movement] . . . on its feet." He reminded his colleagues in the Mapai Center, that

> The power of American Jewry is all the political force we have in the world. . . .
> At the moment we have a chance of taking the Zionist movement in America in hand. The president [Rabbi Wise] is one of our people. . . . Behind us we have an old man [Brandeis] with moral strength. He could swing Hadassah in our direction.

The party leaders responded by sending a delegation to New York to develop a plan of action.[135] But the "insistence of the Laborites" on unification and on open Zionist Congress elections met with general opposition, even from "their man," Wise.[136] In January 1939, Ben-Gurion was once more in America with a familiar message: "The weakness in the Zionist movement in America is due [primarily] to . . . disunity among Zionists." Elsewhere there was "a single Zionist address," but not in the United States. With war clouds on the horizon, that weakness constituted "a great political danger." Again he called for change. Only war would bring it about, however, and then in a halting and temporary fashion: the Emergency Committee for Zionist Affairs founded in 1939 to coordinate Zionist activities and represent the movement during wartime. A weak union of parties at war with each other, the Committee functioned fairly well after 1941 but self-destructed when peace came.[137]

6

While a unified Zionist movement and a united Jewish labor movement remained beyond reach, Ben-Gurion was actually quite successful in the 1930s in cultivating American allies for the *yishuv*, in general, and for his own policies, in particular. Grassroots Zionist sentiment grew steadily, at least in part because of the effective propaganda of the Palestinians. Perhaps even more significant was the cementing of friendships with well-placed sympathizers.

First among these were Brandeis and his associates who returned to power in the ZOA in 1930. The judge's high regard for Ben-Gurion was reciprocated. In 1930 Ben-Gurion still thought of Brandeis as "one [of the] complications" of America, but within a few years he and his close coworker and erstwhile Zionist surrogate, Felix Frankfurter, had become "our faithful friends." In retrospect, he was "the greatest Jew in the United States."[138] Each saw in the other a man of character; they shared a dislike of the wealthy, assimilating Jews like Warburg, despite the fact that Brandeis himself was assimilated and a millionaire; more importantly, they shared sympathy for working people and a social vision, even though Brandeis was a Progressive, not a socialist. From the mid-1930s on, Ben-Gurion consulted regularly with Brandeis (and Frankfurter) in person, by mail, and through intermediaries. The judge not only offered sage advice and money, he and the men of his circle could open doors in Washington, including the portals of the White House, although they were not always willing to do so, and did not always get what they wanted.

From within American Zionism stronger leaders finally began to emerge towards the end of the 1930s: Rabbis Solomon Goldman and Abba Hillel Silver, and Henry Montor, the executive director of the United Palestine Appeal. Henry Monsky, the president of the B'nai B'rith fraternal order, gradually brought his group into the Zionist orbit. Rabbi Wise, who was connected to the Brandeis circle but stood outside the perimeter of the judge's shadow, made his mark much earlier than the others. Not only did he hold major offices in the largest American Zionist and pro-Zionist organizations all during the thirties (except, of course, for Hadassah), he was a significant figure in his own right in the worlds of liberal religion and liberal politics. He and Ben-Gurion did not always agree on policy or even like each other. On occasion Wise found the Palestinian duplicitous, and pined for the "day in Zionist circles [when he would] . . . come upon someone in whom one could place unlimited and unquestioning confidence."[139] Ben-Gurion thought the rabbi sometimes behaved like "a baby" when it came to "political questions"; he saw in him "a typical American tribune" whose "spiritual world [was] . . . limited" and who lacked "political insight"; and like Jabotinsky he found Wise inconstant.[140] But the two cooperated closely on many issues; and Wise proved often to be a valuable political ally.

The early 1930s were a period of preparation for renewed American intervention in Palestine affairs. During the investigatory visit there of Sir John Hope-Simpson in 1930, Katznelson suggested that American Jews be mobilized to counter British pressure on the Zionist Executive in London. Ben-Gurion and others were not yet ready for that step.[141] None of them was aware how jittery the British were about such an eventuality. After the 1929 riots the Colonial Office had attempted to neutralize negative publicity in the United States with its own propaganda program. Albert M. Hyamson, an observant British Jew who, during his service in the Palestine Mandatory government, became a hardened foe of Zionism, was engaged to "provide some material to be used in America for counteracting mendacious abuse of the British Government that was going on there." Although Hyamson admitted to his superiors that his disinformation had not "made the slightest difference to the attitude of American Jews either then or later," serious consideration was given to employing him to try again.[142]

By 1933, Ben-Gurion was prepared for Brandeis and Frankfurter to intercede with the British. Early the next year, he reiterated to the judge his belief that "the friendship of England . . . [is] a necessary condition for our political success." At the same time, he suggested that "America is perhaps in a special position [with regard to Britain], and a hint from its Government [to London] might help us a good deal." Perhaps nervous about Brandeis's reaction, he added that this was "a subject" upon which he was "not qualified to express an opinion."[143] At home, however, he made no effort to conceal the link he saw between "the necessity for political action in America" and the existence there of "Jewish personalities with connections and important positions in the government."[144] Although he was not unwilling to send Frankfurter to act for him, Brandeis guarded his image as a detached jurist. He proved reluctant even to offer Roosevelt advice on the appointment of a minister to Russia who might help Jews there wishing to emigrate to Palestine.[145] "The question" for Ben-Gurion remained, then:

"How to set these political wheels in motion?"[146] During his American visit in 1935, he sought advice from Frankfurter and Brandeis regarding the legislative council proposal. Both felt strongly that nothing could be done in the United States to help; Frankfurter dissuaded the visitor from trying to see Roosevelt.[147]

Wise had spoken of England's "great betrayal" of Zionism already in 1930. By the mid-1930s, Ben-Gurion had also become convinced that the first country to champion the Jewish national movement was turning into its adversary, although many in the Zionist camp refused to acknowledge the change. In January 1936, he spoke of the need for public agitation in the United States against the restriction of immigration to Palestine, and of the need for Frankfurter's intercession in London, where he had "important ties . . . and was known as an intimate of Roosevelt."[148] Only a public outcry would move the British government. In London and New York "large-scale activity . . . [was] required [to] . . . prevent [further restrictive] decrees."[149] In February Rabbi Wise entered the fray, protesting to Roosevelt the nomination as consul in Jerusalem of a person unlikely to be sympathetic to the *yishuv*. The president agreed to reexamine the appointment if the Zionists could provide proof of their allegations.[150] As the leader of Mapai, Ben-Gurion spoke in March of the need for a massive Zionist "offensive" against Britain. Unlike Jabotinsky, who played the Polish card even after the outbreak of war, Ben-Gurion recognized years before that that country's "wretched" Jews could no longer do anything to further Zionist aims. "On whom shall we lean," he asked in March 1936, if not on America?[151]

In response to the Arab riots the next month, he suggested a demonstrative gathering in London of all "our [influential] friends," especially Frankfurter, Lipsky, and Wise; and he asked Brandeis to ensure that Frankfurter, who was in England on sabbatical, would come.[152] This time the crisis was so severe that Brandeis himself intervened with the British government and with Roosevelt—successfully. Although FDR had steadily retreated from his endorsement of a Jewish Palestine during the 1932 elections, he now "pressured London not to curtail the Palestine immigration quota."[153] Wise paid a call on Colonial Secretary William Ormsby-Gore as an official spokesman of American Zionism; Frankfurter planned to see Prime Minister Baldwin and a number of cabinet ministers, "not as a Zionist, [just] . . . to let them know the possible reaction in America should England stray from her obligations."[154] In October, Ben-Gurion reviewed recent events for the Zionist Smaller Actions Committee, the inner circle of the WZO. Among the incidents he recounted was the following: "On the day the cabinet met" in London to discuss the immigration issue,

> an important letter was published from the greats of America, all of them Christian, leaders of trade unions, churches, and charitable agen-

cies . . . a combination that seems weird to us but is usual in America. . . . The prime minister felt obliged to respond . . . and to promise that the government of England would be diligent in preserving the Mandate and in ameliorating conditions.[155]

A few weeks earlier Brandeis had sketched out for Robert Szold what he believed to be the rationale for American submissions (there were several, including those of Hadassah, Junior Hadassah, and the ZOA) to the royal commission headed by Earl Peel, which had been appointed to study the causes of the recent Arab riots. It resembled remarkably Ben-Gurion's conception of America, and the Diaspora in general, as the hinterland of the *yishuv*. "America's deep interest," Brandeis asserted, did "not rest only upon the fact that" it "had the largest Jewish population of any country"; that it had "major investments in Palestine"; or that it had "expended those vast sums" during the formative period of the country and thereby acquired founders' rights. Rather, "the intensity of America's interest

> and its depth of feeling about British action is due in part to the fact that:
> (1) We gave support to the proposed Balfour Declaration in advance, at British solicitation;
> (2) We gave support, largely at British solicitation, to the appointment of Britain as Trustee (as then called) of Palestine."[156]

Here was a rationale for the political partnership of America and her Jews with the *yishuv*. Ben-Gurion and Brandeis had become the parents of a nascent alliance.

More than any other Palestinian, Ben-Gurion anticipated the political role of the American Jewish community, although the vaunted "Jewish lobby" would not come into being for many years yet. Money, he wrote to Wise in January 1937, would be crucial, because "without it we shan't be able to maintain the full strength of the *yishuv*." But it was the "political power" of Jews in the United States, unequalled elsewhere, that would make the difference "in the life and death struggle ahead."[157] He knew there were limits to that power and that there were strong anti-Zionist currents in the country. But nowhere else did Jews have as much access to government, as many of their coreligionists in high places, or the electoral strength in key districts that they had in America.

The following year was marked by the partition debate. Even before the Peel Commission delivered its report, it was assumed that it would recommend the division of Palestine. In the face of widespread opposition to accepting a mini-state, he assured the Mapai Center that the notion was not "fantastic," that with the backing of Roosevelt and Premier Léon Blum of France, who was a member of the Socialist Pro-Palestine Committee and of the Jewish Agency Council, the plan could work. "Without the help of America," however, it would not.[158] In July 1937, with objections to partition mounting, Ben-Gurion defiantly declared all Zionists to be united on one thing: desire for a state of one sort or another.[159] It was not the first time he simply declared his own views to be the consensus. After the Zionist Congress that summer, when it became clear that Hadassah, Wise, and even Brandeis opposed him on partition, he made a flying trip to the United States to twist arms and to repair the strained relationship with Brandeis. He changed only a few minds. But the judge's friendship remained intact, even if his view of current affairs was too "*legalistic*" and not realistically "*political*" (emphasis Ben-Gurion's) to the politician's way of thinking.[160]

7

By 1938, war clouds were gathering. Ben-Gurion had little confidence in "official, gentile America." He was disquieted by the Evian Conference, at which the American delegates had avoided mention of Palestine and seemed to be "distancing [themselves] from foreign 'entanglements.'" He hoped that an aroused public opinion together with pressure on the president by Brandeis, Wise, and Ben Cohen, one of Roosevelt's Jewish advisors, would turn the situation around.[161] Fears that Britain might be preparing to hand over Palestine to the Arabs in the near future prompted his frantic appeal in early October to Rabbi Goldman, the ZOA president, as well as to Wise, Lipsky, and others for help with Roosevelt, and to the Poale Zion for a good word with their Labor friends. Goldman's efforts resulted in newspaper editorials across the country, a flood of telegrams to Washington, and the formation of the National Emergency Committee for Palestine, which eventually included both Zionists and non-Zionists. Brandeis once more interceded personally; and Bernard Baruch, not usually a friend of Zionism, spoke with Churchill.[162]

Later that month encouraged by the activity, Ben-Gurion sent Goldman an outline of the likely approach towards Palestine of His Majesty's Government in the coming months, based on information from a friendly member of the British cabinet. Policy depended on "Neville" (Chamberlain, the prime minister), he wrote, and

> there is only one thing that can influence him—namely, the position of America. If England . . . [can] trade and improve her standing in America because of her relationship to the Jews and Zionism—this he can take into consideration. . . .
>
> England is now negotiating for a commercial agreement. If it . . . [could be made known] that keeping faith with the Jews and [the]

expansion of immigration are able to assist the negotiations and the relations with America—that would be a very great thing.

Everything seemed to depend on America; and it was "necessary somehow to increase pressure" from there. Ben-Gurion cautioned Goldman, that "as far as possible," it should "not become evident that the pressure is organized by the Zionists." On the other hand, "our friends in . . . Government . . . should know how . . . much value is attached to their stand."[163]

As a way of impressing the administration with the broad support for Zionism developing among American Jews and of parading before the world the emerging *yishuv*-America alliance, Ben-Gurion conceived of a plan for a major international conference in support of Zionism to be held in the United States. In December he headed there to promote the event, another attempt at pro-Zionist political theater which bore some similarity in aim to the 1930 Berlin labor congress. Timing was crucial. The British government had summoned Arabs and Jews to a roundtable conference at London's St. James Palace in early 1939. The Zionists anticipated no favorable conclusion to those discussions and wanted the British to know that strong protest from America would follow. Such a threat counted for much just then, Ben-Gurion told the ZOA National Executive Committee: "In case of war . . . [the] fate of England hinges upon the action of America. . . . We think we will be strengthened as far as we can be . . . in this very great struggle, if the British Government will know that the Jewish people in America and, to a certain degree, American public opinion is watching them."[164] There was a Machiavellian aspect to the proposal. Persuaded now that partition would not be implemented and that the doors to Palestine were about to be sealed, the Agency chairman renounced diplomacy in favor of "combative Zionism," which involved, among other things, open illegal immigration, which he expected the British to suppress. The gathering in New York or Washington was meant to highlight the injustice and galvanize the American public and government to press the British to alter their policy.[165]

During his two-and-a-half-week stay he made little headway with the conclave. Brandeis expressed "complete understanding"; Robert Szold was somewhat less enthusiastic. Hadassah was supportive; Cyrus Adler and other non-Zionists were adamantly opposed, suspecting this was just another version of the World Jewish Congress that Stephen Wise and Nahum Goldmann were planning. To Ben-Gurion's chagrin, many Zionists feared attempting to wield Jewish power in public; others thought it would be all but impossible to foment opposition to Britain and Germany at the same time. If lobbying for the conference went poorly, so, too, did the search for "rich Jews who would help" with ships and money for illegal immigration, open or secret. He did, however, manage to establish a working relationship with Henry Montor; and he delivered a rousing address at the Washington conference of the United Palestine Appeal, his first major speech in English.[166]

Notwithstanding his difficulties in organizing the American "front," it remained his strongest suit for the coming St. James Conference. The choreography for the conference called for Rabbi Wise to be the "third speaker on our side," Ben-Gurion wrote to his wife from London. He would "stress America's partnership in the policy of the National Home, and . . . American Jewry's expectations that Britain will stand by its commitments."[167] At the close of the meetings, however, probably at the instance of the less militant and more pro-British Weizmann, Wise undermined his own "side." He declared publicly the impossibility of American Jews' agitating against Britain after years of vociferous opposition to Germany.[168] In the weeks following the conference, Ben-Gurion urged continued lobbying in Washington. "The closer the world is to war," he told the Mapai Political Committee in early April, "the more dependent on America England becomes. And if Roosevelt really wanted to come to our aid, if he would chastise England, he could change a lot."[169]

The president, however, did little; and the British did not flinch. In May 1939, came the white paper intended to pave the way to Palestine's becoming an Arab state. As expected, it severely curtailed Jewish immigration just as Europe's Jews faced annihilation. Frenzied attempts had been made to dissuade Chamberlain from this definitive departure from the Mandate by the leaders of the *yishuv*, by the doggedly pro-English Weizmann, by the League of Nations Mandates Commission, which refused to accept explicit repudiation of the Balfour Declaration, and by Americans of all stripes. Brandeis himself discussed the change at least four times with the British, but all to no avail. In the end, America carried less weight with Chamberlain than Ben-Gurion had been led to believe. The Arabs, with their oil, numbers, and strategic geographical location, were needed in the approaching struggle. Everyone knew the Jews had no alternative but to favor Britain over Nazi Germany. The Agency chairman's repeated warnings not to take the Jews "in Palestine and in America . . . for granted," rang hollow.[170] Sometimes Ben-Gurion appeared to lose heart himself. When he left the United States in January 1939, it seemed to him "all but clear that we had no hope of expecting help from America . . . in our struggle."[171]

The overwhelming odds notwithstanding, the *yishuv* was not about to give up. At the first Mapai Party Center meeting after the invasion of Poland, Ben-Gurion asserted the collective determination not only to survive but yet to succeed in fulfilling the Zionist dream. "Even in normal times, Palestine [still] could not stand on its own feet. . . . Now swift, substantial

David Ben-Gurion

Ben-Gurion as chairman of the Executive Committee of the Jewish Agency for Palestine, holding a press conference on the SS *Berengaria* on his return to America from the Zionist Congress in Geneva, 3 September 1937. (Courtesy of UPI-Bettmann.)

aid from outside is essential; and at this point in time there is no outside other than America." In contrast to Jabotinsky—and Weizmann—the Agency chairman recognized that this war would not be anything like the last. Then America had only to provide food "for a small *yishuv*." Now "large-scale" relief was required for a community of almost half a million people with "a diversified economy." The nature of "the political assistance demanded from America" this time was also very different. Then Zionists "had one simple . . . political claim: recognition of our right to Palestine. Now that right" had been delegitimated. In Ben-Gurion's estimation, such a "complex" situation called for skills and knowledge possessed by no contemporary American Zionist leader, not even Brandeis with his "formidable intellect" and superior knowledge of Palestine. He proposed the immediate establishment in the United States of a Zionist office to be directed by Palestinians "of stature and weight who will impose their opinions and will on American Zionism and on American Jewry" at large.[172] One of those persons "of stature and weight" was Ben-Gurion himself, who spent many months in the United States in the early years of the war activating the hinterland of the *yishuv*.

Although this war might be different, Ben-Gurion did not believe all the Zionist weapons of World War I to be antiquated. Like Jabotinsky, he wanted a Jewish fighting force to help defeat Hitler, to defend the national home, and to renew the claim for spoils, namely Palestine, after the war. Already in 1937, he had toyed with the notion of securing admission to West Point and Annapolis for future *olim*, "not an easy thing for Jews," but "not out of the question with sufficient 'pull' (from senators and congressmen)." Training "officers for Palestine at the expense of the American government" had appeal to the cash-strapped Agency chairman; and he charged Benny Applebaum and another colleague with looking into the matter.[173] It was not, however, a scheme that would appeal to Americans zealous for the good name of Zionism. Whatever their training, Ben-Gurion had "no doubt," he reassured his son, Amos, in the same year, that in the case of war between Jews and Arabs "all of the younger generation in Poland, Rumania, America and other countries will flock to us."[174]

After the failed St. James Conference, he returned to the army idea, informing Colonial Secretary Malcolm MacDonald that if Palestine Arabs could rely on reinforcements from Iraq, the Jews could summon their brethren from Poland and the United States.[175] Here was his notion of American Jewry as a counterweight to the Arab states in a military context. Ben-Gurion conceived of the Jewish Army in two ways: (1) chiefly a local and foreign legion for the defense of Palestine; (2) possibly a unit to fight in Europe like the exile armies of the captive nations, although this notion was more Weizmann's. One of the main reasons for his trip to North America in the fall of 1940 was to lay the groundwork for such a force. Unlike Jabotinsky, he rather quickly perceived the "great legal difficulties" regarding recruitment in America and the lack of "enthusiasm on the part of the Jewish public and leaders." But he, too, refused to abandon the idea altogether, although he did modulate his pitch.[176]

Eager though he was for the army, he refused to cooperate with Peter Bergson and "that gang" in the Revisionist Committee for a Jewish Army and the American Friends of a Jewish Palestine, who had declared independence even from Jabotinsky. In early 1942 he did meet Bergson; he conceded that "these fellows know how to do things," by which he meant duping unwitting gentiles into lending their names, but he remained convinced that "the cause . . . would only suffer from their championship."[177]

Once the United States had entered the war in December 1941, there was no longer any possibility of Americans serving in an army other than that of their own country. Ben-Gurion still hoped, however, that the United States government could convince the British to allow "the maximum mobilisation of the Jews in Palestine for the defense of the country."[178] Towards the end of the war, when Britain finally agreed to a Jewish brigade raised in Palestine, it was allowed to serve only in Europe. Not until Israel's War of

Independence did the kind of foreign legion envisioned by Ben-Gurion and Jabotinsky come into being: Maḥal, the unit of foreign volunteers in which many Americans fought, although they were forbidden to do so according to United States law.

8

Between 1940 and 1942 Ben-Gurion spent over a year on two long visits in the United States. These eventful years included the 1940 elections, the attack on Pearl Harbor, and the American entry into the war. He had resigned his post as Agency chairman because his Mapai colleagues and the Agency Executive had refused to back his anti-British militancy, but no effort was made to replace him, because no one could fill his shoes, and it was hoped that he would soon recant. In the United States he behaved as though still in office. The objectives of these extended visits were several: getting support and recruiting for the Jewish Army; securing backing for a Jewish state or "commonwealth"; firming up the will of American Jews, debilitated, he feared, by life in the Diaspora; unifying American Jewry behind the *yishuv*; and cementing his own alliances within Zionism both to further his policies and to challenge Weizmann's leadership.

During World War I it was Jabotinsky who had seen most clearly the potential of the United States and American Jewry as prods for moving the British in the direction of a pro-Zionist policy. During World War II, it was Ben-Gurion who best understood that the United States had become "the main arena" for Zionists' "efforts outside Palestine" and that, "aside from the *Yishuv* itself," the most "effective" weapon in the battle for Zionism was "the American Jewish community."[179] In mid-March, 1940, Menaḥem Ussishkin of the Jewish National Fund opened a meeting in Jerusalem of the Zionist Inner Actions Committee with a despairing lament that the Jews no longer had any allies on whom they could depend. Ben-Gurion responded with an equally heavy heart about the present, but with a different prognosis for the future and a program of action. He pointed out that there was strong disagreement with Britain's Palestine policies in Britain itself and certainly in the United States. The pro-English sentiments of American Jews had until now been fueled largely by appreciation for the Balfour Declaration. If England was changing course, it would lose American-Jewish support. And since other ethnic groups in the United States, most notably the Irish and the Germans, had a long and vocal tradition of opposing Britain, there could be no conflict between loyalty to America and hostility to Britain. It was an analysis based on familiarity with the American scene.[180]

His first trip, from early October 1940, to mid-January 1941, was devoted to reinforcing "the foundations . . . laid" earlier and to preparing "the ground for the next" visit.[181] Ben-Gurion worked at securing a loan for the Agency, and tried again without success to separate Zionist and general Jewish fund raising.[182] More important for the future, he took careful measure of Zionist leaders as well as the rank and file. The new ZOA president, Edward Kauffman, seemed to be "a very fair-minded Jew" whose only qualification for "head[ing] any movement" whatsoever, was that he "dressed well." Abba Hillel Silver, who chaired the United Palestine Appeal, by contrast, "wielded tremendous influence, and battled for his opinions with courage, obstinacy and enthusiasm." By 1945 Ben-Gurion would view the rabbi as a rival for movement leadership. He came to think of him as a typical American political "boss" and suspected him of "Revisionist-fascist" leanings.[183] Hadassah was too dovish for his taste; and the extent of its success was altogether "a surprise." But he spoke at their convention, explained his views, got a sympathetic hearing, and left with feelings of "the most faithful, honest friendship."[184]

In late November, after the sinking of the refugee ship, *Patria*, with the loss of over two hundred lives, Ben-Gurion shifted into high gear. He addressed the Geverkshaften Campaign convention, which adopted a strong anti-British resolution protesting the recent expulsions from Palestine of illegal immigrants. It was the opening salvo in his American campaign for "combative Zionism"; it found its target and heartened the gunner. Before the Poale Zion Central Committee, Ben-Gurion unveiled his "Program for War and Peace;" it resonated with them, and they became its promoters in the conservative Emergency Committee for Zionist Affairs, along with Rabbi Silver and the Mizraḥi leader, Rabbi Gold.[185] In January, he spoke to the ZOA Administrative Council in Philadelphia, masterfully equating his own militancy with genuine Americanism. The president had just delivered his "Arsenal of Democracy" speech, a landmark of the immediate prewar period that set out the role for the not-yet-belligerent United States in the months to come. Ben-Gurion knew "of no better Zionist message than the message of the President." Now, he said,

> it is for American Jewry to become the champion of the Jewish people as much as the whole of America is going to become the champion of democracy, freedom and justice for the whole world. . . . And just as Franklin Delano Roosevelt, and not Charles Lindbergh, . . . is expressing the true spirit of the United States, it is you . . . who are expressing the real spirit of American democracy and of Jewish democracy, which are one.[186]

When he departed for home some days later, he left behind him a more sympathetic and radicalized community than he had found three months before. "In spite of all the splits and quarrels and weaknesses," he reported to the Mapai Center, "fundamentally there was good Zionism in America."[187]

9

After making "no headway with the British Colonial Office" regarding the Jewish Army, or on selling his maximalism either to Mapai, the Agency Executive, or the WZO Inner Actions Committee, the increasingly well seasoned politician returned to the United States in November 1941. Not pique, but logic, motivated this trip, since his plan of action "was based primarily upon the propaganda possibilities and the power" of the United States.[188] Shortly before leaving, he penned the "Outlines of Zionist Policy," the clearest statement yet of his vision of the alliance and a very prescient document. "Whether America enters the war . . . or not," he wrote with extraordinary foresight,

> the center of gravity of our political work lies . . . in the U.S.A. At the end of the war America will play a major . . . role for the simple reason that she will be less exhausted than the other . . . fighting powers; the welfare of Europe will depend . . . on her economic assistance; and the safeguarding of peace . . . will more than ever depend on the active participation of America in the new arrangements after the war. But whatever the part of America may be in world affairs, in our own affairs she may certainly be decisive. In America it will be easier to win over public opinion for a radical and maximum solution of the Jewish problem in Palestine than it is in England. . . . America is much more disinterested in Palestine than England. . . . She has, moreover, a very large Jewish community . . . which is Palestine-minded and not without influence.

With American backing, he concluded, "all the present difficulties . . . will fade into insignificance. . . . American support for a Jewish State in Palestine is . . . the key to our success."[189]

For ten stormy months in the United States Ben-Gurion pursued the goal of a Jewish state and promoted his own leadership. He relied on tried tactics and new initiatives; he did not hesitate to step on toes; he made enemies and won friends, among the latter, a new romantic interest, Miriam Cohen (later, Taub), a secretary at the Emergency Committee who became his private secretary for a time. (Interestingly, Ben-Gurion's extra-curricular involvements mirror the evolution of his pursuit of international connections for the *yishuv*. The first was Rega Klapholz, a Viennese Jew; the second was Doris May, a British gentile who was Weizmann's secretary in London; the third was Cohen, an American. The relationships were entered into during prolonged absences from Palestine on the continent, in England, and then in the United States.)

These months marked the culmination of Ben-Gurion's orientation towards America and the fixing in stone of the *yishuv*-America alliance.

His stay began dramatically with an address to the Pan-American Zionist Conference in Baltimore during which he so stirred the audience that they rose to sing "HaTikva," the Zionist anthem, when he finished.[190] He was alert now, as always, to the importance of tending the organizational garden. He attempted "to breathe more life" into the Poale Zion and related well to its Habonim youth. He tried again fruitlessly to effect a merger with the Jewish Labor Committee but concluded, in the end, that the party would never fulfill a significant function "in the political life of the Zionist movement."[191] He cultivated Hadassah, especially its "outstanding" president, Judith Epstein, "a dedicated Zionist, wise and resolute." He spoke to the Emergency Committee whose members seemed to have "more penetrating political understanding than a year earlier." At Rabbi Silver's invitation he addressed a United Palestine Appeal meeting in Cleveland where he was introduced by the mayor. And he participated in a Madison Square Garden rally protesting Nazi atrocities.[192]

One of the major projects Ben-Gurion undertook during these months was an updated version of his old unity schemes. This time the aim was a Zionist-non-Zionist union. First he had to overcome his negative feelings about the non-Zionists in the Agency, once more proving he could shift ground for the sake of larger aims. For more than seven months he negotiated with Maurice Wertheim, president of the American Jewish Committee, in an attempt to find terms on which that small, but prominent and moneyed, group would be able to stand behind both the Jewish Army and a Jewish state. At the outset of these negotiations, he "was not sufficiently well-informed" about the Committee, but by early January 1942, he sensed its marginality.[193] He soldiered on nonetheless, partly because he had grown to like Wertheim, partly because the well-connected AJC had the potential for causing trouble with the American government, partly in the hope of acquiring an ally against Weizmann.

Wertheim, the brother-in-law of Secretary of the Treasury Henry Morgenthau Jr. and the son-in-law of the former ambassador to Turkey, had accompanied American aid shipments to the *yishuv* during World War I. Ben-Gurion knew this bit of history but had only a fuzzy notion of his partner's pedigree and thought him a self-made man.[194] Involvement with the Palestine relief missions had left Wertheim with a fond feeling for the National Home, unlike many of the other AJC leaders, who moved away from Zionism during World War II because they opposed Jewish nationalism in principle, or because they feared the double loyalty canard.[195] He and Ben-Gurion established a mutually warm and respectful relationship and arrived at what is known as the Cos Cob Formula (after Wertheim's place of residence) for endorsing a "Jewish commonwealth." Despite their patient labors, however, hard-liners in the Committee refused to accept the concordat. Wertheim proved unwilling to split the group; neither he nor Ben-Gurion could placate the anti-Zionists; and the project was abandoned to the disappointment of both. In 1943 the AJC agreed to join the American Jewish Conference, yet another attempt to achieve a unified American Jewry, but withdrew when the Conference appeared too openly Zionistic. Only after the war, with full awareness of the Holocaust, and with the gates to North America still not open wide, did the AJC and most other non-Zionists begin to cooperate in working towards an autonomous "Jewish commonwealth."[196]

Ben-Gurion's second major initiative, giving the Zionists a forceful voice in Washington, caused added friction with Weizmann and considerable conflict with the American Zionist establishment. From conversations with people in the know, he had learned that the State Department was pro-Arab (and antisemitic), and that FDR, although friendly, "did not consider the Zionist enterprise . . . serious." He—and Mrs. Roosevelt—tended to think of it as "a beautiful" ideal that could never solve the Jewish problem.[197] The "most important political task," then, was "to convince the proper persons that Palestine 'can do it.' " And who better than Ben-Gurion himself for that job?[198] He decided to take up residence in the capital as a representative of the Jewish Agency.

In meetings with the American ambassador, John G. Winant, before leaving London, he had begun the process of trying to obtain an audience with Roosevelt.[199] The purpose was twofold: to convert the president into an active ally and to demonstrate his own primacy in the Zionist movement by overshadowing Weizmann. Although most biographers interpret the anti-Weizmann maneuvering as having to do mostly with ambition and jealousy, one should note that Ben-Gurion strongly believed that his rival was a weak leader whose pro-British policies would bring about the destruction of the *yishuv*.

The Emergency Committee balked at his setting up shop in Washington, viewing it as an invasion of their turf. Weizmann thought the move a usurpation of his authority. Both were right, but Ben-Gurion did as he pleased, after consenting to the nominal supervision of the Committee and obtaining the agreement of the Agency Executive to fund him. He arranged for regular consultations with Justice Frankfurter, who was willing to provide introductions to sympathetic people in government. One such was David Niles, a Jewish presidential aide and a member of the White House inner circle, later a close advisor to President Truman who probably helped persuade Truman to recognize Israel.[200] In Washington, Ben-Gurion was lonely and isolated, except for Miriam Cohen and Frankfurter; and at first he was subjected to a whispering campaign by those who felt encroached upon.[201] But while there, and later in New York, he met with officials, including

Secretary Morgenthau ("friendly, superficial, rash"), Under Secretary of War John J. McCloy, Under Secretary of State Sumner Welles, Coordinator of Information William J. Donovan ("Wild Bill," later head of the OSS, the forerunner of the CIA), William C. Bullitt, a senior diplomat, and others. As well, he "met some people from newly created government agencies [who were] . . . without any special sympathies for Zionism, and even frankly pro-Arab, but all of them . . . honest and open-minded [and] . . . not hopeless when you give them all the facts."[202] He also sought to "enlist . . . the Zionist intelligentsia for the serious examination of political questions"; and Emanuel Neumann, then public relations director for the Emergency Committee, organized a session with a number of younger civil servants.[203]

Ben-Gurion felt drawn to "the progressive circles" around Vice-President Henry Wallace, but it was Weizmann who got to see Wallace a number of times. And it was Weizmann who received the coveted invitation to chat with Roosevelt. Ben-Gurion and Wallace finally met in Jerusalem in 1947, after which occasion the former vice-president praised the future prime minister and his associates for "creating a great state . . . [with] many of the advantages of both socialism and capitalism."[204] In the race to Washington, the Palestinian Laborite had been outrun by the scientist from London; but he had gotten to know some important and useful people; he had learned the workings of the American government; and he had laid the groundwork for capturing the political support the *yishuv* would need in its ultimate battle for independence. He had also gained increased respect for the power, efficiency, and independence of Americans.[205]

Ben-Gurion rightly regarded the Extraordinary or Pan-American Zionist Conference, usually known as the Biltmore Conference after the New York hotel where it took place, as "the most important" of his undertakings during these months.[206] David Shpiro places the Conference in the context of the renewed messianic spirit evident in America even before Pearl Harbor, as the president and others began to search for solutions to world problems in the hope of averting future cataclysms. The first Jewish group to begin postwar planning was the American Jewish Congress; others followed suit, including the Emergency Committee. The direct buildup for Biltmore began in late 1940 with the preparations for the National Conference on Palestine of the United Palestine Appeal, scheduled for January 1941, under the chairmanship of the militant Rabbi Silver. Silver called for "maximal Herzlian Zionism"; and the Conference endorsed large-scale postwar immigration and Jewish independence. The rabbi succeeded in politicizing not only the UPA but also the Keren HaYesod and Keren Kayemet fund drives. By mid-June 1941, the Emergency Committee, Mizraḥi, and the League for Labor Palestine had all accepted the establishment of an autonomous Jewish commonwealth as the immediate postwar Zionist goal. In September the

ZOA fell into line, and in November, Hadassah. The concept was Ben-Gurion's; the term was preferred by Americans to "state," and Ben-Gurion adopted it for tactical reasons.[207]

The "all-Zionist" meeting on May 9–11, 1942, marked the first occasion ever on which all American Zionist groups sat down together.[208] For a few days, at least, Ben-Gurion's long-sought goal of Zionist unity had been achieved. Present were more than five hundred delegates from across America and sixty-seven foreign visitors, including Ben-Gurion and Weizmann. Ben-Gurion reminded the gathering that after World War I the victorious powers had "resolved to undo the historic wrong to the Jewish people and recognize its right to restoration in its ancient homeland [even though] the position . . . was not yet as desperate and hopeless as it will be at the end of this war." With Jews threatened by Nazi Germany, "a leisurely pace" of settlement could no longer be tolerated. Open immigration, a Jewish army, and immediate independence were essential.[209] Weizmann used more temporizing language; and the Conference appeared at the time to belong largely to him as the titular head of the WZO. In fact, it was Ben-Gurion's maximalist vision—dependent on American support, since Britain had already determined to make Palestine an Arab state—that won the day and became the platform for Zionist action known as the Biltmore Program. Among others, Emanuel Neumann recognized that Biltmore had been "a decided success, thanks largely to the influence of Ben-Gurion."[210]

Following the Conference, Ben-Gurion was dismayed by Weizmann's efforts to downplay the Biltmore Program as "just a resolution like the hundred and one resolutions usually passed at great meetings" in the United States, which did no more than reiterate past positions.[211] In any case convinced that Weizmann's irresolute leadership was a calamity for Zionism, Ben-Gurion now turned resentful and thirsty for vengeance. After an ugly and fruitless attempt to discredit Weizmann at a private meeting of American Zionist leaders, he returned to Palestine. There, to the relief of his colleagues he resumed the Agency chairmanship, and to their consternation contemplated a campaign to depose Weizmann.[212]

In the event, such drastic action proved unnecessary, because Weizmann lost the day. Reporting to the Mapai Secretariat in October 1942, Ben-Gurion asserted that at the Biltmore, "the majority of the [American] Zionist movement had accepted . . . [the new program] wholeheartedly." Within a year, it had been formally adopted by most major American Jewish organizations, the deputies of which gathered in the summer of 1943 in a demonstration of solidarity at the American Jewish Conference representing over two-and-a-half million Jews.[213] "Zionist organizations in Palestine and other countries . . . now lagged behind the American[s] . . . in this 'messianic' enthusiasm," a startling reversal for Palestinians accustomed to thinking of their New World *confrères* as weak-kneed.[214]

The Americans enjoyed their new role. "It is certainly encouraging to Zionists here," wrote Carl Alpert, the managing editor of *The New Palestine*, to Ben-Gurion from Washington shortly after his return home, "to know of the high opinion which you hold of the movement in this country." Was it not "a rather new procedure," he inquired tongue-in-cheek, "for the *Yishuv* to take its political line and policy from America?" And, he persisted, was the *yishuv* at last coming to regard America as more than a source of funds?[215] Alpert, of course, was preaching to the converted; his interlocutor had maintained for some time that the primary Zionist role of America was not financial but political.

At this point, Ben-Gurion stood the notion of America as an instrument of Zionism on its head. As he had tried to do during the 1927 orange grove workers' strike, he used the American lever to move his fellow Palestinians. By the end of November 1942, the Inner Actions Committee of the WZO, as well as Mapai, Mizrahi, and the "A" General Zionists had subscribed to Biltmore, although the program contributed to a rift in Mapai that would not be healed for more than a quarter century. In early 1944, Biltmore received the endorsement of the HEC, by a slim majority.[216] The militant, American-oriented policy, rejected by his colleagues four years earlier, now became the policy of most groups in the *yishuv*. The destruction of European Jewry, the failure of the Allies even to attempt rescue, and the impotence of the *yishuv* under the heel of the British had done much to change people's minds. Proclaiming the policy in the United States and first gaining the acquiescence of American Jewry proved to be an effective way to convince the *yishuv* that it could be implemented.

10

In August 1945, just after the cessation of hostilities, a Zionist meeting was held in London to formulate the movement's agenda in the radically altered postwar world. Weizmann was still holding back on statehood, but events had passed him by. Immediate independence became the movement's expressed goal, one that only the United States and American Jewry could ensure. The British were unalterably opposed; the *yishuv*, with a population of some 600,000 could not defeat Britain alone; there were no potential allies other than America. In December of that year the United States Congress went on record in favor of an autonomous Jewish commonwealth in Palestine. There would yet be almost three years of struggle and suffering in the *yishuv* and lobbying in the United States before President Truman made the wish of Congress the policy of the government. But the way had been paved.

The outlines of Ben-Gurion's vision of a Jewish state backed by America began to emerge in the 1920s and early 1930s. The concept had grown out of his assessment of the political potential of the United States and of the character of the country and its people; it may also have been fed by rivalry with Weizmann, the Anglophile. Over the years, it was shaped by his experiences in the New World and by the course of European history. More than any other *yishuv* leader, Ben-Gurion understood the essence of America and its affinity to the *yishuv*. That insight enabled him, more than anyone else, to appeal to the American psyche.

In late 1946 Ben-Gurion was back in the United States arguing his case before the public, buying arms, and organizing Zionists. On Armistice Day, before the Hadassah convention in Boston, he affirmed his confidence in the United States. "The great American people, who twice . . . have fought world wars for freedom [and] for the rights of men and nations," would, he asserted, redeem the "pledge given to the most oppressed and suffering of peoples on earth . . . to reestablish in Palestine a free, democratic Jewish Commonwealth."[217] In a policy speech to the Knesset some years later, he defined the substance of the Israel-America relationship as he conceived it. There were and had always been practical, tactical reasons for an alliance with the United States; but neither that association—nor any other in the realm of international affairs—rested on an "identity of interests. America does not identify with us," nor we with her, he warned. Yet, the two countries had established "an ever-growing partnership." That partnership would last, he believed, because it was not based on common interests, but on a shared commitment to democratic government, to "liberty, . . . freedom of thought, freedom of speech, freedom of debate."[218] It was a noble vision.

CHAPTER

8

Afterword

ALL SIX *yishuv* leaders surveyed here developed extensive relationships with America between 1914 and 1945, each in a different way and in a particular sphere of interest. Three of them, Szold, Meir, and Ben-Gurion, embraced America with rather eager optimism, the other three, Jabotinsky, Bialik, and Katznelson, with resigned pessimism, all six with some reluctance and, at times, even distaste. For the second group, the United States remained a peripheral, if growing, concern; for the first, it became central to their activities during this period. All six contributed to a heightened awareness of the New World in the *yishuv*, the more so because of their prominence.

America had different meanings for each of them and multiple meanings for some. To Jabotinsky, it was the wild, protean frontier, while to Szold it was the birthplace of a civilized—and urban—impulse to reform society. To Bialik, it was first a barbarous wasteland, and later the home of a nascent Hebrew culture movement which might replace the world of Jewish eastern Europe irrevocably damaged during the First World War and the Russian Revolution. To Katznelson, it was the land of business and bluff and the *goldene medine*. Ben-Gurion came to appreciate it as the torchbearer of democracy and defender of the helpless. America was one of the fonts of Szold's values and habits, Golda's first political constituency, and the launching pad for Ben-Gurion's (and Weizmann's) Biltmore Program for achieving statehood.

Looking backward, the Americanization of Israel seems inevitable; and perhaps by the late 1940s it was, in no small part because of the six leaders studied here. Before 1948, however, it was not at all certain, despite the burgeoning links discussed here. The physical presence of Americans in

Palestine was negligible, Szold, Meir, Magnes, the Legionnaires, and others notwithstanding. Fewer *olim* (6396) came from the United States between 1919 and 1945 than from Greece (6931) or Turkey (6610), to say nothing of Yemen (14,454), Germany (39,131), or Poland (137,225).[1] The *yishuv* appeared then to have diplomatic alternatives; and the United States was not always the obvious close ally. At least until the mid-1930s, Britain was the main prop of the Zionist enterprise. Jabotinsky pursued the British option until his death in 1940; and Weizmann continued to do so throughout World War II. Some on the left clung to the hope that Soviet Russia would become the patron of the *yishuv*; and the miniscule Stern Group on the right tried its luck with the Axis powers.[2]

Other political and cultural models were not only available, they appeared to exert far more influence than did America in the interwar years and, except for the Soviet Union, to arouse much less ambivalence. The ideologies of the *yishuv* were grounded in such non-Jewish sources as the nationalisms of central and eastern Europe, European socialism, eastern European populism, and "right-wing radicalism rooted in [the] historical romanticism" of eastern and central Europe. A "wide but differential influence" was exerted by liberalism in its central European and English-speaking forms. The Jewish sources of Zionism were almost entirely eastern European.[3] Americans, as noted earlier on several occasions, tended to be regarded by the leaders of the *yishuv* as ideological lightweights for whom Zionism was a "sport." Some of the more serious American thinkers, Mordecai Kaplan, for example, considered Zionism a religious, more than a political, phenomenon, an approach generally uncongenial to secular Zionists.

There was no ready source of large-scale funding other than the United States, a fact which forced the *yishuv* to take account of that country but also engendered resentment and jealousy, the latter often sublimated. It would have been possible to opt for slower growth, a less advanced economy, or still greater sacrifice. There were voices in the *yishuv* that advocated such a course of action, particularly the philosopher of the labor movement and guardian of its virtue, Aaron David Gordon, who died in 1922. From outside, Brandeis cautioned that heavy reliance on American funds was "not good for . . . [the] health or self-respect" of Zionism.[4] But in those years, American money seemed relatively harmless. Believing in themselves as the vanguard of the nation, creating a state for all Jews everywhere, the men and women of the *yishuv* considered the support they received to be a contribution to the welfare of all Jews and remained largely uncorrupted by it. And in any case, the promise of American largesse remained greater than the reality; despite the dependency, there were never enough resources in these years to meet even the minimal needs of development and defense.

Afterword

"The easy money [that] rolls around like a plague"[5] was not available until long after Israel achieved independence.

None of the six leaders studied here intended to promote the Americanization of the *yishuv*, except, perhaps, Szold, who sought assiduously to introduce American methods and standards in the fields of health care, social work, and education. But she, no less than the others, would have recoiled at the idea of the future state as an American outpost. Jewish patriotism and negative attitudes towards Diaspora life—in some cases, towards the gentile world, in general—motivated the life's work of them all. An American Jewish journalist noted in 1929, that Americans, especially American Zionists, were "not liked in Palestine," because their Zionism was patronizing and philanthropic, because they did not meet their financial obligations, because they came to Palestine, if at all, with a return ticket in hand, and for many other reasons.[6] On the whole, as Thomas Friedman has observed, Israel's founders "consciously rejected" what they knew "of American culture . . . out of the feeling of pioneer moral superiority that prevailed" in the pre-state era.[7]

In 1951, Bernard Rosenblatt, a lifelong American Zionist, one of the leaders of the American Zion Commonwealth, and a former resident of the *yishuv* whose wife had been a founder of Hadassah with Szold, urged Ben-Gurion to pay closer attention to American constitutional and economic models. The prime minister replied that he knew there was "a great deal to learn from America" but that there was "a fundamental difference between learning and imitating. I am prepared," he said, "to learn endlessly the American technical know-how. The rest I will examine according to its merits. If it suits us—I will accept it, if it doesn't—I will not."[8] Such an approach, however, was more easily proclaimed than practiced.

According to Zionist theory, Israel was to be the center of the Jewish world, providing cultural models for the Diaspora periphery to imitate. Instead, as one highly respected Israeli literary and cultural critic noted in 1989, "the Jews of Israel have found a model for emulation in America, so much so that the attractive power of the American center sometimes outweighs that of the Israeli center."[9] Examples abound, from the large number of Israelis who have emigrated permanently to North America—more people, by far, than have moved in the opposite direction—to the weaponry of the army or the tendency of serious Israeli novelists to write with an eye towards American readers. One could point to everyday life, from the many hugely popular American television programs to the proliferation of American fast-food outlets. In 1994, a McDonald's restaurant was launched in Rishon LeZion, that veteran settlement of the Zionist *yishuv*, where in 1882 Yosef Feinberg issued his warning regarding assimilation in America, never imagining that the New World might extend its borders to Rishon. The arrival of the quintessential symbol of the plastic American culture so feared and scorned by the subjects of this study was greeted by patrons as the culmination of Zionist hopes. One diner summed up the feeling of the moment at the opening: "In the days after the *Shoah* [Holocaust], who would have thought a day like this would come? A beautiful place like this, like in Los Angeles, or . . . New York! This is America, but better. . . . Now we have it all."[10]

American technology necessarily came with cultural strings attached; serving a nutritious, healthful, American-style breakfast of oatmeal instead of herring, as Golda did at Merhavya, was not quite as inconsequential as it seemed at the time. Sometimes American money was spent to replicate America, as happened with Hadassah in the earlier years; donors might even stipulate such a requirement. American experts, as a matter of course, acted as conduits of the mores and attitudes of their country, as well as its technology. American freedoms and pluralism could not be emulated without adopting some of the trappings of American political culture. The close personal relationships that developed between *yishuv* leaders—and not only those of the first rank discussed here—and American Jews led to the inevitable exchange of ideas and habits and to ongoing and wide-ranging relationships. And perhaps, too, the brashness and lack of polish of America were more congenial to the rough-hewn Israeli temperament than the urbanity and refinement of Europe.

In the post-World War II era, the popular culture of America captured the imagination of much of the world, even of places far less intimately bound to the United States than Israel. Movies, music, shopping malls, and television have made it almost impossible to escape anywhere in the world the sort of "inflated, hollow" bluff and bluster that Bialik feared would "desecrate his . . . honor," when he visited the United States.[11] (A 1990s apartment complex in Tel Aviv, many of whose residents are of American origin, was named "Golda on the Park." It was not given a Hebrew name.) Large numbers of American tourists to Israel, who had to be made to feel at home because of their importance to the economy, created additional pressure to Americanize, as did the small, but increasing, number of American *olim*. After 1967 Israeli tourists to America brought home their perceptions of New World wonders.

During and before the Second World War, the alternative models and alliances of the interwar era disappeared or became discredited. Britain retreated altogether from its commitment to Zionism; the Soviet Union saw it as a regressive phenomenon at best; the Nazis hated the Jews of the *yishuv* no less than those closer to home; other European countries were too weakened by the war to offer much help even if they had wanted to do so. Itself a client of the Americans, Europe had little to offer in the postwar years

Afterword

except its traditions, which many Israelis viewed as having led to the Holocaust. Most countries outside Europe were either hostile to Zionism or disinclined to become involved. Polish Jewry was destroyed and Soviet Jewry imprisoned behind the Iron Curtain. That left American Jewry as the major community in the Diaspora, as well as the one with the most means and influence, and the United States as the only likely patron of the *yishuv*.

To a tiny country surrounded by hostile neighbors, for most of its history without any reliable allies other than the United States and heavily dependent on American funds, an American alliance has been all the more natural. During the first years of Israeli statehood one of the cardinal principles of Ben-Gurion's "global outlook" was "recognition of the special significance of winning the basic trust of America."[12] For a time after 1948, some Israeli leaders advocated neutrality in the Cold War; and a few on the left still favored the Russians. Not many, however, retained much sympathy for the communist bloc after the open manifestations of virulent antisemitism during the late Stalin years and the revelations of earlier horrors that came with his death. Following the outbreak of the Korean War in 1950, the United States let it be known that it would welcome a contingent of Israeli troops in the battle against the communist invaders. Ben-Gurion favored their dispatch and believed the cabinet had made a serious error in overruling him.[13] In the same year he lectured his Mapai Party colleagues on the historic differences between America and Russia, citing as a reference Alexis de Tocqueville's work of the 1830s, *Democracy in America*, a classic interpretation of America by a sympathetic European aristocrat.[14] Among the leaders of the *yishuv* and of Israel, Ben-Gurion was unique in his appreciation of the virtues of the political culture of the United States.

As the Cold War ground on, Israel became an American client. The Soviets backed the Arabs. After the Six-Day War Israel became "so dependent on the United States for military, economic and political support that . . . some Israelis wonder[ed] aloud whether . . . the Zionist revolution" would end with Israel's becoming "the 51st state."[15]

But Israel's infatuation with America has not been unrequited. Since 1948 American Jews have made Israel the center of their communal life, perhaps the only dogma of their civil religion. Over the years they and the United States government have been willing to an extraordinary extent to proffer financial aid and diplomatic support, their very willingness serving to tighten the bond between the two countries and to accelerate Americanization in Israel. The level of assistance and cooperation suggests "that Israel . . . touches something very deep in the American consciousness."[16]

It is, perhaps, not beside the point that Israel and the United States have in common a unique heritage as countries founded on ideas and ideals. And many of the ideas and ideals most cherished in both countries are shared, as Ben-Gurion perceived. In *Israel in the Mind of America*, Peter Grose puts it this way:

> Americans who are willing to look, see something of themselves in Israel. Even as they go their own way . . . Americans and Israelis are bonded together like no two other sovereign peoples. As the Judaic heritage flowed through the minds of America's early settlers and helped to shape the new American republic, so Israel restored and adopted the vision and the values of the American dream. Each, the United States and Israel, grafted the heritage of the other onto itself.[17]

Whatever their intentions, then, there can be no doubt that these six leaders and their compatriots oriented the *yishuv*, and eventually the state into which it developed, in the direction of America. As a group during the years discussed here, they advanced significantly the development of links in the fields of finance, labor, politics, literature, journalism, public health, education, social welfare, and business, in fact in most important fields of human endeavor except religion, which remained largely impervious to American influences. After 1948, those intricate, manifold connections served as the Israeli foundation of the America-Israel alliance, which developed and deepened under the tutelage of Ben-Gurion as prime minister and of Golda Meir as foreign minister and then prime minister, but no less under Israel's other leaders.

It is easy to point to problems associated with this relationship, especially those that highlight the ways in which Americanization has subverted aspects of the Zionist dream. But there can be no question that Israel's American connection has been of inestimable advantage to it, and, as others have pointed out, to the United States, as well. That American democratic institutions have served as models appears the more fortunate, when one compares Israel to other nations that have gained or regained their independence since 1945. Those sometimes derided values of efficiency and hard work, as well as American know-how, have served Israel well and allowed it to transcend its Third World setting. The significance of the political and economic assistance given by American Jews and of the diplomatic, military, and economic assistance given by the United States government is undeniable. Without such aid the *yishuv* might well have become a minority Jewish community in an Arab Palestine, as the white paper of 1939 intended, or else Israel might not have long survived its birth. It is, then, no exaggeration to say that the many American connections cultivated consciously and unconsciously, carefully and haphazardly, by the outstanding leaders of the *yishuv* in the interwar period had much to do with the "love of Zion" becoming the state of Israel.

Notes

Chapter 1

1. Report of Consul Selah Merrill, Jerusalem, to William F. Wharton, Assistant Secretary of State, Washington, D.C., 3 October 1891, quoted in Ruth Kark, "Annual Reports of United States Consuls in the Holy Land as a Source for the Study of 19th Century Eretz Israel," in *With Eyes Toward Zion*, vol. 2, ed. Moshe Davis (New York: Praeger, 1986), 170. See also, Moshe Maoz, "America and the Holy Land During the Ottoman Period," in *With Eyes Toward Zion*, [1], ed. Moshe Davis (New York: Arno, 1977), 78; Dov Ber Abramowitz et al., "Michtav el HaMa'arechet," *HaIvri*, 9 January 1918; and other sources.
2. Eliezer Ben-Yehuda, "Eretz Yisrael o America?" [Hebrew], *HaHavatzelet*, 5 October 1881, 203. On the generally negative approach of *HaHavatzelet* towards emigration to America, see Frank E. Manuel, *The Realities of American-Palestine Relations* (Washington, D.C.: Public Affairs Press, 1949), 57. All translations unless otherwise noted are the author's.
3. Arthur Ruppin, "The Survival of the Fittest," in *Three Decades in Palestine* (Jerusalem: Schocken, 1936), 68, originally published in German in *Der Jude* [1919?].
4. Yosef Feinberg, "Kruzo shel Yosef Feinberg, Igeret mei'eit Adat HaMoshava HaIvrit HaRishona [Rishon LeZion]" [Hebrew], in *Sefer HaTziyonut*, vol. 2, *Tkufat Hibat Tziyon*, ed. Shmuel Yavnieli (Tel Aviv: Mosad Bialik al yedei Dvir, 1944). The manifesto was originally published in German in *Der Israelit*, 13 September 1882. See also, Ya'akov Kellner, *Lema'an Tziyon: HaHitarvut HaKlal Yehudit BiMtzukat HaYishuv, 1869–1882* [Hebrew] (Jerusalem: Yad Yitzhak Ben-Zvi, 1976), 162–63.
5. Rabbi Avraham Yitzhak HaCohen Kook, Jaffa, letter to Rabbi Evtzinski, 29 Nisan 5672 [1912], in *Igrot HaRa'aya* [Hebrew], vol. 2 (Jerusalem: Mosad Ha-Rav Kook, 1961–65), 74, letter 421; Ya'akov Zerubavel, *Alei Hayim* [Hebrew], vol. 1 (Tel Aviv: Y. L. Peretz, 1960), 372. On Zerubavel's mission to America, see below, chapter 7.
6. One very useful example among many is Peter Grose, *Israel in the Mind of America* (New York: Knopf, 1983).

Notes to Chapter 1

7. Dan Horowitz and Moshe Lissak, *Origins of the Israeli Polity: Palestine under the Mandate*, trans. Charles Hoffman (Chicago: University of Chicago Press, 1978), 46–48, 89.
8. See Shmuel Katz, *Jabo—Biografia Shel Ze'ev Jabotinsky* [Hebrew], vol. 2 (Tel Aviv: Dvir, 1993), 658; Yaacov Shavit, *Jabotinsky and the Revisionist Movement, 1925–1948* (London: Frank Cass, 1988), 45ff.
9. A very useful introduction to the topic can be found in the two volumes of *With Eyes Toward Zion*, mentioned above, and in vol. 3, ed. Moshe Davis and Yehoshua Ben-Arieh (New York: Praeger, 1991).
10. The most complete survey of United States consular activity in Palestine before World War I is Ruth Kark, *American Consuls in the Holy Land, 1832–1914* (Jerusalem and Detroit: Magnes Press, Hebrew University, and Wayne State University Press, 1994). On Cresson, see, among other sources, Yaacov Shavit, " 'Land in the Deep Shadow of Wings' and the Redemption of Israel—A Millenarian Document from Jerusalem, 1847" [Hebrew], *Cathedra* 50 (December 1988): 99–105.
11. Manuel, *Realities*, 6, 76, 90–91, 102–04; Ron Bartur, "Episodes in the Relations of the American Consulate in Jerusalem with the Jewish Community in the 19th Century (1856–1906)" [Hebrew], *Cathedra* 5 (October 1977): 111ff; Mordechai Eliav, "Diplomatic Intervention Concerning Restrictions on Jewish Immigration and Purchase of Land at the End of the Nineteenth Century" [Hebrew], *Cathedra* 26 (December 1982): 121–27; Maoz, "Ottoman Period," in Davis, *With Eyes Toward Zion*, vol. 1, 69.
12. Kark, *American Consuls*, 201–30.
13. Yehoshua Ben-Arieh, "Nineteenth Century Hebrew Periodicals as a Source for America-Holy Land Studies," in Davis, *With Eyes Toward Zion*, vol. 2, 190–91.
14. Letter to Straus from the Jerusalem branch of B'nai B'rith, 1889, quoted in Mordecai Naor, "Oscar S. Straus, U.S. Minister to Turkey, Supporter of Aliya to *Eretz Yisrael*" [Hebrew], *Cathedra* 18 (January 1981): 147. Naor's article offers a good account of Straus's service in Constantinople. See also, Manuel, *Realities*, 59–63; Isaiah Friedman, *Germany, Turkey, and Zionism, 1897–1918* (Oxford: Clarendon, 1977), 44, 49; Jacob M. Landau and Mim Kemâl Öke, "Ottoman Perspectives on American Interests in the Holy Land," in Davis, *With Eyes Toward Zion*, vol. 2, 263; Rabbi Y. L. HaCohen Fishman [Maimon], "Rechusheinu BeEretz Yisrael" [Hebrew], *Halvri*, 5 January 1917, 11–12. For a full account of Straus's life, see Naomi W. Cohen, *A Dual Heritage: The Public Career of Oscar S. Straus* (Philadelphia: Jewish Publication Society, 1969).
15. *Diaries of Sir Moses and Lady Montefiore*, vol. 2, ed. L[ouis] Loewe (Chicago: Belford-Clarke, 1890), 301.
16. Quoted in *The American Hebrew*, 15 July 1898.
17. Shmuel Ettinger and Israel Bartal, "The First Aliyah: Ideological Roots and Practical Accomplishments," *The Jerusalem Cathedra*, 2 (1982): 208; Ben-Arieh, "Hebrew Periodicals," 183; Shmuel Rafa'eli (Rafa'elovitz), "Pe'ulot Ha-Notzrim LeYishuv HaAretz" [Hebrew], *Luah Eretz Yisrael* (5672 [1911–12]): 78–83. See also, V. D. Lipman, *Americans and the Holy Land through British Eyes: 1820–1917* (London: self-published, 1989), 119–49.

Notes to Chapter 1

18. Raḥel Yana'it Ben-Zvi, *Coming Home*, trans. David Harris and Julian Meltzer (New York: Herzl, 1964), 30. On Floyd, see Lipman, *British Eyes*, 145–50, 173.
19. Yana'it Ben-Zvi, *Coming Home*, 147. On the American Colony, see Bertha Spafford Vester's autobiography, *Our Jerusalem: An American Family in the Holy City, 1881–1949* (Garden City, N.Y.: Doubleday, 1950).
20. Manuel, *Realities*, 44–46; Eliyahu Ze'ev Halevi Lewin-Epstein, *Zichronotai* [Hebrew], vol. 1 (Tel Aviv: HaAḥim Lewin-Epstein VeShutafam, 5692 [1932]), 280–85.
21. Margalit Shilo, "On the Way to the Moshav: *Ha-Ikar Hatzair*, the 'American Group' in the Second *Aliyah*" [Hebrew], *Cathedra* 25 (September 1982): 87. See also, Zerubavel, *Alei Ḥayim*, vol. 1, 405.
22. On Yoffe and the Young Farmer group, see Yitzḥak Michaeli, "Reishitah shel Histadrut 'HeḤalutz' BeAmerica" [Hebrew], *Asufot* 6 (December 1989): 107–10; Margalit Shilo, *Nisyonot BeHityashvut: HaMisrad HaEretz Yisraeli, 1908–1914* [Hebrew] (Jerusalem: Yad Yitzḥak Ben-Zvi, 1988); Shilo, "On the Way," 79–98.
23. Sarah Chizick, diary, Milḥamia, Adar, 1915, quoted in *The Plough Woman: Memoirs of the Pioneer Women of Palestine*, ed. Rachel Katznelson Shazar, trans. Maurice Samuel (New York: Herzl Press in conjunction with the Pioneer Women, 1975), 186. (The first English edition of the book appeared in 1932.)
24. On the Achooza movement, see Yossi Katz, "The *Achuza* Projects in Eretz-Israel, 1908–1917" [Hebrew], *Cathedra* 22 (January 1982): 119–44; Bernard Sandler, "The American-Zionist Concept 'Achoozah' and its [sic] Realization in Eretz Israel, 1908–1934" [Hebrew], *Cathedra* 17 (October 1980): 165–82; Sandler, "Efforts and Achievements," 49–64; Shilo, *Nisyonot BeHityashvut*, 99–106, 172–76; Evyatar Friesel, *HaTnua HaTziyonit BeArtzot HaBrit Be-Shanim, 1897–1914* [Hebrew] ([Tel Aviv]: Universitat Tel Aviv and HaKibbutz HaMeuchad, 5730 [1970]), 176; Louis Lipsky, "Early Days of American Zionism, 1897–1929," *Palestine Year Book* 2 (1945–46): 453–54.

    On Merḥavya and the AZC, see below, chapter 7; on Herzliya and the AZC, see below, chapter 6.
25. Landau and Öke, "Ottoman Perspectives," 282, 268; Maoz, "Ottoman Period," 69.
26. Alexander Aaronsohn, *With the Turks in Palestine* (Boston and New York: Houghton, Mifflin, 1916), 3–4; Aaronsohn, "Saïfna Ahmar, Ya Sultan! (Our Swords Are Red, O Sultan)," *Atlantic Monthly*, July 1916, 1–12, and August 1916, 188–96.
27. Louis Marshall, New York, letter to Adolph Lewisohn, New York, 20 November 1909, in *Louis Marshall, Champion of Liberty—Selected Papers and Addresses*, vol 1., ed. Charles Reznikoff (Philadelphia: Jewish Publication Society, 1957), 705; "Aaronsohn's Experiment Station," editorial, *The Maccabaean*, October, 1910; Carol Bosworth Kutscher, "The Early Years of Hadassah," Ph.D. dissertation, Department of Near Eastern and Judaic Studies, Brandeis University, 1976, 73; Saul Katz, "Aharon Aharonson—The Beginnings of Agricultural Science and Research in Eretz Israel" [Hebrew], *Cathedra* 3 (February 1977): 3–29; Allon

Notes to Chapter 1

Gal, *Brandeis of Boston* (Cambridge, Mass.: Harvard University Press, 1980), 178.
28. Jacob Schiff, New York, letter to Julius Rosenwald, Chicago, 27 January 1913, in *Jacob H. Schiff: His Life and Letters*, ed. Cyrus Adler, vol. 2 (Garden City, N.Y.: Doubleday, Doran, 1928), 176–77.
29. Shilo, "On the Way to the Moshav," 84; Friesel, *HaTnua HaTziyonit*, 176.
30. Louis D. Brandeis, Washington, D.C., letter to his brother, Alfred Brandeis, n.p., 7 January 1912, in *Letters of Louis D. Brandeis*, vol. 2 (1907–12), ed. Melvin I. Urofsky and David W. Levy (Albany: State University of New York Press, 1972), 537.
31. See Ben Halpern, "Brandeis' Way to Zionism," *Midstream* 17 (October 1971): 13; and Gal, *Brandeis of Boston*, 178–80.
32. Dr. Shneur Zalman Abramov offered some very helpful comments on Aaronsohn's significance for America-Palestine relations in a personal interview in Jerusalem, 28 December 1990.
33. Kellner, *Lema'an Tziyon*, 11–12.
34. Zvi Shilony, "Changes in the Jewish Leadership of Jerusalem During World War I," [Hebrew], *Cathedra* 35 (April 1985): passim; Nathan Efrati, "The Relationship Between American Jewry and the *Yishuv* in the 1890s" [Hebrew], *Cathedra* 55 (March 1990): 64–65; Manuel, *Realities*, 34–35.
35. Kark, *American Consuls*, 226–30; Efrati, "American Jewry and the *Yishuv*," 81–84; Manuel, *Realities*, 96.
36. Kellner, *Lema'an Tziyon*, 98–99; Ya'acov Kellner, *HaAliyot HaRishonot—Mitos u-Metziut* [Hebrew] (Jerusalem: HaUniversita HaIvrit Birushalayim, Beit HaSefer LaAvoda Sotzialit Al Shem Paul Baerwald, 1982), 46–49; Efrati, "American Jewry and the *Yishuv*," 68–69, 76–79; Shilony, "Jewish Leadership of Jerusalem," 62; and many other sources.
37. Quoted in Friedman, *Germany, Turkey, and Zionism*, 194.
38. Mrs. B. F. [Gertrude] Rosenblatt, Haifa, letter to Henrietta Szold, Jerusalem, 10 August 1934, with a copy of an entry from the author's diary dated 3 December 1912, recording Mrs. Henry Morgentau's gift (sic). The letter is in CZA, File A125/18.
39. Mordecai Ben-Hillel HaCohen, *Milhemet HaAmim (Yoman)* [Hebrew], vol. 2 (Jerusalem and Tel Aviv: "Mizpeh," 5689 [1929]), 69–70.
40. Abraham Elmaleh, *Eretz Yisrael VeSuriya Bimei Milhemet Olam* [Hebrew], vol. 1 (Jerusalem: By the author, 5688 [1928]), 176. See also, 67–69; "Eretz Yisrael veAmerica" and "Hashanim," both in Hebrew in *Luah Eretz Yisrael*, (1914–15), 265–82, and (5675–76 [1915–16]), 252–53, respectively; and Manuel, *Realities*, 117.
41. Telegram, 27 August 1914, from Secretary of State Bryan to Jacob H. Schiff, in *Schiff, Life and Letters*, vol. 2, 277.
42. Maurice Wertheim, "Report of Maurice Wertheim on the Condition of the Jews of Palestine," 21 October 1914, typescript, in CZA, File A125/289.
43. Elmaleh, *Bimei Milhemet Olam*, vol. 2, 194–95.
44. HaCohen, *Milhemet HaAmim*, vol. 1, (Jerusalem and Tel Aviv: "Mizpeh," 5629 [1929]), diary entry for 12 Shvat [1915], 72.

Notes to Chapter 1

45. Ibid., diary entry for 24 Nisan [1915], 94–95; Arthur Ruppin, journal entry, 15 February 1915, in *Memoirs, Diaries, Letters*, ed. Alex Bein, trans. Karen Gershon (London and Jerusalem: Weidenfeld and Nicolson, 1971), 155; Aaronsohn, *With the Turks*, 47–48; Manuel, *Realities*, 124–47.
46. M[enahem] Sheinkin, *Erets Yisroel in Milkhomo Tsayt* [Yiddish] (New York: Federation of American Zionists, 1917), 46; Joseph Rappaport, "Zionism as a Factor in Allied-Central Power Controversy (1914–1918)," in *Early History of American Zionism*, ed. Isidore S. Meyer (New York: American Jewish Historical Society and Theodor Herzl Foundation, 1958), 308.
47. Alexander Aaronsohn, *With the Turks*, 63–64. See also, 85. Aaronsohn was referring specifically to the ship on which he fled from Beirut harbor. His comments, however, reflect the feelings of many other observers.
48. Aaronsohn, "Saïfna Ahmar," 194.
49. Rabbi Y. L. HaCohen Fishman (Maimon), "MeiHatam LeHacha" [Hebrew], *Halvri*, 7 January 1916; HaCohen, *Milhemet HaAmim*, 3 (Jerusalem: Dfus "HaSefer," 5690 [1930]), entry for 21 Teveth [1917], 28–29; Mordecai Naor, "HaRakevet HaYamit SheHitzila Et HaYishuv BeEretz Yisrael BeEit Milhemet HaOlam HaRishona," *Ma'ariv*, 14 April 1976.
50. Elmaleh, *Bimei Milhemet Olam*, vol. 1, 176; "Eretz Yisrael VeAmerica," *Luah Eretz Yisrael* (1914–15). On Rosenwald's pledge, see Alpheus T. Mason, *Brandeis: A Free Man's Life* (New York: Viking, 1946), 447.
51. M[eir] Dizengoff, *Im Tel Aviv BaGola* (Tel Aviv: n.p., 5690 [1931]), 46.
52. Yohanan, "Shana Shel Mashbeir" [Hebrew], *HaPo'el HaTza'ir*, 23 July 1915, 6–7. Other articles praising American charitable endeavors and critical of specifics can be found in *HaPo'el HaTza'ir* for the entire period of the war and in *HaAhdut* for the months before it was closed by the authorities in 1915.
53. Manuel, *Realities*, 134.
54. Vladimir Jabotinsky, London, letter to [Shimon Bernstein], Copenhagen, 4 May 1915, summarized in *Igrot Ze'ev Jabotinsky, Reshima U-Mafteah*, vol. 1 (1901–24) [Hebrew] (Tel Aviv: Chaim Weizmann Center for the Research of Zionism of Tel Aviv University and the Jabotinsky Institute, 5732 [1972]), 39. See also, HaCohen, *Milhemet HaAmim*, vol. 1, entries for 9, 29 Kislev [1914], 37, 52–53; Manuel, *Realities*, 120, 154; Naomi W. Cohen, *Not Free to Desist* (Philadelphia: Jewish Publication Society, 1972), 86–87; Shmuel Katz, *Jabo*, vol. 1, 128.
55. Morgenthau quoted in Ruppin, *Memoirs, Diaries, Letters*, 151.
56. HaCohen, *Milhemet HaAmim*, vol. 2, entry for 28 Elul [1916], 143–45; Joseph Adler, "The Morgenthau Mission of 1917," *Herzl Year Book* 5 (1963): 249–82; Friedman, *Germany, Turkey, and Zionism*, 275; Manuel, *Realities*, 156–58.
57. Ruppin, *Memoirs, Diaries, Letters*, 158–59. See also, Gideon Biger, "The American Consulate of Jerusalem and the 1920–1921 Disturbances" [Hebrew], *Cathedra* 49 (September 1988): 134–35; Manuel, *Realities*, 238.
58. Alexander Aaronsohn, *With the Turks*, 47.
59. HaCohen, *Milhemet HaAmim*, vol. 2, entry for 4 Iyyar [1916], 80–81; David Lior of Tel Aviv, quoted in *Anshei HaAliya HaShniya* [Hebrew], ed. Ya'akov

Notes to Chapter 2

Sharett and Naḥman Tamir, vol. 2 (N.p., 1970–71), 334; Biger, "American Consulate," 134–35; Stuart E. Knee, *The Concept of Zionist Dissent in the American Mind, 1917–1941* (New York: Robert Speller & Sons, 1979), 185–93.

60. HaCohen, *Milḥemet HaAmim*, vol. 1, entry for 10 Nisan [1915], 91–92; Ruppin, *Memoirs, Diaries, Letters*, 159; Naor, "HaRakevet haYamit."
61. "Ba'al haMilon" [Hebrew], *Halvri*, 12 May 1916; Louis D. Brandeis, Washington, D.C., letter to Julian William Mack, n.p., 11 January 1919, in *Brandeis Letters*, vol. 4, 375.
62. Yitzḥak Ben-Zvi, *Poale Zion BaAliyah HaShniya* [Hebrew] (Tel Aviv: Mifleget Po'alei Eretz Yisrael Velḥud Olami Poale Zion [Z. S.] Hitachduth, 1950), 180.
63. Geula Bat-Yehuda [Rafael], *HaRav Maimon BeDorotav* [Hebrew] (Jerusalem: Mosad HaRav Kook, 1979), 223.
64. Aaron Aaronsohn, *Yoman Aharon Aharonson* [Hebrew], ed. Yoram Efrati (Tel Aviv: Sfarim Karni, 1970), entries for 17, 21 November and 11 May 1917, 357–58, 269.
65. Ben-Zvi, *BaAliyah HaShniya*, 184, 186.
66. Rabbi Y. L. HaCohen Fishman, "HaTziyonut HaAmerika'it" [Hebrew], *Halvri*, 9 February 1917; Menaḥem Sheinkin, "Ḥadash veYashan" [Hebrew], in *Kitvei Menaḥem Sheinkin*, ed. A. Ḥermoni (Tel Aviv: Miriam Sheinkin, n.d.), 5.
67. Menaḥem Sheinkin, "Koḥot Yetzira" [Hebrew], *Halvri*, 2 February 1917.
68. Yitzḥak Ben-Zvi, "'HeḤalutz' VeHaHitnadvut LaGdud Halvri BeArtzot HaBrit" [Hebrew], in *Sefer HaAliyah HaShlishit*, ed. Yehuda Erez (Tel Aviv: Am Oved, 1964), 205.
69. Rivka Aaronsohn, on board the *California Limited*, letter to Henrietta Szold, 1 September 1917, in CZA, File A125/325; Yitzḥak Ben-Zvi, New York, letter to Raḥel Yana'it, n.p., 19 March 1918, in BZA, File 1/1/2/13.

Chapter 2

1. Louis Lipsky, *A Gallery of Zionist Profiles* (New York: Farrar Straus and Cudahy, 1956), 102.
2. Vladimir Jabotinsky, "HaEmet" [Hebrew], in *Ktavim* vol. 13 (Jerusalem: Eri Jabotinsky, 1954), 200; id., "Anaḥnu HaBurganim" [Hebrew], in *HaRevisionism HaTziyoni BeHitpatḥuto*, ed. Yosef Nedava (Tel Aviv: Jabotinsky Institute, 1985), 211, originally published in Russian, *Rasswiet*, 17 April 1927.
3. Irma Lindheim, *Parallel Quest* (New York: Thomas Yoseloff, 1962), 377; Jabotinsky, "A Crucible" [Russian], *Russkie vedomosti*, 15 April 1916, translated for me by Prof. Richard Pope; id., *Avtobiografia* [Hebrew], vol. 1 of *Ktavim* (Jerusalem: Eri Jabotinsky, 5707 [1947]), 169.
4. Compare Michael Brown, "A Paradoxical Relationship—American Jews and Zionism," in *An American Historian, Essays to Honor Selig Adler*, ed. Milton Plesur (Buffalo: State University of New York at Buffalo, 1980), 81–97.
5. Jabotinsky, "We Americans" [Hebrew], Haifa *HaZafon*, 4 June 1928, originally published in Yiddish ("Mir Amerikaner") in the New York *Morgn Zhurnal*, 7 May 1926; "The Land of Strong Yearnings" [Hebrew], *HaYarden*, 22 March

Notes to Chapter 2

1935, also published in Yiddish ("Dos Land fun Gigantisher Benkshaft") in the New York *Morgn Zhurnal*, 22 March 1935; and *Avtobiografia*, 21.
6. "Benkshaft," translated for me by Jack Chodoroff.
7. "Mir Amerikaner," translated for me by Jacob Goldfein.
8. "Benkshaft"; Joseph B. Schechtman, *Fighter and Prophet* (New York and London: Thomas Yoseloff, 1961), 588–94.
9. "Mir Amerikaner."
10. Jabotinsky, "HaEmet," 203. Stowe's work was one of the only novels in Ben Gurion's library. Golda Meir (*My Life* [London: Weidenfeld and Nicholson, 1975], 23) and others all mention being influenced by it in their youth.
11. Jabotinsky, "HaEmet," 195–202.
12. Jabotinsky, "Homo homini lupus" [Hebrew], in *Ktavim*, vol. 9 (Jerusalem: Eri Jabotinsky, 5710 [1950]), 256, originally published in Russian in 1910.
13. Ibid., 255.
14. *New York Times*, 5 July 1910. See also 7 July 1910.
15. Jabotinsky, "lupus," 258, 260. See also, Raphaella Bilski Ben-Hur, *Kol Yahid Hu Melech: HaMahshava HaHevratit Shel Ze'ev Jabotinsky* [Hebrew] (Tel Aviv: Dvir, 1988), 29.
16. "Virginia," in *Ktavim*, vol. 6 (Jerusalem: Eri Jabotinsky, 5709 [1949]), 65–81.
17. Schechtman, *Fighter*, 107. For a similar evaluation of Poe by a socialist Zionist contemporary, see M. A., "Unhealthy Literature" [Hebrew], *HaPo'el HaTza'ir*, 18 July 1913.
18. Jabotinsky, "Crucible"; "HaEmet," 195; "lupus," 257.
19. Jabotinsky, "Crucible." In *Kol Yahid*, Ben-Hur claims that "the key to . . . Jabotinsky's thought is the assumption that the individual is the supreme value, followed by the nation" (27).
20. Compare Joseph B. Schechtman, *Rebel and Statesman* (New York: Thomas Yoseloff, 1956), 231–60; Melvin I. Urofsky, *American Zionism from Herzl to the Holocaust* (New York: Anchor, Doubleday, 1976), 183–230; Yosef Gorny, "Zionist Voluntarism in the Political Struggle: 1939–1948," *Jewish Political Studies Review* 2 (Spring 1990): 67–104.

Urofsky writes about the role of America with regard to the Balfour Declaration, but not the Legion. Schechtman essentially ignores this aspect of the Legion. Gorny notes that Jabotinsky "fathered the policy of Zionist pressure" but dates the tactic to a later period. (Schechtman's two books must be read as the works of a disciple.)

21. Isaiah Friedman, *Germany, Turkey, and Zionism, 1897–1918* (Oxford: Clarendon, 1977), 18; Frank E. Manuel, *The Realities of American-Palestine Relations* (Washington, D.C.: Public Affairs Press, 1949), 20, 139–40, 164; Joseph Rappaport, "Zionism as a Factor in Allied-Central Power Controversy (1914–1918)," in *Early History of American Zionism*, ed. Isidore S. Meyer (New York: American Jewish Historical Society and Theodor Herzl Foundation, 1958), 304–05.
22. Jabotinsky, London, letter to Mr. [C. P.] Scott [London], 7 December 1915, in MJ, File 5/2alef.

23. Jabotinsky, London, letter to Viscount Cecil, London, 22 December 1915, PRO, File F.O. 371/2835.
24. Jabotinsky, London, letter to Rt. Hon. C. F. G. Masterman, London, 26 January 1916, PRO, File F.O. 371/2835. See also, his letter to Lord Newton, London, 15 August 1916, summarized in *Igrot Jabotinsky, Reshima U-Mafteah* [Hebrew], vol. 1, 1901–1924 (Tel Aviv: Chaim Weizmann Center for the Research of Zionism of Tel Aviv University and the Jabotinsky Institute, 5732 [1972]), vol. 2 in manuscript in MJ; Shmuel [Samuel] Katz, *Jabo—Biografia shel Ze'ev Jabotinsky* [Hebrew], vol. 1 (Tel Aviv: Dvir, 1993), 136–41, 208–09. Katz's book is an informative, but highly partisan, account that must be used judiciously.
25. See, for example, *The Maccabean*, November-December 1914, May 1915; David Ben-Gurion, Yitzhak Ben-Zvi, and Nahum Slousch, New York, letter to Vladimir Jabotinsky, [London], 23 November 1918, WAR, File 1918; Menahem Sheinkin, "The Jewish Legion" [Hebrew], originally published in Yiddish as a propaganda pamphlet of the Zionist Organization of America in 1918, in *Kitvei Menahem Sheinkin*, ed. A. Hermoni (Tel Aviv: Miriam Sheinkin, n.d.); Schechtman, *Rebel*, 211–12; Friedman, *Germany*, 244. On Szold, see below, Ch. 5, 219–20, 225–27.
26. Quoted in Katz, *Jabo*, vol. 2, 751.
27. Jabotinsky, London, draft letter to [Herbert Samuel], London, 28 June 1916, MJ, File 6/2/1alef; Schechtman, *Rebel*, 231. Wise altered his stance when war was declared.
28. Jabotinsky, London, letter to Rt. Hon. David Lloyd George, P. M., London, 3 April 1917, PRO, File W.O. 32/1539.
29. Jabotinsky, London, letter to Hon. Sir George Perley, K. C., M. C., [London], 1 November 1917, MJ, File 7/2taf.
30. Manuel, *Realities*, 139–40, 164.
31. See, for example, letter by Joseph Trumpeldor, London, on behalf of W. Jabotinsky, to Rt. Hon. P. M. David Lloyd George, 3 November 1917, PRO, File W.O. 32/1539, printed in Hebrew translation in Jabotinsky, *Ktavim*, vol. 18 (Jerusalem: Eri Jabotinsky, 5718 [1958]), 203–04; Jabotinsky, London, letter to Rt. Hon. D. Lloyd George, M. P., London, 29 April 1917, PRO, File W.O. 32/1539; and letters from London, 25 October 1917, to Sir Mark Sykes, Lord Robert Cecil, Leopold Amery, William Ormsby-Gore, Sir Ronald Graham, Philip Kerr, Henry Wickham-Steed, Major D. Dorsett, PRO, File W.O. 39/152; id., *The Story of the Jewish Legion*, trans. Samuel Katz (New York: Bernard Ackerman, 1945), 65–66; Katz, *Jabo*, vol. 1, 114–15.
32. Yitzhak Ben-Zvi, *Poale Zion BaAliyah HaShniyyah* [Hebrew] (Tel Aviv: Mifleget Po'alei Eretz Yisrael velhud Olami Poale Zion (Z. S.) Hitachduth, 1950), 195; Jabotinsky, *Legion*, 21, 151, 164; Zachariah Kay, *Canada and Palestine* (Jerusalem: Israel Universities Press, 1978), 47.
33. See Jabotinsky, letters, summarized in *Igrot Jabotinsky*, to Nahum Sokolow, 15 January 1919 (33/40), to Akiva Ettinger, 1 April 1919 (38/1056) and 19 April 1919 (38/1057), to Zionist Commission, 12 March 1919 (43), and to Harry

Notes to Chapter 2

Friedenwald, 18 May 1919 (38/1059). See also, Jabotinsky, "Kol Korei," [Hebrew] Adar I, 5679 [1919]; and letter, Ludd, to Dr. [David] Eder, 7 July 1919, CZA, File L4/158.

34. G[ershon] A[gronsky, later, Agron, the mayor of Jerusalem], Beirut, letter to Robert Szold, Zionist Commission, Jerusalem, 7 July 1919, in CZA. File A209/12; D. Yaffe, "Demobilization of the Volunteers" [Hebrew], *HaPo'el HaTza'ir* 13 (27 October 1919); Yaffe, "With the Legions" [Hebrew], *HaPo'el HaTza'ir* 13 (5 December 1919); Y.A.y, "From the Legion" [Hebrew], *HaPo'el HaTza'ir* 13 (20 August 1920); Bernard T. Sandler, "The Jews of America and the Resettlement of Palestine, 1908–1934: Efforts and Achievements," Ph.D. dissertation, Bar Ilan University, April 1978, 171–75; "Legion Volunteers From the United States Who Chose Demobilization in Palestine," *Bulletin of the Veterans of the Jewish Legion* 1 (May 1976); Ben-Zvi, *Poale Zion*, 196–97; Shimon Rubinstein, "Efforts to Settle Demobilized Soldiers of the Jewish Legion on Government Lands (1919–1923)" [Hebrew], *HaUmah* 43 (Iyyar, 5735 [1975]).

    There is some evidence that the Zionist Commission and even Jabotinsky himself felt the demobilized soldiers should return to America and allow the few job opportunities in Palestine to be taken by Polish and Russian Jews fleeing their countries. (Yaffe, "Demobilization"; and *Anshei HaAliyah HaShniyah*, vol. 2, ed. Ya'acov Sharett and Naḥman Tamir [Hebrew] [n.p., 1972], 335.) In *A Peace to End All Peace* (New York: Avon, 1990), 386, David Fromkin points out that British troops were rapidly demobilized everywhere, because of the virtual bankruptcy of the government and the eagerness of the men to return to civilian life.

35. N.[aḥum] T.[wersky], "The Question of Our Existence" [Hebrew], *HaPo'el HaTza'ir* 12 (29 August 1919).

36. Ibid.

37. Yaffe, "Legion"; Y.L. n, "Americanism" [Hebrew], *HaPo'el HaTza'ir* 12 (27 Tammuz 1919); Ze'ev Tzaḥor, "David Ben-Gurion's Attitude Toward the Diaspora," *Judaism* 32 (Winter 1983): 13.

38. Jabotinsky, [Ludd], letter to [Robert] Szold, [Jerusalem], 27 June 1919, MJ, File 38/1064. See also, Schechtman, *Rebel*, 275–79.

39. Ibid; Jabotinsky, "On the Mutinies in the Jewish Legion" [Hebrew], speech before the seventh meeting of the Zionist Commission, Jaffa, 15–16 Elul 5679 [September 1919], in *Ktavim*, vol. 4 (Jerusalem: Eri Jabotinsky, 5707 [1947]), 128. See also, Jabotinsky, letters to B.[ezalel] Yaffe, Tel Aviv, 5 July 1919, MJ, File number missing, and to Dr. [David] Eder, [Jerusalem], 17 August 1919, CZA, File L3; id., *Avtobiografia*, 291, 195–96; Schechtman, *Rebel*, 277.

40. Jabotinsky, *Legion*, 21, 164–65; id., *Avtobiografia*, 287–89; id., "Megilat HaGdud" [Hebrew], *Do'ar HaYom*, 17 February 1929. Compare also, Anita Shapira, *Berl*, vol. 1 [Hebrew] (Tel Aviv: Sifriyat Ofakim—Am Oved, 1980), 136; Yitzḥak Ben-Zvi, " 'HeḤalutz' VeHaHitnadvut LaGdud Halvri BeArtzot HaBrit" [Hebrew], in *Sefer HaAliyah HaShlishit*, ed. Yehuda Erez (Tel Aviv: n.p., 1964), 207.

41. *Who's Who in Canadian Jewry*, ed. Eli Gottesman (Montreal: Central Rabbini-

cal Seminary of Canada, 1965), 44; Sharett and Tamir, *Aliyah*, vol. 2, 335; Jabotinsky, New York, letter to Israel Trivus, 9 February 1922, in *Ktavim*, vol. 18, 167–70; Michael Brown, "A Case of Limited Vision: Jabotinsky on Canada and the United States," *Canadian Jewish Studies* 1 (1993): 1–25.
42. Jabotinsky, draft cable, to Judge [Louis] Brandeis, Washington, [1917], MJ, File 7/2/1alef; id., letters, Tel Aviv, to Mr. Edlin, n.p., 2 March 1919, MJ, File 38/1054; [Ludd], to [Robert] Szold, [Jerusalem], 16 June 1919 and 27 May 1919, CZA, File L3; draft letter, [Jerusalem], to ??, 1919, MJ, File 9/2/11alef; untitled flyer [Hebrew], Acco, [5 May 1920], CZA, File A 13/17.
43. Manuel, *Realities*, 209; Schechtman, *Rebel*, 298; George L. Berlin, "The Brandeis-Weizmann Dispute," *American Jewish Historical Quarterly* 60 (September 1970): 47; Katz, *Jabo*, vol. 1, 283, 332–33. Katz claims that Brandeis was sufficiently influenced by Jabotinsky's arguments to raise the issue of antisemitism in the ranks with Balfour, when he met him in Paris on the way home (vol. 1, 334).
44. Deborah Lipstadt, "The Zionist Career of Louis Lipsky, 1900–1921," Ph.D. dissertation, Department of Near Eastern and Judaic Studies, Brandeis University, Waltham, Massachusetts, May 1976, 281–82; Katz, *Jabo*, vol. 1, 406–07, vol. 2, 669.

    In "The American Consulate of Jerusalem and the 1920–1921 Disturbances" [Hebrew], *Cathedra* 49 (September 1988): 136–41, Gideon Biger asserts convincingly that pro-Arab, anti-Jewish officials in the State Department delayed communications between the Zionist Commission and the ZOA and cast doubts on the veracity of reports from the *yishuv*.
45. Z. Jabotinsky, "The Ideal and the Real" [Hebrew], *HaAretz*, 14 December 1919. For an opposing view, see Dr. A. Boehm, "The Ideal in Practice" [Hebrew], *HaPo'el HaTza'ir* 13 (2 January 1920). On the AZMU, see below, Ch. 4, 105; Ch. 5, 140, 145–47, 154–55.
46. A. T. [Jabotinsky], "The Refusal of the American Senate" [Hebrew], *Hadshot HaAretz*, 30 November 1919.
47. Jabotinsky, "On the Mutinies," 135–36; id., "Yearnings;" Schechtman, *Rebel*, 320–21, 363.
48. "The Refusal of the American Senate."
49. Jabotinsky, New York, letter to Israel Trivus, 9 February 1922, in *Ktavim*, vol. 18, 167–70; Schechtman, *Rebel*, 370.
50. Jabotinsky, aboard the RMS *Acquitainia*, letter to mother, Eva Jabotinsky, Jerusalem, 11 November 1921, MJ, File 2/37/2/1gimel. Unless otherwise noted, Jabotinsky's letters in Russian cited herein were translated for me by Yehuda Ben-Ari.
51. Jabotinsky, Kansas City, Mo., confidential letter to Directors, Keren Hayesod Bureau, London, 15 January 1922, WAR, File 1922.
52. Press release of the Keren HaYesod, New York, 18 November [1921], in CZA, File A209/46.
53. *HaDo'ar*, 24 November 1921, 13, 14 January 1922, 28 March 1922. The pages of the then daily *HaDo'ar* from November 1921 to May 1922 give a rather full account of Jabotinsky's itinerary.

Notes to Chapter 2

54. Jabotinsky, letters to his mother, Eva, Jerusalem, from New York, 18 December 1921, MJ, File 2/37/2/1gimel; and from New Orleans, 21 January 1922, summarized in *Igrot Jabotinsky*, 31/61; Berl Katznelson, "Yoman America," entry for 24 November [1921], in *Igrot B. Katznelson*, vol. 5 (5682–5691 [1922–1931]) (Tel Aviv: Am Oved, 1973), 110; "HaMalachut HaTziyonit BeChicago" [Hebrew], New York *HaDo'ar*, 15 December 1921; minutes of meeting of Temporary Executive Committee, American Keren HaYesod, 3 August [1921].

    See also, Jabotinsky's letters to Yona [Machover], London, from New York, 18 December 1921, and [Richard] Lichtheim, London, from Minneapolis, 6 January 1922, both summarized in *Igrot Jabotinsky*, 22/1; W. Gunther Plaut, *The Jews in Minnesota* (New York: American Jewish Historical Society, 1959), 296; editorial, *The New Palestine*, 16 June 1922, quoted in Schechtman, *Rebel*, 394.

55. Jabotinsky, Pittsburgh, letter to [Mina Berlin, Geneva], 13 March 1922, summarized in *Igrot Jabotinsky*, 141/26. See also, Yitzhak Kalugai, Pittsburgh, letter to Yitzhak Ben-Zvi and Aharon Reuveni, Jerusalem, 15 November 1921, BZA, File 1/5/4/26, which talks of the failure of Weizmann and Jabotinsky to raise significant amounts for the Foundation Fund.

56. Jabotinsky, Minneapolis, letter to his mother, Eva, Jerusalem, 6 January 1922, summarized in *Igrot Jabotinsky*, 31/59.

57. On the Weizmann-Brandeis controversy, see Urofsky, *American Zionism*, 209, 231–79, and many other sources.

58. On the disagreement with Brandeis, see, among other sources, Katz, *Jabo*, vol. 1, 454–55. On Jabotinsky's belief that a Jewish state would only be created through political action, see Gorny, "Zionist Voluntarism," 69; Dan Horowitz and Moshe Lissak, *Origins of the Israeli Polity: Palestine under the Mandate*, trans. Charles Hoffman (Chicago: University of Chicago Press, 1978), 126.

59. Julian W. Mack, n.p., letter to Jabotinsky, New York, 29 March 1922, American Jewish Historical Society, Waltham, Stephen S. Wise Collection, Box 113; "Sokolow and Jabotinsky Want to Make Peace with Brandeis" [Hebrew], New York *Di Tsayt*, 9 November 1921; Katz, *Jabo*, vol. 1, 353, 502.

60. Numerous articles in *Di Tsayt*, November and December 1921 and early January 1922. See also, "HaMassa-u-Mattan bein Jabotinsky u-Fetliura" and "Huchhash HaDin-Ve-Heshbon Shel Slavinski al Rezolutzia BaCongress HaTziyoni" [Hebrew], *HaDo'ar*, 8 and 11 December 1921 respectively; minutes of meetings of the Committee of Three, American Keren HaYesod, 1, 2 December 1921; Schechtman, *Rebel*, 399–410; Katz, *Jabo*, vol. 1, 480–88.

61. Jabotinsky, [London], memorandum to Directorium of the Keren Hayesod, [London], 20 November 1920, CZA, File KH 1/172. See also, minutes of meeting of the American Keren HaYesod Committee of Three, 28 November 1921.

62. Jabotinsky, London, letters to Mr. Lipton, 28 December 1920, CZA, File KH 1/172; and to [Arthur] Hantke et al., summarized in *Igrot Jabotinsky*, 20/32, 96–97.

63. Jabotinsky, Kansas City, Mo., confidential letter to Directors, Keren Hayesod

Bureau, London, 15 January 1922, WAR, File 1922; minutes of meeting of the Administrative Committee, American Keren HaYesod, New York, 20 July 1922; "Tafkidei HaMitnadvim Bimei HaHachraza" [Hebrew], *HaDo'ar*, 9 April 1922.
64. "Ze'ev Jabotinsky Hazar LeNew York" [Hebrew], *HaDo'ar*, 6 February 1922; minutes of a meeting of the Temporary Executive Committee, American Keren HaYesod, 20 June [1922].
65. Jabotinsky, New York, letter to the Zionist Executive, England, 13 February 1922, CZA, File A18-47-2. Similar complaints were voiced in letters sent all during his trip, to Richard Lichtheim, London, from New York, 1 March 1922, CZA, File Z4/4026; to Weizmann, from New York, 15 February 1922, WAR, File 1922; to Yona Machover from New York, 9 March 1922, MJ, File 12/2/1gimel; to his wife, Johanna, from New York, 5 May 1922, MJ, File 3/36/2/1gimel.
66. Compare Yitzhak Ben-Zvi, Minneapolis, letter to David Ben-Gurion, n.p., 23 January 1926, BZA, File 1/4/16; Arthur Ruppin, *Pirkei Hayyai* [Hebrew], vol. 3, ed. Alex Bein, trans. A. D. Shafir (Tel Aviv: Am Oved, 1968), diary entry, New York, 26 March 1923; and many other sources.
67. Jabotinsky, New York, letter to Chaim Weizmann, n.p., 25 February 1922, WAR, File 1922.
68. "Alafim u-Revavot Mekablim et Pnei HaMalachut HaTziyonit" and "Agudat Elef HaDollar" [Hebrew], *HaDo'ar*, 13 November 1921 and 5 February 1922 respectively; Jabotinsky, New York, letter to [Richard] Lichtheim, [London], 21 March 1922, CZA, File Z4/4026.
69. Minutes of meetings of the Administrative Committee, Temporary Executive Committee, and Office Committee of the American Keren HaYesod, New York, 12, 26, 31 May and 20 June 1922.
70. Jabotinsky, New York, letter to Chaim Weizmann, n.p., 25 February 1922, WAR, File 1922; id., New York, cable to Zionist Executive, London, 7 March 1922, summarized in *Igrot Jabotinsky*, 456/117; Chaim Weizmann, London, letter to N.[ahum] Sokolow and Jabotinsky, New York, 28 February 1922, WAR, File 1918/47/3; Weizmann, London, draft cable to Sokolow, New York, copied to Jabotinsky and Louis Lipsky, 4 March 1922, MJ, File 10/3/1alef; Weizmann, London, cable to Jabotinsky and Sokolow, New York, 4 May 1922, MJ, 10/3/1alef; Jabotinsky, New York, letter to wife, Johanna, [Bad Kissingen, Germany], 5 May 1922, summarized in *Igrot Jabotinsky*, 27/109; Emanuel Neumann, *In the Arena* (New York: Herzl, 1976), 72.
71. Jabotinsky, letters from Cairo, to [wife, Johanna, London], 3 March 1918, and from [Jerusalem], to [Meir Grossman, London], 20 February 1920, both summarized in *Igrot Jabotinsky*, 12/27 and 38/1076taf respectively; Dr. S. M. Melamed, Chicago, letter to Jabotinsky, New York, 8 May 1922, MJ, File 3/10/1alef; L. E. Miller, New York, letters to Jabotinsky, Berlin, 26 March and 12 March 1923, MJ, File 11/3/1alef; "From a Letter of Jabotinsky," *The Zionist*, 5 November 1926; Schechtman, *Rebel*, 346.
72. "MiPe'ulot Keren HaYesod" [Hebrew], *HaDo'ar*, 2 March 1922; A. Gutman,

Notes to Chapter 2

"Michtav MiMilwaukee, Wis." [Hebrew], *HaDo'ar*, 26 December 1921; ad for Ball of the Jabotinsky Legionnaires, *Di Tsayt*, 16 December 1921; "LeChol HaGduda'im ve-HaHayalim HaIvriyim BeAmerica Kol Korei," Hebrew manifesto signed by Jabotinsky and eight other members of the Temporary National Actions Committee [of Legion Veterans], *HaDo'ar*, 12 February 1922.

73. Jabotinsky, letters, Milwaukee, to Mina and Bella [Berlin, Geneva], 7 December 1921, summarized in *Igrot Jabotinsky*, 140/26; from New York, to [mother, Eva, Jerusalem], 18 December 1921, MJ, File 2/37/2/1alef; from Minneapolis to [mother, Jerusalem], 6 January 1922, and to [sister, Tamar Kopp, Jerusalem], 10 January 1922, both in MJ, File 2/37/2/1alef; from New York, to Israel Trivus, 9 February 1922, in *Ktavim*, vol. 18, 167–70; from Pittsburgh, to [Mina Berlin, Geneva], 13 March 1922, summarized in *Igrot Jabotinsky*, 141/26; Schechtman, *Fighter*, 256; Schechtman, *Rebel*, 394.

74. Jabotinsky, New York, letter to [Richard] Lichtheim, [London], 21 March 1922, CZA, File Z4/4026; id., "Benkshaft;" Schechtman, *Rebel*, 346, 389.

75. Jabotinsky, Berlin, letter to [Frederick H.] Kisch, n.p., 9 December 1923, CZA, File S28/5280.

76. Jabotinsky, "Anahnu HaBurganim," 215–16. See also, Yaacov Shavit, "Ze'ev Jabotinsky and the Revisionist Movement," *Studies in Zionism* 4 (Autumn 1981): 219–36.

    In *Jabo*, vol. 2, 641, Katz claims that Jabotinsky had never toyed with socialist ideas. That assertion, however, makes no sense in light of an exchange between Jabotinsky and Rahel Yana'it and Yosef Sprinzak, which he records just a few pages later (vol. 2, 646). The labor leaders, according to Katz, upbraided Jabotinsky for not having assumed the leadership of the labor movement, which, they said, could have been his for the asking.

77. Yaacov Shavit, *Jabotinsky and the Revisionist Movement, 1925–1948* (London: Frank Cass, 1988), 285ff.

78. Jabotinsky, "What Does America Have to Say?" [Yiddish], New York *Morgn Zhurnal*, 18 June 1926, translated for me by Jacob Goldfein.

79. "Dei'otav HaHevratiyot Shel Hoover" [Hebrew], editorial, *Do'ar HaYom*, 20 March 1929. Although the editorial is unsigned, Jabotinsky was editor of the paper and the only person on the staff likely to have had the knowledge to write the editorial. *Wall Street Journal*, 26 January 1987.

80. Jabotinsky, "Od Al America," [Hebrew], in *Ktavim*, vol. 7 (Jerusalem: Eri Jabotinsky, 5708 [1948]), 195–97.

81. Jabotinsky quoted in "Ze'ev Jabotinsky Hazar leNew York" [Hebrew], *HaDo'ar*, 6 February 1922.

82. Among other sources, see his essays, "Prospect for Plutocratic Rule" and "De Profundis," both originally published in *Rasswiet* in Russian; Jabotinsky, "HaPerspectiva Shel Shilton HaGvirim," *HaAretz*, 13 July 1923; "Jabotinsky on Zionist Policy," *The New Palestine*, 5 February 1926, 141; "The Zionists-Revisionists Programme" [sic], *Palestine Post*, 4 August 1926; M. Ungerfeld, "Massa Jabotinsky BeEiropa" [Hebrew], *HaDo'ar*, 14 January 1927, 164–65; "Jabotinsky Attacks Jewish Agency," *The New Palestine*, 9 September 1927; "Yoman"

[Hebrew], editorial, *Do'ar HaYom*, 3, 17, 24 December 1928 and 17 January 1929; HaSufah [Vladimir Jabotinsky], "Yoman" [Hebrew], *Do'ar HaYom*, 19 April 1929; Shavit, *Jabotinsky, 1925–1948*, 358; Katz, *Jabo*, vol. 2, 589.

83. Altalena [Jabotinsky], "Utilizing Niagara," *The Zionist*, 15 October 1926; Jabotinsky, Paris, letter to *Betar Monthly*, New York, 30 February 1932, MJ, File 1/22/2/1alef. See also, id., "American Zionism," *The Zionist*, 25 June 1926; and "The Secret of Successful Colonization," *The New Palestine*, 12 October 1928, 233–34.
84. Jabotinsky, "Secret of Successful Colonization;" Shavit, *Jabotinsky, 1925–1948*. See also Jabotinsky, "BiShnei Maklot" [Hebrew], *Do'ar haYom*, 22 March 1929.
85. Jabotinsky, "What Does America Have to Say?"
86. "We Americans"; "American Zionism."
87. "We Americans."
88. Jabotinsky, Paris, letter to [Dr. Samuel Perlman, Boston], 17 December 1927, MJ, 33/188taf.
89. Id., "American Zionism."
90. Id., "What Does America Have to Say?"
91. Ibid; Id., "We Americans."
92. Id., "De Profundis," in *HaDerech El HaRevisionism HaTziyoni* [Hebrew], ed. Joseph Nedava (Tel Aviv: Jabotinsky Institute, 1984), 41. The essay was originally published in Russian in *Rasswiet*, 8 July 1923.
93. Jabotinsky, Paris, letter to [Joseph] Brainin, New York, 19 August 1924, MJ, File 14/2/1alef. See also, id., Paris, letter to Elias [Ginsburg], New York, 18 April 1925, MJ, File 15/2/1alef.
94. Id., letters from Paris, to Elias Ginsburg, [New York], 6 June and 16 September 1925, MJ, File 15/2/1alef; and to [Arthur] Adams, Denver, 9 July 1925, MJ, 12/2/1alef. In *Fighter* (46), Schechtman incorrectly states that Jabotinsky and his group were in touch with only one American during this period, Israel Posnansky of New York.
95. Jabotinsky, Vienna, letter to [wife, Johanna, Paris], MJ, File 5/36/2/1alef; id., [Paris], draft cable to Hurok Universal Artists, New York [17 October 1925], MJ, File 15/2/1alef.
96. Robert Silverman, Boston, letter to Dr. Anna Mintz, secretary, Avukah (the student Zionist society), Boston, 21 April 1926, in CZA, File F25/56; "LeVe'idat Bnei Zion," editorial [Hebrew], *HaDo'ar*, 18 June 1926.
97. Jabotinsky, postcard to wife, Johanna, Paris, from Buffalo, 14 February 1926; letter from New York, to wife, [Paris], 17 May 1926, both in MJ, File 6/36/2/1. See also, various letters from February to June 1926 in MJ, Files 1/28/3/1alef and 2/28/3/1alef.
98. Judge Bernard Rosenblatt, New York, letter to Jabotinsky, New York, 2 May 1926, MJ, File 14/3/1; Yitzhak Ben-Zvi, New York, letter to Rahel Yana'it, [Palestine], 5 February 1926, BZA, File 1/4/10/34, which mentions Ben-Zvi's having spoken to Jabotinsky about the "well-known phonographs . . . [and] records," undoubtedly euphemisms for weapons and ammunition.
99. Vladimir Jabotinsky, "Bialik's Poetic Range," *The New Palestine*, 5 February

Notes to Chapter 2

1926; "Large Crowd for the Debate on Zionism and Culture" [Yiddish], New York *Morgn Zhurnal*, 24 May 1926; "Tziyonut VeTarbut" [Hebrew], *HaDo'ar*, 4 June 1926; Shmaryahu Levin, New York, letter to Dr. [Chaim] Weizmann, London, 18 May 1926, in *Igrot Shmaryahu Levin—Mivḥar* [Hebrew] (Tel Aviv: Dvir, 1966), 413. See also, Ch. 3 below.

100. Jabotinsky, "We Americans"; letters, New York, to Rabbi [A. H.] Silver, [Cleveland], 23 March 1926, Temple Library, Cleveland, Abba Hillel Silver Archives, File 6, Drawer 4; to [Julius] Berger, [New York], 14 April 1926, both summarized in *Igrot Jabotinsky*, 37/711taf, 28/79, 28/86; to wife, Johanna, [Paris], 12 March 1926 and 17 April 1926, MJ, File 6/36/2/1alef; Rabbi Stephen S. Wise, n.p., letter to Jabotinsky, New York, 24 March 1926, MJ, File 14/3/1alef; *The New Palestine*, 26 March 1926.

    The atlas was eventually published in Europe. See Katz, *Jabo*, vol. 2, 592–95.

101. Jabotinsky, New York, letter to wife, Johanna, [Paris], 5 May 1926, MJ, File 6/36/2/1alef.

102. Meyer Weisgal, New York, letter to Jabotinsky, [New York], 15 February 1926, MJ, File 14/3/1alef; Jabotinsky, New York and n.p., letters to his wife, [Johanna, Paris], 3 February 1926, 15 June 1926, and 16 November 1926, MJ, File 6/36/2/1alef; id., "Summer Camps and the Holy Tongue" [Yiddish], New York *Morgn Zhurnal*, 26 July 1926; Schechtman, *Fighter*, 85.

103. Jabotinsky, letters to Eva Jabotinsky and Tamar Kopp, Jerusalem, from New York, 3 February 1926, from Chicago, 21 February 1926, from New York, 22 February 1926, MJ, File 4/37/2/1alef. Compare also, Jabotinsky, New York, letter to [wife, Johanna, Paris], 3 February 1926, MJ, File 6/36/2/1alef.

104. Jabotinsky, letters to Johanna, [Paris], 13 February 1926 and 21 February 1926, MJ, File 6/36/2/1alef; and to Rabbi [A. H.] Silver, [Cleveland], 23 March 1926, Temple Library, Cleveland, Abba Hillel Silver Archives, File 6 Drawer 4; Toronto *Globe*, 12 February 1926. In *Jabo* (vol. 2, 650), Katz claims the halls were full. The evidence, however, does not seem to support his contention.

105. Jabotinsky, New York, cable to [Johanna] Jabotinsky, Paris, 22 March 1926, MJ, File 6/36/2/1alef.

106. Robert Silverman, Boston, letter to Dr. Anna Mintz, secretary, Avukah, Boston, 21 April 1926, in CZA, File F25/56.

107. Jabotinsky, letters to his wife, Johanna, Paris, from Buffalo, 13 February 1926, and from New York, 12 March 1926, MJ, File 6/36/2/1alef; "Mr. Jabotinsky's Campaign," London *Jewish Chronicle*, 23 July 1926.

108. Katz, *Jabo*, vol. 2, 649.

109. Jabotinsky, letters to his wife, Johanna, Paris, from n.p., 9 March 1926, MJ, File 6/36/2/1alef; to Shlomo [Jacobi], n.p., 22 March 1927, MJ, File 17/2/1alef. See also, Schechtman, *Fighter*, 53–57.

110. Jabotinsky, "About Cassandra," *The Zionist*, 17 September 1926; "Zionism in America—The Revisionist Movement—Mr. Jabotinsky's Campaign," London *Jewish Chronicle*, 23 July 1926.

    See also, ad in *Dos Iddishe Folk*, 29 January 1926, for Jabotinsky's speech

Notes to Chapter 2

in the Manhattan Opera House two days later, and Dr. Sh[imon] Bernstein's editorial in the same journal, "Jabotinsky's Programmatic Points," 12 February 1926; *The New Palestine*, 26 March 1926; and Marc Lee Raphael, *Abba Hillel Silver: A Profile in American Judaism* (New York and London: Holmes & Meier, 1989), 73.

111. Katz, *Jabo*, vol. 2, 650–51.
112. Jabotinsky, letters to his wife, Johanna, [Paris], n.p., 19 March 1926, Chicago, 21 February 1926, Buffalo, 13 February 1926, MJ, File 6/35/2/1alef; CZA, Files F38/692, F38/755; Louis D. Brandeis, letters, Chatham, Massachusetts, 20 July 1930, and Washington, D.C., 20 October 1929, to J[ulian] W[illiam] M[ack], n.p., in *Letters of Louis D. Brandeis*, vol. 5, ed. Melvin I. Urofsky and David W. Levy (Albany: State University of New York Press, 1978), 437, 408; Naomi W. Cohen, *The Year after the Riots* (Detroit: Wayne State University Press, 1988), 80, 88, 187.
113. Jabotinsky, letter to his wife, Johanna, [Paris], New York 12 March 1926, MJ, File 6/36/2/1alef; Y. P. [Jabotinsky], "HaRevisionism BeArtzot HaBrit," translated by Dr. Nahum Kroll, in Nedava, *BeHitgabshuto*, 243–44, originally published in Russian, *Rasswiet*, 18 July 1926; Schechtman, *Fighter*, 48–49.
114. Jabotinsky, New York, letters to [Jacob Cohen, Warsaw] 22 April 1926, MJ, File 16/2/1alef; to wife Johanna, [Paris], 14 May 1926, MJ, File 6/36/2/1alef.
115. Jabotinsky, New York, 22 June 1926, MJ, File 6/36/2/1alef.
116. Jabotinsky, farewell speech to supporters, in "Farewell to Jabotinsky," *The Zionist*, 16 July 1926; "The Two Conventions," *The Zionist*, 16 July 1926; "Order Sons of Zion Adopts Revisionism," *The Zionist*, 25 June 1926; "Mr. Lipsky's Letter to the Order Sons of Zion," editorial [Yiddish], *Dos Iddishe Folk*, 11 June 1926; "Order Sons of Zion," *The New Palestine*, 9 July 1926; *Palestine Post*, 29 July 1926; "Zionism in America—The Revisionist Movement—Mr. Jabotinsky's Campaign;" Schechtman, *Fighter*, 51–57.
117. Jabotinsky, New York, letters, to Avraham Recanati, Salonika, 17 May 1926, MJ, file number missing; to wife, Johanna, [Paris], 14 May 1926, MJ, File 6/36/2/1alef; to wife, [Paris], 28 May 1926, summarized in *Igrot Jabotinsky*, 28/81; *The Jewish Daily Bulletin Index*, 1925 (New York: Jewish Daily Bulletin, 1925), 158; Jabotinsky, "Utilizing Niagara."
118. Jabotinsky, letters, St. Sauveur [?], to Shlomo [Jacobi, Melbourne], 12 August 1928, and Jerusalem, to Board of Directors, Judea Industrial Corporation, New York, 25 October 1928, both in MJ, File 2/18/2/1alef; Chaim Weizmann, Merano, letter to Frederick H. Kisch, Jerusalem, 23 September 1928, in *The Letters and Papers of Chaim Weizmann*, Series A, vol. 13, ed. Pinhas Ofer, trans. Michael Kisch (New Brunswick, N.J. and Jerusalem: Transaction Books, Rutgers University Press, Israel Universities Press, 1977–78), 485–86; minutes of meetings of the Administrative Committee of the ZOA, 16 May and 8 June 1927; minutes of meeting of the Governing Council of the ZOA, 22 November [1928]. A series of articles in *The Vanguard* during 1929 catalogues the company's difficulties thoroughly.
119. Katz, *Jabo*, vol. 2, 693.

Notes to Chapter 2

120. I[tamar] B[en Avi], "Hitpalalnu LeVoacha, Ish Akko" [Hebrew], *Do'ar HaYom*, 7 October 1928; "Avukah Luncheon, July 2nd," *The New Palestine*, 29 June 1928.
121. In February and March 1929, the paper serialized "The Gold Bug" and "Murders in the Rue Morgue" by Poe, and in April 1929, a story of O. Henry. Although the name of the translator was not given, it was undoubtedly the editor himself. In praise of American free enterprise, there appeared, among other pieces, an unsigned editorial, "Dei'otav HaHevratiyot Shel Hoover," 20 March 1929, and Abba Ahimeir's "HaYozma HaPratit veErkah," 29 March 1929. On the pioneering spirit, see, for example, Jabotinsky's article, "Megilat HaGdud," 17 February 1929.
122. On American Zionists, non-Zionists, and anti-Zionists, see, for example, "BeMa'arechet HaOppozitzia BeAmerica," unsigned editorial, 9 December 1928; Herman Sweet, "Siha im Stephen Wise Lifnei Nas'o MiBerlin," 3 January 1929; Capanella [Jabotinsky?], "H[aAdon] Rosenwald Mitkarev LaTziyonut," 16 April 1919; Meir Grossman, "Madua Anu Mitnagdim?" 19, 21–24, 28 April 1929.
123. See, for example, "Jabotinsky BeArtzeinu" [Hebrew], 7 October 1928; "Likrat HaTa'arucha" [Hebrew], 14 January 1929; "Erev HaTa'arucha" [Hebrew], 7 April 1929.
124. On Jabotinsky's activities as an insurance executive in Palestine, see among other sources, Jacob S. Strahl, Paris, letter to Vladimir Jabotinsky [Paris], 9 July 1928, MJ, File 1/16/3/1alef; Vladimir Jabotinsky, letters, from Paris to Oscar [Grusenberg, Riga], 28 September 1928, summarized in *Igrot Jabotinsky*, 34/252; with Marek Schwartz from Jerusalem, to Board of Directors, Judea Industrial Corporation, New York, 25 October 1928, MJ, File 2/18/2/1alef; Schechtman, *Fighter*, 86ff.
125. Vladimir Jabotinsky, New York, open letter in Haifa *HaZafon* [Hebrew], 28 May 1926.
126. Jabotinsky, "HaRevisionism BeArtzot HaBrit," 149; "Farewell to Jabotinsky."
127. Jabotinsky, speech quoted in "Farewell to Jabotinsky"; id., Lwow, Poland, letter to wife, [Johanna, Paris], 12 March 1927, summarized in *Igrot Jabotinsky*, 28/117.
128. Jabotinsky, London, letter to [Marek Schwartz, Jerusalem], 12 September 1929, MJ, File 2/19/2 1alef.
129. A term of derision used by Jewish social critics of American-Jewish mores to denote what H. L. Mencken called "the booboisie."
130. Jabotinsky, "American Zionism;" id., letters, from New York, to Aaron M. Wilner, Boston, 28 June 1926, MJ, File 16/2/1alef; n.p., to Elias Ginsburg, New York, 19 August 1927, MJ, File 17/2/1alef; from Paris, to Mr. [Mordecai] Danzis, New York, 30 November 1927, MJ, File 17/2/1alef.

    In *Jabo* (vol. 2, 653) Shmuel Katz lays all the blame for lack of follow-up on the disorganized American Revisionists. That judgment, however, must be discounted as apologetics.
131. Jabotinsky, Paris, letters to [Jacob] Ish Kishor, New York, 21 November 1927,

Notes to Chapter 2

MJ, File 17/2/1alef; to Meir Grossman, London, 22 November 1927, summarized in *Igrot Jabotinsky*, 37/749; to Mr. Danzis, New York, 30 November 1927, MJ, File 17/2/1alef.
132. Id., letters, from Paris, to Mr. [Mordecai] Danzis, New York, 30 November 1927, MJ, File 17/2/1alef; from Jerusalem, to [Joseph] Bader, New York, 24 October 1928, MJ, File 2/18/2/1alef.
133. Elias Ginsburg, New York, letter to Shilton, Brith Trumpeldor, Paris, 8 May 1935, in MJ, File 2/23/3/1alef.
134. Katz, *Jabo*, vol. 2, 1124.
135. Jabotinsky, Paris, letter to [Elias] Ginsburg, [Brooklyn], 3 May 1932, in MJ, File 1/22/2/1alef; Abraham Tulin, [New York], letter to Jabotinsky, Paris, 25 March 1931, in MJ, File 19/3/1alef. See also, Jabotinsky, Paris, letter to Meir [Grossman, London], 29 January 1931, summarized in *Igrot Jabotinsky*, 2, 35/424taf.
136. "The Land of Gigantic Longings" [Yiddish] New York *Morgn Zhurnal*, 17 March 1935, and Warsaw *Der Moment*, 22 March 1935, translated for me by Jack Chodoroff; Hebrew, Jerusalem *HaYarden*, 22 March 1935; "Od al America," 203–04.
137. "Tziyonut Ktanah, Mah Hi?" *Ktavim*, vol. 11, 233, originally published in Yiddish in the New York *Morgn Zhurnal*, 3 August 1930; "Echoes" [Russian], *Rasswiet*, 5 June 1932, translated for me by Professor Richard Pope; "The Evacuation that Was Carried Out," originally published in Yiddish in Warsaw's *Der Moment*, 30 June 1939, quoted in Katz, *Jabo*, vol. 2, 117; "Lefi Behirat HaSafran" [Hebrew], Tel Aviv *HaMashkif*, 12, 22 April 1940.

In the last essay, although critical of American prejudice, Jabotinsky praises the country as "an admixture of the best blood of white humanity."
138. Jabotinsky, "Lefi Behirat HaSafran" [Hebrew], *HaMashkif*, 12 April 1940.
139. Id., "Lefi Behirat HaSafran," *HaMashkif*, 22 April 1940.
140. Id., "Gigantic Longings;" "Michtav MeiAmerica" [Hebrew], Jerusalem *HaYarden*, 1 March 1935. See also, Benjamin Akzin, *Mei Riga Lirushalayim, Pirke Zichronot* (Jerusalem: Hassifriya Haziyonit al-yad HaHistradrut HaTziyonit HaOlamit, 1989), 247.
141. Jabotinsky, "Der Bandwagen" [Yiddish], New York *Morgn Zhurnal*, 18 March 1935, and other places. See also, "Michtav MeiAmerica."
142. Id., *The War and the Jew* (New York: Altalena, 1987), 137, originally published in June 1940 as *The Jewish War Front*. See also, 28, 136. For a discussion of the intentions of the American and other governments at Evian, see Irving Abella and Harold Troper, *None Is Too Many: Canada and the Jews of Europe, 1933–1948* (Toronto: Lester & Orpen Dennys, 1982), 16–37 and notes.
143. Schechtman, *Fighter*, 268; Jabotinsky, Paris, letter to Mr. [Mordecai] Danzis, New York, 30 November 1927, in MJ, File 17/2/1alef.
144. *Rassviet* [Russian], 15 April 1934, translation in MJ, File 37/886taf.
145. James Waterman Wise, New York, letter to Jabotinsky, [Paris], 16 November 1933, in MJ, File 21/3/1alef; Stephen Wise, n.p., letter to Jabotinsky, Paris, in MJ, File 22/3/1alef; Ben-Gurion, [Tel Aviv], letter to Dr. Stephen S. Wise, Paris, 4 August 1931, in LAT, File IV-104-29-17bet; Melvin I. Urofsky, *A Voice*

Notes to Chapter 2

that *Spoke for Justice* (Albany: State University of New York Press, 1982), 252–53, 278; Michael A. Meyer, *Hebrew Union College—Jewish Institute of Religion: A Centennial History, 1875–1975*, rev. ed. (Cincinnati: Hebrew Union College Press, 1992), 150.

146. Stephen Wise, n.p., letter to Jabotinsky, Paris, 20 October 1934, in MJ, File 22/3/1alef. In *Fighter* (266–70), Schechtman describes the break but offers no explanation for it. In *Jabo* (vol. 2, 936), Katz claims that Wise aspired to the presidency of the WZO and sought to secure Labor support by breaking with Jabotinsky. He offers no support, however, for this thesis.

147. "Stephen Wise Cracks Down on Jabotinsky," *Jewish Frontier*, April 1935, 6–7; Urofsky, *Voice*, 406; and other sources.

148. Jabotinsky, "Der Bandwagen." The reply was first delivered as a speech in Boston (Akzin, *Riga*, 247).

149. Brandeis, Washington, D.C., letter to S[tephen] S. W[ise], in Brandeis *Letters*, vol. 5, 551; I[srael] Mereminsky (later, Merom), [HEC, Tel Aviv], letter to Dr. [David] Rabelsky, n.p., 14 March 1935, in LAT, File IV-208-1-706; Jabotinsky, Paris, letter to Elias [Ginsburg, Brooklyn], 29 January 1933, in MJ, File 1/23/2/1alef.

150. On the Brandeisists, see J. Lackow, New York, letter to Jabotinsky, [Paris], 16 September 1932, in MJ, File 20/3/1alef; Schechtman, *Fighter*, 258, 261; Katz, *Jabo*, vol. 2, 943. In *HaSochnut HaYehudit—Shanim Rishonot, 1919–1931* [Hebrew] (Jerusalem: Hassifriya Haziyonit, 1990), 255, Yigal Elam suggests that Brandeis's reluctance to enter an anti-Weizmann alliance with Jabotinsky stemmed from the judge's wish to focus on American Zionist affairs, as opposed to Jabotinsky's global aspirations. The reality, however, seems to be more complex.

On the Labor Zionists, see Israel Mereminsky, diary, New York, 27 October 1932, in LAT, File IV-208-1-338bet; id., New York, letter to HEC, Tel Aviv, 27 December 1932, and diary, New York, 5 January 1933, both in LAT, File IV-208-1-407alef; the correspondence between Eliezer Galili, Yosef Sprinzak, and Baruch Zuckerman in New York, and the HEC, Tel Aviv, January-December, 1934, in LAT, File IV-208-1-407bet.

151. Jabotinsky, Pittsburgh, memorandum to the Comité Executif, Paris, 4 March 1935, in MJ, File 1/25/2/1alef; id., letter to Jacob De Haas, 15 June 1935, quoted in Schechtman, *Fighter*, 278; David Ben-Gurion, diary, in BGA, entry for 27 May 1935.

152. Jabotinsky, letters to Shlomo [Jacobi], from St. Louis, 23 March 1935, and Toronto, 28 February 1935, both summarized in *Igrot Jabotinsky*, 2; id., Pittsburgh, memorandum to Revisionist Executive Committee, Paris, 4 March 1935, in MJ, File 1/25/2/1alef; id., quoted in Jerusalem *HaYarden*, 28 April 1935.

153. Id., Paris, letter to Executive Committee, Union of Zionist Revisionists, London, 22 April 1932, in MJ, File 1/22/2/1alef.

154. Id., quoted in Jerusalem *HaYarden*, 28 April 1935.

155. Schechtman, *Fighter*, 256.

Notes to Chapter 2

156. Abraham Tulin, [New York], letter to Jabotinsky, Paris, 25 March 1931, in MJ, File 19/3/1alef. Compare also, the similar assessment of Alon Gal, in *David Ben-Gurion—Likrat Medina Yehudit* [Hebrew] ([Sede Boqer]: Ben-Gurion University of the Negev, Sede Boqer Campus, 1985), 147.
157. "Jabotinsky's International Army," editorial, *Jewish Frontier*, October 1935, 4.
158. Jabotinsky, letters, New York City, to [Akiva] Brun, [Tel Aviv], 19 March 1935, in MJ, File 1/25/2/1alef; Paris, to E[lias] Ginsburg, New York, 29 May 1935, summarized in *Igrot Jabotinsky*, 2, 36/564taf; and Paris, to Elias [Ginsburg, New York], 29 July 1935, in MJ, File 2/25/2/1alef.
159. A[braham] Tulin, [New York], letter to Jabotinsky, New York, 26 February 1935, in MJ, File 1/23/3/1alef; Jabotinsky, New York, letters to his wife, Johanna, [London], 19 March 1940, and 25 April 1940, both in MJ, File 12/36/2/1alef, translated for me by Rahel Halperin.
160. Jabotinsky, Paris, letter to S. S. Wise, New York, 23 July 1930, in Stephen S. Wise Collection, Brandeis University, Waltham, Massachusetts. See also, Schechtman, *Fighter*, 302–04; and Elam, *HaSochnut*, 254.
161. Jabotinsky, [New York], letter to [Executive Council, New Zionist Organization, London], 20 March 1940, in MJ, File 1/30/2/1alef.
162. B[enjamin] Akzin, London, letter to Jabotinsky, n.p., 31 March 1938, in MJ, File 1/26/3/1alef; id., *Riga*, 180; id., "Mediniyut HaHutz shel Jabotinsky" [Hebrew], in his *Sugiyot BeMishpat u-vi-Medina'ut* (Jerusalem: Hotza'at Sfarim al Shem J. L. Magnes, HaUniversita Halvrit, 5726 [1966]), 90, 93; Jabotinsky, London, letter to Akzin, [Washington], 2 January 1939, in MJ, File 1/29/2/1alef; and other sources.
163. Feis, quoted by B[enjamin] Akzin in a letter from Washington, 10 May 1940, to Jabotinsky, New York, in MJ, File 2/28/3/1alef. For Jabotinsky's views, see among other sources, his letters in MJ from New York, to [Shmuel] Katz, [London], 31 May 1940, File 1/30/2/1alef; to Josef [sic] Mirelman, Buenos Aires, 28 June 1940, File 2/30/2/1alef; and to James MacDonald, New York, 16 July 1940, File 40/166. See also, his *aide-mémoire* to the Minister for Foreign Affairs, Provisional Government of the Czechoslovak Republic, New York, 1 August 1940, copy in MJ, 2/30/2/1alef.
164. Jabotinsky, conversation with Dr. Baruch Weinstein in Paris, 1 or 2 September 1939, quoted in Schechtman, *Fighter*, 368. Katz, *Jabo*, vol. 2, 1134, has taken his information from Schechtman.
165. Jabotinsky, Vals-les-Bains, France, letter to Nesiut [Executive, New Zionist Organization], London, 22 July 1939, in MJ, File 2/29/2/1alef.
166. Id., Paris, letter to Elias [Ginsburg, Brooklyn], 27 September 1939, in MJ, File 3/24/2/1alef.
167. Jabotinsky, London, letter to Daniel Syrkis, Haifa, 21 September 1939, in MJ, File 39/181.
168. Id., New York, letters to wife, Johanna, London, 8 April and 8 May 1940, in MJ, File 18/36/2/1alef, both translated for me by Rahel Halperin; id., New York, letter to his sister, Tamar [Kopp, Haifa], 28 July 1940, in MJ, File 11/37/2/1alef.

Notes to Chapter 2

169. Id., New York, letters to [Administrative Council, New Zionist Organization, London], 16 March 1940, in MJ, File 1/30/2/1alef, and to wife, Johanna, [London], 17 March 1940, in MJ, File 12/36/2/1alef.
170. Id., New York, letter to wife, Johanna, [London], 23 March 1940, in MJ, File 12/36/2/1alef, translated for me by Raḥel Halperin.
171. Id., New York, letters to Jacob Daum, [Buenos Aires], 16 April 1940, to [Michael Haskel, Johannesburg], 18 April 1940, and to Dr. [José] Mirelman, Buenos Aires, 16 April 1940, all in MJ, File 1/30/2/1alef.
172. Id., New York, letter to wife, Johanna, [London], 24 June 1940, in MJ, File 12/36/2/1alef, translated for me by Raḥel Halperin.
173. Akzin, *Riga*, 316.
174. On the Irgun-Revisionist split in America and elsewhere, see Eri Jabotinsky, *Avi, Ze'ev Jabotinsky* [Hebrew] (Jerusalem: Steimatzky's Agency, 1980), 157; Akzin, *Riga*, 315; Shavit, *Jabotinsky, 1925–1948*, 100; David Shpiro, "The Role of the Emergency Committee for Zionist Affairs as the Political Arm of American Zionism, 1938–1944," Ph.D. dissertation, Hebrew University, Jerusalem, 1979, vol. 2, 449; Katz, *Jabo*, vol. 2, 1147; and Peter Grose, *Israel in the Mind of America* (New York: Knopf, 1983), 162.
175. Jabotinsky, New York, letter to [his wife, Johanna, London], 19 March 1940. See also, id., [New York], letter to [Executive Council, New Zionist Organization, London], 20 March 1940. Both are in MJ, File 1/30/2/1alef.
176. Id., New York, letters, to Colonel [J. H. Patterson, New York], 11 June 1940, in MJ, File 2/30/2/1alef, and to Dr. Alex Raphaeli, representative of the National Military Organization, New York, 12 June 1940, copy in MJ, File 40/126.
177. "America Seething with Jewish Army Plan," Johannesburg *Jewish Herald*, 21 June 1940; Jabotinsky and Patterson, New York, cable to Winston Churchill, Prime Minister, London, [n.d.], copy in MJ, File 2/30/2/1alef.
178. Jabotinsky, New York, letters to [Administrative Council, New Zionist Organization, London], 16 March 1940, in MJ, File 1/30/2/1alef, and to wife, [Johanna, London], 19 March 1940, in MJ, File 1/30/2/1alef, and 3 June 1940, in MJ, File 12/36/2/1alef; id., letters, all in MJ, London, 2 September 1939, to Anatole de Monzie, Minister of Public Works, Paris, File 2/29/2/1alef; New York, 17 May 1940, to Sir Archibald [Sinclair, Air Secretary, London], File 1/30/2/1alef; [New York], 20 and 21 May 1940, to Prime Minister, Dominion of Canada, Ottawa, File 1/30/2/1alef; [New York], 18 June 1940, to Secretary of State, Washington, D.C., File 40/130; *aide-mémoire*, to Minister for Foreign Affairs, Provisional Government of the Czechoslovak Republic, New York, 1 August 1940, in MJ, File 2/30/2/1alef.
179. Id., *aide-mémoire* to Minister of Foreign Affairs, Provisional Government of the Czechoslovak Republic, New York, 1 August 1940, in MJ, File, 2/30/2/1alef; id., *War and the Jew*, 105–06; Gal, *Likrat Medina*, 77.
180. Extracts from Jabotinsky's address, Manhattan Center, 19 June 1940, PRO, File FO 321/24566; Jabotinsky, New York, letter to wife, [Johanna, London], 11 June 1940, in MJ, File 12/36/2/1alef; Schechtman, *Fighter*, 388–89; Katz, *Jabo*, vol. 2, 1139, 1150; Akzin, *Riga*, 314.

181. Shpiro, "Emergency Committee," vol. 2, 451; Akzin, *Riga*, 314; id., "Mediniyut haḤutz," 105; Urofsky, *Voice*, 312; Katz, *Jabo*, vol. 2, 1141–42.
182. Eri Jabotinsky, *Avi*, 88.
183. Max Raisin, *Groyse Yidn Vos Ich Hob Gekent* [Yiddish] (Paterson, N.J.: New Jersey Branch of the Central Yiddish Culture Organization ("CYCO"), 1950), 130.
184. Akzin, *Riga*, 317.
185. Abraham Revusky, "Vladimir Jabotinsky," *Jewish Frontier*, September 1940; Abe Cahan, New York, letter to Jabotinsky, New York, 17 April 1940, in MJ, File 1/28/3/1alef. See also, Jeanne [Johanna] Jabotinsky, New York, letter to Abraham Cahan, New York, 7 July 1942, in YIVO, Record Group 1139, Folder 170.
186. Jabotinsky, "We Americans."
187. Jabotinsky quoted in Anita Shapira, *Berl: The Biography of a Socialist Zionist*, trans. Ḥaya Galai (Cambridge, England: Cambridge University Press, 1984), 284; and in Gal, *Likrat Medina*, 78.

Chapter 3

1. "Bialik, Greatest of Living Hebrew Poets, Speaks Here," *The Washington Post*, 18 April 1926.
2. Compare Michael Keren, *The Pen and the Sword* (Boulder, San Francisco, and London: Westview, 1989), 26; and Gershon Shaked, "The Great Transition," in *The Great Transition: The Recovery of the Lost Centers of Modern Hebrew Literature*, ed. Glenda Abramson and Tudor Parfitt (Totowa, N.J.: Rowman & Allenheld, 1985), 117–25.
3. David Ben Gurion, *Zichronot*, vol. 1 [Hebrew] (Tel Aviv: Am Oved, 1971), 47; Weizmann, letter, Tel Aviv, 1 October 1924, to his wife, Vera Weizmann, London, in *The Life and Letters of Chaim Weizmann*, Series A, vol. 12, ed. Joshua Freundlich (Jerusalem: Rutgers University, and Israel Universities Press, 1977), 242–43.
4. [Paḥaz], "Bialik Nassa," *HaAretz*, 20 January 1926.
5. Compare Berl Katznelson, "Evel Yaḥid," *Davar*, 13 July 1934; and "Bli Bialik," *Davar*, 7 July 1934, both in Hebrew. On Bialik's influence on his generation, see David Aberbach, *Bialik* (London: Peter Halban, 1988), 15, and the sources cited there.
6. [H. N. Bialik], *"Dvir" Hotza'at Sfarim Leumit Tziburit* (Berlin: Dfus "Ever," 5682 [1922]), 6. This prospectus was signed by Dr. M. Glickson and Dr. Shmaryahu Levin, as well as Bialik. It may be assumed, however, that his colleagues left the task of writing to the poet.

See also, Shalom Spiegel, "Saul Tchernichovsky," *The New Palestine*, 7 December 1928, 463–64, 471; Ya'akov Fichman, "Im Bialik (Zichronot U-Reshimot MiPinkasi)" [Hebrew], *Knesset—Divrei Sofrim Le-Zecher H. N. Bialik*, vol. 2, ed. Ya'akov Cohen and F.[ishel] Laḥover (Tel Aviv: Dvir, 5697 [1937]), 93ff; Aberbach, *Bialik*, 37–55.

Notes to Chapter 3

7. Baruch Benedikt Kurzweil, "The Image of the Western Jew in Modern Hebrew Literature," *Leo Baeck Institute Year Book* 6 (1961): 181.
8. See Joel S. Geffen, "Whither: To Palestine or to America in the Pages of the Russian Hebrew Press, *Ha-Melitz* and *Ha-Yom* (1880–1890), Annotated Documentary," *American Jewish Historical Quarterly* 59 (December 1969): passim; and Harvey Richman, "The Image of America in the European Hebrew Periodicals of the Nineteenth Century (Until 1880)," unpublished doctoral dissertation, University of Texas at Austin, 1971; and other sources.

    Compare also, Hillel Bavli, "Al HaTarbut HaIvrit BeAmerica" [Hebrew], *Moznayim* 1 (20 August 1926). Bavli, an American Hebraist who was visiting in Palestine, told his audience of Palestinian Hebrew writers, that their "notions about America" were conceived in ignorance and "far from the truth." On the date of Bavli's talk, Bialik was still making his way home from America. To an extent, however, Bavli was talking about him, if not to him.
9. As quoted by his son-in-law, Y. D. Berkowitz, in *HaRishonim Kivnei Adam* [Hebrew], vol. 1 (Tel Aviv: Dvir, 1938), 177. On the ambivalent attitude of Sholem Aleichem towards America, see Khone Shmeruk, "Sholem Aleichem and America," *YIVO Annual* 20 (1991): 212ff.
10. Haim Nahman Bialik, "Al America," speech at Bet HaAm, Tel Aviv, [Hebrew], Tishrei, 5687 [1926], in his *Dvarim SheBe'Al Peh*, vol. 2. (Tel Aviv: Dvir, 5695 [1935]), 93–94.
11. K.[alman] Whiteman, "HaRa'ayon HaIvri," *HaToren* 3 (9 February 1917): 3. See also, Michael Brown, "All, All, Alone: The Hebrew Press in America from 1914 to 1924," *American Jewish Historical Quarterly* 59 (December 1969): 138–77.
12. "Dvir," 4.
13. Berkowitz, *HaRishonim*, vol. 2, 262; and Bialik, letter, Odessa, 19 Teveth 1905, to Sholem Aleichem, n.p., in *Igrot Chaim Nachman Bialik*, 5 vols., ed. F.[ishel] Lahover (Tel Aviv: Dvir, 1938 [vols. 1–4], 1939 [vol. 5]), vol. 2, 9. Compare also, the letter of Mendele Mocher Seforim, Geneva, 8 January 1907, to Yehoshua Ravnitzki and Bialik in Odessa, in *Correspondence Between S. J. Abramovitsch, Ch. N. Bialik and Y. Ch. Rawnitzki, 1905–1908*, ed. Chone Shmeruk (Jerusalem: Israel Academy of Science and Humanities, 1976), 89–90; and Bialik's letters from Odessa on 14 Kislev 1905 and 11 Shvat 1906 to S. Ben Zion, n.p., in *Igrot Bialik*, vol. 2, 3–4, 10–12.

    Noah H. Rosenbloom, in "America BeEinei Bialik," in his *Iyunei Sifrut VeHagut* [Hebrew] (Jerusalem: Rubin Mass, 1989), 281–313, claims that Bialik's statement about Russia and Odessa is to be taken at face value and was motivated by his extreme animus towards America. It stretches credulity, however, to believe that Bialik would have sincerely praised Russia as the fairest of countries, when only a few weeks earlier five hundred Jews had been killed and more than three thousand injured in a violent pogrom in Odessa. In fact, the same day he wrote to Sholem Aleichem, Bialik wrote to Y. D. Berkowitz recalling the Odessa pogrom which threatened to put an end to Jewish spiritual and cultural life in the city. About a month later, Bialik wrote to S. Ben Zion:

Notes to Chapter 3

"How fortunate you are . . . to be dwelling in peace . . . in the Alps under the skies of Switzerland, a place without bombs or fear of death or pogroms; we, on the other hand, . . . are like the dead" (letters, Odessa, 19 Teveth and 11 Shvat 1905, in *Igrot Bialik*, vol. 2, 7–8, 10–11).

On Odessa, see Ezra Spicehandler, "Odessa as a Literary Center of Hebrew Literature," in Abramson and Parfitt, *The Great Transition*, pp. 75–90.

14. H. N. Bialik, "Od Al Kinnus HaRuah" [Hebrew], speech at a gathering of the New York Histadruth Ivrith, 1926, in *Dvarim*, vol. 1, 70. See also, Natan Rotenstreich, "Haguto Shel Bialik BeInyenei Tarbut" [Hebrew], *Knesset* (New Series) 1 (5720 [1960]): 208; Aberbach, *Bialik*, 6–7, and the sources cited there.

15. See Keren, *Sword*, 23–25.

16. Sh.[imon] Halkin, "Halton Eretz-HaYisraeli VeHaGola," *Moznayim* 1 (22 March 1929): 9.

17. Quoted in Aberbach, *Bialik*, 4. See also, 58–59. The implications of Bialik's being a small-towner were suggested to me by Shulamith Nardi in a discussion in Jerusalem, 26 March 1991.

18. Bialik, letter, [Berlin], 6 February 1922, to Daniel Persky, New York, in *Igrot Bialik*, vol. 2, 249. See also, Z.[alman] Shneur, *Ch. N. Bialik u-Vnei Doro* [Hebrew] (Tel Aviv: Am Oved, 5713 [1953]), 94.

19. "Bialik Al Reshamav BeLondon," and "Chaim Nahman Bialik BeDarko LeAmerica," both in London *HaOlam* [Hebrew], 29 January 1926; Bialik, letters, London, 26 December 1930, to [Dvir, Tel Aviv], [London], 17 February, 1931, to editorial board of *Moznayim*, Tel Aviv, and [London], 12 February 1931, to Y. H. Ravnitzki, Tel Aviv, in *Igrot Bialik*, vol. 5, 127, 142, 141; Ahad HaAm quoted in Steven J. Zipperstein, *Elusive Prophet: Ahad Ha'Am and the Origins of Zionism* (Berkeley and Los Angeles: University of California Press, 1993), 277. See also, Mordecai Ovadyahu, *MiPi Bialik* [Hebrew] (Tel Aviv: Masada, 5705 [1945]), 28; and Shlomo Shva, *Hozeh Brah!* [Hebrew] (Tel Aviv: Dvir, 1990), 301–03.

20. "Al America," in *Dvarim*, vol. 1, 93; Shmaryahu Levin, letter, n.p., 15 November 1925, to Chaim Weizmann, [London], in *Igrot Shmaryahu Levin—Mivhar* [Hebrew] (Tel Aviv: Dvir, 1966), 411; Bialik, letter, on board ship off Marseilles, [January, 1926], to [Yehoshua] Ravnitzki, [Tel Aviv], in *Igrot Bialik*, vol. 3, 95; Leah Naor, *HaMeshorer—Sipuro Shel Bialik* [Hebrew] (Jerusalem and Tel Aviv: Yad Yitzhak Ben-Zvi and Am Oved, 1991), 200–207. See also, Bialik, letter, Tel Aviv, 15 January 1926, to [S.] Ben Zion, n.p., in *Igrot Bialik*, vol. 3, 92–93; and "Neshef HaPreida LeVialik U-LeDr. S. Levin" [Hebrew], *Davar*, 17 January 1926.

In "Al America" and elsewhere, Bialik speaks of his "*aimah beheimit*" regarding America. Rosenbloom in "America" (289–90) translates the term as "animal fear" and insists that it be understood to refer to a pathological condition. The puckish Bialik, however, may just have liked the rhyme (*aimah shel behaimah*). The phrase could be rendered "blind fear," which would be much less freighted. And, as shown, Bialik feared big cities, in general, not just American cities.

Notes to Chapter 3

21. See Bialik's letter, Tel Aviv, 21 October 1925, to his nephew, Shneur Zalman Bialik, Har[t]ford, [Connecticut], in *Igrot Bialik*, vol. 3, 71–72.
22. Bialik, letter, [The Hague], 23 August 1907, to his wife, Manya, [Odessa], in H. N. Bialik, *Igrot El Ra'ayato, Manya* [Hebrew] (Jerusalem: Hotza'at Mosad Bialik and Dvir, 1955), 21; Judah L. Magnes, "Some Poems of H. N. Bialik," *Hebrew Union College Annual*, 1 (1904).
23. Bialik, letter, Odessa, 8 December 1906, to Sholem Aleichem, New York, in Shmeruk, *Correspondence*, 145. See also, Bialik, letter, [Odessa, November, 1906], to Sholem Aleichem, [New York], *Igrot Bialik*, vol. 2, 27–28; Berkowitz, *HaRishonim*, vol. 2 (1938), 351ff; and Nina Warnke, "Of Plays and Politics: Sholem Aleichem's First Visit to America," *YIVO Annual* 20 (1991): 239–76.
24. Bialik, letter, Odessa, 25 December 1906, to Shmaryahu Levin, [New York], in *Igrot Bialik*, vol. 2, 36.
25. See the exchange of letters in 1906–07 among Bialik and Yehoshua Ravnitzki in Odessa, Mendele in Switzerland, and Sholem Aleichem in New York, in Shmeruk, *Correspondence*, 84–87, 95–96, 120–21, 137–53, 157–60. See also, the Bialik letter cited in n. 23.
26. Bialik, "BiVe'idat HaSofrim," opening address at the Hebrew Writers' Conference, Tel Aviv, Nisan, 1927, [Hebrew], in *Devarim*, vol. 1, 126. On Bialik's relationship with Berkowitz, see Avraham Holtz, *Isaac Dov Berkowitz* (Ithaca: Cornell University Press, 1973).
27. On *HaToren*, its editors, and contributors, see Alan Mintz, "A Sanctuary in the Wilderness: The Beginnings of the Hebrew Movement in America in *Hatoren*," in *Hebrew in America*, ed. Alan Mintz (Detroit: Wayne State University Press, 1993), 29–67.
28. See Z. Fishman, "Haim Nahman Bialik (Biografia U-Vivliografia)," *Ein Ha-Korei* 1 (Nisan-Elul 5683 [1923]); Mintz, "Sanctuary," 49–50; *Bibliography of Modern Hebrew Literature in English Translation*, comp. Yohai Goell (Jerusalem: Executive of the World Zionist Organization, Youth and Hechalutz Department, and Israel Universities Press, 1968); and *Bibliography of Modern Hebrew Literature in Translation*, comp. Yohai Goell (Tel Aviv: Institute for the Translation of Hebrew Literature, 1975).
29. See *HaToren*, 28 April 1916; 12, 19, 26 May 1916; 21 July 1916; 1,8,15 September 1916; Berkowitz, *HaRishonim*, vol. 5 (1943), 1028–29; and Brown, "Alone," 152–57.
30. Simon Ginzburg, "BiChe'eiv Demama Daka" [Hebrew], in *Sefer Zikaron LeB. N. Silkiner*, ed. Menahem Ribalow (New York: Ogen al yad HaHistradruth Halvrith BeAmerica, 5694 [1934]), 26; H. N. Bialik, letter, photocopy, Odessa, n.d., to Simon Ginzburg, New York, in ABTA, File 51-48038a; *Literature in Translation*, 83; and other sources. On Ginzburg (either Simon, Shimon, or Simeon Ginzburg or Ginsberg) see Mintz, *Hebrew*.
31. See Ginzburg, "Bi-Che'eiv," 27; L. Eliav, "Kav Ve-Naki" [Hebrew], in *Silkiner*, 60; Israel Efros, Binyamin Silkiner, Yehuda Even-Shmuel Kaufman, *Milon Angli-Ivri* (Tel Aviv: Dvir, 1929 [reprinted twenty-five times by 1963]). On "Mul Ohel Timura," see [Yosef Haver] Yosef Haim Brenner, "Baltonut U-VaSi-

frut" [Hebrew], *HaPo'el HaTza'ir*, 9 December 1910; and Ezra Spicehandler, "*Ameriqa'iyut* in American Hebrew Literature," in Mintz, *Hebrew*, 75-76. Bialik would certainly have read an article by Brenner, one of the most important Hebrew writers of the day, in one of Palestine's few Hebrew journals, as well as the poem, which was published in Palestine.

32. See Bialik, letters, Tel Aviv, 4 Tishrei [1924], to S. P. Mendelssohn, n.p., in *Igrot Bialik*, vol. 3, 17-18; and Tel Aviv, 4 June 1925, to Ze'ev Rosenblum, editor of the student monthly of the Jewish Theological Seminary, [New York], in *Igrot Bialik*, vol. 3, 35-36.

33. Neumark published two lengthy reviews and a major article on "the new philosophy" in vol. 13 of *HaShiloah* (January-June 1904), a shorter review in vol. 15 (January-June 1905), and a lengthy review of David Philipson's *The Reform Movement in Judaism* in vol. 19 (1908). His scholarly work in Hebrew, *Toldot Halkarim BeYisrael*, was published by Moriah, the first volume in 1912, and the second in 1919. On Neumark at the Hebrew Union College, see Michael A. Meyer, *Hebrew Union College-Jewish Institute of Religion: A Centennial History, 1875-1975*, rev. ed. (Cincinnati: Hebrew Union College Press, 1992), 68-69, 98, 110, 113, 130.

34. See his "HaPilosofia HaAravit VeHashpa'ata Al HaYahadut," *HaShiloah* 15 (1905): 99-115, a continuation of an article that had appeared in vol. 6 (1899): 38-52; and "HaDeot BeMahut HaNefesh Lefi Rabi Sa'adia Gaon," *HaShiloah* 26 (1912): 128-37.

35. "Hoveret Le-Dugma," 14: 381-86. It should be noted that foreign authors from many countries, including Charles Dickens and Gilbert and Sullivan, complained bitterly about American copyright laws, which legalized the piracy.

36. "Kitvei Iteinu," on the American-Jewish press, vol. 14 (1904); "Min HaSifrut HaYehudit BaLashon HaAnglit (Bikoret)," on books by Bernard G. Richards, Rabbi H. Pereira Mendes, and Mary Antin, vol. 15 (1905): 80-86; "Otzar Yisrael (Bikoret)," on the new encyclopedia by J. D. Eisenstein, vol. 19 (1908): 59-70; "Hakirot BeYahadut," on Solomon Schechter's *Studies in Judaism*, Second Series, vol. 21 (1909): 533-34; "HaTziyonut BeAmerica," on American Zionism, vol. 17 (1906): 56-64.

37. A.[braham] S. Waldstein, "Mei-America," *HaShiloah* 13 (1904): 465-72; Bialik, quoted in *The New Palestine*, April 1916, as cited by Gertrude Hirschler in "Bialik's Tour of the United States," *Midstream* 30 (August-September 1984): 31.

38. David Auerbach, "HaAmerikani—(Sipur [a story])," 23 (1910): 298-309; [HaDod Mordecai], "Anashim U-Ma'asim," 25 (1911): 78-86; Menahem Ribalow, "HaNoded," a poem, 27 (1912): 545; Simon Ginzburg, "HaHinuch Halvri BeArtzot HaBrit (Michtav MeiAmerica)," 27 (1912): 270-78; Gedalia Bublick, "Yehudim Ba'alei Homer (Michtav MeiAmerica)," 28 (1913): 81-83; Dr. A. Levinson, "HaStudentim Halvriyim BeAmerica," 28 (1913): 365-72.

39. Mordecai [Max] Z. Raisin, "Mordecai Emanuel Noah" [Hebrew], 13 (1904): 519. See also, 213-22, 313-19, 411-25, 505-19; [Z-S], "Yitronoteihen Shel Artzot HaBrit," 14, 333-43. On Raisin's *Yisrael BeAmerica*, see Bialik letter, Tel Aviv, 19 June 1928 to M. Z. Raisin, New York, in *Igrot Bialik*, vol. 4, 135.

Notes to Chapter 3

40. See H. N. Bialik, circular letter in Hebrew, 28 April 5676 [1916], to Young Judaea, New York, in ABTA, File 51-2098.
41. See Aberbach, *Bialik*, 60–96, and 114ff; and many other sources.
42. "Al Kinus HaRuah," speech at a mass meeting of Hebraists in London, Shvat, 1926, in *Devarim*, vol. 1, 66.
43. "Ne'umo Shel H. N. Bialik" [Hebrew], speech at the Council for Hebrew Culture in Carlsbad, *HaToren*, October 1921, 49–50.
44. See among other sources, "MiSihotav Shel Bialik" [Hebrew], *HaDo'ar*, 21 November 1921; *"Dvir"*, 3; Bialik, "Al Matzav HaYahadut VeHaSifrut HaIvrit BaGola," conversation, Adar Sheni, 5684 [1924], in *Devarim*, vol. 1, 47; Bialik, "Al Hurban HaYahadut BaGola U-Vinyan Eretz Yisrael," speech at a reception held in London for Bialik by the British Zionist Federation, Shvat, 5686 [1926], in *Devarim*, vol. 1, 59; H. N. Bialik, *"Dvir" U-"Moriah"* [Hebrew] (New York: n.p., 5686 [1926]); Emanuel Neumann, *In the Arena* (New York: Herzl, 1976), 73.
45. Speech to the Twelfth Zionist Congress in Carlsbad, Elul, 5681 [1921], in *Devarim*, vol. 1, 30. For another view of the radical effects of World War I on European-Jewish life, see Judah L. Magnes's "Opening Address of the Academic Year of the Hebrew University," 29 October 1939, in *Dissenter in Zion*, ed. Arthur A. Goren (Cambridge, Mass.: Harvard University Press, 1982), 358–59. Magnes quotes there the introduction of Bialik and Ravnitzki to their edition of the poems of Solomon Ibn Gabirol.
46. "Al Hurban HaYahadut BaGola," 60.
47. Chaim Weizmann, letters, London, 22 October 1921, to Bella Berligne, Geneva, and 16 October 1921, to Nahum Sokolow, Berlin, in *Life and Letters*, Series A, vol. 10, ed. Bernard Wasserstein (Jerusalem: Israel Universities Press, 1977), 263, 258; Levin, letter [Hebrew], Berlin, 16 October 1921, to Chaim Weizmann, [London], in *Igrot Levin*, 388; minutes of meeting of the Temporary Executive Committee of the American Keren Hayesod, 3 August [1921], in CZA, File KH7-197. See also, M. Ungerfeld, "Bein Bialik LeWeizmann" [Hebrew], *Moznayim* 9 (July 1959): 151.
48. Bialik, letter, [Hebrew], Berlin, Hoshana Rabba, [1921], to Y. H. Ravnitzki, [Tel Aviv], in *Igrot Bialik*, vol. 2, 220; and as quoted in "Bialik Al Dvar HaSifrut VeHaSofrim HaIvriyim" [Hebrew], *HaDo'ar*, 2 December 1921. See also, Bialik, letter, [Hebrew], Berlin, evening after Yom Kippur, 1921, to [Alter] Druyanov, n.p., in *Igrot Bialik*, vol. 2, 217–18; B. Z. Goldberg, "Bialik, Hebrew Poet and Pioneer," *Der Tog*, English section, 14 February 1926; Aberbach, *Bialik*, 107.
49. Minutes of a meeting of the Committee of Three [Temporary Executive Committee, American Keren Hayesod], 25 November 1921, in CZA, File KH7-189. See also, minutes of meeting, 29 November 1921, File KH7-197; minutes of meetings of Administrative Committee, American Keren Hayesod, 6 July and 11 August 1922, in CZA, File KH7-174; Rabbi Samuel Schulman, copy of letter, New York, 1 November 1921, to Samuel Untermyer, chairman, Reception Committee, New York City, in Papers of Gershon Agron(sky), CZA, File

Notes to Chapter 3

A209-12; "Conference Today About the Reception for the Sokolow Delegation" [Yiddish], New York *Di Tsayt*, 2 November 1921; Shmaryahu Levin, letter, 16 October 1921, [Hebrew], Berlin, to Chaim Weizmann, [London], in *Igrot Levin*, 388; Bialik, letter, [Hebrew], [Berlin], 21 December 1921, to [Yehoshua] Ravnitzki, [Tel Aviv], *Igrot Bialik*, vol. 2, 245.

50. See Fishman, "Biografia," 4; Goell, *English Translation*, 10-18; Abba Ahimeir, "Bialik Shel Mi?" [Hebrew], *HaToren*, Iyyar, 5683 [1923].

51. Ovadyahu, *MiPi*, 89; Bialik, letter, [Hebrew], [Berlin], 6 February 1922, to Daniel Persky, New York, in *Igrot Bialik*, vol. 2, 248. See also, *HaDo'ar*, 27 February 1922, 9, 16 March 1923, and 22 October 1926.

52. Bialik, [Berlin], letter, [Hebrew], 6 February 1922, to Daniel Persky, New York, in *Igrot Bialik*, vol. 2, 248; and his letter in *HaDo'ar* [Hebrew], 31 March 1922. See also, Brown, "Alone," 157-65; and Rosenbloom, "America," 286-87.

53. Bialik, letter, [Hebrew], Tel Aviv, 26 May 1924, to Editorial Board of *Eden*, [New York], in *Igrot Bialik*, vol. 3, 5; id., letter, [Hebrew], Tel Aviv, 17 August 1925, to Editorial Board of *Eden*, New York, in *Igrot Bialik*, vol. 3, 59; Daniel Persky, letter, [Hebrew], New York, 24 April 1924, to H. N. Bialik, [Tel Aviv], in ABTA, File 21/68623/1; A. R. Malachi, "Yetzirat Bialik" [Hebrew], in *Sefer Bialik*, ed. Ya'acov Fichman (Tel Aviv: Shvat, 5684 [1924]), 161. See also, Bialik, letter, [Hebrew], Berlin, 22 July 1924, to his wife, Manya, in *Ra'ayato Manya*, 64-66; id., letters, [Hebrew], Tel Aviv, to Editorial Board, *Eden*, New York, 15 September 1924 and 18 March 1925, in *Igrot Bialik*, vol. 3, 15-16, 26; id., letter, [Hebrew], Tel Aviv, 24 June 1925, to Batsheva Grabelsky, New York, in *Igrot Bialik*, vol. 3, 46-47; advertisement for *Eden* in *HaDo'ar*, 26 December 1924, which highlights Bialik's "regular participation" in the journal; and Rosenbloom, "America," 287.

When the journal ceased publication in 1928, Persky returned to Bialik a number of his unpublished manuscripts. (Bialik, letter, [Hebrew], Tel Aviv, 28 September 1928, to Daniel Persky, [New York], in *Igrot Bialik*, vol. 4, 165-67.)

54. See *HaDo'ar*, 16, 17 November 1921; Bialik, letters, [Hebrew], Berlin, Hoshana Rabba, [1921], to Y. H. Ravnitzki, [Tel Aviv], 6 February 1922, to Daniel Persky, New York, 20 February and 30 March 1922, to Yehoshua Ravnitzki, [Tel Aviv], in *Igrot Bialik*, vol. 2, 218-38, 248-54, 257-62, 264-73.

55. Bialik, letters, [Hebrew], Berlin, [9 Adar Sheni 5684 (1924)?], Tel Aviv, 15 May 1925, and Tel Aviv, 29 December 1925, to Simon Ginzburg, New York, in *Igrot Bialik*, vol. 3, 3-4, 30-32, 87. An original fragment of the second letter can be found in ABTA, File 51-86380a.

56. Bialik, letters, [Hebrew], [Bad Homburg], 20 June 1922, to [Yehoshua] Ravnitzki, [Berlin], in *Igrot Bialik*, vol. 2, 281-84, and Tel Aviv, 14 June 1925, to Y. D. Berkowitz, New York, in *Igrot Bialik*, vol. 3, 41-42.

57. Postcard, [Hebrew], Berlin, 14 January 1923, not signed by Bialik, to S. Maximon, [New York], in ABTA, Letters to Maximon File. Bialik, letters, [Hebrew], Tel Aviv, 19 September 1928 and 19 February 1929 to S. B. Maximon, New York, and 19 September 1928 to [Y. L.] Riklis, [New York], in *Igrot Bialik*, vol.

Notes to Chapter 3

4, 160, 218–19, 161, Tel Aviv, 27 April 1925, to S. B. Maximon, New York, in *Igrot Bialik*, vol. 3, 27; Asher Ginzberg [Ahad HaAm], letter, [Hebrew], Tel Aviv, 25 October 1926, to S. B. Maximon, New York, in *Igrot Ahad HaAm*, vol. 6 (1916–1926), ed. Aryeh Simon (Tel Aviv: Dvir, 1960), 270–71; Bialik, letter, [Hebrew], Tel Aviv, 7 July 1933, to Dr. Joseph Marcus, New York, in *Igrot Bialik BeNogea LeHotza'at Shirei Rabi Shlomo Ibn Gvirol VeRabi Moshe Ibn Ezra BeHosafat Ketaim MiPiyutei Rashbag*, ed. Joseph Marcus (New York: self-published, 1935); Meyer, *Hebrew Union College*, 111, 122.

58. Bialik, letter, [Hebrew], Tel Aviv, 1 June 1925, to Prof. Israel Davidson, New York, in *Igrot Bialik*, vol. 3, 32. See also, letters, [Hebrew], Tel Aviv, 26 July, 7 August, 2 October, and [15 December] 1925, to Prof. Israel Davidson, New York, in *Igrot Bialik*, vol. 3, 53–55, 69, 82–83.

59. Bialik, letter, [Hebrew], Tel Aviv, 10 June 1925, to I. J. Schwartz, n.p., in *Igrot Bialik*, vol. 3, 40; Dov Sadan, introduction to I. J. Schwartz, *Shirat Kentucky* [Hebrew] (Jerusalem: Mosad Bialik, 1962), 7–8. My thanks to Mrs. Shulamith Nardi, the niece of Schwartz, for calling "Kentucky" to my attention.

60. Bialik, letters, [Hebrew], Tel Aviv, 27 Kislev 5686 [1925], to the Zionist Executive, Jerusalem, in Archives of the Political Department of the Jewish Agency, CZA, File S25/527, and 11 November 1925, also to the Zionist Executive, Jerusalem, in *Igrot Bialik*, vol. 3, 74–75.

61. Bialik, as quoted in A. S. Orlans, "Siha Im H. N. Bialik," [Hebrew], *HaDo'ar*, 1 January 1922; Bialik, letter, "Igeret H. N. Bialik Al Dvar Malachut 'Tarbuth' BeAmerica," [Hebrew], London *HaOlam*, 10 October 1924; Bialik, letter, [Hebrew], Tel Aviv, 11 Teveth 5685 [1925], to [Shmaryahu Levin, Chicago], in *Igrot Bialik*, vol. 3, 20–21.

62. Compare, for example, Rosenbloom, "America," and Hirschler, "Tour."

63. Weizmann, London, telegram, 12 November 1925, to Shmaryahu Levin, Tel Aviv, in *Life and Letters*, Series A, vol. 12, 439; Bialik, Tel Aviv, letter [Hebrew], 8 Kislev 5686 [1925], to Chaim Weizmann, London, in M. Ungerfeld, "Bein Bialik LeWeizmann" [Hebrew], *Moznayim* 9 (July 1959): 152; Philip Guedalla, British Zionist leader, quoted in "Bialik in London," London *Jewish Chronicle*, 29 January 1926; Bialik quoted in "Neshef HaPreida LeVialik U-LeDr. S. Levin" [Hebrew], *Davar*, 17 January 1926. See also, Levin, letter, n.p., 15 November 1925, to Chaim Weizmann, [London], in *Igrot Levin*, 410–11; Max Raisin, "Haim Nahman Bialik," [Yiddish], in his *Groyse Yidn Vos Ich Hob Gekent* (Paterson, N.J.: New Jersey Branch of the Central Yiddish Culture Organization ["CYCO"], 1950), 66–69; Hirschler, "Tour," 30.

64. Neumann, *Arena*, 72–73. See also, Neumann, cable, New York, 7 January 1926, to Col. [F. H.] Kisch, Jerusalem, in CZA, File S25-527.

    The original goal of the Joint had been $15 million but the campaign went so well that they raised it to $25 million ("Jews Raise Quota to $25,000,000," *New York Times*, 11 May 1926).

65. Bialik, letter, [Hebrew], Tel Aviv, 24 June 1925, to Batsheva Grabelsky, New York, in *Igrot Bialik*, vol. 3, 46–47, also quoted in Rosenbloom, "America," 288; Bialik, "Al HaBikur BeAmerica" [Hebrew], a talk with reporters on the

Notes to Chapter 3

boat sailing to America, Shvat, 5686 [1926], in *Devarim*, vol. 1, 75. See also, S. P., "Nesiat Bialik LeAmerica," [Hebrew], London *HaOlam*, 29 January 1926.

66. Levin and Bialik quoted in "Neshef Preida LeH. N. Bialik U-LeDr. S. Levin," [Hebrew], *HaAretz*, 18 January 1926. A slightly different and no doubt edited version of Bialik's remarks appears in *Devarim*, vol. 1, 62–63. See also, S. P., "Nesiat;" "Bialik, Greatest of Living Hebrew Poets, Speaks Here," *Washington Post*, 18 April 1926; Reuven Grossman, "Bialik BeAmerica," [Hebrew], *HaTziyoni HaKlali*, 6 January 1933.

67. Bialik quoted in "H. N. Bialik Al Kaf HaMoznayim" [Hebrew], a report of his first speech in the United States at the Mecca Temple in New York, in *HaDo'ar*, 19 February 1926; Bialik, letter, [Hebrew], Tel Aviv, 8 Kislev 5686 [1926], to [Chaim] Weizmann, London, in Ungerfeld, "Bein Bialik," 152. See also, n. 20 above and the sources cited there, as well as other sources.

68. Exchange of cables and letters among Col. F. H. Kisch, member, Palestine Zionist Executive, M. Friedenberg, treasurer, Palestine Zionist Executive, Emanuel Neumann, and Shmaryahu Levin, 11–19 January 1926, in CZA, File S25/527; Israel Malkin, auditor, [ZOA, New York], letter, copy, 4 June 1926, to Schmarya Levin, New York, in ZOA Files, CZA, File F38/437; Minutes of Meeting, Administrative Committee, American Keren Hayesod, 21 June 1926, in CZA, File KH7/178.

The word "sordid" is actually quoted from G.[ershon] A.[gronsky, later, Agron], the former American and future mayor of Jerusalem, then the director of the Press Office of the Palestine Zionist Executive, in a letter from Jerusalem, 10 March 1926, to Neumann in New York, CZA, File S25/527. Since Agronsky is replying to Neumann and defending Bialik, the word conveys more Neumann's sense of the affair than Agronsky's. Neumann's "private" letter to which Agronsky is responding is not in the files.

Hirschler ("Tour," 30) and Rosenbloom ("America," 289) claim that Bialik made the trip unwillingly. They may have been unaware of his own reasons for going.

69. "Applause Delays Bialik," *New York Times*, 11 February 1926; Shva, *Hozeh*, 243. It should be noted that Bialik often received "a royal welcome" when he visited a Jewish community. See, for example, Shmaryahu Levin's description of Bialik's arrival in Warsaw in 1931, in letter, [Hebrew], London, 28 September 1931, to Maurice Samuel, New York, in *Igrot Levin*, 445.

70. The comparison with the press treatment of the arrival in the United States some nine months later of Chaim Weizmann on a similar mission is striking. See, for example, *HaDo'ar*, *New Palestine*, and other publications for November 1926.

71. *HaDo'ar*, 29 January 1926; A. R. Malachi, *Chaim Nahman Bialik* [Hebrew] (New York: Histadruth Ivrith, 5686 [1926]); Meyer W. Weisgal, editor's note, in Chaim Nachman Bialik, *Selected Poems*, trans. Maurice Samuel (New York: The New Palestine, 1926), 5; Hirschler, "Tour," 30; *The New Palestine*, 5 February 1926; "Sabbath Sermons About Bialik in Synagogues and Temples" [Yiddish], New York *Morgn Zhurnal*, 5 February 1926; *Bialik Program*, February 1926, a bilingual brochure with program suggestions for Bialik Week and Bialik

Notes to Chapter 3

Month; [Sfog] S. Tchernowitz, "MiYam Eidim" [Hebrew], *HaAretz*, 9 March 1926; Max Raisin, "Haim Nahman Bialik" [Yiddish], *Tzukunft* 10 (October 1944): 633; Fichman, "Im Bialik," 79; Eliezer L. Sherman, *Der Mensh Bialik, Zikhroynes Un Eyndrukn* [Yiddish] (Philadelphia: Ber-Kay Press, [1936]), 32; interview by the author with Mrs. Shulamith Nardi, Jerusalem, 26 March 1991; "Bialik Received by President Coolidge," *The New Palestine*, 14 May 1926; London *Jewish Chronicle*, 16 April 1926; Raisin, *Groyse Yidn*, 67. See also, A. M. Klein, "Chaim Nachman Bialik, 1873–1934," *Canadian Zionist*, July 1937.

72. Exchange of letters between Meyer Weisgal, secretary of the ZOA, New York, and Max Rhoade, Washington, D.C., 31 January to 2 February 1926, in CZA, File F38-527; "Bialik, Hebrew Poet, Welcomed to America," *New York Times*, 10 February 1926; Raisin, *Groyse Yidn*, 67–68; "From the Heights," *The New Palestine*, 12 February 1926; "Neshef Kabalat HaPanim" [Hebrew], *HaDo'ar*, 12 February 1926; "Applause Delays Bialik," *New York Times*, 11 February 1926; New York *Forverts* [Yiddish], 31 January-11 February 1926; New York *Morgn Zhurnal* [Yiddish], 8–14 February 1926; Hirschler, "Tour," 31; Rosenbloom, "America," 291.

73. See "$75,000 for Jewish Fund," *New York Times*, 15 February 1926; *The New Palestine*, 12 February and 16 April 1926; *HaDo'ar*, 5 March 1926; "$105,000 for Palestine," *New York Times*, 4 March 1926; "Chaim Nahman Bialik in Williamsburgh" [Yiddish], New York *Der Tog*, 18 April 1926; unsigned letter, copy, 23 April 1926, to Shmaryahu Levin, New York, in CZA, File F38/437; and other sources.

74. "Royal Reception to Mark Arrival of Bialik, Hebrew Poet, in Cleveland," *Jewish Review and Observer*, 30 April 1926. Among other sources, see New York *Der Tog*, 1–15, 30 April, 9 May 1926; *The New Palestine*, 12 February, 23, 30 April, 18 June 1926; *HaDo'ar*, 25 February 1926; A.[vraham] Harzfeld, New York, letter to HEC, Tel Aviv, 16 April 1926, in LAT, File IV-208-66b.

75. Louis Lipsky, *A Gallery of Zionist Profiles* (New York: Farrar Straus and Cudahy, 1956), 109. See also, 106, 110. Lipsky mistakenly dates Bialik's visit in 1923. In addition to their official contacts, the Lipskys entertained the Bialiks and Levin at home (unsigned letter, copy, 28 April 1926, to Shmaryahu Levin, New York, inviting him to spend the next Sabbath eve with the Lipskys and the Bialiks, CZA, File F38-437).

76. Minutes of the meetings of the ZOA National Executive Committee, 22 February 1926, in CZA, Section F32; A. Gimel, "Our Future—As Bialik Sees It" [Yiddish], *Dos Iddishe Folk*, 26 February 1926; "President Receives Jewish Poet," *New York Times*, 11 May 1926; "Bialik Received by President Coolidge," *The New Palestine*, 14 May 1926; *Der Tog* [Yiddish], 11 May 1926; "Hirschler, "Tour," 33; Bialik, letter, [Hebrew], Tel Aviv, 30 November 1926, to L. Shapiro, New York, in *Igrot Bialik*, vol. 3, 148–49. Shapiro was an official of the Jewish National Fund in America.

77. "12 Become Rabbis at Seminary Here," *New York Times*, 7 June 1926; "Ve'idat Yehuda HaTza'ir" [Hebrew], *HaDo'ar*, 4 June 1926; "Young Judaea and *Eretz Yisrael*," London *Jewish Chronicle*, 2 July 1926; "Avukah Convention," *The New*

Notes to Chapter 3

Palestine, 9 July 1926; *Der Tog,* 22 February 1926; *The New Palestine,* 18 June 1926; "Tomorrow Evening the Debate Among Bialik, Greenberg, Dr. Levin, and Jabotinsky" [Yiddish], New York *Morgn Zhurnal,* 21 May 1926; Chaim Nachman Bialik, New York, letter to Dr. Cyrus Adler, New York, 10 Nisan 5686 [1926], in JTSA, Record Group 1, Series A, Box 3, Bialik Folder; Meyer, *Hebrew Union College,* 160.

78. "H. N. Bailik BeVeit HaSefer HaLe'umi" [Hebrew], *HaDo'ar,* 28 May 1926; Jacob L. Weinstein, *Solomon Goldman: A Rabbi's Rabbi* (New York: Ktav, 1973), 8–9; "Bialik Al HaShira Halvrit HaTze'ira" [Hebrew], *HaAretz,* 11 April 1926; "Neshef H. N. Bialik" [Hebrew], *HaDo'ar,* 19 March 1926; advertisements in *HaDo'ar,* 12 February 1926; "All Preparations Made for National Education and Culture Conference" [Yiddish], New York *Morgn Zhurnal,* 10 May 1926; "American Zionists Found a National Cultural Corporation" [Yiddish], *Der Tog,* 17 May 1926; Dr. S[amuel] M. Melamed, "At the Cultural Conference" [Yiddish], *Dos Iddishe Folk,* 28 May 1926.

79. Raisin, "Bialik," 633; Bialik, letter, [Hebrew], on board ship, 8 February [1926], to Y. H. Ravnitzki, Tel Aviv, in *Igrot Bialik,* vol. 3, 98, and in *BeNogea,* a.

80. Bialik, letters, [Hebrew], Tel Aviv, 15 December 1925 and 3 Marheshvan [1926], to Alexander Marx, New York, and on board ship, [January, 1926], to [Yehoshua] Ravnitzki, Tel Aviv, in *Igrot Bialik,* vol. 3, 81–82, 122–24, 96; unsigned memo, probably from Alexander Marx, to Cyrus Adler, 14 March 1926, in JTSA, Record Group 1, Series A, Box 3, Bialik Folder. On Marcus, see the exchange of letters between Bialik and him in *BeNogea.*

81. Large advertisement in *Dos Iddishe Folk,* 26 February 1926. The ad was repeated in subsequent weeks but without mention of Bialik. Presumably he had successfully protested the effrontery.

82. New York *Forverts,* 31 January to 11 February 1926. (The paper never greeted him in an editorial.) B. Shelvin, "This Is the Way Yiddishists 'Honor' Bialik" [Yiddish], in *Dos Iddishe Folk,* 19 March 1926; A. S. Orlans, "Proletarion Ruhani" [Hebrew], speech at the same writers' gathering, *HaDo'ar,* 26 March 1926. Compare also, Shva, *Hozeh,* 244.

83. Bialik, letters, [Hebrew], Tel Aviv, 25 November 1925, to Dr. Chaim Weizmann, London, in "Igrot [Bialik]," *Knesset* 5 (1940): 22–23; letters, on board ship off Marseilles [January 1926] to [Yehoshua] Ravnitzki [Tel Aviv], and London, 29 July 1926, to Our Comrades in Dvir, Tel Aviv, in *Igrot Bialik,* vol. 3, 96, 118.

84. Chaim Nachman Bialik, "'Dvir' and 'Moriah,'" *The New Palestine,* 7 May 1926. The same essay appeared in Hebrew, in *Hado'ar,* 30 April 1926, and printed separately as a pamphlet (New York, 1926), both under the same title, "'Dvir' U-'Moriah.'"

85. Advertisements in *HaDo'ar,* 14 May, 18, 25 June 1926, for various booksellers offering Dvir books; Shmaryahu Levin, letters, [Hebrew], New York, 29 April and 20 June 1926, to Eiga Shapiro, [Tel Aviv], New York, 9 May 1926, to Ahad HaAm, Tel Aviv, and [Tel Aviv], 29 December 1926, to Chaim Weizmann, New York, in *Igrot Levin,* 411–16; Bialik, letter, [Hebrew], London, 29 July

Notes to Chapter 3

1926, to Our Comrades in Dvir, Tel Aviv, in *Igrot Bialik*, vol. 3, 112–20. See also, Shva, *Hozeh*, 246–47.

86. "Revival Around Bialik" [Yiddish], *Dos Iddishe Folk*, 19 February 1926; "Birkat HaDerech LeVialik" [Hebrew], editorial, *HaDo'ar*, 9 July 1926; Shmaryahu Levin, n.p., letter, to [Chaim] Weizmann, London, 18 May 1926, in *Igrot Levin* [Hebrew], 413; Neumann, *Arena*, 73; "American Zionists' Activities," London *Jewish Chronicle*, 25 June 1926; Sherman, *Mensh*, 28; Wise quoted in Melvin I. Urofsky, *A Voice That Spoke for Justice* (Albany: State University of New York Press, 1982), 215. Wise was referring to Felix Warburg, the New York banker and Jewish communal magnate, who was a non-Zionist. For a negative assessment by a prominent writer of the *yishuv*, see Sh.[lomo] Tz.[emah], "Birkat HaShalom LeVialik" [Hebrew], in *Mo'adim, Hoveret LeTarbut, Sifrut VeOmanut*, 22 September 1926.

87. Nardi interview; Maurice Samuel, "Chaim Nachman Bialik," *The New Palestine*, 15 July 1934. Compare also, Bialik, "Eretz Yisrael" [Hebrew], excerpts from a lecture in Kaunas, Lithuania, Elul, 1930, in *Devarim*, vol. 1, 153–58.

88. Bialik, letter, [Hebrew], en route from New York to London, 27 Tammuz [1926], to [Ahad HaAm, Tel Aviv], in *Igrot Bialik*, vol. 3, 105. The letter is quoted at length in Hirschler, "Tour," and Rosenbloom, "America," and in full in "As Bialik Saw America in 1926," in *Modern Jewish Life in Literature*, bk. 2, ed. Azriel Eisenberg, trans. Maurice Shudofsky. (New York: United Synagogue Commission on Jewish Education, 1968).

89. "Yenasser Lo Kilevavo," *HaDo'ar*, 23 July 1926. The poem was also published in *HaShiloah* (Bialik, letter, [Hebrew], New York, 21 June 1926, to [Jacob] Fichman, n.p., in *Igrot Bialik*, vol. 3, 102–03).

In "America," Rosenbloom interprets the poem as a cathartic exercise on the part of Bialik, after which he was cleansed of his anti-Americanism. Such a claim requires Rosenbloom to downplay the development of Bialik's relationship to the New World prior to 1926. It also requires a straightforward, rather one-dimensional reading of the poem, which may not be justified.

In "Bialik in America: The Transformation of an Inner Experience" (in *Identity and Ethos: A Festschrift for Sol Liptzin on the Occasion of His 85th Birthday*, ed. Mark H. Gelber [New York, Berne, Frankfurt am Main: Peter Lang, 1986], 267), Efraim Shmueli also claims that as a result of his American visit, Bialik ceased to be "a vehement critic of the American way of life" and became "a most enthusiastic admirer." Shmueli, too, seems unaware of Bialik's earlier connections with the New World.

90. "Bialik BeLondon—Reshamav MiNesi'ato LeAmerica" [Hebrew], London *HaOlam*, 23 July 1926.

91. B.[ernard] G. R.[ichards], "Bialik in America," *The New Palestine*, 15 August 1926; Eli Ginzberg, *Keeper of the Law: Louis Ginzberg* (Philadelphia: Jewish Publication Society, 1966), 206; Bialik, " 'Orah Hayim' Tziyoni" [Hebrew], speech at a Hebrew cultural gathering in America, Adar, 1926, in *Devarim*, vol. 1, 86; "Mishteh 'Shvilei HaHinuch' " [Hebrew], *HaDo'ar*, 16 April 1926; "H. N. Bialik Al HaShavua Halvri" [Hebrew], *HaDo'ar*, 7 May 1926; Bialik,

"Tarbut Yisrael BaGola" [Hebrew], a conversation with the correspondent of *Ketuvim*, Elul, 5686 [1926], in *Devarim*, vol. 1, 90. See also, Bialik, letter, [Hebrew], Tel Aviv, 1 Rosh Ḥodesh Kislev [1926], to Head of the Histadruth Ivrith in America, New York, in *Igrot Bialik*, vol. 3, 129–32.

92. Bialik, " 'Oraḥ Ḥayim' Tziyoni," 85. Bialik's comments on the philanthropic nature of American Zionism can be found in "Divrei Preidah LeYahadut America," 87; "Bialik Leaves the United States," London *Jewish Chronicle*, 16 July 1926; "Zionists in London Plan Syrian Work," *New York Times*, 25 July 1926; and other sources.

93. B. Karpi, "Neshef Preida LiChvod Ḥ. N. Bialik" [Hebrew], *HaDo'ar*, 16 July 1926; Shmaryahu Levin, letter, [Hebrew], New York, 9 May 1926, to Aḥad HaAm, Tel Aviv, in *Igrot Levin*, 412–13; Bialik, letter to Aḥad HaAm cited above, n. 86.

94. Bialik, address to the 29th annual convention of the ZOA in Buffalo, 29 June 1926, in *The New Palestine*, 9 July 1926, and in Yiddish, as "Towards a New Epoch," *Dos Iddishe Folk*, 25 June 1926; id., quoted by Sherman, *Mensh*, 33; id., "If Not Now—When? Concerning Jewish Education," *The New Palestine*, 16 April 1926, and also in the Philadelphia *Jewish Exponent*, 23 July 1926. See also the letter to Aḥad HaAm quoted above, n. 88.

95. "Chaim Nahman Bialik's Declaration on the Education and Cultural Movement" [Yiddish], *Der Tog*, 12 April 1926; Bialik quoted in "American United Palestine Appeal—First Report," London *Jewish Chronicle*, 6 August 1926; Bialik, " 'Eis La'asos' A Word to American Jews" [Yiddish], *Dos Iddishe Folk*, 16 April 1926; id., "Likrat Tekufa Ḥadasha" [Hebrew], *HaDo'ar*, 9 July 1926; Bialik quoted by Solomon [S. Zalman] Abramov, "Problems of Cultural Work," *Avukah Bulletin*, February, 1932. See also, Hirschler, "Tour," and Rosenbloom, "America."

96. "Zionist Convention Opens in Buffalo," *New York Times*, 28 June 1926; Bialik, "Likrat Tekufah Ḥadasha." Bialik spoke of American Jewry as compensation for the lost worlds of prewar Europe on other occasions. See, for example, "Divrei Preidah LeYahadut America," 88; "American United Palestine Appeal—First Annual Report;" letter to Aḥad HaAm, 27 Tammuz [1926], *Igrot Bialik*, vol. 3, 110.

97. Klein, "Bialik"; "Bialik BeLondon—Reshamav MiNesi'otav BeAmerica" [Hebrew], London *HaOlam*, 23 July 1926; "Zionists in London Plan Syrian Work," *New York Times*, 25 July 1926.

98. *HaAretz* ("Ḥ. N. Bialik BeVeit HaAm," 7 October 1926) reported that the crowd numbered over six thousand, *Davar* ("Ḥ. N. Bialik Al Reshamav BeAmerica," 7 October 1926), "several thousands." Both papers offered very full summaries of the poet's hour-and-a-half-long talk. *Do'ar HaYom* and the Palestine *Bulletin*, which leaned towards Revisionism, were preoccupied with Jabotinsky's visit to the *yishuv* and ignored Bialik, who had close ties to the labor sector. See also, Sherman, *Mensh*, 37; Hirschler, "Tour," 32–33; and Shva, *Ḥozeh*, 248–49.

99. The full speech appears in *Devarim*, vol. 1, 92–105. All references here are to that text.

Notes to Chapter 3

100. "Al America" [Hebrew], in *Devarim*, vol. 1, 94, 97–100, 96, 97, 100, 94, 101, 102, 99.
101. Ibid., 102, 104, 103.
102. See, for example, the less than enthusiastic article, "Birkat HaShalom LeVialik," by Sh.[lomo] Tz.[emaḥ],in *Mo'adim*, 1 (22 September 1926), a journal published by the Hebrew Writers' Association. The article was written before Bialik made his speech in Tel Aviv. Although Bialik had helped to found the journal, *Ketuvim*, of which *Mo'adim* was a special issue, he eventually broke with *Ketuvim* and in 1927 with the Writers' Association (Shva, Ḥozeh, 272–74).
103. Morris Rothenberg, quoted in "Bialik Service Is Set For Tomorrow Here," *New York Times*, 15 July 1934.
104. Goell, *English Translation* (1968), 8–18, 64, 85–86, 94. See also, H. N. Bialik, "America HaYehudit" [Hebrew], *HaDo'ar*, 9 March 1928; H. N. Bialik, "Der Koiach Fun HeChalutz" [Yiddish], *Farn Folk*, 30 March 1928; Chaim Nahman Bialik, "Making the Crooked Straight," *The Menorah Journal*, November-December 1930; John Tepper, "Palestinian Personalities" [about Bialik], *Avukah Annual* (1930), 120–21; *HaDo'ar*, 24 February 1933, whole issue devoted to the poet; Bialik, letters, [Hebrew], Tel Aviv, 21 February 1933, and Ramat Gan, 1 Ḥol HaMoed Sukkot [1933], to Israel Osman, Los Angeles, California, in *Igrot Bialik*, vol. 5, 204–05, 321; H. N. Bialik, "Die Legende fun Drei un Fir," trans. Israel Osman, in *Iddisher Kemfer*, 18 May 1934; *A Harvest of Hebrew Verse*, ed. and trans. Harry Herzl Fein (Boston: Bruce Humphries, 1934); Bialik, letter, [Hebrew], Tel Aviv, 7 July 1933, to Leib Glantz, New York, in *Igrot Bialik*, vol. 5, 247; and many other sources.
105. "The Turning of the Tide," *The New Palestine*, 11 November 1927; minutes, meeting of the National Executive Committee of the ZOA, 16 October 1927, CZA, File F38/22; Chaim Weizmann, report to the Zionist Executive, London, 7 November 1927, in *The Letters and Papers of Chaim Weizmann*, Series B, vol. 1, ed. Barnett Litvinoff (Jerusalem and New Brunswick, N.J.: Transaction Books, 1983), 521–24.
106. See, among other sources, Louis [Fischer], letter, Berlin, 30 September 1925, to Gershon [Agronsky, Jerusalem], in CZA, File A209/14; Sh. Dicker, "Reuben Brainin's Impressions of Palestine" [Yiddish], *Dos Iddishe Folk*, 23 April 1926; minutes of the meetings of the ZOA Administrative Committee, 17 August 1926, 27 January 1927, CZA, File F32/90; [Yitzhak], Lamdan, "MiSaviv La 'Braininiada'" [Hebrew], *Ketuvim*, 15 October 1926; minutes of the meetings of the ZOA National Executive Committee, 19 December 1926, CZA, File F32/21; Reuben Brainin, "Anashim Gedolim SheHayu LeKetanim" [Hebrew], Jerusalem *Do'ar HaYom*, 8 February 1928, earlier published in the New York *Der Tog*; Ungerfeld, "Bein Bialik;" Shva, Ḥozeh, 288–90.
107. See, among other sources, 'Ha"Emet" Shel Reuven Brainin Al Russia,' "Gilui Da'at Al Matzav HaYehudim BeRussia," "Meḥa'at Reuven Brainin," all in Hebrew, in Tel Aviv *HaAretz*, 14, 24 May, 25 June 1929; Reuven Brainin, "I Accuse My Judges" [Yiddish], New York *Der Tog*, 17 August 1929; Bialik, letter,

Notes to Chapter 3

[Hebrew], Berlin, 27 September 1929, to Reuben Brainin, Berlin, and the reply, 29 September 1929, in *Moznayim*, 14 (April-May 1962); D. Nissenberg, "Mishpat Brainin" [Hebrew], *HaDo'ar*, 8 November 1929. See also, Israel Cohen, for [World] Zionist Organization, London, cable, 29 January 1929, and follow-up letter, 30 January 1929, to Louis Lipsky, New York, in CZA, File F38/426; and Louis Marshall, letter, copy, New York, 1 March 1929, to Mr. Alexander, [South Africa], in CZA, File S25/1887. The animosity between Bialik and Brainin was so strong that, of their thirty-five-year correspondence, only three letters of Bialik and five of Brainin are extant. The others were apparently destroyed. (Ungerfeld, "Bein Bialik," 454.)

108. Bialik, letters, [Hebrew], Tel Aviv, 5 May 1930, to Dr. Sh.[imon] Rawidowicz, Berlin, in *Igrot Bialik*, vol. 5, 70–71; 27 March 1928, to Dr. Joseph Marcus, New York, in *BeNogea*, 25; 17 February 1927, to Hebrew Union College, Cincinnati, 17 November 1926, and 16 January 1927, to A. Z. Idelsohn, Cincinnati, in *Igrot Bialik*, vol. 3, 189, 139–40, 172; 16 June 1931, and Bad Gastein, 14 September 1933, to Zvi Diesendruck, Cincinnati, in *Igrot Bialik*, vol. 5, 161–62, 294–95. On Diesendruck at the Hebrew Union College, see Meyer, *Hebrew Union College*, 110–11, 130.

109. Bialik, letters, [Hebrew], Tel Aviv, 10 November 1926, to Ḥaim Tchernowitz, New York, in *Igrot Bialik*, vol. 3, 132–33; 19 June 1928, to Dr. M.[ax] Z. Raisin, New York, in *Igrot Bialik*, vol. 4, 135; 2 April 1933, to H[yman] G. Enelow, New York, in *Igrot Bialik*, vol. 5, 212.

110. Bialik, letters, [Hebrew], Tel Aviv, 17 July 1928, to Dr. Joseph Marcus, New York, in *BeNogea*, 28; 22 February 1929, to Prof. Rabbi Levi Ginzberg, Jerusalem, in *Igrot Bialik*, vol. 4, 221; 9 March 1930, to Beit Midrash LeḤochmat Yisrael, New York, 10 March 1930, to Dr. Joseph Marcus, New York, 28 May 1933, to Mr. Stuchinski, Zurich, all in *Igrot Bialik*, vol. 5, 45, 47–48, 232–33; Ginzberg, *Keeper*, 206. See also, Rosenbloom, "America," 303–04.

111. Bialik, letters to Marcus in *BeNogea*; Bialik, letters, [Hebrew], Tel Aviv, to Isaac Rivkind, New York, 14 February 1928, 10 July 1928, 5 June 1929, in *Igrot Bialik*, vol. 4, 89–90, 139–40, 270–71; 4 May 1930, in *Igrot Bialik*, vol. 5, 68–69.

112. Bialik, letters, [Hebrew], Tel Aviv, to David Sasson, London, 27 February 1929, in *Igrot Bialik*, vol. 4, 223; to Joseph Marcus, New York, 11 February 1927, and 24 April 1928, in *BeNogea*, 14, 25–26, and 10 April 1929, in *Igrot Bialik*, vol. 4, 249–50; to Israel Davidson, London, 19 December 1926, and New York, 24 January 1927, 10 May 1927, in *Igrot Bialik*, vol. 3, 156–57, 174–75, 228; 22 February 1928, 12 July 1928, 12 September 1928, 30 May 1928, in *Igrot Bialik*, vol. 4, 83, 151–52, 127; 17 February 1930, 2 April 1930, 27 March 1931, 8 March 1933, 11 May 1933, in *Igrot Bialik*, vol. 5, 30–32, 56–58, 146, 208, 227–28.

See also, Rosenbloom, "America," 301–03. Rosenbloom asserts that the strain in the relationship came in 1930. In fact, however, the correspondence reveals strains at least two years earlier.

113. Bialik, letters, [Hebrew], Tel Aviv, 14 July 1933, to Rabbi Yekutiel Greenwald,

Notes to Chapter 3

Columbus, Ohio, and 20 October 1930, to Dr. H. L. Gordon, New York, in *Igrot Bialik*, vol. 5, 216, 105–06. See also, his letter, [Hebrew], Tel Aviv, 18 March 1930, to Dr. Moshe W. Lewinsohn, Brooklyn, N.Y., in *Igrot Bialik*, vol. 5, 51.

114. Bialik, letters, [Hebrew], Tel Aviv, 2 March 1927, to Shmuel Faigin, Pittsburgh, in *Igrot Bialik*, vol. 3, 192; 15 May 1928, 17 July 1928, 4 December 1928, to Israel Eitan, Pittsburgh, in *Igrot Bialik*, vol. 4, 223, 246, 286; to Nehemiah S. Libowitz, Brooklyn, 15 May 1928, in *Igrot Bialik*, vol. 4, 121, 18 March 1930, 5 June 1931, 10 May 1933, 20 June 1933, in *Igrot Bialik*, vol. 5, 51, 157–58, 225–26, 236–37. The letter of 10 May 1933 appears also in Fichman, *Sefer Bialik*, 51. See also, Sh.[imon] Bernstein, *Nehemiah S. Libowitz (LeYovel Ha-Shiv'im Shelo)* [Hebrew] (New York: Hotza'a Meyuhedet MeiHaDo'ar, 8 Heshvan 5692), 12.

115. Bialik, letters, [Hebrew], Tel Aviv, 20 November 1928, 8 January 1929, 17 February 1919, 19 February 1929, 7 March 1929, and 22 March 1929, in *Igrot Bialik*, vol. 4, 182–83, 196, 213–15, 219–20, 231–32, 237–38.

116. Rabbi Moshe Haim Luzzato, *Migdal Oz* [Hebrew], ed. Shimon Ginzburg (Tel Aviv, 5687 [1927]); id., *Sefer HaMahazot* [Hebrew], ed. Shimon Ginzburg (Tel Aviv, 5687 [1927]); id., *LaYsharim Tehillah* [Hebrew], ed. Shimon Ginzburg (Tel Aviv, 5688 [1928]); Shimon Ginzburg, *HaDvir HaLavan—Osher—Sippurim* [Hebrew] (Tel Aviv, [5687-1927]); id., *Shirim U-Fo'emot* [Hebrew] (Tel Aviv, 5691 [1931]). After Bialik's death Dvir/Mossad Bialik published an additional two editions of Luzzato's work, by Ginzburg, *Rabbi Moshe Haim Luzzato U-Vnai Doro*, ed. Shimon Ginzburg [Hebrew] (Tel Aviv, 5697 [1937]), and *Sefer HaShirim* [Hebrew], ed. Shimon Ginzburg (Jerusalem, 5705 [1945]), and a long poem of Ginzburg's, *Hoshea—Poema* [Hebrew] (Tel Aviv, 5696 [1936]). See also, the many letters of Bialik to Ginzburg, Silkiner, Sho'er, Lissitzky, and others, relating to the Haverim series, in *Igrot Bialik*, vol. 4.

117. Bialik, letters, [Hebrew], Tel Aviv, to Shimon Ginzburg, New York, 16 December 1926, in *Igrot Bialik*, vol. 3, 151–52, 2 November 1927, 30 March 1928, 17 July 1928, in *Igrot Bialik*, vol. 4, 20–21, 104–06, 145, among others. For Bavli's implied criticism of Bialik, see above, n. 8.

Ginzburg was more successful with Bialik than he had been in Odessa. When Bialik was literary editor of *HaShiloah*, he rejected several of Ginzburg's poems, offering a detailed critique. (Shmuel Avneri, "Kavim LeDarko Shel Bialik BeArichat HaShiloah," in *Hallel LeVialik: Iyunim u-Mehkarim Bitzirat Ch. N. Bialik*, ed. Hillel Weiss and Yedidyah Itzhaki [Ramat Gan: Universitat Bar-Ilan, 1989], 286–87).

118. Sh.[imon] Bernstein, "Ata HaIsh!" *HaToren*, Teveth, 5686 [1926]. See also, Bialik, letter, [Hebrew], Tel Aviv, 17 July 1928, to Shimon Ginzburg, New York, in *Igrot Bialik*, vol. 4, 145; and F.[ishel] Lahover, "Polania VeAmerica," in *Ketuvim*, 28 July 1927. The latter article, in a journal with which Bialik was closely associated, compares America most favorably to Poland with regard to Hebrew culture.

119. "Prass Sifruti Shel *HaDo'ar*" [Hebrew], *HaDo'ar*, 28 January 1927; Bialik, let-

Notes to Chapter 3

ter, [Hebrew], Tel Aviv, 5 February 1929, to [Menaḥem] Ribalow, New York, in *Igrot Bialik*, vol. 4, 210–11; id., letter, [Hebrew], Tel Aviv, 24 December 1929, to Av.[raham] Goldberg, [editor of the New York *Der Tog*], in ABTA, File 51-45756a. See also, letters to various Hebrew and Yiddish authors in the United States in *Igrot Bialik*, vols. 4–5.

120. Bialik, letter, [Hebrew], Tel Aviv, 2 November 1927, to Shimon Ginzburg, New York, in *Igrot Bialik*, vol. 4, 20; id., Carlsbad, 14 Elul [1931], to [Yehoshua] Ravnitzki, Tel Aviv, in *Igrot Bialik*, vol. 5, 178–79; id., [Tel Aviv], 22 November 1927, to Y.[itzḥak] Naiditch, Paris, in Fichman, *Sefer Bialik*, 70; id., Tel Aviv, 24 March 1929, to Anna Margolin, New York, in *Igrot Bialik*, vol. 4, 242; and id., Tel Aviv, 15 May 1929, to Naftali Gross, New York, in *Igrot Bialik*, vol. 4, 260. See also various letters of Bialik to Ginzburg, Silkiner, and others, in *Igrot Bialik*, vols. 4–5; and Rosenbloom, "America," 304.

121. Raisin, *Groyse Yidn*, 72. See also, Bialik, letter, [Hebrew], Tel Aviv, 28 September 1928, to Daniel Persky, [New York], thanking him for work he had done for a book on Y. L. Peretz to be published by Dvir, in *Igrot Bialik*, vol. 4, 166.

122. Shmaryahu Levin, letters, [Hebrew], n.p., 8 November 1927 and 16 January 1928, to Y. D. Berkowitz, New York; at sea, 12 August 1927, to H. N. Bialik and Y. H. Ravnitzki, Tel Aviv; in *Igrot Levin*, 424–27; Bialik, letter, [Hebrew], Tel Aviv, 25 January 1928, to Dr. A. Ginzburg, New York, in *Igrot Bialik*, vol. 4, 60–61; audit of Dvir, 2 May 1929, in CZA, File S25/10271; Bialik, letter, [Hebrew], Tel Aviv, 19 February 1930, to Shmaryahu Levin, New York, in *Igrot Bialik*, vol. 5, 36.

123. Bialik, letter, [Hebrew], Tel Aviv, 25 January 1929, to R.[obert] Marwill, Jerusalem, in *Igrot Bialik*, vol. 4, 206; id., "Ptiḥa LeVe'idat HaSofrim" [Hebrew], *Moznayim*, 3 Tammuz 1931, and in *Devarim*, vol. 1, 168–69; id., "Al America," 98. See also, Sh.[lomo] Tzemaḥ, "HaAdam Im Aḥerim" [Hebrew], *Knesset* 4 (1939): 64; Bialik, letters, [Hebrew], Tel Aviv, 25 May 1927, to L. Shapira, New York, in *Igrot Bialik*, vol. 3, 231–32, and 20 June 1929, to Chaim Weizmann, London, in *Igrot Bialik*, vol. 4, 271–72.

124. Ginzberg, *Keeper*, 195; *The New Palestine*, 26 February 1926.

125. Bialik, letter, [Hebrew], Tel Aviv, 24 March 1927, to Herman Bernstein, Naples, in *Igrot Bialik*, vol. 3, 206. See also, his letters from Tel Aviv in Hebrew to Nathan Straus, New York, 2 May 1927, in *Igrot Bialik*, vol. 3, 217–18, and 28 October 1927, in *Igrot Bialik*, vol. 4, 9–11; to Henrietta Szold, Jerusalem, 3 February 1928, and to Po'alei Tel Aviv VeYaffo, 29 May 1929, in *Igrot Bialik*, vol. 4,: 70–73, 263; and Shva, *Ḥozeh*, 277.

126. *American Jewish Year Book* 27 (5686 [1925]): 148; Bialik, letter, [Hebrew], Tel Aviv, 30 April 1925, to the Foundation for the Support of Hebrew Authors, New York, in *Igrot Bialik*, vol. 3, 27–28. See also, id., letters, [Hebrew], to Israel Matz Foundation, New York, 1925–33, in *Igrot Bialik*, vols. 3, 4, and 5; Shva, *Ḥozeh*, 277.

127. Bialik, "Al Te'udat Ohel Shem" [Hebrew], *Devarim*, vol. 2, 163–64; S.[amuel] S.[imon] Bloom, letter, copy, Tel Aviv, to Executive Council of Zionist Organisation, London, 3 April 1927, in CZA, File S25/525. See also, Bialik, "Al

Notes to Chapter 4

'Ohel Shem' Ve 'Oneg Shabbat' " [Hebrew], in *Devarim*, vol. 2, 160–62; id., letter, [Hebrew], Tel Aviv, 5 June 1929, in *Igrot Bialik*, vol. 4, 267–68; *Sefer HaIshim—Lexicon Eretzyisra'eli* [Hebrew] (Tel Aviv: Am Oved, 5697 [1937]), 80–81; Lipsky, *Gallery*, 109–10; Shva, *Ḥozeh*, 260.

128. Bialik, letters, [Hebrew], Tel Aviv, 27 January 1928, to Prof. [P.] Schneurson, New York, and 4 April 1929, to Moshe Carasso and the representative of "Ophir," Mr. Molcho, [Tel Aviv], in *Igrot Bialik*, vol. 4, 70, 245; id., "LeShe'eilat HaTarbut HaIvrit" [Hebrew], lecture at a Mapai seminar, Tammuz, 5692 [1932], in *Devarim*, vol. 1, 192; id., letter, [Hebrew], Tel Aviv, 16 January 1927, to L. Shapiro, New York, in *Igrot Bialik*, vol. 3, 173; id., "HaSifrut VeHaSofer Ha'Ivri" [Hebrew], opening address to the convention of the Association of Hebrew Writers, Tel Aviv, Sivan, 5691 [1931], in *Devarim*, vol. 1, 166–67, also in *Moznayim*, 18 May 1931; id., letter, [Hebrew], Tel Aviv, 14 February 1928, to M.[ax] Lipson, New York, in ABTA, File 51-43694a. For the reaction of Sholem Aleichem to Dolitzky's plight, see Shmeruk, "Sholem Aleichem and America," 217, and the sources cited there.

129. Ch.[aim] N.[achman] Bialik, "On the Tenth Anniversary of the Hechalutz," taken from a speech in Tel Aviv, in *Hechalutz*, ed. Chaim Arlosoroff, Sh.[lomo] Grodzensky, Rebecca Schmuckler (New York: Zionist Labor Party "Hitachduth" of America with the cooperation of Avukah, America Student Zionist Federation, 1929), 15, 19.

130. Chaim Nachman Bialik, "LeShe'eilat HaTarbut Ha'Ivrit," 177, and "The Chalutz," *The New Palestine*, 4 May 1928. See also, his "Lisod 'Agudat Shoḥarei HaUniversita HaIvrit' " [Hebrew], Tel Aviv, 6 Nisan 5693 [1933], in *Devarim*, vol. 2, 79–80.

131. Compare Bialik's statement to the editorial board of *Judisk Tidskrift*, Stockholm, 17 January 1934, in *Igrot Bialik*, vol. 5, 307–08, in which he makes no distinction between Europe and America.

132. Bialik, letter, [Hebrew], Tel Aviv, 24 March 1927, to Herman Bernstein, Naples, in *Igrot Bialik*, vol. 3, 205.

Chapter 4

1. Anita Shapira, *Berl: The Biography of a Socialist Zionist*, trans. Ḥaya Galai (Cambridge, England: Cambridge University Press, 1984), 357.
2. Katznelson, "Our Historical Heritage," in *Revolutionary Constructivism: Essays on the Jewish Labor Movement in Palestine*, trans. and abr. Benny Applebaum and Shlomo Grodzensky (New York: Young Poale Zion Alliance, 1937), 16.
3. Compare, for example, his letters, to David Remez, [December 1919], n.p., and [Tevet, 1920, Palestine], in *Igrot B. Katznelson*, (hereafter, BKL), 6 vols., [Hebrew] (Tel Aviv, 1961–84), vol. 4, 72, 81. All quotations from BKL are translated from the Hebrew version there, regardless of their original language.
4. Katznelson, "HaEḥad BaMa'aracha," introduction to the works of Naḥman Syrkin, in *Kitvei B. Katznelson*, (hereafter, KBK), [Hebrew], 11 vols. (Tel Aviv: Mifleget Po'alei Eretz Yisrael, 5706–13 [1946–53]), vol. 10, 7; and "Bein Adam LaḤavero," introduction to the works of Avraham Liessin, in KBK, vol. 10,

Notes to Chapter 4

115. All translations from *KBK* are translated from the Hebrew version there, regardless of their original language.
5. Katznelson, Bobruisk, letter to brother, Israel, [United States], 30 November 1908, in *BKL*, vol. 1, 84.
6. Id., Vilna, letter to brother, Israel, [United States], 25 January 1908, in *BKL*, vol. 1, 58. See also, Anita Shapira, *Berl (Biografia)*, [Hebrew], 2 vols. (Tel Aviv: Sifriyat Ofakim—Am Oved, 1980), vol. 1, 39–40.
7. Katznelson, Ben Shemen, letter to Hannah Katznelson, [Bobruisk], 26 Shvat [1912], in *BKL*, vol. 1, 327–29.
8. Yosef Haim Brenner, *MiKan U-MiKan* [Hebrew] (Tel Aviv: HaKibbutz Ha-Me'uhad, Sifriat HaPo'alim, 5738 [1978]), 1299, originally published in 1911; [id.], Yosef Haver, "BeHayeinu U-Veltonuteinu" [Hebrew], *HaAhdut*, Kislev, 5672 [1911], 12.
9. See Katznelson, letters, [Bobruisk, 17 Tammuz 1907 and 11 Tishrei 1907], to Israel [Katznelson, United States], in *BKL*, vol. 1, 50, 54.
10. Katznelson, Bobruisk, letters to brother, Israel, [United States], 11 February [1908], n.d. [winter, 1908], [2 January 1908], in *BKL*, vol. 1, 60, 83, 56; Shapira, *Biography*, 40.
11. Shapira, *Berl*, vol. 1, 41.
12. Katznelson, quoted in Baruch Zuckerman, *Zikhroynes*, vol. 2 [Yiddish] (New York: Farlag "Iddisher Kemfer" and Farband Bikher Farlag, 1963), 280–81; and id., "HaEhad BaMa'aracha," 80.
13. Id., Kinneret, letter to Israel Katznelson, [New York], Rosh Hodesh Sivan [1911], in *BKL*, vol. 1, 222. See also, his letter of Erev Lag BaOmer [1911] from Kinneret, to brothers Haim and Israel, [United States], in *BKL*, vol. 1, 218.
14. Id., Ben Shemen, letters to his brother, Israel, [United States], 22 Heshvan 1911, and to his sister-in-law, Batya Katznelson, [United States], 22 Iyar [1912], in *BKL*, vol. 1, 294, 358–59.
15. Id., Ben Shemen, letters, to brothers, Haim and Israel, [United States], 10 Heshvan [1911] and 15 Tevet 1912, in *BKL*, vol. 1, 279, 305.
16. Id., "MiBifnim" [Hebrew], in *KBK*, vol. 1, 14, originally published in *HaPo'el HaTza'ir*, 16 August 1912.
17. See id., letter, [Bobruisk, 14 Nisan 1908], to Israel [Katznelson, United States], in *BKL*, vol. 1, 63; and letter, Jaffa, Rosh Hodesh Eve, 5679 [sic], to Haim [Katznelson, United States], in *BKL*, vol. 3, 269–70.
18. See, for example, Nahman Syrkin, "LaShe'eila HaTerritorialit," *HaAhdut*, 3 (7 Heshvan 5673 [1913]), and "Hasal Sidur Galveston," *HaAhdut*, 5 (1 Av 5674 [1914]).
19. Katznelson, letters, Ben Shemen, Rosh Hodesh Tammuz 1913, to brother, Haim, [United States], and Kinneret, Rosh Hodesh Sivan [1911], to brother, Israel, [United States], in *BKL*, vol. 1, 526, 223; id., "BeHavlei Adam. Al Eliezer Yoffe BeShloshim LeMoto," in *KBK*, vol. 5, 317–18; "LeTnu'at Hehalutz," in *KBK*, vol. 1, 52. The second to last is a letter to Jewish youth outside Palestine originally written in Tishrei, 1917, while the last was originally pub-

Notes to Chapter 4

lished in *Tlamim*, 32 (Kislev-Tevet 5703 [1943]). See also, Shapira, *Berl*, vol. 1, 98–100, 131, 275–80; and Margalit Shilo, "On the Way to the Moshav: Ha-Ikar Hatza'ir, the 'American Group' in the Second *Aliyah*" [Hebrew], *Cathedra* 25 (September 1982): 79–98.

Other Americans with whom he came in contact in these years included A. S. Waldstein and Zvi Hirshfeld, both of whom he liked. (Katznelson, letters, Ein Ganim, 14 Adar 1914, to HaVa'ad HaMerkazi shel Mifleget "Poalei Zion," n.p., in *BKL*, vol. 1, 584, and Jerusalem, 8 Heshvan 5678 [1917], to Sarah Schmuckler, n.p., in *BKL*, vol. 2, 393.)

20. Katznelson, letter, Kinneret, 5 Heshvan [1911], to brother, Israel, [United States], in *BKL*, vol. 1, 182.
21. Id., lecture at the Young Mapai Seminar, May-June 1944, in *KBK*, vol. 11, 198. See also, id., [Hilmiyyeh, Egypt], letters, 7 Av [1918], to Hannah and Rachel Katznelson, Sarah Schmuckler, and Leah Miron, [Palestine], and 6 Elul [1918], to Rachel Katznelson, [Palestine], in *BKL*, vol. 3, 5–6, 32
22. Id., [Tel el-Kabri, Sinai], letter, Sukkot, [1918], to Hannah Katznelson, [Jerusalem], in *BKL*, vol. 3, 64; id., "Ahdut HaAvoda," talk given at first general conference of Ahdut HaAvoda, Petah Tikva, 21 Adar I 5679 [1919], in *KBK*, vol. 1, 113.
23. Id., "Avodateinu BeEretz Yisrael U-Lema'ana," in *KBK*, vol. 1, 317, originally a letter in Yiddish sent to New York's *Di Tsayt* in the late summer of 1920; Shapira, *Berl*, vol. 1, 143. See also, Berl Katznelson, "Beirurim," in *KBK*, vol. 1, 157, first published in *Kuntres* 9 (Tammuz 5679 [1919]).
24. Id., Jaffa, letter, Rosh Hodesh, 5679 [1919, no month given], to brother, Haim, [United States], in *BKL*, vol. 3, 266.
25. Id., "Erev HaCongress HaHamisha-Asar" [Hebrew], in *KBK*, vol. 3, 151, originally published in *Kuntres* 310 (Tammuz, 5687 [1927]); id., "HaMatzav BaAretz U-Va-Tziyonut," in *KBK*, vol. 3, 128, originally published in *Davar*, 14 July 1927; id., letter, [Jaffa?, Nisan-Iyyar, 1921], to [World Association, Poale Zion, Vienna], c/o Shlomo Kaplansky, in *BKL*, vol. 4, 231; id., "Ve'idat London," in *KBK*, vol. 1, 239, originally published in *HaAdamah*, 10–11 (Tammuz-Av 5680 [1920]). See also, id., "Avoda! LaShana HaMitkarevet," in *KBK*, vol. 1, 150–53, originally published in *Kuntres* 5 (Sivan 5679 [1919]).
26. Id., "LaHarada Tziyonit," in *KBK*, vol. 5, 106, originally a speech given in Jerusalem, 23 September 1942; id., Tel Aviv, letter to D[avid Ben-Gurion, Tel Aviv], 4 August 1942, in KABB, Ben-Gurion File.
27. Id., Ismailiya, letter to sister, Hannah Katznelson, [Jerusalem], 4 Heshvan [1918], in *BKL*, vol. 3, 71; id., unpublished notebook in Beit Berl, entry for 4 September [1919]; id., "Bimei Yerushalayim," in *KBK*, vol. 1, 215–16, originally published in *Kuntres* 35 (Iyar 5680 [1920]), signed pseudonymously, "A." Compare also, id., "Likrat HaYamim HaBa'im," in *KBK*, vol. 1, 83–84, originally a talk given at the Seventh Agricultural Conference, Poriya, Palestine, 1918.
28. Id., Vienna, letter to the Executive Committee of Ahdut HaAvoda, [Tel Aviv], 2 August [1920], in *BKL*, vol. 4, 124.

29. Id., letters, Zirlin near Vienna, to Baruch Zuckerman, United States, 27 August [1920]; and Jaffa, to Office of the International Association of Poale Zion, Vienna, 18 Adar Sheni [1921], in *BKL*, vol. 4, 150, 225. See also, id., "MiLifnei HaYetzia," *KBK*, vol. 1, 302–03, originally published in *Kuntres* 51 (Elul 5680 [1920]); and Shapira, *Biography*, 108ff, 132. On the "Tool Campaign" see *BKL*, vol. 4, 221, n. 10.
30. Katznelson, "Avodateinu Be-Eretz Yisrael U-Lema'ana," in *KBK*, vol. 1, 313–18, originally a letter to *Di Tsayt*, n.d. [late summer 1920].
31. Id., letters, Jaffa, 21 November 1920 and 8 Heshvan 5681 [1920], to Ben-Gurion, [London]; 28 March 1921, to [Baruch] Zuckerman, New York; 12 January 1921, to Comrades [Zalman] Rubashov, [Yitzhak] Zaar, and [Berl] Locker, [Vienna]; and 8 February 1921, to Poale Zion in America, all in *BKL*, vol. 4, 170, 159–61, 226–27, 209, 188–91, 170, 209. See also, M. Kramer, Alexandria, Egypt, letter, 21 April 1920, to Katznelson, n.p., in KABB, File Kuf.

    Sometimes, particularly in the first days of the paper, honoraria were paid. See letter of Haim [Hirsch] Ehrenreich, cashier of *Di Tsayt*, New York, to Katznelson, Tel Aviv, 1 January 1921, in KABB, Mosdot File.
32. "Negi'ot," in *KBK*, vol. 1, 188, originally published in *HaAdamah* 1 (Shvat 5680 [1920]).
33. "Ve'idat London," in *KBK*, vol. 1, 245–46, originally published in *HaAdamah*, 10–11 (21 Tammuz 5680 [1920]). See also, letter of Henrietta Szold, quoted in Alpheus T. Mason, *Brandeis: A Free Man's Life* (New York: Viking, 1946), 460.
34. "Ve'idat London," 235–36; Katznelson, letters, London, [early July, 1920], to Leah Miron-Katznelson, [Palestine], and Prague, 19 July [1921], to ?, in *BKL*, vol. 4, 110, 265.

    See also, id., "LaAsefa HaLe'umit," in *KBK*, vol. 1, 205–09, originally published in *Kuntres* 31 (Nisan 5680 [1920]); id., [London], letter to Executive Committee of Ahdut HaAvoda, [Tel Aviv], 28 Tammuz [1920], in *BKL*, vol. 4, 118–19; id., "BaCongress HaShneim-Asar," in *KBK*, vol. 1, 282–84, originally a speech to the twelfth Zionist Congress, Carlsbad, Czechoslovakia, 1 September 1924. Shapira, *Berl*, vol. 1, 173–74, and *Biography*, 74; Israel Kolatt-Kopelovich, "Ideology and the Impact of Realities Upon the Jewish Labour Movement in Palestine, 1905–1919," Ph.D. dissertation, Hebrew University, Jerusalem, 19 June 1964, 316–17; and Frank E. Manuel, *The Realities of American-Palestine Relations* (Washington, D.C.: Public Affairs Press, 1949), 3.
35. Katznelson, "Baltonut," in *KBK*, vol. 1, 143, originally published in *Kuntres* 5 (Sivan 5679 [1919]); Alef. [id.], Jaffa, letter, Rosh Hodesh, 5679 [sic], to Haim [Katznelson, United States], in *BKL*, vol. 3, 266. Among other sources see also, id., "Likrat HaYamim HaBa'im," in *KBK*, vol. 1, 60–86, originally a speech at the Seventh Conference of Agricultural Workers in Palestine, Purim, 1918; id., "Amar Ha'Kuntres,' " in *KBK*, vol. 1, 148–50, originally published unsigned as "LiShe'eilat HaSafot," *Kuntres* 5 (Sivan 5679 [1919]); id., "Beirurim," in *KBK*, vol. 1, 157–68, originally published in *Kuntres* 9 (Tammuz 5679 [1919]).
36. Katznelson, letters, [Mikve Yisrael, end of Iyyar 1919], to Ben-Gurion, n.p., in *BKL*, vol. 3: 318; and [Jaffa?, Nisan-Iyyar, 1921], to [World Association, Poale Zion], c/o Sh. Kaplansky, [Vienna], *BKL*, vol. 4, 231.

Notes to Chapter 4

37. Id., Zirlin near Vienna, letter, 27 August [1920], to Baruch Zuckerman, United States, in *BKL*, vol. 4, 150.
38. Id., "Avodah BeKvish Tverya-Tzemah (Mikhtav MeiEretz Yisrael)," in *KBK*, vol. 1, 318, originally written as a letter to *Di Tsayt* of New York, 21 Heshvan [5681 (1920)]; id., Jaffa, letter, 8 February 1921, to Poale Zion in America, [New York], in *BKL*, vol. 4, 208–09; Ben-Gurion, Vienna, letter to Katznelson, [Tel Aviv], 11 April 1921, in LAT, File IV-104-29-2alef.
39. Katznelson, unpublished notebook in KABB, entry for 5678-Iyyar; and letter, London, to the Executive Committee of Ahdut HaAvoda, [Tel Aviv], 14 September 1919, in *BKL*, vol. 4, 28. See also, id., letter, [Palestine, 2 June 1920], to Zvi Schwartz-Shamir, London, in *BKL*, vol. 4, 97; Shapira, *Biography*, 111; Ya'akov Goldstein, *HaHistadrut U-Fo'alei Artzot HaBrit* [Hebrew] (Tel Aviv: Am Oved, 1984), 10–11.
40. Katznelson, letters, [Tel Aviv], 27 Shvat [1920], to Zvi Schwartz-Shamir, n.p.; Zirlin near Vienna, letter to Baruch Zuckerman, United States, 27 August [1920], in *BKL*, vol. 4, 82–83, 150.
41. Id., quoted in HVHP", 13 October 1927.
42. Id., "El HaPo'alim HaYehudiyim BeAmerica—Michtav LaHaverim," in *KBK*, vol. 1, 285, originally published in *HaDo'ar* and *Di Tsayt*, 1 January 1922.
43. Id., Jaffa, letter to Ben-Gurion, [London], 25 Tevet [1921], in *BKL*, vol. 4, 182.
44. Id., n.p., letter to Executive Committee of the Poale Zion in America, [New York], 4 Shvat [1921], in *BKL*, vol. 4, 194.
45. Id., "Baltonut," in *KBK*, vol. 1, 191, originally published in *Kuntres* 26 (Shvat, 5680–1920). Compare also, id., "Ve'idat London," in *KBK*, vol. 1, 227–61, originally published in *HaAdamah* 10–11 (Tammuz-Av 5680 [1920]).
46. Ben-Gurion, Vienna, letter to Katznelson, [Tel Aviv], 11 April 1921, in LAT, File IV-104-29-2alef; Katznelson, Jaffa, letter, 21 March 1921, to Baruch Zuckerman, [New York], in *BKL*, vol. 4, 222. See also, id., Jaffa, letter, 10 Adar II [1921], to B[en]-G[urion, London], in *BKL*, vol. 6, 1–2.
47. Id., letters to Yekutiel Bahrav, n.p., from [Rafiah, 2 Av 5679 (1919)], [Mikve Yisrael, 23 Tammuz 5679 (1919)], and n.p., [20 October 19?], in *BKL*, vol. 3, 507–08, 475–76; and *BKL*, vol. 4, 59–60; and id., London, letter to Office of the World Union, Poale Zion, [Vienna], 7 Heshvan [1919], in *BKL*, vol. 4, 64–66.
48. Id., Jerusalem, letter, 14 November 1920, to Dr. N.[ahman] Syrkin, [Alexander] Livshitz, and Y.[a'akov] Prozhanski-Ahva, [United States], in *BKL*, vol. 4, 165–66. See also, ibid., 166, n. 2.
49. Katznelson, "Baltonut." See also, id., letters, London, 29 June [1921], to [Executive Committee, Ahdut HaAvoda, Tel Aviv], and Jaffa, 8 Heshvan 5681 [1920], to Ben-Gurion, [London], in *BKL*, vol. 4, 246, 161.
50. Id., letters, London, 2 July [1921], to David Bloch (Blumenfeld), n.p., and Berlin, 22 July [1921], to Manya [Shohat, Paris], in *BKL*, vol. 4, 255, 270; id., quoted in HVHP", 14 June 1921.
51. Compare Katznelson, as quoted in "Poale Zion Party Council Adopts Workers' Bank and Tithe for the Keren Hayesod" [Yiddish], *Di Tsayt*, 28 November 1921.

Notes to Chapter 4

52. Goldstein, HaHistadrut, 15, 40; Katznelson, "Bank HaPo'alim BeEretz Yisrael," in KBK, vol. 1, 350, originally published in Di Tsayt [?], January 1921.
53. Shapira, Biography, 115.
54. Katznelson, Jaffa, letter to London office, World Union of Poale Zion, 24 January 1921, in BKL, vol. 4, 200; Ze'ev Tzahor, "HaHistadrut—Tekufat Haltzuv," Ph.D. dissertation, Hebrew University, Jerusalem, July 1979.
55. Katznelson, quoted in HVHP", 14 June 1921; id., New York, letter to Leah Miron-Katznelson, [Palestine, 2 December 1921], in BKL, vol. 5, 29. See also, Goldstein, HaHistadrut, 21–22; Tzahor, "Tekufat Haltzuv," 137.
56. Katznelson, Cherbourg, letter written just before sailing to New York, to Hannah Katznelson-Nesher, [21 or 22 October 1921], in BKL, vol. 4, 328.
57. Id., "Yoman America," entries for 12, 20, and 30 November, 7, 11–16, 18, and 27 December [1921], 4, 6, 18, and 28 January, 2 and 8 February, and 17 March [1922], in BKL, vol. 5, 101, 107, 112, 114, 117–18, 120–21, 123–24, 127, 129, 132, 138; id., Paris, letter to Leah Miron-Katznelson, [Palestine], 26 June 1921, in BKL, vol. 4, 244; Hado'ar, 19 December 1921; Shapira, Berl, vol. 1, 212–13. See also, J. M. Diamondstone, Montreal, letter to Katznelson, Tel Aviv, 21 March 1933, in KABB, File Dalet.

    Both in Berl (vol. 1, 214–15) and Biography (261, 354), Shapira overstates somewhat the case for Katznelson's abstemiousness. She has overlooked his frequent visits to the Yiddish theater, surely one of the "sights" of America and for him a leisure activity.
58. Katznelson, letters, New York, [2 and 17 December 1921], to wife, Leah Miron-Katznelson, [Palestine], and Winnipeg, 29 March [1922], to sister, Hannah Katznelson-Nesher, in BKL, vol. 5, 28–29, 39, 80–81; id., letter, Winnipeg, 31 March [1922], to Leah Miron-Katznelson, Kinneret, in BKL, vol. 6, 6; id., "Yoman America," entries for 4 February and 17 March [1922], in BKL, vol. 5, 130, 138; and id., unpublished notebooks for 5680–81 [1920–21], in Beit Berl. See also, various other letters and diary entries from the period of his visit.
59. Id., Cherbourg, letter to [Moshe] Beilinson, Trieste, 22 October [1921], in BKL, vol. 4, 334; Nahman Syrkin, "HaMalachut Shel Po'alei Eretz Yisrael BeAmerica" [Hebrew], in HaDo'ar, 15 November 1921.
60. Louis Diamant, chairman, New York Council, the Shiloh League, [November, 1921], to Katznelson, [New York], in KABB, Mosdot File; Katznelson, "Yoman America," entry for 7 January [1922], in BKL, vol. 5, 121–22; id., New York, letter to HEC, [Tel Aviv], 10 January [1922], in BKL, vol. 5, 42.
61. Id., "Yoman America," entries for 12, 26, and 27 November [1921] and 17 March [1922], in BKL, vol. 5, 101, 111, 138; "Bnei Eretz Yisrael Im Tze'irei Histadrut HaOvdim" and "Aseifat Eretz HaYisra'elim" [Hebrew], HaDo'ar, 24 and 29 November 1921; Katznelson, letters, New York, 12 January 1922, to HEC, [Tel Aviv], in LAT, File IV-104-71, and [17 January 1922], to Leah Miron-Katznelson, [Palestine], in BKL, vol. 5, 39; and Cleveland, 22 February [1922], to [David Zakkai, Palestine], in KABB, Correspondence File.

    On the eve of his departure Katznelson also committed himself to work-

Notes to Chapter 4

ing in America for a merger of the Poale Zion with the smaller, non-Marxist, labor-Zionist party, Zeirei-Zion. Apparently in this case, too, he satisfied himself with selling bank shares to the Zeirei-Zion. (Katznelson, Cherbourg, letter to [Israel] Mereminsky [Marom, Warsaw], 22 October 1921, in BKL, vol. 4, 330; "Palestine Workers' Delegation at the Zeirei-Zion" [Yiddish], Di Tsayt, 30 November 1921.) The merger took place some years later without Katznelson's intervention.

62. "Neshef Eivel LeZeicher M. Y. Berdichevsky" [Hebrew], HaDo'ar, 18 December 1921; Katznelson, "Yoman America," entry for 11 December [1921], in BKL, vol. 5, 115.
63. See id., "Tzedek LaUmim," in KBK, vol. 1, 221, originally printed as Ḥoveret, which appeared instead of Kuntres 36 (Iyyar, 5680 [1920]); and Shapira, Berl, vol. 1, 213, and Biography, 122.
64. Katznelson, "Yoman America," entry for 18 November [1921], in BKL, vol. 5, 105.
65. Id., letters, Detroit, to Leah Miron-Katznelson, Kinneret, 3 February 1922, in BKL, vol. 6, 5; and Cleveland, to [David Zakkai, Palestine], 22 February [1922], in KABB, Correspondence File. See also, Yosef Sprinzak, quoted in HVHP", 27 June 1921; and Shapira, Berl, vol. 1, 203, 212.
66. Katznelson, letters, London, 9 Av [1921], to [Baruch] Zuckerman, [New York], in BKL, vol. 4, 288; and New York, 7 December 1921, to Aḥdut HaAvoda, [Palestine], in BKL, vol. 5, 32.
67. Id., "Yoman America," entry for 19 January [1922], in BKL, vol. 5, 125. On 10 February 1922 an op ed piece by Syrkin, "The Workers' Bank in Palestine" [Yiddish], appeared in Di Tsayt.
68. "New York Jewish Workers Give Enthusiastic Reception to the Palestine Workers' Delegation" [Yiddish], Di Tsayt, 11 November 1921.
69. Compare Yosef Baratz, as quoted in HVHP", 5 June 1922.
70. See, among other sources, Katznelson, "Yoman America," 7, 25, 29 November and 7 December [1921], in BKL, vol. 5, 93, 110, 112, 114; id., New York, letter to David Zakkai, [Palestine], 28 November 1921, in BKL, vol. 5, 24. See also, Shapira, Berl, vol. 1, 209–10; Goldstein, HaHistadrut, 28; and id., "Heroine or Traitor? The Controversy over Manya Vilbushevich-Shoḥat and Her Links with Zubatov," Studies in Contemporary Jewry 6 (1990): 287.
71. " 'Farband' Will Aid Palestine Workers' Delegation" and "The Zeirei Zion and the Palestine Workers' Bank," both in Di Tsayt [Yiddish], 12 December 1921; "Tzeirei Zion VeYaḥasam LeVank HaPo'alim BeEretz Yisrael" [Hebrew], Hado'ar, 12 December 1921.
72. Katznelson, "Yoman America," 16 November and 21–25 December [1921], in BKL, vol. 5, 104, 118–19; id., letters, New York, 28 November [1921], to David [Ben-Gurion], n.p., and New York, 15 April [1922], to David (Blumenfeld) Bloch, [Tel Aviv], in LAT, File IV-104-71-3. See also, Yosef Baratz, quoted in HVHP", 5 June 1922.
73. "Enthusiastic Beginning of the Campaign for the Palestine Workers' Bank" [Yiddish], Di Tsayt, 3 January 1922; the New York Times, 2 January 1922; Katz-

nelson, "Yoman America," 1 January 1922, in BKL, vol. 5, 120. See also, Shapira, Berl, vol. 1, 210.

74. "Max Rottenstein off on a Tour for the Workers' Bank" [Yiddish], Di Tsayt, 5 January 1922; "Non-Partisan Committees for the Workers' Bank Already Founded in Many Cities" [Yiddish], Di Tsayt, 8 January 1922; Katznelson, Buffalo, letter to Issachar Bonchik, [New York], 13 January 1922, in BKL, vol. 5, 44–45; and many other sources, especially subsequent letters of Katznelson himself.

75. Id., "Yoman America" and letters in BKL, vol. 5, passim, as well as his datebook for 1922, in Beit Berl; reports in Di Tsayt and HaDo'ar for the period.

76. Katznelson, Buffalo, letter, to David (Blumenfeld) Bloch, [Palestine], 14 February [1922], in BKL, vol. 5, 59; id., "Yoman America," 26 January and 17 March [1922], in BKL, vol. 5, 126–27, 143; "Energetic Work Brings Good Results for the Palestine Workers' Bank" [Yiddish], Di Tsayt, 17 March 1922; Yitzhak Spector, "Malachut HaPo'alim BeChicago" [Hebrew], HaDo'ar, 3 February 1922. See also, Shapira, Biography, 121.

77. See Katznelson, "The First Activities for the Workers' Bank" and "Why Do Workers Need Their Own Bank?" [Yiddish], Di Tsayt, 15 and 26 January 1922; id., Di Arbayter Bank in Erets Yisroel [Yiddish], (New York: American Workers Committee for the Workers' Bank in Palestine, [1922]).

78. Katznelson, New York, letter to David (Blumenfeld) Bloch, [Tel Aviv], 15 April [1922], in LAT, File IV-104-71-3. See also, [id.], Philadelphia, letter fragment, to David [Ben-Gurion], 7 May [1922], in KABB, Ben-Gurion File.

79. Id., [Philadelphia], letter to Leah [Miron-Katznelson, Kinneret, 4 May 1922], in BKL, vol. 6, 7.

80. Ben-Gurion, quoted in HVHP", 5 June 1922; Katznelson, Medling, letter to Nahum Ben-Avi [Brodsky], n.p., in BKL, vol. 5, 149–52. See also, id., New York, letter to David Zakkai, [Palestine], 28 November 1921, in BKL, vol. 5, 23–25. Ben-Gurion's later, more positive assessment, was offered in a letter to Baruch Zuckerman, New York, 26 July 1923, and is quoted in Goldstein, HaHistadrut, 33.

81. Katznelson, New York, letter to Ahdut HaAvoda, [Tel Aviv], 7 December 1921, in BKL, vol. 5, 33. See also, id., letters, New York, to David Zakkai, [Palestine], 28 November 1921, and n.p., n.d. [mid-February 1922], to David Kallai, n.p., both in BKL, vol. 5, 23, 56.

82. Katznelson, New York, letter to David [Ben-Gurion], n.p., 28 November [1921], in LAT, File IV-104-71-3; Zuckerman, Zikhroynes, 2: 283. See also, Hyman J. Fliegel, The Life and Times of Max Pine (New York: By the author, 1959), 13.

83. Katznelson, "Yoman America," 5 November [1921], in BKL, vol. 5, 96.

84. Id., "Yoman America," 17 March [1922], in BKL, vol. 5, 137.

85. Yosef Baratz, quoted in HVHP", 5 June 1922; I.[saac] Hamlin, "The Work for Labor Palestine in America," Labor Palestine 1 (June 1933): 20–21; Shapira, Berl, vol. 1, 217; id., Biography, 124.

86. Katznelson, "Yoman America," 3 November [1921], in BKL, vol. 5, 93; id., Chicago and Buffalo, letter to Ahdut HaAvoda, [Tel Aviv], 30 January and

12 February [1922], in LAT, File IV-104-71-3. See also, Shapira, *Biography*, 120–21.
87. Katznelson, Winnipeg, letter to Leah Miron-Katznelson, n.p., n.d. [late March 1922], in *BKL*, vol. 5, 82; Manya Shohat ("We were not the appropriate people for the delegation"), quoted in HVHP", 24 July 1922; Yosef Baratz ("I arrived there green and foreign"), quoted in HVHP", 5 June 1922.
88. Katznelson, letter, n.p., to Leah Miron-Katznelson, [Palestine, 14 March 1922], in *BKL*, vol. 5, 73. See also, id., letter, New York, to HEC, [Tel Aviv], 10 [January] 1922, in LAT, File IV-104-71-3; and Yosef Baratz, quoted in HVHP", 5 June 1922.
89. Katznelson, speech to Poale Zion Party Council, New York, recorded in "Yoman America," 25 November [1921], in *BKL*, vol. 5, 110. A slightly milder version appeared in *HaDo'ar* ("Mo'etzet HaMiflaga Shel 'Poale Zion' "), 5 December 1921.
90. Katznelson, letters, New York, to David Rahum, n.p., 1 July [1922], in KABB, Miscellaneous File; Boston, to Leah Miron-Katznelson, [Palestine], 4 June [1922], in *BKL*, vol. 5, 92.
91. "El HaPo'alim HaYehudiyim BeAmerica—Michtav LaHaverim," in *KBK*, vol. 1, 285, originally published in *HaDo'ar* and *Di Tsayt*, 1 January 1922.
92. Katznelson, letter, [Philadelphia], to Leah Miron-Katznelson, Kinneret, [4 May 1922], in *BKL*, vol. 6, 8. See also, Shapira, *Biography*, 122.
93. Katznelson, New York, letter to David Zakkai, [Palestine], 28 November [1921], in *BKL*, vol. 5, 24.
94. Id., letters, Buffalo, 13 January 1922, to Issachar Bonchik, [New York], in *BKL*, vol. 5, 44–45; and Detroit, 3 February 1922, to Leah Miron-Katznelson, Kinneret, in *BKL*, vol. 6, 4; id., "Yoman America," entries for 4–6, 7, 23 January and 17 March [1922], in *BKL*, vol. 5, 121, 126, 142. See also, id., letters, Cleveland, 5 March [1922], to Leah Miron-Katznelson, n.p., and 6 March [1922], to Yosef Baratz, n.p.; and Minneapolis, 16 March [1922], to Ahdut HaAvoda, [Tel Aviv], all in *BKL*, vol. 5, 62–63, 76–78.
95. See Yosef Baratz, quoted in HVHP", 5 June 1922; and chapter 2 in this book on Jabotinsky, who participated in the WZO mission.
96. See, among other sources, Katznelson, "Yoman America," 4 November [1921], in *BKL*, vol. 5, 95; *HaDo'ar*, 10, 11, 13 November 1921, and 21 March 1922; A. Kretschmar-Yisraeli, "The Workers' Delegation" [Yiddish], *Di Tsayt*, 26 November 1921.

On the recession in America and its effects on the Workers' Bank Campaign, see Katznelson, Minneapolis, letter to Ahdut HaAvoda, [Tel Aviv], 16 March [1922], in *BKL*, vol. 5, 76–78; Manya [Shohat], Boston, letter to Katznelson, n.p., n.d., in LAT, File IV-104-71-7.
97. Katznelson, Vienna, letter to the HEC, [Tel Aviv], Erev Sukkot, 5682 [1921], in *BKL*, vol. 4, 312–13; id., "Yoman America," 8 and 9 November [1921], in *BKL*, vol. 5, 94; and id., letters, Vienna, to David Zakkai, [Palestine], Day after Fast of Gedaliah [6 October 1921], in *BKL*, vol. 4, 306–10; New York, to Ahdut HaAvoda, [Tel Aviv], 14 November [1921], in *BKL*, vol. 5, 17–18; and

New York, to David Blumenfeld (Bloch), n.p., 15 April 1922, in *BKL*, vol. 5, 87–88. See also, Yosef Baratz, in HVHP", 5 June 1922.

98. Ben-Gurion, Jaffa, memorandum to HaMerkaz HaHakla'i, [Jaffa], 5 Tevet 5682 [1922], in LAT, File IV-104-29-3; Katznelson, letters, New York, to HEC, [Tel Aviv], 10 and 14 January 1922, in LAT, File IV-104-71-3.
99. Katznelson, quoted in HVHP", 15 October 1923.
100. Id., New York, letter to David (Blumenfeld) Bloch, n.p., 15 April 1922, in *BKL*, vol. 5, 87.
101. Id., New York, letter to Ahdut HaAvoda, [Tel Aviv], 14 November [1921], in *BKL*, vol. 5, 18. Also, see chapter 7 in this book on Ben-Gurion.
102. Id., Boston, letter to Leah Miron-Katznelson, [Palestine], 4 June [1922], in *BKL*, vol. 5, 92; id., "Yoman America," entry for 3 November [1921], in *BKL*, vol. 5, 94; id., n.p., letter to David Kallai, n.p., n.d. [mid-February, 1922], in *BKL*, vol. 5, 56; Yosef Baratz, quoted in HVHP", 5 June 1922. See also, Shapira, *Biography*, 119.
103. Katznelson, Boston, letter to Leah Miron-Katznelson, [Palestine], 4 June [1922], in *BKL*, vol. 5, 92.

On Ehrenreich, see also, Katznelson, "Yoman America," 7 and 14 November [1921] and 11–16 January [1922], in *BKL*, vol. 5, 93, 102, 122–23; id., [Chicago], letter to Leah Miron-Katznelson, [Palestine], 28 January 1922, in *BKL*, vol. 5, 47.
104. Id., Buffalo, letter to David (Blumenfeld) Bloch, [Palestine], 14 February [1922], in *BKL*, vol. 5, 58.
105. Id., letters, Minneapolis, [16 March 1922], and Buffalo, 13 January 1922, both to Issachar Bonchik, n.p., in *BKL*, vol. 5, 75, 44. See also, id., New York, letter to David (Blumenfeld) Bloch, [Palestine], 15 April 1922, in *BKL*, vol. 5, 87; id., "Yoman America," entries for 21–25, 27 December [1921], 30, 31 January, 11, 12, 13 February, 17 March 1922, in *BKL*, vol. 5, 118–20, 128, 135, 138–39, 142.
106. Yosef Baratz, quoted in HVHP", 5 June 1922; Berl Katznelson, Boston, letter to Leah Miron-Katznelson, [Palestine], 4 June [1922], in *BKL*, vol. 5, 52.

Baruch Zuckerman, a stalwart of the American Poale Zion Party, claimed that, in fact, the Americans successfully handled the sale of shares in the bank while the delegation was in the United States and afterwards (*Zikhroynes*, vol. 2, 282).
107. Katznelson, "Ta'anot Kineged Eretz-Yisrael," in *KBK*, vol. 1, 324, originally published in *Di Tsayt*, 18 December 1921.
108. Vladimir Medem, "Some Remarks About the Zionist Workers' Delegation" [Yiddish], *Forverts*, 14 December 1921.
109. Katznelson, "Yoman America," entry for 14 December [1921], in *BKL*, vol. 5, 115; id., letters, New York, 15 December 1921 to [Ahdut HaAvoda, Tel Aviv], and Buffalo, 14 February [1922], to David (Blumenfeld) Bloch, [Palestine], both in *BKL*, vol. 5, 36, 59.
110. In "Heroine" (288), Ya'akov Goldstein implicitly criticizes Baratz and Katznelson for not defending their colleague more forthrightly. Shohat considered

Notes to Chapter 4

Katznelson's attacks on Bundists who had cooperated with counter-revolutionary Ukrainian nationalists partly responsible for exposing her vulnerability. (Manya [Shohat, Boston?], letter to Katznelson, n.d., in LAT, File IV-104-71-7.)

111. For examples of support, see "A Statement from Isaac Hourwich on the Accusation of Mrs. Shohat (Manya Vilbushevitz) Against Mr. Vladimir Medem," and "A Statement from the Central Committee of the Poale Zion About Medem's Accusation Against Manya Shohat," both in *Di Tsayt* [Yiddish], 6 and 25 February 1922. From April 19 to 24 *Di Tsayt* published Shohat's own version of the affair, "My Connections with Zubatov" [Yiddish].

    On Katznelson's first fears regarding the damage, see his letter from New York, [17 December 1921], to Leah Miron-Katznelson [Palestine], in *BKL*, vol. 5, 38. On the lingering effects of the affair, see his letter from New York, 15 April [1922], to [David] (Blumenfeld) [Bloch], [Tel Aviv], in LAT, File IV-104-71-3.

    On the affair, in general, see Ya'akov Goldstein, "Heroine" and *HaHistadrut*, and Shapira, *Biography*, 120.

112. Katznelson, New York, letter to Ahdut HaAvoda, [Tel Aviv], 7 December 1921, in *BKL*, vol. 5, 31-33.

113. Katznelson, New York, letters to Ahdut HaAvoda, [Tel Aviv], 14 November [1921], and to David Zakkai, [Palestine], 28 November 1921, in *BKL*, vol. 5, 17-18, 23; id., "Yoman America," 19, 21-22 November, and 10, 12 November [1921], in *BKL*, vol. 5, 106-08, 114-15; "Po'alim U-'Fo'alim' " [Hebrew], *HaDo'ar*, 15 December 1921; Sh.[imon] G.[insburg?], "Kabalat Panim LeMalachut HaPo'alim BeEretz Yisrael" [Hebrew], *HaDo'ar*, 4 January 1922; I. Bonchik, "A Quick Glance at the Condition of the Palestine Workers' Bank Campaign" [Yiddish], *Di Tsayt*, 3 April 1922; Shapira, *Biography*, 119; and many other sources.

114. Katznelson, "Yoman America," entry for 26-27 November [1921], in *BKL*, vol. 5, 110. See also, id., New York, letter to David Zakkai, [Palestine], 28 November 1921, in *BKL*, vol. 5, 25; Yosef Baratz, quoted in HVHP", 5 June 1922.

115. Katznelson, "Yoman America," entries for 15 November, 13 December [1921], in *BKL*, vol. 5, 102, 115; id., New York, letter to Ahdut HaAvoda, [Tel Aviv], 14 November [1921], in *BKL*, vol. 5, 17-18; idem, "Ta'anot Kineged Eretz Yisrael," 325; Haim Zhitlovsky, "Dr. Magnes's Letter to the *Forverts*" [Yiddish], *Di Tsayt*, 10 December 1921; id., "On the 'Job-Faust' Tragedy of the Jewish People" [Yiddish], *Di Tsayt*, 1 January 1922.

116. Katznelson, letters, n.p., to Leah Miron-Katznelson, [Palestine, 14 March 1922], and Minneapolis, to Ahdut HaAvoda, [Tel Aviv], 16 March [1922], in *BKL*, vol. 5, 73, 76-78; id., "How People Falsify Information About Palestine" [Yiddish], *Di Tsayt*, 25 December 1921; id., "Mi Rodef et Mi?" in *KBK*, vol. 1, 337-45, originally published in *Di Tsayt*, 1 January 1922; A[braham] Revusky, New York, letter to Katznelson, [Tel Aviv], 18 May 1933, in KABB, File Resh. See also, Katznelson, letters, New York, 15 December 1921, to [Ahdut Ha-

Avoda, Tel Aviv], and n.p., to Poale Zion Central Committee, New York, n.d. [March, 1922], both in BKL, vol. 5, 37, 84; id., "Yoman America," 29 November and 3 December [1921], 17 March [1922], in BKL, vol. 5, 112–13, 140; Shapira, Biography, 120.

117. Katznelson, [Tel Aviv], letter to Avraham Sharon [Schwadron], [Jerusalem], 19 January 1936, in BKL, vol. 6, 213–15. See also, id., [Tel Aviv], letter to Avraham Sharon [Schwadron, Jerusalem, 6 January 1936], in BKL, vol. 7, 210.

In 1928, unlike many others in the yishuv, Katznelson urged the Hebrew University to accept the donation of a chair of Yiddish ("Katedra HaMeriva," in KBK, vol. 3, 351–56, originally published in Davar, 11 January 1928). Magnes and the university governors finally refused the gift as too contentious.

118. Katznelson, "Shva Mei'ot VeArba'im Halutzim MeiUkraina," in KBK, vol. 1, 344, originally published in Di Tsayt [?], December 1921. Compare also, id., "Yoman America," 21–25, 26 December [1921], and 17 March [1922], in BKL, vol. 5, 118–19, 138; id., letters, Buffalo, 13 January 1922, to Issachar Bonchik, [New York], in BKL, vol. 5, 44, and Winnipeg, 31 March [1922], to Leah Miron-Katznelson, Kinneret, in BKL, vol. 6, 6; Manuel, Realities, 300; Shapira, Berl, vol. 1, 206.

119. Katznelson, letters, Buffalo, to David (Blumenfeld) Bloch, n.p., 14 February [1922], and New York, to Ahdut HaAvoda, [Tel Aviv], 14 November [1921], both in BKL, vol. 5, 58, 17. See also, id., letters, Buffalo, 12 February [1922], to [Ahdut HaAvoda, Tel Aviv], and New York, 15 April 1922, to David (Blumenfeld) Bloch, n.p., both in BKL, vol. 5, 53–54, 87–88; "Poale Zion Members Will Create a 50 Thousand Dollar Fund for the 'Tsayt' by January First" [Yiddish], Di Tsayt, 19 November 1921.

120. Katznelson, Philadelphia, letter to Leah Miron-Katznelson, [Palestine], 8 May [1922], in BKL, vol. 5, 90.

121. Id., "Yoman America," 23 January [1922], in BKL, vol. 5, 126; Shapira, Berl, vol. 1, 216.

122. "Keitzad Mesalfim Yedi'ot MeiEretz Yisrael," in KBK, vol. 1, 332–37, originally published in Di Tsayt, 25 December 1921.

123. Compare, for example, copy of letter from Histadrut Delegation, New York, to HEC, [Tel Aviv], 17 May 1926, in LAT, File IV-208-66gimel; Dov Hoz, [New York], letter to HEC, [Tel Aviv], 23 March [1928], in LAT, File IV-208-121bet; and report of David (Blumenfeld) Bloch on the Histadrut Delegation to America in HVHP", 19 August 1929.

124. Katznelson, "Aharei Esrim Shana," in KBK, vol. 4, 15, originally a speech to Ahdut HaAvoda, 7 Shvat 5689 [1929]; id., "Hachrazato Shel Ormsby-Gore," in KBK, vol. 2, 152, originally published in Davar, 18 June 1925; and id., "Tshuva LaVikuah," in KBK, vol. 3, 52, originally published in Davar, 5 November 1926.

125. Id., "VaAvadetem BaGoyim," in KBK, vol. 3, 309–10, originally published in Davar, 22 July 1928; id., "Delegatim," in KBK, vol. 3, 321, originally published in Davar, 3 September 1928; id., "Aharei Ve'idah Ahat," Davar, 31 July 1928; id., "LeZecher Mocher-Sefarim [Max Shapiro] Yekar HaMetzi'ut," in KBK, vol.

Notes to Chapter 4

3, 307–09, originally published in *Davar*, 22 July 1928; id., Tel Aviv, letters to M.[ordecai/Max] Lipson, New York, 18 February and 29 April 1925, and to Shlomo Kaplansky, Jerusalem, 24 May 1925, all in *BKL*, vol. 5, 195, 212, 215.

For a more positive assessment of the Hebrew movement in America, see id., "Haltonut HaYehudit VeHaShavua HaIvri," in *KBK*, vol. 3, 345–47, originally published in *Davar*, 3 June 1927.

126. Id., "Delegatim," in *KBK*, vol. 3, 322, originally published in *Davar*, 3 September 1928.
127. Id., "Erev HaCongress HaHamisha-Asar," in *KBK*, vol. 3, 154, originally published in *Kuntres* 310 (Tammuz 5687 [1927]).
128. See among other sources, id., "LeHabima," in *KBK*, vol. 3, 358–60, originally published in *Davar*, 27 March 1928; Israel Mereminsky [Marom], New York, letter to HEC, Tel Aviv, 13 June 1928, in LAT, File IV-208-1-121bet; HVHP", 11 August 1927, 30 October 1928; Isaac Hamlin, "In Service of Palestine Labor," *The Vanguard*, December 1928, 51-52; Fliegel, *Max Pine*, 15–20, 31–32, 48; Akiva Ettinger, *Im HaHakla'im HaYehudiyim BaTfutzot* (Merhavya: "Sifriat Po'alim," Workers Book Guild [Hashomer Hatza'ir], 1942), 169; Arthur Liebman, *Jews and the Left* (New York: John Wiley, 1979), 265; Maier Bryan Fox, "Labor Zionism in America: The Challenge of the 1920s," *American Jewish Archives* 35 (April 1983): 53–71.
129. Yosef [Baratz], New York, letter to HEC, [Tel Aviv], 16 January 1926, in LAT, File IV-208-66bet.
130. See, for example, Katznelson, Arza, letter to Dov Hoz, [United States, 23 March 1928], in *BKL*, vol. 5, 252.
131. Id., "LeVo'o Shel Abe Cahan," in *KBK*, vol. 2, 178–79, originally published in *Davar*, 27 September 1925. Compare also, id., "BiMsibat Preida LeAbe Cahan," in *KBK*, vol. 4, 98–99, originally published in *Davar*, 4 October 1929.
132. Id., Arza, letter to Dov Hoz, [New York, 23 March 1928], in *BKL*, vol. 5, 252; Mereham [Israel Mereminsky (Marom) and Isaac Hamlin], New York, telegram to Ovdim Ben-Gurion [Ben-Gurion, HEC], Tel Aviv, 22 May 1928, in LAT, File IV-208-1-121alef; Israel Mereminsky [Marom], New York, letter to HEC, Tel Aviv, 28 June 1928, in LAT, File IV-208-1-121gimel.
133. Katznelson, "LeShe'eilat HaSochnut HaYehudit,' in *KBK*, vol. 2, 58, originally a speech to the thirteenth Zionist Congress at Carlsbad, Czechoslovakia, August 1923; and id., "BaCongress HaHamisha-Asar," in *KBK*, vol. 3, 157–61, originally a speech to the fifteenth Zionist Congress, Basle, Switzerland, 11 September 1927.
134. Id., "Al HaIhud," in *KBK*, vol. 3, 210, originally published in *Kuntres* 320 (Kislev 5688 [1927/28]); id. "Devarim SheHushme'u BeVe'idat 'Ahdut HaAvoda' BeEin Harod—2 Iyyar 5684 (1924)," in *KBK*, vol. 2, 106, originally a speech at the Ahdut HaAvoda conference at Ein Harod, 2 Iyyar 1924; id., "Tshuva LaMitvakhim," in *KBK*, vol. 3, 218–20, originally published in *Kuntres* 321 (Kislev 5688 [1927–28]).
135. Id., "BeYom HaHistadrut HaShishi," in *KBK*, vol. 3, 59, originally a speech given at the Hotel Eden in Jerusalem, on Histadrut Day, 1927.

Notes to Chapter 4

136. On the ways in which Brandeis, in fact, maintained active involvement in Zionism, see Leonard Baker, *Brandeis and Frankfurter: A Dual Biography* (New York: Harper and Row, 1984).
137. Katznelson, "HaBank HaMerkazi LeMosdot Shitufiyim," in *KBK*, vol. 2, 42–44, originally published in *Kuntres* 136 (7 Av 5683 [1923]). On labor's general disdain for American progressives in these years, see Peter Grose, *Israel in the Mind of America* (New York: Knopf, 1983), 102.
138. Katznelson, "BeOchrei Leshoneinu," in *KBK*, vol. 3, 294–96, originally published in *Davar*, 6 September 1928.
139. Id., "HaCongress U-le-Aharav," in *KBK*, vol. 3, 167, originally published in *Davar*, 26 October 1927.
140. Id., "Tshuva LaMitvakhim," in *KBK*, vol. 3, 219–20, originally published in *Kuntres* 321 (Kislev 5688 [1927–28]); id., "Veto," in *KBK*, vol. 4, 71, originally published in *Davar*, 17 April 1929; and id., "BaCongress HaShisha-Asar," in *KBK*, vol. 4, 81–83, originally published in *Davar*, 13 August 1929.
141. On the American Zion Commonwealth, see among other sources, Bernard Sandler, "The American-Zionist Concept 'Achoozah' and Its Realization in Eretz Israel, 1908–1934" [Hebrew], *Cathedra* 17 (October 1980): 165–82; and Leah Doukhan-Landau, "The Haifa Bay Lands and the American Zion Commonwealth Crisis (1925–1930)" [Hebrew], *Cathedra* 41 (September 1986): 173–99.
142. See the exchange of correspondence in 1926 and 1927 between the HEC and its delegates in America in LAT, Files IV-208-1-66gimel and IV-208-1-67alef. See also, Fox, "Labor Zionism," 63.
143. Katznelson, quoted in HVHP", 25 January 1925; id., "Tshuva LeDivrei Haverim," in *KBK*, vol. 2, 241, originally published in *Davar*, 15 February 1926; id., Arza, letter to Dov Hoz, [United States, 23 March 1928], in *BKL*, vol. 5, 251; id., "Veto," in *KBK*, vol. 4, 75, originally published in *Davar*, 17 April 1929; id., "Eser Shnot 'Ahdut HaAvoda,'" in *KBK*, vol. 4, 34, originally a lecture to the Tenth Anniversary Council of Ahdut HaAvoda, Tel Aviv, 12 Nisan 5689 [1929].

    See also, id., "BaCongress HaShisha-Asar," in *KBK*, vol. 4, 85–86, originally published in *Davar*, 13 August 1929; and Katznelson's most spirited defense of the AZC bailout, "Im Ge'ulat Mifratz Haifa," in *KBK*, vol. 4, 48, originally published in *Davar*, 26, 30, 31 December 1928.
144. Id., "Ma'asei Lehatim," in *KBK*, vol. 2, 30, originally published in *Kuntres* 121 (13 Nisan 5683 [1923]).
145. Id., Arza, letter to Dov Hoz, [New York, 23 March 1928], in *BKL*, vol. 5, 252. See also, id., Tel Aviv, letter to Ben-Gurion, [London], 24 July 1924, in *BKL*, vol. 5, 184.
146. Id., "Ma'asei Lehatim," in *KBK*, vol. 2, 30, originally published in *Kuntres* 121 (13 Nisan 5683 [1923]). See also, id., "HaLivyetanim U-Degei HaRakak," in *KBK*, vol. 2, 28–30, originally published in *Kuntres*, 120 (10 Nisan 5683 [1923]); id., "Te'uda Aliva U-Ma'aliva," in *KBK*, vol. 3, 270–78, originally published in *Davar*, 26 June 1928; and id., "Erev HaPtiha Shel HaCongress

HaShisha-Asar," in *KBK*, vol. 4, 76–79, originally published in *Davar*, 9 August 1929.

In fact, Louis Marshall was not a man of great wealth. He was, however, the acknowledged leader and spokesman of American Jewry, and especially of the moneyed Jews, most of whom were of German origin and affiliated with the Reform Movement.

147. Katznelson, "Tshuva LeDivrei Ḥaverim," in *KBK*, vol. 3, 135, originally a lecture to the third Histadrut conference, 18 July 1927. See also, Shapira, *Berl*, vol. 1, 217.
148. Katznelson, quoted in diary of David Ben-Gurion, 22 April 1929, in LAT, File IV-208-1-156. See also, Ben-Gurion diary, 30 April 1929; and Shapira, *Berl*, vol. 2, 388.
149. Katznelson, "Ma'asei Lehatim," 30.
150. Id., quoted in MC", 14–16 April 1939, cited in Allon Gal, *David Ben-Gurion—Likrat Medina Yehudit* ([Sede Boqer]: Ben-Gurion University of the Negev, Sede Boqer Campus, 1985), 35.
151. Katznelson, [Tel Aviv], letter to [Avraham] Regelson, [Tel Aviv, 28 June 1935], in *BKL*, vol. 6, 176–77; id., quoted in MC", 21 November 1933.
152. Id., quoted in MC", 28 March 1933.
153. Id., "Avodateinu HaTarbutit," in *KBK*, vol. 6, 266, originally a lecture to the fourth Histadrut Convention, January 1934. Among other sources, see also, id., "Kabalat Panim LeMishlaḥat HaPo'alim MeiAmerica," in *KBK*, vol. 4, 128, originally published in *Davar*, 24 August 1930; id., New York, letter to Leah [Miron-Katznelson, Tel Aviv], 24 November 1937, in KABB; Shapira, *Berl*, vol. 2, 564.
154. See Shapira, *Berl*, vol. 2, 399.
155. Katznelson, "HaMatzav HaMedini," in *KBK*, vol. 9, 304. See also, id., "HaEḥad BaMa'aracha," in *KBK*, vol. 10, 29–34; and id., "Queries on Jewish Labor," in *Revolutionary Constructivism*, 30.
156. Katznelson, quoted in MC", 29 December 1937. See also, id., letters, New York, to Leah Miron-Katznelson, [Tel Aviv], 30 October [1937], in KABB, and [Tel Aviv], to Avraham Sharon [Schwadron, Jerusalem, 6 January 1936], in *BKL*, vol. 6, 209–10.

Katznelson was aware, of course, that assimilation was not exclusively an American problem. See, for example, his speech, "HaHistadrut HaTziyonit Nitba'at LeFe'ula Tarbutit," in *KBK*, vol. 7, 125–39, originally delivered at the World Zionist Congress, Lucerne, Switzerland, summer 1935, which focuses on assimilation in Poland and elsewhere in the European-Jewish heartland.
157. Katznelson, "Histadrut HaOvdim," in *KBK*, vol. 6, 345–46, originally an address to a conference of young working people, Ḥanukah, 5693 (1932).
158. Id., quoted in HVHP", 19 January 1937; id., "Tvi'a," in *KBK*, vol. 8, 73–78, a second version of the same comments. See also, the Yiddish minutes of the reception speeches, 19 January 1937, in LAT, File IV-208-1-1419; and "Workers' Delegation Goes to Palestine," editorial, *Jewish Frontier*, January 1937, 4–5.
159. Katznelson, "Bameh Nekadeim et HaHityashvut HaOvedet," in *KBK*, vol. 6,

37, originally a talk at the annual Mapai Party conference, Tel Aviv, 31 October 1932; id., "Kaf BeTammuz," in KBK, vol. 4, 125, originally a speech given in Jerusalem in the summer of 1931. See also, Yitzhak Chizik, Chicago, letters to Katznelson, [Tel Aviv], 19 and 22 September 1931, in KABB, File Tzadik-Kuf; "Ma'amada Shel Yehudei America," Davar, 5 September 1934; Katznelson, "BeHagah Shel HaKeren HaKayemet," in KBK, vol. 9, 331–32, originally a speech delivered at a conference of the Keren Kayemet LeYisrael, Tel Aviv, 21 January 1939.

160. Id., "LeVo HaNasi," in KBK, vol. 4, 259, originally published in Davar, 17 March 1931, signed, Mem Dalet.

On the state of American Zionism at the beginning of the 1930s, compare Naomi W. Cohen, *The Year after the Riots* (Detroit: Wayne State University Press, 1988), 84–122.

161. Katznelson, "BaCongress HaShmona-Asar," in KBK, vol. 6, 186, 190, originally a speech at the Zionist Congress in Prague, Czechoslovakia, 24 August 1933; id., "Adama Le'umit VaAvoda Ivrit," in KBK, vol. 7, 103, originally a speech to the Keren Kayemet Conference, Lucerne Switzerland, summer 1935; and B[ernard] Rosenblatt, London, letter to Berl Katznelson, New York, 15 November 1937, in KABB, File Resh.

162. Katznelson, "BaMe Nekadeim et HaHityashvut HaOvedet."

163. Id., quoted in HVHP", 16 December 1937; id., report on trip to America in MC", 29 December 1937. See also, id., New York, letter to Leah [Miron-Katznelson, Tel Aviv], 8 November 1937, in KABB; Shapira, *Berl*, vol. 2, 565–66.

164. Katznelson, "BaCongress HaTziyoni HaEsrim VeEhad," in KBK, vol. 9, 69, originally an address delivered at the twenty-first Zionist Congress, August 1939. See also, Marie Syrkin, "Report of the Zionist Congress," *Jewish Frontier*, September, 1939, 11; David Ben-Gurion, "Why We Placed Our Trust in Britain," *Jewish Observer and Middle East Review*, 18 October 1963, 23; Shapira, *Biography*, 278; Norman Rose, *Chaim Weizmann: A Biography* (New York: Viking-Penguin, 1986), 353; Marc Lee Raphael, *Abba Hillel Silver: A Profile in American Judaism* (New York and London: Holmes & Meier, 1989), 78–79; and Aaron Berman, *Nazism, the Jews, and American Zionism, 1933–1948* (Detroit: Wayne State University Press, 1990), 71.

165. Katznelson, "A New Chapter in Aliya," *Pioneer Woman*, April 1940, 3–4.

166. Ben-Gurion on Katznelson, in BGD, 24 October 1939, quoted in Gal, *Likrat Medina*, 43. See also, Katznelson, Tel Aviv, draft letter to Dr. R[oland] Gittelsohn, Cleveland, 9 January 1938, in KABB; and Shabtai Teveth, *Ben-Gurion: The Burning Ground, 1886–1948* (Boston: Houghton Mifflin, 1987), 675.

167. Personal conversation of the author with Prof. Moshe Davis, Jerusalem, 26 July 1991. Compare also, Daniel Persky, [Tel Aviv], letter to Katznelson, [Tel Aviv], 4 February 1933, in KABB, File Samech-Pei; and Katznelson, New York, letter to Leah [Miron-Katznelson, Tel Aviv], 30 October [1937], in KABB, File 1937. In "Huliya Rishona BaSharsheret," in KBK, vol. 7, 161, originally published in Davar supplement for children, 4 January 1935, signed, "Be'eri," Katznelson wrote about the 75th anniversary of the Motza settlement, which had been

Notes to Chapter 4

rescued from abandonment by the B'nai Brith and the Hovevei Zion, without mentioning that B'nai Brith was an American organization.

168. Katznelson, "Kodmei-Kodmeinu," in KBK, vol. 7, 162–74, originally published in *Davar*, 31 July 1935; id., "Kabalat Panim LeMishlaḥat HaPo'alim MeiAmerica," in KBK, vol. 4, 129, originally a speech to a visiting delegation of American-Jewish labor leaders, Beit HaAm, Tel Aviv, 24 August 1930.

169. In "Goral HaAvoda HaIvrit BeYamim Eile," in KBK, vol. 6, 318, originally a speech to the Aseifat HaNivḥarim, 1 Sivan 5694 (1934), Katznelson spoke of "making Palestine into the California of all this [Middle] East." See also, his "LaTochnit HaAmitit Shel HaTnu'a HaLe'umit HaAravit: HaGoreim HaAngli," in KBK, vol. 8, 193, originally a lecture at a meeting of the Mapai Party, Tel Aviv, 13 June 1936.

170. Katznelson, New York, letter to Leah [Miron-Katznelson, Tel Aviv], 30 October [1937], in KABB; Ben Zion Applebaum [Ilan], "The American Chalutz," *Hechalutz Bulletin* (February 1937), 7–8.

171. Katznelson, "Oraḥ Ḥayav," a eulogy for Shmaryahu Levin, in KBK, vol. 7, 179, originally published in *Davar*, 10 June 1935.

172. Id., London, letter to Zalman [Rubashov-Shazar, Tel Aviv, 22 June 1937], in BKL, vol. 6, 368. See also, id., Tel Aviv, letter to Daniel Fineman, Paris, 26 September 1932, in BKL, vol. 6, 92–93; Yoḥanan Twersky, Boston, letter to Katznelson, [Tel Aviv], 2 November 1935, in KABB, File Tet; Berl Katznelson, [on board ship sailing towards Italy], letter to [Moshe] Braslavsky [Na'an], n.p., [10 August 1935], in BKL, vol. 5, 180; and id., "Hebrew Culture: Immediate Problems," *Jewish Frontier* 2 (November 1935): 17. In his letter to Braslavsky commending to him a poem of B. N. Silkiner, Katznelson did not mention that Silkiner was an American, although he surely knew it.

173. Katznelson, "Kabbalat Panim LeMishlaḥhat HaPo'alim MeiAmerica," 129.

174. Id., "BeVe'idat 'Po'alei Zion' BeGermania," in KBK, vol. 4, 103–04, originally an address to a Poale Zion Party convention, Berlin, 5 January 1930. See also, id., London, letter to Mapai Party Center, Tel Aviv, 31 October [1930], in BKL, vol. 6, 19; and remarks of Zalman Rubashov [Shazar], in HVHP", 26 September 1932.

175. Katznelson, quoted in MC", 7 December 1938. See also, id., quoted in MC", 29 December 1937. Compare also, D[avid] Remez, New York, letter to HEC, [Tel Aviv], 17 May 1926, in LAT, File IV-208-1-66gimel; remarks of Zalman Rubashov, in HVHP", 26 September 1932; chapter 6 below on Golda Meir; and Ben Zion Applebaum, "The American Chalutz," 6–7.

176. See Yitzḥak Chizik, Chicago, letter to Katznelson, [Tel Aviv], 23 May 1932, in KABB, File Tzadik-Kuf; Katznelson, quoted in MC", 5 December 1933; id., quoted in HVHP", 16 December 1937. Compare also, Naḥum Gutman, "Hechalutz in America," in *Arise and Build: The Story of American Habonim*, ed. David Breslau (New York: Ichud Habonim Labour Zionist Youth, 1961), 29.

177. Katznelson, New York, letter to Leah [Miron-Katznelson, Tel Aviv], 24 November 1937, in KABB, File 2. See also, id., quoted in MC", 29 December 1937.

178. Id., "LeAḥar London," in *KBK*, vol. 9, 48, originally a speech to a Mapai Council meeting, 25 Nisan 5699 [1939]. On his experiences with the Histadrut Youth Department, see Shapira, *Biography*, 208–25.
179. See Albert K. Epstein, Chicago, letter to Berl Katznelson, Tel Aviv, 28 February 1939, in KABB, File Alef; Yosef [Baratz], New York, letter to Katznelson, [Tel Aviv], 14 December 1939, in KABB, Institutions File; and the discussions in HVHP", 26 May 1938, 16 March and 13 April 1939.

    The question of how best to reach the youth of America remained a concern for Berl in the forties. See, for example, MS", 18 June 1941.
180. Among other sources, see Katznelson, Trieste, letter to Benny [Applebaum, New York, 1 July 1937], in *BKL*, vol. 6, 376–77; A[vraham] Revusky, New York, letter to Katznelson, [Tel Aviv], 20 September 1934, in KABB, File Resh; and Y. [I. F.] Stone, Library of Congress, Washington, D.C., letters to Katznelson, [Tel Aviv], n.d. [1934 or 1935], in KABB, File Samech-Pei.
181. Katznelson, "Milestones—The First and Second Aliyahs," *Labor Palestine* 1 (June 1933): 6–9; id., "The Unforgettable Arlosoroff" [Yiddish], in *Labor Palestine*, Special Souvenir Number (December 1933): 22–23; id., "The Blockade of the Histadrut" [Yiddish], *Iddisher Kemfer*, 16 March 1934: 11–13; id., "What Obligations Do We Have Towards the Movement?" [Yiddish], *Iddisher Kemfer*, 30 March 1934, 4; id., "War and Peace in Zionism" [Yiddish], *Iddisher Kemfer*, 4 May 1934, 2–4; id., "A Reckoning" [Yiddish], *Iddisher Kemfer*, 5 October 1934, 4–6; id., "Our Reality and Our Goal" [Yiddish], in *Iddisher Kemfer* 5 (November 1937): 4–8, the last published while he was in the United States.

    See also, A. Solodar, editor of *Dorenu*, Chicago, letter to Katznelson, [Tel Aviv], 5 September 1935, in KABB, File Samech-Pei; Berl Katznelson, [Tel Aviv], letter to Ya'akov Shichvitz, [Haifa, 1 December 1931], in *BKL*, vol. 6, 63; and id., Cairo, letter to [Yitzhak] Yatziv, [Tel Aviv], n.d. [March, 1937], in *BKL*, vol. 6, 289–90. The letter to Shichvitz mentions his having written an article for an unidentified "large Christian-American newspaper."
182. E[manuel] N. Mohl, [Jerusalem], letter to Katznelson, [Tel Aviv], 15 June 1938, in KABB, File Mem (Mohl managed various Palestine enterprises of the Brandeis group); D[avid] B[reslau], "Under Fire (1936–1940)," in Breslau, *Arise*, 32. See also, Katznelson, Trieste, letter to Benny [Applebaum, New York, 1 July 1937], in *BKL*, vol. 6, 376–77; and Ben Zion Applebaum, New York, letter to Katznelson, [Tel Aviv], n.d. [1937], in KABB, File Alef.
183. Katznelson, handwritten notebook from 1937 trip, [6, 9, 13, 22, 28 November and 3, 13 December 1937], in KABB. See also, id., New York, letters to Leah [Miron-Katznelson, Tel Aviv], 30 October and 8 November 1937, in KABB, File 1937; and id., quoted in MC", 29 December 1937.

    Shapira again overstates the case somewhat with regard to Katznelson's lack of interest in America during the tour (*Berl*, vol. 2, 564).
184. Katznelson, handwritten notebook from 1937 trip, [13, 18, 27, 19 November 1937], in KABB; id., n.p., letter to Isaac Rivkind, [New York], n.d., in KABB, Correspondence File.
185. Id., speech to the Educators' Council, New York, Kislev, 5699 [1937], in *KBK*,

Notes to Chapter 4

vol. 8, 180; id., quoted in HVHP", 16 December 1937, and MC", 29 December 1937.

186. Id., on board the R. M. S. Queen Mary, letter to M[enaḥem Mendel] Ussishkin, Jerusalem, [13 October 1937], in KABB File 2; Shapira, Biography, 270.

Katznelson did not follow up all leads in this area. Despite the urging of Dr. A. M. Skorodin to visit Chicago on a matter "that if acted upon favorably, our position in Palestine would be strengthened and consolidated," he did not venture beyond the eastern seaboard. (Dr. A. M. Skorodin, Chicago, letter to Katznelson, New York, 12 November 1937, in KABB, File Samech-Pei.) On the other hand, he tried to raise money for Mish'an, the workers' aid fund, and other causes. (Katznelson, New York, letter to H. Breinhandler, n.p., n.d. [1937], in LAT, File IV-104-71-2).

187. Katznelson, [Tel Aviv], letter to Justice Louis D. Brandeis, Washington, 12 March 1931, in BKL, vol. 6, 27. The text quoted is this author's rendering of the translation into Hebrew of the English original in BKL, the only text available to him.

188. Katznelson, handwritten notebook from 1937 trip, undated entry relating to meeting with "the old man" (that is, Brandeis), in KABB; id., New York, letter to Leah [Miron-Katznelson, Tel Aviv], 8 November 1937, in KABB, File 1937; id., quoted in MC", 29 December 1937; Stephen S. Wise, New York, letter to Katznelson, New York, 17 November 1937, in KABB, File Vav; and Maurice Boukstein, New York, letter to Katznelson, New York, 22 November 1937, in KABB, File Mosdot, etc. See also, Shapira, Berl, vol. 2, 565.

In Biography (271) Shapira gives an incorrect quotation from the Wise letter. Rather than consulting Wise's original letter written in English, the translator apparently retranslated into English Shapira's Hebrew translation of it.

189. See, among other sources, A. Dickenstein, Tel Aviv, letter to Katznelson, Tel Aviv, 5 April 1938, in KABB, File Dalet; and Julius Simon, president, Palestine Economic Corporation, New York, letter to Katznelson, The Davar, Tel Aviv, 27 June 1939, in KABB, File Samech-Pei.

On the return journey from New York to Palestine, Katznelson got wind of an impending Arab attack on the yishuv. He drafted a panicky letter to Rabbi Stephen S. Wise to be shown to Frankfurter and Brandeis asking for their intervention with the American government to help avert the disaster. (Katznelson, Venice, draft letter to Rabbi [Stephen S.] Wise, [New York], 11 December 1937, in KABB, File Vav.)

190. Katznelson, quoted in MC", 29 December 1937. See also, id., unpublished notebooks from 1937 journey to America, in KABB; Tamar de Sola Pool, New York, letter to Katznelson, New York, 18 October 1937, and Jeannette N. Label, New York, letter to Katznelson, New York, 4 November 1937, both in KABB, File Institutions, etc; Shapira, Berl, vol. 2, 566–67. See also, Berman, Nazism, 91–93.

191. Katznelson, quoted in MC", 29 December 1937.

192. For the background of the agreement and Ben-Gurion's role in it, see chapter 7, herein.

193. Katznelson, New York, letter to Leah [Miron-Katznelson, Tel Aviv], 8 November 1937, in KABB, Correspondence File.
194. Id., New York, letter to Leah [Miron-Katznelson, Tel Aviv], 24 November 1937, in KABB, Correspondence File.
195. Id., report of his trip to the United States, in MC″, 29 December 1937. See also, Shapira, *Berl*, vol. 2, 565–67. Shapira attributes the failure in large part to Vladeck himself, who, according to her, was lukewarm to Zionism and unwilling to risk prestige in fighting for the agreement. In 1935, in fact, he had accused the WZO of profiting from the misery of German Jews, who exchanged blocked funds in Germany for goods in Palestine ([Isaac] Hamlin, [Joseph] Schlossberg, and [Haim] Feinstone [sic], New York, telegram to Ovdim [HEC], Tel Aviv, 29 October, 1935, in LAT, File IV-208-1-649). On the other hand, as noted below in chapter 7, he acquitted himself well when he visited Palestine.
196. Katznelson, quoted in MC″, 29 December 1937.
197. "Extracts of the Minutes of the Convention for Working Palestine at the Hotel Pennsylvania, 26–28 November 1937" [Yiddish], in *Iddisher Kemfer*, 3 December 1937. See also, "Geverkshaften Campaign" [Yiddish], *Forverts*, 28 November 1937; Katznelson, unpublished notebooks from his 1937 American trip, in KABB, entry for 7 November 1937; *KBK*, vol. 6, 269; [Rabbi] Samuel Wohl, Cincinnati, letter to Katznelson, New York, 28 October 1937, in KABB, File Vav; H[irsch] L. Gordon, [National Commander], American Palestine Jewish Legion, New York, letter to Katznelson, [New York,] 2 November 1937, in KABB, File Gimel; and Emma Harris, Boston, letter to Katznelson, n.p., n.d. [1937], in KABB, File Heh.
198. "On Comrade Katznelson's Departure," editorial [Yiddish], *Iddisher Kemfer*, 3 December 1937.
199. Katznelson, quoted in HVHP″, 19 January 1937. See also, id., "LeVeirur Matzaveinu HaMedini," in *KBK*, vol. 8, 231–32, originally a speech at a Mapai Party Council meeting, Haifa, 23 January 1937.
200. Id., "LeAhar London," in *KBK*, vol. 9, 48, originally a speech to the Mapai Party Council, 25 Nisan 5699 (1939).
201. Id., quoted in MC″, 22 June 1930. See also, Shapira, *Berl*, vol. 1, 322ff.
202. Katznelson, London, letter to Merkaz Mapai, [Tel Aviv], 7 November 1930, in BKL, vol. 6, 20–25. The most comprehensive summary of American reactions to the riots is in Cohen, *Year After*, especially, 13–14, 17–18, 84, 128–29.
203. Katznelson, quoted in MC″, 9 July 1936. See also, MC″, 3 August 1936.
204. Katznelson, quoted MPC″, 31 August 1936.
205. Id., Zurich, letter to [Ben Zion Kunin, his physician, London], 23 August [1937], in BKL, vol. 6, 393. Compare also, correspondence in LAT, Files IV-208-1-1176, 1419.
206. Katznelson, letter of 14 October 1938, read by Moshe Shertok at an off-the-record meeting of the Mapai Political Committee, MPC″, 26 October 1938. See also, id., comments at Mapai Center meeting, 7 December 1938, and at Zionist Inner Actions Committee meeting in London, 20 December 1938, both quoted in Gal, *Likrat Medina*, 12; Shapira, *Berl*, vol. 2, 573; and Gal, *Likrat Medina*, 47, 203, n. 46.

Notes to Chapter 4

207. Katznelson, London, letter to Shaul [Mei'irov-Avigur], n.p., 18 October 1938, in KABB, File alef. Compare also, id., "HaMatzav HaMedini," in *KBK*, vol. 9, 316, originally a lecture delivered at Beit Arlosoroff, Tel Aviv, 23 December 1938.
208. Id., "Al Halkar BeSha'a Zo," in *KBK*, vol. 7, 240, originally a speech at a meeting of the Histadrut Council, 9 February 1936.
209. Compare, id., "Adama Le'umit VaAvoda Ivrit," in *KBK*, vol. 7, 104, originally a speech to the Keren Kayemet Conference, Lucerne, Switzerland, summer 1938.
210. On the Hebrew University, see Katznelson, [Tel Aviv], letter to Miriam [Zimmels, Vienna, 8 February 1933], in *BKL*, vol. 6, 101–02; and Dr. D. W. Senator, administrator, Hebrew University, Jerusalem, letter to Katznelson, London, 7 October 1937, in KABB, File Samech-Pei.

    On writers, see Aryeh Matz, secretary, Israel Matz Foundation, Brooklyn, letter to Katznelson, [Tel Aviv], 15 April [1938?], in KABB, File Mosdot, etc; and Katznelson, Jerusalem, letter to [Zalman] Schocken, [Jerusalem], 26 Tammuz [56]98 [1938], in KABB, File 1938.

    On illegal immigration, see L[ouis] Segal, secretary, Jewish National Workers' Alliance of America, New York, letter to Katznelson, Tel Aviv, 14 April 1938, in KABB, File Samech-Pei; various letters of Lewis J. Ruskin, Chicago, to Berl Katznelson, Tel Aviv, January-March, 1939, in KABB, File Resh; Sophie A. Udin, executive secretary, Va'ad Bitahon, New York, letter to Katznelson, Tel Aviv, 1 February 1939, in KABB, File Yod; Shapira, *Berl*, vol. 2, 572.

    On campaigns to purchase printing machinery for *Davar*, see circular letter of "Davar" Printing Campaign, conducted by printing trades unions, New York, n.d. [1931–32], in LAT, File IV-208-1-337bet; Mayer Kartoff, Bronx, letter to Katznelson, [Tel Aviv], 8 February 1932, in KABB, File Tzadik-Kuf; and notice in *Labor Palestine*, September-October 1933, 13. On enrolling American subscribers to *Davar*, see Martin Fox, Chicago, letter to Katznelson, Tel Aviv, [27 October 1932], in KABB, File Pei; Enzo Sereni, New York, letter to Katznelson, [Tel Aviv], 25 February 1936, in KABB, File Samech-Pei; and other letters in KABB.
211. See, for example, Katznelson, quoted in HVHP", 16 January 1933, and 19 January 1937; and id., quoted in minutes of a meeting of the HEC with a delegation of visiting Americans, 19 January 1937, in LAT, File IV-208-1-1419.
212. Id., speech to a workers' meeting in Tel Aviv, 24 November 1933, in *KBK*, vol. 7, 371; and id., "Mo'etzet HaMehanchim Be New York," in *KBK*, vol. 8, 179–80, originally a speech to the Jewish Educators' Council in New York, Kislev, 5698 [1937].
213. Id., "Likrat Pe'ula Mishkit-Tochnitit," in *KBK*, vol. 6, 94, originally a lecture at the fourth Histadrut Conference, 1933; id., "Kabalat Panim LeMishlahat HaPo'alim MeiAmerica," in *KBK*, vol. 4, 131, originally a speech to the visiting labor delegation from the United States, given in Beit HaAm, Tel Aviv, 20 August 1930.

Notes to Chapter 4

On Katznelson's reservations regarding the wealthy American non-Zionists who participated in the enlarged Jewish Agency after 1929, such as Felix Warburg, see, among other sources, Katznelson, letters, London, 16 January [1930] to [HEC?], and 21 January [1930] to Leah Miron-Katznelson, [Palestine], in BKL, vol. 5, 300–01, 305–06; id., St. Vigilius, letter to [Yisrael] Galili, [Na'an, 30 September 1935], in BKL, vol. 6, 197–98; and id., quoted in HVHP", 9 September 1936.

In "HaNadiv HaYadua," in KBK, vol. 7, 143–57, a eulogy for Baron Edmund Rothschild, originally a speech delivered at a memorial meeting held by the Agricultural Workers' Federation in Tel Aviv, 24 Kislev 5695 [1934], Katznelson argued that Westerners, in general, suffered from superiority feelings that sapped their vigor and spiritual health.

214. Shapira, *Biography*, 310.
215. Katznelson, "BeHavlei Adam," in KBK, vol. 5, 321, originally a eulogy for Eliezer Yoffe published in *Tlamim*, 32 (Kislev-Tevet 5703 [1943]).
216. Id., [Tel Aviv], letter to Sh.[imon] Halkin, Chicago, 15 Av 5703 [1943], in KABB, File Hei.
217. Id., "Le'an Paneinu?" in KBK, vol. 5, 251, originally a speech given at a conference at Afikim, 17 October 1942.
218. Id., "Yetzirato Nimdedet Ach BeAmat-Mida Shel Hazon," in KBK, vol. 9, 300, originally a speech at the opening of the 20th anniversary celebration of the Histadrut, Beit Arlosoroff, Tel Aviv, December 1940. See also, id., "BaVe'ida HaHamishit Shel HaHistadrut," in KBK, vol. 5, 74, originally a response given at the fifth Histadrut Convention, April 1941.
219. Manya [Shohat], Bronx, New York, letter to Katznelson, [Tel Aviv], 19 April 1940, in KABB, Miscellaneous File; Sophie A. Udin, Zionist Archives and Library, New York, letter to Katznelson, Tel Aviv, 24 September 1941, in KABB, File Yod; Katznelson, "Ma BeFinu LeYom Mahar?" in KBK, vol. 5, 11–18, originally a speech at the Unity Council of Poale Zion-Hitahdut, Ayanot, December 1940.
220. Id., quoted in MC", 21 September 1939.
221. Id., "Ahdut Hayaleinu," in KBK, vol. 5, 135, originally a speech at a gathering of Palestine soldiers, 16 August 1942; id., "LeAhar London," 49.
222. MS", 3 November 1942; Gal, *Likrat Medina*, 43.
223. Katznelson, "Begabeinu el HaKir," in KBK, vol. 9, 118–19, originally a speech delivered at Kinusim, 25–29 June 1940.
224. Id., "Ma Lifnim?" KBK, vol. 5, 20, originally published in *Bchor* (Tel Aviv, 5701 [1941]).
225. Id., "The Zionist Situation Today," *Jewish Frontier* 14 (September 1941): 22. Compare also, Gal, *Likrat Medina*, 93–94.
226. Katznelson, unpublished notebooks in Beit Berl, entries for September 1939; id., quoted in MS", 27 September 1939; and id., "Ma BeFinu LeYom Mahar?" 15.
227. See, for example, id., letters to Sh.[imon] Halkin, Chicago, from Tel Aviv, 15 Av 5703 [1943], and from Jerusalem, 29 Tammuz 5704 [1944], in KABB, File

Notes to Chapter 4

1943-44; A. Dickenstein, New York, letter to Katznelson, [Tel Aviv], 15 June 1942, in KABB, File Dalet; Aryeh Tartakower, New York, letter to Katznelson, Tel Aviv, 17 July 1943, in BABB, File Tet; and [Rabbi] Samuel Wohl, Cincinnati, letter to Katzenelson [sic], Tel Aviv, 3 November 1943, in KABB, File Vav.

228. Katznelson, "Nehemia de Lieme," in *KBK*, vol. 9, 282, originally a eulogy delivered at a memorial meeting in Tel Aviv, Kislev 5701 (1940), and printed in *Davar*, 24 December 1940.

229. Id., Tel Aviv, letter to E[limelech] Epstein, Jerusalem, 5 November 1942, to be transmitted to Louis Segal of the Jewish National Workers' Alliance, New York, in KABB, File 1942. See also, letter of Segal to Katznelson, 6 November 1942, in KABB, File Samech-Pei.

230. Katznelson, "Bein Adam LaHavero," in *KBK*, vol. 10, 114–42, originally published as the introduction to the first volume of Liessin's collected works, published by Am Oved, Tel Aviv, 5703 (1943).

231. See MC", 10 July 1944.

232. Katznelson, "BeHitkareiv HaHazit," *KBK*, vol. 9, 99, originally a speech to the Mapai Council, Tel Aviv, 14 June 1940. See also, Shapira, *Biography*, 291–93.

233. Moshe Shertok, quoted in MS", 9 July 1941.

234. Shapira, *Biography*, 312.

235. Katznelson, "Morei HaDor o Bnei Meiroz?" in *KBK*, vol. 5, 47–49, originally published in *Davar*, 19 September 1941, signed, Meshoteit; id., "BeVe'idat HaMitnadvim HaIvriyim," in *KBK*, vol. 5, 124, originally a speech given in Tel Aviv, 24 September 1941.

236. Id., Jerusalem, letter to Sh.[imon] Halkin, Chicago, 29 Tammuz 5704 [1944], in KABB, File 1943-44; A. Dickenstein, New York, letter to Katznelson, [Tel Aviv], 15 June 1942, in KABB, File Dalet.

237. Katznelson, [Tel Aviv], letter to David [Ben-Gurion, Tel Aviv], 4 August 1942, in KABB, Ben-Gurion File. See also, Shapira, *Biography*, 312.

238. See, for example, Katznelson, n.p., letter to Shimshon Meltzer, n.p., 1 Tammuz 5703 [1943], in KABB, File 1943-44; Z[alman] Shneur, New York, letter to Katznelson, [Tel Aviv], 10 February 1943, in KABB, File Shin; Israel [Mereminsky-Marom], New York, letter to Katznelson, [Tel Aviv], 2 June 1943, in KABB, File Mem; Friedrich Torberg, Hollywood, California, letter to Katznelson, Tel Aviv, 12 January 1944, in KABB, File Tet.

239. Katznelson, Jerusalem, letter to Sh.[imon] Halkin, Chicago, 29 Tammuz 5704 [1944], in KABB, File 1943-44.

240. Id., "BaVe'ida HaHamishit Shel HaHistadrut," in *KBK*, vol. 5, 60, originally a speech at the fifth Histadrut Conference, 19 April 1942, published in *Davar*, 22 April and 15 May 1942.

241. Ibid. See also, Shapira, *Biography*, 148.

242. Ben-Zion Ilan, letter to his wife in Afikim, from his base in the British army, 17 August 1944, quoted in his *An American Soldier/Pioneer in Israel* (New York: Labor Zionist Letters, 1979), 50.

243. "Berl Katznelson," editorial, *Jewish Frontier* 11 (September 1944): 6. See also,

Notes to Chapter 5

"Berl Katznelson," editorial, *Pioneer Woman*, October 1944, 3; and Ginzberg, *Keeper of the Law*, 206.
244. MC", 14 August 1945.

Chapter 5

1. See, for example, Frederick Painton, "Henrietta Szold—American," typescript, in CZA, File A125/29; Louis Lipsky, *A Gallery of Zionist Profiles* (New York: Farrar Straus and Cudahy, 1956), 142; Joan Dash, *Summoned to Jerusalem: The Life and Times of Henrietta Szold* (New York: Harper & Row, 1979), 224-25; and Sylva M. Gelber, *No Balm in Gilead* ([Ottawa]: Carleton University Press, 1989), 52, 191.

    Dash's work is the most complete biography of Szold to date. Gelber, who had a career as a distinguished senior civil servant in Canada, lived in Palestine for some time and was the first graduate of the school of social work established by Szold.

2. See, for example, [Gershon] A.[gronsky?], "A Life of Dedication," *Palestine Post*, 14 February 1945.
3. The works which come closest to appreciating the American dimension of Szold's work in Palestine are Irving Fineman's *Woman of Valor* (New York: Simon and Schuster, 1961); and Carol Bosworth Kutscher, "The Early Years of Hadassah," Ph.D. dissertation, Faculty of the Graduate School of Arts and Sciences, Department of Near Eastern and Judaic Studies, Brandeis University, April 1976.
4. Ernst Akiba Simon, "Henrietta Szold—Meḥanechet HaAm," in *Henrietta Szold 5621-5705. Divrei Azkara SheNe'emru BeYom 3 BeIyar 5705 Al Yedei Prof. Sh. Adler VeDr. E. Simon BaUniversita HaIvrit* [Hebrew] (Jerusalem: HaUniversita HaIvrit, 1945), 7.
5. Richard Hofstadter, *The Age of Reform from Bryan to F.D.R.* (New York: Knopf, 1956), 5.
6. See, among other sources, Robert H. Wiebe, *The Search for Order, 1877-1920* (New York: Hill and Wang, 1967), 144-59.
7. Among other sources on Rabbi Szold, see Shmaryahu Levin, "MiSefer Ḥayyai" [Hebrew], *HaAretz*, 25 May 1934.
8. Szold, speech to Aliyat Noar, Ben Shemen, Palestine, 24 December 1940, in CZA, File A125/188. See also, Simon, "Meḥanechet," 8; and Arnold Zweig, "Henrietta Szold on Her Return Today from America," *Palestine Post*, 5 February 1936.
9. Partial record book of Szold's reading, in CZA, File A125/250.
10. Szold, Jerusalem, letter to sisters, Bertha [Levin] and Adele [Seltzer], n.p., 7 August 1936, in CZA, File A125/265.
11. Gelber, *Balm*, 193.
12. Szold, New York, letters, to "Mamma and All," n.p., 30 July 1914, and to "Mamma," [Maine], 3 August 1914, both in CZA, File A125/275.
13. Id., New York, letter to Dr. [Richard] Gottheil, [New York], 13 May 1917, in CZA, File A125/302; minutes of meeting of Provisional Executive Committee

Notes to Chapter 5

for General Zionist Affairs, New York, 23 September 1917, stenographic draft. See also, Dash, *Jerusalem*, 118; and Kutscher, "Early Years," 162–63.

14. Szold, [Jerusalem], letter to Mrs. Edith Gann Kniberg, Newark, N.J., 17 June 1934, in CZA, File A125/95.
15. Id., "Extension Work Meeting," handwritten notes for speech [?], n.d., CZA, File A125/285.
16. Ibid.
17. Gelber, *Balm* 190. In an interview with the author in Jerusalem, 6 July 1986, Szold's longtime personal secretary, Emma Ehrlich, denied that her employer had ever attempted to apply American notions of any sort in Palestine. Rather, Ehrlich asserted, she had merely responded pragmatically to the needs of the hour. Such a view, however, is not tenable.
18. Szold, Jerusalem, letter to her sisters, Bertha [Levin] and Adele [Seltzer], n.p., 17 February 1939, in CZA, File 125/267.
19. Id., letters, Jerusalem, to "dear Family," [United States], 22 November 1920, in CZA, File A125/256; en route to Marseille [sic], to Sisters, n.p., 17 June 1930, in CZA, File A125/262; and Jerusalem, to sister, Adele [Seltzer], n.p., 8 December 1933, in CZA, File A125/263; and Jerusalem, to Ellis Radinsky, League for Labor Palestine, New York City, 28 January 1943, in CZA, File A125/62. See also, transcript of her address to the *The Survey Graphic*, New York, January 1936, typescript, in CZA, File A125/83.
20. Szold, Maine, letter to Elvira Solis, New York City, 16 August 1915, in CZA, File A125/309; id., Boston, letter to family, [Baltimore], 10 August 1885, in CZA, File A125/275.
21. See Louis D. Brandeis, letters, Boston, 11 March 1916, and Washington, 6 November 1925, both to Julian W. Mack, n.p., in *Letters of Louis D. Brandeis*, vol. 4, ed. Melvin I. Urofsky and David W. Levy (Albany: State University of New York Press, 1975), 115, 191–92.
22. Szold, Baltimore, letter to her sister, Rachel [Jastrow], n.p., 25 October 1891, in CZA, File A125/17. See also, her eulogy for Brandeis, delivered on Palestine radio, 9 October 1941, the typescript of which is in CZA, File A125/15.

    On Brandeis as a Progressive, see, among other sources, Allon Gal, *Brandeis of Boston* (Cambridge, Mass.: Harvard University Press, 1980); and Melvin Urofsky, *Louis D. Brandeis and the Progressive Tradition* (Boston and Toronto: Little, Brown, 1981).
23. Szold, Jerusalem, letter to "dear Ones" (that is, her sisters and their families in the United States), 29 March 1926, CZA, File A125/260.
24. Id., Rishon le-Zion, [Palestine], letter to "dear Ones," 14 April 1922, in CZA, File A125/258.
25. Id., Jerusalem, letter to sister, Bertha [Levin, Baltimore], 15 April 1938, in CZA, File A125/266.
26. Id., Baltimore, personal letter to Miss [Elvira] Solis, New York, 1 March 1901, in CZA, File A125/308.
27. Id., Jerusalem, letters, to sisters, Bertha [Levin] and Adele [Seltzer], n.p., 6 January 1939, in CZA, File A125/267; to sister, Bertha [Levin], n.p., 4 December 1942, in CZA, File A125/274.

28. Id., Jerusalem, letter to sisters Bertha [Levin] and Adele [Seltzer, United States], 31 May 1935, in CZA, File A125/265. See also, her letters from Jerusalem, to "Sisters," n.p., 8 September 1933; and to sister, Adele [Seltzer], n.p., 8 December 1933, both in CZA, File 125/263.
29. Id., [Jerusalem], letter to Wendell Willkie, New York City, 27 March 1944, in CZA, File A125/63.
30. Id., Jerusalem, letter to sister, Bertha [Levin, Baltimore], 18 July 1940, in CZA, File A125/267.
31. Sylva Gelber, personal interview with the author, Ottawa, 24 January 1988.
32. See Dash, *Jerusalem*, 39–79.
33. Szold, "Tsu Haim Arlosoroff's Ershten Yortsayt" [Yiddish], *Pioneer Woman*, June 1934, 15.
34. Id., Jerusalem, letter to "My dear Ones" [her family in the United States], 26 January 1922, in CZA, File A125/258.
35. See Dash, *Jerusalem*, 196–99, 216–17.
36. Szold, address to a special meeting of the ZOA Administrative Committee, Hotel Astor, New York City, 9 January 1936, typescript, in CZA, File A125/315.
37. Id., Jerusalem, letter to Mrs. Edgar J. Wachenheim, New Rochelle, New York, 30 May 1920, in CZA, File A219/4. See also, Simon, "HaMeḥanechet," 9; and Joan Dash, "Doing Good in Palestine: Magnes and Henrietta Szold," in *Like All the Nations? The Life and Legacy of Judah L. Magnes*, ed. William H. Brinner and Moses Rischin (Albany: State University of New York Press, 1987), 103–04.
38. Shulamith Schwartz Nardi, personal interview with the author, Jerusalem, 26 March 1991.
39. Szold, Jerusalem, letter to her sisters, [United States], 15 April 1932, CZA, File A125/263.
40. Id., [Jerusalem], letter to Mrs. David Greenberg, chairman, National Youth Aliyah Committee, New York, 15 May 1939, in CZA, File A125/59.
41. Id., Jerusalem, letter to M[oshe] Shertok, Jerusalem, 8 July 1941, in CZA, File S25/1125.
42. Yosef Sprinzak, Haifa, letter to daughter, Naomi Sprinzak [Raanan], n.p., 2 Kislev 5703 [1943], in *Igrot Yosef Sprinẓak*, vol. 2 (1929–1947), ed. Yosef Shapira (Tel Aviv: Ayanoth, 1969), 415–20.
43. Id., letter to Edwin Samuel, 5 January 1930, quoted in Susan Lee Hattis, *The Bi-National Idea in Palestine During Mandatory Times* (Haifa: Shikmona, 1970), 171–72.
44. F.[rederick] H. Kisch, *Palestine Diary* (London: Victor Gollancz, 1938), 30–31.
45. Szold, on board the *S. S. Esperia*, letter to Dr. and Mrs. J. L. Magnes, [Jerusalem], 10 October 1937, in CZA, File A125/30.
46. Dash, *Jerusalem*, 171; Hattis, *Bi-National Idea*, 259; Anita Shapira, *Berl: The Biography of a Socialist Zionist*, trans. Ḥaya Galai (Cambridge, England: Cambridge University Press, 1984), 282; M[oshe] S[hertok (later, Sharett), Jerusalem], letter to Szold, Jerusalem, 17 September 1941, in CZA, File S25/1125;

Notes to Chapter 5

Nahum Goldmann, New York, letter to Ben-Gurion, [Jerusalem], 26 October 1942, in CZA, File S25/237b. On the Biltmore Program, see below, chapter 7.
47. Szold, "Ershten Yortsayt," 15.
48. Id., Jerusalem, letter to sisters, Bertha [Levin] and Adele [Seltzer], n.p., 5 June 1936, in CZA, A125/265.
49. Id., Jerusalem, letter to "dear Sisters," [United States], 22 June 1934, File A125/264.
50. Id., Jerusalem, letter to sisters, Bertha [Levin] and Adele [Seltzer], n.p., 9 July 1937, in CZA, File A125/266.
51. See Michael Brown, "Some Early Nineteenth-Century [should be Twentieth-Century] 'Travelers' to America: Sources and Contexts," in *With Eyes Toward Zion*, vol. 2, ed. Moshe Davis (New York: Praeger, 1986), 243.
52. Simon, "Meḥanechet," 11.
53. Szold, Jerusalem, letter to sisters, Bertha [Levin] and Adele [Seltzer], n.p., 25 February 1938, in CZA, File A125/266.
54. Id., Jerusalem, letter to her sisters in the United States, 22 July 1931, in CZA, File A125/263.
55. BGD, 14, 15 December [1923].
56. I. J. Kligler, "Builder and Leader of Hadassah," Palestine *Post*, 20 December 1940. The article appeared as a tribute to Szold on her eightieth birthday.
57. Among other sources, see *Report* of the Activities of the American Zionist Medical Unit from July, 1919 to August, 1920—Director: I. M. Rubinow, n.p., n.d; Emanuel Neumann, *Causes of the Conflict* (New York: New Maccabean, [1921]); BGD, 15 December [1923]; Sophie Udin, "Henrietta Szold," *Pioneer Woman*, January 1931, 5; and contemporaneous reports in the Palestine press (*Do'ar HaYom* and *HaPo'el HaTza'ir*, for example).
58. Szold, Jerusalem, letter to Administrative Committee, ZOA, New York, 21 December 1927, in CZA, File A125/51.
59. Ben-Gurion quoted in minutes of meeting between the HEC and the Palestine Zionist Executive, 12 December [1927], in LAT, File IV-208-67bet, and in HVHP", 5 December 1927.
60. See, for example, Katznelson, "Veto" [Hebrew], and "BaCongress HaShisha-Asar" [Hebrew], both in *KBK*, vol. 4, 71–75, and 79–86. These essays appeared originally in *Davar*, the first on 17 April 1929, and the second on 13 August 1929. For Szold's reactions to the ZOA, see among other sources, her letter from Jerusalem to the Administrative Committee of the ZOA, New York, 21 December 1927, in CZA, File A125/51; and "Miss Szold's Message" to the recent ZOA convention in Pittsburgh, *The New Palestine*, 13–20 July 1928.
61. "Turning the Tide," *The New Palestine*, 1 November 1927, 348. See also, "Honoring Henrietta Szold," *The New Palestine*, 28 October 1927.
62. Szold, Jerusalem, coded cable to the ZOA, New York, 30 November 1927, in CZA, File F38/509. See also, her follow-up letter from Jerusalem to the Administrative Committee, ZOA, New York, 23 December 1927, in the same file.
63. Moshe Smilansky, "HaKedosha VeHaTehora" [Hebrew], *HaAretz*, 20 February 1945.

64. Szold, Jerusalem, letter to "dear Girls" [Alice and Annie Jastrow, Philadelphia], 2 May 1921, in CZA, File A125/257. The Jastrow "girls" were the sisters of Joseph Jastrow, Rachel Szold's husband, and childhood friends of Henrietta. On Szold's attraction to the ḥalutzim, see Dash, "Doing Good" 104.
65. Judah Magnes, "Henrietta Szold—LiGvurot" [Hebrew], *Davar*, 20 December 1940; and many other sources.
66. Benjamin Akzin, *MeiRiga Lirushalayim Pirke Zichronot* [Hebrew] (Jerusalem, 1989), 297–98. Also, compare the treatment of Szold's seventieth birthday in *Do'ar HaYom* (19 December 1930) and of her eightieth birthday in *HaMashkif* (24 December 1940) with that in *Davar*, the Labor daily, or in the unaligned *HaAretz*.
67. Udin, "Henrietta Szold," 5.
68. Szold, New York, letter [Hebrew] to HEC, Tel Aviv, 20 February 1931, in LAT, File IV-208-336alef.
69. Hannah Thon, "Sheva Shanim Shel Binyan" [Hebrew], *Davar*, 6 February 1939.
70. Judd L. Teller, "America's Two Zionist Traditions," *Commentary* 20 (October 1955): 351. Compare also, Dorothy Kahn, "Henrietta Szold Stands Fast at Wartime Post," Philadelphia *Jewish Exponent*, 20 December 1940.
71. Simon, "Meḥanechet," 11.
72. Szold, [Jerusalem], letter to Mrs. David B. Greenberg, Hadassah, New York, 27 March 1938, in CZA, File A125/95.
73. Lipsky, *Gallery*, 137.
74. Rose Halpern, "Henrietta Szold," *Jewish Frontier* 12 (March 1945): 9–10.
75. Szold, Jerusalem, letter to Elvira Solis, New York City, 10 April 1923, in CZA File A125/310.
76. Sara Feder, "Henrietta Szold Serves the Yishuv," *Pioneer Woman*, January 1941, 7.
77. Wiebe, *Order*, 122.
78. Szold, Baltimore, letter to Miss [Elvira] Solis, New York, 17 February 1896, in CZA, File A125/308.
79. Id., "The Future of Women's Work for Palestine," Jerusalem, 30 May 1930, typescript, 12–13, in CZA, File A44/35. (The paper was a proposal to Hadassah and WIZO for the transfer of welfare activities from the Jewish Agency to the Va'ad Le'umi.)
80. Louis D. Brandeis, Woods Hole, Massachusetts, letter to J[ulian] W[illiam] M[ack], J[acob] d[e] H[aas], S[tephen] S[amuel] W[ise], F[elix] F[rankfurter], and A[bba] H[illel] S[ilver, his minions in the ZOA], n.p., in *Brandeis Letters*, vol. 5, 8. See also, Szold, Jerusalem, letter to "Family," [United States], 10 July 1921, in CZA, File A125/257.
81. "Early Years," 253.
82. See, for example, her letter, from Jerusalem to her family in America, 31 July 1921, in Marvin Lowenthal, *Henrietta Szold, Life and Letters* (New York: Viking, 1942), 185–86; and her letter of 14 March 1927 to the National Board of Hadassah, recorded in the minutes of the meetings of the ZOA Administrative Committee, 14 April 1927.

Notes to Chapter 5

83. Szold, [Jerusalem], letter to the Delegates to the Convention of Hadassah, St. Louis, 4 October 1938, in CZA, File A125/58.
84. Id., Jerusalem, letter to Mrs. Lindheim, New York City, 29 June 1926, in CZA, File A125/22.
85. Id., Rehobot, letter, to her sister, Adele [Seltzer], n.p., 28 April 1921, in CZA, File A125/257.
86. Id., Jerusalem, letter to Family, [United States], 3 June 1920, in CZA, File A125/256.
87. Id., "Women's Work;" and letter from R. M. S. *Caronia*, en route to Zionist Congress, to Elvira Solis, Twin Mountains, New Hampshire, 17 August 1927, in CZA, File A125/310.
    Compare also, her letter from Jerusalem, to "dear Sisters," 22 June 1934, in CZA, File 125/264; and Michal Hagitti, "A Rest-Home for Agricultural Laborers in Jerusalem, 1919–1923" [Hebrew], *Cathedra* 30 (December 1983): 99.
88. Szold, Jerusalem, letter to Miss Pinczover, [Jerusalem], 25 May 1921, in CZA, File A125/321. Many other sources could also be cited.
89. See, for example, id., Jerusalem, letter to "dear Ones" [family in the United States], 28 November 1922, in CZA, File A125/258.
90. See, for example, id., [Jerusalem], letter to Zionist Executive, London, 10 January 1928, in CZA, File S25/997. On behalf of the Palestine Executive, Szold protested the Londoners' requesting that Felix Warburg alter the terms of a large donation which was intended for the educational system in Palestine.
91. F[rederick] H. Kisch, [Jerusalem], memorandum to Dr. [Werner] Senator, [Jerusalem], 20 April 1930, in CZA, File S25/1594.
92. Szold, on board the S. S. *Amazonia* sailing from Marseille [sic] to Jaffa, letter to [Louis] Lipsky, [president of the ZOA, New York], 24 November 1927, in CZA, File F38/509.
93. Id., "The Task of the Executive," address to the Cleveland Conference of the United Palestine Appeal, published in *The New Palestine*, 11 November 1927. On the Progressives and the city manager concept, see Harold U. Faulkner, *Politics, Reform and Expansion, 1890–1900* (New York: Harper Tarehbooks, 1963), 27–28; and Wiebe, *Order*, 168.
94. Szold, Jerusalem, letter to Gisela Warburg, New York, 31 July 1943, in CZA, File A125/111.
95. Id., [Jerusalem], letter to Mrs. Edward Jacobs, president, Hadassah, New York City, 8 June 1936, in CZA, File A125/94.
96. Moshe Shertok, typescript of speech [Hebrew] given at the Jewish Agency Building, Jerusalem, 12 December 1940, on the occasion of Szold's eightieth birthday.
97. Aaron Aaronsohn, Copenhagen, letter to Judge Julian W. Mack, n.p., 9 October 1916, in *Yoman Aharon Aharonsohn* [Hebrew], ed. Yoram Efrati (Tel Aviv: Hotza'at Sfarim Karni, 1970), 112. See also, Extracts from the Diary of Gertrude Goldsmith Rosenblatt, entry for 16 January 1913, in CZA, File A125/18; Aaron Aaronsohn, Washington, D.C., letter to [Henrietta Szold], n.p., 4 January 1917, in CZA, File A125/325; and Kutscher, "Early Years," 73.

Notes to Chapter 5

98. See Wiebe, *Order*, 113–17.
99. Irma L. Lindheim, *Parallel Quest* (New York: Thomas Yoseloff, 1962), 169. Lindheim succeeded Szold as president of Hadassah and subsequently herself emigrated to Palestine.

    Among other sources with references to "American standards," see Henrietta Szold, letters, Jerusalem, 18 August 1921, in CZA, File A125/257; Jerusalem, 1 November 1922, in CZA, File A 125/258, both to "dear Ones" [family in the United States]; and her letter from Jerusalem published as a supplement to the *Hadassah News Letter*, 13 May 1920.
100. "Mitoch Ne'umah HaAḥaron Shel Henrietta Szold" [Hebrew], *HaAḥot*, December 1945. See also, Dash, "Doing Good," 100.
101. Mrs. B. A. [Gertrude] Rosenblatt, Haifa, letter to Szold, Jerusalem, 10 August 1934, including notes from Rosenblatt's diary, in CZA, File A125/18. Rosenblatt was one of Szold's early compatriots in Hadassah. See also, *American Zionist Medical Unit for Palestine* (New York: ZOA, 1919), 6; and Dash, *Jerusalem*, 108–09.
102. Kutscher, "Early Years," 131.
103. Extracts from the Diary of Gertrude Goldsmith Rosenblatt, 19 May 1913, in CZA, File A125/18. On Addams and her Progressive context, see Samuel P. Hays, *The Response to Industrialism, 1885–1914* (Chicago and London: University of Chicago Press, 1957), 76–83; and Gunther Barth, *City People* (Oxford and New York: Oxford University Press, 1980), 7–8ff.
104. Szold, [New York], letter to Mamma, Rachel, and Joe [Jastrow, Madison, Wisconsin], 4 November 1913, in CZA, A125/275; and Louis D. Brandeis, Washington, letter to Alfred Brandeis, n.p., n.d. [1924], in *Brandeis Letters*, vol. 5, 107. See also, Charles A. Hawley, State University of Iowa, Iowa City, letter to Szold, Jerusalem, 16 December 1935, in CZA, File A125/160; and Fanny Goldstein, "Jewry Honors Its Chaucer [Mendele Mocher Sefarim] and Its Jane Addams," Boston *Evening Transcript*, 21 December 1935.
105. *American Zionist Medical Unit for Palestine*, 30, 35. See also, *Report* of Activities of the American Zionist Medical Unit from July, 1919 to August, 1920—Director: I. M. Rubinow (n.p., n.d.), 7; *Twenty Years of Medical Service to Palestine, 1918–1938* (Jerusalem: Hadassah Medical Organization, 1939), 7, 24, 27, 47; and Dash, *Jerusalem*, 116, 132.
106. *Twenty Years*, 25. See also, Szold, Jerusalem, letters to "Family," [United States], 7 October 1921, and to Miss [Jane?] Friedenwald, [Baltimore], 4 January 1921, both in CZA, File A125/257.
107. *Hadassah Medical Organization Third Report—September, 1920-December, 1921* (Jerusalem, 1922), 39–40.
108. *Twenty Years*, 17, 65, 67; Gelber, *Balm*, 103.
109. "Dr. Yassky's Review of Post-War Medical Needs of the Yishuv," August 1944, mimeograph, in CZA, File F32/120.
110. Szold, "Jewish Palestine in the Making," speech delivered at the Hadassah reception in her honor at the Hotel Pennsylvania, New York City, 30 April 1923, typescript, in CZA, File A125/9.

Notes to Chapter 5

111. Program of the Women's Centennial Congress, Hotel Commodore, New York City, 26 November 1940. Szold was the only woman honored who was identified as a Jew.
112. Alexander Dushkin, "Impressions of Henrietta Szold as a Jewish Educator," *Hadassah News Letter*, December 1945.
113. Szold, "Jewish Palestine in the Making."
114. See undated fund-raising brochure for the School of the Parents' Education Association, as Kallen's school came to be called. In addition to Szold's, the brochure carries the endorsement of Rabbi Stephen S. Wise, Prof. John Dewey, and others. Among the alumni of the school were members of elite families of the *yishuv*, including the general, politician, and archaeologist Yigal Yadin and his brother, actor Yossi Yadin. Judy Hollander of Jerusalem was kind enough to share with me information on Kallen and her school.
115. Szold, Jerusalem, letter to Miss Pinczover, [Jerusalem], 25 May 1921, in CZA, File A125/321.
116. Id., Jerusalem, letter to "dear Ones," [United States], 4 February 1922, in CZA, File A125/258.
117. Id., Jerusalem, letter to ZOA Education Committee, New York, 7 December 1927, in CZA, File F38/509. See also, Dash, *Jerusalem*, 198–200.
118. Szold, Jerusalem, letter to Executive Committee, Junior Hadassah, New York, 1 January 1928, in CZA, File A125/51.
119. Kutscher, "Early Years," 19; and Henry Franc Skirball, "Isaac Baer Berkson and Jewish Education," Ed.D. dissertation, Teachers' College, Columbia University, 1976, 115.
120. Szold, on board the *R. M. S. Carmania*, letter to "Sisters," [United States], 18 November 1927, in CZA, File A125/261.
121. Id., Jerusalem, letter to Col. F.[rederick] H. Kisch, Johannesburg, 24 April 1928, in CZA, File S25/1594. Kisch and Harry Sacher were Szold's two colleagues on the Executive.
122. Id., near Alexandria on the way to Berlin, letter to "Sisters," [United States], 13 July 1928, in CZA, File A125/262.
123. Id., [Jerusalem], letter to Mrs. Stephen S. Wise, New York City, 14 October 1928, in CZA, File A125/68.
124. See, for example, id., Jerusalem, letters to ZOA Administrative Committee, New York, 21 December 1927, in CZA, File F38/509; and to London Zionist Executive, London, 10 January 1928, in CZA, File S25/997; "Brief News from the Homeland," *The Vanguard*, April 1928; and Naomi W. Cohen, *The Year after the Riots* (Detroit: Wayne State University Press, 1988), 65.
125. Szold, Jerusalem, letter to "Sisters," [United States], in CZA, File A125/262.
126. Skirball, "Berkson," 129. See also, 180–81.
127. I. B. Berkson, "Reorganization of the Haifa Technical Institute," 2 February 1931; Skirball, "Berkson," 150–51.
128. Szold, *en route* to Marseille [sic], letter to "Sisters," [United States], 17 June 1930, in CZA, File A125/262.
129. Id., Jerusalem, letter to Sisters, [United States], 6 February 1930, in CZA, File

Notes to Chapter 5

A125/262. See also the letter cited in n. 124. In fact, Warburg and Szold had clashed even before she left for Palestine. (See Yigal Elam, *HaSochnut HaYehudit—Shanim Rishonot, 1919–1931* [Hebrew] [Jerusalem: Hassifriya Haziyonit, 1990], 183, 207.)
130. Quoted in Skirball, "Berkson," 181.
131. Shoshana Persitz, "HaOvedet" [Hebrew], *Hed HaHinuch*, 15 Iyyar 5690 [1930].
132. See Dash, *Jerusalem*, 214–17.
133. Dr. I. B. Berkson, "Sirtut LiDmutah Shel HaGv. Szold" [Hebrew], *Hed HaHinuch*, 15 Iyyar 5690 [1930].
134. Gelber, *Balm*, 55–56.
135. Szold, Jerusalem, letters to her sister, Bertha [Levin, Baltimore], 26 September 1941, and 16 October 1942, in CZA, Files A125/268, and A125/274.
136. Id., Jerusalem, letters to sister, Bertha [Levin, Baltimore], 12 November 1943, and 10 March 1944, in CZA, File A125/274.
137. Id., quoted in *The Maccabean*, July 1913.
138. Id., transcript of address to the *Survey Graphic* Association in New York, January 1936, in CZA, File A125/83; Gelber, *Balm*, 53.
139. Szold, quoted in Kutscher, "Early Years," 127.
140. Id., Haifa, letter to Rachel [Jastrow], n.p., 6 November 1920, in CZA, File A125/256.
141. Haim Yaphet, *Tet-Vav Shnot Sherut Sotziali BiKnesset Yisrael* [Hebrew] (Jerusalem, 5707 [1947]), 8. See also, Dash, *Jerusalem*, 181.
142. Szold, quoted in "Rashei HaYishuv Mechabdim et Henrietta Szold" [Hebrew], *HaAretz*, 24 December 1940. See also, "H. Szold Al Darka LaTziyonut UvaTziyonut" [Hebrew], *Davar*, 25 December 1940.
143. Szold, n.p., letter to Jacob H. Margowski, Philadelphia, 31 December 1912, in CZA, File A125/287. Margowski, had failed to acknowlege a donation from Szold for the United Aged Home of Jerusalem. To her "American mind" the oversight was "of the greatest importance."
144. Minutes of the meetings of the Administrative Committee of the ZOA, 29 December 1926.
145. Szold, Jerusalem, letter to the Executive Committee of Junior Hadassah, New York City, 1 January 1928, in CZA, File A125/51. See also, *Twenty Years*, 8.
146. Szold, letters, Jerusalem, to Mr. and Mrs. Nathan Straus, Mamaroneck, New York, 14 May 1926, and New York City, 2 March 1928, both in CZA, File A125/39; and Jerusalem, to her sister, Rachel [Jastrow, Madison, Wisconsin], 7 July 1926, in CZA, File A125/260. See also, Miss Sarah Katz, "Report of Soup Kitchen Investigation," Jerusalem, 1926/1927.
147. See her letter, Jerusalem, to I. Braude, Straus Soup Kitchen, Jerusalem, 11 March 1929, in CZA, File A125/40.
148. Szold, Jerusalem, letter to Dr. Maurice B. Hexter, the Jewish Agency, Jerusalem, 3 November 1931, in CZA, File A125/45. On the halukah system, see David Ben-Gurion, "LeShe'eilat HaYishuv HaYashan" [Hebrew], *HaAhdut*, Av, 5670 [1910], reprinted in *Ketavim Rishonim* (Tel Aviv: Ahdut, 5722 [1962]), 20.

Notes to Chapter 5

149. Szold, Jerusalem, letter to Mrs. Irving Lehman, New York City, 29 July 1931, in CZA, File A125/47; minutes of meetings held in December 1931, in an effort to establish an investigating committee for the Straus Soup Kitchen, in CZA, File A125/44; Henrietta Szold, Jerusalem, letters to Mrs. Irving Lehman, New York, in CZA, File A125/41, and to Harry I. Viteles, New York, 15 August 1932, in CZA, File A125/43. See also, "An Inquiry into the Activities of the Nathan Straus Soup Kitchens, Jerusalem, Conducted by Harry I. Viteles, December, 1931, to February, 1932." Viteles, an American, was the local representative of the Palestine Economic Corporation.
150. Szold, Jerusalem, letters to Mrs. Irving Lehman, New York, 4 August and 30 October 1932, in CZA, Files A125/41 and A125/43.
151. F.[rederick] H. Kisch, Palestine Zionist Executive, [Jerusalem], letter to [Bernard Stone], Executive Secretary of the United Palestine Appeal, New York, 18 December 1928, in CZA, File S25/1885.
152. See, for example, Szold, Jerusalem, letter to the Administrative Committee, ZOA, New York, 21 December 1927, in CZA, File F38/509.
153. Henrietta Szold, "The Future of Women's Work," 7–8.
154. Id., talk given at the Hadassah National Board meeting, New York, 2 January 1936, draft typescript, in CZA, File A125/12. See also, her address to the students of the Jewish School for Social Work, New York, 13 January 1936, in the same file.
155. "Al HaPerek. LeHizuk HaVa'ad HaLe'umi" [Hebrew], *HaAretz*, 4 May 1931.
156. Szold, "Avoda Sotzialit BiShe'at Herum" [Hebrew], *Dvar HaPo'elet*, 27 December 1940; and "The Future of Women's Work," 2.
157. Thon, "Sheva Shanim."
158. I. Braude, [director, Straus Soup Kitchen], Jerusalem, letter to Mrs. Irving Lehman, [New York], 14 August 1931, in CZA, File A125/41.
159. Yaphet, *Tet-Vav Shnot*, 14.
160. Szold, Jerusalem, letter to Mrs. Irving Lehman, New York, in CZA, File A125/41.
161. Id., Jerusalem, letter to Mrs. Irving Lehman, New York, 28 March 1932, in CZA, File A125/41.
162. Id., Women's Day address at the Levant Fair, Tel Aviv, 31 May 1934, typescript, in CZA, File A125/315.
163. Rose Luria Halpern, "Portrait of Hadassah," *Jewish Frontier*, August 1937, 18.
164. A.[vraham] Katznelson, "Henrietta Szold" [Hebrew], *HaPo'el HaTza'ir*, 27 December 1940. See also, Mayor Dahan, Tiberias, letter to Henrietta Szold, [Jerusalem], 22 December 1940, in CZA, File A125/179.
165. "Henrietta Szold Completes a Job," Palestine Post, 19 January 1939.
166. National Executive Committee, Brit HaTziyonim HaKlaliyim, Tel Aviv, letter to Henrietta Szold, Jerusalem, in CZA, File A125/175.
167. Yaphet, *Tet-Vav Shnot*, 15.
168. Szold, Jerusalem, letters to Sisters, [United States], 8 September, and 1 September 1933, both in CZA, File A125/263.
169. Id., transcript of address to *Survey Graphic* Association, New York, January 1936, in CZA, File A125/83.

170. Id., address to a special meeting of the ZOA Administrative Committee, New York, 9 June 1936, typescript, in CZA, File A125/83.
171. Id., "Avoda Sotzialit."
172. Dash, *Jerusalem*, 235–38.
173. See, for example, Szold, Jerusalem, letters to Harry I. Viteles, New York, 26 September 1932; to her sisters, Bertha [Levin] and Adele [Seltzer, United States], 4 February 1938; and to Yosef Baratz, Degania, 6 December 1939, all in CZA, Files A125/43, A125/266, and A125/59, respectively. See also, her notes for a discussion on children at a conference in Tel Aviv, February 1938, in CZA, File A125/34.
174. Zena Herman, "Henrietta Szold and Youth Aliyah," typescript, n.p., [1945].
175. MS", 6 October and 23 December 1942; Szold, New York, letters to Mrs. David Ben-Gurion, Brooklyn, 17 March and 23 June 1919, in LAT, File IV-104-29-7. See also, Shabtai Teveth, *Ben-Gurion: The Burning Ground, 1886–1948* (Boston: Houghton Mifflin, 1987), 127, 857.
176. MS", 6 October and 23 December 1942.
177. Szold, address sent to delegates to the 22nd Annual Hadassah Convention, Philadelphia, 18–20 October 1936, typescript in CZA, File A125/83.
178. Id., Jerusalem, letter to Mrs. David B. Greenberg, n.p., 2 November 1938, in CZA, File A125/34. See also, Herman, "Henrietta Szold."
179. Id., Jerusalem, letter to her sister, Adele [Seltzer], n.p., 18 September 1934, in CZA, File A125/264. See also, her letters, New York, 5 November 1911, to Boris Kazmann, Battle Creek, Michigan; and Jerusalem, 26 March 1944, to her sister, Bertha [Levin], n.p., in CZA, Files A125/283, and A125/274 respectively.
180. Id., on the train between Houston and Beaumont, Texas, letter to Elvira Solis, New York City, 18 January 1918, in CZA, File A125/309.
181. Id., Jerusalem, letter to Administrative Committee, ZOA, New York, 21 December 1927, in CZA, File A125/51.
182. Id., Jerusalem, letter to sisters, Bertha [Levin] and Adele [Seltzer, United States], 22 February 1935, in CZA, File A125/265, and many other letters.
183. Id., Jerusalem, letter to "dear Ones" [her family in the United States], 13 July 1921, in CZA, File A125/257.
184. Id., Jerusalem, letters to Family, [United States], 22 June and 18 August 1921, both in CZA, File A125/257.
185. Id., Jerusalem, letter to Sisters, [United States, August 1928?], in CZA, File A125/262. See also, the extract of her letter from Jerusalem, 17 August 1928, to Mrs. A. H. Vixman, Pittsburgh, in CZA, File A125/223.
186. Id., New York, letter to sister, Bertha [Levin, Baltimore], in CZA, File A125/263.
187. Id., New York, letter to Messrs. [Frederick] Kisch, [Arthur] Ruppin, and [Werner] Senator, Executive, Jewish Agency, Jerusalem, 6 February 1931, in CZA, File S25/1594.
188. Id., Jerusalem, letter to Sisters, [United States], 28 December 1934, in CZA, File A125/264. See also, her letters to her sisters, Bertha [Levin] and Adele

Notes to Chapter 5

[Seltzer], from Trieste, 27 August 1937, and from Jerusalem, 10 September 1937, both in CZA, File A125/266; and Nardi interview.

189. Quoted by Katznelson in a letter from New York to his wife, Leah [Miron-Katznelson, Tel Aviv], 24 November 1937, KABB, File 2.

190. Szold, Jerusalem, letter to Mrs. Edward [Rose] Jacobs, New York, 7 June 1943, in CZA, File A125/35. See also, Dash, *Jerusalem*, 219–20.

191. Id., typescript of notes for an address to the Zionist Congress, Zurich, summer 1937, in CZA, File A124/13.

192. Judah Magnes, quoted in "Rashei HaYishuv Mechabdim et Henrietta Szold," *HaAretz*, 24 December 1940. A partial transcript of Magnes's remarks, which were delivered at an eightieth birthday celebration for Szold at the Jewish Agency, 22 December 1940, mentions not the 1882 pogroms but the Kishinev pogrom "of 1905 or 1906" (CZA, File A125/188). The later version in *HaAretz* is assumed to be correct.

193. H. Yaffe, "Di Amerikaner froi vos hot gebracht Erets Yisroel keyn America un America keyn Erets Yisroel" [Yiddish], New York *Der Tog*, 21 December 1935.

194. Szold, letter from Jerusalem, supplement to the *Hadassah News Letter*, 13 May 1920.

195. Id., Jerusalem, letter to "dear Ones" [family in the United States], 16 April 1926, in CZA, File A125/260.

196. Id., Jerusalem, letter to Executive Committee, Junior Hadassah, New York, 1 January 1928, in CZA, File A125/51.

197. Id., Jerusalem, letter to the Administrative Committee of the ZOA, New York, 21 December 1927, in CZA, File A125/51.

198. Id., [Jerusalem], letter to Mrs. David Greenberg, chairman, National Youth Aliyah Committee of Hadassah, New York, 20 March 1939, in CZA, File A125/59.

199. Id., "The Future of Women's Work," 19.

200. Id., "Jewish Palestine in the Making," an address delivered at the Hadassah reception in her honor, Hotel Pennsylvania, New York City, 30 April 1923, typescript in CZA, File A125/21.

201. Gertrude Rosenblatt, Haifa, letter to Szold, Jerusalem, December 1927; and Henrietta Szold, Jerusalem, letter to Mrs. B. A. Rosenblatt, Haifa, 1 January 1928, both in CZA, File A125/57.

202. Szold, Jerusalem, letters to Sisters, [United States], 6 February and 8 August 1930, both in CZA, File A125/262.

203. See, for example, "Review of Activities of Kupat Holim Center, 1 September–15 November 1928," [Hebrew], mimeo, in LAT, File IV-208-146aleph; "Pe'ulot Hadassah," [Hebrew], mimeo, Jewish Agency Executive Circular #15, [1930]; Szold, Jerusalem, letter to Harry I. Viteles, Kitzbühl, Austria, 7 August 1932, in CZA, File A125/43; and other sources.

204. Szold, Jerusalem, letter to Mrs. Jacobs, [New York City], 18 September 1930, in CZA, File A125/35.

205. Id., [Jerusalem], letter to Mrs. Lola Hahn-Warburg, Arbeitsgemeinschaft, Berlin, 14 September 1936, in CZA, File A125/94. See also, her letter from Jerusa-

Notes to Chapter 6

lem, to Mrs. David [Tamar] de Sola Pool, president, Hadassah, New York City, 16 July 1941, in CZA, File A125/61. Although she had lived many years in America de Sola Pool was a native of Palestine.
206. Id., [Jerusalem], letter to Mrs. David B. Greenberg, chairman, National Youth Aliyah Committee, New York City, 1 December 1940, in CZA, File A125/60.
207. Szold, on board the S. S. *Esperia*, memorandum to the Agency Executive, Jerusalem, 11 October 1937, in CZA, File S25/1125.
208. Id., Jerusalem, letter to sister, Bertha [Levin, Baltimore], 12 July 1940, in CZA, File A125/267.
209. Dash, "Doing Good," 99.
210. "HeArot" [Hebrew], *HaAretz*, 16 February 1945.
211. Lotta Levensohn, "Henrietta Szold," *Moznayim* 2 (25 December 1930): 4; *HaAretz*, 19 December 1930.
212. Meir Dizengoff, mayor, Tel Aviv, letter to Szold, Jerusalem, 17 December 1935, in CZA, File A125/159; Moshe Athiash, "LiDmutah Shel Henrietta Szold Limlot Lah Shiv'im VeḤamesh Shana" [Hebrew], *Do'ar HaYom*, 22 December 1935.
213. Szold, en route from Trieste to Alexandria, letter to Elvira Solis, New York, 1 January 1929, in CZA, File A125/310.
214. Id., on the Mediterranean between Alexandria and Trieste, letter to "dear Ones" [family in the United States], 28 November 1909, in CZA, File A125/276.
215. Id., "The Future of Women's Work," 12.
216. Id., address to special meeting of the ZOA Administrative Committee, New York, 9 June 1936, typescript, in CZA, File A125/83.

Chapter 6

1. Meir, in a radio interview in Hebrew in 1969, as quoted in *A Land of Our Own: An Oral Biography of Golda Meir*, ed. Marie Syrkin (New York: Putnam's Sons, 1973), 31.
2. Meir was the Hebrew name she assumed in 1952. Myerson (or Meyerson) was her marriage name. In later life her first name was usually rendered "Golda," although earlier "Goldie" and even "Golde" were more common. All are used interchangeably here.
3. Compare, for example, Margaret Davidson, *The Golda Meir Story* (New York: Charles Scribner's Sons, 1976), 1–9, 66; Laird O'Brien, *Golda Meir: A Perspective on the Woman and Her Times* (London, Ont.: London Life Insurance Company, 1978); Yigal Allon, radio interview, 12 January 1979; Ya'akov Ḥazan, *Em BeYisrael*, (n.d.); *Golda—Kovetz LeZichrah* [Hebrew], ed. Naḥman Tamir (Tel Aviv: Am Oved, 1981), 33; personal interview with Sylva Gelber, Ottawa, 24 January 1988; Ralph G. Martin, *Golda Meir: The Romantic Years* (New York: Charles Scribner's Sons, 1988), 99; Meron Medzini, *HaYehudiya HaGei'a* [Hebrew] (Jerusalem: Edanim, 1990), 17, 39–41.
4. There are several difficulties in evaluating Meir's career. The most important of these is the sparse written record she left behind. She was neither a letter

Notes to Chapter 6

writer nor a diarist. As a result there are not many sources on which to base such an evaluation. Moreover, her autobiography, *My Life* (London: Weidenfeld and Nicolson, 1975), the several biographies written during her lifetime, and interviews with her all repeat the same few biographical details, which have about them the air of myth. The autobiography of her sister, Sheyna Korngold, *Zikhroynes* [Yiddish] (N.p.: Farlag Idpis, [1968]), is not much more revealing. All of these sources seem to conceal Meir's serious thoughts about her American experience and about other aspects of her life as well. Finally, most of the sources date from the latter part of her life and were colored by her later experiences.

5. Meir, *Beit Avi* [Hebrew] ([Tel Aviv]: Hakibbutz Hame'uchad, 1972), 18; id., quoted in radio interview in Hebrew, 1969, in Syrkin, *Land*, 17–18; Korngold, *Zikhroynes*, 130.
6. Meir, *My Life*, 17; Martin, *Golda*, 35.
7. Compare, for example, Meir, *My Life*, 4–7 and *Beit Avi*, 43–44; Davidson, *Meir Story*, 53–54; Korngold, *Zikhroynes*, 104; Martin, *Golda*, 16; and Medzini, *HaYehudiya*, 29. All translations are the author's unless otherwise noted.
8. Meir, *My Life*, 45, 214. See also, Meir interview in Syrkin, *Land*, 23.
9. Meir, *My Life*, 23; id., "MiShlihut HaHistadrut LeShlihut HaMedina" [Hebrew], report to the HEC on her visit to the United States, before leaving for the USSR (as Israeli minister designate), 1948, in her *BeDegel HaAvoda*, [Hebrew], (Tel Aviv: Am Oved, 1972), 237; Marie Syrkin, *Golda Meir; Woman with a Cause* (New York: G. P. Putnam's Sons, 1963), 24; Davidson, *Meir Story*, 71; personal interview with Sarah Rahabi, Tel Aviv, 2 September 1985.

   Compare also, Michael Brown, "Some Early Nineteenth-Century [should be Twentieth-Century] Holy Land 'Travelers' to America: Sources and Contexts," in *With Eyes Toward Zion*, vol. 2, ed. Moshe Davis (New York: Praeger, 1986), 243; and id., "The New Zionism in the New World: Vladimir Jabotinsky's Relations with the United States in the Pre-Holocaust Years," *Modern Judaism* 9 (February 1989): 84.
10. Meir, quoted in HC", 21 July 1941; in MC", 20 May 1942 and 10 July 1944; and in MS", 21 October 1947; Rahabi interview; Korngold, *Zikhroynes*, 125; "Bet Avi" [Hebrew], transcript of interview by Dan Raviv with Mrs. Golda Meir and Mrs. [Sheyna] Korngold, in GMM, 22–23; Meir interview in Syrkin, *Land*, 27–28.
11. Personal interview with Regina Medzini, Jerusalem, 29 August 1985.
12. Meir, quoted in "The Banquet for Comrades Zuckerman on the 24th of September, 1932" [Yiddish], *Iddisher Kemfer*, 27 September 1932; id., *My Life*, 38; id., "Yamim Rishonim BaKvutza" [Hebrew] (N.p., 1969), [originally a talk at Kibbutz Revivim, Pesach, 1969], 3; Yitzhak Greenberg, interview with Yitzhak Elam, 26 June 1989, (transcript in GMM), 1; Meir, *Beit Avi*, 58. Elam was Golda's close coworker for many years.
13. Menahem Meir, *My Mother Golda Meir* (New York: Arbor House, 1983), 14–15; Gelber interview; Medzini, *HaYehudiya*, 29.
14. Baruch Zuckerman, "Golda Meir" [Yiddish], in his *Essayen un Profilin* (Tel Aviv: I. L. Peretz, 1967), 423.

15. Meir, "Tnu'at HaPo'alim BeMivḥan" [Hebrew], *HaPo'el HaTza'ir*, 3 August 1944, 6. Compare also, id., "BeLev Shalem U-VeSimḥa" [Hebrew], remarks at a reunion of Third Aliyah veterans in Tel Aviv, n.d., in *Sefer HaAliyah HaShlishit*, vol. 2, ed. Yehuda Erez (Tel Aviv: Am Oved, 1964), 910–13.
16. Id., "BeHargashat HaYe'ood VeHaAḥrayut" [Hebrew], talk given at the fiftieth anniversary conference of the Histadrut, 9 December 1969, quoted in Tamir, *Kovetz*. 140; id., "We Are Rooted in the Soil," statement on receiving an honorary doctorate of humane letters from the Hebrew Union College Biblical and Archaeology School, Jerusalem, 13 October 1970, in Syrkin, *Land*, 177–78.
17. Meir, quoted in *The Canadian Zionist*, April 1934, 11; id., quoted in "A New Approach to Zionism," *Avukah Bulletin*, February 1932, 2; id., quoted by Sophie A. Udin, "The Fourth Convention," in *Pioneer Woman*, December 1932, 1; id., "BeLev Shalem," 911.
18. Syrkin, *Woman*, 57.
19. Robert Slater, *Golda: The Uncrowned Queen of Israel* (New York: Jonathan David, 1981), 26.
20. Meir, letter written from Merḥavya, 24 August 1921, quoted in Syrkin, *Land*, 240–41.
21. Id., quoted in "Discussion about the Land of Israel and the Diaspora" [Yiddish], condensed minutes of a session of the annual convention of the Poale Zion-Zeire Zion Party, Baltimore, 17 September 1932, in *Iddisher Kemfer*, 7 October 1932.
22. Id., speech on the dedication of a new neighborhood on the banks of the Yarkon, 22 October 1939 [Hebrew], manuscript in her hand, in GMM, file of unsorted material.
23. Id., "The Face of the Histadruth," comments delivered at a meeting of the HEC held to welcome Richard Crossman, 27 March 1946, [Hebrew], quoted in her *BeDegel*, 166. See also, Meir, "Rooted."
24. Greenberg interview with Elam, 9 July 1989, transcript in GMM, 17. Compare also, Meir's "Report to America," an address to the National Press Club, Washington, 11 December 1956, in *This Is Our Strength: Selected Papers of Golda Meir*, ed. Henry M. Christman (New York: Macmillan, 1962), 61.
25. President Yitzḥak Navon and Shimon Peres, chairman of the Labor Party, press releases after the death of Golda Meir, quoted in Aryeh Ḥashavya, *Golda Meir* (Jerusalem: Agaf HaNo'ar/HaMaḥleka LeḤinuch Ḥevrati, 1978), 31–32.
26. Compare Yitzḥak Ben-Zvi, diary, entry for 28 Tammuz 1915, New York, quoted in his *Poale Zion BaAliyah HaShniya* (Tel Aviv: Mifleget Po'alei Eretz Yisrael VeIḥud Olami Poale Zion (Z. S.) Hitachduth, 1950), 186.
27. Goldie [Meyerson], Winnipeg, letter to [Chaim] Arlazaroff [sic, Jerusalem], 1 March 1932, in CZA, File S25-793.
28. Id., at a Mapai Center meeting, 22 August 1940, ISAMP, Division Bet, File 23/40. Compare also, Golda Meir, "BeLev Shalem," 910; Dr. Yisrael Eldad, "Golda" [Hebrew], in Tamir, *Kovetz*, 56; Yitzḥak Elam, "BiMḥitzatah Shel Golda: Siḥot Im Yitzḥak Elam," transcript in GMM, conversations with Drora

Notes to Chapter 6

Beit-Or, September 1985–February 1986, 12–13, 25; Yehudit Simḥoni, interview with Drora Beit-Or and Sarah Rahabi, 5 April 1987, transcript in GMM; Elam interview with Greenberg, 26 June 1989, 5; Korngold, Zikhroynes, 106; Medzini, HaYehudiyah, 95.
29. Meir, Beit Avi, 33.
30. Id., at a meeting of the Histadrut Council, 28 January 1941, ISAHC, File 62/810aleph. Compare also Menahem Meir, My Mother, 11; Slater, Uncrowned Queen, 19, 22; Eliyahu Agress, Golda Meir: Portrait of a Prime Minister, trans. Israel I. Taslitt (New York: Sabra, [1969]), 12; Terry Morris, Shalom, Golda (New York: Hawthorn, 1971), passim; Martin, Golda, 56, 73, 87; and Medzini, HaYehudiya, 31–32, 36, 38.
31. Zuckerman, "Golda Meir," 423–24.
32. Regina Medzini interview.
33. Meir, My Life, 60; and Korngold, Zikhroynes, 139. See also, Korngold, Zikhroynes, 58–59, 68–69; Meir, Beit Avi, 61, 66; Slater, Uncrowned Queen, 29; Martin, Golda, 108–09; Mollie Keller, Golda Meir (New York: Franklin Watts, 1983), 37.
34. Syrkin, Woman, 53.
35. Meir, at a meeting of the Histadrut Council, 28 January 1941, in ISAHC, File 62/810alef.

These guilt feelings seem to have intensified after the Holocaust, although by then they were less associated with the United States. In 1946, at a ceremony welcoming Zivia Lubetkin, one of the few survivors of the Warsaw Ghetto Uprising, to Palestine, Meir spoke of the bond between Lubetkin and the Laborites in the yishuv: Although of the same movement, "often we could not but feel that we were unworthy of your stand; that we as parents, had not deserved such children." Meir asked of Lubetkin that she "work with us in such a way as to reawaken our faith that we are worthy of you." (Quoted in "Zivia Lubetkin Welcomed by Yishuv," Pioneer Woman, June 1946, 7.)
36. Meir, My Life, 53, 59; customs official quoted in Medzini, HaYehudiya, 41; Golda Meir, "How I Made It in My Kibbutz," in Syrkin, Land, 12; Korngold, Zikhroynes, 139.
37. Korngold, Zikhroynes, 139; and Golda Meir, "BeLev Shalem," 45; and many other sources.
38. Berl Repetur, interview with Drora Beit-Or, 5 March 1985, transcript in GMM, 11–12.
39. Meir, quoted in MC", 11 August 1942.
40. Id., "My Kibbutz," 39; and "BeLev Shalem," 911–12. See also, id., Beit Avi, 59; Syrkin, Woman, 77; Medzini, HaYehudiya, 45.
41. Meir, "My Kibbutz," 39–40. See also, id., My Life, 64; and Morris, Shalom, Golda, 49.
42. Meir, "From the Words of Golda Meir—From Milwaukee to Merhavya" [Hebrew], in Sefer Merhavya, HaCo'operatzia (Tel Aviv: Hotza'at Vatikei HaCo'operatizia 1961), 235. See also, Syrkin, Woman, 73; Slater, Uncrowned Queen, 29; Morris, Shalom, Golda, 47; Martin, Golda, 81.

43. Sarah [Rahabi] and Menaḥem [Meir], "Imma" [Hebrew], in Tamir, Kovetz, 66; Menaḥem Meir, My Mother, 14–15.
44. Shabtai Teveth, Ben-Gurion: The Burning Ground, 1886–1948 (Boston: Houghton Mifflin, 1987), 501; Goldie Myerson, "Hadassah and the Zionist Congress," Pioneer Woman, May 1933.
45. Meir, Beit Avi, 47–49; id., radio interview in Syrkin, Land, 34; Raviv interview, 21, 25–26; Korngold, Zikhroynes, 154, 161; Slater, Uncrowned Queen, 26, 31; Morris, Shalom, Golda, 45; Martin, Golda, 169.
46. Israel Mereminsky (Merom), [HEC, Tel Aviv], letter to A. Koller, New York, 20 May 1932, in LAT, File IV-208-1-337bet.
47. Repetur, interview, Beit-Or, 16–19.
48. Berl Repetur, "Im Golda BeFe'ilut Histadrutit" [Hebrew], in Tamir, Kovetz, 96; Golda Meir, letter [Hebrew photocopy], Tel Aviv, 17 September 1928, to Comrades, Mishkei VeḤavurot HaPo'alot, in GMM, File of unsorted materials; id., speech at the second convention of the Histadrut, Tel Aviv, 21 Shvat 1923, quoted in Hebrew translation in Ben-Gurion, Zichronot [Hebrew], vol. 1 (Tel Aviv: Am Oved, 1971), 214. See also, Medzini, HaYehudiya, 52.
49. Elam, interview with Greenberg, 26 June 1989; Elam, "BiMhitzatah," 9.
50. In HaYehudiya, (52), Medzini claims that Meir expressed such an opinion at a leadership meeting of the Working Women's Council in December 1922. Although the view is consistent with her later statements, and although she only rarely altered her views, the source cited by Medzini is incorrect. Further verification is therefore needed.
51. Meir, at a meeting of the HEC, Tel Aviv, 14 May 1925, in ISAHVHP, File 32/810aleph (1). See also, Medzini, HaYehudiya, 58.
52. BGD, 5 May 1924; Jüdische Rundschau, 28 May 1924; Vienna Arbeiter Zeitung, 8 August 1928.
53. Yosef Sprinzak quoted in HVHP", 24 October 1923.
54. Remez quoted in HVHP", 4 September 1928.
55. See especially, HVHP", for meetings of 3, 4, 17, 20 September 1928.
56. Eliyahu Golomb quoted in HVHP", 4 September 1928.
57. See letters [Yiddish] of Leah Biskin, secretary, Pioneer Women's Organization, New York, 3, 23 October 1928, 9 November 1928, to Working Women's Council, Tel Aviv, in LAT, File IV-208-1-137; Isaac Hamlin, national secretary, National Labor Committee, letter [Yiddish], New York, 19 November 1928, to HEC, Tel Aviv, in LAT, File IV-208-1-121gimel; HVHP", 20 September 1928.
58. See minutes of meeting of the Working Women's Council Enlarged Secretariat, 10 September 1929. Golda insisted that a delegate be sent to America no later than the end of that month.
59. Isaac Hamlin, letter [Yiddish], New York, 15 December 1928, to HEC, Tel Aviv, in LAT, File IV-208-1-121aleph.
60. "Decision to Raise $300,000 for Jewish Workers in Palestine," New York Morgn Zhurnal [Yiddish], 31 December 1928. See also the less enthusiastic account in the New York Forverts [Yiddish], "Workers' Convention Decides to Raise $300,000 to Help Palestine Workers," 31 December 1928.

Notes to Chapter 6

61. Budget of Working Women's Council for 5689 (1928–29), in LAT, File IV-208-1-174; Leah Biskin, secretary, Pioneer Women's Organization, New York, letter, [Yiddish], to Working Women's Council, Tel Aviv, 3 July 1928, in LAT, File IV-208-1-137; I[srael] Mereminsky, [HEC, Tel Aviv], letter, [Yiddish], to Pioneer Women's Organization, [New York], 25 December 1930, in LAT, File IV-208-1-174. See also, Golde Myerson, "The Working Women's Movement in Palestine" [Yiddish], in *Palestine Souvenir on the Occasion of the Fifth Anniversary of the Geverkshaften Palestine Campaign and the Fourth National Labor Convention for Palestine Held in New York, December 29/30, 1928*, 35.

62. Ibid; id., "The Pioneer Women's Organization," *Labor Palestine*, June 1933, 22; and Yehudit Simḥoni, leader of the Working Women's Council, in an interview with Drora Beit-Or and Sarah Rahabi, Tel Aviv, 5 April 1987, transcript in GMM.

63. Leah Biskin, New York, letter [Yiddish], 17 January 1929, to Working Women's Council, in LAT, File IV-208-1-137. See also, in the same file, her letter [Yiddish] of 8 May 1929, also to Working Women's Council; Israel Mereminsky, letter [Hebrew], New York, 7 February 1929, to HEC, Tel Aviv, in LAT, File IV-208-1-121alef; "We Stand Pledged," editorial, *Pioneer Woman*, December 1928; ad for farewell banquet in honor of the "Palestine Labor Delegation, Israel Mereminsky, David Bloch, Golde Myerson," and "The Poale-Zion Program," *The Vanguard*, June 1929; Golde Myerson, "Women's Workers Movement"; Medzini, *HaYehudiya*, 69.

   On male chauvinism in American Labor Zionism at the time, see Golda Meir, "Travel Impressions" [Yiddish], *Iddisher Kemfer*, 2 May 1932.

64. Quoted in Martin, *Golda*, 188.

65. Meir, *My Life*, 104.

66. Id., quoted in HVHP", 3 September 1930.

67. Id., speech to the Geverkshaften Campaign Convention, New York, 30 December 1928, quoted in Moshe Rivlin, "At the Convention of the Jewish Workers for Palestine" [Yiddish], in New York *Morgn Zhurnal*, 1 January 1929.

   In *HaYehudiya* (68), Medzini claims that on her 1928 trip Golda perceived a gap between herself and American Jews of which she had not previously been aware. He offers no evidence, however, for this assertion.

68. Meir, quoted in HVHP", 3 September 1930. See also, HVHP", 23 September 1929, 8 September 1930; and MC", 18 October 1930, ISAMP, File 23/30, section 2; Medzini, *HaYehudiya*, 74.

69. Simḥoni interview with Beit-Or and Rahabi.

70. Raḥel Yana'it, report on her work in America for the Pioneer Women's Organization in HVHP", 4 September 1928.

71. Meir, quoted in HVHP", 3 September 1930; Martin, *Golda*, 167–68.

72. Meir, "Ma She-Lo Asinu BeZurich U-Ma She Od Mutal Aleinu La'asot" [Hebrew], *Davar*, 10 January 1930. Medzini claims in *HaYehudiya* (68) that Golda felt frustrated during her American stay because she had no access to the wealthy, acculturated Jews. He offers no evidence for the claim, however.

73. Meir, quoted in HVHP", 3 September 1930; id., *My Life*, 105.

Notes to Chapter 6

74. Quoted in HVHP", 8 September 1930.
75. Menaḥem Meir, *My Mother*, 14–15.
76. Ibid., 32; Berl Katznelson, notebook from 1937 trip to the United States, entry for Friday, [9 November 1937], in KABB.
77. David (Blumenfeld) Bloch, report on the delegation to America, HVHP", 19 August 1929.
78. Israel Mereminsky, letter [for the HEC, Tel Aviv], 29 May 1930, to Pioneer Women's Organization, New York, in LAT, File IV-208-1-174. See also, Mereminsky letter [for the HEC, Tel Aviv], 11 July 1930; D[avid] R[emez], letter [for the HEC, Tel Aviv], 10 February 1930, [Yiddish], to Pioneer Women's Organization, [New York], c/o Leah Biskin; [Leah Biskin, for the] Pioneer Women's Organization, letter [Yiddish], New York, 28 April 1930, to Working Women's Council, Tel Aviv; all in LAT, File IV-208-1-174.
79. [Leah Biskin], Pioneer Women's Organization, [New York], letter to Working Women's Council, Tel Aviv, 28 April 1930, in LAT, File IV-208-1-174.
80. Leah Biskin, secretary, Pioneer Women's Organization, New York, letter to I[srael] Mereminsky, HEC, Tel Aviv, 14 August 1930, in LAT, File IV-208-1-174.
81. Elam interview with Greenberg, 9 July 1989, 14. See also, report of David Bloch on the delegation to the United States, in HVHP", 19 August 1929.
82. Meir, "Women's Movement," 35.
83. Compare HVHP", 1929–31. Sometimes, even at crucial junctures, Ben-Gurion left her on her own. See, for example, HVHP", 3 and 15 September 1930.
84. D[avid] B[en-Gurion], "At the Imperial Laborers' Conference," [Hebrew], *Ha-Po'el HaTza'ir*, 15 August 1930. Ben-Gurion used identical language in describing the event in a letter to his wife, Paula, quoted in Medzini, *HaYehudiya*, 71. See also, memo [Hebrew], Working Women's Council, Tel Aviv, to HEC, [Tel Aviv], 18 September 1929, in LAT, File IV-208-1-174. Compare, as well, Martin, *Golda*, 170; Medzini, *HaYehudiya*, 70.
85. Ada Fishman (Maimon) and Raḥel Katznelson (Rubashov), Working Women's Council, Tel Aviv, letter, [Hebrew], to Golda Meyerson, Tel Aviv, 30 August 1931, in LAT, File IV-208-1-281alef; MS", 23 September 1931.
86. Menaḥem Meir, *My Mother*, 31; Martin, *Golda*, 176–77.
87. Ben-Gurion, quoted in MS", 23 September 1931. Shortly after her arrival in New York, she complained bitterly that her colleagues in the *yishuv* were not giving her and the Americans working on their behalf the support to which they were entitled. See Golda [Meyerson], New York, telegram to Ovdim [HEC], Tel Aviv, 21 October 1931, in LAT, File IV-208-1-336bet.
88. Golde Meyerson, open letter, [Yiddish], in *Pioneer Woman*, October 1931, 4.
89. Menaḥem Meir, *My Mother*, 33. On Golda's work on behalf of aliyah, see, among other sources, Golda Meir, New York, letter to [Eliyahu] Dobkin, [HEC, Tel Aviv], 19 October 1932, in LAT, File IV-208-1-338bet; minutes of a meeting of HaVa'ad Lema'an HeḤalutz, New York, 6 June 1934; and HVHP", 18 August 1934.
90. "Facts About the Division of Certificates," *Hechalutz Bulletin*, January-February 1935, 3–4.

Notes to Chapter 6

91. Golda Meyerson, "Ma She-Lo Asinu BeZurich"; id., quoted in HVHP", 3 September 1930, a meeting held with visitors from America. See also, HVHP", 23 September 1929.
92. Meir, quoted in HVHP", 16 June 1931.
93. Id., "Rishmei Masa BeAmerica" [Hebrew], *Davar*, 25 May 1932. See also Elam interview with Greenberg.
94. "In the Pioneer Women's Organization" [Yiddish], *Iddisher Kemfer*, 13 April 1934; Golda Meyerson, New York, letter to [Working Women's Council, Tel Aviv], 27 April 1932, in LAT, File IV-208-1-281bet; id., *My Life*, 111. Her itinerary is recorded in the pages of the *Pioneer Woman* and the *Iddisher Kemfer* for these years.
95. Bella Collier, for the National Executive of the Pioneer Women's Organization, New York, letter to Working Women's Council, Tel Aviv, 25 June 1932, in LAT, File IV-208-1-281bet; Elisheva [Kaplan], Cincinnati, letter to Bebe Idelson, [Tel Aviv], 30 January 1935, in LAT, File IV-208-1-816bet; *Iddisher Kemfer*, 27 October 1933 and 23 March 1934.
96. Meir, *My Life*, 109; Morris, *Shalom, Golda*, 65.
97. Golde Meyerson, "Our Organization" [Yiddish], *Pioneer Woman*, June 1934, 3. See also, id., "Travel Impressions" [Yiddish], *Iddisher Kemfer*, 2 May 1932.
98. "HaPe'ulah HaPolitit," summary report of Working Women's Council, mimeo, [1932], in LAT, File IV-230-5-14alef.
99. Yosef Sprinzak, n.p., letter to Merkaz Mapai, Tel Aviv, 2 Tammuz 5694 [1934], in *Igrot Yosef Sprinzak*, vol. 2 (1929–1947), ed. Yosef Shapira (Tel Aviv: Ayanoth, 1969), 274–75; Golde Meyerson, "Travel Impressions"; Bella Collier, for the national executive of the Pioneer Women's Organization, New York, letter to Working Women's Council, Tel Aviv, 2 May 1932, in LAT, File IV-208-1-281bet.
100. Golda Meyerson, "Rishmei Masa"; id., report on her mission to the United States in HVHP", 16 August 1934.
101. "On Golda Meyerson's Departure for Eretz Yisroel," *Pioneer Woman*, June 1934, 3.
102. "Comrade Meyerson Visits Chicago" [Yiddish], *Pioneer Woman*, December 1933, 12; "Welcome Goldie Myerson," *Pioneer Woman*, April 1937. See also, "Comrade Meyerson's Tour" [Yiddish], *Iddisher Kemfer*, 12 January 1934, 14–15.
103. Ada Fishman and Ben-Gurion quoted in MC", 8 August 1934; Elisheva Kaplan quoted in mimeographed excerpts from her letters, n.d., in LAT, File IV-208-1-816alef.
104. Meir, speech to the Histadrut Council, 28 January 1941, in ISAHC.
105. In letters to the Working Women's Council, Tel Aviv, 13 January 1936, 10 April 1936, both in LAT, File IV-208-1-816bet, Sophie A. Udin, national secretary of the Pioneer Women's Organization, [New York], complained mildly about Meir's inattention. Rubashov, on the other hand, reported that she busied herself to a considerable extent with the Pioneer Women (HVHP", 24 September 1936). See also, Bert Goldstein, member, National Praesidium,

Notes to Chapter 6

Pioneer Women's Organization, New York, letter to Goldie Meyerson, Jerusalem, 1 August 1947, in CZA, File S25-825.

106. See among other sources, Israel Mereminsky, "Yoman," entry for 2 October [1932], in LAT, File IV-208-1-338bet, and letter from [New York] to Merkaz Kupat Ḥolim, Tel Aviv, in LAT, File IV-208-1-407alef.

107. Goldie Meyerson, New York, letter to [Working Women's Council, Tel Aviv], 27 April 1932, in LAT, File IV-208-1-281bet; Zalman Rubashov, report on activities in America, in HVHP", 26 September 1932. See also, Meyerson, Winnipeg, letter to [Chaim] Arlazaroff (sic), [Jerusalem], 1 March 1932, in CZA, File S25/793.

108. Yosef Sprinzak, report on his activities in America, HVHP", 16 August 1934.

109. Goldie Meyerson, report on activities in America, HVHP", 7 July 1932; "The Call from the Histadrut" [Yiddish], an open letter to American Jews, n.d. (1932), from Goldie Meyerson, Shimon Kushiner, and Zalman Rubashov.

110. Shimon [Kushiner], New York, letter to [Israel] Mereminsky [HEC, Tel Aviv], 17 June 1932, in LAT, File IV-208-1-337bet. See also, Kushiner letter from New York to HEC, [Tel Aviv], 9 February 1932, in the same file.

111. Goldie Meyerson, report on America, HVHP", 7 July 1932. Her trips for the Campaign are catalogued in the pages of the *Iddisher Kemfer*.

112. E[liyahu] D[obkin for the HEC, Tel Aviv], letters to Yisrael [Mereminsky, New York], 2 November 1932, and 17 July 1933, in LAT, Files IV-208-1-338bet, and IV-208-1-407bet, respectively.

113. Goldie Meyerson, report on America, in HVHP", 7 July 1932; id., [Tel Aviv], letter to Avukah, New York, 8 March 1935, in LAT, File IV-208-1-705; id., in MC", 18 October 1930. See also, her comments in HVHP", 16 August 1934.

On Mereminsky, see, among other sources, his letter on behalf of the HEC in Tel Aviv, to HaHanhaga HaRashit Shel HaShomer HaTza'ir, New York, 26 January 1932, in LAT, File IV-208-1-337alef; "Histadruth Leader Sees Time Ripe for New Migration Movement to Palestine," *Jewish Daily Bulletin*, 2 September 1932.

114. Celia Monowitz, "Camp Kvutzah," *Pioneer Woman*, October 1933, 3; Ruth Bondy, *HaShaliaḥ* [Hebrew] (Tel Aviv: Am Oved, 1974), 240–41; correspondence and memoranda between Goldie Meyerson and Dr. Emanuel Gamoran, director of education for the Union of American Hebrew Congregations in Cincinnati, and other American-Jewish educators, 1935, in LAT, File IV-208-706; Rivka Markovitz, "The Young Poale Zion Convention," *Pioneer Woman*, October 1932.

115. Goldie Meyerson, quoted in MC", 4 August 1931.

116. *The New Palestine*, 31 May 1929, 16 June 1933; *Avukah Bulletin*, May 1929, December 1931, February 1932, April 1932; *Pioneer Woman*, May 1933; Yitzḥak Chizik, "MiPe'ulot Mishlaḥat HaHistadrut BeAmerica" [Hebrew], *Davar*, 15 January 1932. See also, correspondence between Meir and officers of Avukah in LAT, Files IV-208-1-1174 and 1175alef.

117. Monowitz, "Camp Kvutzah"; *Iddisher Kemfer*, 26 August 1932, 11 November 1932, 4, 18 August 1933; Jacob Lemberger, "Accord-1933," in *Adventure in*

Notes to Chapter 6

Pioneering, ed. David Breslau (New York: CHAY Commission of the Labor Zionist Movement, 1957), 19.

118. H. Giladi, HaVa'ad Lema'an HeHalutz, New York, letter to HEC, Tel Aviv, 5 October 1932, in LAT, File IV-208-338bet.

119. Israel Mereminsky (Merom), diary entry for 30 August 1932, in LAT, File IV-208-338alef; Golda Meyerson, quoted in HVHP", 3 September 1930.

120. Among other sources, see Avraham Zeiger and Y. Leibner, HaShomer HaTza'ir, New York, letter to HEC, Tel Aviv [Hebrew], 14 June 1932, in LAT, File IV-208-337alef; minutes of meetings of HaVa'ad Lema'an HeHalutz in America, 16 May 1932 and 22 September 1932, in LAT, Files IV-208-337bet and IV-208-338alef respectively; Mae Bere (Mereminsky) and Goldie Meyerson, [New York?], letter, to HaHanhaga HaRashit [Leadership], HaShomer HaTza'ir BeArtzot HaBrit VeCanada, New York, n.d. [after 8 February 1933], and E. Galili, New York, letter to HEC, [Tel Aviv], 13 July 1934, both in LAT, File IV-208-407alef.

121. Goldie Meyerson, review of her recent activities in America, in HVHP", 6 August 1936; id., quoted in HVHP", 20 June 1945. The latter quotation is reprinted in "Shlihim le'HeHalutz' " [Hebrew], Meir, *BeDegel*, 211–12.

122. Meir quoted in MS", 31 August 1932 and 18 December 1945. See also, her letter from New York to the [Working Women's Council], 27 April 1932, in LAT, File IV-208-1-281bet; Israel Mereminsky, diary entry for 14–18 September 1932, in LAT, File IV-208-1-338bet; and Yosef Sprinzak, New York, letter to [Berl] Locker, [London], 4 February 1934, in LAT, File IV-208-1-407bet.

123. Israel Mereminsky, New York, letter to HEC, Tel Aviv, 30 August 1932, and Meyer Brown, secretary, Poale Zion-Zeirei Zion, New York, letter to Israel Mereminsky, Tel Aviv, 15 April 1932, both in LAT, Files IV-208-1-338bet, and IV-208-1-337bet respectively. Maximilian Hurwitz claimed the League was conceived by Ben-Gurion and launched at the 1930 Congress of Friends of Palestine Labor held in Berlin ("Why a League for Labor Palestine," *Labor Palestine*, September-October 1933, 15). Joseph Schlossberg, the American-Jewish labor leader, believed the League was founded in order to bring onside people who could not be reached by the Geverkshaften Campaign (minutes of the first session of the National Executive of the League for Labor Palestine, New York City, 25 June 1937, in LAT, File IV-208-1-1176).

124. Golda Meyerson, quoted in minutes of a meeting of the Poale Zion-Zeire Zion Party, New York, included in a letter from Israel Mereminsky, New York, to the HEC, Tel Aviv, 12 October 1932, in LAT, File IV-208-1-338bet; Yosef Sprinzak, New York, letter to HEC, [Tel Aviv], 28 Sivan 5694 [1934], in *Igrot Sprinzak*, vol. 2, 271.

125. "About Golda's Visit" [Yiddish], *Iddisher Kemfer*, 2 March 1934; Golda Meyerson, report on activities in America, HVHP", 6 August 1936; Dr. Alexander S. Kohanski, Report of the National Secretary [of the League for Labor Palestine], for the Year 1936–37, 20 July 1937; I[saac] Hamlin, "League Activities," *Labor Palestine*, February 1934, 13; Joseph Schlossberg, general secretary of the Amalgamated Clothing Workers of America, New York, letter to Israel Mere-

minsky, Tel Aviv, 14 September 1936, in LAT, File IV-208-1-705; Avis Shulman, [Highland Park, Illinois, 1 February 1937], letter to Goldie Myerson, [Tel Aviv], in LAT, File IV-208-1-1178alef; minutes of the Administrative Committee of the League for Labor Palestine, special *Jewish Frontier* emergency session, 23 November 1937; Golda Myerson, "Pe'ulat HaHistadrut BeḤoref 5696 [1936] BeAmerica," in *BeDegel*, 226–28; Shlomo Tzemaḥ, quoted in HVHP", 16 September 1937; Michael A. Meyer, *Hebrew Union College-Jewish Institute of Religion: A Centennial History, 1875–1975*, rev. ed. (Cincinnati: Hebrew Union College Press, 1992), 130.

126. See, for example, remarks of Golda Meir, MC", 4 August 1931 and HVHP", 7 July 1932; Israel Mereminsky (Merom), diary entries for 14–18 September 1932 and 28 May 1936, in LAT, Files IV-208-1-338bet and IV-208-1-753bet respectively; and Bondy, *HaShaliaḥ*. Bondy quotes a report to the HEC sent from Los Angeles by Enzo Sereni in February 1937.

127. Goldie Meyerson, [Tel Aviv], letters to Dr. Samuel Wohl, Cincinnati, 21 January [May?] 1935, and [Pinḥas] Cruso, [New York], 18 December 1936, in LAT, Files IV-208-706 and 754bet respectively. Wohl, a Reform rabbi, was the first professional head of the League. Cruso was its national secretary for a time.

128. "Palestine Aid Event Sunday," Los Angeles *B'nai B'rith Messenger*, 6 March 1936; Golda Meir, "Skirah al HaPe'ulah BeAmerica," HVHP", 6 August 1936; Alexander S. Kohanksi, national secretary of the League for Labor Palestine, New York, letter to Israel Mereminsky (Merom), HEC, Tel Aviv, 28 January 1938, in LAT, File IV-208-1-1177; "League For Labor Palestine," *Jewish Frontier*, March 1938, 30; letter of Pinḥas Cruso, national secretary, League for Labor Palestine, New York, to Goldie Myerson, Tel Aviv, 21 June 1935, and minutes of meetings on 29 August 1935 and 28 August 1936 of the Secretariat of the HEC, all in LAT, Files IV-208-1-752bet and IV-208-1-754alef; Goldie Myerson, [HEC, Tel Aviv], letter to Rabbi Samuel Wohl, [executive secretary, League for Labor Palestine], Cincinnati, 21 May 1935, in LAT, File IV-208-1-706; Israel Mereminsky, diary entry for 14 September 1937, in LAT, File IV-208-1-1419; minutes of a meeting on 23 November 1937 of the Administrative Committee of the League for Labor Palestine, Special *Jewish Frontier* Emergency Session.

129. "Greetings from the Delegation," [Yiddish], *Iddisher Kemfer*, 13 May 1932; "Golde Myerson Visits Another Few Cities," [Yiddish], *Iddisher Kemfer*, 27 May 1932; "Pioneer Women's Organization," [Yiddish], *Iddisher Kemfer*, 10 June 1932.

130. Yosef Sprinzak, New York, letter to HEC, Tel Aviv, 28 Sivan 5694 [1934], in *Igrot Sprinzak*, vol. 2, 271–73. On these negotiations, see chapters 4 and 7 of this book.

131. Israel Mereminsky, Boston, letter to Comrades [HEC, Tel Aviv], 18 November 1932, in LAT, File IV-208-1-338bet; Goldie Myerson, "Hadassah and the Zionist Congress, *Pioneer Woman*, May 1933, 5–6; id., "To Break—Pious and Not so Pious," [Yiddish], *Pioneer Woman*, February 1934, 7.

132. Letters, D[avid] B[en]-G[urion], for the HEC, Tel Aviv], to I[srael] Mereminsky

and G[oldie] Myerson, New York, 1 December 1932; [Israel] Mereminsky, New York, to E[liyahu] Dobkin, Tel Aviv, 12 January 1933; and E[liyahu] D[obkin for the HEC, Tel Aviv], to [Israel] Mereminsky, [New York], 31 January 1933, in LAT, Files IV-208-1-338bet, and IV-208-1-407alef.
133. MC″, 21 October 1934.
134. *Iddisher Kemfer*, 21 July 1933 and 4 August 1933. Partly because of lack of funds, Meir did not attend the Congress.
135. Meir, foreword to Alexander Manor, *Commitment and Creative Action: The Life and Work of Israel Merom (Mereminsky)*, trans. and adapted S. Leshner-Shapira (Tel Aviv: Sponsoring Committee, 1978), vii. For similar assessments of Meir by others, see Menaḥem Meir, *My Mother*, 114; and Yehudit Simḥoni, interview with Drora Beit-Or and Sarah Rahabi, 5 April 1987, transcript in GMM, Oral History Section.
136. Meir, "Ezrah Hadadit Bimei Mashbeir," lecture to the Histadrut Study Seminar, 1941, in Meir, *BeDegel*, 53. See also, id., "Darkei Ha'Ezrah HaHadadit BeKerev Tzibur HaPo'alim" [Hebrew], *HaPo'el HaTza'ir*, 24 December 1939, 6–9; MC″, 22 August 1940; and Elam, interview with Greenberg (transcripts in GMM), 9 July 1989. To Meir's comments compare the remarks of Irma Lindheim to the convention of the National Labor Committee for Palestine, quoted in the *New York Times*, 29 November 1937.
137. Compare Melech Epstein, *Jewish Labor in the U.S.A.*, vol. 2 (1914–1952) (New York: Trade Union Sponsoring Committee, 1953), 161–62, 262, 354, and elsewhere.
138. HVHP″, 7 January 1942.
139. Yosef Sprinzak, Chicago, letter to Hannah Sprinzak, n.p., 2 Nisan 5694 [1934], in *Igrot Sprinzak*: vol. 2, 257–58.
140. Yosef Sprinzak, report on his eight months in the United States, in HVHP″, 16 August 1934. See also the debate between Sprinzak and Meir Ya'ari, HVHP″, 23 August 1934.
141. Quoted in *HaPo'el HaTza'ir* 30 (1937): 22.
142. Quoted in MS″, 28 September 1938.
143. See among other sources, E[liyahu] Dobkin, [HEC, Tel Aviv], letters to Israel [Mereminsky, New York], 17 November 1932, and to [Eliezer] Galili, [New York], 16 January 1934, both in LAT, Files IV-208-1-338bet and IV-208-1-407bet respectively; Shimon Kushiner, New York, letter to HEC, [Tel Aviv], 9 February 1932, in LAT, File IV-208-1-337bet; HVHP″, 9 August 1934.
144. See remarks of Meir in HVHP″, 16 August 1934.
145. Goldie Myerson, [HEC, Tel Aviv], letter to Mrs. Belle T. Daiches, Chicago, 11 February 1936, in LAT, File IV-208-1-706alef. Daiches was a travel agent and an active member of a Reform synagogue that arranged tours to Palestine through her.
146. Among other sources, see the letters to Goldie Myerson, Tel Aviv, of Isaac Hamlin, national secretary of the National Labor Committee for the Jewish Laborers of Palestine, New York, 20 February 1935, Nathan Guttman, acting secretary, Young Poale Zion Alliance, New York, 29 June 1935, and Rabbi

Edward L. Israel, Baltimore, 4 October 1935, all in LAT, Files IV-208-1-752alef, IV-208-1-700, and IV-208-1-706 respectively.

147. Goldie Myerson, [Tiyur ve-Tiyul, Tel Aviv], letter to Mr. Rosen, Palestine Oriental Tours, [New York], 2 May 1935, in LAT, File IV-208-1-705, regarding a projected young people's tour to be organized by his firm. See also the letters exchanged by Golda with Mr. Weiss of the Compass Travel Bureau, New York, and with John Rothschild, director of the Open Road, New York, regarding youth tours, in LAT, Files IV-208-1-705 and 706.

148. See Goldie Myerson, [HEC, Tel Aviv], letters to S[amuel] W. Rulnick, Hartford, 3 April 1935, to Samuel Lefcovits, Chicago, 30 July 1935, and to others in LAT, File IV-208-1-706.

149. Goldie Myerson, "Memorandum on Tourist Activity in the Settlements," to the Jewish Agency Executive, Jerusalem, 18 January 1935, in LAT, File IV-208-1-758bet.

150. HVHP", 25 August 1937. See also, "News from Palestine," *Hechalutz Bulletin*, October 1934,

151. See letters and telegrams from Golda to American Jewish labor leaders, from William Green, president of the American Federation of Labor, to Edward Canavan of the British Trade Union Congress, and from Sir Walter Citrine of the Congress to David Dubinsky, president of the International Ladies Garment Workers, in LAT, Files IV-208-1-706alef and 754bet.

152. I[saac] Hamlin, New York, letter to Goldie [Myerson, HEC, Tel Aviv], 24 December 1936, in LAT, File IV-208-1-1419. He had sent a similar letter to the committee two days earlier.

153. Yosef Sprinzak, Tel Aviv, letter to Yosef Baratz, [United States], 2 Adar 5697 [1937], in *Igrot Sprinzak*, vol. 2, 331–33; Goldie Myerson, [HEC, Tel Aviv], letter to Isaac Hamlin, [New York], 2 March 1937, in LAT, File IV-208-1-1419; MC", 16 January and 5 February 1937; Ben-Gurion, *Zichronot*, vol. 4 (1937) (Tel Aviv: Am Oved, 1974), 66.

154. Max Zaritsky, quoted in HVHP", 19 January 1937.

155. HVHP", 19 January 1937.

156. Quoted in HVHP", 16 September 1937. Yosef Baratz (MM", 25 May 1937) reported that the delegation might have been more effective fund raising in the United States, if some of its members hadn't stumbled into an unfortunate battle with the Bund over one of its campaigns. Golda also acknowledged that the unionists were less helpful than she had hoped with regard to fund raising.

157. For a discussion of the Campaign in other than Labor circles, see chapter 2 of this book.

158. Letters of Malkah Goodlow, Totzereth Haaretz Consumers' League, Inc., New York, and of Sara Feder, [secretary], Pioneer Women's Organization, New York, July–September 1938, to Goldie Meyerson, Israel Mereminsky, and Jacob Efter, Tel Aviv, in LAT, Files IV-208-1-1173 and 1177; Yosef Baratz, quoted in HVHP", 8 June 1939.

159. Rubashov, quoted in HVHP", 24 August 1931; Lubianiker, quoted in MS", 28 September 1938.

Notes to Chapter 6

160. Meir quoted in MS", 28 September 1938.
161. MC", 3 August 1936.
162. Yisrael Mereminsky, [HEC, Tel Aviv], letter to General Secretariat, Jewish Agency, Jerusalem, 3 November 1935, in LAT, File IV-208-1-649.
163. Quoted in *Forverts*, 28 November 1937.
164. "Pioneer Women's Organization' [Yiddish], *Iddisher Kemfer*, 10 December 1937.
165. Meir, speech to the Council of Jewish Federations, Chicago, 21 January 1948, in Syrkin, *Land*, 76.
166. Exchange of correspondence among Caiserman, Dov Hoz, and Heschel Frumkin, March-June 1935, in LAT, File IV-208-1-705; David Ben-Gurion, "Call of the Sea," *Jewish Frontier*, August 1935, 22–25; id., "Realization of Zionism," speech to the 19th Zionist Congress, in *Jewish Frontier*, October 1935, 24–31; Elam interview with Greenberg, 19 September 1989, transcript in LAT, GMM; Medzini, *HaYehudiya*, 82–83.
167. Correspondence in LAT, File IV-208-1-706bet.
168. Ovdim [that is, HEC, Tel Aviv], telegram to Ampoalim [that is, National Labor Committee for the Jewish Workers in Palestine], New York, 28 February 1937, in LAT, File IV-208-1-1419.
169. See chapter 4 of this book.
170. "Jewish Labor Leader To Give Address At Y.M.H.A.," *Scranton Times*, 11 November 1937; "Pioneer Women's Organization" [Yiddish], *Iddisher Kemfer*, 12 November 1937; "League for Labor Palestine," *Jewish Frontier*, January 1938; "Golde Myerson Will Appear in Brooklyn, Bronx, and Newark" [Yiddish], *Iddisher Kemfer*, 4 February 1938; League for Labor Palestine—Report of the National Secretary for the Year 1936–1937, 20 July 1937; MC", 14 March 1938.

    Meir had tried to avoid conflict with the UPA and had gone to see Wise and Lipsky before she began her tours. She thought she had gained their consent for her efforts, but that proved not to be the case (HVHP", 16 September 1937).

171. HVHP", 16 September 1937.
172. HVHP", 16 September 1937; MC", 14 March 1938; minutes of meeting of the Naḥshon administration, 11 August 1938.
173. Meir, quoted in HVHP", 16 September 1937.
174. Id., quoted in minutes of Naḥshon administration meeting, 11 August 1938.
175. HVHP", 13 April 1939.
176. D[avid] Remez, [HEC, Tel Aviv], letter to The President, American Academy of Political and Social Science, West Philadelphia, 17 February 1936, in LAT, File IV-208-1-705; exchange of correspondence between Myerson, Tel Aviv, and J. R. Carskadon, *New Republic*, New York, August-September 1936, in LAT, File IV-208-1-1080; Goldie Myerson, [Tel Aviv], letter to Charles [Brown, Los Angeles], 2 March 1937, in LAT, File IV-208-1-1178bet; id., [HEC, Tel Aviv], letters to William Green, Washington, D.C., 25 October 1936 and 23 October 1938, in LAT, Files IV-208-1-701 and 1176 respectively; Yeruḥam Meshel, "Mofet LeRoch Enoshi U-LeKashyut Oref Yehudit," in

Notes to Chapter 6

Tamir, *Kovetz*, 49; Melvin I. Urofsky, *American Zionism from Herzl to the Holocaust* (New York: Doubleday Anchor, 1976), 388.

177. For example, Avner Yaniv, "All That Glitters Is Not Golda," *Jerusalem Report*, 3 January 1991, 50. In *HaYehudiya*, Medzini implies as much.
178. Meir, quoted in Julie Nixon Eisenhower, *Special People* (New York: Ballantine, 1977), 10.
179. Id., quoted in minutes of meeting of the secretariat of the Poale Zion World Union, 11 April 1940, and in HVHP", 27 January 1938. The latter is quoted in Medzini, *HaYehudiya*, 86–87. On Jabotinsky, see chapter 2 of this book.
180. Meir, *My Life*, 131.
181. Quoted in Medzini, *HaYehudiya*, 87.
182. See the chapters on those three herein.
183. Meir, speech to the Histadrut Council, either 28 or 29 January 1941 (the typescript of her speech in GMM, LAT is dated 29 January; in the collected speeches in the Israel State Archives the date of 28 January is given).
184. See, for example, MC", 9 April 1940.
185. Meir, quoted in the minutes of a consultation on the political situation of the Mapai Political Committee, 26 February 1939.
186. HVHP", 31 July 1941. See also, HVHP", 2 October 1941, and Medzini, *HaYehudiya*, 96.
187. Myerson and David Remez, [HEC, Tel Aviv], cable to [Moshe] Shertok, London, n.d. [1943]. See also, their cable to Berl Locker, London, 10 May 1943; Medzini, *HaYehudiya*, 99; and Dina Porat, *The Blue and Yellow Stars of David: The Zionist Leadership in Palestine and the Holocaust, 1939–1945*, trans. David Ben-Naḥum (Cambridge, Mass.: Harvard University Press, 1990), 57. On the Revisionist petition of the 1930s, see Joseph B. Schechtman, *Fighter and Prophet: The Last Years* (New York and London: Yoseloff, 1961), 212–13. On the Bermuda Conference, see Irving Abella and Harold Troper, *None Is Too Many* (Toronto: Lester and Orpen Dennys, 1982), 126–58; and David S. Wyman, *The Abandonment of the Jews* (New York: Pantheon, 1984).
188. HVHP", 23–24 February 1944; Myerson, "Tnu'at HaPo'alim BeMivḥan" [Hebrew], *HaPo'el HaTza'ir*, 3 August 1944. See also HVHP", 16 February 1944.
189. See, for example, her report in HVHP", 27 January 1938; and her speech to the Histadrut Council, 29 January 1941, the text of which is in LAT, File IV-104-754-9.
190. "This Is Our Strength," *Dvar HaPo'elet*, 3 May 1939, reprinted and translated in Christman, *Our Strength*, 5.
191. Golda Meir, in HC", 21–24 March and 3–7 July 1944.
192. MC", 3 August 1936, and 14 April 1941. See also 9 November 1939.

    Meir's moment of greatest exasperation with Wise came at the Zionist Congress held in August 1939, just before the outbreak of war. It was increasingly clear that Jews trapped in Europe would suffer a terrible fate. Yet Wise spoke out against illegal immigration to Palestine, the only hope then for Europe's Jews denied legal immigration almost everywhere (Menaḥem Meir, *My Mother*, 55–56). See above, pp. 121–22.

Notes to Chapter 7

193. MC", 22 August 1940. See also, her speech to the Histadrut Council, 29 January 1941, the text for which is in LAT, File IV-104-754-9.
194. MS", 18 December 1945.
195. MC", 22 August 1940.
196. Meir, quoted in HC", 28 January 1941.
197. HVHP", 25 August 1939; HC", 28 January 1941. Medzini (HaYehudiya, 92) claims Meir was optimistic and simple-minded regarding American volunteers. The record shows, however, that while she thought recruitment possible, she did not think it would be at all easy.
198. Quoted in MC", 14 November 1945.
199. Meir, quoted in MS", 18 December 1945.
200. MS", 17–18 December 1945.
201. Meir, speech to a visiting delegation of Histadrut Campaign leaders, in HVHP", 6 August 1947; also in Meir, BeDegel, 230–32.
202. JAE", 28 September 1947.
203. Meir, speech to the Council of Jewish Federations and Welfare Funds, 25 January 1948, quoted in Syrkin, Land, 78, and Keller, Golda Meir, 74.
204. See, for example, her report to the HEC, HVHP", 4 August 1948. Compare also, MC", 10 September 1950.
205. Ben-Gurion, letter to Dr. Israel Goldstein on the occasion of the awarding to Golda Meir of the Stephen Wise Award, 25 July 1957, in Tamir, Kovetz, 11, also quoted in Menaḥem Meir, My Mother, 95.

Chapter 7

1. Transcript of Ben-Gurion's speech to the third conference of the Student Federation, Tel Aviv, 12 January 1944, in CZA, File S25/1483; id., "Yisrael ve-HaGola" [Hebrew], Shnaton HaMemshala (1958), quoted in Ze'ev Tzahor, "David Ben-Gurion's Attitude Toward the Diaspora," Judaism 32 (Winter 1983): 21.
2. In David Ben-Gurion—Likrat Medina Yehudit [Hebrew] (Sede Boqer: Ben-Gurion University of the Negev, Sede Boqer Campus, 1985) and elsewhere, Allon Gal offers the fullest treatment of the issue for the years 1938 to 1941. The English version of Gal's book is David Ben-Gurion and the American Alignment for a Jewish State (Bloomington and Jerusalem: Indiana University Press and Magnes Press, 1992). References herein are to the Hebrew text.

    Shabtai Teveth's monumental biography, Ben-Gurion: The Burning Ground, 1886–1948 (Boston: Houghton Mifflin, 1987), based on his three-volume Hebrew work, Kin'at David (Tel Aviv and Jerusalem: Schocken, 1977, 1980, 1987), contains a great deal of information on Ben-Gurion and America for the entire pre-state period. Among other scholars who offer important insights and whose works will be cited herein are Avraham Aviḥai, Michael Bar-Zohar, Yosef Gorny, Menaḥem Kaufman, Yisrael Kolatt, Matityahu Mintz, Monty Penkower, David Shpiro, and Ze'ev Tzahor. More popular biographies, such as Dan Kurzman's Ben-Gurion, Prophet of Fire (New York: Simon and Schuster, 1983), also address the question.

Notes to Chapter 7

3. Ben-Gurion, *Zichronot* [Reminiscences], 6 vols. [Hebrew] (Tel Aviv: Am Oved, 1971–1987), vol. 1, 10. The *Zichronot* are not memoirs in the usual sense but rather a collection of documents and diary extracts edited by Ben-Gurion. They must be read judiciously.
4. See Teveth, *Burning Ground*, 1–88, and other sources.
5. Teveth, *Burning Ground*, 48.
6. A.[haron] R.[euveni], "Shvitat HaHayatim," 11 Nisan 5673 [1913].
7. Avner [Yitzhak Ben-Zvi], "HaHagira VeTafkidah," Av, 5670 [1910], 46.
8. K.[arl] Kautsky, untitled article, 23 Kislev 5615 [1914]; N. Wagman [Aharon Reuveni], "Te'alat Panama," 18 Heshvan 5673 [1912]; "MiSipurei Nosei Itonim BeNew York," 6 Tammuz 5672 [1912]; Yosef Haver [Yosef Haim Brenner], "BeHayeinu U-Veltonuteinu," 19 Teveth 5672 [1912]; id., "BeHayeinu U-Veltonuteinu," 10 Kislev 5672 [1912]; A. Kretschmar-Yizra'eli, "Avoda Nochriya," 12 Heshvan 5615 [1914]. Kautsky, of course, was a well-known German/Austrian socialist whose article was reprinted from another journal.
9. "Chronika," 17 Sivan 5672 [1912]; N.[ahman] Syrkin, "HaHityashvut Ha-Co'operativit Ve-HaAhva," 4 Sivan 5674 [1914]; Avner [Yitzhak Ben Zvi], "HaHagira Ve-Tafkideinu," Av, 5670 [1910]; "Chronika," 7 Heshvan 5673 [1913]; "Michtav MiKineret," 26 Tammuz 5672 [1912].
10. [A. S. Waldstein?], "Eretz Yisrael VeAmerica," 3 Heshvan 5675 [1914]; N.[ahman] Syrkin, "Hasal Sidur Galveston," 1 Av 5674 [1914].
11. "Chronika," 1 Adar 5674 [1914]. On Aaronsohn, see chapter 5 of this book.
12. "Chronika," 19 Kislev 5673 [1912]; A.[haron] R.[euveni], "America U-Mexico," 12 Iyyar 5674 [1914]; Yosef Haver [Yosef Haim Brenner], "BeHayeinu U-Veltonuteinu," 19 Teveth 5672 [1912]. See also, Wagman, "Te'alat Panama;" "Chronika," 29 Av 5671 [1911]; and "Chronika," 10 Teveth 5673 [1913].
13. R.[euveni], "Shvitat HaHayatim BeAmerica"; Katriel [Leon Hazanowitz], "BeOlameinu Halvri," 17 Iyyar 5673 [1913]. See also, "Chronika," 21 Shvat 5672 [1912]; "Chronika," 21 Tammuz 5672 [1912]; and A. Shalmon [A. S. Waldstein], "MeiHayei HaYehudim BeAmerica," 2 Tevet 5673 [1913]; A[braham] Liessen, "Yovel HaAgudot HaOmanutiyot HaYehudiyot BeNew York," 24 Adar 5674 [1914], originally published in *Tsukunft*.
14. "Chronika," 26 Av 5672 [1912]; "BeOlameinu," 23 Iyyar 5673 [1913].
15. [Waldstein?], "Eretz-Yisrael VeAmerica."
16. "Chronika," 8 Sivan 5673 [1913]; "Chronika," 18 Tevet 5674 [1914].
17. Untitled editorial, 14 Tishrei 5675 [1914].
18. "MiYeshivat Misrad HaAvoda," 3 Heshvan 5675 [1914]; "Chronika," 12 Heshvan 5675 [1914]; "Chronika," 2 Kislev 5675 [1914]; "Chronika," 19 Kislev 5675 [1914]; Y.[a'akov] Z.[erubavel], "Michtav MiYafo," 13 Teveth 5675 [1914].
19. "HaMa'azan Shel HaKapa'i" and "HaVe'ida HaOlamit HaShlishit BeVina," both in the issue of 8 Elul 5671 [1911]; "Chronika," 19 Heshvan 5672 [1911]; "BeOlameinu," 28 Nisan 5674 [1914]; "BeOlameinu," 18 Sivan 5674 [1914]. See also, "Chronika," 21 Iyyar 5671 [1911]; "BeOlameinu," 7 Adar I 5673 [1913]; "HaVe'ida HaOlamit HaRevi'it BeCrakow," 24 Elul 5673 [1913].
20. Ya'akov Zerubavel, *Alei Hayim* [Hebrew], 2 vols. (Tel Aviv: I. L. Peretz, 1960),

Notes to Chapter 7

vol. 1, 364. See also, 375 and 403. Reports of Zerubavel's trip in *HaAhdut* include "Chronika," 10 Tevet 5673 [1913]; "BeOlameinu," 28 Adar II 5673 [1913]; and "HaVe'lda HaOlamit HaRevi'it BeCracow."

21. Zerubavel, *Alei Hayim*, 1, 325.
22. Syrkin, "HaHityashvut HaCo'operativit." See also, D. Yizraeli, "Ha'Ahva' V-Isodotehah," 12 Iyar 5674 [1914]; and Bernard I. Sandler, "The Jews of America and the Resettlement of Palestine, 1908–1934: Efforts and Achievements," Ph.D. dissertation, Bar Ilan University, April 1978. For a critique of the Ahva as an American model inappropriate to Palestine, see "LeTochnit 'Ahva,'" 14 Sivan 5674 [1914].
23. Ben-Gurion, speech, quoted in "HaVe'ida HaOlamit HaRevi'it BeCracow."
24. Yosef Aharonowitz, "Bifnei HaMe'ora'ot," *HaPo'el HaTza'ir*, 20 October 1914, 5.
25. Yisrael Kolatt-Kopelovich, "Ideologia U-Metzi'ut BiTnu'at HaAvoda BeEretz Yisrael, 1905–1919," Ph.D. dissertation, Hebrew University of Jerusalem, June 1964, 285; Isaiah Friedman, *Germany, Turkey, and Zionism, 1897–1918* (Oxford: Oxford University Press, 1977), 224; Zvi Shilony, "Changes in the Jewish Leadership of Jerusalem During World War I" [Hebrew], *Cathedra* 35 (April 1985): 58–90; Teveth, *Burning Ground*, 92; and Matityahu Mintz, "Ben-Gurion and Po'alei Zion in the United States During World War I," in *David Ben-Gurion: Politics and Leadership in Israel*, ed. Ronald Zweig (London and Jerusalem: Frank Cass and Yad Izhak Ben-Zvi, 1991), 57–58. In *A Peace to End All Peace* (New York: Avon, 1990), 211, David Fromkin claims that Ben-Gurion and Ben-Zvi agitated in the United States for the formation of a pro-Ottoman Jewish army; but he offers no evidence.
26. Ben-Zvi, *BaAliya HaShniya*, 156. Ben-Zvi erroneously claimed that their goal from the start had been to form a "Hebrew Legion." See also, Rahel Yana'it Ben-Zvi, *Coming Home*, trans. David Harris and Julian Meltzer (New York: Herzl, 1964), 245.
27. BGD, 16 Iyyar [30 April 1915]. Diary entries cited herein are from sections located at BGA, CZA, and LAT. Citations from printed diary entries note the work in which they appear.
28. Ibid., 29 Iyyar [13 May 1915]; 20 Sivan [2 June 1915].
29. Ibid., 3 Sivan [16 May 1915]; 26 Tammuz [8 July 1915]; 28 Tammuz [10 July 1915].
30. Ibid., 4 Sivan [17 May 1915]; 10 Sivan [19 May 1915]; 22 Sivan [4 June 1915]; 14 Tammuz [26 June 1915]. Teveth (*Burning Ground*, 99) notes only the few unfavorable remarks of Ben-Gurion and claims his initial reaction to the New World was negative.
31. BGD, 20 May 1935. To his wife, Paula, he wrote more prosaically of "the most interesting flight," although he conceded that "the two great cities from a great height [were] the grandest sight" he had "ever seen." (Letter, 20 May 1935, in *Letters to Paula*, trans. Aubrey Hodes [London: Valentine-Mitchell, 1971], 72.)
32. BGD, 14 Nisan [should be Sivan, 27 May 1915]; 13 Sivan [26 May 1915].
33. Ben-Zvi, *BaAliyah HaShniya*, 162. See also, his "'HeHalutz' VeHaHitnadvut

LaGdud HaIvri BeArtzot HaBrit," in *Sefer HaAliyah HaShlishit* [Hebrew], ed. Yehuda Erez (Tel Aviv: n.p., 1964), 202–08; and id., "America SheHikdima et Eiropa," *Davar*, 3 February 1928.

34. BGD, 19 Iyyar [3 May 1915]. On *HeHalutz*, see among other sources, "The Principles of *HeHalutz*," undated pamphlet in Yiddish from the World War I period, in BZA, File 1/4/13/47; Circular No. 18, Poale Zion Central Committee, New York, 28 June 1915; and Teveth, *Burning Ground*, 105. On the burgeoning Hebrew press in America in these years, see Michael Brown, "All, All Alone! The Hebrew Press in America, 1914–1924," *American Jewish Historical Quarterly* 59 (December 1969).

35. Ben-Gurion, open letter to Central Committee, Poale Zion in America, New York, 5 Shvat 5678 [1918], in *Igrot David Ben-Gurion*, 3 vols. [Hebrew], ed. Yehuda Erez (Tel Aviv: Am Oved and Tel Aviv University, 1972), vol. 1, 335–36.

36. BGD, 16 Sivan [29 May 1915], and 17 Sivan [should be Tammuz, 29 June 1915]; Teveth, *Burning Ground*, 99–103.

37. BGD, 23 Tammuz [5 July 1915]; 24 Tammuz [6 July 1915]; 26 Tammuz [8 July 1915]; 16 Av [26 July 1915]; 22 Av [2 August 1915]; Selig Adler and Thomas Connelly, *From Ararat to Suburbia* (Philadelphia: Jewish Publication Society, 1960), 302; Teveth, *Burning Ground*, 103–04.

38. BGD, 29 Av [9 August 1915]; Baruch Zuckerman, *Zikhroynes* [Yiddish], vol. 2 (New York: Farlag "Iddisher Kemfer" and Farband Bikher Farlag, 1963), 206.

39. Ben-Gurion, letters to H.[irsch] Ehrenreich, secretary of the Poale Zion of the United States, New York, from Youngstown, Ohio, 19 Teveth 5676 (1916), and Columbus, Ohio, 1 Shvat 5676 (1916), in *Igrot Ben-Gurion*, vol. 1, 328–29, 333; id., New York, letter to Ben-Zvi, [Washington, D.C.], 22 June 1916, quoted in Matityahu Minc [Mintz], "David Ben-Gurion's Correspondence with Izhak Ben-Zvi in America, 1915–1916" [Hebrew], *Cathedra* 44 (June 1987): 93; Teveth, *Burning Ground*, 107–08.

40. Golda Meir quoted in Meron Medzini, *HaYehudiya Ha'Gei'a* [Hebrew] (Jerusalem: Edanim, 1990), 35; Minc, "Correspondence with Ben-Zvi," 85; Ze'ev Tzahor, "David Ben-Gurion's Attitude Toward the Diaspora," *Judaism* 32 (Winter 1983): 12; BGD, 13 Tishrei [21 September 1915].

41. Ben-Gurion, "Min HaTzad" [Hebrew], *HaToren*, 21 July 1916.

42. David Ben-Gurion, *Zichronot*, vol. 1, 85; Teveth, *Burning Ground*, 109.

43. Among the pamphlets were *The Palestine Workers' Fund* and *Palestine as a Land of Jewish Colonization* by Ben-Zvi; *The National Fund—What It Is and What It Has Accomplished* and *Who Will Give Us the Land?* of Ben-Gurion; and the coauthored *"HeHalutz," Its Tasks at the Present Moment*.

44. On the dispute between Ben-Gurion and the *Kemfer*, see the exchange of correspondence between him and Ben-Zvi in Minc, "Correspondence with Ben-Zvi," 92–94; Teveth, *Burning Ground*, 110.

45. See Brown, "All, All Alone!" Among Ben-Gurion's articles in *HaToren*, the most widely read American Hebrew journal of the day, were "Zechuyoteinu HaLe'umiyot BeTurkiya U-VeEretz Yisrael," 2, 9, 23 June 1916; "Likrat He-

Notes to Chapter 7

Atid—LiShe'eilat Eretz Yisrael," August 1915; and "Min HaTzad." Ben-Zvi wrote or coauthored twenty-two articles, three pamphlets, and two books in Yiddish and Hebrew during his stay (*Kitvei Yitzhak Ben-Zvi, Bivliografia, 5664–5718 [1904–1958]* [Hebrew], ed. Shlomo Shunami [Jerusalem: n.p., 5718 (1958)]).

46. Ben-Gurion, New York, letter to Ben-Zvi, [Washington], 19 July 1916, quoted in Minc, "Correspondence with Ben-Zvi," 96.
47. Jonathan Frankel, "The 'Yizkor' Book of 1911—A Note on National Myths in the Second Aliya," in *Religion, Ideology and Nationalism in Europe and America: Essays Presented in Honor of Yehoshua Arieli*, ed. H. Ben-Israel et al. (Jerusalem: Historical Society of Israel and Zalman Shazar Center for Jewish History, 1986), 381–83; Zuckerman, *Zikhroynes*, vol. 2, 265; Minc, "Correspondence with Ben-Zvi," 85–88, 91, 95–96; Teveth, *Burning Ground*, 109–18.
48. Minc, "Correspondence with Ben-Zvi," 90, 93–94; BGD, 11 Sivan [24 May 1915]; H. Komunoff, "HaVe'ida HaIvrit HaRishona" [Hebrew], *HaIvri*, 16 February 1917.
49. Teveth, *Burning Ground*, 152; Zuckerman, *Zikhroynes*, 2: 223; Komunoff, "HaVe'ida"; Melech Epstein, *Jewish Labor in the U.S.A.*, 2 vols. (New York: Trade Union Sponsoring Committee, 1950, 1953), vol. 2, 82–83.
50. Gal, *Likrat Medina*, 5; Teveth, *Burning Ground*, 115–16; Yitzhak Ben-Zvi, New York, letter to Rahel Yana'it, Jerusalem, 31 January 1918, in BZA, File 1/1/2/12.
51. BGD, 29 November and 16 December 1917; "Poale Zion, HaSnif HaIvri," *HaIvri*, 21 December 1917; resolutions quoted in Teveth, *Burning Ground*, 115. Teveth says there were 2,000 people at the Cooper Union meeting. In his diary, Ben-Gurion claims only 580.
52. Teveth, *Burning Ground*, 115–16, 123–24.
53. Ben-Gurion, Egypt, letter to Shmuel Kaplansky, n.p., 15 Heshvan 5679 [1918], in *Igrot Ben-Gurion*, vol. 2, 1–2; Ben-Zvi, New York, letter to Rahel Yana'it, [Jerusalem], May 1918, in Yitzhak Ben-Zvi, *HaGdudim HaIvriyim—Igrot Yitzhak Ben-Zvi* [Hebrew] (Jerusalem: Yad Yitzhak Ben-Zvi, 1968), 2.
54. Ben-Gurion, Cincinnati, letter to Comrade [Hirsch] Ehrenreich, [New York], 2 Shvat 5676 [1916], in Ben-Gurion, *Zichronot*, vol. 1, 84–85. See also, Mintz, "World War I," 61–65.
55. Friedman, *Germany, Turkey, and Zionism*, 291; Y. L—n, "Likrat Ve'idat HaShalom" [Hebrew], *HaPo'el HaTza'ir*, 23 June 1915, 5.
56. Ben-Zvi, " 'HeHalutz' VeHaHitnadvut," 205. Baruch Zuckerman, a Poale Zion stalwart who went on aliyah and in Palestine supported the Labor establishment, made similar claims (*Zikhroynes*, vol. 2, 190, 223–24). Accounts of the Congress sessions, however, and of the planning before in the *The American Hebrew* (29 December 1916), *HaIvri* (throughout 1916 and 1917), and elsewhere are most reticent regarding Palestinian involvement. The "Report of Proceedings" of the Preliminary Conference of the American Jewish Congress, March 26–27, 1916 (New York, n.d.), does not list Ben-Gurion or Ben-Zvi as a delegate, although it records that they volunteered a donation from the floor (29).

Notes to Chapter 7

57. In his diary entry for 17 Sivan, 27–30 May [1915], Ben-Gurion noted that he had spoken with Rutenberg and the topic of the conversation, but he offered no comment. See also, Michael Bar-Zohar, *Ben-Gurion*, trans. Peretz Kidron (London: Weidenfeld and Nicolson, 1978), 33–34.
58. Tzahor, "Ben-Gurion's Attitude," 37; Zuckerman, *Zikhroynes*, vol. 2, 226.
59. Ben-Gurion, *Zichronot*, vol. 1, 85–86, 98, 393; id., New York, letter to his daughter, Renana, n.p., 8 January 1939, in BGA, correspondence file; id., "About the Author," in *The A.B.C. of Zionist Policy* (New York: Habonim Labor Zionist Youth, 1945), 2; Jabotinsky, letter to Colonel [Patterson], n.p., 30 May 1920, in LAT, File IV-104-29-6alef.
60. Ben-Gurion, *Zichronot*, vol. 1, 86–87; "A Summons to Jewish Youth in America," draft circular letter in Yiddish, 5 March 1918, signed by fifteen members of the American Jewish Committee for a Jewish Palestine Legion, including Ben-Zvi, Nahman Syrkin, Haim Zhitlovsky, Reuben Brainin, and Ben-Gurion; Teveth, *Burning Ground*, 114–26.

    In *Zikhroynes*, vol. 2, 196, Baruch Zuckerman estimates that 60 percent of the Legionnaires (perhaps 1,500 men) were HeHalutz alumni. In the *Hechalutz Bulletin* in January 1934, however, David Yaroslavsky ("Links in the Chain," 9–13) states only that most of the approximately 150 members of HeHalutz recruited by Ben-Gurion and Ben-Zvi during the war joined the Legion. The figure is probably closer to Yaroslavsky's, but there seems to be no ready method of determining it with any precision.
61. Zuckerman, *Zikhroynes*, 2: 228; Ehrenreich quoted in Teveth, *Burning Ground*, 125.
62. Transcript of Ben-Gurion's speech to the National Council of the Maccabi Federation, 1 April 1943, in CZA, File S25/1483.
63. Anita Shapira, *Berl (Biografia)*, 2 vols. [Hebrew] (Tel Aviv: Sifriyat Ofakim—Am Oved, 1980), vol. 1, 148; Kolatt-Kopelovich, "Ideologia u-Metziut," 321, 334; Teveth, *Burning Ground*, 139.
64. Ben-Gurion, Jaffa, letters to the Central Committee of Poale Zion in America, [New York], 16 Tishrei 5720 [1919], in *Igrot Ben-Gurion*, vol. 2, 8–13; and to Comrades [Ahdut HaAvoda? American Poale Zion?], n.p., 21 Elul 5679 [1919], in LAT, File IV-104-29-3; Nellie Strauss, n.p., letter to [David] Ben-Gurion, [Jaffa], 5 September 1919, in LAT, File IV-104-29-7; Teveth, *Burning Ground*, 148–51.
65. Ben-Gurion, n.p., letter to B.[erl] Katznelson, Vienna, in *Igrot Ben-Gurion*, vol. 2, 69–70. In "America's Two Zionist Traditions," *Commentary* 20 (October 1955): 344, Judd Teller claims erroneously that Ben-Gurion and Ben-Zvi returned to Palestine full of heady enthusiasm for the United States, which misled them in the years to follow. In fact, they returned quite sober.
66. Bar-Zohar, *Ben-Gurion*, 48. An inventory by the present author of Ben-Gurion's library housed in his Tel Aviv home and at Sde Boker revealed scores of books on various aspects of American life. Most of these, however, were acquired considerably later. Some of them were gifts of the authors and perhaps not read by Ben-Gurion. Most, however, one can assume he read.

Notes to Chapter 7

67. Yisrael Kolatt, "Ben-Gurion: Image and Reality," in Zweig, *Politics and Leadership*, 17.
68. Shlomo Avineri, "Ideology and Pragmatism in Ben-Gurion's Leadership: Lessons for the Future," in *Towards the Twenty-first Century: Judaism and the Jewish People in Israel and America*, ed. Ronald Kronish (Hoboken, N.J.: Ktav, 1988), 29. See also, Allon Gal, "The Sources of Ben-Gurion's American Orientation, 1938–1941," in Zweig, *Politics and Leadership*, 120; and Ze'ev Sternhell, "Ḥazon Medumeh Shel Ḥevra Shivyonit" [Hebrew], *HaAretz*, 31 May 1991.
69. Ben-Gurion quoted in Y. Bankover and Y. Lufbin, Mapai Party Center, "confidential and private" memo, [Hebrew], to H[aver] Y[akar], that is, Dear Comrade], Tel Aviv, 21 October 1937, in LAT, File IV-104-29-5bet.
70. Teveth, *Burning Ground*, 252, mentions a 1924 trip. There is no evidence that such a visit ever took place, nor does the chronology of his travels in that year make it plausible.
71. Ben-Gurion, *Zichronot*, vol. 1, 211.
72. Id., Alexandria, letter to the Central Committee of the Poale Zion in America, [New York], 1 December 1924, in *Igrot Ben-Gurion*, vol. 2, 273; Kolatt, "Image and Reality," 18–19; Shmuel Sandler, "Ben-Gurion's Attitude Towards the Soviet Union," *Jewish Journal of Sociology* 21 (December 1979); Avraham Avihai, *Ben-Gurion, State-Builder* (New York, Toronto, and Jerusalem: John Wiley and Sons-Israel Universities Press, 1974), 214; Teveth, *Burning Ground*, 240–41.

   For his comments on Harding, see BGD, 4 August 1923. On Jabotinsky and Harding, see chapter 2 of this book.

   In "Ideology and Pragmatism" (31), Shlomo Avineri describes Ben-Gurion as "a rather orthodox Marxist" with pronounced Leninist tendencies in the 1920s, who left Marxism largely behind by the late 1930s in the search for allies for Zionism. But whatever his theoretical stance, he did not turn his back on capitalist America even in the 1920s.
73. Ben-Gurion, letter to Eliyahu Golomb, 10 October 1927, in *Igrot Ben-Gurion*, vol. 2, 360–61; A.[vraham] Harzfeld, [New York], letter to M.[enahem] M.[endel] Ussishkin, [Jerusalem], 14 May 1926, in LAT, File IV-208-66gimel; David Bloch quoted in HVHP", 19 August 1929.
74. Ben-Gurion, letters, London, 10 February 1921, to Central Committee, Poale Zion in America, [New York]; 15 June 1921, to B[erl] Katznelson; and Carlsbad, to members of the Aḥdut HaAvoda Executive Committee, 29 August 1922, all in *Igrot Ben-Gurion*, vol. 2, 55, 69–70, 114.
75. Id., *Zichronot*, vol. 1, 209.
76. HEC, Tel Aviv, letter to Mission Members in America, 16 March 1927, in LAT, File IV-208-67alef; summary memorandum of meeting between Hadassah delegation consisting of Henrietta Szold, Mrs. Jacobi [sic], and Comrade [Irma] Lindheim, with HEC representative David Ben-Gurion and Kupat Ḥolim representatives, Drs. Noak, A. Pearlson, Y. Kanivsky, and R. Sinker, 7, 13 April 1927, in LAT, File IV-104-29-17bet; Teveth, *Burning Ground*, 242–43, 261, 357–58.

77. Ben-Gurion, n.p., letter to Baruch Zuckerman, n.p., 30 March 1928, in *Igrot Ben-Gurion*, vol. 2, 364–65; id., speech to the International Conference on Immigration, Prague, September 1924, in *Zichronot*, vol. 2, 290–94.
78. Medzini, *HaYehudiya HaGei'a*, 48.
79. Ben-Gurion, London, letters, to Dr. N.[aḥman] Syrkin, New York, 2 December 1920, in LAT, File IV-104-29-2alef; to Moshe [Shertok], n.p., 20 May 1921, in LAT, File IV-104-29-6gimel; HVHP", 22 November 1921, 6 January 1922, 7–8 April 1924. See also, Ben-Gurion, letters, London, to Misrad HaAvoda, Jaffa, 23 November and 16 December 1920; and n.p., to People's Relief Committee, New York, 25 July 1922; all in *Igrot Ben-Gurion*, vol. 2, 36–38, 49, 108; and to Berl Katznelson, 11 April 1921, in LAT, File IV-104-29-2alef.
80. HEC, Tel Aviv, letter to Histadrut Mission Members, [New York], 9 February 1927, in LAT, File IV-208-67alef; HVHP", 11 August and 13 October 1927, 23 April 1929; Ben-Gurion, [Tel Aviv], letters to [Israel] Mereminsky, [New York], 9, 15 May 1929, in LAT, File IV-208-1-121alef; Teveth, *Burning Ground*, 332ff.
81. Kolatt-Kopelovich, "Ideologia U-Metziut," 334.
82. Bar-Zohar, *Ben-Gurion*, 49.
83. Ben-Gurion quoted in HVHP", 10 January 1924, and 2 December 1925.
84. Ben-Gurion, "US Jewry on the Threshold of Unity," *Jewish Observer and Middle East Review*, 3 April 1964, 17.
85. Id., telegram to Geverkshaften Campaign, recorded in BGD, 26 December 1928. See also, his letters to Baruch Zuckerman, New York, 7 January and 9 March 1924, in *Igrot Ben-Gurion*, vol. 2, 189–91, 204.
86. Id., quoted in HVHP", 5 November 1928; id., n.p., letter to Baruch Zuckerman, n.p., 30 March 1928, in *Igrot Ben-Gurion*, vol. 2, 364.
87. See HVHP", 25 April 1927, 13 February 1928, and 20 March, 1925; Ben-Gurion, [Tel Aviv], letter to Israel Mereminsky, [New York], 15 May 1929, in LAT, File IV-208-1-121alef.
88. Teveth, *Burning Ground*, 164, 174.
89. BGD, 22 April 1929; HVHP", undated discussion [1923].
90. HVHP", 24 October 1923; 10 January 1924; 7, 22 December 1925; 21 February 1928; 16, 23 April 1928; 25 June 1928; and many other dates; minutes of a meeting between the HEC and the Palestine Zionist Executive, 12 December [1927], in LAT, File IV-208-67bet.
91. BGD, 15 November 1928.
92. BGD, 27 June 1928; id., Warsaw, letter to the Mapai Party Center, [Tel Aviv]. 9 July 1933, in *Igrot Ben Gurion*, vol. 3, 323–26; id., [Tel Aviv], letters to I[srael] Mereminsky, [New York], 4 March and 15 May 1929, both in LAT, File IV-208-1-121alef; Teveth, *Burning Ground*, 391.
93. Ben-Gurion, diary entry for 20 July 1937, in *Zichronot*, vol. 4, 309.
94. Among many sources, see, Ben-Gurion, London, confidential report to [HEC, Tel Aviv], 3 Tammuz 5690 [1930], in LAT, File IV-104-29-17bet; id., London, letter to Zalman [Rubashov] Shazar, [United States], 31 May 1936, in his *Zichronot*, vol. 3, 221–25; id., diary entry, 17 July 1937, in his *Zichronot*, vol. 4,

Notes to Chapter 7

302; BGD, 24, 26, 31 May 1935, 1, 3, 5, 13 June 1935, 15 July 1936; Naomi W. Cohen, *The Year after the Riots* (Detroit: Wayne State University Press, 1988), 163; Menaḥem Kaufman, "Ben Gurion and the American Non-Zionists," in Zweig, *Politics and Leadership*, 125–26; Teveth, *Burning Ground*, 619–20.

95. See, for example, Ben-Gurion's comments at the 12 September 1939 meeting of the Mapai Party Center. See also, Gal, *Likrat Medina*, 94.
96. Ben-Gurion, *Zichronot*, vol. 1, 124.
97. Ben-Gurion, n.p., letter to the Trade Union Center of the Jewish Workers in America, 24 July 1923, in *Igrot Ben-Gurion*, vol. 2, 132–39. The letter was an invitation to send a study mission of labor leaders to Palestine, as suggested by Baruch Zuckerman. (Zuckerman, *Zikhroynes*, vol. 2, 286–89; HVHP", 15 July 1923; and Ben-Gurion, n.p., letter to Baruch Zuckerman, New York, 26 July 1923, in *Igrot Ben-Gurion*, vol. 2, 142.) The mission was not undertaken at that time.
98. Ben-Gurion, [Tel Aviv], letter to National Labor Committee, New York, 27 December 1928, in LAT, File IV-208-1-121gimel. Ben-Gurion was expressing thanks on behalf of the Histadrut to the Jewish group for its role in securing the AFL statement of support.
99. BGD, 21 January 1924; HVHP", 26 March 1928. See also, Ben-Gurion, London, letter to Dr. N.[aḥman] Syrkin, New York, 2 December 1920, in LAT, File IV-104-29-2alef, also in *Igrot Ben-Gurion*, vol. 2, 47–48.
100. Teveth, *Burning Ground*, 157, 350.
101. Ben-Gurion, diary, 7 December 1930, in *Igrot Ben-Gurion*, vol. 3, 175–80.
102. El[iezer] Galili, New York, letter to HEC, [Tel Aviv], 13 July 1934, in LAT, File IV-208-1-407bet, and many similar letters in the Histadrut letter files; Ben-Gurion, diary, 8 December 1930, in *Igrot Ben-Gurion*, vol. 3, 175–80.
103. Ben-Gurion, on board the *Ile de France*, sailing from New York to Europe, letter to his wife, Paula, 14 September 1937, in his *Letters to Paula*, 143.
104. Id., "New Perspectives on Zionism," *Jewish Frontier*, June 1935, 21. See also, Allon Gal, "Zionist Foreign Policy and Ben-Gurion's Visit to the United States in 1939," *Studies in Zionism* 7 (1986): 69–71.
105. Ben-Gurion, n.p., letter to Dr. Chaim Weizmann, n.p., 26 October 1933, in *Igrot Ben-Gurion*, vol. 3, 360.
106. Id., quoted in MPC", 9 March 1936; Dalia Ofer, "HaAliyah, HaGola VeHaYishuv" [Hebrew], *Cathedra* 43 (March 1987): 77.
107. Ben-Gurion, remarks at a meeting of the Mapai Party Political Committee, in MPC", 26 January 1936.
108. Ben-Gurion, diary entries, 7, 10, 11, 25, 27 December 1930, and letter, Berlin, to Comrades [HEC, Tel Aviv], 24 January 1931, all in *Igrot Ben-Gurion*, vol. 3, 175–82, 196.
109. Ben-Gurion, [Jerusalem], letter to Golda [Myerson], Zalman [Rubashov], and [Baruch] Zuckerman, [New York], in *Zichronot*, vol. 3, 75; BGD, 6, 8, 11 June 1935, 10 January 1939; Gal, *Likrat Medina*, 115; Teveth, *Burning Ground*, 690–91.

Notes to Chapter 7

110. Ben-Gurion, quoted in MC", 16 January 1937; id., on board the *Ile de France* sailing from New York to Europe, letter to Eliezer [Kaplan, Jerusalem], 14 September 1937, in CZA, File S25/1481.
111. MC", 15 December 1937; Teveth, *Burning Ground*, 640-41.
112. Lewis J. Ruskin, Chicago, letter to [Berl] Katznelson, n.p., 26 January 1939, in KABB, File resh; exchange of cables between Ben-Gurion and Rabbi Solomon Goldman of the ZOA, 22-24, 29 May, 1 June 1939, in CZA, File F/38/473; *Letters of Louis D. Brandeis*, vol. 5, ed. Melvin I. Urofsky and David W. Levy (Albany: State University of New York Press, 1978), 532, n. 1. See also, David Shpiro, "The Role of the Emergency Committee for Zionist Affairs as the Political Arm of American Zionism, 1938-1944," 2 vols., Ph.D. dissertation, Hebrew University, 1979, vol. 1, 132; Jacob J. Weinstein, *Solomon Goldman: A Rabbi's Rabbi* (New York: Ktav, 1973), 62; Yitzḥak Avnery, "Immigration and Revolt: Ben-Gurion's Response to the 1939 White Paper," in Zweig, *Politics and Leadership*, 109.
113. Rose G. Jacobs, National President, Hadassah, New York, letter to Ben-Gurion, Jerusalem, 30 April 1936, in CZA, File S44/250. See also, Bengurion, [Jerusalem], cable to Hadassah, New York, 24 April 1936, in CZA, File S25/4525.
114. HVHP", 9 June 1930; Ben-Gurion, [for the HEC, Tel Aviv], telegram to [Louis D.] Brandeis, Washington, D.C., 4 April 1932, in LAT, File IV-208-1-337alef, and the reply of Julius Simon, 13 April 1932, in the same file; Louis D. Brandeis, Chatham, Massachusetts, letter to Robert Szold, n.p., 23 June 1935, in *Brandeis Letters*, vol. 5, 558-59; Melvin I. Urofsky, *American Zionism from Herzl to the Holocaust* (New York: Anchor, Doubleday, 1976), 315; Teveth, *Burning Ground*, 497.
115. Louis D. Brandeis, Washington, D.C., letter to S[tephen] S[amuel] W[ise, New York], 2 June 1936, in *Brandeis Letters*, vol. 5, 571-72.
116. Ben-Gurion, Warsaw, letter to Israel Merom-Mereminsky, [New York], in *Igrot Ben-Gurion*, vol. 3, 296-97. See also, id., in MC", 15 March 1933, and 7, 15 April 1937; and id., "The Nature of Collective Bargaining," *Jewish Frontier*, May 1933.
117. Ben-Gurion, [Tel Aviv], letter to [Baruch] Zuckerman, [New York], 30 March 1928, in LAT, File IV-208-1-121bet. Exactly the same terminology was used by Berl Katznelson in a letter from Arza to Dov Hoz, [New York, 23 March 1928], in BKL, vol. 5, 252.
118. Ben-Gurion, remarks in HVHP", 7 May 1928, and in MC", 18 October 1930; id., report of World Congress of Workers for Labor Palestine, 6 October 1930, in *Igrot Ben-Gurion*, vol. 3, 160-61; Teveth, *Burning Ground*, 392-98.
119. Id., [New York], diary entry, 31 December 1930, in *Igrot Ben-Gurion*, vol. 3, 184; BGD, 25 May and 8 June 1935; id., on board the *Ile de France*, sailing from New York to Europe, letter to Eliezer [Kaplan], n.p., 14 September 1937, in CZA, File S25/1481; Teveth, *Burning Ground*, 627.
120. J. S. Hertz, *50 Years of the Workmen's Circle in Jewish Life* [Yiddish] (New York: National Executive Committee of the Workmen's Circle, 1950), 261.
121. BGD, 1, 7, 8, 12, 13 June and 7 July 1935.

Notes to Chapter 7

122. Stephen S. Wise, New York, letter to [David] Ben-Gurion, Jerusalem, 15 April 1936, in CZA, File S34/36.
123. Mereminsky remarks in HVHP", 9, 24 September 1936.
124. On the Vladeck visit, see CZA, File S25/4300. On Rubashov [Shazar], see his letter from New York, 16 June 1936, to Ben-Gurion, in Ben-Gurion, Zichronot, vol. 3, 274.
125. BGD, 10 September 1937; Ben-Gurion, on board the Ile de France, sailing from New York to Europe, letter to Eliezer [Kaplan, Jerusalem], 14 September 1937, in CZA, File S25/1481; Y. Bankover and Y. Lufbin, Mapai Party Center, confidential memorandum to D[ear] C[omrade], 21 October 1937, in LAT, File IV-104-29-5bet; Teveth, Burning Ground, 628–29. On Katznelson's attempts to conclude the agreement, see chapter 4 of this book.
126. Ben-Gurion, "United States Jewry on the Threshold of Unity," *Jewish Observer and Middle East Review*, 3 April 1964, 18; id., remarks in MS", 17 December 1945; Alexander Manor, *Commitment and Creative Action: Life and Work of Israel Merom (Mereminsky)*, trans. and adapted S. Leshner-Shapiro (Tel Aviv: Sponsoring Committee, 1978), 165–200.
127. Ben-Gurion, Washington, D.C., letter to Berl Locker, London, 4 January 1942, in CZA, File S25/60. See also, BGD, 9, 12 December 1941; Ben-Gurion remarks in MC", 23 June 1943.
128. Ben-Gurion, dairy entry, 7 December 1930, in *Igrot Ben-Gurion*, vol. 3, 175–80.
129. Ibid., 31 December 1930, 184–85. On Golda's involvement with HeHalutz and HaShomer HaTza'ir, see chapter 6 of this book.
130. Teveth, *Burning Ground*, 501; BGD, 17 May 1935.
131. BGD, 19, 21, 23 May 1935.
132. Teveth, *Burning Ground*, 502; BGD, 25, 19 May, 5 June 1935. See also, Ben-Gurion, Milwaukee, letter to [Dr. Selig] Brodetsky, [London], 21 May 1935, in LAT, File IV-104-29-2alef.
133. Ben-Gurion, New York, letter to his wife, Paula, [Tel Aviv], 1 June 1935, in *Letters to Paula*, 72.
134. Id., quoted in MC", 26 July 1935; Zalman [Rubashov], New York, letter to Ben-Gurion, [Jerusalem], 31 March 1936, in CZA, File S44/250.
135. Ben-Gurion, remarks quoted in MC", 9 July 1936.
136. [Rabbi Stephen S.] Wise, New York, letter to Dr. Chaim Weizmann, London, 18 June 1937, in CZA, File S25/1874.
137. Id., quoted in minutes of the ZOA National Executive Committee, 11 January 1939. See also, Teveth, *Burning Ground*, 690; Gal, *Likrat Medina*, 22.
138. Ben-Gurion quoted in HVHP", 10 February 1930; id., [Tel Aviv?], letter to Zionist Executive, London, 25 March 1936, in his *Zichronot*, vol. 3, 97–98; id., "A Month in a Flying Clipper," *Jewish Observer and Middle East Review*, 14 February 1964, 21. See also, Gal, "Ben-Gurion's Visit," 44; and id., "Eulogy and Policy: David Ben-Gurion's Address at a Memorial Meeting Honoring Louis D. Brandeis, London, October 21, 1941" [Hebrew], *Cathedra* 44 (June 1987): 108–9.

Notes to Chapter 7

139. Stephen S. Wise, New York, letter to Gershon Agronsky, [Jerusalem], 22 September 1931, in CZA, File S25/794. The context of these remarks is not clear from the letter, but the feelings expressed were not limited to this instance, as the rabbi's rage over Ben-Gurion's deal with Vladeck demonstrates.
140. Ben-Gurion, quoted in Gal, *Likrat Medina*, 18, and Teveth, *Burning Ground*, 693. On Jabotinsky and Wise, see chapter 2 of this book.
141. Anita Shapira, *Berl: The Biography of a Socialist Zionist*, trans. Ḥaya Galai (Cambridge, England: Cambridge University Press, 1984), 178.
142. Albert Hyamson quoted in memorandum of O. G. R. Williams, 12 August 1931, in PRO, File CO 733 209/13.
143. Felix Frankfurter, letter to Ben-Gurion, 12 October 1933, quoted in Ben-Gurion, *Zichronot*, vol. 1, 668; Yehuda Even-Shmuel, Philadelphia, letter to HEC, [Tel Aviv], 3 Adar Sheni [1932], in LAT, File IV-208-337bet; MC", 2 January 1934; Ben-Gurion, n.p., letter to Justice Louis D. Brandeis and copied to Louis Lipsky in New York, 9 January 1934, in CZA, File F38/1192.
144. Ben-Gurion, quoted in Yosef Sprinzak, New York, letter to [Berl] Locker, [London], 4 February 1934, in LAT, File IV-208-1-407bet.
145. Ibid; exchange of correspondence between Eliezer Galili, New York, and Eliyahu Dobkin, Tel Aviv, November 1933-January 1934, in LAT, File IV-208-1-407bet.
146. Ben-Gurion, quoted in MPC", 5 August 1934.
147. BGD, 20, 21, 30, 31 May and 1 June 1935; Ben-Gurion, Milwaukee, letter to [Dr. Selig] Brodetsky, [London], 21 May 1935, in LAT, File IV-104-29-2alef. See also, Gal, *Likrat Medina*, 16; Kaufman, "American Non-Zionists," 125.
148. Ben-Gurion, quoted in minutes of meeting of the Jewish Agency Executive, 19 January 1936, cited in *Zichronot*, vol. 3, 28. See also, Teveth, *Burning Ground*, 515-17.
149. Ben-Gurion, quoted in MC", 29 January 1936.
150. Stephen S. Wise, New York, letter to Ben-Gurion, Jerusalem, 25 February 1936, in CZA, File S25/6617.
151. Ben-Gurion, MPC", 9 March 1936, cited in his *Zichronot*, vol. 3, 87.
152. Minutes of Jewish Agency Executive meeting, 29 April 1936, quoted in *Zichronot*, vol. 3, 132.
153. Ben-Gurion, diary entry for 8 June 1936, in his *Zichronot*, vol. 3, 249; Zalman [Rubashov-Shazar], n.p., letter to Ben-Gurion, [London], 18 July 1936, also quoted in *Zichronot*, vol. 3, 344ff; Ben-Gurion, remarks in MC", 11 September 1936; Selig Adler, "The Roosevelt Administration and Zionism: The Pre-War Years, 1933-1939," *Herzl Year Book* 8 (1978): 133-34.
154. BGD, 24 June 1936; Urofsky, *Voice for Justice*, 283.
155. Ben-Gurion, quoted in the minutes of a meeting of the Zionist Smaller Actions Committee, Zurich, 14 October 1936, in CZA, File S25/1775.
156. Louis D. Brandeis, Chatham, Massachusetts, letter to [Robert Szold], n.p., 5 September 1936, in *Brandeis Letters*, vol. 5, 578.
157. Ben-Gurion, n.p., letter to Dr. [Stephen S.] Wise, [New York], 11 January 1937, quoted in his *Zichronot*, vol. 4, 24-25.

Notes to Chapter 7

158. Id., quoted in MC", 5 February 1937.
159. Id., diary entry, 20 July 1937, in his *Zichronot*, vol. 4, 309.
160. Teveth, *Burning Ground*, 589. 593, 601, 608, 625–27, 681; Gal, *Likrat Medina*, 17; Ben-Gurion, on board the *Ile de France*, sailing from New York to Europe, letter to Eliezer [Kaplan, Jerusalem], 14 September 1937, in CZA, File S25/1481; id., "Flying Clipper," 23.
161. Id., report to the Zionist Executive, Jerusalem, 3 October 1938, quoted in Gal. *Likrat Medina*, 7.
162. Gal, *Likrat Medina*, 8–9; Teveth, *Burning Ground*, 683.
163. Ben-Gurion, London, letter to [Rabbi Solomon] Goldman, n.p., 21 October 1938, in CZA, File F38/?. In the file is an English translation of the original "confidential" Hebrew letter. The file number has been misplaced.
164. Ben-Gurion, address to the ZOA National Executive Committee, New York, 11 January 1939, in minutes of the meeting, CZA, File F38/473. On the genesis of the conference, see Gal, *Likrat Medina*, 9–10, 202, n.33; and id., "Ben-Gurion's Visit," 41.
165. Kaufman, "American Non-Zionists," 126; and Avnery, "Immigration and Revolt," 99–100.
166. Ibid; BGD, 4, 8 January 1939. See also, Avnery, "Immigration and Revolt," 102; Gal, *Likrat Medina*, 19–25; Kaufman, "American Non-Zionists," 127–28; Teveth, *Burning Ground*, 686–90, 708–09.
167. Ben-Gurion, London, letter to wife, Paula, n.p., 6 February 1939, in *Letters to Paula*, 219–20. From the follow-up discussion in the Mapai Center, it is apparent that Wise followed the plan (MC", 22 February 1939).
168. Gal, *Likrat Medina*, 27–29.
169. Ben-Gurion, quoted in MPC", 5 April 1939.
170. Id., "Additional Notes on the Present Situation," 17 May 1940, in CZA, File Z4/14632. Useful summaries of the events leading up to the white paper can be found in Urofsky, *From Herzl to the Holocaust*, 387–90; and Howard M. Sachar, *A History of Israel* (New York: Knopf, 1976), 222–26.
171. Ben-Gurion quoted in MC", 5 July 1939.
172. Id., quoted in MC", 12 September 1939. See also "Looking Ahead," an English translation of his speech to the Va'ad Le'umi, 17 September 1939, in CZA, File S25/1484.
173. Ben-Gurion, on board the *Ile de France* sailing from New York to Europe, letter to Eliezer [Kaplan, Jerusalem], 14 September 1937, in CZA, File S25/1481.
174. Id., letter to his son, Amos, 5 October 1937, quoted in Teveth, *Burning Ground*, 629.
175. Teveth, *Burning Ground*, 700.
176. MPC", 29 October and 21 November 1940; MC", 19 February 1941; Ben-Gurion, "On the Road to the State—I Try to Arouse U.S. Zionists," *Jewish Observer and Middle East Review*, 7 February 1964. See also, MS", 27 September 1939; MPC", 27 November 1939; Ben-Gurion, "A Jewish Army," *Jewish Frontier*, November 1940; BGD, 9 November 1940; Gal, *Likrat Medina*, 67, 88, 107; Shpiro, "Emergency Committee," vol. 2, 363.

Notes to Chapter 7

177. BGD, 29 November 1941; Ben-Gurion, Washington, D.C., letter to Berl Locker, London, 4 January 1942, in CZA, File S25/41. See also, id., statement to press conference held by the Zionist Emergency Committee, New York, 14 November 1940, mimeograph, in CZA, File S25/1494; Shpiro, "Role of the Emergency Committee,". vol. 2, 392; Yosef Gorny, "Ben-Gurion and Weizmann During World War II, in Zweig, *Politics and Leadership*, 90.
178. Ben-Gurion, New York, letter to Judge Louis E. Levinthal, Emergency Committee, New York, 29 June 1942, in CZA, File S25/1458. See also, Ben-Gurion, New York, letters, to Moshe Shertok, Jerusalem, 3 July 1942, and to Judge [Louis] Levinthal, n.p., 2 September 1942, both in CZA, Files Z4/14632 and Z5/1219 respectively.
179. Id., "On the Road to the State—We Look Towards America," *Jewish Observer and Middle East Review*, 31 January 1964, 16. See also, his "Lord Lloyd Proposes an Arab-Jewish Federation," *Jewish Observer and Middle East Review*, 6 December 1963, 20–23.
180. For a summary of the interchange between Ussishkin and Ben-Gurion, see Gal, *Likrat Medina*, 60–61.
181. Teveth, *Burning Ground*, 768.
182. Ben-Gurion, New York, cable to [Eliezer] Kaplan, Jewish Agency, Jerusalem, 13 November 1940, in CZA, File S25/1494; id., New York, cables to Berl Locker, [London], 28 October and 13 December 1940, both in CZA, File Z4/14632; id., report on last ten months in England and America, MC", 19 February 1941; id., "Flying Clipper," 23.
183. Ben-Gurion quoted in MC", 19 February 1941; id., "Flying Clipper," 23; id., quoted in MS", 17 December 1945.
184. Id., MC", 19 February 1941.
185. Gal, *Likrat Medina*, 98–99, 109–13, 171–73; Monty N. Penkower, "Ben-Gurion, Silver, and the 1941 UPA National Conference for Palestine: A Turning Point in American Zionist History," *American Jewish History* 69 (September 1979): 72–74.
186. Ben-Gurion, speech to the Administrative Council of the ZOA, Philadelphia, 5 January 1941, printed in Gal, *Likrat Medina*, Appendix 6, p. 174.
187. Id., MC", 19 February 1941.
188. J. H. Pollock, "Profile of Ben-Gurion," *National Jewish Monthly*, January 1942, 163; David H. Shpiro, "The Political Background of the 1942 Biltmore Resolution," *Herzl Year Book* 8 (1978): 170.
189. Ben-Gurion, "Outlines of Zionist Policy," 15 October 1941, marked "Private and Confidential," typescript, in CZA, File Z4/14632.
190. BGD, 20, 24 November 1941.
191. Ben-Gurion, report on eight months in England and the United States, in MPC", 6 October 1942. See also, D[avid] B[reslau], "The Beginning of the War (1941–1942)," in *Arise and Build: The Story of American Habonim*, ed. David Breslau (New York: Ichud Habonim Labour Zionist Youth, 1961), 42; the letter of Breslau, New York, to Ben-Gurion, Washington, 7 January 1942, in CZA, File S25/10237; and Shpiro, "Role of the Emergency Committee," vol. 2, 371–72.

192. BGD, 28 November, 16, 29 December 1941; Teveth, *Burning Ground*, 840.
193. Ben-Gurion, Washington, D.C., letter to Berl Locker, London, 4 January 1942, in CZA, File S25/60.
194. BGD, 16 December 1941.
195. Naomi W. Cohen, *Not Free to Desist* (Philadelphia: Jewish Publication Society, 1972), 249–50.
196. There is very ample documentation of the Ben-Gurion-Wertheim negotiations in the sources, especially accounts in Ben-Gurion's letters in CZA and elsewhere. Useful summaries can be found in Ben-Gurion, remarks in MPC", 3 May 1943; id., "Threshold of Unity," 16–17; Cohen, *Not Free*, 252ff; Kaufman, "American Non-Zionists," 124–32; and other sources.
197. BGD, 8, 21 December 1941. The latter entry was made following a visit with Justice Frankfurter, which Ben-Gurion had requested.
198. Ben-Gurion, New York, letter to Arthur Ruppin, Jerusalem, 28 April 1942, in CZA, File S25/4754. See also his remarks in MC", 6 October 1942.
199. Ben-Gurion, "Three New Friends for Zionism," *Jewish Observer and Middle East Review*, 13 March 1964, 20; Gal, "Eulogy and Policy," 114; Teveth, *Burning Ground*, 794.
200. BGD, 21, 23, 28–31 December 1941; Shpiro, "Role of the Emergency Committee," vol. 2, 366–71. On Weizmann's response, see Gorny, "Weizmann and Ben-Gurion," 90.
201. See letter of I[srael] Mereminsky, New York. to Ben-Gurion, [Washington], 9 January 1942, in CZA, File S25/10237, in which he quotes to Ben-Gurion a report from the Toronto *Iddisher Zhurnal* about Ben-Gurion's rebellion against the Zionist authorities; Teveth, *Burning Ground*, 803ff.
202. Ben-Gurion, Washington, letter to Berl Locker, London, 26 January 1942, in CZA, File S25/41.
203. William J. Donovan, Washington, letter to Ben-Gurion, New York, 8 December 1941, in CZA, File S25/10237; BGD, 6 January 1942; Shpiro, "Role of the Emergency Committee," vol. 2, 392; Teveth, *Burning Ground*, 833–34.
204. BGD, 7 December 1941; H[enry] A. Wallace, Jerusalem, letter to Ben-Gurion, [Jerusalem], 29 November 1947, in CZA, File S44/424; Teveth, *Burning Ground*, 821, 833–34.
205. Ben-Gurion, report on his visits to England and America, in MS", 6 October 1942.
206. Ben-Gurion, quoted in JAE", 4 October 1942.
207. Shpiro, "Background of the Biltmore Resolution," 166ff. See also, id., "Role of the Emergency Committee," vol. 1, 313; Penkower, "A Turning Point," 74–76.
208. Ben-Gurion, quoted in JAE", 4 October 1942.
209. Id., "Test of Fulfillment—Can Zionism Be Achieved?" address to the All-Zionist Conference, Biltmore Hotel, 10 May 1942, typescript, in CZA, File S25/1493.
210. Neumann, *In the Arena*, 168. See also, Shpiro, "Role of the Emergency Committee," vol. 1, 319–23, 340.
211. Weizmann, quoted by Meyer Weisgal, . . . *So Far, An Autobiography* (New

Notes to Chapter 8

York: Weidenfeld and Nicolson and the Ma'ariv Book Guild, 1971), 173–74. See also, Gorny, "Ben-Gurion and Weizmann," 94; Teveth, *Burning Ground*, 817–21.

212. See, for example, Stephen S. Wise and Louis Levinthal, [New York], cable to Ben-Gurion, n.p., 6 October 1942, in CZA, File Z5/1219, telling him that an attempt to unseat Weizmann would be "catastrophic for [the] movement and completely unwarranted by [the] situation or facts." See also, Norman Rose, *Chaim Weizmann: A Biography* (New York: Viking-Penguin, 1986), 378–79; Shpiro, "Role of the Emergency Committee," vol. 2, 397–412; Teveth, *Burning Ground*, 832–43.

213. Ben-Gurion, report on his trip to England and the United States, MS", 6 October 1942; Monty Noam Penkower, "American Jewry and the Holocaust: From Biltmore to the American Jewish Conference," *Jewish Social Studies* 47 (Spring 1985): 102–03; Amitzur Ilan, *America, Britannia, VeEretz Yisrael—Reishitah Ve-Hitpathutah Shel Me'oravut Artzot HaBrit BaMediniyut HaBritit BeEretz Yisrael, 1938–1947* [Hebrew] (Jerusalem: Yad Yitzhak Ben-Zvi, 5739 [1979]), vii–viii.

214. Amitzur Ilan, "From the Hebrew Press, America, Britain, and Palestine," *Jerusalem Cathedra* 1 (1981): 330.

215. Carl Alpert, Washington, letter to Ben-Gurion, Jerusalem, 20 November 1942, in CZA, File S44/250.

216. Susan Lee Hattis, *The Bi-National Idea in Palestine During Mandatory Times* (Haifa: Shikmona, 1970), 250; Shapira, *Biography of a Socialist Zionist*, 331–32; Teveth, *Burning Ground*, 842–43; Porat, *Blue and Yellow Stars*, 258.

217. Ben-Gurion, speech at the 32nd annual Hadassah Convention, Boston, 11 November 1946, in BGA.

218. Id., quoted in Avineri, "Ideology and Pragmatism," 32–33.

Chapter 8

1. Dan Horowitz and Moshe Lissak, *Origins of the Israeli Polity: Palestine under the Mandate*, trans. Charles Hoffman (Chicago: University of Chicago Press, 1978), Appendix 2.
2. Yehuda Bauer, *From Diplomacy to Resistance: A History of Jewish Palestine, 1939–1945*, trans. Alton M. Winters (Philadelphia: Jewish Publication Society, 1970), 131–32.
3. Horowitz and Lissak, *Origins of the Israeli Polity*, 150ff.
4. Brandeis quoted in Alpheus T. Mason, *Brandeis: A Free Man's Life* (New York: Viking, 1946), 460. On Gordon and his attitude towards foreign funds, see Ya'akov Kellner, *HaAliyot HaRishonot—Mithos U-Metzi'ut* [Hebrew] (Jerusalem: HaUniversita HaIvrit Birushalyim, Beit HaSefer LaAvoda Sotzialit Al Shem Paul Baerwald, 1982), 41–42.
5. Zvi Bahur, an old settler in Bat Shlomo, decrying the decline of morality in Israel after 1967, quoted in Amos Oz, *In the Land of Israel*, trans. Maurie Goldberg-Bartura (San Diego, New York, and London: Harcourt, Brace, Jovanovich, 1983), 209.

Notes to Chapter 8

6. Lotta Levensohn, "The American Jew in Palestine," *The New Palestine*, 7 June 1929, 485.
7. Thomas L. Friedman, "America in the Mind of Israel," *New York Times Magazine*, 25 May 1986, 24.
8. Ben-Gurion, Jerusalem, letter to [Bernard] Rosenblatt, n.p., 24 December 1951, in Bernard A. Rosenblatt, *Two Generations of Zionism* (New York: Shengold, 1967), 244.
9. Gershon Shaked, "Can Israeli Culture Survive the American Challenge?" *Moment*, August 1989, 58.
10. Quoted in Russell Miller, "Dining on McTreif," *Forward*, 23 September 1994. On Feinberg, see chapter 1 of this book.
11. Chaim Naḥman Bialik, "Al America" [Hebrew], address at Beit HaAm, Tel Aviv, Tishrei, 5687 (1926), in *Dvarim SheBe'al Peh*, 2 vols. (Tel Aviv: Dvir, 5695 [1935]), vol. 2, 58; id., Tel Aviv, letter to Chaim Weizmann, London, 8 Kislev 1926, in M. Ungerfeld, "Bein Bialik LeWeizmann" [Hebrew], *Moznayim* 9 (July 1959): 152.
12. Uri Bialer, "Facts and Pacts: Ben-Gurion and Israel's International Orientation, 1948–1956," in *David Ben-Gurion: Politics and Leadership in Israel*, ed. Ronald Zweig (London and Jerusalem: Frank Cass and Yad Izḥak Ben-Zvi, 1991), 232–33.
13. Teddy Kollek with Amos Kollek, *For Jerusalem* (London: Weidenfeld and Nicolson, 1978), 96–98; Moshe Zak, "Tzahal—Shtei Etzba'ot MiMilḥemet Korea" [Hebrew], *Ma'ariv*, 22 April 1988.
14. Shmuel Sandler, "Ben-Gurion's Attitude Towards the Soviet Union," *Jewish Journal of Sociology* 21 (December 1979): 153.
15. Friedman, "Mind of Israel," 23.
16. Ibid., 26.
17. Peter Grose, *Israel in the Mind of America* (New York: Knopf, 1983), 316. My son, Joshua, called my attention to the fact that Israel and the United States both have ideas at the root of their experience.

Glossary

Aḥdut HaAvoda
a labor political party formed in Palestine in 1919 through the merger of the Marxist Poale Zion Party and nonparty socialist groups. Ben-Gurion and Katznelson were its outstanding leaders. In 1930 it merged with the non-Marxist party, HaPo'el HaTza'ir, to become the Mapai Party. The name Aḥdut HaAvoda was used again in the 1940s and 1950s by a breakaway leftist group from Mapai.

aliyah
immigration to the land of Israel. An immigrant is called an *oleh*, *olim* in the plural.

Diaspora
the Jewish communities outside the land of Israel.

Emergency Committee for Zionist Affairs
the World War II committee that coordinated the activities of most Zionist organizations in the United States.

Hapo'el Hatza'ir
a non-Marxist labor party in Palestine that merged with Aḥdut HaAvoda in 1930 to form the Mapai Party. In the United States most of its members belonged to Zeire Zion, which first federated with the Poale Zion and then merged into it. In Palestine the party journal was also known as *HaPo'el HaTza'ir*.

Histadrut
the National Labor Federation in Palestine and then Israel, founded in 1920. In addition to organizing laborers, it sponsored cooperative enterprises and provided health care and other welfare services to its members.

Jewish Agency
the quasi-governmental executive body for the *yishuv* that dealt chiefly with land acquisition, settlement, and external relations. From 1929 it operated as the executive body in Palestine of the World Zionist Organization. From that date its executive committee and governing council included representatives of the WZO and

Glossary

non-Zionists. Since 1948 it has dealt chiefly with the settlement of immigrants in Israel and educational work in the Diaspora.

Keren HaYesod
the fund-raising arm of the World Zionist Organization and the Jewish Agency known in English as the Palestine Foundation Fund.

Keren Kayemet
the land acquisition and settlement arm of the World Zionist Organization and the Jewish Agency known in English as the Jewish National Fund.

Knesset Yisrael
the organized Jewish community of the *yishuv* during the British Mandate. In effect, it was the government of the state in the making.

Kupat Holim
the Histadrut sick fund, which offers a full range of medical services and operates medical institutions.

Mapai
the Workers' Party of the Land of Israel. Formed in 1930, it was the forerunner of the Labor Party of Israel. (See above, Ahdut HaAvoda.)

Mizrahi
a political party of Othodox Zionists.

New *Yishuv*
the community of Zionist Jews in Palestine. They were the overwhelming majority of Jews in the post-World War I period.

Old *Yishuv*
the community of pietist Jews in Palestine, most of whom believed Jews should dedicate their lives to prayer and await the Messiah. Generally they opposed Zionism.

oleh (pl. *olim*)
an immigrant to Palestine.

Palestine Zionist Executive
the operational arm in Palestine of the World Zionist Organization between 1921 and 1929.

Poale Zion
a Zionist-Marxist political party, in Palestine merged into Ahdut HaAvoda in 1919. In the Diaspora the next year its communist-oriented left wing split off and became the Left Poale Zion.

Provisional Executive Committee for General Zionist Affairs
the committee formed during World War I in the United States to run Zionist affairs on behalf of the World Zionist Organization, which was rendered largely impotent

Glossary

because its members were divided by allegiance to the different sides in the conflict. The committee was headed by Louis D. Brandeis.

Smaller (Inner) Actions Committee
the executive committee of the World Zionist Organization.

Va'ad Leumi
the elected legislative body of the Knesset Yisrael.

World Zionist Organization
the worldwide organization founded by Theodor Herzl in 1897 to implement the Jewish nationalist program, which looked forward to reconstituting a Jewish state in the ancient land of Israel. Its representative body was the Zionist Congress.

yishuv
the Jewish community of Palestine in the pre-state era. In this book it generally means the New Yishuv.

Zionist Commission
the international group appointed by the World Zionist Organization after World War I to act as an executive authority in Palestine during the transitional period.

Selected Bibliography

Archives

Ben-Gurion Archive, Sde Boker
Ben-Gurion House, Library, Tel Aviv
Ben-Zvi Institute, Jerusalem
Central Zionist Archives, Jerusalem
Genazim, Machon Bein-Bibliografi al Shem Asher Barash, Tel Aviv
Golda Meir Memorial Association at the Lavon Labor Archive
Israel State Archives, Jerusalem
Jabotinsky Institute, Tel Aviv
Jewish Theological Seminary Archives, New York
Katznelson Bequest, Beit Berl
Mapai Archive, Beit Berl
Pinḥas Lavon Labor Archive, Tel Aviv
Public Record Office, London
YIVO (Jewish Institute for Historical Research) Archive, New York

Interviews, Minutes, and Other Unpublished Materials

Abramov, Shneur Zalman. (Scholar formerly active in politics.) Interview by Michael Brown. Jerusalem, 28 December 1990.
Allon, Yigal. Interview on Israel Army Radio, 12 January 1979. Transcript in GMM.
Ben-Elissar, Eliahu. (Member of the Knesset, and head of its Foreign Affairs and Defense Committee.) Interview by Yaron Ronen. Broadcast on Israel Television, 26 June 1991.
Ben-Gurion, David. Yoman [Diaries]. In Ben-Gurion Archives, Sde Boker. Diaries division, Ben-Gurion section.
"Bulletin of Events." Jewish Agency for Palestine, Child and Youth Immigration Bureau. Stencil. Jerusalem.
Davis, Moshe. (Founding head of the Institute of Contemporary Jewry, Hebrew University.) Interview by Michael Brown. Jerusalem, 26 July 1991.

Bibliography

Ehrlich, Emma. (Longtime secretary of Henrietta Szold.) Interview by Michael Brown. Jerusalem, 6 July 1986.

Ehrlich, Emma. "Notes and Impressions." Typescript. CZA, File A125/29.

Elam, Yitzhak. (Coworker of Golda Meir.) "BiMḥitzatah Shel Golda." Conversations between September 1985 and February 1986 with Drora Beit-Or. Transcript in GMM.

———. Interviews by Yitzhak Greenberg. N.p., 13, 19, 29 August 1985; 7, 29 November 1985; 6, 20, 27 December 1985; 17, 24, 30 January 1986; 26 June 1989; 9 July 1989; 19 September 1989. Transcripts in GMM.

Gelber, Sylva. (First graduate of Szold's School of Social Work and Palestine resident from 1932 to 1948.) Interview by Michael Brown. Ottawa, 24 January 1988.

HaPo'el HaTza'ir. Minutes of Central Committee meetings.

Herman, Zena. "Henrietta Szold and Youth Aliya." N.p., [1945?]. Typescript in CZA, File A125/91.

Histadrut National Labor Federation. Annual balance sheets of the Executive Committee.

———. Minutes of the Annual Meeting.

———. Minutes of Council meetings.

———. Minutes of Executive Committee meetings.

———. Minutes of Executive Committee Secretariat meetings.

Hollander, Judy. "Deborah Kallen, on American Education in Eretz Yisrael," draft paper.

———. (Scholar, researching Deborah Kallen.) Interview by Michael Brown. Jerusalem, 5 July 1986.

Jewish Agency Executive. Minutes of meetings.

Kadar, Lou. (Secretary of Golda Meir.) Interview by Michael Brown. Jerusalem, 28 August 1985.

Kolatt-Kopelovich, Yisrael. "Ideologia U-Metzi'ut BiTnu'at HaAvoda BeEretz Yisrael, 1905–1919" [Hebrew]. Ph.D. dissertation, Hebrew University of Jerusalem, 1964.

Kutscher, Carol Bosworth. "The Early Years of Hadassah," Ph.D. dissertation, Brandeis University, 1976.

Lenroot, Katherine F., Chief, Children's Bureau, U.S. Department of Labor. "Henrietta Szold—Social Pioneer," speech at Szold Memorial Meeting, Baltimore, 29 April 1945. Typescript in Central Zionist Archives, File A125/235.

Lipstadt, Deborah E. "The Zionist Career of Louis Lipsky, 1900–1921." Ph.D. dissertation, Brandeis University, 1976.

Mapai Party. Minutes of Annual Meeting.

———. Minutes of branch meetings.

———. Minutes of Center meetings.

———. Minutes of Council meetings.

———. Minutes of Political Committee meetings.

———. Minutes of Secretariat meetings.

Medzini, Regina. (Friend of Golda Meir.) Interview by Michael Brown. Jerusalem, 29 August 1985.

———. Interview by Drora Beit-Or. N.p., 29 September 1986. Transcript in GMM.

Bibliography

Meir, Golda, and Sheyna Korngold. "Beit Avi." Interview by Dan Raviv. N.p., 1 January 1967. Transcript in GMM.
Naḥshon. Minutes of Directorate meetings.
Nardi, Shulamith. (Scholar and former assistant to presidents of Israel.) Interview by Michael Brown. Jerusalem, 26 March 1991.
Painton, Frederick. "Henrietta Szold—American," [1944]. CZA, File A125/29.
"Proceedings of the Louis D. Brandeis Memorial Meeting held under the auspices of the Palestine Economic Corporation at Ein Hashofet, Palestine, October 16, 1941" (mimeo).
Rahabi, Sarah. (Daughter of Golda Meir.) Interview by Michael Brown. Tel Aviv, 2 September 1985.
Repetur, Berl. (Coworker of Golda Meir.) Interviews by Drora Beit-Or. N.p., 5, 10 March 1985; 10, 17 April 1985. Transcripts in GMM.
Richman, Harvey. "The Image of America in the European Hebrew Periodicals of the Nineteenth Century until 1880." Ph.D. dissertation, University of Texas at Austin, 1971.
Rosenblatt, Gertrude Goldsmith. (A founder of the Daughters of Zion with Henrietta Szold and the wife of Judge Bernard Rosenblatt of the American Zion Commonwealth.) Extracts from her diary. CZA, File, A125/18.
Sandler, Bernard I. "The Jews of America and the Resettlement of Palestine, 1908–1934: Efforts and Achievements." Ph.D. dissertation, Bar Ilan University, 1978.
Shpiro, David. "The Role of the Emergency Committee for Zionist Affairs as the Political Arm of American Zionism, 1938–1944" [Hebrew]. Ph.D. dissertation, Hebrew University of Jerusalem, 1979.
Simḥoni, Yehudit. (Associate of Golda Meir.) Interview by Drora Or-Beit and Sarah Rahabi. N.p., 5 April 1987. Transcript in GMM.
Skirball, Henry Franc. "Isaac Baer Berkson and Jewish Education." Ed.D. dissertation, Teacher's College, Columbia University, 1976.
"Summary of the Position of the Zionist Organization of America in Conference with Dr. Weizmann and Associates." Submitted by the president of the Zionist Organization of America to, and adopted by, National Executive Committee at meeting of 19–20 March 1921.
Szold, Henrietta. "The Future of Women's Work for Palestine." Jerusalem, 30 May 1930. Typescript in CZA, File A44/35.
Tzaḥor, Ze'ev. "HaHistadrut—Tekufat HaItzuv." Ph.D. dissertation, Hebrew University of Jerusalem, 1979.
Wertheim, Maurice. "Report" of Maurice Wertheim on the Condition of the Jews of Palestine. N.p., 21 October 1914. Typescript in CZA, File A125/289.
World Zionist Organization. Minutes of Zionist Executive Committee meetings.
Zionist Organization of America. Minutes of Administrative Committee meetings.
———. Minutes of National Executive Committee meetings.

Newspapers and Journals

HaAretz, Tel Aviv (before December 1919, *Ḥadshot HaAretz*)
Activity Bulletin, Chicago League for Labor Palestine

Bibliography

HaAhdut, Jerusalem
HaAhot, Jerusalem
The American Hebrew, New York
Die Arbeiter Zeitung, Vienna
Avukah Annual, New York
The Avukah Bulletin, New York
Ba-Ma'ala, Tel Aviv
Baltimore *Sun*
HaBoker, Tel Aviv
Bulletin, Veterans of the Jewish Legion, Baltimore and Avihail
Bulletin of Events of the Jewish Agency for Palestine, Child and Youth Immigration Bureau (stencil), Jerusalem
Bustenai, Rehovot
The Canadian Zionist, Montreal
CCAR Yearbook
Davar, Tel Aviv
HaDo'ar, New York
Do'ar HaYom, Jerusalem
Dvar HaPo'elet, Tel Aviv
Farn Folk, New York
Forverts, New York
Di Frayhayt, New York
Gerverkshaften Kampayn Zhurnal [Palestine Labor Journal]
Hadassah News Letter, New York
Halvri, New York
HaHavatzelet, Jerusalem
Haynt, Warsaw
Hechalutz Bulletin, New York
Hed HaHinuch, Tel Aviv
Hed Yerushalayim, Jerusalem
Dos Iddishe Folk, New York
Der Iddisher Kemfer, New York
Jerusalem Post (before 1950, the *Palestine Post*)
The Jewish Chronicle, London
Jewish Daily Bulletin, New York
Jewish Frontier, New York (before December 1934, *Labor Palestine*)
The Jewish Herald, Johannesberg
The Jewish Monitor, Fort Worth, Texas
Jewish Observer and Middle East Review, London
The Jewish Review and Observer, Cleveland, Ohio
The Jewish Tribune, New York
Jüdische Rundschau, Berlin
Kongress Zeitung [Iton HaCongress HaTziyoni]
The Labor Zionist, New York
Labor Zionist News Letter of the Hechalutz Organization of America with the Collaboration of the League for Labor Palestine

Bibliography

Luah Eretz Yisrael, Jerusalem
The Maccabaean, New York
HaMashkif, Tel Aviv
Mo'adim, Tel Aviv
Der Morgn Zhurnal, New York
Moznayim, Tel Aviv
The New Palestine, New York
New York Times
HaOlam, London
Opinion: A Journal of Jewish Life and Letters, New York
Palestine Bulletin (incorporated into the Palestine Post in 1932)
Palestine Souvenir on the occasion of the Fifth Anniversary of the Geverkshaften Palestine Campaign and the Fourth National Labor Convention for Palestine Held in New York, 29/30 December 1928
The Pioneer Woman, New York
HaPo'el HaTza'ir, Jaffa, then Tel Aviv
Rasswiet, Paris
Reshumoth, Odessa, then Tel Aviv
HaShilo'ah, Odessa, then Cracow
New York Sun
Scranton Times
Scranton Tribune
Der Tog, New York
HaToren, New York
Di Tsayt, New York
HaTzafon, Haifa
HaTziyoni HaKlali, Jerusalem
The Vanguard, New York
Washington Post
HaYarden, Jerusalem
Yediot HaMercaz Shel Mifleget Po'ale Eretz Yisrael, Tel Aviv
The Zionist, New York
The Zionist Revisionist Fortnightly, New York

Works by Subjects of this Book

N.B. Most articles in the above journals are not listed separately here.

David Ben-Gurion

Ben-Gurion, David. *The A.B.C. of Zionist Policy*. New York: Habonim Labor Zionist Youth, 1945.

———. *Igrot David Ben-Gurion* [Hebrew]. Comp. Yehuda Erez. 3 vols. Tel Aviv: Am Oved and Tel Aviv University, 1972.

———. *Ktavim Rishonim* [Hebrew]. Tel Aviv: Aḥdut, 5722 [1962].
———. *Letters to Paula*. Trans. Aubrey Hodes. London: Vallentine-Mitchell, 1971.
———. "A Month in a Flying Clipper," *Jewish Observer and Middle East Review*, 14 February 1964, pp. 21, 23–24.
———. "On the Road to the State—I Try to Arouse U.S. Zionists," *Jewish Observer and Middle East Review*, 7 February 1964, pp. 12–15.
———. "On the Road to the State—We Look Towards America," *Jewish Observer and Middle East Review*, 31 January 1964, pp. 14–16.
———. "Three New Friends for Zionism," *Jewish Observer and Middle East Review*, 13 March 1964, pp. 18, 20, 22, 24.
———. "United States Jewry on the Threshold of Unity," *Jewish Observer and Middle East Review*, 3 April 1964, pp. 14–16.
———. "Why We Placed Our Trust in Britain," *Jewish Observer and Middle East Review*, 18 October 1963, pp. 19, 21–23.
———. *Zichronot* [Hebrew]. 6 vols. Tel Aviv: Am Oved, 1971–87.
Ben-Zvi, Yitzḥak, and David Ben-Gurion. *Oyfgabn in Yetztign Moment* [Yiddish]. New York: n.p., 5678 [1918].

Chaim Nachman Bialik

Bialik, Chaim Nachman. "As Bialik Saw America in 1926." In *Modern Jewish Life in Literature*, bk. 2. Ed. Azriel Eisenberg. Trans. Maurice Shudofsky. New York: United Synagogue Commission on Jewish Education, 1968.
———. *Bialik on the Hebrew University*. Jerusalem: Palestine Friends of the Hebrew University, 1935.
———. *Devarim SheBe'al Peh*. 2 vols. Tel Aviv: Dvir, 5695 [1935].
———. *"Dvir" U-"Moriah"*. New York: n.p., 5686 [1926].
———. "Igrot." *Knesset* 5 (1940): 19–25.
———. *Igrot Bialik Benogei'a LeHotza'at Shirei Rabi Shlomo Ibn Gvirol VeRabi Moshe Ibn Ezra BeHosafat Keta'im MiPiyutei Rashbag* [Hebrew]. Ed. Joseph Marcus. New York: Privately by Joseph Marcus, 1935.
———. *Igrot Chaim Nachman Bialik*. Ed. F[ishel] Laḥover. 5 vols. Tel Aviv: Dvir, 1938–39.
———. *Igrot El Ra'ayato Manya* [Hebrew]. Jerusalem: Mosad Bialik and Dvir, 5716 [1955].
———. *Selected Poems of Chaim Nachman Bialik*. Trans. Maurice Samuel. New York: New Palestine, 1926.
Bialik, Chaim Nachman, Dr. H. Glickson, and Dr. Shmaryahu Levin. *"Dvir," Hotza'at Sfarim Le'umit Tziburit"* [Hebrew]. Berlin: Dfus "Ever," 5682 [1922].
Ovadyahu, Mordecai. *MiPi Bialik* [Hebrew]. Tel Aviv: Masada, 5705 [1945].
Shmeruk, Khone, ed. *Correspondence Between S. J. Abramowitsch, Ch. N. Bialik and Y. Ch. Rawnitzki, 1905–1908*. Jerusalem: Israel Academy of Science and Humanities, 1976.

Bibliography

Ze'ev Jabotinsky

Jabotinsky, Ze'ev. *HaDerech el HaRevisionism HaTziyoni* [Hebrew]. Ed. Joseph Nedava. Tel Aviv: Jabotinsky Institute, 1984.

———. *Igrot Ze'ev Jabotinsky, Reshima u-Mafteah* [Hebrew]. Vol. 1, 1901–24. Tel Aviv: Chaim Weizmann Center for the Research of Zionism of Tel Aviv University and the Jabotinsky Institute, 5732 [1972]. Vol. 2, 1924–40, in manuscript in MJ.

———. *Kitvei Ze'ev Jabotinsky, 5657–5700/1897–1940* [Hebrew]. Ed. Yisrael Yevarovitch. Tel Aviv: Machon Jabotinsky, 1977.

———. *Ktavim* [Hebrew]. 18 vols. Jerusalem: Eri Jabotinsky, 1948–59.

———. *HaRevisionism HaTziyoni BeHitgabshuto* [Hebrew]. Ed. Joseph Nedava. Tel Aviv: Jabotinsky Institute, 1985.

——— [Vladimir]. *The Story of the Jewish Legion*. Trans. Samuel Katz. New York: Bernard Ackerman, 1945.

———. "Tigel" [A Crucible]. *Russkie vedomosti* [Russian], 15 April 1916.

———. *The War and the Jew*. New York: Altalena, 1987.

Berl Katznelson

Katznelson, B[erl]. *Di Arbayter Bank in Erets Yisroel* [Yiddish]. New York: American Workers Committee for the Workers' Bank in Palestine, [1922].

———. *Igrot B. Katznelson* [Hebrew]. 6 vols. Tel Aviv: Am Oved, 1961–84.

———. *Kitvei B. Katznelson* [Hebrew]. 11 vols. Tel Aviv: Mifleget Po'alei Eretz Yisrael, 5706–13 [1946–53].

———. *Revolutionary Constructivism: Essays on the Jewish Labor Movement in Palestine*. Trans. and abr. Benny Applebaum and Shlomo Grodzensky. New York: Young Poale Zion Alliance, 1937.

———. "Ve'idath London" [Hebrew]. *HaAdama* 1 (Tamuz-Av, 5680 [1920]): 453–76.

Golda Meir

Meir, Golda. *BeDegel HaAvoda* [Hebrew]. Tel Aviv: Am Oved, 1972.

———. *Beit Avi* [Hebrew]. [Tel Aviv]: Hakibbutz Hame'uchad, 1972.

———. "BeLev Shalem U-VeSimḥa." In *Sefer HaAliyah HaShlishit*, vol. 2. Ed. Yehuda Erez. Tel Aviv: Am Oved, 1964.

——— [Golde Meyerson]. *Likrat Ha-Congress Ha-22*. [Tel Aviv]: Mifleget Po'alei Eretz Yisrael, 1946.

———. *My Life*. London: Weidenfeld and Nicolson, 1975.

———. "Yamim Rishonim BaKvutza" [Hebrew]. From a talk at Kibbutz Revivim. N.p., 1969.

Christman, Henry M., ed. *This is Our Strength: Selected Papers of Golda Meir*. New York: Macmillan, 1962.

Shenker, Israel, and Mary Shenker, eds. *As Good As Golda.* New York: McCall, 1970.
Syrkin, Marie, ed. *A Land of Our Own: An Oral Biography of Golda Meir.* New York: Putnam's Sons, 1973.

Henrietta Szold

Lowenthal, Marvin. *Henrietta Szold, Life and Letters.* New York: Viking, 1942.

Related Printed Primary Works

Aaronsohn, Aaron. *Yoman Aharon Aharonson* [Hebrew]. Ed. Yoram Efrati. Tel Aviv: Hotza'at Sfarim Karni, 1970.
Aaronsohn, Alexander. *With the Turks in Palestine.* Boston and New York: Houghton, Mifflin, 1916.
———. "Saïfna Ahmar, Ya Sultan! (Our Swords Are Red O Sultan!)." *Atlantic Monthly,* July 1916, 1–12; August 1916, 188–96.
Ahad HaAm [Ginzberg, Asher]. *Igrot Ahad Ha-Am* [Hebrew], 6 vols. (1916–1926). Ed. Aryeh Simon. Tel Aviv: Dvir, 1960.
Akzin, Benjamin. *MeiRiga Lirushalayim, Pirkei Zichronot* [Hebrew]. Jerusalem: Hassifriya Haziyonit Al-Yad HaHistadrut HaTziyonit HaOlamit, 1989.
American Zionist Medical Unit for Palestine Maintained by the Zionist Organization of America and the Joint Distribution Committee of the American Funds for Jewish War Sufferers, June, 1916–June, 1919. New York: ZOA, 1919.
Arlosoroff, Chaim, ed. *Ahduth HaAvodah, 1930–1932.* Tel Aviv: n.p., 1930.
———. *Kitvei Chaim Arlosoroff* [Hebrew]. 6 vols. Tel Aviv: Alef Yod Shtibel, 5694 [1934].
———. *Surveying American Zionism.* New York: Zionist Labor Party "Hitachduth" of America, 1929.
———. *Jews, Arabs and Great Britain.* The Young Jew Series, no. 4. Winnipeg: "Hitachduth" of Winnipeg, 1930.
———. *To the Jewish Youth.* Address of Dr. Chaim Arlozoroff Before the Washington Chapter of "Avukah." New York: Zionist Labor Party "Hitachduth" of America and Canada, 1928.
———. *Yoman Yerushalayim* [Hebrew]. [Tel Aviv]: Mifleget Po'alei Eretz Yisrael, 1949.
Arlosoroff, Chaim, S. Grodzensky, and Rebecca Schmuckler, eds. *Hechalutz.* New York: Zionist Labor Party "Hitachduth" of America with the cooperation of Avukah, America Student Zionist Federation, 1929.
Bar-Ilan [Berlin], Meir. *Igrot HaRav Meir Bar-Ilan* [Hebrew]. Ed. Nathaniel Katzburg. Ramat Gan: Bar Ilan University, 5736 [1976].
———. *MiVolozhin ad Yerushalayim* [Hebrew]. 2 vols. Tel Aviv: Jalkut, 1939, 1940.
Bat-Yehuda [Rafael], Geula. *HaRav Maimon BeDorotav* [Hebrew]. Jerusalem: Mosad HaRav Kook, 1979.

Bibliography

Ben-Zvi, Raḥel Yana'it. *Coming Home.* Trans. David Harris and Julian Meltzer. New York: Herzl, 1964.

[Ben-Zvi, Yitzḥak?]. *Colonizatsions Grupen far Erets Yisroel* [Yiddish]. New York: Tsiyonistishe Palestina Byuro, 5677 [1917].

Ben-Zvi, Y[itzḥak]. *HaGdudim HaIvriyim-Igrot Yitzḥak Ben-Zvi.* Jerusalem: Yad Yitzḥak Ben-Zvi, 1968.

———. "HaKomuna'im BeAvodatam" [Hebrew]. *Kuntres,* 18 June 1926, 3–5.

———. " 'HeḤalutz' VeHaHitnadvut LaGdud HaIvri BeArtzot HaBrit" [Hebrew]. In *Sefer HaAliyah HaShlishit.* Ed. Yehuda Erez. Tel Aviv: n.p., 1964.

———. "Od Al Tnu'ateinu BeAmerica" [Hebrew]. *Kuntres,* 20 August 1926, 4–9.

———. *Poale Zion BaAliyah Hashniya* [Hebrew]. Tel Aviv: Mifleget Po'alei Eretz Yisrael VeIḥud Olami Poale Zion (Z. S.) Hitachduth, 1950.

———. "Tnu'ateinu BeAmerica" [Hebrew], originally a lecture given at the Aḥdut HaAvoda Council, Tel Aviv. *Kuntres,* 24 July 1926, 8–11.

Berkowitz, Y. D. *HaRishonim Kivnei Adam* [Hebrew]. 5 vols. Tel Aviv: Dvir, 1938, 1943.

Bernstein, Sh[imon]. *Neḥemia Shmuel Libowitz (LeYovel HaShiv'im Shelo)* [Hebrew]. New York: Hotza'a Meyuḥedet MeiHaDo'ar, 8 Ḥeshvan 5692 [1932].

Brandeis, Louis D. *Letters of Louis D. Brandeis.* Vols. 1–5. Eds. Melvin I. Urofsky and David W. Levy. Albany: State University of New York Press, 1971–1978.

Brenner, Yosef Ḥaim. *MiKan U-MiKan* [Hebrew]. In *Yosef Ḥaim Brenner, Ktavim,* vol. 2. Tel Aviv: HaKibbutz HaMe'uḥad, Sifriyat HaPo'alim, 5738 [1978], pp. 1263–1440. (Originally published in 1911.)

Brinner, William M., and Moses Rischin, eds. *Like All the Nations? The Life and Legacy of Judah L. Magnes.* Albany: State University of New York Press, 1987.

Carpi, Daniel, Attilio Milano, and Umberto Naḥon, eds. *Scritti in Memoria di Enzo Sereni.* Milan and Jerusalem: Fondazione Sally Mayer and Scuola Superiore di Studi Ebraici, 1970.

Dizengoff, M[eir]. *Im Tel Aviv BaGola* [Hebrew]. Tel Aviv: n.p., [1931].

Elath [Epstein], Eliahu. *Zionism at the United Nations: A Diary of the First Days.* Trans. Michael Ben-Yitzḥak. Philadelphia: Jewish Publication Society, 1976.

Elmaleh, Avraham. *Eretz Yisrael VeSuria Bimei Milḥemet Olam* [Hebrew]. 2 vols. Jerusalem: By the author, 5688 [1928] (vol. 1); Jerusalem: Mizraḥ U-Ma'arav, 5689 [1929] (vol. 2).

Fichman, Ya'akov. "Im Bialik (Zichronot U-Reshimot MiPinkasai)." In *Knesset: Divrei Sofrim LeZecher H. N. Bialik,* 2. Ed. Ya'akov Cohen and F[ishel] Laḥover. Tel Aviv: Dvir, 5697 [1937], 53–104.

———, ed. *Sefer Bialik* [Hebrew]. Tel Aviv: Va'ad HaYovel BeHishtatfut Hotza'at "Omanut," Shvat, 5664 [1924].

———. *Sofrim BeḤayeihem* [Hebrew]. Tel Aviv: Sifryiat Rimon, Masada, 1942.

Fishman [Maimon], Yehuda Leib HaCohen. *Artzeinu.* New York: Hotza'at HaMizraḥi, 5678 [1918].

———. *HaColonialfund Shel HaMizraḥi, Te'udato U'Matrato* [Hebrew]. New York: Hotza'at HaMizraḥi, 5676 [1916].

———. *Dvarim Aḥadim Odot HaTaḥkemoni She-BeIr HaKodesh Yafo* [Hebrew]. New York: Lishkat HaMizraḥi, 5676 [1916].

Bibliography

———. *Igrot HaRav Maimon*. Jerusalem: Mosad HaRav Kook, 1979.

———. *Sarei HaMe'a* [Hebrew]. 6 vols. Jerusalem: Mossad HaRav Kook, 5703–5716 [1943–56].

———. *Te'udath HaMizrahi* [Hebrew]. New York: HaMizrahi Publications, 5679 [1919].

———. *Toldot HaMizrahi* [Hebrew]. Jerusalem: "HaTor," 5687 [1927].

Frankfurter, Felix. *From the Diaries of Felix Frankfurter*. Ed. Joseph P. Lash, assisted by Jonathan Lash. New York: Norton, 1975.

Gelber, Sylva M. *No Balm in Gilead*. [Ottawa]: Carleton University Press, 1989.

Gilner, Elias. *War and Hope*. New York: Herzl Press, 1969.

HaCohen, Mordecai Ben Hillel. *Milhemet HaAmim (Yoman)* [Hebrew]. 3 vols. Jerusalem and Tel Aviv: Hotza'at Sfarim "Mizpeh," 5689 [1929] (vols. 1–2); Jerusalem: Dfus "HaSefer," 5690 [1930] (vol. 3).

"Hechalutz in America." New York: Mercaz Hechalutz, 1934.

Henrietta Szold, 5621–5705 [1860–1945]. Divrei Azkara SheNe'emru BeYom Gimel BeIyar, 5705, Al Yedei Prof. Sh. Adler VeDr. E. Simon BaUniversita HaIvrit [Hebrew]. Jerusalem: HaUniversita HaIvrit, 1945.

Hoofien, S[igfried]. *Report of Mr. S. Hoofien To the Joint Distribution Committee of the American Funds for Jewish War Sufferers*. rpt., New York: Arno Press, 1977.

Ilan, Ben Zion [Benny Applebaum]. *An American Soldier/Pioneer in Israel*. New York: Labor Zionist Letters, 1979.

Jabotinsky, Eri. *Avi, Ze'ev Jabotinsky* [Hebrew]. Jerusalem: Steimatzky's Agency, 1980.

Japhet, Chaim. *Tet-Vav Shnot Sherut Sotziali BeKnesset Yisrael* [Hebrew]. Jerusalem: HaVa'ad HaLe'umi LiKnesset Yisrael BeEretz Yisrael, HaMahleka LaAvoda Sotzialit, 5707 [1947].

Katznelson-Shazar, Rachel, ed. *The Plough Woman: Memoirs of the Pioneer Women of Palestine*. Trans. Maurice Samuel. New York: Herzl Press in conjunction with the Pioneer Women, 1975.

Kisch, F.[rederick] H. *Palestine Diary*. London: Victor Gollancz, 1938.

Kollek, Teddy, with Amos Kollek. *For Jerusalem*. London: Weidenfeld and Nicolson, 1978.

Kook, Avraham Yitzhak HaCohen. *Igrot HaRa'aya*. 3 vols. Jerusalem: Mosad HaRav Kook, 5722–25 [1961–65].

Korngold, Sheyna. *Zikhroynes* [Yiddish]. N.p.: Farlag Idpis, [1968].

Levin, Shmaryahu. *Bimei HaMa'avar (Kovetz Ma'amarim)* [Hebrew]. New York: Hotza'at Asaf with the participation of the Chicago Zionist Centre, 1919.

———. *Forward From Exile*. Trans. and ed. Maurice Samuel. Philadelphia: Jewish Publication Society, 1967.

———. *Igrot Shmaryahu Levin-Mivhar* [Hebrew]. Tel Aviv: Dvir, 1966.

———. *MiZichronot Hayai*. vol. 4, *BaOlam HeHadash* [Hebrew]. Tel Aviv: Dvir, 5701–2 [1941–42].

Lewin-Epstein, Eliyahu Ze'ev Halevi. *Zichronotai* [Hebrew]. 2 vols. Tel Aviv: HaAhim Lewin-Epstein VeShutafam, 5692 [1932].

Lindheim, Irma L. *Parallel Quest*. New York: Thomas Yoseloff, 1962.

Bibliography

Lipsky, Louis. "Early Days of American Zionism, 1897–1929." *Palestine Year Book* 2 (1945–46): 447–88.
Lissitzky, Ephraim E. *In the Grip of Cross Currents*. Trans. Moshe Kohn and Jacob Sloan. New York: Bloch, 1959.
Locker, Berl. *MiKitov Ad Yerushalayim* [Hebrew]. Jerusalem: Hassifriya HaTziyonit, 5730 [1970].
Magnes, L. Y. [sic]. *Azkara LeNishmat Henrietta Szold, Masa Hesped BeYom Gimel, 7 BeAdar 5705, 20 February 1945*. Jerusalem: n.p., n.d.
Maimon [Fishman], Ada. *Women Build a Land*. Trans. Shulamith Schwarz-Nardi. New York: Herzl, 1962.
———. *Hamishim Shnot Tnu'at HaPo'alot, 1904–1954*. Tel Aviv: Sifriyat Ayanot-Hotza'at Am Oved, 1958.
Marshall, Louis. *Louis Marshall, Champion of Liberty—Selected Papers and Addresses*. 2 vols. Ed. Charles Reznikoff. Philadelphia: Jewish Publication Society, 1957.
Meir, Menahem. *My Mother Golda Meir*. New York: Arbor House, 1983.
Montefiore, Moses, and Judith Montefiore. *Diaries of Sir Moses and Lady Montefiore*. 2 vols. Ed. L[ouis] Löwe. Chicago: Belford-Clarke, 1890.
Neumann, Emanuel. *Causes of the Conflict*. New York: New Maccabean, [1921].
———. *In the Arena*. New York: Herzl, 1976.
Nordau, Max. B. *Ktavim Tziyoniyim* [Hebrew]. 4 vols. Ed. B. Netanyahu. Jerusalem: HaSifriya HaTziyonit, 5720 [1960].
Palestine on Brandeis. Jerusalem: n.p., 1937.
Preliminary Conference of the American Jewish Congress. *Report* of Proceedings, March 26 and 27, 1916, Philadelphia, Pa. New York: Executive Organizing Committee, American Jewish Congress, n.d.
Ribalow, Menahem, ed. *Sefer Zikaron LeB. N. Silkiner* [Hebrew]. New York: Ogen Al Yad HaHistradruth Halvrith BeAmerica, 5694 [1934].
Rosenblatt, Bernard A. *An American Solution of the Palestine Problems*. Jerusalem: n.p., 1937. (Two essays originally published in *Palestine Review*, 7 August 1936, and 26 February 1937, and replies to suggestions.)
———. *Two Generations of Zionism*. New York: Shengold, 1967.
Ruppin, Arthur. *Memoirs Diaries, Letters*. Ed. Alex Bein. Trans. Karen Gershon. London and Jerusalem: Weidenfeld and Nicolson, 1971.
———. *Pirkei Hayai* [Hebrew]. 3 vols. Ed. Alex Bein. Trans. A. D. Shafir. Tel Aviv: Am Oved, 1968.
———. *Three Decades in Palestine*. Jerusalem: Schocken, 1936.
Rutenberg, Pinhas. *Tehiyat HaLe'umiyut Shel HaAm HaYehudi*. Haifa: n.p., 1942. (Trans. from booklet that appeared in Yiddish in New York, 1915.)
Sampter, Jessie. "A Confession." In *Self Fulfillment Through Zionism*. Ed. Shlomo Bardin. New York: American Zionist Youth Commission, 1943. (Originally published in *The Reconstructionist*.)
Samuel, Maurice. *Little Did I Know: Recollections and Reflections*. New York: Knopf, 1963.
Schiff, Jacob H. *Jacob H. Schiff: His Life and Letters*. 2 vols. Ed. Cyrus Adler. Garden City, N.Y.: Doubleday, Doran, 1928.

Bibliography

Schwartz, Y. Y. *Shirat Kentucky* [Hebrew]. Jerusalem: Mosad Bialik, 1962.
Sereni, Chaim Enzo. *HaAviv HaKadosh* [Hebrew]. Tel Aviv: Am Oved, 5707.
Sharett [Shertok], Moshe. *Yoman Medini* [Hebrew], vols. 1–3. Tel Aviv: Am Oved, Hassifriyah Haziyonit, 1968, 1971, 1972.
Sheinkin, M[enaḥem]. *Erets Yisroel in Milkhomo Tsayt* [Yiddish]. New York: Federation of American Zionists, 1917.
———. *Kitvei Menaḥem Sheinken* [Hebrew]. Ed. A. Ḥermoni. Tel Aviv: Miriam Sheinkin, n.d.
Sherman, Eliezer L. *Der Mensh Bialik: Zikhroynes un Ayndruken* [Yiddish]. Philadelphia: Ber-Kay Press, [1936].
Shunami, Shlomo, ed. *Kitvei Yitzḥak Ben-Zvi, Bivliografia, 5664–5718 [1904–1958]* [Hebrew]. Jerusalem: n.p., 5718 [1958].
Spizman, L., ed. *A Quarter Century of the Histadruth* [Yiddish]. New York: National Committee for Labor Palestine, 1946.
Sprinzak, Yosef. *Igrot Yosef Sprinzak* [Hebrew]. 3 vols. Ed. Yosef Shapira. Tel Aviv: Ayanoth, 1965, 1969.
Stenographisches Protokoll der Verhandlungen des IV. Zionisten Congresses in London, 13., 14., 15. und 16. August 1900. Vienna: Verlag des Vereines "Erez Israel," 1900.
Twenty Years of Medical Service to Palestine, 1918–1938. Jerusalem: Hadassah Medical Organization, 1939.
Weisgal, Meyer. *. . . So Far, An Autobiography.* London and Jerusalem: Weidenfeld and Nicolson and the Ma'ariv Book Guild, 1971.
Weizmann, Chaim. *The Letters and Papers of Chaim Weizmann.* General editor, Meyer Weisgal. New Brunswick, N.J. and Jerusalem: Transaction Books, Rutgers University, Israel Universities Press, 1977–.
Yavne'eli, Shmuel. *Masa leTeiman, BiShliḥut HaMisrad HaEretz Yisraeli Shel HaHistadrut HaTziyonit BiShnot 5671–5672, 1911–1912* [Hebrew]. Mifleget Po'alei Eretz Yisrael, 5712.
Zerubavel, Ya'akov. *Alei Ḥaim* [Hebrew]. 2 vols. Tel Aviv: I. L. Peretz, 1960.
Zuckerman, Baruch. *Essayen un Profilin* [Yiddish]. Tel Aviv: I. L. Peretz, 1967.
———. *Oyfn Veg* [Yiddish]. New York: Yiddisher Kemfer, 1956.
———. *Zikhroynes* [Yiddish]. 3 vols. New York: Farlag "Iddisher Kemfer" and Farband Bikher Farlag, 1962, 1963, 1966.

Selected Secondary Works

Books

Aberbach, David. *Bialik*. London: Peter Halban, 1988.
Adler, Selig, and Thomas Connelly. *From Ararat to Suburbia*. Philadelphia: Jewish Publication Society, 1960.
Agress, Eliyahu. *Golda Meir: Portrait of a Prime Minister*. Trans. Israel I. Taslitt. New York: Sabra, [1969].

Bibliography

Avihai, Avraham. *Ben Gurion, State-Builder.* New York, Toronto, and Jerusalem: John Wiley and Sons and Israel Universities Press, 1974.
Avineri, Shlomo. *Arlosoroff.* London: Peter Halban, 1989.
Bar-Zohar, Michael. *Ben-Gurion.* Trans. Peretz Kidron. London: Weidenfeld and Nicolson, 1978.
Bardin, Shlomo. *Pioneer Youth in Palestine.* New York: Bloch, 1932.
Ben-Hur, Raphaella Bilsky. *Kol Yahid Hu Melech: HaMahshava HaHevratit Shel Ze'ev Jabotinsky* [Hebrew]. Tel Aviv: Dvir, 1988.
Berman, Aaron. *Nazism, the Jews and American Zionism, 1933–1948.* Detroit: Wayne State University Press, 1990.
Breslau, David, ed. *Adventure in Pioneering.* New York: CHAY Commission of the Labor Zionist Movement, 1957.
———. *Arise and Build: The Story of American Habonim.* New York: Ichud Habonim Labour Zionist Youth, 1961.
Brinker, Menachem. *Ad HaSimta HaTveriyanit* [Hebrew]. Tel Aviv: Sifriyat Ofakim, Am Oved, 1990.
Cohen, Naomi W. *American Jews and the Zionist Idea.* [New York]: Ktav, 1975.
———. *Not Free to Desist.* Philadelphia: Jewish Publication Society, 1972.
———. *The Year after the Riots.* Detroit: Wayne State University Press, 1988.
Cornfeld, Peretz, ed. *Palestine Personalia 1947.* Tel Aviv: "Palestine Personalia," 1947.
Dash, Joan. *Summoned to Jerusalem: The Life of Henrietta Szold.* New York: Harper & Row, 1979.
Davidson, Margaret. *The Golda Meir Story.* New York: Charles Scribner's Sons, 1976.
Davis, Moshe, ed. *With Eyes Toward Zion* [vol. 1]. New York: Arno, 1977.
Eisenhower, Julie Nixon. *Special People.* New York: Ballantine, 1977.
Elam, Yigal. *HaSochnut HaYehudit—Shanim Rishonot, 1919–1931* [Hebrew]. Jerusalem: Hassifriya Haziyonit, 1990.
Epstein, Melech. *Jewish Labor in the U.S.A.* 2 vols. New York: Trade Union Sponsoring Committee, 1950, 1953.
Ettinger, Akiva. *Im Hakla'im Yehudiyim BaTfutzot.* Merhavia: "Sifriyat Po'alim," Workers Book Guild (Hashomer Hatzair), 1942.
Feinstein, Marnin. *American Zionism 1884–1904.* New York: Herzl, 1965.
Fineman, Irving. *Woman of Valor.* New York: Simon and Schuster, 1961.
Fliegel, Hyman J. *The Life and Times of Max Pine.* New York: By the author, 1959.
Friedman, Isaiah. *Germany, Turkey and Zionism, 1897–1918.* Oxford: Clarendon, 1977.
Friesel, Evyatar. *HaTnu'a HaTziyonit BeArtzot HaBrit BaShanim, 1897–1914.* [Tel Aviv]: Universitat Tel Aviv and HaKibbutz HaMeuchad, 5730 [1970].
Fromkin, David. *A Peace to End All Peace.* New York: Avon, 1990.
Gal, Allon. *Brandeis of Boston.* Cambridge, Mass.: Harvard University Press, 1980.
———. *David Ben-Gurion—Likrat Medina Yehudit* [Hebrew]. [Sede Boqer]: Ben-Gurion University of the Negev, Sede Boqer Campus, 1985.
Ginzberg, Eli. *Keeper of the Law: Louis Ginzberg.* Philadelphia: Jewish Publication Society, 1966.
Goell, Yohai, comp. *Bibliography of Modern Hebrew Literature in English Translation.*

Jerusalem: Executive of the World Zionist Organization, Youth and Hechalutz Department, and Israel Universities Press, 1968.
———. *Bibliography of Modern Hebrew Literature in Translation*. Tel Aviv: Institute for the Translation of Hebrew Literature, 1975.
Goldstein, Ya'akov. *HaHistadrut U-Fo'alei Artzot HaBrit* [Hebrew]. Tel Aviv: Am Oved, 1984.
Goren, Arthur A., ed. *Dissenter in Zion*. Cambridge, Mass.: Harvard University Press, 1982.
Grose, Peter. *Israel in the Mind of America*. New York: Knopf, 1983.
Hadassah—History of Organization—Present Status. Mimeograph. N.p., [1925?].
Hashavya, Aryeh. *Golda Meir* [Hebrew]. Jerusalem: Agaf HaNo'ar/HaMahleka LeHinuch Hevrati, 1978.
Hattis, Susan Lee. *The Bi-National Idea in Palestine During Mandatory Times*. Haifa: Shikmona, 1970.
Hazan, Ya'akov. *Em BeYisrael* [Hebrew]. N.p., n.d.
Hertz, J. S. *50 Years of the Workmen's Circle in Jewish Life* [Yiddish]. New York: National Executive Committee of the Workmen's Circle, 1950.
Holtz, Avraham. *Isaac Dov Berkowitz*. Ithaca: Cornell University Press, 1973.
Horowitz, Dan, and Moshe Lissak. *Origins of the Israeli Polity: Palestine under the Mandate*. Trans. Charles Hoffman. Chicago: University of Chicago Press, 1978.
Hurgin, Ya'akov, ed. *Sifriyat Rishonim*. Vol. 1, no. 10, *Israel Belkind*. Tel Aviv: n.p., 1943.
Ilan, Amitzur. *America, Britannia VeEretz Yisrael—Reishitah VeHitpathutah Shel Me'oravut Artzot HaBrit BaMediniyut HaBritit BeEretz Yisrael, 1938–1947* [Hebrew]. Jerusalem: Yad Yitzhak Ben-Zvi, 5739 [1979].
Kark, Ruth. *American Consuls in the Holy Land, 1832–1914*. Jerusalem and Detroit: Magnes Press, Hebrew University, and Wayne State University Press, 1994.
Katz, Shmuel. *Jabo—Biografia Shel Ze'ev Jabotinsky* [Hebrew]. 2 vols. Tel Aviv: Dvir, 1993.
Kaufman, Menahem. *An Ambiguous Partnership: Non Zionists and Zionists in America, 1939–1948*. Jerusalem and Detroit: Magnes Press, Hebrew University, and Wayne State University Press, 1991.
Keller, Mollie. *Golda Meir*. New York: Franklin Watts, 1983.
Kellner, Ya'akov. *HaAliyot HaRishonot—Mithos U-Metzi'ut* [Hebrew]. Jerusalem: HaUniversita HaIvrit Birushalayim, Beit HaSefer LaAvoda Sotzialit Al Shem Paul Baerwald, 1982.
———. *Lema'an Tziyon: HaHitarvut HaKlal Yehudit BiMtzukat HaYishuv, 1869–1882* [Hebrew]. Jerusalem: Yad Yitzhak Ben-Zvi, 1976.
Keren, Michael. *The Pen and the Sword*. Boulder, San Francisco, and London: Westview, 1989.
Knee, Stuart E. *The Concept of Zionist Dissent in the American Mind, 1917–1941*. New York: Robert Speller & Sons, 1979.
Kolatt, Israel. *Avot U-Meyasdim* [Hebrew]. Tel Aviv: Institute of Contemporary Jewry [of] the Hebrew University of Jerusalem [and] Hakibbutz Hameuchad Publishing House, 1975.

Bibliography

Lipsky, Louis. *A Gallery of Zionist Profiles*. New York: Farrar Straus and Cudahy, 1956.

Livneh, Eliezer. *Aharon Aharonsohn, Halsh U-Zmano*. Jerusalem: Mosad Bialik, 1969.

———. *Is the American Diaspora a Second Babylonia?* Mimeograph. Jerusalem: American Jewish Committee, 1973.

Mann, Peggy. *Golda: The Life of Israel's Prime Minister*. London: Valentine, Mitchell, 1972.

Manor, Alexander. *Commitment and Creative Action: Life and Work of Israel Merom (Mereminsky)*. Translated and adapted by S. Leshner-Shapiro. Tel Aviv: Sponsoring Committee, 1978.

Manuel, Frank E. *The Realities of American-Palestine Relations*. Washington D.C.: Public Affairs Press, 1949.

Martin, Ralph G. *Golda Meir: The Romantic Years*. New York: Charles Scribner's Sons, 1988.

Mason, Alpheus Thomas. *Brandeis: A Free Man's Life*. New York: Viking, 1946.

Medzini, Meron. *HaYehudiya HaGei'a* [Hebrew]. Jerusalem: Edanim, 1990.

Meyer, Isidore S., ed. *Early History of American Zionism*. New York: American Jewish Historical Society and Theodor Herzl Foundation, 1958.

Meyer, Michael A. *Hebrew Union College-Jewish Institute of Religion: A Centennial History, 1875–1975*. Rev. ed. Cincinnati: Hebrew Union College Press, 1992.

Mintz, Alan, ed. *Hebrew in America*. Detroit: Wayne State University Press, 1993.

Morris, Terry. *Shalom, Golda*. New York: Hawthorn, 1971.

Morris, Ya'akov. *Pioneers from the West*. Jerusalem: World Zionist Organization, 1953.

Naor, Leah. *HaMeshorer—Sipuro Shel Bialik* [Hebrew]. Jerusalem and Tel Aviv: Yad Yitzḥak Ben-Zvi and Am Oved, 1991.

Nobel, Iris. *Israel's Golda Meir: Pioneer to Prime Minister*. Folkstone: Bailey Brothers and Swinten, 1972.

O'Brien, Laird. *Golda Meir: A Perspective on the Woman and Her Times*. London, Ont.: London Life Insurance Company, 1978.

Oz, Amos. *In the Land of Israel*. Trans. Maurie Goldberg-Bartura. San Diego, New York, and London: Harcourt, Brace, Jovanovich, 1983.

Plaut, W. Gunther. *The Jews in Minnesota*. New York: American Jewish Historical Society, 1959.

Porat, Dina. *The Blue and the Yellow Stars of David: The Zionist Leadership in Palestine and the Holocaust, 1939–1945*. Trans. David Ben-Nahum. Cambridge, Mass.: Harvard University Press, 1990.

Raisin, Max. *Groysè Yidn Vos Ikh Hob Gekent* [Yiddish]. Patterson, N.J.: New Jersey Branch of the Central Yiddish Culture Organization ("CYCO"), 1950.

Raphael, Marc Lee. *Abba Hillel Silver: A Profile in American Judaism*. New York and London: Holmes & Meier, 1989.

Rose, Norman. *Chaim Weizmann: A Biography*. New York: Viking-Penguin, 1986.

Sarna, Jonathan D. *JPS: The Americanization of Jewish Culture, 1888–1988*. Philadelphia: Jewish Publication Society, 1989.

Schechtman, Joseph B. *Fighter and Prophet*. New York and London: Thomas Yoseloff, 1961.

Bibliography

———. *Rebel and Statesman*. New York: Thomas Yoseloff, 1956.
Sefer Merhavya, HaCo'operatzia [Hebrew]. Tel Aviv: Hotza'at Vatikei HaCo'operatzia, 5721 [1961].
Shapira, Anita. *Berl (Biografia)* [Hebrew]. 2 vols. Tel Aviv: Sifriyat Ofakim—Am Oved, 1980.
———. *Berl: The Biography of a Socialist Zionist*. Trans. Haya Galai. Cambridge, England: Cambridge University Press, 1984.
Sharett, Ya'akov, and Nahman Tamir, eds. *Anshei HaAliyah HaShniya* [Hebrew]. 4 vols. N.p., 1970–72.
Shavit, Ya'akov. *Jabotinsky and the Revisionist Movement, 1925–1948*. London: Frank Cass, 1988.
Shavit, Ya'akov, Ya'akov Goldstein, and Haim Be'er, eds. *Leksikon HaIshim Shel Eretz Yisrael, 1799–1948*. Tel Aviv: Am Oved, 1983.
Shilo, Margalit. *Nisyonot BeHityashvut: HaMisrad HaEretz Yisraeli, 1908–1914* [Hebrew]. Jerusalem: Yad Yitzhak Ben-Zvi, 1988.
Shneur, Z[alman]. *Ch. N. Bialik U-Vnei Doro* [Hebrew]. Tel Aviv: Am Oved, 5713 [1953].
Shva, Shlomo. *Hozeh Brah!* [Hebrew]. Tel Aviv: Dvir, 1990.
Slater, Robert. *Golda: The Uncrowned Queen of Israel*. New York: Jonathan David, 1981.
Sobel, Zvi. *Migrants from the Promised Land*. New Brunswick, N.J.: Transaction, 1984.
Sokolow, Nahum. *History of Zionism, 1600–1918*. 2 vols. 1919; rpt., New York: Ktav, 1969.
Syrkin, Marie. *Golda Meir: Woman with a Cause*. New York: G. P. Putnam's Sons, 1963.
Tamir, Nahman, ed. *Golda—Kovetz LeZichrah* [Hebrew]. Tel Aviv: Am Oved, 1981.
Teveth, Shabatai. *Ben-Gurion: The Burning Ground, 1886–1948*. Boston: Houghton Mifflin, 1987.
Tidhar, David. *Antziklopedia LeHalutzei HaYishuv U-Vonav* [Hebrew]. 19 vols. Tel Aviv: By the author, 1946–70.
Tzahor, Ze'ev. *Shorshei HaPolitica HaYisra'elit*. [Tel Aviv and Beersheba]: HaKibbutz Hameuchad Publishing House and Ben Gurion University of the Negev, 1987.
Urofsky, Melvin I. *American Zionism from Herzl to the Holocaust*. New York: Anchor, Doubleday, 1976.
———. *A Voice That Spoke For Justice*. Albany: State University of New York Press, 1982.
Weinstein, Jacob J. *Solomon Goldman: A Rabbi's Rabbi*. New York: Ktav, 1973.
Wistrich, Robert. *Between Redemption and Perdition: Modern Antisemitism and Jewish Identity*. London and New York: Routledge, 1990.
Yavne'eli, Shmuel, ed. *Sefer HaTziyonut*. Vol. 2, *Tkufat Hibat Tziyon* [Hebrew]. Tel Aviv: Mosad Bialik Al Yedei Dvir, 1944.
Zipperstein, Steven J. *Elusive Prophet: Ahad Ha'Am and the Origins of Zionism*. Berkeley and Los Angeles: University of California Press, 1993.
Zweig, Ronald W., ed. *Ben-Gurion: Politics and Leadership in Israel*. London and Jerusalem: Frank Cass and Yad Izhak Ben-Zvi, 1991.

Bibliography

Articles

Adler, Joseph. "The Morgenthau Mission of 1917." *Herzl Year Book* 5 (1963): 249–82.
Adler, Selig. "The Roosevelt Administration and Zionism: The Pre-War Years, 1933–1939." *Herzl Year Book* 8 (1978): 132–48.
Akzin, Benyamin. "Mediniyut HaHutz Shel Jabotinsky" [Hebrew]. In Binyamin Akzin, *Sugiyot BeMishpat U-ViMdina'ut*. Jerusalem: Hotza'at Sfarim Al Shem J. L. Magnes, HaUniversita Halvrit, 5726 [1966].
Avineri, Shlomo. "Ideology and Pragmatism in Ben-Gurion's Leadership: Lessons for the Future." In *Towards the Twenty-first Century: Judaism and the Jewish People in Israel and America*. Ed. Ronald Kronish. Hoboken, N.J.: Ktav, 1988.
Avneri, Shmuel. "Kavim LeDarko Shel Bialik BeArichat *HaShiloah*" [Hebrew]. In *Hallel LeVialik: Iyunim U-Mehkarim Bitzirat Ch. N. Bialik*. Ed. Hillel Weiss and Yedidyah Itzhaki. Ramat Gan: Universitat Bar-Ilan, 1989.
Barshai, Bezalel. "The Hebrew University of Jerusalem, 1925–1935" [Hebrew]. *Cathedra* 53 (September 1989): 107–22.
———. "The Hebrew University of Jerusalem from the Plan to Reality" [Hebrew]. *Cathedra* 25 (September 1982): 65–78.
Bartur, Ron. "Episodes in the Relations of the American Consulate in Jerusalem with the Jewish Community in the 19th Century (1856–1906)" [Hebrew]. *Cathedra* 5 (October 1977): 109–43.
Ben-Arieh, Yehoshua. "Nineteenth Century Hebrew Periodicals as a Source For America-Holy Land Studies." Vol. 2 of *With Eyes Toward Zion*. Ed. Moshe Davis. New York: Praeger, 1986.
Berlin, George L. "The Brandeis-Weizmann Dispute." *American Jewish Historical Quarterly* 60 (September 1970): 37–68.
Biger, Gideon. "The American Consulate of Jerusalem and the 1920–1921 Disturbances" [Hebrew]. *Cathedra* 49 (September 1988): 133–59.
Brown, Michael. "All, All Alone! The Hebrew Press in America from 1914 to 1924." *American Jewish Historical Quarterly* 59 (October 1969): 138–77.
Doukhan-Landau, Leah. "The Haifa Bay Lands and the American Zion Commonwealth Crisis (1925–1930)" [Hebrew]. *Cathedra* 41 (December 1986): 173–99.
Efrati, Nathan. "The Jerusalem Lodge of B'nai B'rith, 1888–1919" [Hebrew]. *Cathedra* 50 (December 1988): 140–66.
———. "The Relationship between American Jewry and the Yishuv in the 1890s" [Hebrew]. *Cathedra* 55 (March 1990): 63–88.
Eliav, Mordechai. "Diplomatic Intervention Concerning Restrictions on Jewish Immigration and Purchase of Land at the End of the Nineteenth Century" [Hebrew]. *Cathedra* 26 (December 1982): 117–33.
Ettinger, Akiva. "HaHityashvut HaHaklа'it Shel HaYehudim BeArtzot HaBrit" [Hebrew]. *HaSadeh* 14 [1934].
Ettinger, Shmuel, and Israel Bartal. "The First Aliyah: Ideological Roots and Practical Accomplishments." *Jerusalem Cathedra* 2 (1982): 197–227.
Fein, Leonard. "Who is a Jew? Covenant and Contract." *Forum* 62 (Winter/Spring 1989): 27–38.

Bibliography

Fishman, Z. "Chaim Nahman Bialik (Biografia U-Vivliografia)" [Hebrew]. *Ein Ha-Koreh* 1 (Nisan-Elul 5683 [1923]).

Fox, Maier Bryan. "Labor Zionism in America: The Challenge of the 1920s." *American Jewish Archives* 35 (April 1983): 53–71.

Fox, Nili. "Balfouriya: An American Zionist Failure or Secret Success?" *American Jewish History* 78 (June 1989): 497–512.

Frankel, Jonathan. "The 'Yizkor' Book of 1911—A Note On National Myths in the Second Aliya." In *Religion, Ideology and Nationalism in Europe and America: Essays Presented in Honor of Yehoshua Arieli.* Ed. H. Ben-Israel et al. Jerusalem: Historical Society of Israel and Zalman Shazar Center for Jewish History, 1986.

Friedman, Thomas L. "America in the Mind of Israel." *New York Times Magazine,* 25 May 1986, 22–30, 50.

Friesel, Evyatar. "Brandeis' Role in American Zionism Historically Reconsidered." *American Jewish History* 69 (September 1979): 34–59.

Gal, Allon. "Eulogy and Policy: David Ben-Gurion's Address at a Memorial Meeting Honoring Louis D. Brandeis, London, October 21, 1941" [Hebrew]. *Cathedra* 44 (June 1987): 108–15.

———. "Zionist Foreign Policy and Ben-Gurion's Visit to the United States in 1939." *Studies in Zionism* 7 (1986): 37–50.

Geffen, David. " 'A Visit to the Land of the Patriarchs'—The Diary of William Topkis, 1923" [Hebrew]. *Cathedra* 13 (October 1979): 71–94.

Geffen, Joel S. "Whither: To Palestine or to America in the Pages of the Russian Hebrew Press, Ha-Melitz and Ha-Yom (1880–1890), Annotated Documentary." *American Jewish Historical Quarterly* 59 (December 1969): 179–200.

Goell, Yoḥai. "Aliyah in the Zionism of an American Oleh: Judah L. Magnes." *American Jewish Historical Quarterly* 65 (December 1975): 99–120.

Goldstein, Ya'akov. "Heroine or Traitor? The Controversy over Manya Vilbushevich-Shoḥat and Her Links with Zubatov." *Studies in Contemporary Jewry* 6 (1990): 284–305.

Gorny, Yosef. "Zionist Voluntarism in the Political Struggle: 1939–1948." *Jewish Political Studies Review* 2 (Spring 1990): 67–104.

Govrin, Nita. "The Encounter of Exiles from Palestine with the Jewish Community of Egypt During World War I as Reflected in Their Writings." In *The Jews of Egypt.* Ed. Shimon Shamir. Boulder and London: Westview Press, 1987.

Hagitti, Michal. "A Rest-Home for Agricultural Laborers in Jerusalem, 1919–1923" [Hebrew]. *Cathedra* 30 (December 1983): 91–110.

Halpern, Ben. "Brandeis' Way to Zionism." *Midstream* 17 (October 1971): 3–13.

Hirschler, Gertrude. "Bialik's Tour of the United States." *Midstream* 30 (August–September 1984): 30–34.

Ilan, Amitzur. "From the Hebrew Press, America, Britain and Palestine." *Jerusalem Cathedra* 1 (1981): 328–35.

Ivey, Sara. "Golda Meir—One of the World's 10 Greatest Women." *Dixie Business* (Summer 1973).

Kark, Ruth. "Annual Reports of United States Consuls in the Holy Land as a Source for the Study of Nineteenth-Century Eretz Israel." In *With Eyes Toward Zion,* vol 2. Ed. Moshe Davis. New York: Praeger, 1986.

Bibliography

Katz, Saul. "Aharon Aharonson—The Beginnings of Agricultural Science and Research in Eretz Israel" [Hebrew]. *Cathedra* 3 (February 1977): 3–29.

Katz, Yossi. "The *Achuza* Projects in Eretz-Israel, 1908–1917" [Hebrew]. *Cathedra* 22 (January 1982): 119–44.

———. "The Plans and Efforts of the Jews of Winnipeg to Purchase Land and to Establish an Agricultural Settlement in Palestine before World War I." *Canadian Jewish Historical Society Journal* 5 (Spring 1981): 1–16.

Klein, A. M. "Chaim Nachman Bialik, 1873–1934." *Canadian Zionist* (July 1937).

Kurzweil, Baruch Benedikt. "The Image of the Western Jew in Modern Hebrew Literature." *Leo Baeck Institute Year Book* 6 (1961): 170–89.

Kutscher, Carol Bosworth. "From Merger to Autonomy: Hadassah and the ZOA, 1918–1921." *Herzl Yearbook* 8 (1978): 61–78.

Landau, Jacob M., and Mim Kemâl Öke. "Ottoman Perpsectives on American Interests in the Holy Land." In *With Eyes Toward Zion*, vol. 2. Ed. Moshe Davis. New York: Praeger, 1986.

Lavsky, Hagit. "The Financial Policy of the Zionist Commission, 1918–1921" [Hebrew]. *Cathedra* 16 (July 1980): 57–73.

Levensohn, Lotta. "A School Where Art Is Life." *Jewish Tribune* 5 (September 1924).

Michaeli, Yitzhak. "Reishitah Shel Histadrut 'HeHalutz' BeAmerica." *Asufot* 6 (December 1989): 107–10.

[Mintz] Minc, Matityahu. "David Ben-Gurion's Correspondence with Izhak Ben-Zvi in America, 1915–1916" [Hebrew]. *Cathedra* 44 (June 1987): 81–96.

———. "Pinchas Rutenberg and the Establishment of the Jewish Legion in 1914." *Studies in Zionism* 6 (1985): 15–26.

Naor, Mordecai. "Oscar S. Straus, U.S. Minister to Turkey, Supporter of *Aliya* to *Eretz Yisrael*" [Hebrew]. *Cathedra* 18 (January 1981): 130–55.

———. "HaRakevet HaYamit SheHitzila et HaYishuv BeEretz Yisrael BeEit Milhemet HaOlam HaRishona" [Hebrew]. *Ma'ariv*, 14 April 1976.

Nash, Shlomo. "Noah H. Rosenbloom—Mashkif Matun U-Mekori Al Sifrut VeHagut." *HaDo'ar*, 27 April 1990, 20–22.

Neustadt-Noy, Isaac. "Toward Unity: Zionist and Non-Zionist Cooperation, 1941–1942." *Herzl Year Book* 8 (1978): 149–65.

Niederland, Doron, and Zohar Kaplan. "The Establishment of the Hebrew University—Hadassah Medical School in Jerusalem" [Hebrew]. *Cathedra* 48 (June 1988): 145–63.

Ofer, Dalia. "HaAliyah, HaGola VeHaYishuv" [Hebrew]. *Cathedra* 43 (March 1987): 69–90.

Panitz, Esther. "Louis Dembitz Brandeis and the Cleveland Conference." *American Jewish Historical Quarterly* 65 (December 1975): 140–62.

Parzen, Herbert. "The Magnes-Weizmann-Einstein Controversy." *Jewish Social Studies* 32 (July 1970): 187–213.

Penkower, Monty. "American Jewry and the Holocaust: From Biltmore to the American Jewish Conference." *Jewish Social Studies* 47 (Spring 1985): 95–114.

———. "Ben-Gurion, Silver and the 1941 UPA National Conference for Palestine:

A Turning Point in American Zionist History." *American Jewish History* 69 (September 1979): 66–78.

———. "The 1943 Joint Anglo-American Statement on Palestine." *Herzl Year Book* 8 (1978): 212–41.

Raider, Mark A. "Zion and America. The Utopian Vision of American Labor Zionism." *Jewish Frontier*, March/April 1993, 16–22.

Raisin, Max. "Chaim Nachman Bialik" [Yiddish]. *Tsukunft* 49 (October 1944): 632–37.

Rosenblum, Chanoch (Howard). "The New Zionist Organization's Diplomatic Battle Against Partition, 1936–1937." *Studies in Zionism* 11 (Autumn 1990): 154–81.

Rosenblum, Noah H. "America BeEinei Bialik" [Hebrew]. In *Iyunei Sifrut VeHagut*. Jerusalem: Rubin Mass, 1989.

Rotenstreich, Natan. "Haguto Shel Bialik BeInyenei Tarbut" [Hebrew]. *Knesset* 1 [new series] (5720 [1960]): 207–14.

Rubinstein, Shimon. "Aaronson's Proposal for the Development of Uncultivated Lands Between Jaffa and Rafah" [Hebrew]. *Cathedra* 28 (June 1983): 77–118.

———. "HaNisyonot Leyashev Meshuḥrarei HaGdudim HaIvriyim Al Karka'ot HaMemshala (1919–1923)" [Hebrew]. *HaUma* 43 (Iyar 5735 [1975]): 1–12; and 44 (Elul 5735 [1975]): 1–10.

Sandler, Bernard. "The American Zionist Concept 'Achoozah' and Its Realization in Eretz Israel 1908–1934" [Hebrew]. *Cathedra* 17 (October 1980): 165–82.

Sandler, Shmuel. "Ben-Gurion's Attitude Towards the Soviet Union." *Jewish Journal of Sociology* 21 (December 1979): 145–60.

Shaked, Gershon. "Can Israeli Culture Survive the American Challenge?" *Moment* 14 (August 1989): 57–59.

Shavit, Ya'akov. " 'Land in the Deep Shadow of Wings' and the Redemption of Israel—A Millenarian Document from Jerusalem, 1847" [Hebrew]. *Cathedra* 50 (December 1988): 98–110.

———. "Ze'ev Jabotinsky and the Revisionist Movement." *Studies in Zionism* 4 (Autumn 1981): 219–36.

Shilo, Margalit. "On the Way to the Moshav: Ha-Ikar Hatzair, the 'American Group' in the Second *Aliyah*" [Hebrew]. *Cathedra* 25 (September 1982): 79–98.

Shilony, Zvi. "Changes in the Jewish Leadership of Jerusalem During World War I" [Hebrew]. *Cathedra* 35 (April 1985): 58–90.

Shmeruk, Khone. "Sholem Aleichem and America." *YIVO Annual* 20 (1991): 211–38.

Shmueli, Efraim. "Bialik in America: The Transformation of an Inner Experience." In *Identity and Ethos: A Festschrift for Sol Liptzin on the Occasion of His 85th Birthday*. Ed. Mark H. Gelber. New York, Berne, Frankfurt am Main: Peter Lang, 1986.

Shpiro, David H. "The Political Background of the 1942 Biltmore Resolution." *Herzl Year Book* 8 (1978): 166–77.

Sternhell, Ze'ev. "Ḥazon Medumeh Shel Ḥevra Shivyonit" [Hebrew]. *HaAretz*, 31 May 1991.

Bibliography

Teller, Judd L. "America's Two Zionist Traditions." *Commentary* 20 (October 1955): 343–52.

———. "Zionism, Israel and American Jewry." In *The American Jews: A Reappraisal*. Ed. Oscar Janowsky. Philadelphia: Jewish Publication Society, 1964.

Tzaḥor, Ze'ev. "The Controversy Amongst the Eretz-Israel Labour Parties Concerning Enlistment in the 'Jewish Legion' " [Hebrew]. *Cathedra* 3 (February 1977): 30–39.

———. "David Ben-Gurion: From Socialism to Statehood." *Midstream* 32 (January 1986): 36–39.

———. "David Ben-Gurion's Attitude Toward the Diaspora." *Judaism* 32 (Winter 1983): 9–22.

Tzemaḥ, Sh[lomo]. "HaAdam Im Aḥerim" [Hebrew]. *Knesset* 4 (1939): 52–69.

Warnke, Nina. "Of Plays and Politics: Sholem Aleichem's First Visit to America." *YIVO Annual* 20 (1991): 239–76.

Zak, Moshe. "Tzahal—Shtei Etzba'ot MiMilḥemet Korea" [Hebrew]. *Ma'ariv*, 22 April 1988.

Geographic and Name Index

Aaronsohn family, 200
Aaronsohn, Aaron, 23–25, 31–33, 145, 199
Aaronsohn, Alexander, 24, 28, 31–32, 251n. 47
Aaronsohn, Rivka, 32–33
Addams, Jane, 145
Adler, Cyrus, 227
Adler, Felix, 111
Afula, 119
Agnon, S. Y., 139
Agronsky (Agron), Gershon, 276n. 68
Ahad HaAm (Asher Ginsberg), 71–72, 80, 88–89
Akzin, Benjamin, 66–67
Alexandria, Egypt, 37, 52
Alpert, Carl, 238
Andrews, Eliza Frances, 135
Ann Arbor, Michigan, 179
Applebaum, Benny (Ben-Zion Ilan), 122–23, 132, 230
Arkansas, 33
Arlosoroff, Chaim, 137, 139, 164, 171
Athlit, 24, 199
Atlantic City, 124, 158
Australia, 41, 104
Austria, Austro-Hungary, 30, 76
Avineri, Shlomo, 210

Babbitt, George, 49, 57
Balak, 82
Baldwin, Stanley, 224–25
Balfour, Arthur, Lord, 256n. 43
Baltimore, 27, 83, 134–35, 186, 234
Baratz, Yosef, 109–10, 112, 115, 210, 294n. 110, 332n. 156

Baron, Professor Salo, 129–30
Barton, Clara, 145
Baruch, Bernard, 226
Bavli, Hillel, 94, 269n. 8
Beirut, 251n. 47
Belgium, 144
Belkind, Israel, 32, 151
Ben-Avi, Itamar, 55
Ben-Gurion, Amos, 230
Ben-Gurion, David, 62, 101, 157, 189, 193; and American culture, 162, 198, 201–02, 205, 239, 253n. 10, 340n. 66; and American politics, 191, 197, 223–36, 239, 241, 245–46; Bialik and, 70; early life, 198–202; exile in America, 28, 32, 104, 163, 179, 201; and fund-raising, 119, 198, 205, 212, 219, 232; Jabotinsky and, 208, 231; Katznelson and, 17, 104–05, 107–08, 111–13, 119, 122, 126–28, 131, 154–55, 209–11, 217, 223; Meir and, 17, 154, 163, 169, 175, 177, 191, 195, 203, 220; as prime minister, 198, 243–46; Szold and, 139–40, 154–55, 211; and youth and pioneering, 201–02, 210–11, 216, 220. *See also* aliyah, Ben-Zvi, Biltmore Conference, Brandeis, Britain, Geverkshaften Campaign, Hadassah, Hebrew, HeHalutz, Histadrut, Jewish Agency, Jewish Army, Jewish Legion, Keren HaYesod, Labor Zionism, Lipsky, Mack, Magnes, Mapai, Marxism, Poale Zion, Revisionism, Russia, socialism, Turkey, Warburg, Weizmann, Wise, WZO, Yiddish, ZOA
Ben-Gurion (Munweis), Paula, 155, 203, 208, 216, 228

Geographic and Name Index

Ben-Gurion, Renana, 211
Ben-Yehuda, Eliezer, 16, 31–32, 55, 199
Ben Zion, S. (Simḥa Alter Gutman), 71, 269n. 13
Ben-Zvi, Yitzḥak, 21, 28, 46, 199, 339n. 45; Ben-Gurion and, 32, 179, 198, 200–208; and Histadrut, 169; Jabotinsky and, 52; and Jewish Legion, 32–33, 104–05, 129; Katznelson and, 104–05; Meir and, 163; and Poale Zion, 32, 106, 113, 202
Berdichevsky, Michah Yosef, 110
Bergman, Professor Shmuel Hugo, 139
Bergson, Peter, 230
Berkowitz, Y. D., 73–74, 78–79, 86, 97, 269n. 13
Berkson, Isaac B., 148–50
Berlin, 72, 77, 92, 135
Berlin (Bar-Ilan), Rabbi Meir, 32
Berman, Simon, 21
Bernstein, Simon, 93–94
Bialik, Chaim Naḥman, 118, 124, 157, 197, 241; in America, 80–87; and American culture, 70–73, 77, 86, 88–90, 97, 136, 155, 270n. 20, 279n. 89; and American politics, 83–84; editor (see Dvir, HaShiloaḥ, Moriah); and fund-raising, 76, 79–81, 83, 87, 95–97; Jabotinsky and, 52, 71, 84; and literary circle in Russia, 70–72, 78; poetry of, 74–79, 82–83, 88, 91; reputation in America, 74, 77, 79–84, 87, 91; Szold and, 91, 96, 160. See also aliyah, Ben-Gurion, Brandeis, Britain, Germany, Hebrew, Keren HaYesod, Labor Zionism, Shmaryahu Levin, Lipsky, Mack, Magnes, Russia, Weizmann, Wise, WZO, Yiddish, yishuv (culture), ZOA
Bialik, Manya (wife), 73, 81, 84
Binghamton, New York, 189
Bloch (Blumenfeld), David, 171, 211
Bloom, Samuel Simon, 95–96, 99
Bloom, Sol, 83
Bluestone, Dr. E. M., 146, 157
Blum, Léon, 225
Bobruisk, Belarus, 102–04, 109–10, 124
Booth (Luce), Claire, 67
Boston, 24, 83, 123, 136, 179, 193, 207, 239
Brainin, Joseph, 51
Brainin, Reuben, 92, 282n. 107
Brandeis, Louis, 22, 24, 60, 111, 146–47, 181, 242; Ben-Gurion and, 204, 213, 217–18, 221–27; Bialik and, 82; Jabotinsky and, 39, 41–42, 45–50, 54, 62, 106, 256n. 43, 265n. 150; Katznelson and, 106–08, 118, 121, 124, 130, 303n. 189; Szold and, 118, 135–36, 141–42, 145, 155–56. See also Palestine Economic Corporation, Progressive Party, ZOA
Brenner, Yossef Haim, 102–03, 272n. 31
Britain, 15, 31, 109, 138, 184, 190, 195, 200–201, 214, 238, 244; American Jews and, 38–41, 47, 67, 191, 223, 227–28, 231; Arabs and, 42, 54, 126, 216, 226–28, 237, 246; Ben-Gurion and, 126–27, 131, 215–18, 223–35; Bialik and, 76, 84; and immigration to Israel, 58, 106, 127, 175, 190–91, 212, 215–16, 220, 224, 227–30; Jabotinsky and, 17, 38–42, 46–49, 55, 58–60, 63–64, 67, 126, 231, 242; Jews in, 38–39, 41, 44, 72, 76, 81, 104; Katznelson and, 107, 120, 124–27, 131, 223; labor in, 110, 169, 175, 192; Meir and, 131, 175, 187, 190–92, 194; press in, 38, 215; Revisionism and, 58–59; Russia and, 26, 38; Szold and, 136; Turkey and, 26, 30–31; U.S. government and, 41–42, 126–27, 136, 195, 223–31, 238. See also Balfour Declaration, Jewish Legion, Mandate, Palestine, Weizmann, World War I, WZO
Bronx, New York, 205
Brooklyn, New York, 93
Brussels, 170
Bryan, William Jennings, 27, 30
Buber, Martin, 138–39
Buenos Aires, 64
Buffalo, New York, 89, 111, 113, 201, 203
Bullitt, William C., 236
Bumppo, Natty, 57

Cahan, Abe, 67, 115, 117, 123, 169, 219. See also Forverts
Caiserman, H. M., 189
California, 33, 48, 156, 176
Camus, Albert, 69
Canada, 41, 50, 67, 176, 211
Canton, Ohio, 203
Carlsbad, Czechoslovakia, 76, 117
Caruso, Enrico, 49
Catskills, 111
Cecil, Robert, Lord, 39
Chamberlain, Neville, 226, 228

Geographic and Name Index

Chicago, 31, 44, 111, 128, 145, 150, 195, 202, 221, 303n. 186
Chizik, Yitzḥak, 123
Churchill, Winston, 66, 226
Cincinnati, 31, 203
Cleveland, 53, 83, 86, 111, 113, 216, 234
Cohen, Ben, 226
Cohen, Dr. Frances, 147
Cohen, Lionel, 214
Cohen (Taub), Miriam, 233, 235
Columbus, Christopher, 108, 111
Columbus, Ohio, 93, 109, 111
Constantinople, 198. *See also* Turkey
Coolidge, Calvin, 82
Cooper, James Fenimore, 36, 52
Coughlin, Father Charles, 59–61
Cracow, 200
Cresson, Warder (Michael Boaz Israel), 18
Crèvecoeur, J. Hector St. John, 90
Crimea, 80, 92
Cruso, Pinḥas, 330n. 127
Czechoslovakia, 62, 67, 69

Daiches, Belle T., 331n. 145
Davidson, Israel, 79, 86, 93
Davis, Moshe, 122
De Haas, Jacob, 39, 62
Decker, Captain (USS *Tennessee*), 28
Denver, 163
Detroit, 62, 109, 111, 114, 193, 203
Dewey, John, 89, 148–49, 315n. 114
Dickens, Charles, 272n. 35
Diesendruck, Zvi, 92
Dizengoff, Meir, 30, 81
Dobkin, Eliyahu, 178
Dolitzky, Menaḥem Mendel, 97
Donovan, William J., 236
Doyleston, Pennsylvania, 21
Druyanov, Alter, 92
Dubinsky, David, 125
Dubinsky, Meir, 168
Dubnow, Simon, 71
Duluth, Minnesota, 111
Dushkin, Alexander, 147–48

Egypt, 28–30, 56, 90
Ehrenreich, Hirsch, 113, 208, 211
Eilat, 218
Einstein, Albert, 44
Eitan, Israel, 93

Elkus, Abraham I., 26
Elmaleh, Abraham, 27–28
Emerson, Ralph Waldo, 89
Enelow, Hyman G., 93
Epstein, Judith, 234

Faigin, Samuel, 93
Feder, Sara, 142
Feinberg, Yosef, 16, 243
Feinman, Professor Chaim, 190
Feis, Herbert, 64
Ferber, Edna, 59
Finn, Huck, 36, 57
Fischer, Louis, 109
Fishman (Maimon), Ada, 169, 177
Fishman (Maimon), Rabbi Yehuda Leib, 28, 32–33, 177, 205
Floyd, Rolla, 21
Fox (Fuchs), Shmuel, 198
France, 26, 44, 49, 67, 69, 76, 127, 214, 225
Francis Joseph (Franz Jozef), 135
Frankfurter, Felix, 124, 222–24, 235, 303n. 189
Friedenwald, Dr. Harry, 42, 107
Friedman, Thomas, 243

Galilee, 24
Galili, Eliezer, 185–86
Garfield, James, 20
Garibaldi, Giuseppe, 35
Geneva, 66, 229
Germany, 43, 59, 216, 218; American Jews and, 38, 206, 227–28; Bialik and, 72, 76–78; education in, 74, 135, 137; emigration from (to Palestine), 16, 20, 137, 150, 155, 175, 217, 242; emigration from (to U.S.) 231, 299n. 146; Jews in, 38, 44, 49, 72, 75, 120, 304n. 195; language, 72; literature, 74; Russia and, 38, 129; Turkey and, 26, 30, 206. *See also* Berlin, Hitler, Nazism, World War I, World War II
Gilbert and Sullivan, 272n. 35
Ginsburg, Elias, 41–42, 59, 64, 67, 109
Ginzberg, Professor Louis, 88, 93, 137
Ginzburg, Simon, 74–75, 78, 86, 94, 283n. 117
Glazebrook, Otis, 31
Glick, Sammy, 57
Goethe, Johann Wolfgang von, 70
Gold, Rabbi Wolf, 232

Geographic and Name Index

Golden Horn, 201
Goldman, Rabbi Solomon, 112, 121, 217, 222, 226–27
Goldmann, Naḥum, 227
Goldsmid, Osmond d'Avigdor, 214
Goldstein, Bert, 177
Golomb, Eliyahu, 171
Gordon, Aaron David, 242
Gordon, Yehuda Leib (Y. L.), 97
Gorky, Maxim, 76
Grabelsky, Batsheva, 78, 81
Grand Island, New York, 75
Grant, Ulysses S., 122
Greece, 242
Green, William, 190
Greenberg, Ḥaim, 123
Greenberg, Rabbi Simon, 179
Greenwald, Rabbi Yekutiel, 93
Grey, Zane, 52
Griffith, D. W., 36
Grodzensky, Shlomo, 123
Grose, Peter, 246
Gunther, John, 67

HaCohen, Mordecai Ben–Hillel, 28
Ḥadera, 188
Hagai, Yosef, 114
The Hague, 73
Ḥaifa, 18, 64, 119, 153
Halkin, Shimon, 72, 94, 128
Hamilton, Ontario, 111
Hamlin, Isaac, 186–87
Hapgood, Norman, 83
Harding, Warren G., 44, 47, 49, 210
Harlem, 77
Harte, Bret, 36, 52
Harzfeld, Avraham, 53, 211
Ḥashin, Alexander, 204
Havel, Vaclav, 69
Hebron, 27
Heifetz, Yascha, 83
Henry, O., 263n. 121
Herzl, Theodore, 35, 62, 236
Herzliya, 23, 119, 169
Hexter, Maurice, 214
Higger, Michael, 93
Hirshfeld, Zvi, 287n. 19
Hitler, Adolf, 98, 120, 129, 131, 135, 137, 154, 184, 193, 218, 230
Hofstadter, Richard, 134

Homer, 70
Hoover, Herbert, 49, 144
Hope-Simpson, Sir John, 126, 223
Hoz, Dov, 119, 175
Huerta, Victoriano, 199
Hugo, Victor, 35
Hungary, 135
Hurok, Sol, 51–53
Hurwitz, Maximillian, 329n. 123
Hyamson, Albert M., 223

Idelsohn, Abraham Zvi, 92
Iraq, 230
Isaacs, Professor Nathan, 83
Israel, Rabbi Edward L., 186
Italy, 35, 58–59, 93

Jabotinsky, Eri, 47, 67
Jabotinsky, Eva (mother), 44, 47, 53
Jabotinsky, Johanna (wife), 47, 53–54, 64, 67
Jabotinsky, Vladimir, 17, 30, 73, 89–90, 157, 197, 229–30; and aliyah, 48, 64; and American culture, 36–37, 47–53, 55, 57, 59, 68, 136; and American literature, 35–37, 50, 52, 59, 63, 253n. 10, 263n. 121; and American politics, 35–36, 43, 46–49, 58–60, 64, 191; and Arabs, 39, 42; and blacks, 36–37, 48, 59, 162, 264n. 137; and economics, 49–51, 55, 263n. 121; as editor (see Do'ar HaYom, HaSefer); and frontier (pioneering), 36–38, 41, 48–51, 55, 57, 59, 241; and fund-raising, 45–48, 56, 112, 211; as the "Jewish Garibaldi," 45; as journalist and writer, 37, 43, 47, 52, 55–56, 59, 63; Katznelson and, 44, 68; Meir and, 181; as translator, 36, 47, 52, 70, 263n. 121; in U.S., 43–48, 51–56, 60–67, 81. See also Ben-Gurion, Ben-Zvi, Bialik, Brandeis, Britain, fascism, Hadassah, Hebrew, Jewish Agency, Jewish Army, Jewish Legion, Keren HaYesod, Labor Zionism, Lipsky, Mack, Magnes, Poland, Revisionism, Russia, socialism, Nathan Straus, Warburg, Weizmann, Wise, WZO, ZOA
Jacobs, Rose, 156, 158–59
Jaffa, 16, 18, 27–31, 113, 139, 146, 164, 189
Japan, 199
Jefferson, Thomas, 36
Jemal Pasha, 31
Jerusalem, 15, 18–21, 25–31, 44, 53, 75, 81,

382

Geographic and Name Index

92, 121–22, 146–47, 150–53, 156, 159, 193, 199, 231, 236
Johannesburg, 64
Joseph, Bernard (Dov Yosef), 193

Kallen, Deborah, 147, 315n. 114
Kallen, Horace, 147
Kanter, Cantor, 83
Kaplan, Eliezer, 129
Kaplan, Elisheva, 177
Kaplan, Mordecai, 242
Katz, Shmuel, 53–54
Katznelson, Berl, 157, 197; and American culture, 102–04, 109, 117, 120, 124, 128–29, 155–56, 241, 306n. 213; and American politics, 126–27, 130–32, 191, 303n. 189; and Arabs, 139; editing and writing (see Am Oved, Davar, Di Tsayt, Kuntres); fund-raising, 106–13, 116, 119–20, 124, 127–28, 130, 158–59; Meir and, 17, 123–24, 130–31, 169; Szold and, 118–19, 139–40, 154–56; in U.S., 108–16, 124–26; and wife, 109, 111–12; and youth/pioneering, 103–08, 111, 122–23, 302n. 179. See also, aliyah, Ben-Gurion, Ben-Zvi, Brandeis, Britain, capitalism, Geverkshaften Campaign, Hadassah, Histadrut, Jabotinsky, Jewish Agency, Jewish Legion, Keren HaYesod, Kinneret Training Farm, Labor Zionism, Lipsky, Mack, Magnes, Mapai, Poale Zion, Poland, radicalism, Russia, socialism, Weizmann, Wise, Workers' Bank, WZO, Yiddish culture, ZOA
Katznelson, Haim, 102–03, 110
Katznelson, Hannah, 102, 105, 109
Katznelson, Israel, 102–03
Katznelson, Isser, 102–03
Kaufman, Edward, 232
Kiev, 162
Kilpatrick, W. H., 148–49
Kishinev, 36
Klapholz, Rega, 233
Kolatt, Yisrael, 210
Kook, Rabbi Abraham Isaac HaCohen, 16, 137
Kopp, Tamar (Jabotinsky's sister), 47, 53
Korngold, Sheyne, 161–62, 168–69
Kushiner, Shimon, 178
Kutscher, Carol Bosworth, 142

Lansing, Robert, 214
Latvia, 216, 221
Lebanon, 56
Lehman, Herbert, 111
Lehman (Straus), Sissie, 151, 153
Lenin, Vladimir Ilych, 76, 210
Lerner, Max, 131
Lévi, Sylvain, 214
Levin, Louis, 27
Levin, Shmaryahu, 32, 72–73, 77, 80–81, 87, 95, 122, 277n. 75
Levinsky, David, 57
Lewin-Epstein, Eliyahu, 39, 107
Lewis, John L., 184
Lewis, Sinclair, 49–50
Libowitz, Nehemiah Samuel, 93
Liessin (Walt), Abraham, 130
Lincoln, Abraham, 35–36, 43, 57, 90, 134–35, 205
Lindbergh, Charles, 232
Lindheim, Irma, 143
Lipsky, Louis, 22, 62; Ben-Gurion and, 224, 226; Bialik and, 81–83, 86, 88, 91, 277n.75; Jabotinsky and, 35, 42, 46, 53–55, 67; Katznelson and, 121; Meir and, 333n.170; Szold and, 141. See also ZOA
Lissitzky, Ephraim, 94
Lithuania, 62, 167, 216
Litvinovsky, Pinhas, 94
Lloyd, Harold, 50
London, 17, 38–39, 42, 44, 63, 67–68, 72, 76–77, 89–90, 106–08, 127, 187, 212, 214, 223–24, 228, 233–36
London, Meyer, 205
Long, Huey, 59
Longfellow, Henry Wadsworth, 70
Los Angeles, 244
Lothian, Lord, 67
Lubetkin, Zivia, 323n.35
Lubianiker (Lavon), Pinhas, 188
Luzzato, Moshe Haim, 78, 94

Mabovitch (Zipke), Clara, 169, 173
Mabovitch, Moshe, 161–62
MacDonald, Malcolm, 230
Mack, Julian W.: Ben-Gurion and, 204, 217; Bialik and, 82; Jabotinsky and, 45, 48, 50, 54; Katznelson and, 118–21; Szold and, 118, 153
MacPherson, Aimee Semple, 59

Geographic and Name Index

Magnes, Rabbi Judah, 54–55, 161, 242; Ben-Gurion and, 215; Bialik and, 73; Jabotinsky and, 39; Katznelson and, 111–12, 296n. 117; Szold and, 133, 138–41. *See also* pacifism, Sons of Zion
Maimon. *See* Fishman
Malachi, A. R., 81
Malter, Henry, 74
Marcus, Joseph, 86–93
Margowski, Jacob H., 316n. 143
Marshall, Louis, 111, 119, 173, 213, 299n. 146
Marwill, Robert, 95
Marx, Professor Alexander, 86, 93
Masterman, C. F. G., 39
Matz, Israel, 95–96
Maximon, Shalom Ber, 79
May, Doris, 233
McCloy, John G., 236
McKinley, William, 136
Medem, Vladimir, 115, 118
Mediterranean Sea, 27
Medzini (Hamburger), Regina, 168
Meir, Golda, 15, 133, 142, 157, 197, 241–42; and American culture, 162–67, 172, 174, 182–84, 190–95; as foreign minister, 190, 246; and fund-raising, 46, 162, 166, 169–77, 188–90, 195, 332n. 156; growing up in U.S., 161–63, 166, 174; as "minister of American affairs," 184–86; parents, 23, 161–62, 169; as prime minister, 161, 246; Szold and, 154; and youth/pioneers, 123, 164, 167–68, 172, 176, 178–80, 186, 188, 194, 220. *See also* aliyah, Ben-Gurion, Ben-Zvi, Britain, Geverkshaften, Hadassah, Hebrew, Histadrut, Jabotinsky, Jewish Agency, Katznelson, Labor Zionism, Lipsky, Mapai, Merḥavya, Morris Myerson, Pioneer Women's Organization, Poale Zion, Sarah Rahabi, Revisionism, Russia, Warburg, Weizmann, Wise, Working Women's Council, Yiddish, Youth Aliyah, ZOA
Melamed, Dr. S. M., 47
Mendele Mocher Sforim (Shalom Jacob Abramovitch), 71, 73
Mereminsky (Merom), Israel, 171, 178, 180–82, 185, 212, 219
Merḥavya (Kibbutz), 23, 167–68, 209, 244
Merril, Selah, 15–16, 20–21
Mesopotamia, 136

Mexico, 199
Milwaukee, 111, 162–63, 203, 221
Minneapolis, 111
Miville, Alfred J., 189
Molière, 70
Monsky, Henry, 222
Montefiore, Sir Moses, 20, 25
Montor, Henry, 222, 228
Montreal, 62
Moore, George Foote, 97
Moorehead, Alan, 131
Morgenthau, Henry, 26–27, 30–31, 39
Morgenthau, Henry Jr., 234, 236
Moscow, 140, 162
Moseley, Sir Oswald, 63
Moses, 28, 81
Mossinsohn, Ben-Zion, 32
Mount of Olives, 25
Mount Sinai, 59
Mumford, Lewis, 131
Mussolini, Benito, 58
Myerson, Morris, 167–68, 174

Naples, 164
Neumann, Emanuel, 80–81, 87, 236–37, 276n. 68. *See also* Keren HaYesod
Neumark, David, 74, 92, 272n. 33
New England, 136
New Jersey, 180
New Orleans, 25
New York City, 27, 44, 46–48, 52–53, 57, 66–67, 73, 82–88, 90, 94–95, 107–15, 117, 124–28, 136, 146–48, 150, 152, 155–57, 172, 174, 176, 181, 187, 189, 193, 195, 201–06, 212, 221, 224, 227, 235, 244
New York State, 67, 145, 185
Niagara Falls, 109, 201
Niagara River, 75
Niger, Shmuel, 109, 117
Niles, David, 235
Noah, Mordecai Manuel, 75, 102
Norwich, Connecticut, 44

Odessa, 48, 70–72, 74, 78, 93–94, 269n. 13, 283n. 117
Omaha, 44, 177, 189
Orloff, L. A., 128
Ormsby-Gore, William, 224
Ottawa, 67
Owens, Jesse, 135

Geographic and Name Index

Palestine (Holy Land, Israel): American diplomacy in, 18, 23, 26–32; American Jews in, 18–23 (*see also* immigration, Jewish Legion, Magnes, Meir, Szold); British in (*see* Mandate); Christian interest in, 18–20, 122; defense of, 52, 215 (*see also* Jewish Army, Jewish Legion); emigration from, 15–16, 23, 26, 28, 32, 40, 105, 110; Hebrew press in, 92, 272n. 31; hydroelectric station in, 46, 109; illegal immigration, 58, 121–22, 127, 159, 194, 217, 227, 232, 334n. 192 (*see also* Aliyah Bet); immigration 15, 18, 23, 41, 218, 237 (*see also* aliyah, Britain, Germany, Nordau Plan, Poland, Russia, Youth Aliyah); independence/statehood of, 17, 130, 194–95, 197, 205, 219–37 (*see also* Biltmore Conference); medical care in, 21 (*see also* Hadassah; Medical Organization, Kupat Holim); products and exports, 26, 50, 125, 187, 210; shipping, 188–90. *See also* Arabs, Va'ad Le'umi, *yishuv*
Panama, 199
Paris, 57, 256n. 43
Patterson, Colonel J. H., 65–66
Peel, Earl, 225
Perlman, Dr. Samuel, 52
Persitz, Shoshana, 149
Persky, Daniel, 77–78, 86, 274n. 53
Petaḥ Tikva, 27, 153, 204
Petliura, Simon, 45, 115
Philadelphia, 44, 48, 95, 232
Pine, Max, 112, 117
Pinsk, 162, 166
Pinsky, David, 111, 130
Pittsburgh, 93, 95, 111, 113, 182
Plonsk, Poland, 198, 202
Poe, Edgar Allan, 36–37, 263n. 121
Poland, 95; emigration from (to Palestine), 21, 120, 164, 175, 242, 255n. 34; invasion of, 58, 228; Jabotinsky and, 17, 51, 56–59, 62–63, 67–68, 224; Jews in, 44, 76, 179, 216, 221, 230, 245; Katznelson and, 299n. 156; Revisionists and, 62, 66, 118, 184. *See also* Bund/Bundists
Poriya, 23, 27
Proskerov, 166

Qantara, 167

Rabin, Neḥemiah, 168–69
Rabin, Rosa, 169
Rabin, Yitzḥak, 168
Rahabi (Myerson), Sarah, 175
Raisin, Max, 75, 86, 93, 102
Ramat Gan, 73
Ravinitzki, Yehoshua, 72, 78, 92, 95
Reid, Mayne, 36
Remez, David, 53, 169, 171, 185, 189, 191, 212
Repetur, Berl, 167
Reuveni, Aharon, 199
Revusky, Abraham, 115
Rishon LeZion, 16, 243
Rivkind, Isaac, 93
Rochester, 111, 203
Rock Island, Illinois, 111, 113
Roosevelt, Eleanor, 235
Roosevelt, Franklin D., 59–62, 127, 131, 136–37, 182–84, 190–91, 223–28, 232, 235–36
Roosevelt, Theodore, 36, 38, 43, 57
Rosenblatt, Bernard, 243
Rosenblatt, Gertrude, 158, 243
Rosenbloom, Sol, 95–96
Rosenwald, Julius, 24, 28, 199
Rosenwald, Lessing, 56, 95
Rothenburg, Morris, 91, 221
Rothschild, Baron Edmund, 148, 306n. 213
Rubashov (Shazar), Zalman 175, 178, 188, 190, 220–21, 327n. 105
Rumania, 36, 120, 179, 230
Ruppin, Arthur, 16, 23, 30–31, 46
Russia (Soviet Union): American Jews and, 39, 80, 86, 163, 191, 206; Arabs and, 245; Ben-Gurion and, 140, 210–11, 215, 245; Bialik and, 70–72, 76, 86, 92, 96, 269n. 13; emigration from (to Palestine), 16, 20–23, 26, 28, 164, 167, 198, 200, 211, 215, 223, 255n. 34 ; emigration from (to U.S.), 21, 38–39, 73, 103, 110, 162–63; Jabotinsky and, 35–39, 49, 63, 210; Jews and Jewish culture in, 38, 44, 76, 139, 199, 210, 215, 245; Katznelson and, 102, 121, 130–32; language, 36, 51, 72, 219; literature of, 70; Meir and, 161–62, 191–92; press in, 37, 47; U.S. government and, 39, 199 (*see also* Cold War); and Zionism, 44, 92, 131, 162, 210, 215, 242, 244. *See also* Bolshevism, Britain, communism, Crimea, Germany,

Geographic and Name Index

Odessa, Pale of Settlement, pogroms, Russian Revolution, Turkey, World War I
Rutenberg, Pinhas, 46, 109, 206

Salant, Rabbi Shmuel, 20
Sampter, Jesse, 138
Samuel, Herbert, 42
Samuel, Maurice, 54, 82, 88
Sarona, 23
Sartre, Jean-Paul, 69
Schechter, Solomon and Mathilda, 137
Schiff, Jacob, 24, 27, 30
Schlossberg, Joseph, 111–12, 117, 329n. 123
Schwartz, I. J., 79
Scott, C. P., 38
Scranton, Pennsylvania, 189
Sejera, 204
Shakespeare, William, 69
Shapira, Anita, 101
Sheinkin, Menahem, 33
Shelley, Percy Bysshe, 70
Shertok (Sharett), Moshe, 131, 144, 218
Shlisskey, Yossele, 83
Sho'er, Avraham, 94
Shohat, Manya, 109–10, 112, 115, 129, 210, 294n. 110
Sholem Aleichem (Rabinovitch), 70–71, 73, 79, 86
Shpiro, David, 236
Silkiner, Benjamin, 74, 86, 94, 301n. 172
Silver, Rabbi Abba Hillel, 52–53, 121–22, 222, 232, 234, 236
Silverman, Robert, 53
Simon, Ernst, 134, 139–41
Skorodin, Dr. A. M., 303n. 186
Smilansky, Moshe, 141
Snowden, Phillip, 169
Sodom and Gomorrah, 72
Sokolow, Nahum, 44, 82
Solis, Elvira, 155
Soloveitchik, Rabbi Joseph, 123
South Bend, Indiana, 111, 113
Spain, 20, 74, 86, 93, 200, 202
Spiegel, Professor Shalom, 93, 179
Sprinzak, Yosef, 171, 176, 178, 184, 259n. 76
Stalin, Joseph, 245
Steinbeck, John, 59
St. Louis, 180
Stowe, Harriet Beecher 52, 253n. 10
Straus, Lena, 95, 151

Straus, Nathan, 24, 95; Jabotinsky and, 42, 52–53; Szold and, 96, 138, 145, 151
Straus, Oscar, 20, 24
Strauss (Mochenson), Nellie, 209
Switzerland, 71, 270n. 13
Syracuse, New York, 111
Syrkin, Marie, 166
Syrkin, Nahman, 103–04, 110–11, 163, 166, 200, 212
Szold, Adele, 143
Szold, Rabbi Benjamin, 135
Szold, Bertha, 156
Szold, Henrietta, 22, 24, 27, 33, 96, 161, 166, 186, 197, 209, 241–43; and American politics, 136–37 (see also Progressive Party); and Arabs, 134, 138–41, 155; and blacks, 134–35, 138–39; and education, 142, 147–50, 313n. 90; fund-raising, 140, 155–56, 158–60; growing up in U.S., 133–36, 157; pacifism of, 39, 135, 138, 141, 155, 159; and pioneering, 141, 150–51; and refugees and immigrants, 134–37, 152–53 (see also Youth Aliyah); and religion, 135, 137–38, 141; and social work, 142, 146, 150–54; views of U.S., 135, 150–51, 155–56. See also Ben-Gurion, Bialik, Brandeis, Britain, Daughters of Zion, Hadassah, Hebrew, Histadrut, Jabotinsky, Jewish Agency, Katznelson, Keren HaYesod, Labor Zionism, Lipsky, Mack, Magnes, Meir, Revisionism, Nathan Straus, U.S. (efficiency), Warburg, Weizmann, Wise, WZO, ZOA
Szold, Rachel, 151
Szold, Robert, 42, 107, 225, 227

Tchernichovsky, Shaul, 70
Tchernowitz, Haim (Rav Tza'ir), 93
Tel Aviv, 28–30, 70, 72, 80–81, 90, 92, 94, 122, 139, 149, 153, 167–69, 244
Teveth, Shabtai, 205
Texas, 48, 155, 176
Tocqueville, Alexis de, 90, 245
Toronto, 41, 61, 111
Touro, Judah, 25
Truman, Harry S. 194, 235, 238–39
Tulin, Abraham, 62–64
Turkey (Ottoman Empire, Porte), 76; Ben-Gurion, 200, 206–08; "capitulations system," 18; expulsion of Jews from Palestine, 28–32, 37, 205; Jews of, 242; Palestine and,

386

Geographic and Name Index

30–32, 38, 200–201, 208; Russia and, 26, 31, 200. *See also* Armenians, Britain, Germany, United States, World War I
Twain, Mark, 36, 102. *See also* Huck Finn
Twersky, Yoḥanan, 78, 94

Udin, Sophie A., 327, n.105
Ukraine, 45, 71, 110, 115, 162, 295n. 110
United States: American dream, 36, 103, 246; and Arabs, 15, 126, 131, 235, 256n. 44; blacks in, 36–37, 95, 162, 198–99 (*see also* Jabotinsky, Szold); consuls in Palestine, 15–18, 20–21, 24–27, 30–31, 39, 164, 224; economy of, 44, 49–50 (*see also* capitalism, Great Depression); education in, 16, 49, 75; efficiency of, 46, 96, 143, 146, 171, 201, 205; film, 36, 50–51, 63, 109, 244; fund-raising for *yishuv* in, 16, 24–28, 242–46 (*see also* Ben-Gurion, Bialik, Jabotinsky, Katznelson, Meir, Szold); gentile expatriates in Palestine, 21, 25; Hebrew culture in, 53, 69–98, 123, 131, 199, 241; Hebrew press in, 32, 75, 77, 204; immigration, 15, 43, 135, 154, 235; isolationism of, 31, 120, 126; Jewish immigration into, 60, 63, 75, 122, 131, 154, 166, 199, 211 (*see also* Palestine, Russia, Szold, Yiddish); Jewish labor in, 33, 110, 112, 115–16, 121–24, 126, 129, 166, 181, 184, 199, 201–02, 210–15 (*see also* Geverkshaften, Schlossberg Poale Zion: American); Jewish press in, 52, 56, 60, 64–66, 77, 91–92, 103, 123; labor movements in, 102–03, 110, 131, 190, 192; as land of dollars 44, 56, 78, 88, 124 (*see also goldene medine*); literature of, 70 (*see also* Jabotinsky); pioneering in (*see* Achooza, Jabotinsky, Szold); press in, 36, 47, 73, 97, 190, 215; science and technology, 17, 24, 103–04, 109, 131, 145–46, 160, 244 (*see also* Progressivism); and Turkey, 18–20, 23, 26, 30–31, 38, 214, 234; warships of, 27–28; Yiddish press in, 32, 75, 77, 86, 97, 204. *See also* aliyah, antisemitism, assimilation, Britain, Hebraism, Jewish Legion, Russia, Spanish-American War, World War I, World War II
Ussishkin, Menaḥem, 124, 187, 211, 231
Utah, 48

Verne, Jules, 36

Vienna, 63, 105–06, 170, 233
Villard, Oswald Garrison, 215
Viteles, Harry, 118, 157
Vladeck, Baruch Charney, 117, 125, 219–20, 304n. 195

Waco, Texas, 86
Waldstein, Abraham S., 75, 83, 287n. 19
Walker, Jimmy, 82
Wallace, Edwin S., 25
Wallace, Henry, 236
Wallace, General Lew, 20
Warburg, Felix, 54, 88, 219; Ben-Gurion and, 214, 217, 222; Jabotinsky and, 56; Meir and, 173; Szold and, 148–49, 313n. 90. *See also* Jewish Agency
Warsaw, 128, 198
Washington, Booker T., 135
Washington, D.C., 63, 124, 177, 189, 227–28, 235, 237
Washington, George, 90
Waterbury, Connecticut, 189
Weisgal, Meyer, 54, 81
Weizmann, Chaim, 17, 31, 39, 44, 60–62, 76, 87, 118, 197, 228–30, 233, 241–42; Ben-Gurion and, 213–14, 216, 231, 234–39; Bialik and, 70, 77, 80, 82, 95, 97, 121; Jabotinsky and, 42, 45–50, 53–55, 95, 119, 269n. 150; Katznelson and, 119, 121, 127, 130; Meir and, 187; Szold and, 139, 156. *See also* Britain, Jewish Agency, WZO, ZOA
Welles, Sumner, 236
Wertheim, Maurice, 27, 234–35
Wilkes-Barre, Pennsylvania, 86
Willkie, Wendell, 137
Wilson, Woodrow, 27, 31, 33, 199
Winant, John G., 235
Wise, James, 60
Wise, Rabbi Stephen S., 22, 39, 254n. 27; Ben-Gurion and, 60, 217, 219–28; Bialik and, 79, 82–83, 88; Jabotinsky and, 45, 52, 60–63, 67, 223, 265n. 150; Katznelson and, 121–22, 303n. 189; Meir and, 193, 333n. 170, 334n. 192; Szold and, 145, 158, 315n. 114. *See also* WZO, ZOA
Wohl, Dr. Samuel, 330n. 127
Woodbine, New Jersey, 21
Worcester, Massachusetts, 77

Yadin, Yigal and Yossi, 315n. 14

Geographic and Name Index

Yana'it (Ben-Zvi), Raḥel, 21, 33, 171, 173, 259n. 76
Yassky, Dr. Ḥaim, 146
Yehoash (Solomon Bloomgarden), 82
Yemen, 242
Yoffe, Eliezer Lippe, 23, 104

Zaritsky, Max, 187

Zemaḥ, Shlomo, 198
Zerubavel, Ya'akov, 16, 200, 204
Zhitlovsky, Ḥaim, 107, 111, 115, 118
Zhitomir, Ukraine, 72
Zichron Ya'akov, 23–24
Zuckerman, Baruch, 106–07, 110, 163, 294n. 106, 343n. 97

Subject Index

Achooza, 23–24, 27, 200
Agricultural and Botanical Explorations in Palestine (Aaron Aaronsohn), 24
Agricultural Experiment Station, 24, 145, 199
Agricultural Workers' Federation, 306n. 213
Agudat Bialik, 77
Agudath Israel, 83
Aḥdut HaAvodah, 105–06, 109–10, 117–18, 120, 209, 220. *See also* Mapai Party
Aḥva, 200, 203
aliyah (*olim*), 242; from America, 48, 121–22, 125, 165, 169, 175–76, 180, 184, 186, 193–94, 198–200, 202, 205–08, 211–12, 216–17, 244; Ben-Gurion and, 205–08, 211–12, 216–17, 230; Bialik and, 70; Katznelson and, 105, 110, 121–22, 125; Meir and, 169, 172–73, 175–76, 184, 186, 193–94. *See also* Palestine: immigration, Second Aliyah, Third Aliyah
Aliyah Bet, 67. *See also* Palestine: illegal immigration
Allies, 38–40, 191, 238. *See also* World War I, World War II
Amalgamated Clothing Workers of America, 112, 184. *See also* Schlossberg
American Academy of Political and Social Science, 190
American Archaeological Instititute (Jerusalem), 31
American Assistance Council ("American Fund"), 30
American Colony (Jerusalem), 21
American Economic Committee for Palestine, 124
American Exploration Society, 24

American Federation of Labor, 110, 117, 190, 192, 215
American Friends of Jewish Palestine (New York Irgun), 66, 230
"American Group." *See* Young Farmer society
Americanism, 134, 157, 232
American Jewish Committee, 27, 206, 213, 234–35
American Jewish Conference, 235, 237
American Jewish Congress, 117, 166, 204, 206, 219, 236
American Jewish Joint Distribution Committee (JDC), 80, 111, 205, 213, 275n. 64
American Oriental Society, 32
American Red Cross, 145
American Relief Committee, 108
American School for Oriental Studies, 24
American Zion Commonwealth (AZC), 23, 119, 121, 169, 209, 243
American Zionist Medical Unit (AZMU). *See* Hadassah: Medical Organization
Am Oved Publishing House, 101, 128, 130–31
antisemitism, 15, 41, 58, 67, 178, 210, 217, 245, 256n. 43; in United States, 31, 39, 120, 155, 157, 162, 190–92, 206, 235. *See also* fascism, pogroms
Apollo Theater (New York), 77
Arabs, 28, 177, 195; blockade of Jaffa, 139, 189; and Histadrut, 124, 218; and Palestine, 15, 39, 54, 124–25, 138, 188, 195, 216; riots, 42, 54, 58, 105, 109, 123, 126–27, 131, 138, 186–87, 215–16, 221, 224–25, 303n. 189; schools, 148. *See also* Ben-Gurion, Britain, Iḥud, Jabotinsky, Katznelson, Russia, Szold, United States
Arbayter Ring, 210, 219

389

Subject Index

Arlington National Cemetery, 124
Armenians, 27–31
"Arsenal of Democracy" (Roosevelt), 232
assimilation, 35, 49; in United States, 16, 70–71, 79, 102, 116–17, 120–21, 199–200, 222, 243, 299n. 15
Attica prison, 52
Avukah, 84, 179
Axis, 131, 242. *See also* World War II

Balfour Declaration, 33, 40, 47, 84, 131, 205, 208, 225, 228, 231
Beit Berl, 132
Beit HaAm (Tel Aviv), 90
Beit Ya'akov Synagogue (Jerusalem), 20
Ben Hur (Wallace), 20, 97
Betar, 61
Bezalel School of Art (Jerusalem), 148
Biltmore Program/Conference (New York), 139, 155, 234–37, 241
Birth of a Nation (Griffith), 36
Blue Laws, 48
B'nai B'rith, 222, 301n. 167
Board of Health (New York), 145
Board of Jewish Education (Chicago), 148
Bolshevik Revolution, 45
Bolshevism/Bolsheviks, 44, 47, 73, 76, 86, 92, 115, 132, 136
Brandeis Group, Brandeisists. *See* Brandeis
Brit Shalom, 138–39
Bund/Bundists, 107, 115, 218–19, 295n. 110, 332n. 156
Bureau of Jewish Education (New York), 148

Canadian Jewish Congress, 189
capitalism, 49, 60, 199, 236; Katznelson and, 102, 129, 131
Carnegie Hall (New York), 44, 60
Central Bank for Co-Operative Institutions, 111, 118
Central Community Younger Clubs (Brooklyn), 179
Cimarron (Ferber), 59
City College of New York, 179
Civil War, 36, 135
Clinton Hall (New York), 208
Cold War, 162, 245
Colonial Office (Britain), 223, 233
Columbia University, 129
communism, 86, 115, 131, 173, 180; American Jews and, 92, 123, 130, 178. *See also* Russia, Third International
Congress (U.S.), 145, 238–39
Congress of Industrial Organizations, 192
Conservative Jews/Judaism, 82, 88, 112, 117. *See also* Jewish Theological Seminary
Cooper Union Hall (New York), 83, 110, 205
Cooperative League, 110
"Cos-Cob formula" (Wertheim and Ben-Gurion), 234
Council of Jewish Federations and Welfare Funds, 189, 195
cultural pluralism, 89, 135, 137, 147–48

Daily Jewish Courier (Chicago), 47
Daughters of Zion, 27, 145. *See also* Hadassah
Davar, 90, 101, 115–19, 122–31, 141, 187
Democracy in America (Tocqueville), 245
Department of Agriculture (U.S.), 24
Der Iddisher Kemfer, 125–26, 198, 204, 208
Der Morgn Zhurnal (New York), 47, 52, 115, 181
Der Tog, 52
Der Yiddisher Farmer, 103–04
Di Frayhayt, 86
Di Tsayt (New York), 45, 106–07, 111, 115–17, 130
Divine Comedy (Jabotinsky trans.), 47
Di Warheit (New York), 47
Do'ar HaYom, 55, 159, 259n. 79
Dos Iddishe Folk, 93, 107, 278n. 81
Dropsie College for Jewish and Cognate Studies (Philadelphia), 74
Dvir Publishing House, 72, 74, 77–78, 81, 87, 92–95

Eden (New York), 78
Emancipation, 69
Emergency Committee for Zionist Affairs, 193, 222, 232–36
Entente, 206–08
Ethical Cultural Society, 111
Evian Conference, 60, 190–91, 226
Ex-Lax Company, 95
Ezra, 198

fascism, fascists, 51, 55, 58–60, 63, 73, 136. *See also* Revisionism
"Fifth Avenue ghetto" crowd, 50
Final Solution, 191

390

Subject Index

Ford Motor Company, 109
Foreign Office (Britain), 42
Forverts (New York), 86, 107, 112, 115, 117, 123, 125, 130, 169, 210, 219
Free Synagogue (New York), 60
"The Future of Woman's Work for Palestine" (Szold), 151

Gettysburg Address (Lincoln), 205
Geverkshaften (Trade Union) Campaign, 323n. 123; Ben-Gurion and, 212–13, 217, 219, 232; Katznelson and, 117, 125, 128; Meir and, 170–73, 178, 186–88, 194
Golda on the Park (Tel Aviv), 244
"The Gold Bug" (Poe), 263n. 121
goldene medine, 15, 102, 121, 127, 162, 167, 241
"Golden Fleece," 76
Gone with the Wind, 63
Gordonia, 179
Grace Church (New York), 157
The Grapes of Wrath (Steinbeck), 59
The Great Betrayal (De Haas and Wise), 62
Great Depression, 49, 62, 95, 121–22, 127, 136, 151, 172, 182, 215

HaAdamah, 106
HaAhdut, 16, 103, 198–201, 203
HaAretz, 70, 82, 90, 159
Habonim, 234
Hadassah, 180, 223, 225, 243–44; Ben-Gurion and, 155, 211, 217, 221, 226–27, 232, 234, 237, 239; Hospital (Jerusalem), 146; Hospital (Safed), 143; Jabotinsky and, 42–43, 46, 221; Katznelson and, 105–06, 124–25, 155, 211; Medical Organization (American Zionist Medical Unit), 26, 42–43, 46, 105–06, 140, 142, 145–47, 153–57, 168–69; Meir and, 168–69, 172, 176, 181; National Board, 124, 138, 152, 158; School Luncheon Fund, 151; Szold and, 133, 138, 140, 142–59, 211. See also Junior Hadassah
HaDo'ar (New York), 77–78, 87–88, 94
Hadshot HaAretz, 43. See also *HaAretz*
HaHavatzelet, 16, 20
Halvri, 32
HaKoach (Palestinian soccer team), 82
haluka, 151
HaMashbir, 101, 212

Hapo'el HaTza'ir, 109, 220. See also Mapai Party
HaPo'el HaTza'ir, 30, 40, 198
Harvard Law School, 124
Harvard University, 83, 97, 179
HaSefer, 52
HaShiloah, 74–75, 83, 283n. 117
HaShomer HaTza'ir, 179–80
Hat and Capmakers' Union of America, 187
"HaTikva," 234
HaToren, 74
HaTzefira (Warsaw), 77
Haverim (book series), 94
HaYarden (Jerusalem), 59
Hebraism/Hebraists, 70–77, 82; in America, 71, 73, 86, 91, 117, 124. See also Eden, Ha-Do'ar, Halvri, HaShiloah, HaToren, HaTzefirah, Hebrew Writer's Association, Histadruth Ivrith
Hebrew, 16–17, 32, 40, 123, 244; Ben-Gurion and, 104, 122, 198, 202–05, 209, 213; Berkson and, 148–49; Bialik and, 52–53, 70, 72, 76–77, 84–87, 92–93; Ginzberg and, 88; Jabotinsky and, 52, 84; Katznelson and, 208; Lipsky and, 83, 89; Meir and, 163; Szold and, 150, 157; Viteles and, 118. See also Ben-Yehuda, Diesendruck, Hebraism, Hebrew culture, Russia, United States
Hebrew Cultural Garden. See Shakespeare Garden
Hebrew culture and literature, 115, 127; Bialik and, 69–98; Katznelson and, 101, 110, 131. See also Ahad HaAm, Reuben Brainin, Halkin, Hebraism, Hebrew, Russia, Schwartz, Silkiner, United States
Hebrew/English Dictionary (Silkiner), 74
Hebrew Geographical Atlas (Perlman and Jabotinsky), 52
Hebrew Health Station for Bacteriological Research, 24
Hebrew Publishing Company (New York), 78
Hebrew Teacher's College (Boston), 52, 123
Hebrew Union College (Cincinnati), 74, 86, 92–93, 181
Hebrew Union College Annual, 92
Hebrew University, 39, 73, 86, 92, 96, 122, 127, 296n. 117
Hebrew Writer's Association, 91, 159, 281n. 102

Subject Index

Hebrew Youth Association (Histadrut Ha-No'ar Halvri), 122
Hed HaHinuch, 149
HeHalutz, 179–80, 202–03, 208
Herzliya Gymnasium (Tel Aviv), 32
Histadrut: Ben-Gurion and, 111–13, 140, 175, 209–19, 232, 238; convention (4th), 120; Council, 127, 177, 185, 193; Executive Committee (HEC), 141, 169, 171, 178, 184, 186–90, 211–12, 215, 219, 238; Katznelson and, 101, 108–13, 119–31, 170, 209–12; Meir and, 169–94, 212, 216; "study month," 128; Szold and, 140–41, 211; Youth Department, 123. See also Am Oved, Arabs, Geverkshaften Campaign, Kupat Holim, Nahshon, Solel Boneh, Tiyur veTiyul, Working Women's Council, Yachin
Histadruth Ivrith, 81, 205
Histadrut Nashim Ivriot (Federation of Hebrew Women), 151
Holocaust, 58, 194, 235, 244–45, 323n. 35. See also Nazism in, World War II
Holy Landers, 18
Horace Mann School (New York), 149
Hotel Astor (New York), 83
Hotel Pennsylvania (New York), 188
Hovevei Zion, 301n. 167
Hull House, 145

Ihud, 139
Imperial Labor Conference (London), 175
Indians (American), 59, 74
Institute of Contemporary Jewry (Jerusalem), 122
International Health Board, 146
International Ladies' Garment Workers' Union, 125, 181, 184
International Longfellow Society, 157
Irgun (National Military Organization), 66
Irish Americans, 231
Iron Curtain, 245
Israel in the Mind of America (Grose), 246

jazz, 50, 57
Jewish Agency, 54, 129, 139, 144, 175; Ben-Gurion and, 154, 184, 195, 213–17, 220–21, 227–37; Bialik and, 95; Council, 213–14, 217, 226; Executive, 101, 154, 158–59, 195, 213–17, 220, 229, 231, 233, 235; Jabotinsky and, 49, 55–56, 95, 119, 213; Katznelson and, 101, 119, 128, 154; Meir and, 173, 190, 195; Szold and, 149, 152, 154, 158–59. See also Warburg, Weizmann
Jewish Army, 58, 64–67, 230–34, 237
Jewish Brigade, 67
Jewish Educator's Council (New York), 125
Jewish Encyclopedia, 74
Jewish Frontier, 130, 181–82, 216
Jewish Herald (Johannesburg), 66
Jewish Instititute of Religion (New York), 60, 79, 84, 93
Jewish Legion, 19, 26, 33, 168, 188, 242; Ben-Gurion and, 32, 40, 104–05, 129, 204, 206–09; Jabotinsky and, 37–42, 48, 51, 58, 64, 67–68, 105, 109, 129, 206–09, 255n. 34; Katznelson and, 104–06, 108–10, 125, 129, 208–09. See also Jewish Army
Jewish Marine School, 58
Jewish National Fund (Keren Kayemet), 52, 83, 119, 124, 178, 187, 231, 236
Jewish National Home. See Palestine
Jewish People's School (Milwaukee), 165
"The Jewish Problem and How to Solve It" (Brandeis), 135
Jewish Question, 130
Jewish Telegraphic Agency Bulletin, 52
Jewish Theological Seminary (New York), 79, 84–86, 88, 92–94, 124, 135, 137, 179
Jewish unions. See Geverkshaften Campaign, United States: Jewish labor in
Johnson-Jeffries prize fight, 36
Joint Congressional Resolution (1922), 47, 84
Judea Insurance Company, 55–56, 68
Junior Hadassah, 148, 157, 225

"Kentucky," (Schwartz), 79
Keren HaYesod (Palestine Foundation Fund), 81, 178, 211, 236; Ben-Gurion and, 213; Bialik and, 77, 80, 83–84; Jabotinsky and, 43–46, 48, 59; Katznelson and, 119; Szold and, 158
Ketuvim, 281n. 102
kibbutzim, 101, 154, 186. See also Merhavya
King-Crane Commission, 131
Kinneret Training Farm, 23, 103–04, 129
Knesset, 171, 239
Knesset Yisrael, 150, 152; Social Service Department, 153–54

Subject Index

Kolel America, 25
kolelim, 25
Korean War, 245
Ku Klux Klan, 48, 50
Kuntres, 101, 105, 108, 117–19, 209
Kupat Holim, 155, 168, 178, 211

labor movement. *See* Britain, Geverkshaften Campaign, Histadrut, Labor Zionism, Mapai Party, Poale Zion, United States
Labor Party (Israel), 105, 120. *See also* Histadrut, Mapai Party, Poale Zion
"The Labor Problem in Palestine" (Ben-Gurion), 204
Labor Zionism, 81, 168–69; American, 45, 62, 75, 123, 127, 142, 176, 193, 203, 220, 226 (*see also Di Tsayt*, Geverkshaften Campaign, League for Labor Palestine); Ben-Gurion and, 107, 154, 175, 211–13, 216–221, 226, 236, 329n. 123; Bialik and, 101; Jabotinsky and, 45, 59, 62, 66–67; Katznelson and, 105–10, 113–121, 125–29, 131–32; Meir and, 170–72, 174–86, 189–93, 323n. 35; and Revisionists, 62, 181–82, 215; Szold and, 139–41, 149, 152–53, 159. *See also* HaAhdut, Hapo'el HaTza'ir, Poale Zion
Labour Party (Britain), 187, 194
The Land of Israel in Past and Present (Ben-Gurion and Ben-Zvi), 204
League for Labor Palestine, 170, 180–82, 186, 221, 236, 329n. 123, 330n. 127
League of Nations, 43, 46–47, 228
Lexington Avenue Armory (New York), 44
Liberals (Britain), 38
Library of Congress, 124
Likud Party, 35
"Little Mother" circles, 145
Luah Eretz Yisrael, 28

Macy's Department Store (New York), 20
Madison Square Garden, 234
Mahal, 231
Manchester *Guardian*, 38
Mandate, Mandatory Government, 21, 47, 56, 84, 127, 136, 148, 169, 212, 223, 225, 228
Mandates Commission, 228
Manhattan Center, 65
Manhattan Opera House, 111

Manifesto Against Internal Terror, 139
Mantrap (Lewis), 50
Mapai Party, 220; Ben-Gurion and, 216–17, 221, 224–25, 228, 231–33, 237–38, 245; Center, 126, 176, 178, 184, 221, 225, 228, 232; Central Committee, 184; Conference (1932), 121; Council, 126, 130–31; Katznelson and, 120–21, 123, 126–28, 130–31; Meir and, 167, 175–76, 178, 180, 184; Political Committee, 217, 228; Secretariat, 237
Marxism, Marxists, 50, 107, 199; Ben-Gurion and, 198, 202, 341n. 72
Masonic Temple (Cleveland), 83
Mayflower, 193
McDonald's, 243–44
Mecca Temple (New York), 62, 82
Medical Sanitary Expedition (HMO), 146
Menorah Society, 179
Menorat HaMa'or, 93
Metropolitan Museum of Art, 49, 124
Metropolitan Opera, 49
Mikan u-Mikan (Brenner), 102
Min HaSafa VeLifnim (Diesendruck), 92
Mish'an, 303n. 186
Mizrahi, 28, 32, 137, 232, 236, 238
Mo'adim, 281n. 102
Moriah Publishing House, 74, 76–78, 87, 272n. 33
Mormons, 48
moshavei ovdim (smallholders' settlements), 23, 101, 186
Motza settlement, 301n. 167
Moznayim, 159
Mul Ohel Timura (Silkiner), 74
"Murders in the Rue Morgue" (Poe), 263n. 121

Nahshon, 189
Nathan and Lena Straus Health Center (Jerusalem, Tel Aviv), 96, 151
Nathan Straus Soup Kitchen, 151–52, 158
The Nation, 136, 215
National Arbayter Farband, 125
National Committee for the Jewish Workers in Palestine, 187
National Conference on Palestine, 236
National Council of Jewish Women, 176, 180
National Cultural Corporation (ZOA), 86

Subject Index

National Emergency Committee for Palestine, 226
National Hebrew School (New York), 86
National Jewish Labor Commitee, 125, 219, 234
National Labor Committee for Palestine, 172
National Labor Delegation, 186
National Recovery Act (1935), 137
Nazism, 60, 63–64, 73, 120, 129, 139, 142, 150, 152, 190, 214–15, 228, 234, 237, 244
Nettie Lasker Foundation (New York), 153
New Deal, 60, 137, 182–84
The New Palestine, 42, 52, 75, 81–82, 238
New Yishuv. See yishuv
New York Kehilla, 205
The New York Times, 81
New Zionist Organization, New Zionist Party. See Revisionism
Nordau Plan, 64
North American Relief Society for the Indigent Jews in Jerusalem, 25
Northwest Passage, 63

The Occident, 25
Ohel Shem (Tel Aviv), 96, 99
Okies, 59
Old Yishuv, 25, 151
Opinion, 60
Orthodox Jews/Judaism, 82, 93, 137, 155, 200. See also Agudath Israel, Mizrahi, Old Yishuv
OSS, 236
Ottoman Empire. See Turkey
"Outlines for Zionist Policy" (Ben-Gurion), 233

pacifism, 39, 208. See also Magnes, Szold, Wise
Pale of Settlement, 102, 104
Palestine Economic Corporation, 121, 157
"Palestine or America?" (Ben-Yehuda), 16
Palestine Settlement Office, 16, 23, 31, 103
Palestine Workers' Fund, 200
Palestine Writer's Asociation, 96
Palestine Zionist Executive (WZO), 45, 101, 118–19, 140–41, 144, 147–52, 157, 212–13, 223, 276n. 68, 313n. 90
Pan-American Zionist Conference. See Biltmore Conference
Passover, 27, 135
Pearl Harbor, 129, 131, 231, 236

Peel Commission, 225
People's Relief, 205, 212
Pioneer Women, 122, 176
Pioneer Women's Organization, 171–78, 182–83, 187, 221, 327n. 106; Consumers' League, 187
Pittsburgh Program (ZOA), 106, 118
Poale Zion (Labor Zionist party), 105; Action Committees, 205; American, 32, 106–18, 130, 166, 180–81, 189, 200, 202–11, 216, 218–21, 226, 234, 294n. 106; Ben-Gurion and, 32, 106, 113, 125, 182, 198–212, 216, 218–20, 226, 232, 234; Central Committee (American), 202, 208–09, 232; Katznelson and, 106–18, 125, 130, 220, 291n. 61; Left Poale Zion, 107, 115, 220; Meir and, 166, 171–72, 179–82; Palestine Committee (American), 202, 205–06; Workers' Council, 205. See also *Der Iddisher Kemfer*, *Di Tsayt*, *HaAhdut*
Poale Zion-Zeire Zion Party, 125, 171–72, 182, 220, 291n. 61
pogroms, 46, 72, 108–09, 164; in Russia, 16, 36, 102, 157, 161–62, 269n. 13; in Ukraine, 45
Polo Grounds (New York), 82
Porte. See Turkey
"Program for War and Peace" (Ben-Gurion), 232
Progressive Party, 24, 134–36, 139–50, 153–54, 160, 209, 222. See also Brandeis, Szold
Prohibition, 48, 50, 90
Provisional Executive Committee for General Zionist Affairs (WZO), 22, 27, 32, 135, 205

Quakers, 141

radicalism, 49, 101, 106
"The Raven" (Poe), 36
Reconstruction Era, 36
Reform Jews/Judaism, 74, 82, 88, 112, 137, 155, 211, 299n. 146, 331n. 145. See also Hebrew Union College, Jewish Institute of Religion, Magnes, Silver, Wise)
"Report on the Condition of the Jews in Palestine" (Wertheim), 27
Reshumot, 92–93
Revisionism (New Zionism), 17, 118, 179, 184; in America, 57, 62–64; Ben-Gurion and, 218, 232; Executive Committee, 62,

Subject Index

230; Jabotinsky and, 41, 51–67; Meir and, 181–82, 191–92; Szold and, 141. *See also* Britain, *Do'ar HaYom*, Jewish Army, Labor Zionism, Poland
Revolutionary Constructivism (Katznelson), 123
"roaring twenties," 50, 82
Rockefeller Foundation, 146
Romans, 76
Rothschild Hospital (Jerusalem), 146
Royal Fusiliers, 40
Russian Revolution, 204, 241

Salvation Army, 201
Schools Hygiene Department (Jerusalem), 146
Scopes Trial, 50
Sears Roebuck, 24, 56
Second Aliyah, 23, 103–05, 129
Senate (U.S.), 43
Sephardim, 20, 25, 28
Shakespeare Garden (Cleveland), 83, 85
Shaw Commission, 126
Shirim (Silkiner), 74
Six-Day War, 245
Social Gospelists, 141
socialism, 15, 21, 40; in America, 80, 113–15, 122, 166, 200; Ben-Gurion and, 205, 212–13, 218–20, 222, 236; Jabotinsky and, 49, 259n. 76; Katznelson and, 101–03, 121, 124, 126, 129–32; in *yishuv*, 106, 242; and Zionism, 42, 50, 103, 180, 208, 210. *See also* Cahan, *Forverts*
Socialist Party of America, 181, 219
Socialist Pro-Palestine Commitee, 225
Social Reformers, 141
Solel Boneh Construction Company, 169, 212
Sons of Zion, 54–55, 57
Spanish-American War, 20, 135–36
S.S. Berengaria, 229
S.S. Patria, 159, 232
Standard Oil Company, 136
State Department (U.S.), 28, 31, 44, 63, 235, 256n. 44
Statue of Liberty, 201
Stern Group, 242
St. James Conference (London), 227–28, 230
Supreme Court (U.S.), 39, 118, 124, 137
The Survey Graphic, 136, 154

Talmud Torah (Minneapolis), 111

Tammany Hall, 206
Teacher's College (Columbia University), 149
Technical Institute (Technion), 149
Tel Aviv Council, 159
Tel Aviv Exposition, 55
Theories of Americanization (Berkson), 148
Third Aliyah, 164
Third (Communist) International, 106
Third World, 43, 246
Thomas Cook's Tours, 21
Thorndike-Terman measurement system, 149
Tiyur veTiyul (Sightseeing and Touring), 186
Toldot HaIkarim BeYisrael (Neumark), 272n. 33
Tom Sawyer (Twain), 102
"Tool Campaign," 106
"Torah of Monroe," 43
Totzeret HaAretz, 187
Town Hall (New York), 52
Trade Union Congress (Britain), 187
Trade Union Council (Britain), 186
Triple Alliance, 206

Uncle Tom's Cabin (Stowe), 36, 162, 198
"Under the Cross" (Berkowitz), 78
United Aged Home (Jerusalem), 316n. 143
United Fruit Company, 190
United Hebrew Charities, 153
United Hebrew Trades, 117, 170. *See* Geverkshaften Campaign
United Jewish Appeal, 217
United Mine Workers of America, 184
United Palestine Appeal, 87, 91, 189, 219, 222, 228, 232, 234, 236, 333n. 70
United States Naval Academy (Annapolis), 230
University of Chicago, 179
University of Wisconsin, 163
Up from Slavery (Washington), 135
USS North Carolina, 27
USS Tennessee, 28–29

Va'ad Le'umi (National Council in Palestine), 17, 101, 154
vegetarianism, 50
Versailles, Treaty of, 43, 214
"Virginia" (Jabotinsky), 37

Wall Street, 141
Wall Street Journal, 49

Subject Index

War of Independence (Israel), 193, 230–31
Warsaw Ghetto Uprising, 323n. 35
The War Time Journal of a Georgia Girl, 1864–65 (Andrews), 135
The Washington Post, 69
"We Bourgeois" (Jabotinsky), 49
Weizmann Institute (Rehovot), 81
Wellington House, 39
West Point Academy, 230
White House, 44, 82–84, 222, 235
Wisconsin Normal School, 179
women's liberation, 117
Workers' Bank, 108–116, 118, 189, 209, 212, 291n. 61, 294n. 106
Working Women's Council (Histadrut), 169–70, 172, 174–77
Workmen's Circle, 181
World Congress for Labor Palestine (Berlin), 218–19, 227, 329n. 123
World Jewish Congress, 219, 227
World War I, 15, 21, 26–31, 38–40, 43, 75–76, 90, 98, 104, 121, 128–29, 131, 135, 144–45, 166, 191, 200–201, 210, 230, 231, 234, 237, 241. See also Jewish Legion
World War II, 58, 64, 105, 130, 146, 162, 184, 190–94, 197, 222, 228–34, 242, 244. See also Holocaust, Nazism
World Zionist Congress, 92, 201, 218, 221; 1907, 73; 1923, 117; 1927, 118–19, 148; 1929, 149, 172–73; 1933, 121, 181; 1935, 182, 189; 1937, 138, 225, 229; 1939, 121, 334n. 192
World Zionist Organization (WZO), 82, 108, 118, 237, 304n. 195; Ben-Gurion and, 154, 206–09, 212–13, 219, 224, 231, 233, 238; Bialik and, 77, 90; Jabotinsky and, 42, 44–45, 48, 50–51, 53, 58–60, 63, 113, 255n. 34; Katznelson and, 105–07, 109; Szold and, 140–41, 144, 147–49, 151–52, 157, 313n. 90. *See also* Palestine Settlement Office, Palestine Zionist Executive, Zionist Commission, Zionist Smaller Actions Committee

Yachin, 178
Yahoodim, 49
Yeshiva University, 80
Yeshurun Synagogue (Jerusalem), 138
Yiddish, 35, 70, 75; Ben-Gurion and, 202, 204, 208–09, 213; Meir and, 163, 168, 173; in U.S., 113–16; in *yishuv*, 107. *See also* United States: Yiddish press in, Yiddish culture
Yiddish culture, Yiddishists, 40, 78, 82; in America 86, 91, 94, 103–04, 113–15, 131, 174; Bialik and, 78–79, 86, 91, 94, 97; Katznelson and, 109, 131, 296n. 117. *See also* Berkowitz, Bialik, Liessin, Niger, I. J. Schwartz, Sholem Aleichem, Yehoash
yishuv: agriculture in, 16, 21–24, 106–08, 145 (*see also* Aaron Aaronsohn, Kinneret Training Farm, Merhavya); culture in, 52, 72, 79, 89–91, 94–97, 106, 131; education in, 21, 91 (*see also* Berkson, Hebrew University, Szold); pioneers in, 16, 103–04 (*see also* Achooza, Ben-Gurion, Jabotinsky, Katznelson, Meir, Szold, Young Farmer society); spiritual life, 16, 137–38. *See also* Palestine, socialism, Yiddish
Yizkor, 204
Y. L. Peretz Writer's Association (New York), 86
YMCA, 151
Young Farmer society, 21–24
Young Judea, 84
Young Poale Zion, 179
Youth Aliyah, 138, 141–42, 154–59; National Youth Aliyah Committee, 159

Zeire Zion. *See* Poale Zion-Zeire Zion Party
Zionist Commission (WZO), 40, 42, 107, 206–09, 255n. 34, 256n. 44
Zionist Federation, Zionist Organization of America (ZOA), 60–61, 92, 219, 222, 225, 256n. 44; Administrative Council, 232; Ben-Gurion and, 213, 217, 219, 221, 226–27, 232, 237–38; Bialik and, 80–86, 89, 91; Education Department, 147; Jabotinsky and, 39–42, 44–47, 52–55, 62, 89; Katznelson and, 106–07, 112, 117–18, 121; Meir and, 189, 193; National Executive Committee, 83, 221, 227; Szold and, 83, 91, 136, 140, 147, 151, 156–58. *See also* American Zion Commonwealth, Brandeis, *Dos Iddishe Folk*, Solomon Goldman, Lipsky, *The New Palestine*, Pittsburgh Program, Silver, Weizmann
Zionist Smaller (Inner) Actions Commitee (WZO), 219, 224, 231, 233, 238

www.ingramcontent.com/pod-product-compliance
Lightning Source LLC
Chambersburg PA
CBHW050849160426
43194CB00011B/2091